HOME GUNSMITHING DIGEST

By Tommy L. Bish

Gun Digest Publishing Company
Northfield, Illinois

DEDICATION

To my lovely, trusting wife, Evelyn, who will readily volunteer to fire the first shot from any rifle I might build, be it elephant caliber or a flintlock muzzleloader. Greater love hath no man.

ACKNOWLEDGEMENTS

A book such as this doesn't just happen. It is the result of countless hours of hard work and plain old sweat over a workbench, typewriter and camera. However, there have been others who have contributed immeasureably to the production of this book.

Had it not been for the masterful hand of Jack Lewis in editing my sometimes unjournalistic copy for these past ten years, and encouragement by his partner, Ray Rich, this work still would be just an idea.

Bob and Frank Brownell, Rick Fajen, Bo Randall, George Cooper, Redfield Gun Sight, Leupold, Bausch & Lomb, Turner Kirkland, Val Forgett, George Brothers, Birchwood Casey, Bishop Stocks, Maynard P. Beuhler, Dale Edwards, Timney Triggers, Frank Pachmayr, Bill Dyer, Jerry Evans and many more all have shared in the production of this book. To these, as well as those not listed, my most sincere thanks. — **TLB**

Cover photos by Chuck Tyler
Art direction by Lloyd Haynes

CONTENTS

Introduction To A Gunsmith

Some ten years ago, about the time that Ray Rich and I were starting GUN WORLD Magazine, we repaired to a Southern California range with a replica black powder handgun and an unformed idea of doing a story about it.

At a nearby shooting station, a sun-burned man in cowboy boots and ten-gallon hat was working with a pair of single actions, seemedly preoccupied at first with what he was doing. But the more involved we became with our black powder efforts, the less interest this individual seemed to take in his shooting. Finally, he came over to watch for a moment.

And this is how we met Tommy L. Bish, who has spent the entire decade — and more — of GUN WORLD's existence as its technical editor.

Tommy Bish is more than just another firearms enthusiast. Guns of one kind or another have made up most of his life from the days in the mid-Thirties, when he was a machine gunner with the Marines in China. He was an Air Force armorer and aerial gunner in World War II and, between, a gunsmith, saddlemaker and motion picture stuntman.

But perhaps most important of all, at least for the readers of this book, is the fact that Bish is a hunter; he has been a hunter all of his adult life and the practical knowledge he has gained in the field, looking through the sights of a rifle, has been put to equally practical use in planning this volume. In short, Bish has set out to create a book of practical gunsmithing for the gunowner

In considering this book for the home gunsmith and what should go into it, we spent long hours of acceptance and rejection of ideas. It will be noted, for example, that there is little mention of shotguns. It is deliberate. Tommy Bish feels that there is not really a great deal that the home gunsmith can do to a shotgun; not of a constructive nature, at least. And, for the man without professional training, there is a good deal that can be done to damage a scattergun. Bish does touch on some jobs for the shotgun enthusiast, but for the most part, this book is devoted to rifles, handguns and what to do about them.

A good deal of type metal has passed through the printers since Bish volunteered his help with that initial story. In the decade or so in which we have been associated, he has built a following among shooting enthusiasts around the world; they respect his knowledge, his ability and his plain-spoken manner in explaining a specific project on improving or repairing a favorite firearm.

Tommy Bish will be the first to say he is not a journalist; that he is a gunsmith. But as the one who has put the commas in the right place for him over the years, I can only contend that there are a lot more journalists than there are gunsmiths. And Bish is one of the best!

Jack Lewis

Covina, California
February, 1970

Jack Lewis
Co-Publisher &
Editorial Director
GUN WORLD Magazine

tools for home
GUNSMITHS

It Doesn't Take Fortune A
If You Learn To Master A Few Of
The Basic Requirements!

A protractor level is invaluable for installation of sights, to level a gun in a vise tc drill it.

Over the years, I have found one thing to be true in the field of gun craftmanship, be it on a professional or amateur scale. It isn't the quantity of tools that makes a true craftsman. It is ability and know-how with only a few tools that is the mark of a true artisan.

I have seen any number of gun hobbiests working in their own homes with a minimum of costly and specialized gunsmithing tools, who turn out work that would rival that of even the best known gun shops.

On the other hand, I have visited professional gunsmithing shops that had a multitude of the finest in gunsmithing tools — and no one who knew how to use them properly!

Most professionals are aware of the necessary basic tools for even a small shop, so this is directed at amateur craftsmen in need of information as to just what consitutes basic tools for the home gun mechanic.

One of the first items mandatory for acqustion of good gunsmithing tools is a catalog listing gunsmith tools and supplies. Perhaps the best of these are those put out by Brownell's of Montezuma, Iowa, and Frank Mittermeier of New York City. Out of these two catalogs one can furnish and supply completely the finest gunshop with everything needed. Supplies, such as bluing salts, soldering and welding materials and other similar items used in a gun shop, have been tested for suitability and quality before being included in either catalog. All gun components supplied by these sources are of equal quality.

The first consideration for the establishing of a good home shop for gun work is a solid workbench. This should be made from substantial woods and well anchored either to a wall or the floor When you build a workbench for gunsmithing, build it solid. Otherwise, the first time you try to pull a barrel from a rifle action, you are apt to end up with a demolished workbench.

The second prime need will be a husky bench vise with jaws at least 4½ inches in width. It is also advisable, when securing this vise, to make sure it has a swivel base that will allow the vise to be rotated once it is bolted to the workbench. Never purchase a cheap vise.

The next consideration should be adequate racks and/or shelves on which to place and hang the various handtools.

But we'll assume that you have a good work bench and vise, as well as a reasonable assortment of the more common handtools, such as pliers and a few screw drivers. The more specialized tools that will prove invaluable to even the most amateur of home gun craftsmen are by a no means those designed with the amateur in mind. Instead, they are full fledged professional gunsmithing tools that are a must for even the neophyte in custom gun craft.

As a rule, the first type of amateur gunsmithing attempted is converting some military rifle into a full-fledged sporter. The first tool one should acquire for this type of work is a set of stockmakers' hand screws. These screws come in sets of two and each set is designed to fit a particular type, make and model rifle. In ordering, be sure to specify the rifle such as Mauser, Springfield, Enfield, ad infinitum. These screws are a must in hand-

*Such specialized tools as jigs to install ramps,
stockmaker hand screws, gunsmith levels,
carbide drills are some of the gunsmithing needs.*

fitting a semi-finished stock to the action.

In 1939, there was no tool on the market for the easy installation of front sight ramps attached by the soldering method. Then it was a matter of by guess-and-by golly in attempting to hold the ramp in precisely the exact location while applying flame from the torch to melt the solder. When the solder flowed, so did the ramp! Following one such incident with a temperamental ramp, I decided to do something about it. I put together a somewhat crude jig with a clamp attached that allowed me to locate the ramp in precisely the right location, tighten the clamp and go on with the soldering with no sweat or slippage!

Today Brownell's has a ramp soldering jig available t $4.95. This jig eliminates ramp slippage under heat

from the torch and is designed to last practically forever.

About the same is true with another modern piece of gunsmithing equipment. For many years, the installation and removal of front sights from elevated ramps was a gunsmith's headache. It required extreme care to prevent damaging or marring of the ramp during this operation.

The Williams Gun Sight Company came to the gunsmith's rescue on this problem by manufacturing what is known as a front sight pusher, a screw-operated affair that neatly and efficiently installs or removes dovetailed front sights with no fuss or muss.

One of the lesser known improvements in the area of sight mounting is the gunsmith level. The type I use most often is produced by Brownell's for $3.20. This level incorporates a magnet in its base for secure attachment to any part of the rifle's receiver or barrel. It comes equipped with a protractor which adjusts easily for any degree of angle. This level also is great for perfect leveling of a rifle receiver on a drill press table when drilling for a scope mount.

Possibly the least understood of all tools by amateur gunsmiths are the metal checkering files. Some of the questions I've been asked regarding these files by amateurs would be substance for a complete story in itself. Many have the mistaken idea that actual checkering of steel with these files is a complex operation only for gunsmiths who have been in the business for at least a hundred years! Don't you believe it!

Metal checkering files are used for checkering hammer spurs, bolt handles, back straps of pistols and revolvers and for serrating straps and ribs. These files require a little practice to master before perfect work can be expected and they are expensive! However, I always have figured that one single job of checkering a bolt handle would pay enough to buy at least three additional files, so I never considered their cost as a detriment to their worth.

Also in the file department — and every gun hobbiest should have at least a few in varying sizes — are screw head files. These files are designed for renewing or recutting the screw driver slots in screw heads. Nothing can do the job as professionally as these files, although I

Sturdy machinist's tool box should be available to serious gun worker for the care of precision tools.

The front sight pusher made by Williams Gun Sight is safe way to install dovetail sight without mars.

have seen some who open up a peened in screw slot with a hacksaw! This is the rank amateur's way of doing it and the resulting slot is a sad looking affair, indeed.

Screw head files cut only on the edges and are used either to deepen existing slots or cutting new ones in unslotted screw blanks. They cut a slot that is neat and professional looking. These files are available in thicknesses of .043 inches for large screws; .035 especially for sight base screws, and .027 for smaller screws. Their cost is under a dollar apiece.

Swiss needle files, sight base files, pillar files are but a few others that are needed and each should be on hand in varying sizes. Then there are fine mill files, half-round, rasps, stockmaker's wood rifflers and barrel inletting rasps that, in time, will become must items with the serious custom gun builder.

It is best to buy files as you have a need for them. In this way, you can build up a collection that suits your type of specialized work. For a working gunsmith to have several hundred files on hand, all in varying styles, is not unusual.

Regardless of the type of customization being done by the home gun craftsman, a complete set of high speed

number drills is another must. A set from size No. 1 through No. 60 will handle about nine-tenths of all gun work, including scope and sight mounting jobs. When buying high speed drills, buy the best. The cheapies aren't worth carrying into your shop!

One problem facing the first-time builder of a surplus military rifle into a sporter is in drilling the receiver to accept scope base screws. The receivers of some of these rifles are so case-hardened that an ordinary high speed drill will only burn up when attempts are made to pierce the hard coating. What is needed here is a solid carbide drill.

These drills are available in two sizes for gun work, No. 31 (6x48) and No. 28 (8x40) and are the only drills to use on a hard receiver. While quite expensive — about $5 each — they will last for years under normal and careful use and are a lot cheaper than having someone spot anneal the receiver to accept a high speed drill.

Once the receiver of a rifle is drilled for scope bases, it is ready for tapping. The two standard thread sizes for American-made scope bases are either 6x48 or 8x40 and it will be one or the other of these sizes in taps that must be used. Both sizes are special gun taps and are not found usually in hardware stores or regular tool shops. They must be ordered from a gunsmith supplier. Price is about $3 each.

The tools described here will prove to be invaluable to the man doing gun work as a hobby. It is a start in the right direction. The accumulation of a good set of tools for gun work is one that should take place over a period of several years. In this manner, only those tools actually needed are acquired.

I once knew a fellow who inherited quite a wad of dough and decided to open a gun shop. He spent several thousand dollars on a pile of specialized gunsmithing tools, most of which he didn't even know how to use.

This fellow died two years ago and I inventoried his shop equipment for his wife. Over three-quarters of the new tools he had purchased some ten years before never had been used! They were still in their original waxed wrappers! The moral is to buy only those tools you actually need. Learn to use them properly, then buy more as needed. You will have a far better understanding of the uses of each tool in your shop and will appreciate them more.

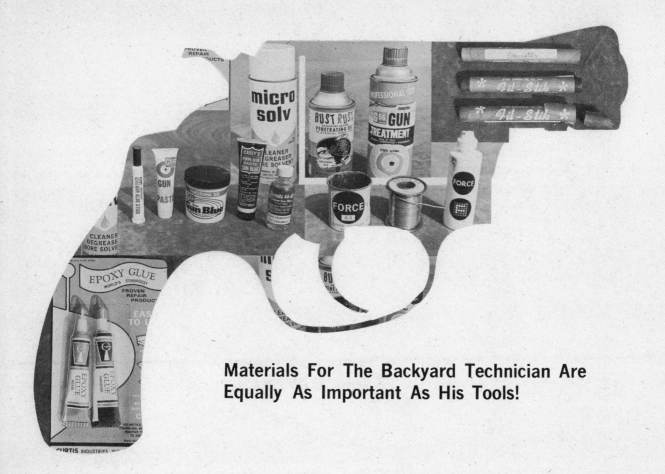

Materials For The Backyard Technician Are Equally As Important As His Tools!

The second most important phase of the gunsmithing trade, regardless of whether as a hobby or professional basis, concerns the specialized materials needed. Over the years, professional gunsmiths have tried about every concoction known to man in an effort to bring their work closer to perfection and possibly make it a little easier.

Let's take, for instance, methods used in years gone by in the finishing of a gunstock. I remember when I would spend as long as several weeks in applying a finish to a gunstock. Today, this process should be completed in two days at most and a far better finish is obtained, due to the improvements made in stock finishing materials.

Today there are any number of excellent preparatives for the finishing of a gunstock. These not only seal the entire stock against moisture, but coat it in a tough sheath of glass or plastic that is extremely tough and durable. Too, finishes of this type literally accentuate the full beauty and grain of a good stock wood. Some of these finishes are comparatively easy to use; others require some fairly expensive equipment, such as a compressor-type spray gun. As a rule, the finishes easily applied seldom are as durable as those that require more elbow grease.

Take, for instance, those with glass or plastics as a base. With careful use, these stock finishes can be applied by hand, until the pores of the stock are filled thoroughly, then sanded glassy smooth and another coating applied. Finally, when the pores are filled and the finish appears glassy smooth, the entire stock is well rubbed with a compound, such as lava stone pumice, until it takes on a mirror-like appearance. Then it is waxed and given a final polish with a soft cloth.

Stock finishing kits of this type are available at most gunshops and are produced by such gunsmith supply houses as Brownell's, Williams Gun Sight and Herter's. The Brownell kit is known as **Acraglas.** The Williams kit goes by the name **Williams Commercial Stock Finish** and the Herter's kit is known as the **Satinsilicol Stock Finishing Kit.** Another excellent preparation, produced by the Anderson Gun Shop of Yakima, Washington, is known as **Glascoat.** I have used all of these finishes with excellent results in each case. All are capable of producing a hard, glass-like finish to any gunstock if properly applied. All are extremely durable and stand up under the hardest use. Of equal reputation, but of a different principle, are the compounds by G-66, Birchwood-Casey and George Brothers Company.

The same applies to stock bedding kits, which are available from most of the sources mentioned above, as well as from Micro Sight Company of Belmont, California. Known as **Micro-Bed,** this is an easily mixed preparation that comes in two tubes.

Stock preparations for both finishing and bedding are possibly one of the biggest headaches to the amateur gun craftsman. But there are other headaches, too. Among these are the proper method and materials for installing ramps and sights with solder. In my opinion, there are at least two proper procedures to follow in this phase of gun construction — and especially in building custom rifles.

For many years I used low-temp silver solder for the installation of both ramps and some types of sights. Just recently I tried a product known as **Force 44,** a silver-bearing soft solder that flows easily at 400 degrees and is unaffected by hot bluing baths. This solder eliminates

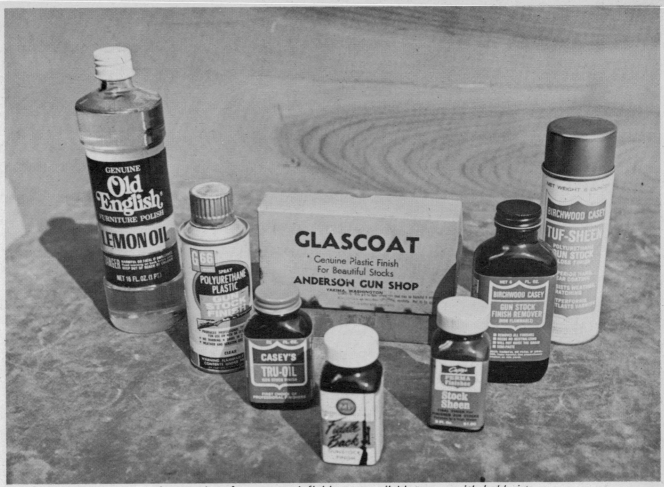

*Any number of proven stock finishes are available to gunsmith hobbyists.
All are capable of producing durable finish, if applied under directions.*

the need for expensive heating equipment, such as oxy-acetylene torches, and has a strength of 14,000 to 25,000 psi.

The list of needed materials for a well equipped gun-shop can be endless, so I mention only a few of those considered basic for the home gun mechanic. All are proven, professional materials.

Building a sporting rifle — or even a set of custom pistol grips — requires hours of sanding. For this, the finest grades of paper should be purchased in at least three grits: #3/0 for rough finishing, #6/0 for semi-smooth finishing and "whiskering" and #8/0 for a smooth, London-type finish.

These garnet papers are fairly expensive, but are the cheapest to use in the long run, if beautiful woodwork is desired. Those for putting the final finish on a stock are known as wet-or-dry papers and a supply in grits of from 220A (very fine), to 600 grit (ultra fine) should be on the shelves, be it an amateur operation or the most professional gun shop. In addition, steel wool is a must. This material is invaluable for removing rust, scouring, polishing, burnishing and cleaning all gun parts and woodwork. Steel wool is available in several grades, from 0000 (super fine) to Grade 3, which is coarse. I have found that either the three-0 or four-0 grades fill the bill for most jobs around a gunshop.

In the more specialized lines, engine-turning abrasives, epoxy glues, touch-up cold blues, lubricants, liquid rust removers, buffing compounds, case hardening compounds, shellac sticks and a multitude of other materials are necessities around a gun shop.

The engine-turning abrasive is used to produce a jewel-like appearance on bolts, hammers, triggers and side plates. This process is accomplished with an engine-turning brush chucked in a drill press. The brush is coated liberally with a mixture of oil and the abrasive. With the drill press running, the coated brush is lowered onto the work to be jeweled in a uniform manner. When properly done, the gun part will take on a beautiful jeweled finish, increasing the value and eye appeal of the arm.

Epoxy glues of the type used most around a gun shop are available in kits containing two tubes. Equal portions from each tube are mixed thoroughly, then applied to the part to be welded.

While glues of this type require approximately twenty-four hours for complete curing and hardening, this process can be greatly accelerated with the use of a common desk lamp. Situate the glued part as near to the light bulb as possible. In an hour's time, the weld should be completed and the epoxy thoroughly cured. As a rule, repairs such as this are the strongest part of the wood, whether a rifle stock or a broken pistol grip. Quite naturally, though, glues of this type are reserved solely for mending wood or plastics. They never should be applied to metal parts of any firearm!

Cold bluing solutions are fairly well known to all persons interested in firearms repair or rebuilding. Solutions of this type are used primarily for touching up minor wear areas or scratches on the metal of firearms. They never should be used for complete blue jobs on any arm, as they are not sufficiently durable.

Solutions of this type are produced by a number of manufacturers, including G-66.

Important around any shop are proper lubricants, whether it be for oiling machinery, such as lathes and drill presses, or for firearms use. In my opinion, the best all-around lubricating oil is pure sperm oil. I have found, in the years that I have used this type of oil, that it does not gum up or dry out. It is a pure natural lubricant with

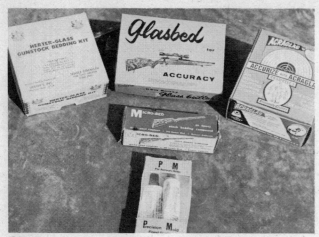

Glass bedding is another important phase of the art of gunsmithing. These kits are used by professionals.

Fastest, surest way to hone bolt and action of rifle or shotgun is use of abrasive such as Crystolon 600B.

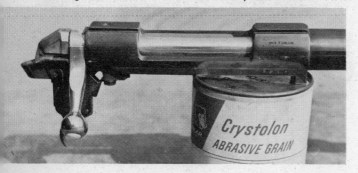

Every gunshop, amateur or pro, should have on hand oils for guns and leather goods. Recommended by author: sperm oil for guns, neatsfoot for leather.

no additives. Too, for many years I have used **Rig** gun grease with excellent results on both firearms and as a preservative for many of my better tools. Available today are any number of so-called special firearms lubricants. Many of these are filled with such additives as powdered graphite and mica dust. Use your own judgment on these lubricants.

Liquid rust removers are self explanatory. Preparations of this type are used for removing rust from metal parts and for loosening stubborn screws and pins in firearms.

Some of these preparations are mild, but others act quite severely on blued surfaces and sometimes will either streak the bluing of an otherwise finely finished arm or remove the bluing completely. I have found **WD-40** to be one of the best of these.

In using any of these solutions for the first time, first try them out on a scrap barrel or other gun part before applying them directly to a nicely blued arm. Fine surface rust is best removed with nothing more than 4-0 steel wool. This will not impair, remove or damage the original blued surface. The more the blued surface is rubbed with the wool, the prettier it will become!

Buffing compounds, varying from emery or black through tripoli, reddish in color, and white finishing compounds, are essential for metal refinishing. These compounds are applied to various types of buffing wheels and are capable of producing finishes from a dull, satin appearance to a gleaming high luster. Emery compound cuts fast and is used usually where heavy rust removal is required. Tripoli is used in preparing the metal for the final buffing with the white compound. Tripoli, properly used, removes minor scratches left by emery papers, thus preparing it for the final finish.

White or finishing compound is used in the final preparation of the metal for bluing or plating.

Varying pressures of the metal parts against the buffing wheel, will produce different finishes. A light buffing with white compound will produce a highly polished chrome-like finish, while additional pressure with this same compound brings a slightly duller gleam to the metal. Buffing of any firearm correctly requires countless hours of experience. Otherwise fine guns have been completely ruined at the buffing wheel!

Of the materials essential to either advanced amateur or professional gunsmiths is some sort of case-hardening compound. These concoctions are used where new parts are handmade from mild steels and must be hardened, or for old parts that have been repaired and the original case-hardening removed by heating with a torch. Case-hardening compounds are sometimes a little difficult for the home gunsmith to locate, but are available under such trade names as **Kasenit** and **Hard 'N Tuff.** Either of these compounds is capable of hardening such items as firing pins, hammer davits, trigger pins, sears, et al. The only requisite is to follow the directions to the letter.

Shellac sticks are used for patching stocks that might be dented, deeply scratched or gouged. These sticks are available in colors ranging from ivory through light, dark and Circassian walnut, as well as black. Shellac sticks are applied with heat to the damaged part, smoothed out, then allowed to cool and harden. The area then is sanded to the surface of the wood and finished along with the stock. If correctly done, a repair of this nature is hardly noticeable.

As with tools, I would suggest that specialized materials associated with gunsmithing be acquired only as needed. There is no sense in purchasing materials that you may never use as a gun building hobbyist.

11

Chapter 2

WHAT CONSTITUTES CUSTOM

Some Controversial Opinions On What Is Good Taste, Too!

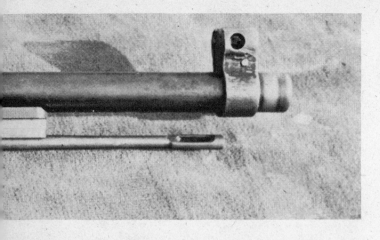

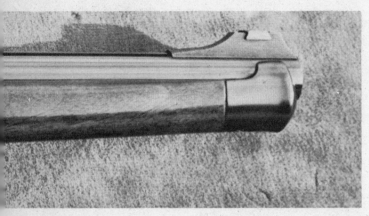

A Mannlicher-type bolt handle and custom trigger with thumb safety are two improvements that might be incorporated on surplus rifle to change look.

Pistol grip caps of exotic materials such as stag horn, elephant ivory and rare woods can be made and installed to give the firearm some individuality.

A rifle is a rifle, but for a truly custom-built sporting job, this rather simple classification applies less strictly.

Over the years, I have been shown many rifles that their proud owners tabbed as being "custom-built" simply because they were converted military surplus weapons. Conversion, in most cases, meant a new sporter stock, possibly a recoil pad, perhaps a custom trigger and a thin application of some commerical stock finish.

In a great number of cases, workmanship on these home-built conversions was above average, while on others it was plain lousy! However, the application of a new sporter stock and a few other necessary components certainly does not place that old military rifle in the custom class.

Custom refers to something not readily available on the market or that is made exclusively to special order. A truly custom-built rifle is all these things. It must be, in order to be classed as custom and the workmanship exercised in its finish has to be far above average.

A custom-built rifle certainly requires more than the mere installation of a new stock, regardless of how fancy the wood might be, or adding of a few standard features such as a custom set-trigger and such. For the most part, those contemplating the conversion of a military rifle into a custom sporter, whether it be any of the Mauser models, an '03 Springfield or even the lowly M1 carbine, are not aware that those little things that can turn a plain rifle into a custom job are, for the most part, the cheapest part of the entire conversion!

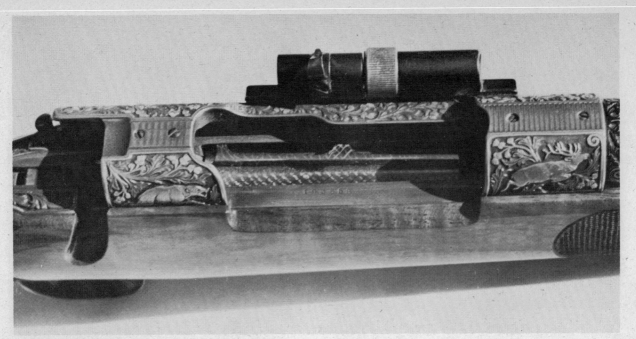

*Elaborate engravings can run up price of any firearm,
as they usually are done by specialists in this art;
it is hardly a project for the average gun owner.*

Customizing features, such as inlays, grip caps, cartridge traps, bolt handles and similar items can be made entirely by hand by the astute builder of a custom rifle and all of these accessories can be made with a small outlay of hard cash.

Certainly no one building a fine sporting rifle wants to leave that old military bolt handle on the finished job. There are commercial bolt handles available at most gun shops. Some of these are rather plain, solid-head affairs which a few custom rifle builders might prefer. On the other hand, there are custom bolt handles available with hollow heads, beautifully knurled, that sell for less than five bucks. These particular handles are worthy of even the finest custom-built sporters when properly welded in place.

I always have made it a practice to fill the hollow heads of this type handle with elephant ivory.

There are those who might prefer a spoon or Mannlicher-type bolt handle in lieu of the round knob. These are made easily from either cold-rolled or tool steel in about an hour's time, using a hacksaw and a few files. This Mannlicher-type handle is welded in place on the bolt and bent to the proper shape to assure ease of operation. Such a bolt handle both reduces the finished weight of the rifle and eliminates the bulkiness created by the round knob type of handle.

The trigger guard of military rifles as a rule are too wide, too square and too thick for a custom sporting rifle. Alterations here not only further reduce the weight of the finished rifle, but will add that all important feature we are after: customization.

The trigguer guard should be tapered from the rear of the front, making it slightly wider on the front bow. Then the entire guard should be thinned and given a rounded contour.

Floor plates of military rifles — speaking principally of Mauser and Springfield models — are equipped with a

*Trigger guards and floor plates also can be engraved
with various motifs, including game animals, but
this type of work is becoming more rare, expensive.*

release that must be actuated with the point of a cartridge. Being converted to sporting purpose means that, for the most part, the same rifle will be shooting soft or semi-soft nose ammunition.

To attempt to release a standard military floor plate with ammunition of this type would result in malformed bullets. However, it is a simple matter to manufacture a knurl-headed push button release that can be installed in the existing hole in the floor plate.

(The complete process for manufacturing one of the floor plate buttons is covered later in the book.)

Custom caps for pistol grips comprise another feature

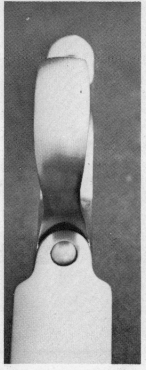

Hollow head bolt handles can be made more attractive by inserting rare woods or ivory in void, then polishing it.

Reshaping the trigger guard and installation of floor plate release button should be on the list of anyone customizing rifle from Mauser, Springfield action.

that easily sets a rifle apart from all others. There is an infinite number of commercially available pistol grip caps and they aren't expensive either. However, neither are they custom, as I interpret the word.

Grip caps of elephant ivory, stag horn, steer or cow horn, big horn sheep and rare woods, when handmade, are for the custom-built sporting rifle. All of these materials are worked easily with a hacksaw and files, then the final high luster polish is attained with a muslin buffing wheel using white rouge. The whole idea is to

Silver or gold monogram plate inlaid into heel of stock adds custom touch not found in commercial guns.

The bolt release area of the stock can be reinforced with black or brown fiberglass sheeting for appearance.

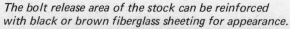

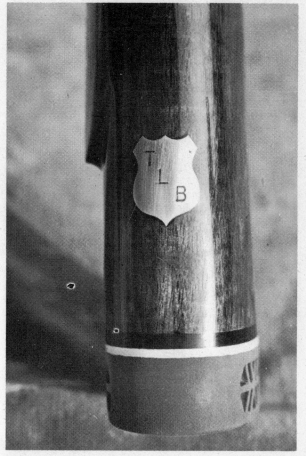

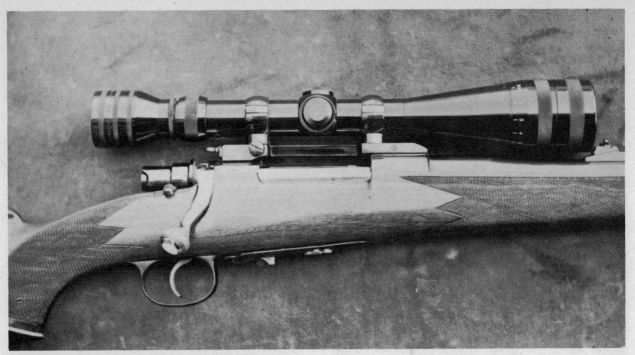

The installation of a scope, with replacement of the military-type bolt sleeve with a FN style, adds to the finished appearance of the custom-worked rifle.

have equipment on your rifle that cannot be bought at the local gun shop or sporting goods store.

The finish and final contouring of the stock most certainly will set yours aside as either a custom-built rifle or one that has been haphazardly cobbled together. This is especially true where the receiver and butt sections of the stock are concerned.

The wood in the area where the bolt handle fits into its slot in the stock should be tapered gracefully to meet the slot, not just filed flat. The leading edge of the wood adjoining the area where cartridges are loaded into the magazine of the rifle should be slotted gracefully downward or left with a crisp, sharp edge. The wood of the stock that adjoins the tang and trigger guard should be absolutely flush with the metal surfaces.

The stock's pistol grip should be contoured tastefully. By this, I mean that it should be shaped classically and minus the ugly hook found on too many commercial stocks today. Any knowledgeable rifleman will confirm the fact that hook-shaped pistol grips serve no worthy purpose other than to make the rifle ugly and to act as an excellent brush hook!

If a half-stock sporter is being build, the forend should be rounded over nicely in lieu of the undercut type that joins the barrel, making still another excellent brush hook. If a full Mannlicher-type stock is used, a custom forend cap should be employed. These are made easily in a few minutes.

Possibly the most important part of a rifle is the butt section. The cast and drop of the butt must be proportioned to fit the individual perfectly so that no neck craning is necessary in aligning either scope or open iron sights. The cheek rest should be shaped and contoured to meet the individual's requirements and facial structure. Finally, the cheek rest can be given that extra custom look never found on commercial rifles, by pro-

viding a raised sculptured effect with files and diligent use of fine garnet paper.

Any number of other customizing features might be applied to a sporting rifle. Inlays of ivory or rare woods sometimes are desired by the man building his own custom rifle. However, it always has been my idea that a custom sporting rifle can be beautiful without the gaudiness being inlaid into an otherwise beautiful piece of stock wood!

I long have been an avid exponent of glass bedding. If properly done, nothing can equal it for bringing out the potential accuracy of any rifle, at the same time adding

A deluxe checkering job not only makes rifle handle more easily, but adds to the value, when completed.

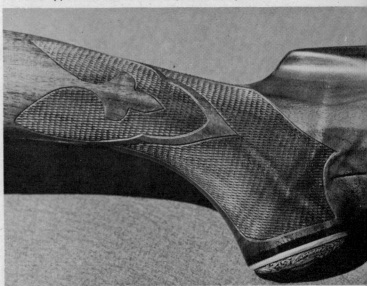

A sculptured effect can be given the cheek rest with use of files, garnet sandpaper, bit of elbow grease.

Solid head bolt knobs can be flattened, checkered as shown here to provide a better gripping surface.

Hinged floor plates are available for 98 Mauser and '03 Springfield, replacing original military types.

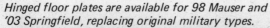

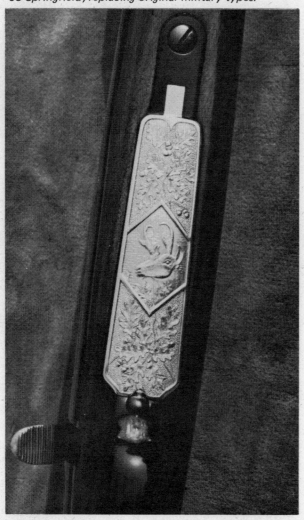

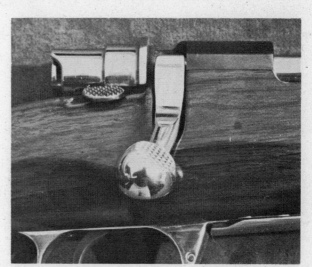

FN bolt sleeve has cleaner lines than military type. Installation requires custom trigger, thumb safety.

strength to the stock itself and preventing warping in damp weather.

On rifles of magnum calibers, it is sane thinking to inlay a steel lug into the recoil shield of the stock, then glass it in place. When properly done, the stock is capable of withstanding the most severe recoil without damage.

For final stock finishing, thorough sanding with 400 paper to remove even the most minute whiskers should be accomplished. Then the pores of the stock are filled with a good commercial filler made for the purpose, left to dry for at least twenty-four hours, then resanded lightly before the final finish is applied. When completely finished, no open pores in the wood should be visible.

In building a custom rifle, keep it simple; include only those custom features that will add to the rifle's attractiveness and usefulness. Above all, careful, painstaking workmanship is important.

Chapter 3

Burred Heads & Bird Brains

For Those Who Attack Tiny Screws With Tools Built To Repair Steam Shovels!

THERE'S nothing more disheartening to the firearms fancier than to examine an otherwise fine sporting arm that has the screw heads badly burred up through the use of an ill-fitting screwdriver.

Just recently, I bought several fine guns from a hard-pressed friend. Each of these guns was in near-new condition, but someone in the past had loused up several of the screw heads in each. Luckily, most of these screws were saved by carefully redressing the heads to their original appearance, then rebluing them. Several had to be discarded and replaced, so badly were they burred.

The seemingly insignificant and inexpensive screwdriver is one of most important tools used by any gunsmith, but this one tool can make all the difference in whether a custom gun is beautiful in overall appearance or has been slopped together with no precaution taken as to tool fit.

In the past thirty years or so, to my knowledge, little has been written in the majority of gunsmithing books regarding the proper use, design and correct grinding of the lowly screwdriver. For the most part, a screwdriver simply is taken for granted. Occasionally it will be mentioned that ''the bit of the screwdriver should fill the width of the screw slot.'' Then the most important phase of bit-fit to screw slot is left to the readers' imagination. The result usually is burred or ruined gun screws.

Not only must the bit of the screwdriver fill the width of the slot, but it must conform perfectly to the contour of the slot interior, both for size and shape. The matter of proper pressure on the screwdriver usually is overlooked. Too light a pressure on a tight gun screw can only result in a burred head!

A thick book could — and probably should — be written concerning the proper use of screwdrivers in gunsmithing. Seemingly overlooked facets concerning the screwdriver include proper steels, types, sizes and shapes of bits, correct grinding, handle materials and sizes, tempering, degree of angle of the bit, bit length, various screw types, including both foreign and domestic.

The one field of gun screws that causes the greatest consternation for even the most practiced gunsmith involves

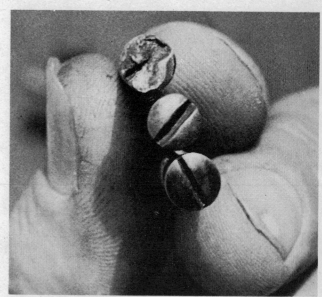

Burred screw (top) contrasts with damaged one in center and new screw ready for use as replacement.

those with extremely narrow slots in their heads. While screws of this type are found in the finest sporting rifles, pistols and shotguns of European origin, such as W.W. Greener, Purdey, Holland & Holland, Merkel, Ferlach, Hammerli and others, it is nearly impossible to buy a complete set of drivers in this country that will fit them all. Screwdrivers for these must be handmade by the gunsmith or good screwdrivers must be ground and reshaped to fit the extra narrow slots of these European screws.

No less than a hundred screwdrivers could be assembled

Screw driver should fill screw slot. Bit of this driver is too narrow for adjustment of rear sight.

in a few minutes around my own non-commercial gunshop, I buy screwdrivers in half-dozen lots, having them on hand to regrind to fit specific off-size screw slots. For the most part these drivers cost less than half a dollar each — less than the cost of some gun screws — and each is capable of unwinding hundreds of odd-ball sized gun screws before they are worn out or ground to a nubbin!

Screwdrivers are about the cheapest investment a gun-smith or gun hobbiest can make, if it will preserve the full value of fine sporting arms. I always have figured that, if I could loosen one stubborn screw from one fine gun with a single screwdriver, that instrument paid for itself — providing the screw wasn't burred in the process.

Gun screws comprise a small part of the types encountered by anyone doing gun work. There are scope mount and ring screws, sight and ramp screws and numerous others encountered in everyday gun work. Big screws hold the stocks to the receivers of some shotguns and rifles and small screws are found on micrometer-type hunting and target sights, while minute screws are incorporated on some buckhorn rear sights with interchangeable reticles. While the overall head size of many of these gun-related screws may appear identical (such as those found on many scope rings), the slots can vary considerably in width. This requires a screwdriver with a bit of the proper thickness and correct bottoming contour.

As stated, a screwdriver filling the width of a screw slot doesn't assure removal of a tight screw without burring. The bit must completely fill the interior of the screw slot in a snug fit to assure positive and maximum pressure, when the driver is turned by hand. A certain amount of pressure must be exerted downward at the same time the rotating

Screws in many European firearms have narrow, thin slot and require screw drivers be especially ground.

motion is executed. This will prevent the bit of the screwdriver from crawling out of the slot under pressure. This is possible, when the screw is of soft steel, allowing the metal flanking the slot to give under pressure of the hardened screwdriver bit.

When soft screws are encountered in any gun, they should be removed and either hardened or replaced. These basics refer both to the removal or tightening of any gun-related screw, be it in a scope mount, a receiver screw or one that holds the stock to the action.

Basic? True, but every day fine guns are ruined by those who don't understand these simple rudiments.

Gun hobbyists are not the only offenders, as I have seen more screwed-up screws come out of established gunshops in recent years than one would imagine! Guns with newly mounted scopes often have the scope ring screws so burred that they appear to have been attacked by steel-eating termites!

Aside from gun screws proper, scope mount and ring screws probably receive more punishment under the screwdriver than do all others. Take, for instance, mounts with windage adjustment screws at the rear of the scope base. These screws have fairly large heads, most measuring roughabout three-eighths inch in diameter by about one-fourth inch in thickness. I had to remove hundreds that were broken off in the mount through excessive tightening.

Windage adjustment screws of this type are designed to accomodate a coin, such as a nickel or a twenty-five-cent piece for tightening or adjustments. So what do some use? A large, heavy duty screwdriver capable of twisting the

Top: Barrel weight screws of High Standard pistol have been burred by an ill-fitting screw driver. (Below) Same screws after they have been redressed by the author and touched up with G-66 cold blue.

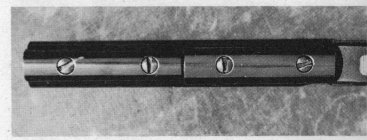

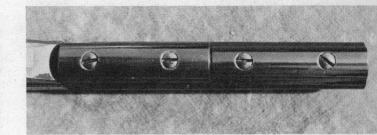

To avoid marring, screws in pistol grip cap and this cartridge trap require screw driver of perfect fit.

Various makes of rear sights require variety of screw driver sizes be available for individual use.

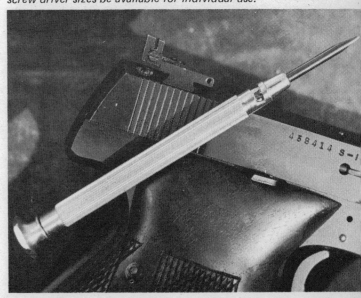

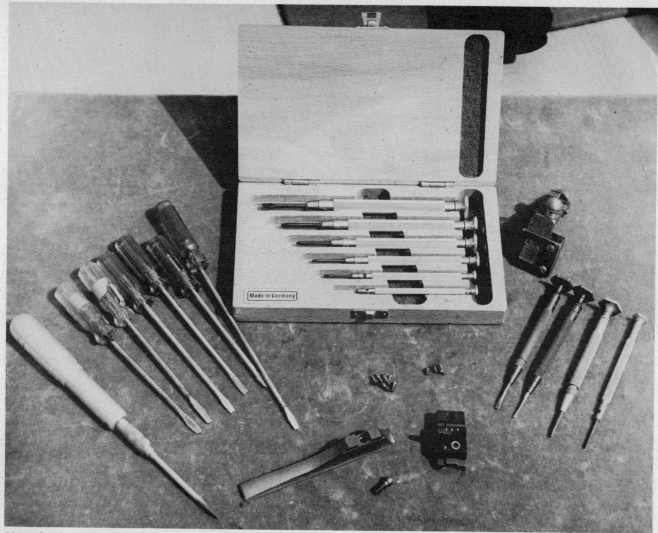

Musts for gun craftsmen are screw drivers of many sizes, shapes, including those for precision work.

Screw on left has thin, narrow slot common to the European arms. Other has standard American slot.

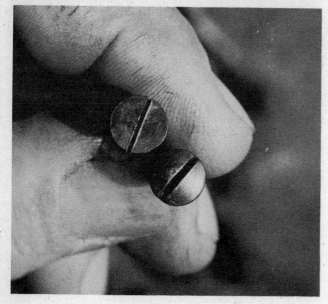

head completely off. If the head doesn't pop off its threaded shank, it is so burred it is unsightly, yet a coin will get these screws as tight as is necessary.

For most gunsmithing purposes, screwdrivers with so-called hollow ground bits serve best for all screw removal or tightening purposes. This type will stand up under greater stress and exerted strain than will those with long, tapered bits, providing they are shaped properly to fit the screw slot. Screwdrivers of this type available to gunsmithing supply houses usually are products of Grace Metal Products of Michigan or are imported from Germany. These are available in sets containing as many as twenty-five bits in various sizes and shapes with one handle that fits them all. The bits are available at about three for a dollar, while the interchangeable handle is priced at $3 or so, with one bit. Invaluable to the working gun hobbiest is a set of instrument screwdrivers, which comes in a hinged wooden box. These are ideal for working on sights of all types and for all scope work. This set is a product of Germany.

In spite of the number of screwdrivers one might have on hand, there always will be that screw that none will fit properly. For this, I keep on hand a supply of fairly inexpensive drivers of good quality steel that can be ground in a few minutes to an exact fit. This is a good method, when you consider that one four-bit screwdriver is fully capable of taking care of countless screws that would cost as much as a dollar apiece to replace. Many European screws cannot be replaced at any price.

A fine gun is well worth the extra effort.

Chapter 4

NO COST GUNSMITHING

**That "Worthless" Looking Barrel
May Be In Perfect Condition!**

DELEADING of a seemingly shot-out barrel has saved many a fine barrel from being discarded. The method discussed here, while a simple one, can be used as a last resource to remove stubborn lead that has resisted all other means of cleaning. This method consists of but three steps to possibly restore your barrel to a good, accurate shooter.

The first step is to dismantle the pistol or rifle, removing the barrel from the receiver if possible, making certain that all springs and hardened metal parts are removed from the barrel assembly, itself. The heating can be done on a common kitchen stove, using your wife's hot pads as hand protectors. The melting point of lead is quite low, so it is only necessary to heat the barrel to that point just when the lead reaches a molten state and can be "bounced" out of the barrel as illustrated. It may be necessary to bounce the barrel several times between heatings to determine when the lead has reached its melting point. At any rate, when molten lead splatters and powder residue appear on the "bouncing board," the job is done.

Now the bore may be brushed with a fine steel wool wrapped around a bristle or bronze brush to remove any residue still left in the bore. This deleading process can be accomplished without in any way harming the blue on the barrel. The trick is to move the barrel back and forth in a rotating manner to assure proper heat distribution over the entire surface.

RUST REMOVAL — Rust occurs only from long neglect and improper cleaning, or with the wrong use of greases and oils. Rust begins in the pores of the steel and works much like a cancerous growth; as long as it is there, it is working, regardless of how much oil and grease are applied. The only way to kill it is to remove it completely!

An oldtime preventative for rust was to heat the barrel to the temperature of boiling water, then cover it with a good copal varnish, letting it stand for one-half hour, then rubbing off the varnish with a soft cloth. The theory was that the varnish "sealed" the pores of the steel, locking rust out.

If your pistol or rifle has a film of rust covering it, but the blue is still visible, the best solution is to completely dismantle the gun, cleaning each part with dry, fine steel wool, rubbing until the rust disappears. Many persons believe that steel wool will remove the blue and case hardening left on the gun, but the use

of steel wool will only bring out a luster that the gun hasn't had since it left the factory. Steel wool, if used in one of the finer grades, will completely remove the rust in spite of the rust being over the blued surface, it will actually bring back that blue as it was before the rust began.

DISMANTLING — This operation, while simple, is one of the most abused practices in firearms care. For instance, a person obtains an arm with which he is not familiar; before this arm is disassembled it should be studied closely and its mechanical parts analyzed as to purpose and what part they might play in the correct procedure for dismantling.

For example, several European arms are manufactured without the use of screws to "hold the gun together." These arms were so precisely fit into a seemingly jig-saw pattern that sometimes hours of study are necessary to determine which part goes where, where to disengage this, to release that, all of which makes for a complex situation.

A good thing to remember about almost any modern firearm is that it is a precision instrument and was built to be dismantled easily. The use of a bench vise in the disassembly of arms is another abused point to bring out here. How many barrels of rifles and pistols have you seen that were deeply pocked with vise jaw marks? When using a bench vise to hold your gun, be sure to use either felt or cork jaws to protect both the finish and to prevent gouging of the metal. Vise jaws are of hardened steel and play havoc with the milder steel of gun barrels.

Gun screws are the next important feature to consider when taking your gun apart for cleaning or minor repairs. Be certain that the screw driver is a perfect fit in the screw slot; if it isn't, grind or stone it to fit. An ill-fitting screw driver can mean burred and ragged screw heads on your gun. It is good practice to buy as many as ten inexpensive screw drivers and grind them to fit the screws of your particular guns, then use them. This is covered in depth elsewhere.

Drive pins are used on some guns to retain such parts as triggers, springs and barrel stabilizers. These pins are, as a rule, a tight fit and must be removed with a pin punch of the correct size to prevent the peening over of the ends of these pins. When this happens, the pin is almost "welded" into the hole and to remove it sometimes means distortion of the pin hole and a marred gun results.

In dismantling a firearm, use extreme care, take your time, use the proper tools and above all, know what you are doing by studying the assembly of the gun itself. Do it correctly and it will come apart easily.

KILLING "DINGS" — It is disheartening to suddenly discover that your favorite gun has suffered a bad dent during a sudden slip or fall in the field. Such dents, in gun stocks, while usually minor, detract from the gun's appearance and removal can be accomplished easily by the following tried and true method.

First, rub the immediate area of the dent with fine steel wool to remove any varnish or other resinous substances present on the wood in the form of stock finish. A dent is nothing more than compressed wood, and the trick is to "decompress" this wood back into its original position on the gun stock with the use of steam and heat, the theory being that wood does expand while wet. It expands more so when that "wet" is in the form of hot steam. Steel wooling the area will allow the steam to penetrate the wood more readily.

After the light steel wooling of the dent area, lay the stock on a soft surface, dent-side up. Place a dampened kitchen towel (folded to one quarter-inch thickness) over the dent area only. With your wife's electric iron heated to "cotton" temperature, place the iron on the dent area and let steam rise for a few seconds, then lift the cloth to observe what progress the steam is making on the dent. If the dent has not risen to its proper level, apply the iron and steam

Should checkering become filled with stock finish, a toothbrush, dipped in turpentine, will renew pattern.

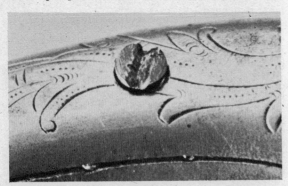

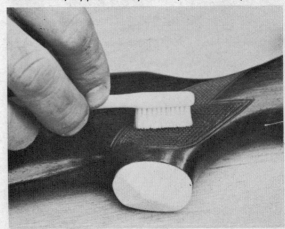

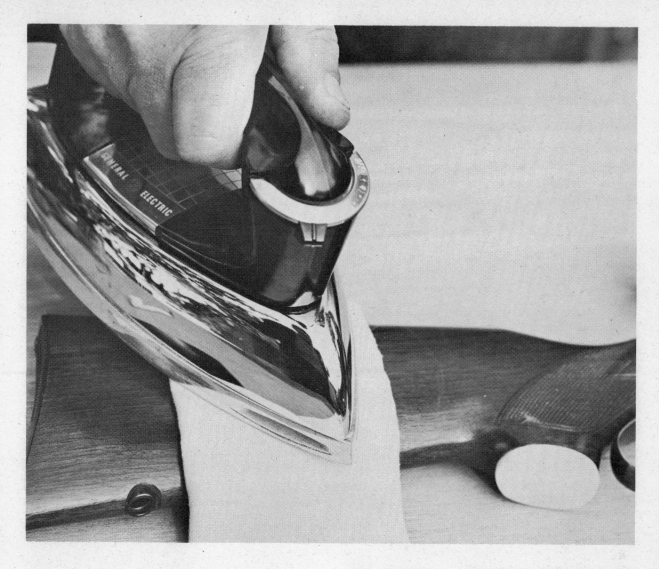

again. Repeat until the dent has "decompressed" itself to its proper level.

With the dent gone, the area will seem a little on the rough side. This is caused by action of the steam upon the wood fibers. Let the stock stand until completely dry, then sand lightly with 0000 granet sandpaper. If the dent area seems a trifle lighter in color than the rest of the stock, it must be touched up with the proper wood stain, using care not to overdo it.

With the dent raised, the spot lightly sanded and restained to proper color, you may apply any good commercial stock finish or linseed oil. If care and patience has been exercised, the dent in your favorite rifle has been removed, and is undetectable.

Chapter 5

where
the ACTION is!

Surprising though it may seem, one of the most important facets of gunology — one that can make the difference between hits and misses on both targets and game — is most neglected by gun writing bards. This is probably because there are few writers in the field who know what they are talking about, when it comes to the actual insides of a gun's mechanism. Be it rifle, shotgun, pistol or revolver, this important facet of gun craftsmanship is known as action honing.

There is one firearms writer who took a trip into the Canadian wilds after moose, caribou and bighorn sheep. He got his chance at a trophy head at about 150 yards, but his rifle refused to fire! He returned to the States empty handed simply because his knowledge of a rifle's action was so limited he couldn't detect the cause of a malfunction that could have been corrected in thirty seconds!

Honing a firearm's action, whether a rifle, pistol, shotgun or revolver, is done basically in the same manner. To some, the seeming mysteries of action honing sounds so complex that they never have dared tackle the job themselves.

True, action honing is one gun job that requires at least a reasonable knowledge of what makes any gun tick. One must be capable of dismantling a firearm, honing the action and properly oiling it, then reassembling the gun correctly without burring screw heads

Entire frame of revolver or receiver of shoulder arm is cleaned thoroughly before, after honing, then given light coat of oil before reassembly.

Equipment for honing includes abrasive hones, an Arkansas hard stone, correct oils and, for rifles and shotguns, emery flours like Crystolon 600B.

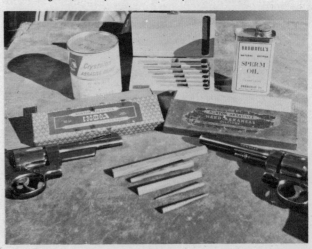

or bending delicate parts all out of shape.

In a nut shell, the honing of anything metallic means simply that, using the proper abrasives, stones, powdered emery, flour emery, rouges, carborundum and aloxite sticks, all minute roughness on the metal surfaces is removed; literally polished away. In the case of a firearm, the idea is to remove all microscopic roughness from the surfaces of all moving parts where friction is encountered with other moving parts. The type of materials needed depends upon the type of action being honed. Flour emery, such as **Crystolon 600 B,** supplied by Brownells of Montezuma, Iowa, generally is used for honing bolt action rifles and in arms having a sliding breech block riding on steel guide rails.

The first consideration for honing any firearm action is the tools and materials needed. Screwdrivers to correctly fit the screws of the particular gun being worked on are mandatory. Be certain that the bit of the screwdriver completely fills the slot in the screw in a snug fit. The entire action of the arm is disassembled and cleaned thoroughly. While various cleaning solvents will do this job adequately, I prefer lacquer thinner. This vaporizes quickly and will loosen stubborn dirt and grime on the working parts of the action.

When thoroughly cleaned, all parts of the action are laid out on a clean paper or shop rag.

Fine grit carborundum or aloxite sticks are available in shapes varying from square, triangular, half round, round and tapered rounds, which come to a point. A complete set of these should be on hand. Next, one should have a good hard Arkansas oil stone for putting a highly polished finish on such items as the sides of revolver hammers. The hard Arkansas is also invaluable for honing sears and trigger assemblies. Flour abrasives, such as optical emery and Crystolon 600B, are used by some for a quick hone job on pistols and revolvers, but the correct method is to use nothing but stones for honing handgun actions.

The next need for a first class honing job is the correct type of oil. I always have preferred to use nothing

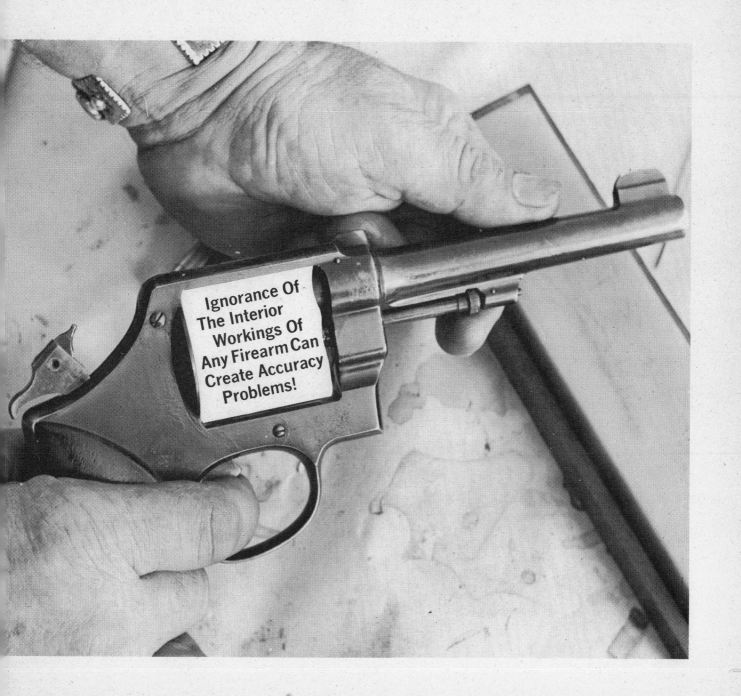

Ignorance Of The Interior Workings Of Any Firearm Can Create Accuracy Problems!

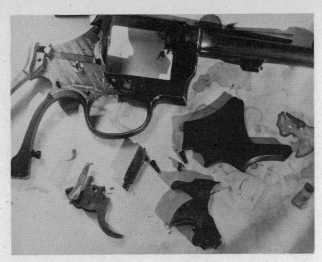

The parts of the gun's mechanism are laid out on a clean paper or cloth to await individual honing.

Removal of screws in side plates requires screw drivers of correct size, shape to prevent burring.

Abrasive hones of varying shapes are available; each is for part best matching its conformation.

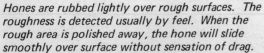

Hones are rubbed lightly over rough surfaces. The roughness is detected usually by feel. When the rough area is polished away, the hone will slide smoothly over surface without sensation of drag.

but **Pike** oil or pure sperm oil for all of my lubrication needs. Oils of this type will not become gummy or dry out after a few weeks or months. **Rig** gun grease is also an excellent gun lubricant and works well on abrasive oil stones.

In honing any firearm, cleanliness is a must. Should even a minute particle of hard-grained grit or dust be ground into the surface by the fine honing stone being used, then a scratch, will result. Keep the work as clean as possible during honing.

Honing a revolver action requires that, prior to complete disassembly, but with the side plate off the frame, the action is studied to determine what parts need to be honed. This examination may not be necessary for someone totally familiar with the gun being smoothed up, but it is a must for those doing the job for the first, second or even third time.

With the gun disassembled and all parts thoroughly cleaned, each part is honed as needed, is cleaned thoroughly again, is oiled, then laid aside temporarily. When all parts have received this treatment, they are

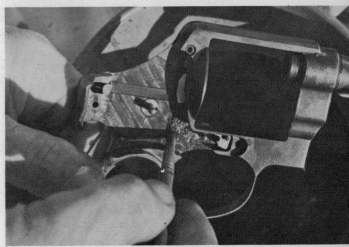

Gun is disassembled with care and each part then cleaned thoroughly, using brush to wash in solvent.

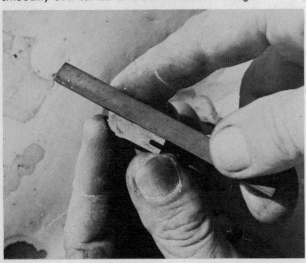

reassembled into the frame and tested for smoothness. If done correctly, the action should feel smoother and more crisp than before.

Remember that the whole theory behind honing is to remove completely any roughness from moving surfaces. While this roughness often is not visible to the naked eye, under a microscope it sometimes has the appearance of a rough mountain range in miniature! It is this rough surface on working parts that makes a

Well honed actions offer an increase in efficiency for target work and when put to use in game fields.

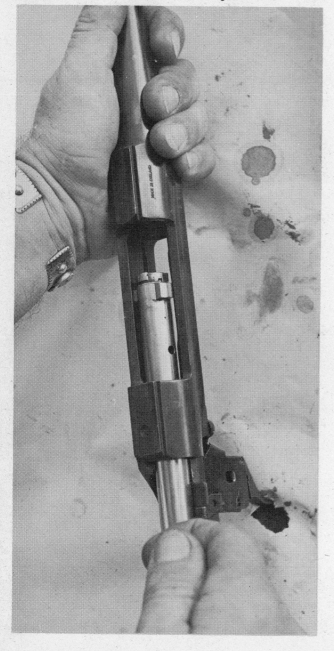

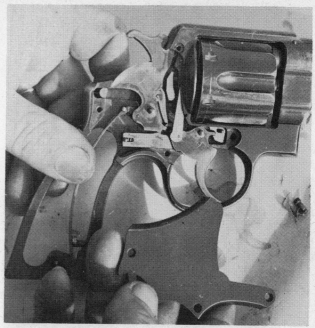

Regardless of the type of firearm, each part, after honing, should be cleaned again thoroughly, lightly oiled, then reassembled into the action of the gun.

pistol action feel as though it is lubricated with sand! Remove this minute roughness and you have a smooth gun.

In the case of bolt action rifles or a shotgun with a sliding breech block, each firearm will have certain characteristics to be corrected during honing, but basically they are the same. Take, for instance, a bolt action rifle that has a rough lift to the bolt handle. This means that there is rough metal on the guide rails, the outer surfaces of the bolt or on the camming surfaces of the bolt's interior.

I have found that a mixture of Crystolon B and sperm oil, mixed into a thin paste, works quite well in giving the bolt a satiny smooth pull. The surfaces of the bolt are painted with the mixture, then the bolt is worked in and out of the receiver about twenty or thirty strokes, depending upon how much roughness is present. Then it is cleaned thoroughly, buffed and oiled, again tested for smoothness. If it is found that stubborn roughness is still present, repeat the operation. A small amount of the mixture painted on the inner parts of the bolt has a tendency to further increase the smoothness of operation. The same basic principle is used in smoothing up breech blocks in shotguns.

Trigger mechanisms of all sporting firearms are treated the same in honing. The entire job is done with abrasive hones or stones. However, there is one class of firearms that will not satisfactorily accept tuning-up or honing by even the expert in this phase of gunsmithing. Arms in this classification include many of the extremely cheap modern foreign revolvers and pistols. For the most part, such guns are constructed of inferior materials and the finish is so rough that, by the time they are correctly honed and all roughness removed, there isn't much left of the gun! There are a few American-made revolvers which fall into this same classification. No amount of honing will smooth them up to any extent.

If correctly done, a honing job on any quality firearm should increase its efficiency considerably, both for target work and in the game fields.

STEP BY STEP

STEP ONE:

Completely dismantle the action of the gun to be honed, laying the parts and screws preferably on a clean white cloth. (This prevents them from sliding or rolling off the bench.) All parts should be cleaned of grease and gum in a good cleaning solvent; if lacquer thinner is available, this makes an excellent cleaner and evaporates almost immediately, leaving the parts clean and dry.

With all of the dismantled parts and your tools arranged before you as illustrated here, you now are ready to begin the actual honing.

The tools necessary for the job are simple and easily acquired, consisting of several hones in varying sizes and shapes as seen in the accompanying photos; several good screw drivers that fit exactly the screws of the gun to be worked over; a can of Pike oil, and a great deal of care and patience.

STEP TWO:

Starting with the hammer, run your fingers along all edges lightly. If the edges feel sharp and cutting, they need honing. A honed edge will feel smooth and will not have this jagged, cutting feel against your flesh.

Select the hone most suited to the surface to be

worked on, one that will follow the contour of the metal. By rubbing at first lightly, slowly applying more pressure, you will actually be able to feel the hone removing the coarse, jagged edges.

Care must be taken to remove only the burrs; when the hone slides smoothly and evenly across the edge and it feels finger-smooth, the honing is completed.

You must continue this procedure on all working and bearing surfaces, being extremely careful to remove only the knife-like edges—nothing more. (Removing too much metal can easily throw your gun out of smooth working adjustment!)

It should be pointed out that no files of any type or coarse abrasive stones ever should be used in this honing of a gun's action unless you are looking for a valid excuse to buy a new gun. Only the finest grit hones and stones are utilized. Polishing — more than cutting — is the secret to a sweetly tuned gun.

STEP THREE:

When all parts have been stoned, wash them again in a clean solvent and dry thoroughly. Apply a thin coat of good gun grease to all parts, as they are re-assembled into the frame of the firearm.

If care and patience have been exercised in your honing project, you no doubt will find that the piece will operate a great deal more smoothly than before.

With a little practice, this entire operation should take no more than half an hour and you can rest assured the time spent will be many times repaid with bullets in the black!

THERE are several trains of thought regarding the altering of an otherwise fine, serviceable revolver into a blank-shooting fast draw gun. Being entirely open minded about this situation and still not wishing to see any good revolver deliberately butchered to the point that it never again can be used as a serviceable sidearm, let us take a middle-of-the-road stand and attempt to handle a somewhat delicate situation in such a way that it will be acceptable to all concerned.

The typical fast draw guns used in blank-popping contests against time usually are altered so drastically that most are unsafe for firing live ammunition. These alterations usually consist of bending the hammer spur upward, then welding on an extension to form the so-called "fanning" type of

spur. The front sight, in most cases, is ground entirely from the gun's barrel to reduce holster friction, while the main spring is ground to about half its original thickness. The trigger and bolt spring is replaced usually with one made from piano wire.

In some cases, a trigger shoe either is welded or screwed onto the trigger to increase its width and the front half of the trigger guard is ground away to facilitate fast entry of the trigger finger.

In addition to these alterations, the revolver is gone over completely to remove all sharp edges, especially on the top of the hammer face where there is the possibility of suffering a badly gashed hand during some hot and heavy fanning. Each individual will make other alterations to suit his particular style. Special grips and altering of the gun's timing mechanism are but two of the changes made to turn a bullet shooting gun into one solely for popping primers in fast draw.

But it is not necesary to completely ruin a good gun to alter it for fast draw purposes. Such ruin can be alleviated by simply obtaining a few spare parts such as an extra hammer, an extra main spring and any other parts that are to be altered by grinding or otherwise changing their shape or strength. These extra parts are the ones that will be used in turning that Colt into a race horse while the original parts from the gun are laid aside for future use in returning the gun to its original condition.

The Colt SAA Revolver is the gun that we will be dealing with in this article and all alterations will pertain to the parts used in this particular revolver. We will assume that the Colt is in reasonably good shape and that all original parts are intact and in perfect condition. We also have at hand our extra parts that we have obtained solely for the purpose of alterations.

WITH THE REVOLVER DISMANTLED, the frame of the gun then is completely cleaned of all grease and dirt, as are all the original parts that are to be saved for later use.

The first major alteration is on the extra hammer. This hammer is clamped into a bench vise, with the base of the hammer between the vise jaws and shielded by either sheet copper or brass to protect it from being marred. This, too, will prevent the temper from being withdrawn from the vital hardened surfaces of the sear area of the hammer (the three small notches at the base of the hammer). A welding torch then is played over the area of the hammer spur until it is cherry red color, at which moment the spur is bent to an almost perpendicular position.

A HAMMER EXTENSION consisting of a small piece of mild steel should be placed on top of the hammer spur and firmly welded into place. This extension later will be filed down to the proper proportions of the "fanner" type of hammer spur.

The hammer now is allowed to cool in the vise to the point that it can be removed with the fingers and placed in water. Do not douse the hammer with water while it is very hot as this may harden it to a degree that it cannot be filed.

Again clamp it into the vise and shape the extension with a combination of rat-tail and mill files and, finishing it with a half round Swiss needle file, emery cloth, and finally buffing it on a cloth wheel to a high luster.

During the shaping and welding process, one should bear in mind the limitations in building up the height of the hammer extension. National Fast Draw Association rules call for a hammer being no higher than one-half inch above the gun's top strap (that bridge of metal in the gun's frame that crosses the cylinder). A simple gauge will simplify this measurement greatly.

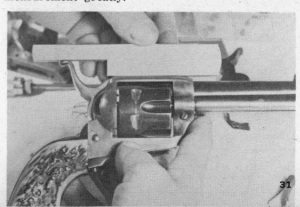

Extremes in altering Colt's Single Action for fast draw are reflected in these three specimens. Note the variations in hammers, triggers and even the absence of a front sight on one gun.

With the hammer spur finished to our satisfaction, we will next thin down our spare main spring to the proper tension for use in the finished fast draw gun. A grinder or disc sander may be used, but great care must be taken to grind the spring evenly over its entire working length. This does not include the lower portion of the spring where the screw holds it to the gun's grip strap. Do not grind here at all.

Grind the spring with a sweeping motion of the hands, so that it is evenly reduced in thickness; also, douse it in water after every two or three sweeps to prevent the spring from over-heating and losing its temper. With the spring ground to approximately one half its original thickness, it then is buffed to a high luster and all weakening scratches removed.

THE TRIGGER AND BOLT SPRING of an original gun is a flat, two-pronged affair which may be thinned by grinding as was the main spring.

However, most seasoned veterans of fast draw prefer to have this spring made from a short piece of spring or piano wire of about .045 thickness because of its durability. This trigger and bolt spring is made easily in only a few minutes, using a pair of spring bending or needle nose pliers. Care should be taken to make this spring to the exact proportions to assure proper contact on both the trigger step and on the back of the cylinder locking bolt.

The three major operations in turning a revolver into a fast draw gun have been covered: The hammer alteration, grinding down of the main spring and manufacturing a new trigger and bolt spring from spring or piano wire. It is best to now assemble the gun after carefully honing all working parts of the action to assure silky smooth operation upon completion.

With the gun completely assembled, work the action to test the tension of the ground down main spring. If it is still too heavy, remove it and repeat the grinding operation, testing it in the gun periodically to assure that you do not remove too much metal. This main spring should have a tension strong enough to detonate a primer properly — and no more.

There are various means of turning a gun into a first class fast draw revolver. Each variation serves a purpose for the individual developing it. Too, each individual will want various other changes to meet with his particular requirements. Some gunmen like to alter the timing of the gun slightly so that the locking bolt falls prematurely. Others will alter the hand spring, making it extremely light, and still others will alter the hand, itself, to the point that in normal cocking, the gun will not properly function. These alterations are necessary for fanning a revolver. The hammer is literally slapped to the rear in less than a twinkling of the eye, so the individual alterations of the cylinder locking bolt, hand and other components are certainly necessary for this type of gun handling.

With your Colt Single Action Army Revolver altered into a truly fast draw gun as we have done here, you are ready for competition.

THE ALTERING OF THE RUGER Single Six and the Black Hawk models is accomplished in much the same manner as is the Colt SAA but with the following exceptions:

The springs of the Ruger are of the coil type instead of the flat type found in the Colt. For this reason, there are variations in the spring lightening process. It stands to reason that coil springs cannot be ground down in thickness to ease their tensile strength to that necessary in a fast draw type of revolver.

The most widely accepted manner of reducing the strength of Ruger coil springs is to shorten them in length. This process is a touchy one and must be handled with the greatest care lest the springs be cut so short that they render the gun totally inoperative. This is accomplished by cutting off very short lengths — not over one coil at a time — from the spring, then reinstalling it into the pistol and testing it. You will know by "feel" when the spring has been cut to the proper length.

As in the Colt SAA, all internal parts of the Ruger should be honed with a hard Arkansas oil stone to a satiny smoothness if maximum speed is to be expected from the finished gun. A great deal of care and no little amount of patience are prime requisites in the chore of turning a proposed fast draw gun into one with a silky smooth and lightning fast action.

Chapter 6

Build Your Own Checkering Cradle

For An Investment Of A Few Dollars You Can Make Life A Lot Easier Around Your Gun Shop

Rotating bolt is locked rigidly into place in the large nut mounted on socket. This allows the socket to rotate as the lever is turned. The socket is fashioned of pine.

The checkering cradle used in checkering gunstocks is a specialized tool of the gunsmithing trade. It is a piece of shop equipment usually constructed by the individual gun craftsman to his own specifications meeting his particular needs, be he a professional or a gun-building hobbiest.

To describe the purpose of a checkering cradle, it is a relatively simple piece of gunshop equipment designed so that a gunstock can be mounted in it for checkering. The stock is mounted between screw-adjusted centers, and by merely turning one of these screws, the stock may be rotated at will so that the area to be checkered always will be convenient for the gunsmith's work.

The cradle must be constructed so that it will accept gunstocks of all sizes and lengths between its centers. It must have locking features to assure that the stock will remain rigid between the centers when a particular area of the stock is being worked upon. It may be constructed in such a manner that it may be clamped in a bench vise or mounted permanently on a stand of either metal or hardwood. If shop space is limited, then the vise mounted version is the most desirable. The cradle built to illustrate this article is of that type.

A good, durable checkering cradle may be built for about $3 total cash outlay.

Needed materials are: A 2 x 4 of hardwood such as oak, birch, ash or hard fir measuring fifty-four inches in length; two pieces of the same measuring seven inches in length to be used for head and tail stocks. Hardware needed: six ½-inch machine nuts; one ½ x 2½-inch machine bolt: two ½ x 4½-inch machine bolts, four one-half-inch steel washers, two aluminum or steel plates measuring an eighth inch in thickness by 3½ x 4½ inches, and finally, two pieces of half-inch hardwood doweling, each four inches in length.

The main beam — or bed — of the cradle is made from the fifty-four-inch 2 x 4. A slot is milled into this beam using a half-inch router chucked in a drill press. It is into this slot that the headstock locking bolt will slide, allowing full longitudinal adjustment of the headstock. This slot is milled exactly one and a quarter inches from the bottom-side of the beam to center and should extend to within fifteen inches of the stationary tail-stock. This will allow even the shortest carbine or shotgun stocks to be centered between the two stocks.

With the longitudinal adjustment slot milled into the bed, we now shape and assemble both the head and tail stocks. The shape of these stocks may vary according to

Cost of the basic materials is minor, but the finished product can save any gunsmith many hours of hard labor.

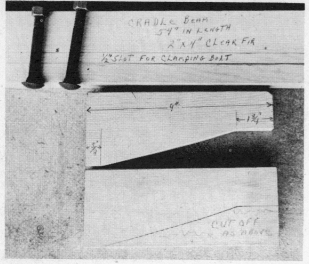

The slot to accept the sliding bolt of the head stock may be milled with half-inch router bit on a drill press.

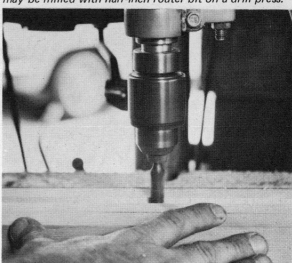

Easily constructed, the head stock consists of socket for holding the butt, the locking screw, the rotating screw with lock nut and the upright with the aluminum plates screwed into place. Simple, it can save one work.

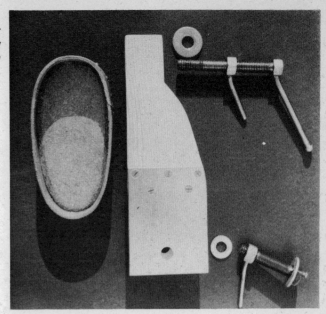

Steel nuts are inlaid into the facing surfaces of the head and tail stocks to prevent undue wear as pressure is applied to the stock centered between these points.

Tail stock is adjustable for length and forearm socket may be lined with leather or rubber to protect finish.

Aluminum plates are attached to each side of head stock, allowing it to slide freely along main beam of the cradle.

The tail stock, designed to hold the forend of the rifle or shotgun stock, should have a cup-shaped insert lined with leather. This is meant to protect the stock wood.

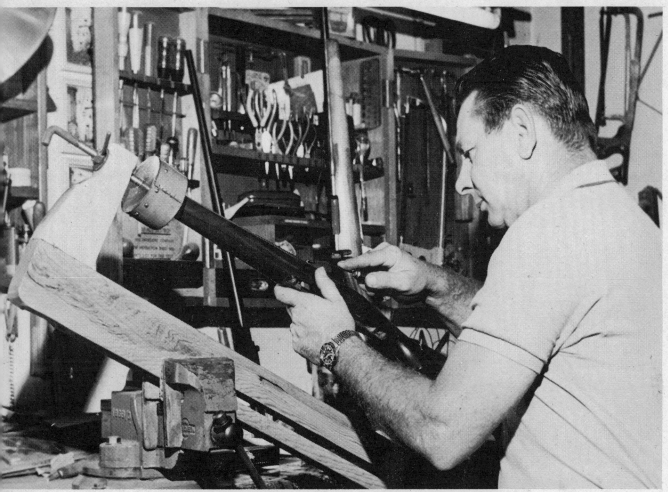

When completed, the new checkering cradle may be mounted in bench vise or special stand can be constructed for it.

each builder's taste, but contour should follow quite closely those shown in the photos accompanying this article. A half-inch hole is drilled into each stock exactly one inch from the top. The square machine nuts then are inlaid into each stock flush with the surface, then disc sanded smooth.

The tail-stock is doweled and glued to the end of the bed, making certain that this union is strong enough to accept extreme pressures when in use. If in doubt, a steel angle-iron may be screwed into place to prevent possible breakage of this joint.

The two slide plates then are screwed onto the head-stock, filed and sanded smooth on the inside. This will assure that they will slide smoothly over the cradle bed when adjustments are made. These plates are then drilled with a half-inch drill to accept the ½ x 2½-inch machine bolt mentioned earlier.

Be especially careful during the drilling of these holes to assure that they will be in perfect alignment with the milled slot in the cradle bed, thus allowing the headstock to slide freely up and down the bed with the bolt in place. This bolt will act as the headstock lock when the nut is in place and tightened.

The head and tail-stock centers consist of the two half-inch machine bolts four and a half inches in length. Used in this article were half-inch bolts with thirteen threads to the inch (½ x 13 machine bolts). This allows faster adjustments than would be possible with bolts having finer threads.

As it is the custom for a gunstock to be completely finished before it is checkered, it is best to forget about pointed centers as were used some years ago and make, instead, socket-type holders for the butt and forend of the stock. These sockets are made over-sized to assure that all stocks, regardless of size or shape, may be held in the cradle. The sockets are cut from ordinary hardwood and a slip-proof wall of saddle leather is glued and tacked to the outer edge of the socket. The holes are drilled to accept the center bolts and finally, a half-inch of firm-textured foam rubber is cut to shape and inserted into each socket to protect the gunstock and to prevent it from slipping while being worked with the checkering tools.

The checkering cradle, when finished, should have great versatility of movement. However, all rotating of the gunstock should be done from the headstock alone. The tail-stock socket should be designed so that it will rotate freely as the gunstock is turned from the opposite end.

The lock nuts used on the cradle may be drilled and a short piece of steel rod silver-soldered into place. This eliminates the necessity of using a wrench each time these nuts are loosened or tightened.

The bed of the cradle, after its final finish of varnish or lacquer, should be well waxed with a good paste wax to assure that the headstock will slide smoothly during adjustments. With a little practice in its use, a checkering cradle could become one of the handiest tools in your shop. It may be used for applying the final finishes to the stock, for sanding and even for final inletting chores.

GET FRESH WITH YOUR STOCK

**Freshing Out Old Checkering
Can Give That
Shoulder Arm New Beauty
And A Better Feel!**

CHECKERING on rifle or shotgun stocks and pistol grips is certain to become dull and smooth with any amount of use under hunting conditions. Too, the grooves forming the minute diamonds in checkering often become filled with a variety of stock oils, waxes and natural oils and grimes from the shooter's own hands. When this happens, the checkering becomes ineffectual for its intended purpose—that of providing a positive gripping surface —which is particularly important in handling and shooting the majority of today's modern high-powered rifles.

So what can be done to restore this checkering to its original sharp condition?

Chapter 7

First: The tools necessary for recutting checkering that has lost its feel are few and inexpensive. However, in performing this restorative measure, it is imperative that the craftsman undertaking the job have a world of patience and the ability to follow a straight line with a checkering tool. Good eyesight is also a must in performing this intricate retracing job with the use of tiny file-like cutters.

Needed for the job are four basic tools which might include one Dem-Bart F-1 checkering tool, one Dem-Bart Special S-1 tool, a stiff-bristled tooth-

Needs for recutting old checkering are few, inexpensive. Denatured alcohol is used for washing stubborn grime and dirt from the old checkering prior to start of recutting.

brush and a small three-cornered Swiss needle file. The file should be slightly bent at the tip for getting into the tight corners. Also needed is a small bottle of denatured alcohol and a pad of extra-fine steel wool.

For best results and ease of handling, the barrel and receiver section of the firearm should be removed from the stock. It sometimes is desirable, due to bad dings and scratches, to completely refinish the stock before attempting to re-cut the worn checkering. Dents in the stock may be raised by steaming with a damp cloth and your wife's electric iron. Most scratches probably are not as deep as they appear and may be removed with a

little diligent sanding with first a medium-coarse garnet sandpaper, then finishing with 600 grit paper.

Following the sanding operation—during which the checkered areas should be avoided—the stock is given several coatings of any one of several known good stock finishes, then set away in a dust free area to thoroughly dry. About twenty-four hours is usually sufficient.

During the stock refinishing operation, and immediately prior to final sanding, the worn checkered areas should be scrubbed briskly with a toothbrush dipped repeatedly in alcohol. This will loosen and remove the grime, oils and waxes that have accumulated in the fine cuts and will result in a much nicer appearing job when the checkering is freshed-out.

To eliminate this brushing often will result in

Cutting heads of Dem-Bart checkering tools are precisely made. They are kept clean by constant brushing, and are capable of creating real artistry, if utilized correctly.

dark streaks appearing in the recut checkering. These streaks are nothing more than grime and residue, so for a perfect job, be sure that these are removed before starting to recut the old checkering.

Assuming that the stock either has been refinished, or at least cleaned up, it is ready for re-checkering. It is placed in the padded jaws of a bench vise. Better yet, if you built a checkering cradle by following my instructions you are all set to begin the actual job of making that old, worn checkering

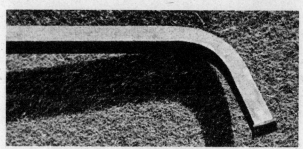

The C-1 Dem-Bart tool is designed for close work in tight corners, as in the points of small diamond shaped cuts.

look and feel just like new.

With the stock firmly clamped between the centers of the checkering cradle or in a bench vise, starting at the outermost edge of the worn design, the F-1 tool is placed into the groove of the checkering and carefully worked back and forth the full length of the groove until it is recut evenly. This is repeated line after line until all of the grooves paralleling the starting point are identically recut. Now move your F-1 tool over to the uncut lines or grooves, which cross the ones you have just finished. Recut these lines in the same manner and to

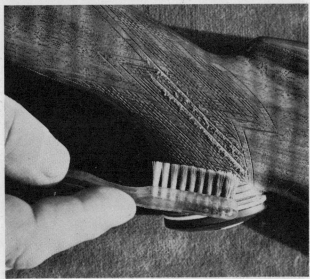

Constant brushing away of wood dust assures more precise work, allowing a clear vision of the work at all times.

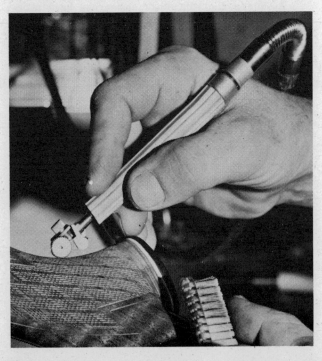

the same depth until perfect, sharp-pointed diamonds are formed over the entire surface of the checkered design.

It is best not to attempt to run the tool too closely to the outside border of the design which may result in unsightly over-runs. For this purpose the Dem-Bart Special S-1 tool was designed with a much shorter head for getting into close places where it is not practical to use the F-1. The S-1 is particularly valuable when complicated designs in checkering are encountered and is the only such tool manufactured today for this particular type of close work.

When the old checkering has been completely recut and precisely pointed-up, the F-1 tool again is taken in hand and the entire design is border-cut. During this operation, a single-line border is created and any slight overruns should disappear under the fine cutting of the tool. This single-line border should be cut only slightly deeper than those used in the actual checkering to assure an attractive and professional looking job when finished.

With the old checkering recut and outlined so

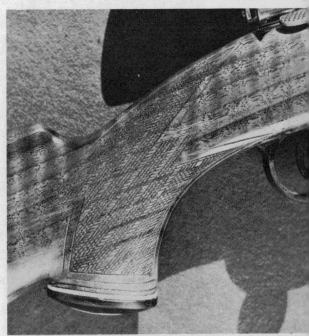

Prior to recutting, the old checkering has a lifeless, dull appearance and provides poor surface for holding.

Dem-Bart electric checkering tool greatly speeds any checkering job. It can be mastered in a short time.

After recutting, the worn checkering takes on the appearance of being new. Brushing with lemon oil completes job.

that it looks—and feels—like new, the pad of steel wool then is rubbed briskly over the checkered surface. It is surprising how this will polish the diamonds of the checkering and remove any minute wood fuzz. During the actual checkering, the work must be constantly brushed clean with the toothbrush. This not only makes the work easier but assures a finer job.

Should you own an electric checkering machine, this job will be duck soup for you and can be per-

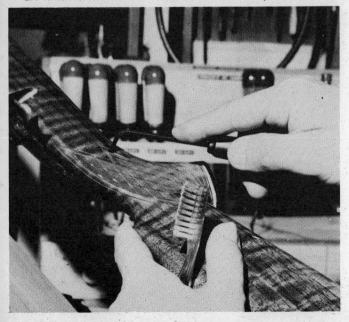

When the recutting is partially completed, the points are finished with the C-1 tool manufactured by Dem-Bart.

formed in an hour or less. Until recently, all of my checkering jobs have been done strictly by hand. However, that bag-toting bearded gentleman who visits us every December was kind enough to leave a spanking new Dem-Bart electric checkering machine in my sock. Whereas it once took me hours to completely checker one stock, I now can do five in the same amount of time and do a better job!

But getting back to the job at hand, there is nothing more disturbing than to throw a rifle or shotgun to my shoulder and discover that the checkering on the pistolgrip and forearm are as slick as a greased hog! When I run into this situation, and the gun belongs to me, I waste no time in re-cutting the checkering, as outlined here.

Time was when the finer checkering—from 22 to 32 lines per inch—was relegated to shotguns only, but nowadays there seems to be a trend to putting this type of checkering on hunting rifles. It does give a little more attractive appearance to the stock, but you can't hold onto it!

To my way of thinking, checkering is put on a rifle, first, to provide a good gripping surface, and second, for appearance. For this reason, I strongly prefer checkering on a rifle that is no coarser than eighteen lines per inch nor finer than twenty lines per inch. It is possible to recut old checkering—should it be extremely fine—to either eighteen or twenty lpi by following the instructions outlined here but by substituting the F-1 tool for a set of three tools designated as #2, #3 and #4 in the lpi desired. This amounts to doing a complete re-checkering job, with the old, worn checkering providing the master lines for you to follow.

When the chore of freshing out the old checkering has been completed, it is given a light coating of either boiled linseed oil or lemon oil. Should linseed oil be used, wipe away all of the excess not absorbed by the wood. To leave excess oil on the checkering would defeat your purpose, as it would harden and again fill up the checkering cuts.

I have made it a practice, after coating the checkered section with linseed oil, to thoroughly brush it with a toothbrush, thus removing any excess oil that may remain in the bottoms of the cuts. This applies to new checkering as well as to checkering that has been re-cut.

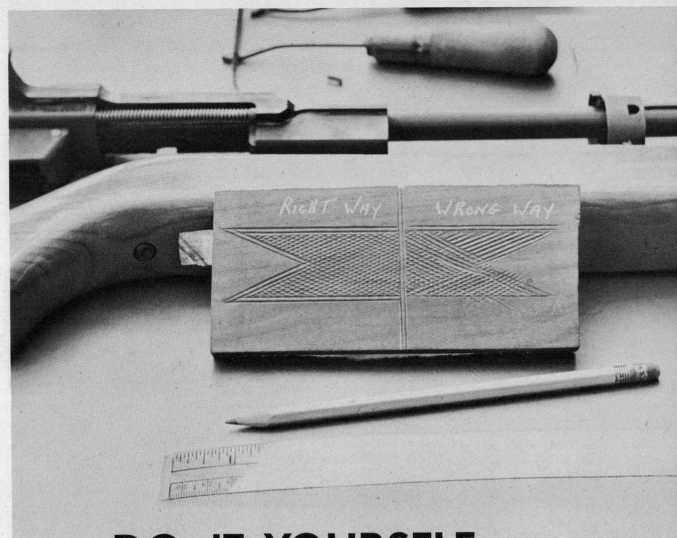

DO-IT-YOURSELF CHECKERING

The checkering of gun stocks and pistol grips is an art of the gunmakers' trade and never should be attempted by the amateur without first doing considerable practicing on blank pieces of wood similar in density to those of most stocks.

The beginner first should obtain a flat, smooth piece of seasoned walnut and on this wood learn the art of handling a checkering tool so that it will perform the job properly.

After considerable practice in handling the few tools necessary for a good checkering job, the amateur then may proceed in laying out a simple design — still using a practice piece of wood — then completely checkering this design and edging it into a finished product.

While this practice on a piece of blank wood may seem like wasted time, it will pay off when the actual gunstock is checkered and will result in a more profes-

sional looking job. The mistakes made on the blank piece of walnut during the practice-checkering session should be kept in mind when the actual job is started on your rifle stock or pistol grips.

Tools needed for checkering may vary with the individual's taste. Some may want to obtain a set of the fine Swedish-made professional checkering tools which are available only from a few sources in this country. Others may decide to use the type of tools available at their local gunshop. It is with this latter notion that the highly efficient line of Dem-Bart checkering tools will be utilized in this article. They are conveniently available, are inexpensive, yet will produce a professional looking job, if properly used.

Checkering requires a great deal of patience and the ability to concentrate upon your work. If your patience is limited, your ability to concentrate poor and you are

Chapter 8

Patience, Concentration and Good Eyesight Are Required

unwilling to undertake a job that will bring no little amount of sweat to your brow, then read no further!

We will assume that you possess the necessary requisites outlined above and want to enhance the beauty and value of one or more of your favorite guns; that you are eager to learn just how this may be accomplished by an amateur. Before any facet of the gunsmithing trade can be undertaken, tools for that particular job must be given first consideration. Without the proper tools, the job is best left undone.

There are many makes and types of checkering tools available on the market; some are excellent, some are good and others aren't worth carrying home. Not to confuse the man doing his first checkering job, I will keep the tools required to a minimum and will utilize only those readily available at no great cost.

The checkering cradle, used by professional gunsmiths and stockmakers, is a tool which greatly simpli-

Practicing on a walnut block is a prerequisite to actual checkering of a gun stock. Once the feel of the tool has been mastered by the craftsman, quality work is possible.

5. A silver-lead blueprint pencil for stock marking.
6. One soft bristled brush for cleaning out checkering.
7. Several sheets of ordinary paper for pre-drawing of checkering designs.

With tools assembled, we proceed to the actual laying out of the checkering design on the gun stock preparatory to the actual checkering. This is best accomplished if the stock is completely removed from the gun's

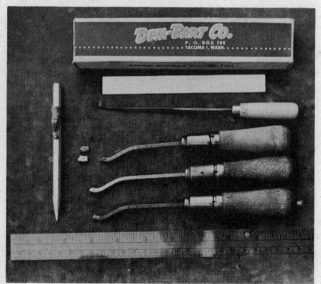

For the beginner at checkering, the basic tools should include three professional checkering cutters; a bent Swiss needle file; clear plastic ruler; white lead pencil.

fies checkering, but this device would require prolonged explanation as to its construction and use. For this reason, we will utilize the common bench vise instead. The basic tools required by the beginner in checkering must consist of:

1. One set of checkering tools, including left and right edgers and beading tools.
2. One three-sided Swiss needle file bent as shown in illustration.
3. A bench vise equipped with either cork or felt protective jaws for holding the gun stock.
4. A flexible, transparent twelve-inch ruler for laying out checkering designs on stock.

Various configurations of the cutting heads are apparent. Each is designed for a specific purpose explained in text.

action. The stock then is placed in the cork or felt-lined jaws of the bench vise and determining of the checkering design begins. Bear in mind that all designs should be in harmony with the general contour of the stock itself. For example, a diamond-shaped design when placed on an extreme curved surface such as the pistol grip of a rifle will appear to be nothing more than a chopped off square from a side view. Again, be particular about your design and its relationship to the part of the stock on which it is to be applied.

When you have completed your experiments with checkering designs, it is time to transfer them to the stock. This is accomplished with the flexible ruler and the blueprint pencil. Only one section of the stock is worked on a time. With the outline of the design clearly penciled onto the stock, use the bent three-cornered needle file to lightly cut the guide lines. These guide lines are utilized solely as slots in which the checkering border tool will be guided for the final finishing of the checkering job. These lines mean stop for the checkering tools when cutting the actual checkering within them. Do not overrun these lines or a great deal of clean-up work will be necessary when the checkering is finished and final bordering of the design is done.

The checkering tools are so designed that, if properly used, they will cut perfect little diamonds, in perfect alignment, providing that the workman has used the tool properly and has used good sense in his lay-out design. Too, the cross-cut, which actually forms the diamonds when the cutter is passed across other lines at a fifteen-degree angle, must be made carefully. Care should be taken to make certain that cutters are kept clean. This assures that none of the tiny diamonds are chipped out due to clogged checkering tools.

The professional method of outling a purposed checkering design is to completely cut outline with a veining chisel. However, work of this type should be limited to the more advanced craftsman.

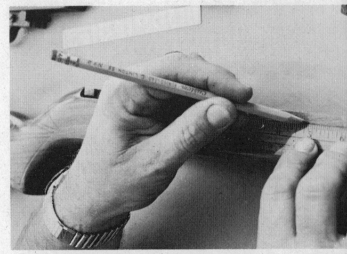

The laying-out of the checkering design is accomplished with clear plastic ruler and templates principally designed by the individual.

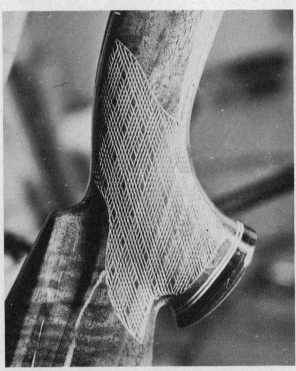

Skip-line checkering is possible for the advanced novice but requires additional specialized tools.

Novel effect can be gained by differing the space between lines

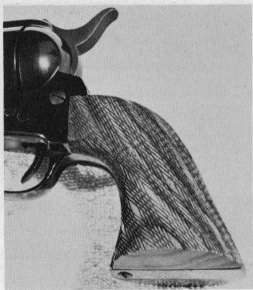

Some factory checkering now is being done with a roll-on die. It is more durable than standard checkering, some say, due to inverted diamond design, but less attractive.

The author's tool lay-out for checkering consists of a Dem-Bart Electric tool plus hand cutters in various sizes, from 18 lines per inch to 28 lines per inch. Various beaders and edger sizes are included.

The stock of this Savage 99 was home-checkered to give it a more custom appearance. The pistol grip was done at factory, cleaned up, then detailed for appearance's sake.

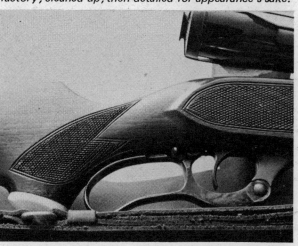

A well layed out design will produce a matting of hundreds of tiny diamonds upon the surface. This can be accomplished only if three things are kept in mind: First, the angle of cross-cut must be compatible with those that they cross in order to form perfect diamonds. Second, checkering tools (cutters) must be kept clean by brushing often with either a suede brush or an old toothbrush. Third, the checkering, itself, must be kept free from wood dust and cuttings by brushing often with an old toothbrush. If these three requisites are followed, a beautiful, professional appearing job will result.

There is no limit to the checkering designs that may be created by the individual for application to gun stocks, but simple, attractive ones should be utilized when starting, and these should first be drawn to actual size on paper before being transferred to the stock.

The cutting heads are used with a short, gentle stroke on the first cutting, then this stroke is lengthened as the cut is deepened.

With each stroke of the cutters, gentleness of touch is absolutely necessary. Otherwise the small diamonds being formed under the cutter will be torn out and a sloppy job will result — if not a ruined gun stock!

When the final bordering cut is finished and the corners all are squared up by using the needle file, the checkering then is given a careful brushing to rid it of wood dust and cuttings. A mild stock dressing then is applied to the raw wood. Never use a thick stock dressing, as this has a tendency to fill the slight cuts forming the diamonds, rendering the checkering ineffectual for providing a better holding area on the gun's stock.

Checkering tools come in sizes of so many lines to the inch. The fewer lines to the inch, the larger the diamonds. Therefore it has long ago been established that the coarser checkerings, or fewer lines such as fourteen through eighteen lines to the inch, are best applicable to sporting rifles, while twenty to as fine as twenty-eight lines to the inch are best applied to shotguns.

The tools utilized in this article are manufactured by Dem-Bart Company of Tacoma, Washington, and are available in most gunshops in a variety of sizes. The cutting heads may be bought separately and pin-attached to the handles.

Stock on left has steel plate inserted in mortise prior to inletting. Stock at right has the plate inletted, sealed with glass bedding compound.

HERE'S AN EASY CURE FOR YOUR SICK SHOOTING STICK

A BEDTIME STORY

Let's say that you have spent many hours over a hot workbench busily restocking either a military surplus or commercial rifle action with a new sporter-type stock that cost you good loot.

You have completed your restocking job, have even gone to the trouble of adding some inlays and checkering just to dress it up a bit. Now, on the range, you find that it does not shoot worth a hoot. Each shot is literally sprayed onto the target as though from the bore of a shotgun shooting double O buckshot! Your groups are that loose, no matter how carefully you hold and squeeze each shot. Nine chances out of ten, your rifle is suffering from beddingitis.

Countless times I have had occasion to note rifles so poorly bedded that they were as erratic as a feather in a windstorm. The amount of hard work expended in restocking these rifles by the owners, usually was apparent in the many extras that they had so painstakenly added, such as inlays, and it was beyond

Chapter 9

Barrel channel of the stock is relieved to allow full clearance of the barrel, using sharp chisel or a rasp.

their comprehension as to why this labor of love wouldn't shoot at least a reasonable group. They had overlooked that most important factor that makes the difference between a rifle that consistently shoots tight groups and one that has all of the qualities of a spray gun: Bedding.

So that the amateur gunstocker might better understand what is meant by "proper bedding" of a rifle barrel and receiver into a new stock, I will attempt to explain this phase of the gunmaker's art in brief.

Let's assume that you have purchased a new semi-inletted sporter stock that you intend to use on your barreled action. The term, "semi-inletted," means that this stock was turned on a stockmaking lathe or pantograph machine to fairly close tolerances. However, this stock is far from being finished simply by sanding and varnishing the exterior and bolting the action into the ill-fitting recesses in the stock. The correct finishing of the stock requires that the gunstocker, with a variety of chisels, files and stocker's gouges, finish-fit this particular stock to his particular rifle action until everything fits precisely.

The most important phase of finishing a semi-inletted rifle stock requires the correct and precise fitting of the barreled action so that it seats perfectly into the stock. The barrel, in particular, must be set into the stock with such precision that it slides into the barrel channel of the stock in an almost glove-like fit. Great care must be taken to assure that there are no high spots in this channel. These may create a pressure-point on part of the barrel's surface and it is at these high spots and pressure points that warpage will occur when the rifle is fired to any extent. Erratic shooting and scattered groups result invariably.

The correct bedding of a rifle barrel into a stock is an involved procedure and actual experience is perhaps the best teacher of how this one phase of gun building must be done. However, we will again assume that you have already stocked your rifle and it shoots poorly.

On the market today, and usually available through most gun shops of any size, are commercially made units known as stock bedding kits. These kits, if properly utilized, can completely eliminate the pressure points created by poorly or improperly finished stocks.

The basic use of the two components contained in these kits is to fill in all low spots of an improperly inletted barrel channel, thus eliminating the pressure points that have a tendency to warp a rifle barrel as it is fired. The kit selected for this article is a product of the Micro Sight Company of Belmont, California and is labeled as the Micro-Bed.

It is necessary first to remove the complete barreled action from the stock. Following this, the barrel channel

of the stock is examined closely for any high spots that actually contact the barrel when it is in the stock. These high spots, or pressure points, must be shaved down with a sharp chisel until there is a clearance of at least one thirty-second inch between the barrel and the channel. This space will allow for a complete and even coverage of the bedding compound once it is introduced to the wood of the barrel channel. The basic idea is to build up all low or uneven spots of this channel, thus giving the barrel full support in the stock.

With all high spots in the barrel channel removed with the use of a half-round chisel, we now turn our attention to the recoil lug recess. This recess should be enlarged only enough to allow a thorough coverage by the epoxy bedding compound.

Included in the Micro-Bed Kit are two tubes. One contains an adhesive which makes the finished mixture harden. The contents of these two tubes, when mixed in

Fit of the barreled action to the stock must allow at least 1/32-inch clearance for the glass bedding.

equal and sufficient amounts, will afford your gunstock a perfect barrel bed, making it a far more accurate arm.

Mix equal parts of the Tube Number 1 and Number 2 in a container, such as an old jar lid. Mix only a sufficient amount to do the job, as this compound, once mixed, cannot be saved for future use. Stir the mixture until all streaks have disappeared and the mixture turns a walnut color. Use extreme caution to avoid getting this compound into the eyes and do not allow prolonged contact with the skin. While I applied the compound with my right index finger with no ill effects, this may not prove true with persons having less sensitive skin. Should you use your fingers for application, wash thoroughly with soap and hot water to remove compound.

The next step is to apply a liberal coating of paste wax to those parts of the barrel and receiver that will be contacted with the compound. This one phase is an important one in that, if paste wax or some other releasing agent is not used, the entire action will be glued literally to the stock and great difficulty experienced in getting these two components apart. Do not overlook this one most important operation.

With the bedding epoxy mixture all stirred and the rifle stock securely clamped in a vise, using protective cork or felt jaws, apply the mixture liberally to the entire area of the barrel channel and recoil lug recess. Following this, the barrel and receiver unit is replaced in the stock and the retaining screws firmly tightened.

As the barrel and receiver screws are tightened down, the bedding compound will be squeezed up and out of the crack between the barrel and the stock channel. This

Bedding of action is done in two stages. First the barrel, then lug section are sealed thoroughly in well cured glass.

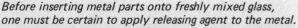
The bedding compound is mixed, according to directions, until it becomes a smooth, consistently colored mixture.

Before inserting metal parts onto freshly mixed glass, one must be certain to apply releasing agent to the metal.

Compound then is applied either with a finger or spatula of wood. Be certain to wash hands, removing toxic material.

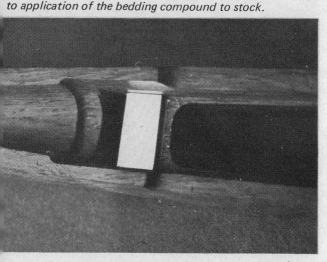

As discussed, steel recoil plate must be in place prior to application of the bedding compound to stock.

The barrel and action are placed in stock and tightened in place. Excess bedding compound is wiped off with paddle.

With barrel, action secured in the newly glassed channel, excess compound wiped off, it is allowed to cure, harden.

Full clearance of barrel in stock channel may be checked by sliding business card length of barrel. If it does not move freely, this means you must remove more wood.

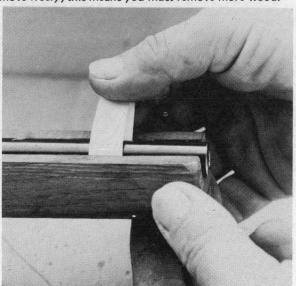

excess is scraped off carefully with a piece of wood, making certain that no compound is left on the outer surfaces of the stock or barrel. This compound, once set, is extremely difficult to remove, so use care that no streaks or lumps are left on exposed surfaces. The workable period for freshly mixed compound is one hour, more than sufficient time in which to do this operation correctly.

With all surplus compound removed from stock and barrel, the entire rifle then is set aside for a minimum of twelve hours. The Micro-Bed epoxy compound will set hard in this time; however a period of from 24 to 48 hours should elapse before shooting the newly bedded rifle.

At the end of twelve hours, the retaining screws may be removed and the barrel lifted from the stock. This may be accomplished by tapping the underside of the barrel with a rubber or soft wooden mallet until it frees itself from the tight fit of the epoxy compound. After which the stock and barrel are cleaned of any adhering compound and reoiled

Following the 24 to 48 hours waiting period for the compound to thoroughly dry, the rifle then is reassembled. It will undoubtedly be found, following this bedding operation, that it will require zeroing-in. The only difference will be that now the rifle will hold its zero instead of your shots wandering all over the target as they did prior to this operation.

Your rifle is now properly bedded. The barrel lies in a perfect cradle of hardened epoxy. It no longer has pressure points to warp the barrel each time it is fired. You soon will realize that this one section of the stock is truly the heart of the rifle's shooting capabilities.

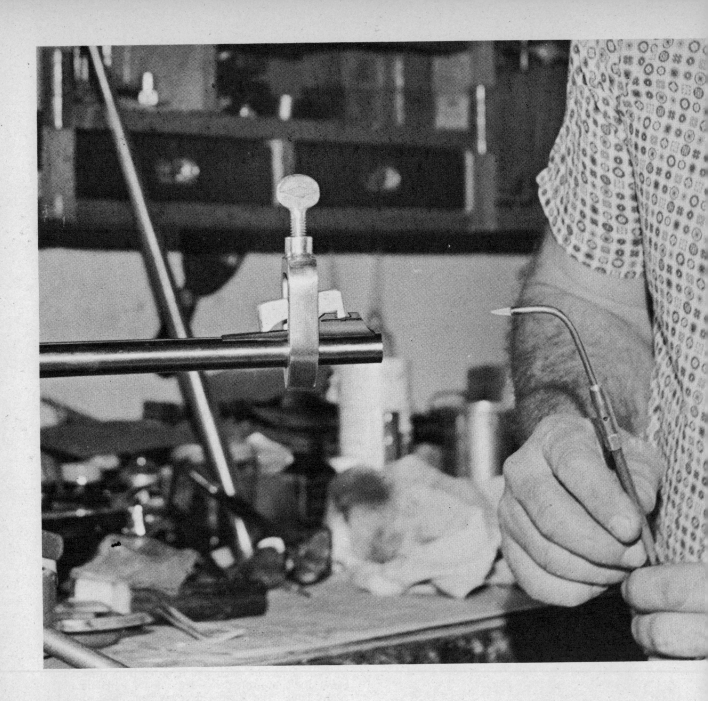

THE term, sweating, when used in conjunction with metals, means the joining or fusing together of two metals through the use of a bonding agent. This agent can be a combination of soft solder and soldering paste, silver solder and flux, or the welding process known as brazing. The process should not be confused with the commoner soldering method of bonding; if properly done, sweating is far stronger and by far the neatest looking of the two.

The many phases of soldering, brazing and welding would fill a technical manual, so this article will concentrate upon the sweating process used by gunsmiths in the installation of sights, scope mounts, ramps, etc. Soft solders are those containing specific amounts of lead and tin; the higher the tin content, the higher will be the melting point. If there are ten parts tin and ninety parts lead, the melting point will be approximately 620 degrees Fahrenheit. If the tin content is increased, then so must be the heat required to melt the mixture.

Lead wire can be purchased at most hardware stores in varying ratios of lead-tin content. The best, and most often used by gunsmiths, is a blend of thirty parts tin to seventy parts lead, as this combination is best suited to barrel and sight work. In addition to this lead-tin combination, a small can of soldering paste is an absolute necessity as is a small propane heating torch. Inexpensive propane torches are available in hardware stores with disposable tank units and are both compact and handy around the home workshop.

As in plating or bluing a firearm, cleanliness is a prime necessity, if you want a strong, first class job. All contacting pieces of metal to be sweating together must be completely cleaned of all grease, rust, pits and gun bluing. The presence of any amount of blue finish will prevent the solder from taking hold and will result in a loose joint.

To install a ramp front sight on a brightly blued rifle barrel, the ramp is placed in the exact position on the

Chapter 10

HERE'S A SIMPLE METHOD FOR INSTALLING ACCESSORIES WITH A MINIMUM OF TOOLS

No Sweat With SWEATING

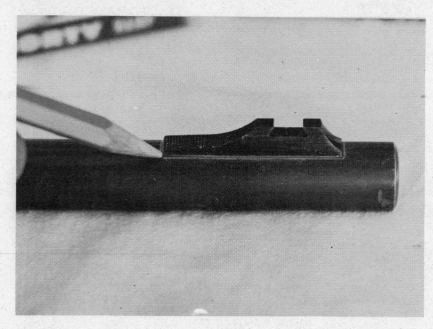

The outline of ramp is traced on barrel, using either steel scribe or silver lead pencil.

Author has found that Force 44 silver-bearing solder is excellent for sweat soldering.

barrel and perfectly aligned. With a sharp scribe or pointed metal marking pencil, the ramp then is outlined on the barrel. Be careful that the ramp does not slip, causing you to mark an area too large for the ramp to cover when the job is finished.

With the ramp outlined on the barrel, it then is removed and, with a fine ten-inch mill bastard file, we brighten up that area just within the outlined area on the barrel. Extreme care should be exercised not to overrun the penciled or scribed lines. Remove all of the blue finish possible within the lines without excessive cutting of the metal itself. This filed area should not be a polished finish, but left rough with the file marks giving the solder something to hold to.

With the area well cleaned and the blued finish removed, check the bottom side of the ramp. This will undoubtedly be nicely blued, but the finish must be

With flux applied to surface, solder is melted and flowed onto areas of both ramp and barrel in a smooth, even coat.

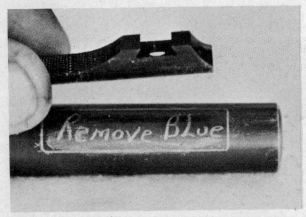

With outline of the ramp traced on barrel, the blued surface is removed to assure positive bond to metal.

Properly done, the ramp and barrel should be joined in a perfect union of bonded steel. Trim away overflow solder.

Underside of ramp also is cleared of any bluing, foreign matter so as to insure perfect overall contact on barrel.

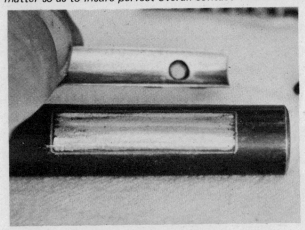

removed by wrapping a piece of fine emery paper around a wooden dowel, then carefully cutting away all of the finish on the surface of the ramp that will be in contact with the barrel.

Tinning consists of applying the solder to the contact area of the two pieces of metal to be joined. Apply a thin coat of soldering paste (No-Ko-Rode is one of the best) to both the brightened area on the barrel as well as to the underside of the ramp. Then light your torch and heat the barrel just to the point that the wire solder, held in the other hand, will melt and flow freely onto it. When the area is well covered with solder — and the torch still directing heat in the area — wipe it lightly with a piece of cloth to remove the excess solder, leaving only a thin coating. (Be sure that no excess solder is left on the brightened area, as this results in unnecessary work later.)

With the area on the barrel thinly coated with a bright layer of solder, turn your attention to the ramp and coat the underside in the same manner as with the barrel. With both barrel and ramp plated with solder, allow them to cool slightly. I find it best to give these areas another light coating of soldering paste before going on to the final operation.

Making certain that there are no lumps or foreign matter in the solder-covered areas, the ramp then is placed on the barrel in the precise position and firmly clamped in place with a ramp soldering jig. Extreme tightening of this jig is not necessary and may result in a gouged barrel or ramp. In snuggly tightening the jig, be

This is one method by which double barrels can be held in proper position to repair a minor separation of the rib.

Loose ribs on shotguns can be resoldered, using method described in text, but cleanliness of metal is mandatory.

sure that the ramp does not slip from its correct placement on the barrel.

With the ramp clamped in perfect alignment on the barrel, the torch again is fired up and the flame played over the entire area in a circular motion. When the solder turns a shiny, bright color, this indicates it is molten. At this point, remove the torch and allow the barrel to cool until the solder turns a dead color, which signifies that it has hardened sufficiently to apply water slowly, thus completely cooling the area. A very small amount of bead solder may have escaped along the edge of the solder line, and this may be removed by carefully cutting it away with a sharp knife or chisel, leaving only a fine line of solder visible. This may be blued with a cold touch-up gun bluing solution.

The sweating process just described is done with what is commonly known as "soft solder" of lead and tin content, but if properly done, will hold any joint till hell takes on a sub-zero look. If a joint is likely to receive extra wear or abuse, it may be desirable to do the job with what is known as "hard" or silver soldering, which consists of a mixture of copper, silver and zinc or brass. This type of soldering is superior to the above in that it is much stronger when used on small parts repair.

As with soft solder, the content of the different components of silver solder will vary with the job, but as a rule those solders carrying the trade names of Easy Flow or Low Temp are well suited to most gun work, particularly in the installation of scope bases, ramps and the like.

Hard soldering is done in much the same manner as is soft soldering, but with these exceptions: A proper silver soldering flux (borax in paste form is best) must be applied to the areas to be fused together instead of the regular soft soldering paste. Secondly, hard soldering calls for a much higher degree of heat to flow the harder alloys. While there are available various mixtures of copper, zinc and silver in the form of silver solder, the best for all around gunsmithing work consists of fifty percent silver, thirty-five percent copper, and fifteen percent zinc. In the old days, silver coins often were melted down and utilized as silver solder on small jobs.

Sweating, as a means of joining pieces of metal together into a lasting, strong joint, calls for a minimum amount of heat during the process to prevent unnecessary burning or discoloration of existing blue on the arm and to prevent the possible change of the metal's molecular structure or temper.

Opinions and methods having to do with the sweating-on of various gun accessories will vary from one gunsmith to the next, but I have come to feel that some additions such as ramps, scope bases, sights and other items that come equipped with screws for installation should instead be sweated on and the screws thrown into the parts box. This is especially true if a novice is doing the job, for a slip with a high speed drill can ruin either a gun barrel or a receiver.

Installing a ramp on the front of a rifle barrel, with screws is a mighty touchy job, especially if the barrel is one of the newer lightweight models. Here a slip of the drill can puncture the bore. The barrel then would have to be shortened one or two inches to salvage it. A sweat-on ramp is both more stable and far safer with no screws to loosen through hard use of the gun.

Like all crafts related to gunsmithing, the chore of sweating requires a certain amount of actual practice before one attempts this means of installing a sight or ramp on his favorite rifle. It would be best that you first do a little practicing on scrap metal. I feel that nine-tenths of a successful soldering or sweating job is in having the work spotlessly clean, removing the blue in the work area. Solder will not cling to a blue surface and this is where many novices fall down on an otherwise simple project.

INSTALL YOUR OWN TARGET SIGHTS

THIS PROJECT REQUIRES A MINIMUM OF TALENT AND TOOLS TO BUILD MORE ACCURACY INTO YOUR GI .45

The installation of new sights on the Colt Government Model .45 automatic pistol can be accomplished easily by almost anyone with a minimum of tools. The basic purpose of installing new sights on a gun such as this quite naturally is to improve its accuracy, so some thought must be given to the selection of these sights.

The standard factory sights on the .45 Government automatic pistol, acceptable to some, leave a lot to be desired by the serious shooter and the dyed-in-the-wool accuracy hound. These factory sights consist of a low, rounded front sight, while the rear sight is a stationary bar-type Partridge variation that may be adjusted for windage only by tapping slightly either to the right or left. These sights, designed primarily for combat use, have proven so inaccurate that their use generally is a by-guess and by-golly affair in firing at ranges in excess of twenty-five yards. Thus, the installation of up-to-date target sights is a prerequisite to improved accuracy.

With periodical release of large numbers of these pistols to the American shooting public, the demand for more accuracy has become so prevalent that countless thousands of dollars are spent yearly by shooters in attempts to accurize these guns into some semblance of shooting quality. It is to these owners that this article is directed; a do-it-yourself project that will save money as

Chapter 11

well as result in more personal satisfaction in the paper-punching department, when the pistol is fired on the range.

Through the results of many tests involving various types of sights best suitable for just this gun and purpose, I found several that adequately filled the bill. Some of the sights tested were a little too difficult for home installation, and therefore are all but useless for consideration in an article such as this. My final selection narrowed down to one that I feel encompasses all qualities necessary for fine accuracy. Of fine workmanship and materials, I wanted to use a sight that could be

The original front sight blade is filed to the contour of the receiver, taking care not to cut receiver proper.

installed properly at home with a minimum of mechanical knowledge and the ability to use simple hand tools.

My choice was the Micro pistol sights manufactured by the Micro Sight Company.

The first step, prior to the actual mounting of these sights, is to remove the slide (barrel housing) from the pistol. Then remove the follower, bushing, sleeve, recoil spring and barrel from the slide. In other words, strip it of all parts except the extractor and firing pin assembly.

Place the slide securely in a vise with lined jaws of cork, lead or even a thick layer of cloth to protect it from being marred. The vise jaws are tightened only enough to hold the slide snuggly. Do not "over squeeze" the slide, as it can be crushed or distorted to the point that it is no longer useable. With the slide held firmly in the padded vise jaws, remove the factory front sight using a ten-inch mill bastard file. File this sight until it is perfectly flush with the slide surface, taking great care not to file into the slide, itself. Remove only the sight blade without touching the curved surface of the slide.

Following the filing down of the front sight, the exact center of the filed area must be determined and lightly center-punched. It will be noted that the new front sight furnished in the Micro Sight kit has a small "fin" on the under side. This is for the purpose of locking the newly installed sight to the slide by peening this fin over from the inside of the slide housing, where it

With the front sight filed perfectly flat, it is center-punched, drilled and slotted as outlined in the text.

protrudes through the slot that is to be cut into this area.

However, this peening type of installation may be too difficult for the novice whose supply of tools is limited, but this method is unnecessary when there is a simpler and equally as strong means of installation.

With the exact center of the front sight area determined and center-punched, a hole then is drilled with a 1/32-inch drill, going completely through the thickness of the slide. This hole then is enlarged lengthwise with

Area to be tinned must be clean and a thin coating of a soldering paste or flux applied before applying the torch.

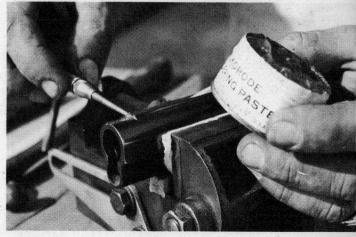

the use of a fine, flat Swiss needle file until it snugly accepts the fin of the new sight. Following the drilling and slotting of the sight area, the new sight should seat perfectly upon the slide. Should the sight not seat perfectly, further minor filing is necessary to remove any minute bumps that may be present.

With the new front sight seated and fitted to the slide, it then is removed and set aside until the next step is accomplished.

This phase is to lightly coat the clean-filed area with soldering paste, followed by tinning the area with either a soldering iron or a small Presto-Lite torch (as illustrated). The solder should be of a mixture of ninety-five percent tin and five percent lead, available in most hardware stores. The use of Low-Temp silver solder creates an extremely tough joint and may be used instead of the tin-lead solder, but silver-solder flux must be used instead of soldering paste if this method is used.

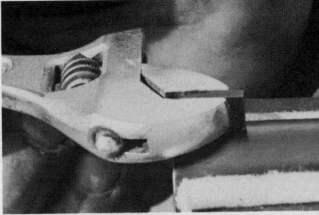

Should newly installed blade not be perfectly straight on the receiver, it may be straightened slightly by using duck bills or a small crescent wrench, as shown.

The filed area then is tinned with solder, leaving a smooth, even coating of solder over the filed area.

The new target front sight is inserted in the slot, is tapped into position and heat is applied until solder is molten. After this step, allow it to cool in the air.

When installation is completed, the new sight should be checked for perfect alignment horizontally, vertically.

Regardless of which method is used, it must be remembered that, in any type of metal bonding, the surfaces to be joined must be absolutely free from any foreign matter to assure a strong, perfect joint.

The sight area now is tinned and ready for the actual sight installation. The new front sight is placed between the jaws of a pair of pliers for ease of holding, then given a light coating of soldering paste (or flux, if silver solder is used) around the entire underside of the base. With the flame playing on the tinned area and the front sight simultaneously until the solder becomes molten, the front sight and fin are pushed into place, making certain that it is closely aligned and as perfectly perpendicular as possible.

Allow sufficient time and heat for the solder to become molten and free-flowing, for this is the secret of a good, strong solder job.

The original rear sight is removed by tapping from slot, using brass or copper rod, even a copper hammer.

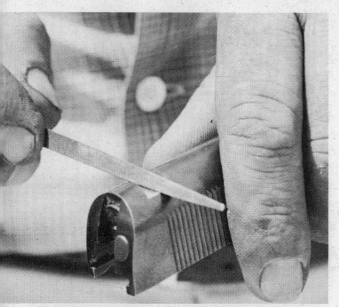

If necessary, existing slot in pistol's receiver can be enlarged slightly to accept target sight in a snug fit.

The new sight is tapped carefully into slot, until it is centered on the receiver. Care is needed not to harm it.

With installation completed, the two retaining screws in the Micro Sight are tightened to prevent slipping should the handgun be bumped or from the recoil, when fired.

With the sight firmly soldered into place, it should be cooled slowly, then doused in water. This is followed by dressing-up any excess solder that may have shouldered around the sight base. This may be trimmed away with a sharp knife or chisel, taking precaution not to scratch the existing blue on either the sight or the slide. Should there to a fine hair line of solder visible around the sight base, this is dressed up easily with Formula 44-40 instant gun blue, which is available in most gun shops.

The last step in the front sight installation is to check inside the slide to determine whether or not the fin of our newly mounted sight has protruded. If so, this is easily removed with a small half-round file, filing the fin until it is flush with the inside surface of the slide housing.

The installation of the Micro rear sight is a more simple chore. It is necessary only to remove the factory bar-type sight by tapping it out — to the right — with a brass or copper rod. The existing slot in the side will likely be slightly undersized in width, so it will be necessary to file this area lightly with a small three-cornered file, enlarging it sufficiently to accept in a snug, slide fit the new Micro sight.

With the slot correctly enlarged and the new rear sight firmly in place, align it with the dead center of the slide, then lock it in place with the two locking screws located on either side of the main, large headed adjusting screw.

With your new Micro sights installed, it is time to take a trip to the range to zero in. You undoubtedly will find, following the final sight adjustments, that you are shooting better scores than ever before, and that your old .45 auto has taken on a new personality. It isn't the "inaccurate clunk" you once considered it to be.

Most of all, there will be that feeling of knowing that it was your own efforts, and a few minutes work, plus the expenditure of only a few dollars, that made your pistol into one that is a pleasure to shoot. However, unless fully accurized, it still will never qualify as a serious target gun. New sights comprise only the first step in the necessary full treatment.

*WITH
MINIMUM
MONEY
AND
MAXIMUM
ELBOW
GREASE,
YOU CAN
BUILD
THIS
GAME
GETTER!*

SPORTERIZE
THAT LATIN MAUSER

SOME months ago, while browsing through the gun racks of a large retail gun dealer, I was somewhat surprised to discover that one of these long racks in particular was filled to capacity with Mauser rifles of the Model 98 pattern. For the most part, these rifles were in apparently unused condition. The bores were perfect and none were rust pitted.

Close inspection proved these rifles to be of the German Gewehr 98 pattern with only slight modifications. All were manufactured for the Argentinian and Peruvian governments and are known more correctly as the Model 1909 and Model 1935 Argentine or Peruvian Mauser military rifle. They were, back in those days, available in 7.65mm and .30/06 caliber and ranged in price from $25 for a short action to as high as $50 for one in .30/06 caliber with the long action.

The rifles examined were beautifully finished, all parts blued with the exception of the bolt and receiver. It was apparent that one of these would be ideal for customizing into a fine sporting rifle and that such a job could, for the most part, be done by the home craftsman with a minimum outlay of cash and countless hours of careful and enjoyable labor.

Such a rifle could be sporterized in its original caliber or rebarreled to a more popular, and more potent, caliber, at the discretion of the builder.

The 7.65mm cartridge, when loaded with a spitzer-type bullet, is capable of velocities approaching 2800 feet per second. Too, the four-groove barrel of this Mauser is well known for accuracy. It is possible to obtain one of these rifles chambered for the popular .30/06 cartridge. However, in this caliber, the rifle will have that initial cost of around $50 as compared to the $25 to $29 for a short actioned 7.65 caliber.

These rifles are available in the so-called long receiver and the short receiver. The less expensive short receiver version is ideal, providing the craftsman plans on leaving the rifle in its original 7.65mm, or rebarreling to any one of the newer, short case cartridges. Should the builder wish to rebarrel to one of the magnum calibers, such as the 7mm Remington magnum employed on the rifle built to illustrate this chapter, then the long action is absolutely necessary to handle the longer magnum cartridge.

The Argentine and Peruvian Mauser rifles are basically identical. Both use a five-round staggered-row box magazine, a Barleycorn front sight and a tangent leaf rear sight. One version of this rifle has a barrel measuring a fraction over twenty-nine inches while another version of the M/1935 has a barrel only 23½ inches in length and with modifications only slightly different from those of the M/1909.

It is best to decide the exact style in which you wish to customize your rifle: Leave it in its original caliber,

Chapter 12

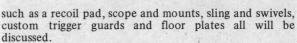

Model 1909 Peruvian Mauser, this one in 7.65mm, can be rebarreled to one of the modern magnum cases. (Left) In converting it to one of the larger magnum calibers, the 1935 Peruvian Mauser must have rails opened up in receiver to accept the larger cases. Author checks altered action for smooth feeding.

After original military sight has been disassembled, locking screw is removed before starting next step.

utilizing the original barrel — or have the action rebarreled to a more popular caliber by a competent gunsmith. The type and style of stock also should be decided before work is begun on the conversion.

Should one wish to go whole hog, as much as several hundred dollars can be spent in sporterizing this military rifle. Or the job can be done inexpensively by utilizing the original barrel and investing in new sights and an inexpensive sporter-type stock.

A new barrel, installed and chambered by a gunsmith, as was the Douglas Premium grade barrel used on this rifle, can run as high as $65 but there are other less expensive barrels in popular calibers that can be threaded and chambered to your action.

In addition to the Douglas Premium barrel, it was decided to utilize a Bishop stock in one of the finer grades. This stock would be redesigned in contour to that of a custom-built European sporter of Mannlicher design.

For adding a scope, the alteration or complete replacement of the military bolt handle is necessary for low mounting of the scope. Experience has proved that it is best either to purchase a custom bolt handle, or manufacture one yourself, and have it welded, replacing the military version. This operation will be covered more thoroughly later on.

The installation and costs of additional accessories,

such as a recoil pad, scope and mounts, sling and swivels, custom trigger guards and floor plates all will be discussed.

When first purchased, both the Argentinean and the Peruvian Mauser rifle will most likely be well saturated with a thick preservative grease. This should be removed by first completely disassembling the rifle and thoroughly washing all parts to be used in the conversion in cleaning solvent.

After disassembling and degreasing the rifle, if the original barrel is to be retained as a part of the finished rifle, the rear sight sleeve must be removed. This is accomplished by first disassembling the elevator section of the rear sight, which will expose a small set screw. Remove this screw.

With the barrel firmly clamped in protected vise jaws, the flame of a torch is played over the entire surface of

Sleeve of military sight is heated, until solder is melted; it is tapped from barrel with copper hammer.

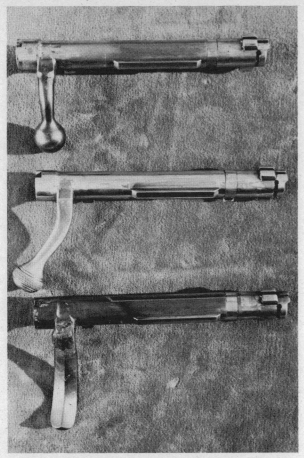

At top is standard Mauser bolt handle, which must be replaced or altered extensively in order to clear a low-mounted scope. (Center): The custom knob-type bolt handle offered by Williams. (Bottom): Hand-made spoon version that shows rough weld before filing.

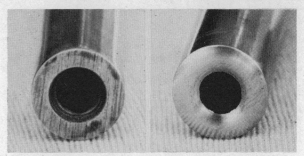

The new barrel must be crowned precisely, polished for assured accuracy. On left is the freshly cut muzzle, while properly crowned muzzle is at right.

filing will remove all scratches and machine marks from the barrel with careful, precise application and emery cloth. Then buffing, first on a medium-course, then fine, buffer will remove all minor scratches left by the draw filing operation.

With the barrel surface smoothed up and ready for its final finish-buffing, we turn our attention to the all-important receiver section. It is possible, but not absolutely necessary, to remove the Peruvian or Argentine insignia, or crest, from the receiver ring by carefully cutting it away on a belt sander — or it may be left intact. This is the choice of the individual however, care must be taken not to weaken the structure of the receiver ring by the removal of too much metal during

Should new barrel be used, it can be contoured to desired shape on lathe, being dressed down with a variety of files, emery cloth to pre-buffing state.

the sleeve until it becomes sufficiently hot for molten solder to bubble from the area where the sleeve contacts the barrel. At this point, the sleeve is tapped forward lightly with a brass hammer, until it slides free of the soldered area. Slide the sleeve far enough forward to completely clear the solder-tinned area of the barrel, otherwise it will be necessary to reheat the area to free the sleeve. Following the removal of the rear sight sleeve, it will be noticed that the barrel is tinned in this area with soft solder. This must be removed completely with emery cloth or by buffing to assure that this area will accept a perfect blue job later on.

In all probability, the twenty-nine-inch barrel will prove to be too long for the ideal sporting rifle and that cutting and recrowning the barrel to either twenty-two or twenty-four inches will result in the finished rifle having a far better balance. Should a lathe be available, shortening and recrowning the barrel is a simple matter. However, in the absence of a lathe, this operation may be done with a hacksaw and files, great care being taken to assure that the muzzle of the barrel is perfectly squared-up, when the recrowning operation is completed. Should you have a new barrel installed by a gunsmith, the shortening and recrowning of the barrel will be done as a part of the rebarreling job.

While a metal turning lathe will hasten the job of contouring and preparing the barrel for final finishing on a buffer, this work may be executed by careful hand-work, emery cloth and an assortment of files. Draw-

this operation. In either case, the serial numbers of the rifle must be left intact.

Should the rifle be rebarreled to one of the larger magnum calibers such as the 7mm Remington magnum, it is necessary to widen the cartridge rails and guide ramp of the receiver, until they will freely accept the larger diameter magnum case. Again, this will be a part of the gunsmith's job, should you have the rifle rebarreled. Should the rifle be left in its original caliber, this operation is unnecessary.

To rebarrel the rifle for this article, it was taken to a gun shop where a new Douglas Premium barrel was threaded, chambered and installed. Lacking a lathe, it was necessary that I have this one operation performed outside of my own shop. The widening of the rails and smoothing-up of the guide ramp were accomplished with a small electric hand grinder, the Dremel.

You may choose to have your local gunsmith do this vital chore as a part of the rebarreling operation, but it must be brought out that this intricate job of widening the rails must be done correctly the first time to assure that the finished rifle will feed cartridges into the chamber smoothly and correctly. To grind away too

The Mannlicher-type spoon bolt handle can be made from raw cold-rolled steel bar, sawed and filed.

Should rifle be rechambered to large magnum caliber, cartridge guide rails must be opened to accept them.

The face of the bolt also must be enlarged if it is to accept the larger diameter of the magnum case.

It was decided to employ the spoon-type bolt handle inasmuch as the finished rifle would be of the Mannlicher-type and this spoon would add that extra custom look.

The spoon bolt handle was made from tool steel, hand shaped with the use of files and a hacksaw and checkered with a three-cornered Swiss needle file.

Removal of the old bolt handle is accomplished with a carbide cut-off wheel mounted on a grinder. Being exceptionally hard, it is impossible to cut this bolt handle from the housing with a hacksaw. If it is possible to cut the handle with a hacksaw, it is far too soft to perform its job and should be recase hardened for safety's sake.

The new handle may be held carefully in place with a pair of large pliers and firmly tack-welded, after which it is thoroughly welded in place, being certain that its cast

The new bolt handle, whether spoon or ball type, is welded securely to bolt sleeve in a perfect bond.

much metal in this area will ruin the receiver. In addition to widening the rails to accept the larger magnum cases — the face of the bolt and the extractor must be "opened up" to accept the larger magnum rims. This also is done best by a competent gunsmith.

It is necessary, should a low-mounted scope be desired, that the old bolt handle be either extensively altered or replaced by one of commercial manufacture or one that you have designed and built yourself. It is possible to install a new bolt handle of either one or two designs on your custom rifle. The popular knob-type is manufactured and sold by the Williams Gun Sight Company in a solid-head unpolished version, while there also is the hollow-headed knurled type. You may prefer one of the racy "spoon-type" bolt handles found on the finest of European Mannlicher-type sporting rifles.

Mortise in stock to accept bolt release lever is lined with sheet fiberglass in black or brown shade.

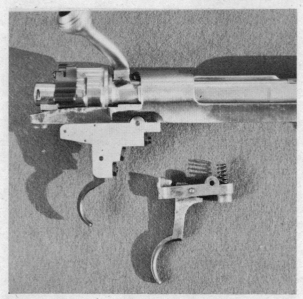

The issue trigger can be honed, used in conversion, but the Timney custom trigger, already in place in photo, was substituted; it's more crisp, adjustable.

The original trigger guard and magazine assembly may be retained as a part of the finished rifle after being thoroughly polished and the trigger guard recontoured to a more pleasing shape.

This is accomplished by rounding over the squared outer edges of the guard with files or disc sander and tapering it from front to rear. Approximately one-eighth inch may be removed from each side of the rear portion of the trigger guard, then tapering the guard gracefully to its full width at the front. This results in a custom-looking trigger guard after polishing and bluing.

It is possible to replace the original military trigger guard and magazine assembly for one having a hinged floor plate. Michael's Of Oregon produces an attractive customized trigger guard with either a plain anodized black floor plate. as well as one with either a gold or silver plate, and engraved with such animals as a prong horn antelope or a deer.

is such that it will clear a low mounted scope when placed in the receiver.

With the new bolt handle welded in place, care is taken in dressing up the welded area with the use of files and emery cloth. The finished and polished weld should be invisible and pleasingly contoured into the bolt handle, whether it be of the knob or spoon type. Following the dressing up of the welded area of the bolt, the entire bolt must be honed and polished to satin smoothness. It is well not to over-buff the sections of the locking lugs with too coarse a buffing compound. They must retain their snuggness in the locking grooves of the receiver. To over-buff a bolt with coarse compound can result in it becoming sloppy and ill-fitting in the receiver.

In addition to the new bolt handle installation, it is important that the safety catch be replaced with one that will not interfere with low-scope installation. For this replacement one of the fine Buehler Low-Safety units will be found to be ideal from a standpoint of easy installation and attractive appearance. Easily followed instructions for installation accompany each safety.

As-issued military trigger guard and floor plate can be replaced with custom type at minor expense.

These custom trigger guard and floor plate assemblies are made of tough lightweight aluminum alloy and not only will add to the appearance of the finished rifle, but will aid greatly in keeping the weight of the finished rifle to a minimum.

Whether or not you use the original trigger guard or one of the custom versions, the original magazine spring and follower must be retained as a part of the finished rifle. Neither of these components are furnished with the Michael's trigger guard, but will require no major alterations with the exception of a thorough cleaning and polishing of the follower.

In addition to the possibility of using a custom trigger guard, the rebuilder might also obtain one of the streamlined bolt sleeves used on commercial FN sporting rifles. This sleeve, while adding that custom look, necessitates the installation of a thumb or side-type safety, as they are not equipped with a safety.

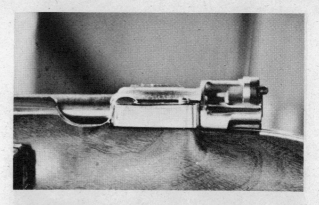

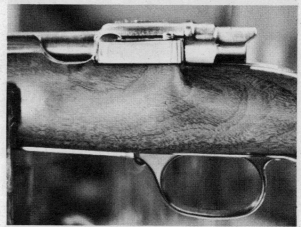

Top: Military bolt sleeve may be retained with the installation of more efficient Buehler safety. The lower photo shows a streamlined FN bolt sleeve in place, requiring special trigger with thumb safety.

Top photo is military receiver prior to alterations. Beneath it is same receiver after the hump on the rear bridge has been removed, with military insignia.

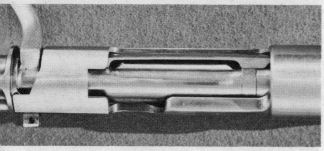

A simple method of finding dead-center of the top of the receiver is with two steel squares, as shown.

By grinding away the clip ears on the receiver and installing this FN-type bolt sleeve, then installing one of the Timney Target Master triggers with thumb safety, your rifle receiver will lose much of it's military appearance and take on a contour similar to that of a commercially built FN action. No fitting is necessary, as these sleeves readily replace the old, safety catch-type bolt sleeve on all M/98 type Mauser bolts in a matter of seconds.

While there are bound to be numerous points of views on any given subject, I have long stuck to the procedure of semi-finishing all metal work first, when building a sporting rifle. It is my feeling, gained from a few years at a gunsmith's bench, that all metal work, namely the barrel and receiver section of a firearm, should have all contouring and alterations completed — with the

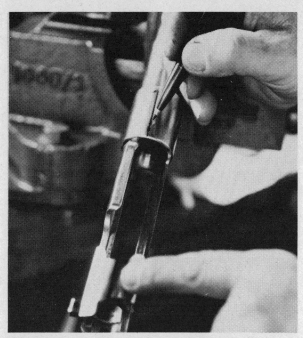

Once the top center of receiver is determined by use of squares, it is marked preparatory to placing the mount in position and center-punching for drilling.

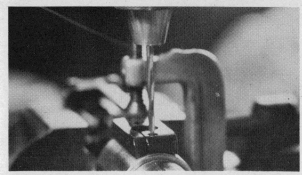

The scope base is clamped to receiver, used as a drilling jig. This prevents the possibility of the drill walking out of proposed screw hole location.

exception of the final light buffing prior to bluing — before fitting of these components to the stock is begun. This also includes the installation of such accessories as scope mounts and sights.

To assure a perfect inletting job on the stock, the metal work of the barrel, receiver, trigger and magazine assembly must be as nearly finished as possible to prevent the removal of additional metal after the stock is fitted.

In the event that open sights are preferred to a scope, or if a combination of both scope and open sights are desired, there are numerous variations from which one might choose. A micrometer rear sight, such as those produced by both Lyman and Williams is ideal if a peep-type sight is desired. The front sight should be mounted on a ramp, several styles of which are available from Lyman and Williams. Should you be building a Mannlicher-type carbine, then one of the Williams Shorty Ramps is an ideal choice. Topped with a gold bead sight, this ramp makes an ideal combination for any type of micrometer or buckhorn rear sight.

The installation of ramp-type front sights is thoroughly explained and illustrated in Chapter 11.

Should a scope be desired, either as the only sight, or in combination with open sights, the choice of scope, power, make, type of base and rings is up to individual taste.

To assure that it will zero properly when the rifle is fired, the proper mounting of a scope requires a minimum of specialized tools, but know-how in the intricacies of proper scope mounting. Neither the Peruvian nor the Argentine Mauser (nor any other M/98 Mauser, for that matter) are ready-drilled and tapped to accept any of the American-made scope bases.

Mounting a scope properly requires precision workmanship. It is preferable that a drilling jig be utilized in performing this all-important operation, but on the other hand, if one is capable of careful workmanship, a scope base may be mounted correctly with the use of nothing more than two machinist squares, the proper size drills and taps, a drill press and drill press vise.

By first placing the squares as illustrated, you will be able to determine the exact center of those portions of the receiver that are to accept the scope base. Mark this center carefully with a felt-tipped marking pencil.

After determining and marking the dead center of the receiver rings, the scope base then is placed carefully on the receiver so that the holes in the base will be in perfect alignment with the ink markings and in alignment with the bore of the rifle.

The base then is clamped to the rifle's receiver making certain that it doesn't shift its position. Using the scope base as a drilling jig, a number 28 drill is used to drill all holes to the proper depth. This is determined by the length of threaded screw that protrudes from the bottom of the base, with the screw fully seated in the hole provided. The holes then are tapped out, usually with a 6x48 gunsmith's tap and bottom-out with a bottoming tap.

In some cases, the receivers of these rifles are case hardened to the point that an ordinary high-speed drill will not penetrate. In this event, there are two courses of procedure. The first is to grind away the case-hardened skin in the immediate vicinity of the proposed screw holes, using a small electric hand tool chucked with a

The holes then are tapped out. Use of a drill press assures perpendicular threaded holes for scope base.

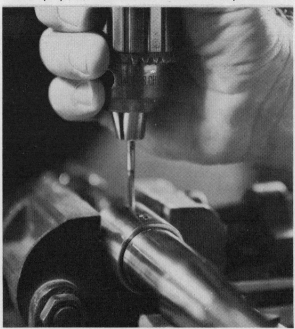

pointed carbide stone. This will permit the drill to enter the surface. The other course, and perhaps the simplest, is to obtain a carbide drill which will readily penetrate the case-hardened skin. However, these drills are quite expensive, and in most cases, are available only from a gunsmith supply house. The grinding method was used in the preparation of this article.

With the receiver drilled and tapped, using the scope base as a drilling jig, the newly tapped holes are cleaned thoroughly and the slight burrs around the edges removed with a Swiss needle file. The rings then are placed on the scope and the scope mounted on the action. During this operation, it is best to have the action firmly clamped in the bench vise. When the base, scope and rings have been securely tightened in place, the bore of the rifle barrel is centered on a small object.

Once the rifle receiver is drilled, tapped, the scope base is tightened in place. However, this means it must be checked thoroughly for alignment.

I use a telephone pole insulator at about one hundred yards distance. In adjusting the scope to dead center on the target, all windage adjustments should be taken in the scope base, itself, not in the scope. The elevation adjustments, if the base has been properly mounted, should only be minute in the scope turret. Should you find that too much elevation adjustment from the scope turret is necessary, it is possible that shims will have to be used under one end or the other of the scope base to true it up. The shimming-up of scope bases is a fairly common procedure when scoping certain military rifles due to irregularities in receiver sizes.

The best policy in mounting a scope is to take up as little adjustment as possible in the scope turret during the initial stages of bore sighting. This will eliminate the possibility of the cross-hairs being badly off center in the tube, when it is minuted-in on the rifle range.

With all major metal work completed, the new bolt handle welded in place to clear a low mounted scope, the barrel gracefully tapered and the trigger mechanism honed, if the original trigger is being used or the custom set-trigger adjusted to your satisfaction, the scope base holes drilled and tapped and the sights mounted and all parts given a semi-finish polish, we are now ready to go into perhaps the most crucial phase of building a sporting rifle that will be both rugged and accurate, when

taken on a tough hunting expedition.

Available to the custom rifle builder is a selection of stock material varying through a rough-turned blank, a partially finished blank or a stock that is ninety percent finished, needing only a good sanding, filling and application of the stock finish which may vary from epoxies or linseed oil to any of those special preparations made for the sole purpose of giving a hard, durable and waterproof finish to gunstocks.

The stock used for this article is by Bishop Stocks of Missouri, and when received, was inletted in the receiver section only as a rough-turned blank. The barrel channel was not inletted due to the fact that a custom Douglas barrel was utilized, but for those planning to use the original barrel in their conversions, Bishop can furnish

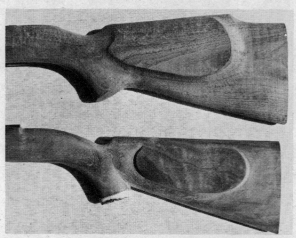

Top: Semi-finished Bishop stock utilized a full Monte Carlo comb and cheek rest. It was removed to attain full classic design shown beneath it.

stocks fully inletted to accept both barrels and actions of almost any rifle popularly used in converting to sporters.

Many American gunmakers build a stock that is more like a club than part of a hunting rifle. They leave too much wood. I favor the sleek, graceful lines common to the sporting rifles by such makers as Holland & Holland, Purdey, Griffith & Howe and a few others.

I would completely eliminate the so-called Monte Carlo hump on the backbone of the stock and made a few other innovations that are typical of a sleek, racy looking, stocked-to-the-muzzle Mannlicher-type hunting rifle. Any stockmaker knows that a rifle can be fitted with a piece of wood that will serve all purposes, providing it is built to the individual. I have never cared for a Monte Carlo-type stock, so I used a wood plane to remove it.

In shaping the Bishop stock, rest assured that there will be sufficient wood from which to build and shape it until it fits you perfectly. It is possible to give this stock a reasonable amount of either left or right cast-off should you need such an innovation due to facial structure or irregularities in eyesight. However, as cast-off in gun stocks is the exception rather than the rule, we won't dwell on this phase.

Needed for inletting and final fitting of the barreled action to the stock will be a minimum of tools. A wood rasp and several files of finer cut will be necessary for final shaping and contouring of the exterior, while an assortment of chisels and gouges will be needed for the inletting of the barrel. Lastly, sheet after sheet of fine garnet paper in grits from medium coarse to 600 extra fine will be needed to work the stock down and give it a glassy surface in the final stages of completion.

Of classic design, the stock sports a stag pistol grip cap, inlaid silver initial plate and Pachmayr White Line recoil pad. Wood is finished with Tru-Oil.

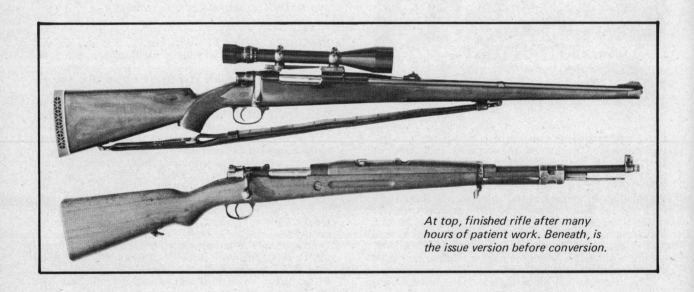

At top, finished rifle after many hours of patient work. Beneath, is the issue version before conversion.

ANY RIFLE IS ONLY AS GOOD AS ITS WOODWORK; AND HERE'S THE KNOW-HOW FOR FINISHING A WINNER!

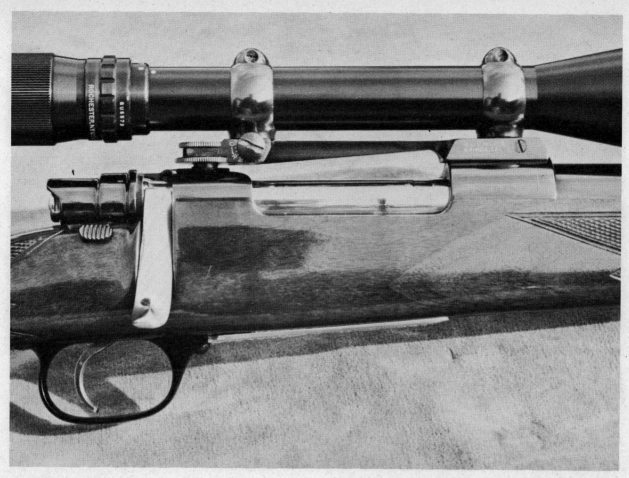

Incorporated in finished product are FN bolt sleeve, spoon bolt handle. Improvised thumb button on thumb safety was created by Bish. Also utilized on Mauser were Balvar scope, Buehler mount, Williams sights.

We have reached the point that we are ready for the woodwork; fitting the action to a new Mannlicher stock, which makes it appear an entirely different rifle from the surplus bargain with which we started.

The Bishop Mannlicher stock we decided to use in this article was inletted nicely in the area accepting the receiver, trigger and magazine assembly and required only minor fitting. The barrel channel will be in accordance with your initial order of the new stock. Bishop stocks may be ordered fully inletted in the barrel channel so as to accept the original, as-issued military barrel or left uncut so that you might inlet it to accept a custom barrel of your choice. In either case, there will still be hours of work to be done on both the interior and exterior surfaces before the stock is completed.

The first step is to bed the receiver and barrel so these components are a snug fit in their mortises. If inletting is necessary for the bedding of a gunsmith-installed custom barrel, it is best to have on hand a small assortment of barrel inletting rasps to both speed up the job and to assure that a good job of inletting will be the end result. These rasps are available from Frank Mittermeier's, Gunsmith Supplies, Brownell's or your local gun shop may have them on hand.

To start inletting the barrel into the stock, the barreled action is placed atop the stock so that the receiver section is in exact alignment with the mortises.

The barrel then is outlined on the stock with a soft-lead pencil, making certain that the pencil is held in a perpendicular position to the outer edge of the barrel during this tracing. Once this outlining is completed and the barreled action lifted from the stock, a perfect out-

Outline of barreled action is traced carefully onto stock wood prior to inletting. This assures a more precise job of mortising of the metal to the wood.

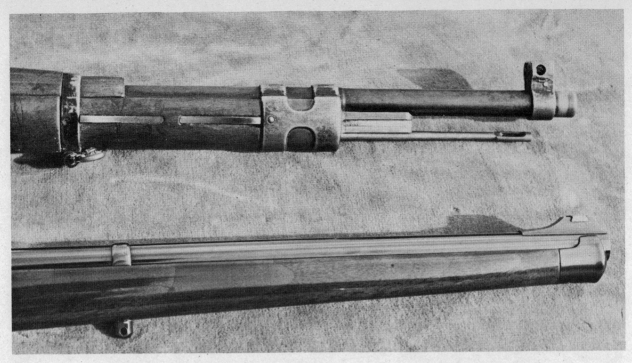

Above is the Peruvian Mauser in as-issued condition. Beneath is finished product, which features a Bishop Mannlicher stock, Williams sight, Michael's barrel band.

line of the barrel's contour should appear on the wood.

It is possible to rough-route this area by chucking a rotary wood rasp or core box bit in a drill press and carefully routing out the channel by sliding the forearm of the stock on the drill press table. This is a ticklish job and requires perfect control of the stock to prevent over-running the traced lines. This method will give the barrel channel depth in which to begin the use of inletting rasps. Do not attempt to do the entire inletting job in this manner as it is probable that you will ruin the stock for any purpose other than firewood!

After rough-routing the barrel channel, it then is carefully deepened and shaped by hand to its proper proportions with the barrel inletting rasps. Extreme care must be practiced to prevent cutting too deeply. The use of Prussian blue or other marking substances should be used continuously during this barrel-to-stock fitting if perfect inletting is to be expected.

Knowing the difficulty and added expense of obtain-ing many of the specialized tools of the gunsmithing profession, it is possible to improvise many of these tools. If one tool won't do the job, then try something else that will.

Let's say that you have done the best you know how in performing the job of inletting the stock with the tools at hand. In spite of your careful workmanship, the barrel channel is still a pretty rough proposition and the barrel seemingly seats in a bed of rough, splintery wood. In short, the barrel channel is just plain lousy! We will correct these mistakes in inletting later on so that they will be completely unnoticed in the finished rifle and it will still possess the accuracy and ruggedness you desire.

Assuming that the wood-to-barrel fit leaves a lot to be desired, that there are numerous bearing surfaces which could easily result in the rifle being inaccurate, take the inletting rasp in hand once more and rasp away all wood in the channel that might contact the barrel. During this corrective operation, it is necessary to have a clearance

Upper stock shows barrel channel, receiver section after being glass bedded completely. Note that recoil lug has been reinforced greatly by use of the glass compound. The lower stock is shown prior to bedding.

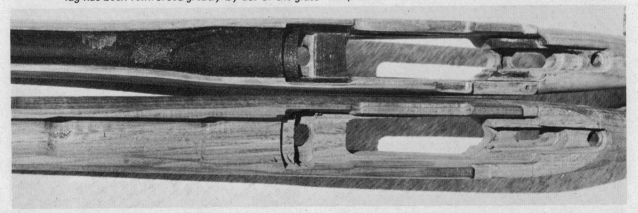

The barrel encircling ears of the metal snobble may be reshaped, as shown in shaded area, for a custom look, then installed on stock's forearm as outlined.

of about one-sixteenth inch between barrel and wood for the full length of the channel. (Check Chapter 9, which concerns glass bedding of troublesome stocks.)

By following the directions and illustrations in this article, you will have no trouble in turning that rough looking barrel channel into one that is glassy smooth and one that will result in your rifle being both accurate and attractive in appearance.

Immediately following the inletting and glass bedding of the barreled action to perfection, it may be sent off for bluing.

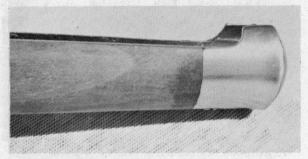

When installation is complete, the wood to metal fit should show only a hairline. Unsightly open cracks detract from the craftsmanship and value of rifle.

With or without the aid of glass bedding, we can assure that the inletting now is completed and we proceed to the exterior surfaces of the stock. My personal schedule in building a stock, following the inletting, is to install such accessories as the forend snobble — if building a Mannlicher-type rifle — and as work progresses, the recoil pad or butt plate, pistol grip cap and sling swivels. The installation of the Mannlicher-type forend snobble, (see Chapter 21) usually a well shaped hollow steel cap is accomplished in the following manner.

The forearm is cut to the exact length of the finished barrel, then one inch is measured back and marked with a lead pencil. I have found that, by placing a piece of masking tape immediately to the rear of the penciled line, then using this as a cutting guide, the union of the wood and the edge of the snobble contacting it will be a perfect hairline fit.

A medium course file is used in removing the bulk of the wood from the area to accept the snobble. The final fitting is done with a ten-inch mill bastard file. The end of the snobble-accepting area of the wood must be con-

toured to fit the interior shape of the metal snobble in an exacting fit to assure permanence of installation. It must be a precision fit where the rear portion of the snobble contacts the wood to eliminate the possibility of an unsightly crack between wood and metal.

With the snobble or forend cap securely mounted and the necessary retaining nut and screw in place, we turn our attention to the contouring and shaping of the entire outer surface of the stock.

As stated earlier, it is my opinion that far too much wood is left on rifle stocks by many modern day gunmakers. However, due to the varying tastes in rifle design, I will leave the final contouring of the stock to the individual.

It is advisable that the novice study the mechanics of stock design by closely examining photographs of rifles in gun catalogs, then after selecting a stock design that appeals to him, transferring this configuration to his own rifle.

One of the most critical points in building a rifle stock is the correct contouring of the pistol grip area. It is this area that must absorb much of the rifle's recoil, and should it be in one of the more potent magnum calibers, the strength of this vital area will mean the difference between a broken stock and one that will tolerate the pounding of even the most potent handloads

During initial stages of shaping the stock, coarse wood rasps are used to remove excess wood. As work progresses, stock taking shape, finer files are used.

that can be fired safely through the rifle's action. In shaping this area, make certain that sufficient thickness is left in the wrist of the stock to safely handle the recoil of the cartridge being used. Do not cut the rear portion of the pistol grip section too deeply into the stock. To deviate from either of these customary and sane rules of stock design often will result in a stock that is unattractive and weak — to say nothing of it being a potential danger to the shooter.

Wood rasps are used extensively in rough shaping the stock to near perfect proportions. Files of fine cut are utilized in eliminating the marks and cuts left by the rasps. Finally, garnet sandpapers in medium-coarse, fine and extra-fine grades are used in preparing the stock for its first coat of epoxy or other finish.

Both the rubber recoil pad or hard rubber plate and

Above: Outline of semi-finished stock is traced onto hard backing of recoil pad. Excess rubber is removed with coarse disk sander in first stage of fitting. (Below) In final stages of recoil pad installation, mask off stock wood to prevent sandpaper scratches.

The stock requires many sandings before final finish is attained. Author sands walnut with 400 grit preparatory to applying next coat of stock finish.

the pistol grip cap should be installed just before the stock receives its final sanding in order for both to be blended into the lines and contour of the stock, itself. The recoil pad in particular should follow the straight lines of both heel and toe of the stock for pleasing appearance. To round over these points of the pad will result in an unattractive and amateur job.

When all rasp marks have been removed from the stock's surface with files of fine cut, then sanded smooth, the stock may be dampened or steamed to raise "whiskers" on the surface of the wood. These whiskers are sanded off with extra-fine garnet paper and the dampening repeated until these whiskers cease to rise on the surface of the stock.

It is considered unnecessary by many stockmakers to exercise this de-whiskering process when modern day stock preparations are used. Stock finishes, such as the G96 Gun Stock Finish, produced by Jet-Aer Corporation and George Brothers Lin Speed Oil are excellent for producing a lasting glassy finish to wood, making it both waterproof and mar-resistant. Both of these products are available in larger gunshops.

In application of stock oils or finishes, it is best to mask ribber recoil pad. This will prevent added labor in cleaning the pad, when stock is completed.

When the surface of the stock has taken on a glass-like smoothness, it is time to start the application of the liquid stock finish. The stock must be thoroughly dust-free, dry and the finish applied in a dust-free room at about seventy-five degrees for best results. The finish should be applied sparingly and spread in a thin, even layer over the entire surface.

The rubber recoil pad should be masked off with masking tape to prevent it from becoming saturated and coated with the liquid stock finish. This will eliminate the necessity for later cleaning up the recoil pad. When the stock is finished completely, the masking tape may be removed, leaving the pad in perfect condition.

I have always used the palm of my hand to quickly rub in the above mentioned preparatives and have found this method to be unequalled for obtaining a glass-like finish. However, in using the palm of the hand for this purpose, it must be done quickly before the stock finish becomes tacky and begins to set-up.

After the first application, allow the stock to dry at least twenty-four hours. The stock then is sanded with 600-grit paper and another coat of finish applied. I have found that at least three coats are necessary to fill the

Interior areas of stock should be protected against possible dampness from rain or snow by brushing all of these surfaces with stock finishing preparation.

are coated with either soap or wax and tightened into the hole until seated squarely on the stock. The forward swivel, in most cases, is held in place with a counter-sunk nut on the inside of the barrel channel. This is accomplished by first locating the position of the swivel on the forearm, drilling a clearance hole for the swivel screw, then counter-boring this hole in the barrel channel to accept the swivel retaining nut.

In the case of the rifle built for this article, a barrel band containing the nut was used, which necessitated counter-boring the stock to accept this entire nut section of the barrel band assembly. The front swivel screw is threaded into this barrel band assembly, thus securing the stock to the barrel at this point.

During the final stages of sanding, and prior to the application of any stock finish, one may wish to inlay a small monogram or initial plate into the stock. This may be hand-cut from sheet silver or gold with a jeweler's saw, the edges dressed up with Swiss needle files, then inletted just below the surface of wood. This will add to that customized look, especially if the shield is engraved with your initials.

The customary locations for this ornamentation is either on the comb of the stock near the butt, or below the sling swivel, near the toe of the stock so it will be visible when a leather sling is installed.

Some craftsmen are prone to checker a stock before it has received its final coat of stock finish. This method if not recommended, because much of the effect of checkering is lost during the application of sometimes thick, fast drying stock oils and finishes which fill up the tiny cuts forming the diamonds, thus rendering the checkering ineffectual for its original purpose — that of providing a gripping surface for the hands. For this reason it is best to do the checkering as the final phase of stock building.

Gold or silver initial plates are inlaid easily into the stock. This is done before applying the finish.

pores of most walnut. However, some open-grained woods will require more. When the pores are completely filled, the final finish is applied and the stock put away in a dust-free area to thoroughly dry. I allow the stock to dry and harden at least a week before rubbing it down with rottenstone and waxing it. Birchwood-Casey stock wax is my personal choice for the final protective finish to be applied to the finished stock.

It is well to seal the interior surfaces of the stock with the same preparation used on the exterior. This is not necessary in a barrel channel that has been glassed, but is highly desirable on those raw interior surfaces of the receiver section capable of absorbing moisture. A small artist's brush will prove excellent for coating such surfaces with stock finish, thus sealing it from moisture and dampness.

When the final finish has been rubbed down and waxed, it is time to install the sling swivels. The swivels used here are the quick detachable European-type by Michaels of Oregon, and like most swivels, are installed on the stock with the use of a quarter-inch electric drill motor chucked with a drill of the correct size. The lower, or butt swivel is installed by first locating its position near the toe of the butt, usually within two inches of the toe, then drilling a hole approximately three-quarters of an inch deep with a drill smaller in diameter than the screw threads.

With the hole drilled, the threads of the swivel screw

Used to checker the rifle was a set of Dem-Bart checkering tools in a size measuring twenty lines to the inch. These tools are quite inexpensive and may be obtained in sizes ranging from sixteen lines per inch up to thirty-two lines per inch. With careful workmanship, they are capable of producing fully professional checkering. (This is covered fully in Chapter 8.)

During this exacting operation, take your time. It can mean the difference between an attractive rifle, when finished, or one that was ruined during the final stages of completion. Give the new checkering a good brushing with an old tooth brush, a brisk rubbing with fine steel wool to polish the diamonds, then coat it lightly with either linseed oil or lemon oil.

The rifle is ready for final assembly, zeroing and its first trip afield for game.

Chapter 13

DOUBLE DUTY FOR THAT RECOIL PAD

PROPERLY FITTED, IT ABSORBS SHOCK — AND LENGTHENS THAT TOO SHORT STOCK

Installing a recoil pad without shortening the stock could result in stock being too long as shown at left. Properly installed, stock shortened in order to compensate for pad thickness, the stock length now allows shooter easy access to the trigger (right).

THERE can be several reasons for the installation of a recoil pad on either a rifle or shotgun. The most prevalent reason, of course, is for the absorption of some of the kicking ability of the particular gun. It can be taken for granted that a good recoil pad does absorb a great deal of the mule-like recoil of some big bores, but the usefulness of the recoil pad doesn't end there.

Take, for instance, the case of one hunter who had purchased a new magnum shotgun only to find that the stock was much too short for his extra long arms. The recoil of the gun didn't bother him in the least, but the short stock was aggravating to the point that most of his shots on game birds were misses. It was found that by only adding one inch to the length of this gun's stock, it would fit perfectly.

One danger is in installing the pad in such a manner that the pitch and drop of the stock are completely changed; this results in a stock that is ill-fitting and uncomfortable. The sloppy way is to install and finish the pad in such manner that it appears a completely foreign part of the gun. The pad is ground down in such a fashion that it is left with ridges and bumps, the toe and heel of the stock lines are rounded over. A job such as this certainly does nothing for appearance or serviceability, to say nothing of the value of the gun.

To install a recoil pad and do it correctly requires a minimum of tools, the most important being a disc sander of some sort. I personally use a small size sander, which is chucked onto a one-third horsepower electric motor. This one tool will do all but the final finishing for a well mounted pad.

Assuming that you have selected a recoil pad that will give good service as a recoil absorber or as a stock lengthener, (in this instance, I used the Pachmayr Whiteline pad), here are simple steps to follow:

STOCK PREPARATION

Remove the stock from the action for easier handling during installation. If the stock is of correct length, a section equaling the thickness of the recoil pad must be cut from the butt section of the stock. Assuming your recoil pad is one inch in thickness, this much wood must be removed carefully from the stock after first scribing a line completely around the butt. This is best done by

While epoxy cements are used for pad installation, certain glues of less strength often are preferred; this makes it easier to remove the pad if need be.

using a simple stock marking block, a piece of wooden block with a steel scribe protruding from one side so that the point of the scribe is exactly one inch above bench level during the operation..

The stock is held firmly in a perpendicular position, while the other hand carefully guides the scribe completely around the butt, marking a perfect line, as illustrated. Bear in mind that the inch to be removed includes the thickness of the original hard rubber or steel butt plate. This butt plate should be removed only after the scribed line is accomplished. With this line as a guide, be extremely careful not to overrun the line or to chip the stock with the saw. (Use a fine toothed mitre saw, if possible.)

MARKING AND GRINDING PAD

With the one-inch section removed from the butt, make certain the sawed surface is perfectly flat, then place the recoil pad in the correct position on the butt and mark screw holes where they will hold the pad in

Prior to actually cutting the stock, it is marked to desired length with a marking block mounted with a sharp awl. Cut is made on line with fine-tooth saw.

perfect alignment when tightened. With screw holes marked, drill starter holes with a one-eighth-inch drill to a depth of about one inch, then replace the pad and screw it down tightly. Do not glue the pad in place.

With the pad tightly in place, take a sharp scribe and mark the contour of stock onto recoil pad, then remove the pad for disc sanding. With the scribed line as a guide, dressing down the rubber pad now begins.

This one operation can mean the difference between a perfectly mounted pad and one that is sloppy and rough. It is best to do the majority of the disc sanding with a medium coarse disc and finishing up with a fine grit surface.

In the absence of a table rest on your disc sander, it is best to sand the pad while it is held in a perpendicular rather than horizontal position, as this is less likely to leave rough ridges and sander marks on the fiber backing or the rubber of the recoil pad. Disc sand only up to the scribed line, using a fine grit disc.

Location of pad screws is determined by placing them through holes in the pad, then pressing or even tapping them, as pad is held in exact spot on butt.

Before beginning the sanding operation, bear in mind the contour of the stock in relation to the recoil pad, particularly the toe of the stock. Do not round over the toe of the recoil pad at this point, but be careful to carry out the plane of the stock line. Keep the lines of the finished recoil pad in perfect relation to those of the stock.

With this excess material removed from the pad, it

Contour of the butt section of the stock is traced onto recoil pad, using white or silver lead pencil.

Excess rubber of pad can be removed with a coarse disk sander. This is followed by finer grained disk, as visual inspection shows a perfect fit is near.

now should be an almost perfect fit on the butt and the screws tightened. If slight overlap is evident in the pad, this can be removed carefully with a fine mill file, taking care not to mar or scratch the stock wood.

Another method of fitting the pad for older guns or those needing stock refinishing is as follows:

If a stock is to be refinished, it is sometimes best to dress the recoil pad down while it is permanently installed on the stock. In this way, the pad may be sanded absolutely flush with the wood of the stock, then finished and polished by hand, using fine garnet paper. This method is recommended over the first method, but does

Once cemented in place, the screws tightened, the stock should be placed in a clamp to assure bonding.

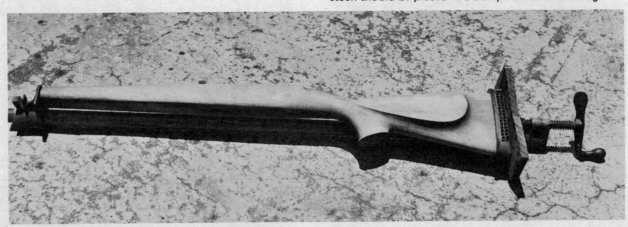

Final finish of pad-to-stock fit is accomplished with fine garnet paper and mill files. It is best to mask wood of finished stock, preventing scratches.

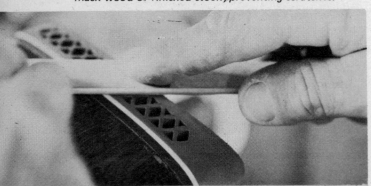

call for complete refinishing of the stock wood.

In some cases, the installation of a recoil pad will not add enough length to the stock to satisfy the user. In this situation, it is possible to install spacers between the pad and stock. These spacers can be made from a great variety of materials such as plastics in ivory or black color, rare woods, fiber or hard rubber These spacers are fitted and installed in precisely the same manner as the recoil pads, but it is often wise to use reinforcing dowels of hard wood where spacers are over one-half inch in the thickness.

The installation of recoil pads, like all other phases of gunsmithing, can add both beauty and value if properly done. Improperly accomplished, this same job can turn a once beautiful gun into a monstrosity that is ugly to look at and certainly no pleasure to shoot.

Chapter 14

Chipped tang sections of stocks are direct result of loose action screws, poorly fitting recoil lugs, allowing action to slide to rear under heavy recoil.

SURE CURE FOR MANGLED MAGNUM STOCKS

That section of stock to receive steel reinforcing bar is relieved to allow about 1/16-inch covering of the glass bedding to extend over entire plate.

Here's One Method For Insuring That Your Pet Wood Doesn't Turn Into Toothpicks!

WITHOUT a doubt there will be those who have devised various methods for preventing a magnum stock from splitting under the heavy recoil of calibers over .300 magnum and on through the .458s and .460s. However, for the benefit of those not familiar with the comparatively simple chore of reinforcing the stock on a big magnum rifle, you can eliminate the chance of it splitting under the terrific recoil.

I have seen far too many stocks of high-powered rifles that either were badly split in the area of the front recoil lug or a large chip knocked out of the stock where the rear receiver tang is inletted, all due to one factor: negligence on the part of the man who owned that particular rifle! He hadn't taken the precaution of tightening the trigger guard screws sufficiently to hold the barreled action tightly in the stock. A free-floating barrel and action is one thing — but loose scews are ridiculous!

A friend of mine bought a brand new magnum rifle in .458 caliber. On the first shot, the stock split the entire length of the forearm and back to the pistol grip. Close examination revealed that the trigger guard screws had been sufficiently tight to prevent any end-play in the barrel or action due to the rifle's recoil when fired. The only possible conclusion was that the recoil lug of the stock was not in any way reinforced to accept the hammering of so potent a caliber. This, and the fact that the walnut of the stock was not suitable for magnum calibers due to its softness, resulted in my friend having to purchase a new magnum stock at considerable expense — to say nothing of having run the risk of possible injury when that old stock let go!

I explained my method of reinforcing such a stock in such a manner that it was undetectable. This method requires about an hour or less of actual

The outline of steel plate is traced onto the lug section. This acts as template for wood removal.

The all-important recoil lug section of stock, unless reinforced properly, can crack, break under recoil.

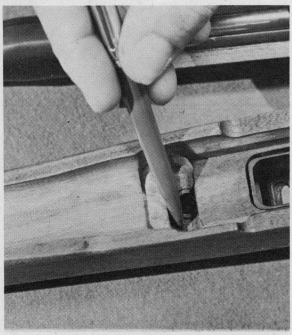

working time and the only cost is for the glass bedding. I use Micro-Bed, a product of the Micro-Precision Corporation. Anyway, I proceeded to steel and glass the recoil lug of his new stock. This is the section of the stock that takes all of the beating when the rifle is fired.

Needed for this job, in addition to the glass bedding compound, will be a small piece of tool steel — even cold-rolled will do — measuring five-eighths of an inch in width, one-eighth of an inch in thickness by one and an eighth inch in length. When this steel plate is cut to exact size so it is a snug fit in the mortised cut-out of the stock, a chisel then is used to cut away sufficient wood from the recoil lug to allow the steel plate to be force-fitted into the cut-out.

This steel plate is inlaid into the wood of the recoil lug of the stock in a tight fit — and just below the original surface of the wood to allow for at least a sixteenth-inch of glassing compound to cover it.

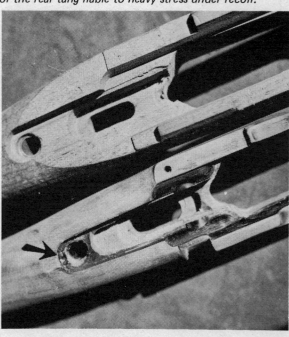

Lightened area denotes wood that craftsman must remove for inletting of reinforcing steel plate.

Added strength can be attained by glassing sections of the rear tang liable to heavy stress under recoil.

Some military rifles, such as versions of Model 98 Mauser, were issued with steel reinforcing bars in recoil area (left). Stock at right is a commercial sporter with steel plate under fiberglass bedding.

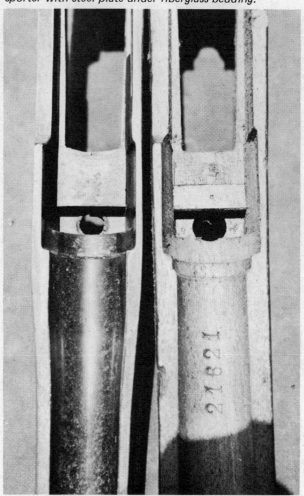

With the steel plate inlaid into the recoil lug section of the stock, we are ready to glass bed the entire area surrounding, and including, the inlaid plate. The barrel and receiver section of the rifle are coated liberally with a good releasing agent (to prevent the glass from binding to the metal) then the glassing compound is mixed as per directions on the box and applied to the recoil lug of the stock. Be certain that sufficient glass is used to thoroughly cover the inlaid steel plate — and be especially sure that you have applied the releasing agent to the barrel and receiver section.

With the glass applied, the barrel and receiver section is placed into the stock, the trigger guard installed, then the two guard screws are tightened until the barrel and receiver are fully seated in the stock. During this operation one often will notice excess glassing compound oozing from the stock. Wipe this excess off with a small piece of wood. Set the rifle away for at least twenty-four hours for the bedding compound to set and harden, after which the barrel and receiver may be removed from the stock and the excess glass cleaned up with fine files and garnet paper.

The entire recoil lug section of the stock now is encased in strong bedding compound and re-inforced with the steel plate. This will be the last place your stock will ever let go from recoil; that is, providing you have tightened those trigger guard screws as they should be.

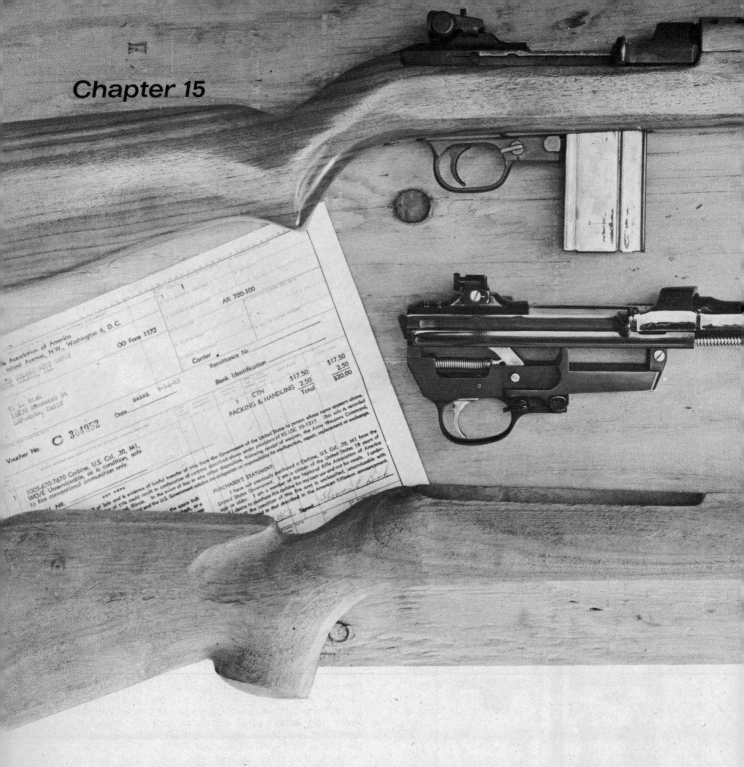

Chapter 15

REBUILDING THE G.I.

You Can Dress Up That Carbine Yourself...
Inexpensive If You Know How.

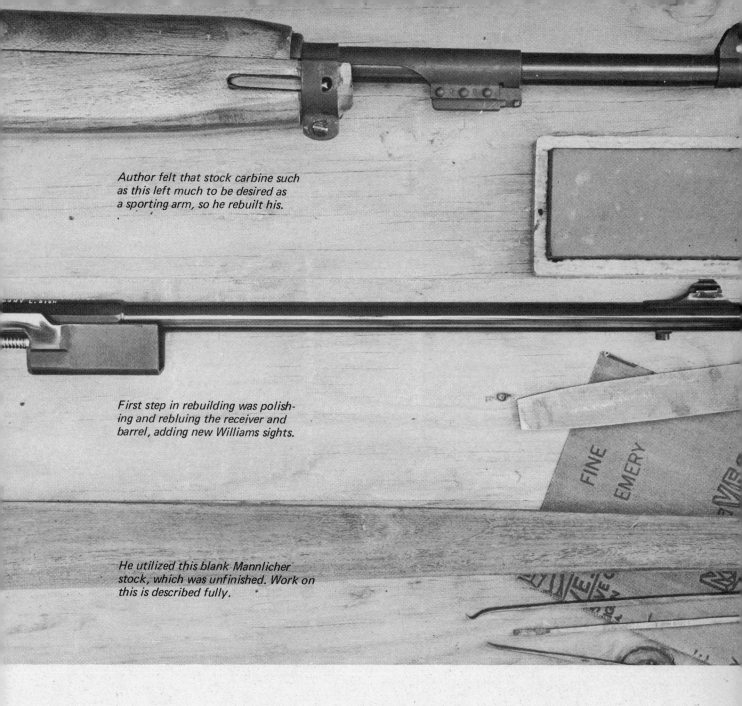

Author felt that stock carbine such as this left much to be desired as a sporting arm, so he rebuilt his.

First step in rebuilding was polishing and rebluing the receiver and barrel, adding new Williams sights.

He utilized this blank Mannlicher stock, which was unfinished. Work on this is described fully.

FINE EMERY

CARBINE

E VER since those early days of World War II, when I was an instructor in the various phases of aerial gunnery for the U. S. Army Air Corps, and still later, while on detached duty as a range master at a major air base, I had, for some reason yet unknown to me, a yen to own one of the crudely constructed little M1 carbines.

Actual experience with one of those little boogers had taught me that they weren't worth their salt at ranges much over a hundred yards. The sights on the as-issued jobs left a lot to be desired, and that all in all, they were just what they were — a crudely built wartime military weapon. However, after hours of studying countless of these little semi-autos, I came to the conclusion that, in spite of their rough appearance on the outside, they had the potential of being a worthy little sporting weapon, providing the time was taken to polish and hone them up a bit.

When the NRA announced several years ago that they were arranging for the release of thousands of these

Does That Surplus M1
Live Up To Your
Expectations?
If Not,
Here's How To
Improve Its Looks
And
Limitations!

or shooting qualities, but I still am pleased that mine is marked with Winchester

The exterior surfaces of the new arrival had the appearance of a gun still in the intermediate stages of manufacture. All tooling and lathe marks were in evidence on the outer surfaces of the barrel, but the bore was perfect. The receiver, trigger group and bolt, as well as all other components, still bore the rough surfaces common to steel castings of this type.

When I ordered this carbine, I thought it might be a nice piece to leave in its original state and to accumulate accessories such as a bayonet, web sling strap, oiler, fifteen and thirty-shot magazines and even a flash hider. These accessories could add greatly to the gun's desirability in future years — or so I thought before seeing it.

But after examining the carbine, new though it was, I knew I was in for some hard labor, dressing the carbine into one that I wouldn't be ashamed to add to my gun rack.

There are two methods of converting the M1 carbine from its rough "as issued" state into a more desirable specimen. The first, and easiest, is to leave the gun strictly "G.I." but to completely refinish the metal and wood into something more appealing to the eye.

The second method consists of completely revamping its entire design into that of a super sporter; turning it from a work horse into a racer, so to speak. This operation can be accomplished by the tool-wise in his own home workshop, the only costs being the price of a new semi-finished sporter stock, sights, sling swivels and the fee for having the metal parts reblued.

The first step is to completely strip the carbine down, depositing all small parts in a container where they won't be lost. It is not necessary during the operation to remove the barrel from the receiver. We will assume that the majority of home workshops do not have a metal cutting lathe, and that all work will be done by hand with a variety of files, emery cloth and buffing wheels.

carbines to members at something like fifteen bucks a throw, I lost no time in submitting my application and the required loot to cover both the carbine and shipping costs. In about six weeks, the carton arrived and I tore into the box to remove the M1 carbine that had been classified as "serviceable."

The carbine itself appeared to be in new, unused condition and I was elated to notice that on the receiver was the magic word: Winchester.

I had been told by several friends, who had received carbines quite early, that theirs carried names of various contract companies not usually connected with firearms manufacturing. An unlikely manufacturer, of course, doesn't necessarily detract from the carbine's reliability

Before and after: Showing the improvements made in the muzzle section of the carbine barrel.

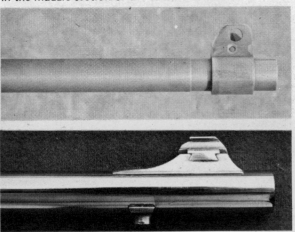

But the shop must have a good bench vise with protective jaws of either lead or cork in which to hold the various carbine parts for working.

We begin by removing the combat type front sight from the barrel. This is accomplished by first driving out the round retaining pin with a pin punch of the proper size, driving the pin from the left to emerge from the right side. The front sight then is tapped with a brass hammer until it is free of the front sight key, and will slide freely from the barrel. The front sight key is removed by tapping slightly on one end. The rear sight is

Authors carbine was marked Winchester, making it additionally worthy of sporterizing.

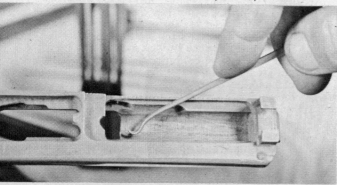

The interior of the action is quite rough. May be smoothed up with die sinker files, stones, hones.

removed by driving it from its slot in the receiver, again, from left to right.

With the receiver and barrel stripped of their combat sights, one of the most critical of our revamping operation is removal of all tool and lathe marks from the barrel's exterior surfaces. Using a twelve-inch mill bastard file, it is necessary first to draw-file all lathe marks from the barrel. This work is done evenly over the entire surface lest we end up with a barrel that has flat appearing spots on its surface.

In the draw filing operation, the file is held in both hands and pushed the length of the barrel in an even stroke. For the next stroke, the file is lifted from the barrel, returned to its starting point and pushed again. By constantly turning the barrel in the vise jaws so that the filing is done evenly and around the entire surface of the barrel, the tool and lathe marks will disappear. Keep in mind that draw filing the barrel is solely to remove the rings left by the lathe, so remove only these rings.

If you want only a dolled up G.I. version, remove as little metal as possible in the immediate vicinity of the front sight area. Removing too much can cause the original sight to be loose and wobbly when reinstalled. If you intend to install a ramp type front sight, the shoulder or step in the barrel, located approximately an inch and a half from the muzzle, must be completely removed by carefully blending this step into the general lines of the barrel. Draw file carefully to leave no hump in this section, thus allowing the new ramp sight to seat perfectly on the barrel.

The trigger assembly requires several hours of honing to assure custom-like performance in carbine.

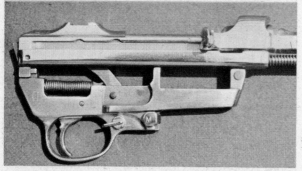

With the barrel free of lathe marks, we further work down the barrel with emery cloth to remove any minute marks. This is done by wrapping the twelve-inch file with a strip of 4/0 emery cloth. Repeat the draw filing operation, only this time have the file wrapped in emery paper; let the emery paper do the cutting.

This treatment is continued until the barrel is absolutely free of any minute scratches left by the file, and until the barrel takes on a soft luster.

The outer surfaces of the receiver are quite rough in appearance and must be smoothed out by draw filing and the use of other hand tools before they can be attractively blued. The milled cut-outs in the receiver, especially the one to accommodate the operating slide, are extremely rough in the majority of "as issued" carbines. This must be honed out for the carbine to operate smoothly, as well as for appearance's sake when the gun is reblued.

This honing and smoothing necessitates the use of a variety of hand tools including a small electric hand tool such as the Dremel and several die sinker's files.

In the case of the rear sight base area, a piece of emery cloth wrapped around a three-quarter-inch wooden dowel will work fine to polish after first removing the excess roughness with a half-round file. Small abrasive rubber wheels mounted in the electric hand tool are ideal for honing out the milled channels and other hard-to-get-at places. Die sinker's files will prove their worth in getting into the corners and channels of the inner receiver.

Slack in trigger is taken up by adding metal buffer.

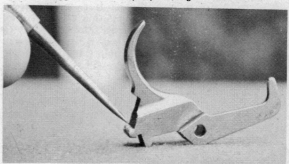

It is not necessary to polish that section of the barrel extending from the gas cylinder back to the forward edge of the receiver. This section is covered with the wooden hand guard. This is also true of the entire upper portion of the trigger assembly group, which is hidden in the stock.

After removal of all tool and casting marks from the barrel and receiver, these parts are polished, first on a muslin wheel, using a general purpose emery compound such as Tripoli, then comes a final buffing on a cloth wheel using 400 grit emery compound. How well this is done, will be the deciding factor in the finish, when the gun is blued.

The trigger housing, trigger, sear, hammer, magazine catch and safety all are castings that never have been honed. The trigger pull on my M1, when received, was no less than fourteen pounds.

I had never had an occasion to experiment on the trigger mechanism of the M1, but found that it wasn't difficult at all to cut down the pull to a respectable weight by careful honing of two critical points. These are the sear that actually engages the hammer, and the hammer notch, itself. In addition to honing these two points, I also cut approximately one-eighth inch from the length of the sear spring and honed that section of

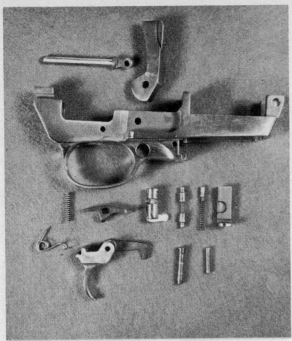

Most components of the carbines mechanism require thorough honing to remove the sand blast finish.

the rear portion of the trigger that engages the sear, as well as the underside of the sear.

It is possible to remove all creep from the trigger by building up the seat on the underside of the trigger where it seats on the trigger housing. It was necessary to build up this section an additional .025 inch for my particular carbine, but it is a certainty that others will vary in the additional height necessary to completely remove trigger creep. This operation is a simple one and may be accomplished by soft soldering a piece of thin brass at this point, then dressing down to the proper dimensions. Brass will suffice here, as there is no wear at this point; the brass acts merely as a seat for the trigger.

Prime requisite to the smoother functioning of the M1 carbine action is to thoroughly polish all bearing surfaces with an Arkansas hard oil stone. The hammer spring plunger was found to be rough enough to cause friction, even if ever so slight, against the plunger spring, so it was highly polished. The sides of the hammer, trigger, and sear should be polished to decrease friction against the walls of the trigger housing. The

The Williams rear sight was installed in the existing slot that accomodated the GI carbine version.

housing walls, themselves, were smoothed up to assure that there was no abrasive action against working parts.

I chose for a front sight a Williams "shorty" ramp in three-sixteenths-inch height. This was topped with a Lyman gold bead, which I felt suited the M1 because of its small, compact lines. This ramp can be centered and sweat soldered onto the barrel in a matter of a few minutes, but locate the ramp so that it covers the slot cut into the barrel for the front sight key.

At first, I felt the combat rear sight would be adequate, but its limited adjustments, especially in elevation, determined a need for something more versatile. Williams' Model FP receiver sight is made especially for the M1 carbine and priced at $9. This sight was meant to be mounted on the extreme rear portion of the receiver in the area of the recoil plate, but I had other ideas. Instead of mounting this sight far back on the receiver, leaving the original carbine sight base hump and dove tail, I decided to utilize these characteristics to improve stability.

Such an installation creates a sleek appearance to the overall carbine. Shown here is the right side view of the newly installed Williams sight.

The first step in installation was to hack saw and file out the existing dove tail on the carbine receiver until it would accept, in a precision fit, the cross bar of the commercial sight.

The two mounting screw holes were located on the left side of the receiver, then drilled and tapped out to 6-48 thread.

The new sight then was screwed into place, the cross bar firmly in the newly cut slot.

In my opinion, this is the strongest method of installing this type of receiver sight on an M1 carbine.

Instead of purchasing new sights, the originals may be reinstalled after complete polishing and bluing, should you want your gun to retain its military lines.

With action, barrel and trigger group polished to perfection and the sights of your choice ready for reinstallation, the gun is ready for the actual rebluing. This is best left to one set up with a complete tank-type bluing outfit, so it is best to patronize your local gunsmith on this job.

You can use one of the commercial cold bluing solutions and do the job yourself, but this method is not recommended if durability of finish is desired. Having your barrel and action reblued professionally shouldn't run much over five dollars, providing the gunsmith does not have to touch up your polishing job. Completing that operation with care, it can save you money.

In having my own carbine blued, I left the internal parts of the trigger and hammer assembly at home. Being highly polished, they would function better than if blued.

After bluing, the parts are carefully reassembled and lightly lubricated with a good gun grease and the bore given a thorough cleaning.

But don't get the idea that you can finish the job in one evening. A complete honing and polishing job is a big job, when done entirely by hand, so you can plan on having your evenings taken up for a week or so.

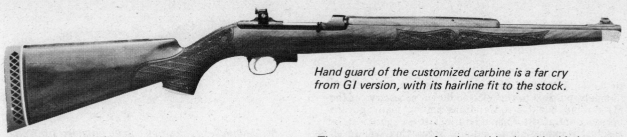

Hand guard of the customized carbine is a far cry from GI version, with its hairline fit to the stock.

The neat appearance of action — blued and bedded — into finished stock suggests time, craftsmanship.

Whether to refinish the G.I. stock or replace it with a new sporterized version is up to each individual, but if you want to refinish the G.I. stock, it generally will be found that the wood is so soaked with oil that creating a high luster finish will be nearly impossible. Due to this heavy oil content, few — if any — commerical stock finishes will prove effective.

Several individuals have told me that they have thoroughly washed these oil-soaked stocks in cleaning solvent or carbon-tetrachloride, allowed them to dry thoroughly, then applied stock finishes with good results.

In personally examining these same stocks, I found that in each case, the deeply penetrated oil in the wood was bleeding through the satiny finish. When the stock was rubbed with the palm of the hand, the fine finish was literally rolled off.

To eliminate hours of useless labor in attempts to refinish a piece of wood sodden with oil, and to add additional beauty, you may decide to turn this weapon into a customized sporter by purchasing a new semi-inletted stock of sporter design.

To convert my carbine into a completely revamped sporter of Mannlicher design, I turned to a semi-finished Mannlicher type stock made especially for the M1 carbine. "Semi-finished" means that these stocks require complete finishing of the exterior surfaces and minor fitting of the action and barrel to the stock.

The stock I received was strictly run-of-the-mill Claro walnut with a Monte Carlo cheekpiece. I have yet to find a Monte Carlo stock to fit me perfectly, so with an eleven point carpenter saw, I cut the "hump" off my new stock!

In addition, I gave the comb a little more pitch than it originally had and thinned out the cheek rest until I could comfortably align the sights with my right eye without craning my neck. Then I went to work with wood rasps and files to slim the entire stock to dimensions that pleased my eye.

In turning these stocks, Fajen follows rigid specifica-

Trim lines of completed forearm are a far cry from the rough military original with which we started.

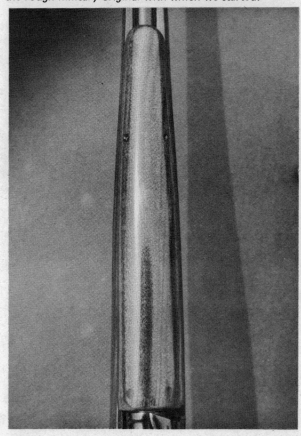

tions. Their pantograph machine is set as closely as is humanly possible to the inletted design necessary for the M1 carbine, but due to variations among many government contractors manufacturing these guns, it is absolutely impossible to cut one stock that will fit all carbines perfectly. Therefore, a happy medium may be expected in commercial sporter stocks of this type.

It may be found that some wood will have to be removed from the bed of the stock for the barrel and receiver to properly seat into position. The most critical

The Mannlicher-type stock can be obtained from any of several sources, but this one was furnished by Fajen. Wood was chosen for its matching quality.

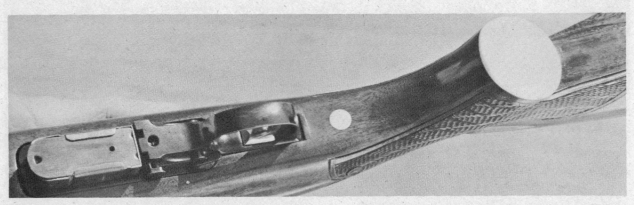

Precise fitting of the action to the stock, plus installation of ivory pistol grip cap, added to the attractiveness of the carbine when finished.

Author tries his reconstructed prize for fit. He utilized elephant ivory for forend snobble, pistol grip cap, recoil pad spacer. Pad added more length.

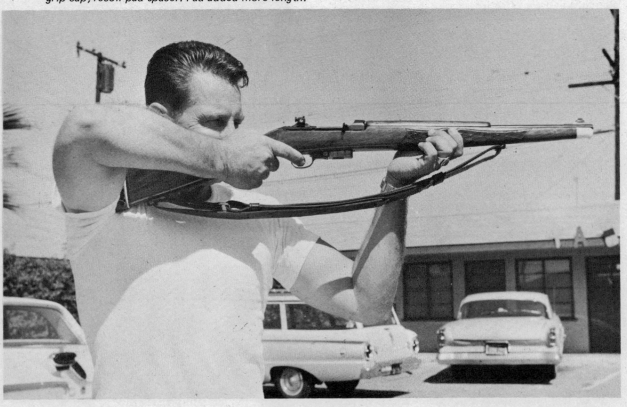

Bish checks the stock for possible warp before he begins the inletting and complicated contouring.

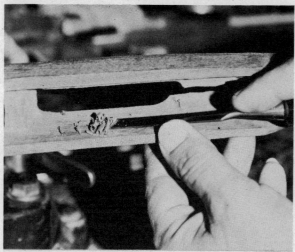

Minute shavings of wood are removed from receiver section of stock to allow exacting fit of action.

of the carbine's metal parts to be fitted to the stock is the recoil plate. This plate must be set into the stock with such precision that the barrel and receiver section will not "cock off" to one side or the other when inserted into this recoil plate and lowered into position in the stock. The recoil plate must be inletted perfectly straight, in alignment with the barrel, and still be mounted at the right pitch for the entire gun's action and barrel to slide properly into the inletted sections of the stock.

With the carbine used, it was necessary to remove minute sections of shavings from the area of the stock that accepts the receiver and trigger assembly. This is

All of the mortises to accept the receiver section must be chiseled out for a precise fit. Here, the inletting is completed for the recoil plate.

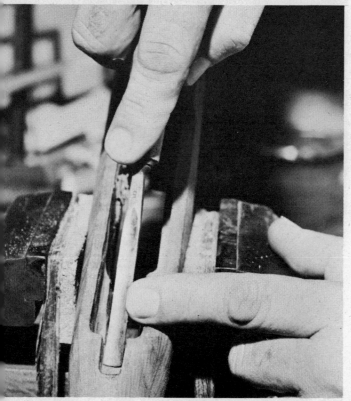

The forend cap was fashioned from elephant ivory. It is held in place by a dowel, epoxy for strength.

best accomplished with small sharp chisels of the type used by stock makers, but those used in model making or wood carving will prove satisfactory for this one job.

Make it a practice to remove only minute shavings from the bedding sections of the stock, then place the action into the stock, checking each time for proper clearance. It may be necessary to repeat this action-fitting procedure many times before reaching perfection of inletting, but it is the only satisfactory method.

As this article is aimed at the average home workshop mechanic using the normal tools found in his shop, we will dispense with explaining tools used by professional stockmakers such as highly specialized scrapers, channel gouges, and the many and varied types of chisels.

The job of setting the recoil plate and inletting the action will prove the biggest chore, and each stock and each action will present a different problem in fitting so take your time.

The final shaping of the stock's exterior, contour and finish are up to individual tastes, but it is best to follow accepted stock designs. Mannlicher stocks usually are equipped with a forend snobble of some type. Many are made from stag horn, some are pre-formed metal caps, and still others are fashioned from rare woods such as rosewood, lignum vitae, birdseye maple and the many other suitable materials. In the case of the illustrated carbine, elephant ivory was utilized for both the forend

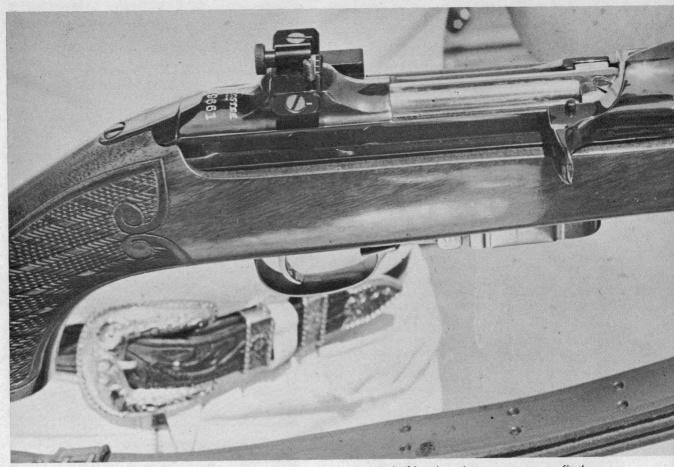

snobble and the pistol grip cap. It is best to use the same type of material for both of these stock parts on an individual gun.

The snobble is attached to the stock by a hardwood or a steel dowel, then cemented firmly into place, while still unfinished and slightly oversize. This part, as well as the pistol grip cap, is dressed down to shape after the cement has dried, and during the usual shaping, sanding and finishing of the stock. If you use a metal fore end cap, this is merely slid over the fore end which had been inletted to accept this cap. A single screw holds it in place.

Fast removal of excess wood from the stock is best achieved with the use of a coarse rasp, but this rasp should be exchanged for one of finer cut as the stock nears its proper proportions. It finally should be smoothed up with a large mill file before the sanding operations.

The wooden hand guard furnished with Fajen stocks must be worked down as a part of the stock itself for this important piece to be a perfect fit on the finished stock. The permanent attachment of this hand guard may be accomplished by utilizing the original barrel band or by two screws. The metal cleat must be riveted to the hand guard in the same manner as on the original G.I. version.

With the stock rasped and filed to correct contour, it then is given a thorough sanding, beginning with a medium coarse garnet paper and sanding until all signs of file marks are removed. Following this, the sand paper is reduced in coarseness and the stock again thoroughly sanded with a finer paper until a paper of 400 grit is utilized.

A rubber recoil pad may be installed after cutting the

There are several good stock finishes available at most gun shops and like all things, what one man will swear by, another man will swear at, so use your own judgment or the recommendations of your favorite gunsmith.

After applying the stock finish of your chocie, it is time to consider the final stock decoration — the checkering.

For the checkering on this carbine, the only chore that I did not perform on the entire gun was done by Fred Shaw of Anaheim, California, who has built an excellent reputation for himself for his outstanding work on custom rifles.

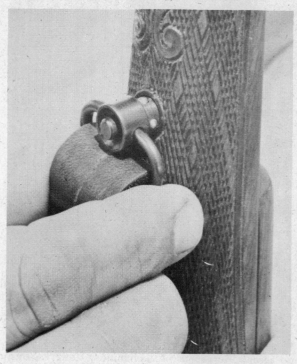

Detachable sling swivels were installed on forend and toe of the stock. These, author feels, are the most practical swivels for this type of conversion.

When stock checkering has been completed, the new cuts are coated liberally with lemon oil. Author prefers this to bring out beauty of wood, the design.

stock the proper length and deducting for the thickness of the pad. This should be installed after the stock has been completely finish-shaped and before any sealer or stock finish has been applied. In this way, no refinishing of the finished stock will be necessary in the area of the recoil pad.

Methods of finishing a rifle stock will vary greatly from one stockmaker to the next; even from one section of the country to the other. Stockmakers located in wet, damp climates find that oil hand-rubbed finish is best suited to their area. On the other hand, one located in a hot, dry climate will choose a stock finished with a synthetic.

The age-old method of dampening a new stock to raise the "whiskers" is pretty much a thing of the past due to the many perfected wood sealers now on the market. These sealers not only completely waterproof the fibers of the wood, but prevent the rough fibers from popping out on a stock, when it is soaked in a sudden rain storm.

Following the sanding of this stock, a commerical wood sealer was swabbed on until the wood would absorb no more, then the stock was allowed to dry for twenty-four hours. After drying, the stock again was sanded with 400 grit paper. By this time the pores of the wood were well filled with the transparent sealer and the stock was ready for its final finish.

After discussing the design, I settled for the one shown on these pages as the most attractive and best suited to this particular type of stock. Two weeks later, when I returned, Shaw was putting the finishing touches to the stock. The way this man can handle a carving chisel is amazing and it was fascinating to watch as his hands guided that razor sharp chisel over invisible lines, carving his own design with no visible pattern.

Some craftsmen will want to attempt checkering their own gunstocks which is entirely possible. Checkering is within the ability of most "tool-wise" men and is discussed at length in Chapter 8.

Checkering a rifle stock should be done after the finish has been applied. Following the checkering and the final clean-up, lemon oil should be applied to highlight the cuts and accentuate the design to the highest degree.

With the checkering oiled, it is now time to assemble the carbine into a complete unit. We now have a crude weapon of war turned into a beautiful sporting rifle.

To install sling swivels on your carbine, make certain that the forward sling swivel is placed forward of that area of the stock that houses the gas port and operating lever, as this section of the wood is quite thin.

THAT SURPLUS ARM MAY BE ILLEGAL UNLESS YOU SHORTEN THE CLIP

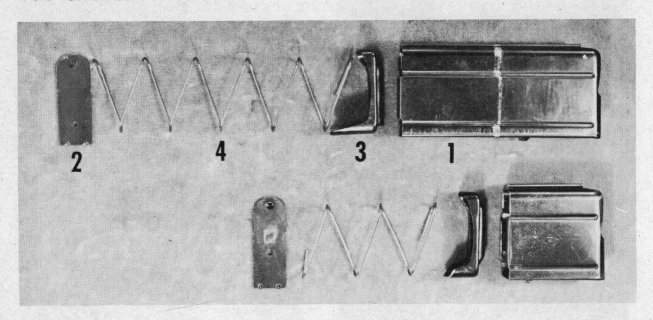

This project can be termed most aptly "from fifteen to five in twenty," which simply means that you can convert a standard fifteen-round M1 carbine magazine to accept only five rounds in twenty minutes — or less, if you are adept in the use of tools.

This conversion may be accomplished simply by inserting a pre-shaped wooden block into the full-size magazine, allowing only enough room for the magazine to accept five rounds of ammunition. However, this is not the most desirable method, if cleanness of contour is desired in the carbine when the magazine is installed.

This project requires that a portion of the magazine be cut away, the follower spring shortened and the follower "tail" cropped slightly to allow smooth loading of the magazine to full capacity of five rounds. The basic reason behind this operation is the fact that in many states a carbine or rifle having a magazine capacity of more than five rounds is strictly illegal. Other than this, the shortening of the magazine tends to give the carbine a more trim and sleek look.

The first step in shortening the magazine is to completely strip it down by first removing the plate at the base of the magazine. This plate is held in place by a small retaining nub. When this nub is raised slightly — enough to clear the forward edge of the magazine — it may be slid free of the housing, which, in turn, will release both the follower and the follower spring.

In order to eliminate confusion, each part is numbered in the photo above:
1. Magazine Housing
2. Base Plate
3. Follower
4. Follower Spring

Following the field stripping of the magazine, all parts are thoroughly cleaned of grease and any rust with the use of cleaning solvent and a light rubbing with steel wool.

The next step in the actual shortening operation on the magazine will be to take the housing in hand and measure exactly two inches up from the bottom, drawing a line completely around the housing at this measured distance with a white leaded blueprint pencil, so that it can be easily seen during the cutting operation.

The housing then is placed (but not too tightly) in a vise and where the measured section is cut off with a fine toothed hacksaw or, if a pipe cutting abrasive wheel is available, this may be utilized. Following the removal

The unaltered clip is compared to one shortened by Bish, with follower before and after treatment.

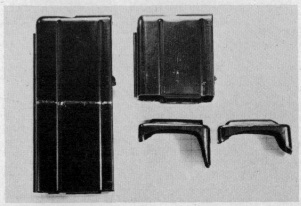

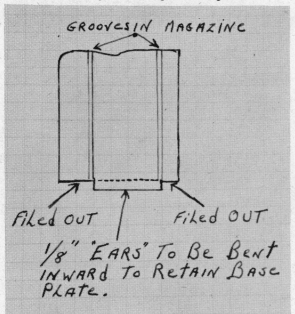

Diagram illustrates method in filing clip to form base plate retaining ears, with grooves as guide.

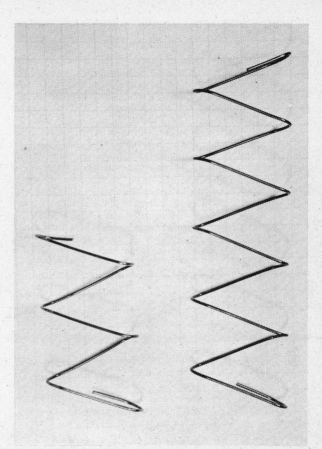

The follower spring is cut in two parts of equal length. One section can be retained as a spare.

of the lower part of the housing, a file is then used to smooth up the cut.

The next step is to form the "ears" which will be bent over to retain the base plate in place, when the magazine is reassembled. This is accomplished by using the grooves in the sides of the housing as measuring devices, between which the ears will be located.

The ears are formed by filing both rear and front sections of the housing down exactly one-eighth of an inch, leaving the ears intact between the two grooves (as per illustration). These ears then are carefully bent over to form the retainers for the base plate.

With the base plate retaining ears formed and bent to perfection, we now cut the follower spring into two equal parts. One part is to be used in the magazine, while the other may be used as a spare.

The tail or lower section of the follower must be shortened a quarter inch to prevent bottoming on the base plate with five rounds loaded in clip.

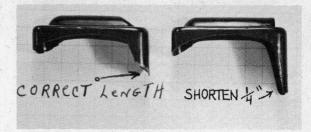

After careful filing, the two ears then are bent to accept the base plate in a snug fit as on original.

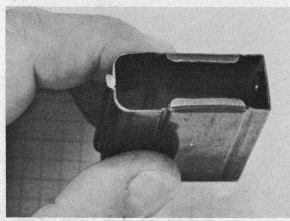

The final step is to shorten the tail on the follower so that when five rounds of ammunition are loaded into the magazine this tail does not seat on the base plate prematurely, rendering the magazine incapable of accepting five rounds. One quarter-inch removed from this area is about right, but this may vary slightly from one follower to the next.

With the retainer ears cut and bent, and the spring shortened as well as the tail of the follower bobbed, you are now ready to reassemble your new five-shot carbine magazine. If you took care in each simple operation, your magazine should function perfectly, and with one round in the chamber of the carbine, you have six shots.

When my GI carbine was first received, I had no idea of going to such limits in order to turn out a fairly attractive and yet more servicable weapon. The labors of almost two months, in my spare time, are climaxed in the carbine and case illustrated on these pages and when "reconstruction" was first started on this $20 new arrival, it was with the idea of simply cleaning up the metal and installing one of the Mannlicher-type stocks.

But as time progressed, I went whole hog and added a few extras, just to give the carbine that distinctive look of individuality, a one of-a-kind. One thing led to another until the $20 carbine had progressed to the point of becoming an almost entirely different arm than it originally had been.

When the final oil had been applied to the stock and well rubbed in, and the gold initial plate installed on the ivory pistol-grip cap, the carbine was literally finished. But was it? Here was a carbine dressed in a new stock and a fine blue job, trimmed with elephant ivory, deluxe checkering and a gold name plate, but still something seemed amiss.

What this rebuilt carbine needed to really set it apart from all others was a plush, velvet-lined, compartment case sporting ivory handled and gold-plated accessories, etc. So it was off to the local lumber yard to search for a suitable hardwood from which to manufacture such a case.

Walnut was priced first, but this idea was discarded in a hurry after hearing the going price of the precious wood, so a well-grained mahogany in half-inch thickness finally was selected. This mahogany ran nine inches in width, which was ideal for the size case to be built. The finished case was to measure thirty-eight inches in length by nine inches in width with a depth of 3½ inches.

The case was formed by first building a framework of these dimensions which would form the sides and ends of the case. This framework was of mahogany "slats" cut to three inches in width. By mortising the top and bottom surfaces into this framework approximately one-quarter inch there was an inside depth of 2½ inches; just right for holding the carbine securely in place. All joints and the mortised top and bottom surfaces were glued into place, then securely clamped until dry. (It is best to use no nails or screws).

When one has gone to this much work to rebuild any arm, it deserves the type of setting described here.

The lid section is marked off, measuring down from the proposed top exactly 1¼ inches for planned cut.

A well equipped woodworking shop is not necessary to turn out such a gun case if care is taken. In the assembling of the case, no woodworking tools other than a common eight-point carpenter's saw and a wood plane were used, since my shop boasts no tools other than those used in gunsmithing. The mortising of the top and bottom surfaces was done on a drill press with use of a routing tool.

With the case assembled and glued into a solid block-like affair, and the glue thoroughly dried, the case then is sanded until it is glassy smooth. Following this sanding, the lid is marked at 1¼ inches in thickness and sawed off. Cutting the lid off is best accomplished with a table saw if available, but it may be cut by hand, and with reasonable precision, using a sharp eight-point carpenter's saw.

With the lid cut and the saw marks carefully sanded

Prior to cutting off lid, entire box is thoroughly sanded, using sanding block. It then is marked as described and lid is cut free with fine-tooth saw.

away, the case then is given a good coating of clear wood sealer and allowed to dry overnight. I strongly feel that the hardware for such a case should be of good quality, and for this reason, solid brass should be utilized. This brass may be gold plated to add even greater appeal and desirability to the finished product.

With the sealer thoroughly dried, the case again is sanded with 400 grit garnet paper. Be extremely careful that the lid is in its proper position during sanding to avoid lid-fit distortion. Sand both lid and bottom part of case as a single unit.

The velvet lining is installed over contoured pine forms, using transparent glue; pins hold for drying.

It is best to utilize the concealed type of hinge in preference to the outside, visible screw type, which may be removed by merely removing the exposed screws. A good drawer-type lock can be utilized instead of a common hasp-and-padlock type for both attractiveness and future value. Care should be exercised in the installation of lock and hinges so that a neat, precise job results. The application of brass protective corner plates will add to the finished case in both attractiveness and durability.

The most trying of all steps in the building of a compartmented gun case is the installation of the interior. This may be accomplished in several different ways. One may line the entire case with velvet, which first has been glued to pre-measured and appropriately sized pieces of stiff cardboard. This is glued into place on the bottom, top and sides of the case. Following this, stiff partitions of velvet-covered cardboard are carefully glued into proper position to form the desired compartments for gun and accessories.

It was found, in the case of the M1 carbine and accessories, that in preference to the partitioned-type case, a contoured type of inletted blocking would be better suited. For this, several pieces of lightweight sugar pine were used on which the carbine and all accessories were placed in exactly the positions that they would occupy in the finished case. Around each item was traced an outline, to be either cut out with a saw or chiseled to conform to the contour of each accessory.

Special compartments can be cut in sugar pine forms prior to lining. These can be lined with velvet that is glued over strips of cardboard of correct size.

Holder for gold-plated cleaning rod is made from small pieces of elephant ivory, held by one screw.

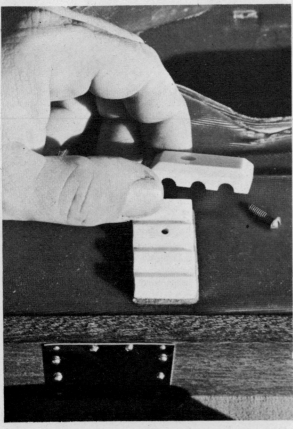

With these pine blocks — two in number — cut to proper dimensions and inletted for each accessory, they then were carefully covered with a fine grade of red velvet, which was firmly glued to the underside of the blocks. Care must be taken during this phase to allow no glue to be spilled or rubbed onto the exposed surfaces of the velvet as it is impossible to remove without leaving an unsightly smear.

A lidded compartment may be pre-cut into the pine blocking. The velvet lining covering is cut from corner to corner of this space, then the entire interior of this compartment is lined with velvet-covered cardboard which is glued into place on all four sides and bottom. The inside of the lid may be of wood, highly polished, or tightly covered with velvet glued into place. This compartment, in addition to being a lidded accessory box, also may be utilized as storage for two fifteen-shot magazines by merely removing the lid. This compartment should measure five inches in length by 1¼ inches in width before lining.

In the preparation of the ivory-handled and gold-plated accessories such as the screw driver, gas port wrench, and three-section cleaning rod, I again found the plating kit, produced by Wisconsin Platers Supply Company to be invaluable. It was no chore to produce a professional type of gold plating on these tools in a matter of minutes, after the metal had first been properly polished. I have used this plating kit for several years now and have had excellent results from it. It is simple and inexpensive and produces quality plating in gold, silver, copper, brass and nickel. As something of an afterthought, I nickel-plated the trigger of the carbine. The brass corner plates, locks and other metal trim of a gun case may be easily and quickly plated.

The lining of the interior of a gun case requires forethought and preparation. Velvet readily shows any glue smear or hand smudge, so care must be taken to prevent such an occurence if a perfect job is to be the final result.

The laying-out of the case's interior may vary with

Cartridge block is fashioned from highly figured lignum vitae. Gas port wrench and the screw driver are gold-plated, with ivory handles then installed.

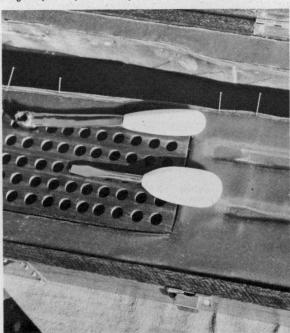

personal taste, but in the case of the illustrated outfit, I featured a solid brass (gold-plated) cleaning rod which is held in place by ivory blocks. In addition to this, and the screw driver and gas port wrench, I made a special cut-out to accommodate a fine Randall hunting knife. Last but not least, a cartridge block made from lignum vitae, and holding fifty highly polished .30 M1 carbine cartridges completes the case.

It is not wise to add too much decoration to the exterior of the case as this can easily cheapen the entire job.

The exterior may be finished by applying a smooth

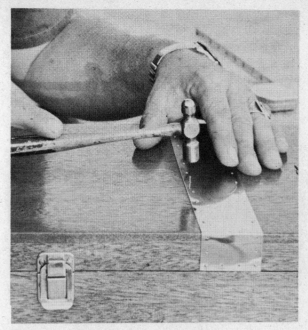

The metal strips binding the case first are bent to fit corners perfectly, then installed with brads.

The case can be bound with brass or copper strips, adding to its appearance, also to its durability.

coat of varnish, rubbing it down and applying another coat until the case is glassy smooth. I found that by using Birchwood Stock Finish, produced by the Birchwood-Casey Company of Minnesota, much of the labor of a varnish job was eliminated and a more durable finish resulted.

There are any number of finishing touches that may be made to such a case; one of the most appropriate would be to have a brass or silver plate inletted into the lid which indentifies the man who customized the carbine and built the case; the date of completion also is appropriate.

A hundred years from now, some collector may drool over your craftsmanship in completely customizing an antique M1 carbine and casing it in a one-of-a-kind box.

Finished case contains necessary accessories such as screw driver, gas port wrench, cleaning rod. The matching hunting knife also is handled with ivory.

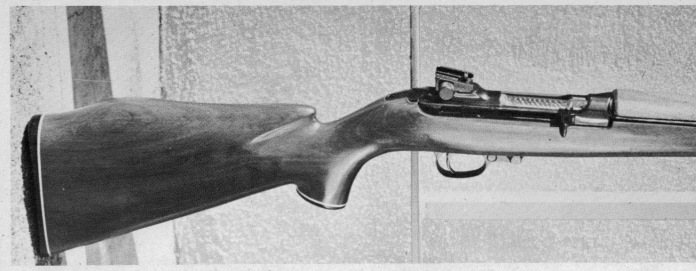

Restocking did much to change the image of the M-1 carbine from a military arm to one that boasts the lines of a sporter.

The M-1 carbine is old enough to be either a legend or a classic; the only thing that keeps it from being both is the number still in use.

However, for those seeking to give their own pets a bit of individuality, there are numerous approaches to customization that can be taken. This chapter has dealt at great length with one approach. On the following pages, are illustrated several other ideas that one might use, depending upon the amount of money he wants to spend; the amount of time involved, and the ultimate purpose.

THE EASIEST WAY — if not the least expensive— of customizing that war surplus M-1 carbine is to send it out to the experts. On these two pages the GI-issue has been turned into a sleek, well balanced little sporter that retains the action of the original and little else.

This carbine was revamped and restocked by Bain & Davis Sporting Goods of San Gabriel, California, for approximately $85. The stock was carved from a special Fajen blank which is cut specifically for carbines. The rest of the work, though, was done strictly by the San Gabriel outfit. Not only was the stock cut with an eye to pleasing flow and design, but the hand-guard, which covers the top of the barrel was redesigned. On the original GI model, this bit of wood fit loosely so that it would absorb heat under rapid-fire combat firing. The Bain & Davis conversion fits tightly, and the metal band at the forend of the guard is one of their own design. Thus, a single screw through the bottom of the stock goes into the band, holding the gun and stock together.

Fajen supplied the basic stock for this conversion to sporter, featuring a redesigned hand guard.

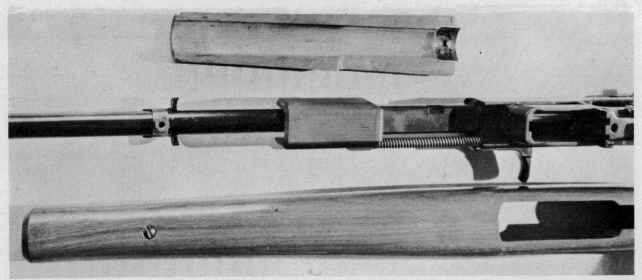

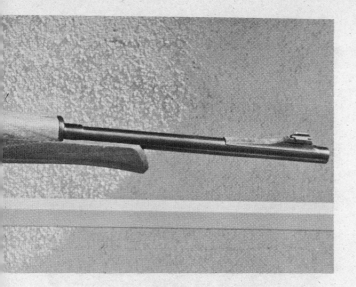

Approaches In Customizing The M-1 Carbine Cover A Wide Range Of Imagination, Goods, Prices!

A Williams ramp front sight replaces the winged GI version, but the orginal "L" rear sight was left on the gun. The bolt was jeweled for great beauty, and the entire barrel and action were reblued after the metal had been hand-polished. As the wood on the forward edge of the stock is rather thin, it was fiberglassed inside to provide added strength.

The proof of any gun is in the shooting, and when this surplus item had been rebuilt as pictured here, Keith Davis found he was able to shoot two-inch groups at a hundred yards.

The bolt of the government-issue carbine was jeweled for appearance, rather than to improve functioning.

Metal band at forend of hand guard is of special design. Single screw through the stock goes into band, holds stock to metal.

Basket weave pattern on stock was costly and may
appear out of place to some on this firearm,
but it was in keeping with the owner's desires.

This carbine — with Mannlicher stock — is owned by
Christopher Rivera of Tijuana, Mexico, who had it
customized by the Krasne Gunshop of San Diego,
California, at a cost of $329. The stock is of myrtle-
wood, which has been beautifully finished and carved.
Inlays are of molded catalyn, a variety of extremely hard
plastic.

The pistol grip cap also is of catalyn, while the clip
has been reduced to a five-round magazine from its
original fifteen-round capacity. The gunsmith, in order
to stock it with the Mannlicher model, cut down the
slide of the carbine action.

The muzzle has been equipped with a steel forend cap
from an old .45-70 Springfield "trap door" musket.
Perhaps the greatest innovation is in the sights. The
original rear sight has been removed and a folding model

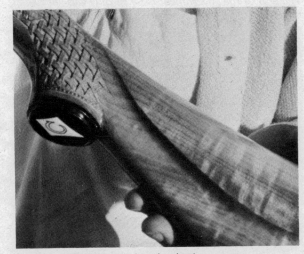

Special initial inlay in the pistol grip cap gave
this carbine the mark of pride in ownership that
was wanted. The stock was fashioned of myrtlewood.

Forend cap is of steel and is from an old .45-70
Springfield musket; sights have been replaced, too.

Top: Muzzle brake from a Johnson automatic rifle was welded to carbine barrel to give it additional length. (Below) Trigger shoe was incorporated, plus simple, easily installed initials of the carbine's owner.

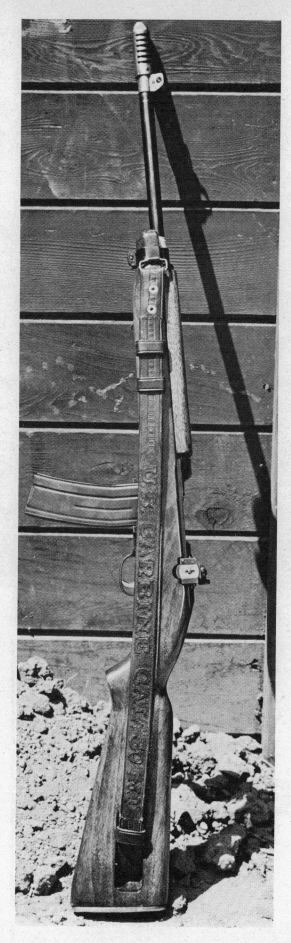

placed forward on the barrel, while a ramp front sight has been substituted forward.

The basket weave carving is clean and concise, while the plain sections of the wood have been so highly polished as to catch reflections.

A conversion which you can do yourself is the type accomplished here by John Bianchi. Retaining the original stock, he used commercial wood bleach to lighten the color of the walnut. In applying this, one should do it outdoors on a hot sunny day, as sunlight hastens the action upon the wood.

The muzzle brake is from a Johnson auto rifle and is not too practical unless welded to the barrel. The reason for it being installed was that the barrel was too short to be legal and this added length made the gun lawful.

Unlike the other carbines shown, this one has retained the wing-type front sight, but a Lyman peepsight has been installed at the rear. The initials on the stock are those which can be purchased at nearly any jewelry store, adhering directly to the wood with a plastic adhesive.

After the color of the wood had been lightened with bleach, Bianchi then treated it with hot linseed oil, and finally applied a coat of hard automobile wax to give it sheen. He completely honed the entire action, then hand-polished the bolt and all moving parts, finally rebluing.

As customized, he has found the gun to be excellent for varmit shooting at a hundred yards. He uses regular government issue ammo, but grinds off a portion of the steel jacket on each bullet to expose the lead.

And this type of customizing can be done on a tight budget. Cost of polishing and bluing the gun was $16, while the rear sight cost $8. Price of the muzzle brake was $4, and the bottles of wood bleach cost approximately $1. Total: $29.

Chapter 16

DRESS-UP FOR THE REMINGTON 600

When Tom Fry, Remington Arms representative, first mentioned the intention of the Remington people to turn out the compact little Model 600 in 6mm caliber, I immediately envisioned this little carbine as having great possibilities as a Mannlicher sporter. Of course Remington didn't at that time — nor do they yet — produce this carbine in a stocked-to-the-muzzle version, but I still was curious about how such a restocking job would work out using the 600 barreled action.

That conversation with Fry regarding this then new 6mm caliber Model 600 took place way back in April, 1964, at the National Rifle Association convention in Los Angeles. For several years my ideas of converting the 600 to a Mannlicher-type sporter lay dormant in the back of my mind.

I still had visions of some day tackling this job just to see what it would look and handle like when finished. That day came when I ordered a barreled action in 6.5mm Remington magnum. A call to Reinhart Fajen, Incorporated, the stockmakers in Warsaw, Missouri, produced a semi-finished Mannlicher-type stock for the 600. Then my job of conversion began.

The Model 600 carbine, either in the 6.5mm Rem. mag or the .350 Rem. mag caliber, is a sweet little rifle. The trigger pull leaves little to be desired and the action is a honey, but, to my way of thinking, there are several items about this little shooter that bear redoing. These things I planned to alter or change in my own conversion.

While there are those who are thrilled with that ventilated rib on the 600, it leaves me cold! And that dog's hind leg bolt handle just had to go! One other thing about the stock 600 that doesn't exactly meet my personal requirements is the trigger guard. The trigger guard is rather small and a man hunting in cold weather and wearing a pair of thick gloves could

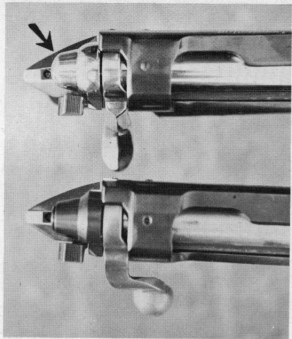

The sharp outer edges of the bolt sleeve used were recontoured to afford a more custom look to carbine.

The new bolt handle was sawed and filed to shape, then cut from the steel bar and welded to the bolt.

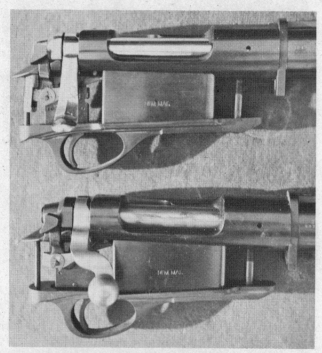

Author replaced the original S-shaped bolt handle with a Mannlicher-type, which he designed himself.

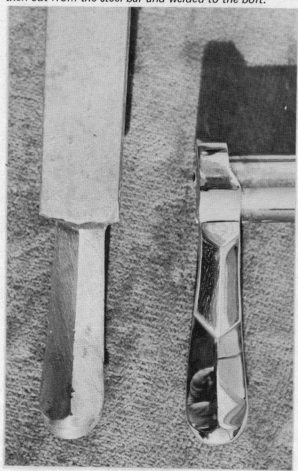

experience trouble getting his finger onto the trigger. Eventually I want to manufacture a steel plate which will be inletted into the existing trigger guard mortise and topped with a shotgun-type trigger guard.

The first thing I considered in starting the conversion job on my 600 was whether to leave that ventilated rib on the barrel. I went to the trouble of countersinking those blister-like screw heads holding the rib to the barrel. This gave the rib a smoother appearance, but for some reason, I felt it just wouldn't look right on a stocked-to-the-muzzle Mannlicher-type rifle. I removed the rib and hacksawed the steel studs off the barrel, then dressed them with a file until they were undetectable. While this operation necessitates the rebluing of the entire barreled action, it still gave the trim lines I wanted in the finished product. The removal of the entire ventilated rib left the barrel with no sights but this was easily remedied by installing a Williams Shorty ramp on the front and a Williams Fool-Proof sight on the rear.

The next step was to do something about that S-shaped bolt handle. No self-respecting Mannlicher-styled rifle should have anything but a Mannlicher bolt handle. This handle, often referred to as a *spoon*, is made easily from a bar of steel first by hacksawing it to shape, then grinding, polishing and finishing, while it still is attached to the steel bar for ease of handling. Finally, the new spoon-type bolt handle is bent to the proper angle, cut free of the steel bar and welded to the bolt. Following the installation of my bolt handle, I overlayed the upper portion of the shank with 14-carat gold plate which added a flamboyant but custom look to the overall job.

The installation of a new bolt handle on the Remington 600 is a touchy job. The entire bolt handle is brazed or silver-soldered to the bolt, itself, so this section must be clamped carefully and tightly to prevent it from coming loose when the welding torch is applied in installing the new handle. I clamped the upper section of the bolt handle in a drill press vise be-

The Mannlicher-type stock must offer clean, straight lines of contour in forend area. Bish checks this contour before beginning final shaping and finishing.

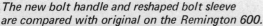

The new bolt handle and reshaped bolt sleeve are compared with original on the Remington 600.

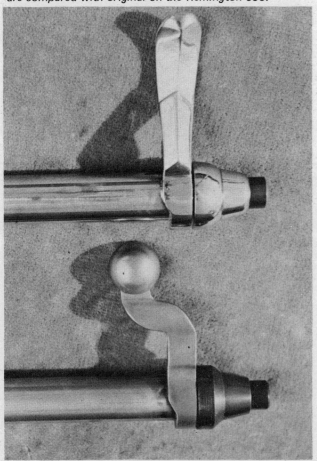

fore attempting to weld on the new spoon.

The bolt sleeve on the standard Model 600 is well-shaped but I feel that by rounding over those sharp shoulders, a more custom-like job will result. After all, when building a custom rifle, I feel that every safe and sane innovation that will enhance the appearance of the finished product should be accomplished. This rounding over of the bolt sleeve is a minor chore but in the finished rifle all of these little innovations will add up to a rifle that is highly customized and individualistic.

The walnut stock sent by Rick Fajen from the family plant was typical of their fine craftsmanship in good stock design. This semi-finished stock was of the full Mannlicher-type especially designed for use on the Model 600 Remington and is available in the utility grade or the superbly figured AAA fancy grade.

It was necessary to do major inletting around the tang area of the new stock to accept the rear receiver tang and for smooth operation of the safety. This done and the barrel inletted into the stock, I completely glass bedded the barrel and receiver with *Micro-Bed*. While there are those who frown upon glass bedding a rifle stock, I have found that it is the only way to be assured of top accuracy and little or no stock warpage. This goes double for a Mannlicher-type rifle.

In early stages of redesign, modifications of the front sight, plastic rib were attempted. However, both were discarded as unsuitable for such change.

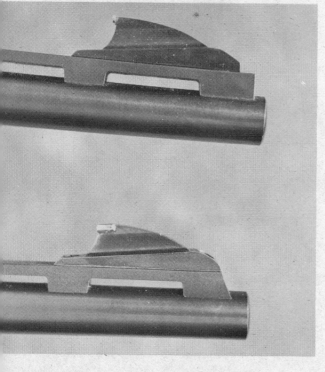

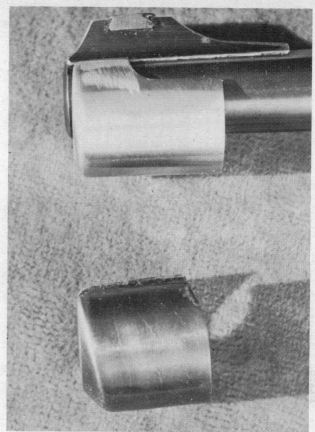

At top is the hand-made snobble or forend cap that was made by Bish. It is compared with the standard version that normally is furnished with Fajen stock.

The bolt release lever of Remington Model 600 can be inconvenient in removing the bolt. Bish devised push button release mounted on the side of the stock.

While the folks at Fajen included both models of their forend caps, the standard and the Sweptline, I have long preferred to make my own caps from sheet black iron. The caps I make are much smaller in diameter, thus allowing the finished forend of the stock to be slimmer, just as a well-built Mannlicher forend should be. These caps are made easily by first bending a correctly sized piece of mild sheet iron to the desired contour, then welding the end caps in place. The barrel cut-out may be drilled with the proper size drill prior to welding in place, then filed and finished later.

It also is my feeling that a truly custom-built forend cap should be equipped with protruding arms that go up and around the contour of the barrel, thus locking the barrel to the forend cap when the cap is slid on and the retaining screw installed.

The installation of a forend cap is covered in Chapter 12.

Following the installation of the metal forend cap — and not before — the shaping of the entire forearm section of the stock begins. It must be kept in mind during this operation that the stock must retain a perfectly straight line from the front tang of the trigger guard up to the forend cap. Don't leave a belly, either in or out, in the forearm if a well-shaped Mannlicher design is expected.

Custom Model 600 has all-steel trigger guard and floor plate, push botton bolt release, other one-of-a-kind innovations.

Original Designers Would Have To Take A Good Look To Recognize Their Carbine After This Custom Going Over!

Several months ago I finished a Springfield conversion rechambered to accept the potent .308 Norma magnum cartridge, quite naturally, a full-stocked Mannlicher. On this rifle I had used a Fajen stock redesigned to my own tastes. The Monte Carlo hump on the comb was removed for better fit and, in the final stages of completion. I mounted a fine Leupold 4X scope on a Conetrol mount. Today this rifle will group under one-inch at a hundred yards in the hands of a good benchrest shooter.

Again using a Fajen Mannlicher stock, I glass-bedded the Model 600 barreled action, making especially certain that the recoil lug area of the stock was reinforced with a steel plate prior to the glassing operation. It is my opinion that all magnum rifles should be reinforced in this manner before any extensive use afield.

The exterior finishing of a rifle stock is a stan-

Customizing done, Redfield scope is collimated to the axis of the bore prior to zeroing on the range.

dard procedure; however, in building a Mannlicher-type stock be sure that the forend is slimmed down far more than for a conventional sporting, or half-stock rifle. In shaping the cheekpiece it always is desireable to give it a sculptured look by leaving a slight bead around the outer edge. This is accomplished, after the cheekpiece has been finish-sanded, with a mill bastard file. I find that one of my wife's fingernail emery boards works great for the final touch-up sanding of this operation.

One notable irritation I found with the Model 600 is in attempting to remove the bolt from the receiver. There is no visible bolt release lever, so it is necessary to "go fishing" with a small pry bar alongside the bolt to depress the bolt lock. In my book this is a poor arrangement. After all, who wants to fumble around with a pry bar to remove a rifle bolt in the dark?

I prefer the mere touch of a lever or button to

Forearm of the Fajen stock was slimmed down to compliment the proportions of the Model 600 barrel.

Improvement in appearance is apparent with new steel trigger guard, floor plate. Original version of the guard and plate, at right, seem crude by comparison.

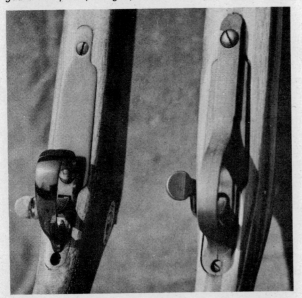

remove a bolt from any rifle, so I derived a simple lever-button arrangement operating much like the button type slide safety as found on fine W. W. Greener firearms. This consists of an oval plate of German or sterling silver. The knurled thumb button is recessed into this plate so that only the knurling of the button protrudes above the surface of the plate. The button shank extends into the interior of the stock where it contacts the rounded under side of the bolt lock. When the button is pushed to the rear, it depresses the bolt lock, instantly releasing the bolt from the receiver.

The silver plate containing the push button is inlaid into the stock at the proper location and is held in place by two small flat-head screws. Precise workmanship must be exercised in the placement of the plate to assure that the shank of the thumb button will make an exacting contact with the front edge of the bolt locking lever. It took me over an hour to locate this position on the stocks exterior before attempting to inlay the plate containing the push button.

The shank of the button should be threaded to about 6 x 32 to accept a quarter-inch threaded brass sleeve. This sleeve may be filed and cut in size for an exacting fit against the bolt lock. When the bolt release button and plate have been recessed into the stock, there is ample clearance between the trigger assembly and the walls of the stock to accept a simple wire return spring necessary to return the push button to the locked position. While this bolt release button assembly may sound like a simple affair, it took me over six hours to perfect the prototype used on my carbine. It's an addition to a Model 600 Remington that is functional as well as adding that customized flavor.

After much deliberation, I decided to eliminate both the ventilated rib on the barrel as well as the plastic trigger guard. I found it impossible to place my finger on the trigger while wearing gloves without firing the rifle. This can prove disconcerting in cold weather where heavy hunting gloves are worn.

Replacing the ventilated rib is a Williams shorty ramp and Williams Guide rear sight. For a new trigger guard and plate, I manufactured these parts from a bar of tool steel. The outline of the original trigger plate was laid out on the steel, and cut out with a hacksaw, then finished with a disc sander and files to fit exactly the pre-mortised cut-out in the stock. The trigger guard — another custom feature — was patterned after the shotgun-type guard found on the finest European sporting rifles. While the manufacture of both trigger plate and guard entail considerable handwork and several hours, it will all add up to a highly customized job when the rifle is completed.

In eliminating the ventilated rib from the barrel, it was necessary to remove the steel studs protruding from the barrel so that it might be buffed and reblued. These studs are quite hard but a sharp hacksaw removed them quickly. The stumps of the studs then are

Above: with standard Model 600 carbine, to release bolt, it is necessary to reach catch inside action. (Below) Push button was installed to make it more simple to remove the bolt when one wishes.

From top: Bish's custom Norma magnum; custom Model 600; basic factory-version Remington carbine.

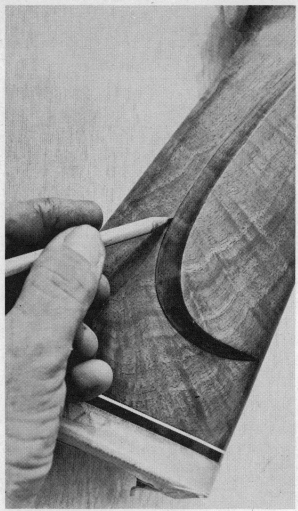

Raised cheek piece on the stock can be given this sculptured effect through the use of several types of small files, as well as one's infinite patience.

Head of original screw for trigger guard and floor plate was too large. It was dressed to size of smaller dimensions, which had neater appearance.

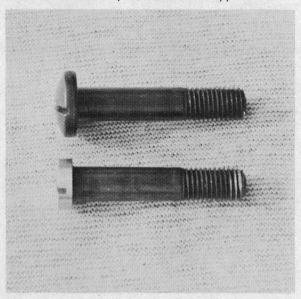

ground or filed until flush with the barrel's surface before the entire barrel and receiver section are polished and reblued. During the rebluing, it is necessary to remove the trigger assembly. This is accomplished simply by removing the steel retaining pins holding the assembly to the receiver.

While commercial forend caps are available, I prefer to manufacture my own from sheet black iron. In this way I get a much trimmer, smaller and more streamlined version than those furnished with semi-finished Mannlicher-type stocks. There's nothing wrong with the commercial version, mind you — I just like to roll by own.

The recoil pad and pistol grip cap are pretty much matters of personal choice. I made the pistol grip cap on my M/600 from a piece of American bison horn and covered the retaining screw with a piece of rounded elephant ivory. The recoil pad is a Pachmayr.

The overall finish of the stock and metal will determine just how good a job you have done in revamping your little 600 Remington into a custom rifle. If you have no bluing setup, have this job done by a competent gunsmith, but make damned sure he is competent! I have seen some mighty sad blue jobs turned out by some who should be knitting instead of butchering guns!

Most home craftsmen will want to finish their own wood. The first stock is always the hardest, and they get easier as you go along. The most important phase of stock finishing is in the final sanding, removing all of those minute file marks and scratches left by coarse sandpaper during the earlier shaping.

There are several good commercial stock finishes on the market that one might choose from. Tru-Oil, George Brothers and Birchwood brands all are good for producing a beautiful and lasting finish on a stock if properly applied. Follow the directions furnished with each bottle and you can't go wrong.

Once the finish has been applied and properly rubbed down with rotten stone and waxed to a glass-like surface, the stock is ready for checkering.

The Mannlicherized M/600 shown on these pages was checkered by Pete Thacker who currently is doing much of the custom checkering for Los Angeles' Pachmayr Gun Works. As Thacker could do the job in about half the time it would take me, I took the stock to him after the final rub-down and polishing and in about three hours he returned it with a plain, but attractive pattern on the pistol grip and forearm. For my customized M/600 I chose a Redfield scope base with the new peep-sight on the rear and one of the latest 4X 4-P CCH Redfield scopes. After checking the alignment with a Sweany Site-A-Line, the revamped M/600 Remington was ready for its first hunting trip.

Little Daddy and Big Daddy — the 6.5 Rem. mag and the big .308 Norma magnum Springfield — complement each other. I have every confidence in the world in both of these hunting rifles. That's partly because I built them and know what's in 'em, and because I know that either of these calibers will down anything on the American Continents, as well as most of the soft-skinned animals in Africa!

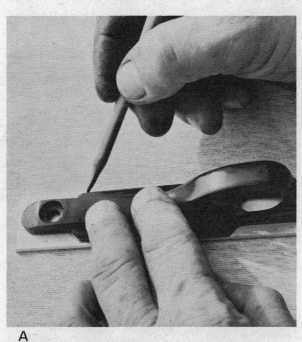

A

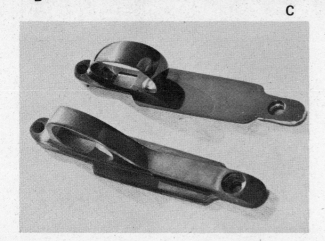

B

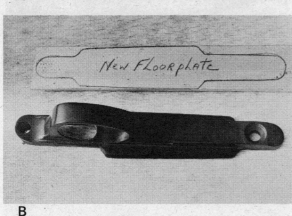

C

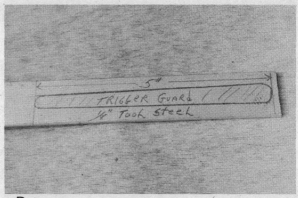

D

E

A. *Old floor plate was outlined on raw metal, as author did not like original.* B. *Once traced, the floor plate assembly could be cut out of metal.* C. *Trigger guard assembly at bottom is standard unit, while the one above it was made by Bish of tool steel to meet his personal need.* D. *The trigger guard for his custom unit also was traced on tool steel, then cut out.* E. *The trigger guard was properly shaped before being attached to floor plate.* F. *Factory version of the Model 600 shows the impressed checkering, factory-produced trigger guard.* G. *Reworked model has clean lines, and shows imagination.*

F

G

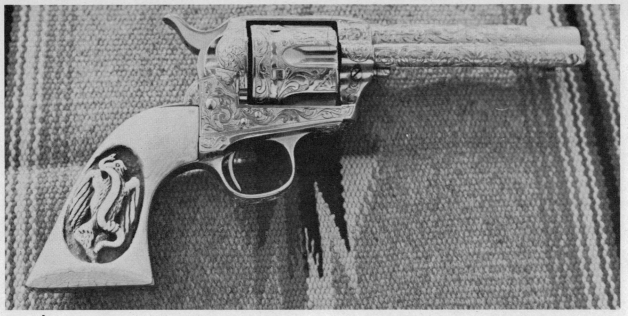

A

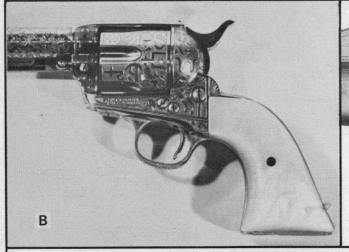

B

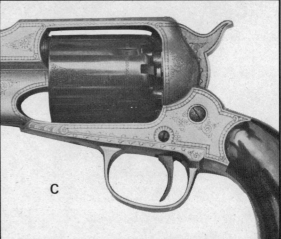

C

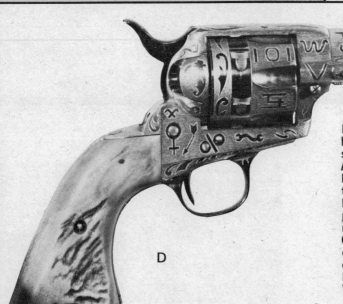

D

Illustrated are various styles, designs of both engraving, etching. Beginners should start with simple patterns.

A Colt SA has both floral and scroll work by modern artist. Extensive use of matting tool is used in this type.

B Cattle brand engravings have great appeal, are easiest. This one by Kornbrath is most famous of this design.

C Delicate engraving on this pistol is not overdone, but difficult. It was accomplished in Italy.

D Machine engraving as on this Great Western is clean, lacks originality.

Chapter 17

DRESS-UP YOUR FAVORITES

ETCHING:

E

F

E Combining relief etching and bold engraving, this S&W is work of art. Grip is by Tiffany's, overlaid with silver.
F Floral engraving on .380 Browning auto is classic type of art from Europe today.

T HE beautifying of firearms by etching, engraving, inlaying and other forms of decoration is nearly as old as gunpowder itself. Etching, as a form of decorative art on metal, has been practiced since the time of the ancient Egyptians.

This type of arms decoration requires that the student possess no little amount of artistic ability, plus a working knowledge of a few simple tools necessary for the successful completion of the etching project. It requires that the workman be able to combine artistic as well as manual skill in the execution of his labor.

The fundamentals of etching are difficult to put down on paper; they are best learned by actual practice; therefore this will deal only with the rudiments of etching, necessary tools, acids, mordants, stopping-out var-

Needed for sketching design on gun surface through protective wax or varnish coating are needles, pin vise, awl, oil stone for keeping needles sharp and small artist's brush for touching up the over-runs.

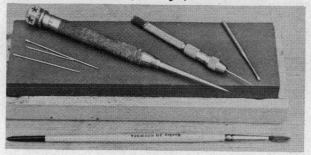

nishes, etc. This is meant for those who would enjoy experimenting in this art of firearms decoration, but it is recommended to begin with, that the novice practice on scrap metal such as sheet iron instead of his nice new pistol or rifle — learning to walk before you run is especially true in this situation.

The tools necessary for even the finest job of etching are simple ones and can be assembled by almost any person right in his own home. Worn dental burrs can be obtained from the family dentist and ground to desired shape, then supplied with handles of hard wood. For scroll work common sewing needles can be inserted into wooden handles and used as etchers; these needles may be shaped according to need by honing on an oil stone, then reshaped in the same manner as they are worn down through use. An excellent holder for needles is the small scribe holder manufactured by various leading tool manufacturers. The etching needle should be perfectly round and blunt to prevent it from catching and skipping on the metal as it cuts through the varnish in tracing its design. This bluntness of the needle also allows the hand to travel in any direction without the needle snagging on the metal surface. Practice alone will lead to perfection in the handling of the etching needle.

Stopping-out varnishes are used to protect the steel parts that are not to be etched when the gun is placed in the necessary acid bath. Beeswax has been used unsuccessfully in etching due to the fact that in the process of the actual etching operation with the needle etchers, the wax has a tenency to flake off, leaving the exposed raw steel where etching is not desired. Stopping-out liquid should be applied with a brush, then allowed to dry thoroughly before the actual etching begins. One of the proven formulas for this type of spirit varnish is as follows:

      4 oz. white shellac
      8 oz. pure grain alcohol
      45 gr. methyl-violet dye

Mix alcohol with shellac, allow the shellac to dissolve completely, then add dye. This formula is ideal, as it

Basic etching supplies can be bought locally. Shellac is diluted as explained in text. Ammonia is used to prevent burns, if acid is spilled on clothing or hands.

Before scribing design, brush on shellac with soft-haired brush. If necessary, reshellac flaws and redo.

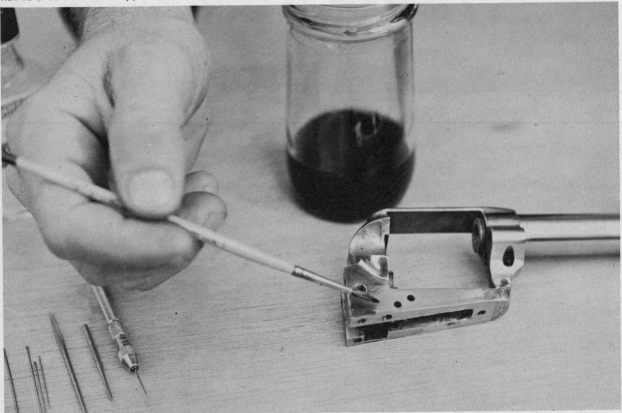

provides the proper color necessary to correctly detail the etched designs. This mixture is painted over the entire metal surface to be etched and allowed to dry.

A well laid out design should be drawn on paper first to give the workman a concise pattern to go by; too, it will help in deciding what type of ornamentaion is best suited to the area to be covered. Floral designs, intricate scroll work, names and scenes are but a few of the recommended designs to be applied by the artist.

Following the application of the stopping-out varnish and with a clear picture in mind of the design wanted, the artist will proceed to "cut" his design into the varnish, making certain that he completely penetrates the varnish coating down to bare metal. This is an absolute must in order for the acid to bite into the metal during the acid bath.

Great care must be taken in laying out the design on the varnish surface; any undue scratches or slips of the etching needles must be touched up with varnish and allowed to dry before proceeding. The design should be as intricate as possible and as beautiful as is the artist's ability to apply it.

A word of caution at this point to prevent one from receiving acid burns in his first attempt at gun etching. Always have close at hand a bottle of liquid ammonia to apply to acid spots on skin or clothing. Water is the next best thing to counteract acid should it be spilled or splattered. The use of rubber gloves is a must, while giving the metal parts their acid bath in the actual etching process. Use the greatest care in handling etching acids, as they can be dangerous. The fumes alone can turn bright, clean tools to rust in short order, so use the acid bath in a well ventilated room and away from other metal objects.

The theory of etching is the ability to enhance the beauty of metal objects by the use of acids; to eat that metal immediately surrounding the design away, leaving a raised effect to the scroll, floral or other scenes used. The use of stopping-out varnishes is to prevent the eating away of metals that will comprise the design itself; it is well to keep in mind that where there is not stopping-out varnish, the acid will eat, and the longer the metal is in the acid bath, the deeper the metal is eaten away.

To prepare metal such as gun frames, barrels, cylinders, etc., they first must be thoroughly cleaned, removing all grease, oil and fingerprints before applying the stopping-out varnish. Plugs must be made of wood to be inserted in both ends of barrels to be given an acid bath. All threaded screw holes must be coated well with varnish inside and out and all wooden plugs liberally coated with varnish at the point where they enter the barrel or cylinder holes.

The type of agent most prominently used in etching work is nitric acid. This is available at most drug stores at nominal cost. It is impossible to state just how soon the eating action will begin on the metal, as there are numerous factors involved. For example, the tempera-

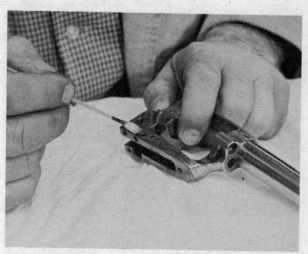

If etching small area, use clean cotton swab to coat section repeatedly with acid until desired depth is reached. Surrounding metal is covered with shellac.

ture of the acid will affect its power in etching.

The acid bath, itself, consists of a tray or vessel large enough to receive the parts being etched. This tray must be of some material that will not be affected by the eating action of the acid; baked enamel, porcelain or crockery make good acid bath trays.

Into this vessel is poured only enough acid to completely cover the metal being etched. As stated earlier, the length of time this metal remains in the bath will determine just how deeply it is etched by the acid; visual inspection is a good indication of this phase. All parts should be suspended in the bath by wires for easy removal. (Never use string or cord for this purpose, as the acid will soon burn through, allowing the metal parts to drop to the bottom of the tank or tray. The resultant splash may be damaging to both the workman and to the surrounding tools and materials.)

The novice should select only the simplest designs to begin with, gradually working into the more complicated scroll and floral designs, as he progresses in his ability and understanding of the art. The worker must have considerable artistic ability, but regardless of this ability it is best to begin with practice. A finely etched gun or other metal object is the result of having the etching needles properly honed at all times during the cutting of the design. Improperly sharpened needles result in coarse, rough lines, which in turn, result in a poor job.

Take your time, never try to cut corners in order to finish the job sooner. Etching especially is an art that requires utmost care and patience, but careful workmanship can easily increase the value of an arm many times both artistically and monetarily.

During hand scribing the design, it is best to steady the cutting hand with the forefinger of the opposite hand. This insures finer cuts, more accurate work.

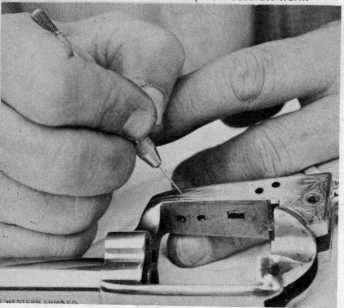

CUSTOM GRIPS:

GUESS who I don't like, more than practically anybody I can think of?

I don't like people who come at me with cigar boxes in their hands.

No, I don't have a psych problem. Old Bish has nothing against cigar boxes. To coin a phrase that some tobacco company will probably steal, it's what's inside that counts.

A few years ago I finally lost count of the number of times I have been approached by some clown carrying a cigar box containing the mortal remains of a new pistol. The story was always the same: He had stripped it completely down, badly burring the slots in all the screws. Parts that didn't come out

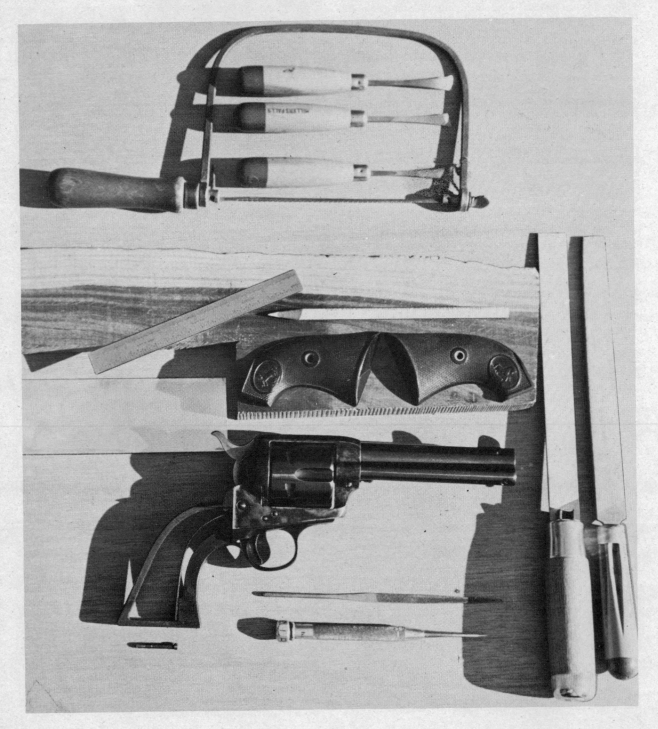

easily, he pried out. Some had to be pried pretty hard, too, because "they seemed to be a force-fit." And would Old Bish mind putting it back together?

What Old Bish would really like to do in such cases is have a little force-fit himself, such as forcing the guy's head to fit inside a gaspipe. But everybody knows how calm and forgiving Old Bish is; how he always tries to look at the good side of everything.

What good side, do you ask? Well, the only redeeming feature about these #$!&/*X misguided people is that they usually would like to do some work on their new gun, but they don't know how. So being the naturally inclined good samaritan type, I have decided not to run amok the next time I see a man coming toward me with a cigar box in his hands. Instead I will take him quietly aside, speak with sweet reasonableness about leaving complicated work to expert gunsmiths, and suggest that he start with something simple, such as making a new set of custom grips. Only **then** will I hit him with a gaspipe.

I have often wondered how much real gun knowledge these destructive neophytes gain from almost

And outline of original grips is traced on proposed grip materials; grain runs longitudinal in pattern.

ruining guns that were in top working order prior to their carnage. They seem to prefer starting their gun education by wrecking new guns, then expecting some poor gunsmith to put them back in factory-condition for nothing, or at most, for a couple of bucks.

Well, it just doesn't work out that way any more. Most gunsmiths have come to the conclusion that these cracker-jack gun mechanics are just going to have to pay for their experimentations — and they are right! Why should a competent, working gunsmith have to bear the expense of their ignorance?

This narrative is not to go into all of the fallacies of those prone to wrecking good firearms in order to satisfy their own curiosity. Instead it is for those who would like to start out by doing some sort of gun work without ruining the guns they might own.

Possibly one of the most important parts of a

pistol or revolver is its wooden grips. Should these grips not fit the shooter to a T, poor shooting can be expected. In many cases, pistol owners want a pair of pistol grips that are unique — one-of-a-kind so to speak — so it is necessary either to have them custom-made by a person specializing in this type of work, or to make them himself.

For the most part, fancy custom-made pistol grips in semi-precious materials such as elephant ivory, gold or silver and even rare woods are made

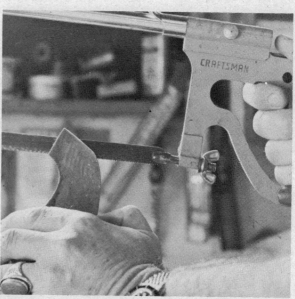

The material, preferably double thickness, is cut to provide left and right grip, the grain matching.

by men who specialize in gun engraving. These grips usually are made only on special order and can run in price from $45 to as high as several thousand dollars if gold, silver and even inset diamonds are desired by the customer.

However, as this article is directed mainly at those who would like to do some sort of work on their own guns, without ruining them, by making a custom pair of pistol grips for their favorite pistol or revolver, I will explain the basic steps necessary for those building their first grips in wood.

First, the selection of wood is vital in making a set of pistol grips. Not only should they be beautiful when finished, they must be durable. Elephant ivory also may be used, and while somewhat harder to work than even the finest burl walnut, it may be handled in basically the same way with allowances being taken for its hardness.

Woods for custom grips should be limited to those having close grain and a reasonably hard — but not brittle — texture. For my own purposes, I usually select a piece of root growth, commonly called burl, in either French or Circassian walnut having a well-figured, dark grain. In most cases I obtain this wood from scraps left over from shotgun or rifle stocks, but pieces large enough for pistol grips may be purchased from rare wood dealers for a dollar or so.

The grip blanks should be sawed oversize and slightly more than twice the thickness needed for a single grip. This blank should measure roughly over an inch in thickness for most pistols. This blank then is cut in two with a fine-toothed saw, after which the two halves are reversed — the freshly sawed inner surfaces becoming the outer, or exposed side, of the finished grips. In this way the grain pattern of the wood will match, thus adding greatly to the "custom" appearance of the finished grips.

The tools necessary for making pistol grips are simple: A few files, consisting of a medium rasp and a couple of half-round files, a coping saw, an eleven-tooth (or finer) carpenter's saw, a bench vise, several grades of garnet sandpaper for finishing and

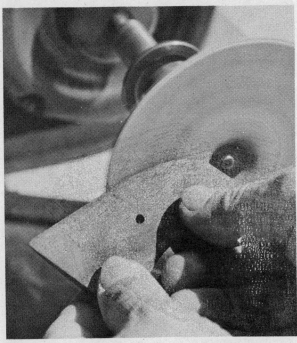

Excess material can be removed with a disc sander; it is used on the rounded outer surfaces of grips.

a drop or two of good stock finish or varnish for the finish coat.

I might add that a little careful workmanship in fitting the grips to the pistol's straps will make the difference in whether the finished grips have that truly custom look, or are just another pair of cobbled-up pieces of wood slung together by some neophyte! The fitting of the grips — in a precise fit — will be the deciding factor in just how "custom" the grips really are!

In same cases it may be desired to have the grips larger in proportion than that provided by the grip straps of the pistol. In this case it is necessary to inlet the straps into the new wood grip blanks. Each grip should be inletted until exactly one-half of the steel grip strap seats into each of the two wood grips. Oversized grips of this type may be cut, filed and shaped to the individual requirements of the maker, and may even include finger grooves and a thumb rest.

It is quite apparent that custom-made pistol grips must be fitted perfectly to the frame of the gun before the outer surfaces are ever touched with a file for final shaping. In this way — the only cor-

rect way — the exact contour of the grip straps of the pistol may be traced onto the wooden grips with a sharp, soft-lead pencil then dressed to a perfect fit with mill bastard files and garnet paper.

The rounded contours of the grip surface are obtained by using mild wood rasps and half-round files in those areas immediately to the rear of the trigger guard. For the most part, this work should be done with the wood grips off the pistol to prevent marring the blued surfaces. It is possible, with a great deal of care, to finish-fit the wood grips while they are in place on the gun, but this is a tedious chore and requires skilled handling of both files and sandpaper.

It will be noticed during the final sanding with from 400 to 600 grit garnet paper that the grain of the wood will become increasingly apparent. The finer the finish, the more beautiful will be the grain of the wood. Finally, when the gun stock finish or varnish is applied, the grain of the wood should take on a sheen that you can actually look down into — just as though the surface of the wood had become transparent, exposing all of the interior grain. Should the wood have a dead look to it, then it is not properly finished or sanded.

Possibly the most important factor in making a set of pistol grips is in getting the grain of the wood running in the right direction! On more occasions than I care to remember I have seen beautifully finished and carefully made grips that had the grain running the width of the grips instead of the length! It stands to reason that these grips will split in two should the pistol be bumped or accidentally dropped. The pressure of the retaining screws alone, in many cases, has caused cross-grained grips to fall apart. So when you draw up your patterns, make certain that the grain is running the length of the grips, not the width! This is more correctly determined by visually drawing a line from the heel of the grip straight up the grip to its highest point, and at the same time following the general angle of the grip section in relation to that of the gun barrel. Better yet, just examine the direction of the

With excess material removed, the rounded surfaces are finished with a fine file and garnet paper.

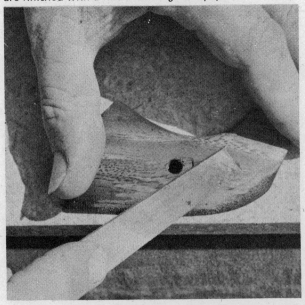

wood grain in your pistol's factory grips.

When your custom grips are finish-sanded, it is time to add such niceties as silver or gold inlays in the form of initial plates or butt caps, but this is still another phase which we must take up at some later date. The inlaying of precious metals, ivory, rare woods horn, bone and even brass and copper into the wood of pistol grips is far too complicated to merely glance over in a few lines here. Too, it is possible to do this inlaying after the grips are finished, requiring only that a complete new coating of stock finish or varnish be applied to the grips when the inlaying job is finished.

To assure perfect fit, grips are placed on handgun frame. Overhanging material can be felt easily with finger, dressed down with fine garnet paper.

One-piece grips for early models of Colt revolvers require the same basic procedure as outlined here.

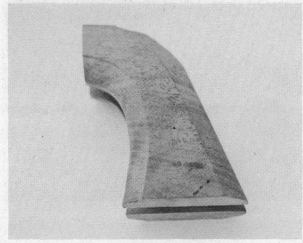

Instead of tinkering with the insides of their new guns, it might be best for those interested in increasing their knowledge of guns to first build a simple pair of pistol grips. While this job of gunsmithing is one of the simplest for a learned gunsmith, the novice might have a surprise in store for him in attempting to build his first pair.

It certainly is not as simple as it sounds, and in order to turn out a set of pistol grips that one can be proud of, a lot of time, sweat and effort — to say nothing of careful workmanship — will be exercised before the grips are ready for use.

Top (from left): original hard rubber; big horn sheep horn; burl walnut; elephant ivory. The one-piece grips beneath are of zebra wood, more elephant ivory, silver inlaid walnut and bison horn.

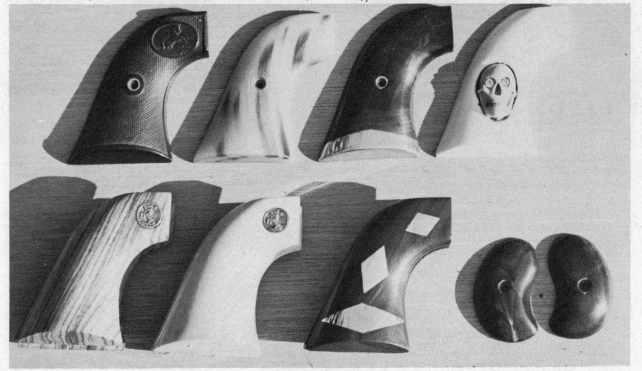

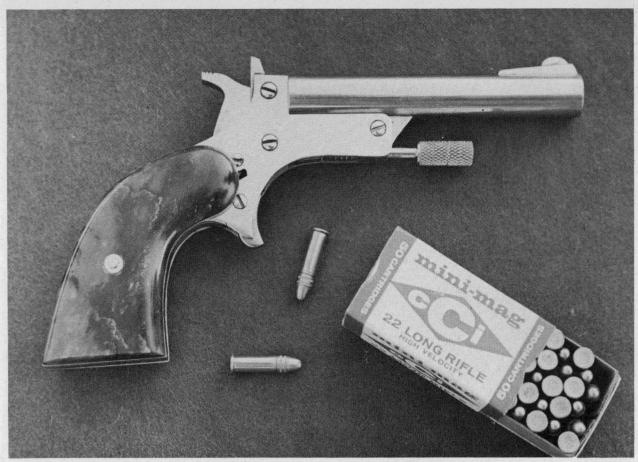

Handcrafted for .22 rimfire ammo, pistol has unique locking, trigger mechanism, as well as jade grips.

DRESS-UP YOUR FAVORITES

THE JADED LOOK

To The Best Of Our Knowledge This Is The First Pair Of Handgun Grips Ever Made From This Semi-Precious Stone!

Piedra de Yjada, refers to a particular stone that has for centuries been regarded as a sure cure for pains in the side. This stone was merely rubbed on the aching area and **presto,** no aches!

The name of this stone also has been applied to loose and disreputable women and even horses that have seen better days. However, we today simply refer to this rare, beautiful green stone as jade, in spite of its claimed colic curing powers.

Regardless of its superstitious past, and the various names tacked on it by peoples of other countries, jade is regarded as a rare gem material capable of being used in finger rings, brooches and as lavaliers to hang around the neck. The Chinese for centuries have carved jade into exquisite statuettes.

This Wyoming jade is in raw chunk and slabbed form. Polished, this type of jade takes on a dark green shade, which is mottled with a white smoky pattern for beauty.

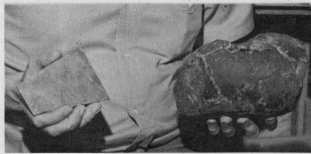

Jade is an extremely hard gemstone and in my thirty-plus years in the gun game, I've never heard of it being used in the ornamentation of firearms. I have seen a few minor inlays on ancient oriental matchlock firearms but this was about the extent of it. Jade is, and has always been, considered nothing more than a gemstone. Its application to firearms is almost unheard of. That is, until I was sitting in a dentist chair one day a few weeks ago being worked over by a practitioner of dental gymnastics, one Doctor Gerald Lowdermilk.

As is usual during one of these dental sessions — and I think most maulers of the molars get their kicks this way — Jerry was asking me questions about various firearms in which he was interested, knowing full well

Again using the diamond cutting wheel, the grips are roughed out, cutting to the outside of the traced line.

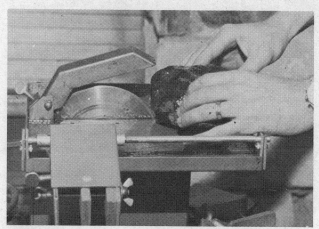

Slabbing of the natural jade is accomplished with a rock cutting saw, which is impregnated with diamond dust.

that it was impossible for me to answer him due to various contraptions of the trade he had stuffed into my mouth!

Continuing a running jargon of patter concerning guns, and at the same time drilling with a dental burr until my head rattled, he mentioned that he was building a pistol and when finished, he planned to make a set of solid jade grips for it.

In spite of the dental burr, I managed to gargle something about jade pistol grips being a real rarity and that I would be interested in covering all phases of their construction.

Several days later, I drove down to my dentist's home, was introduced to his attractive wife, Margo, and

The inner curves of the grips are cut in this manner due to the hardness of the jade. After chipping, the area is ground to the exact contour with stone-cutting wheel.

Once in slab form, the material for the jade grips is marked with the outline, using aluminum or silver pencil.

retired to what he refers to as his hobby room. Margo not only does metal sculpturing with a welding torch, but also does stained glass leading and a variety of other artistic endeavors aimed at beautifying the home. Jerry occupies his spare time in rock cutting and polishing, metal casting, sealing rattlesnakes and tarantulas in clear plastic blocks, and collects guns and knives.

I arrived at the Lowdermilk home just as he was beginning work on his jade pistol grips. The jade was still in its crude rock form. It looked like any other rock that one might pick up in the mountains or on the desert, however, it was dark in appearance. Lowdermilk informed me that this was an especially fine piece of jade he had just acquired from the state of Wyoming. It is a dark green in color with mottlings of white and black jade.

The first step in building a set of pistol grips from the raw jade stone entails the cutting of the stone through the center, then following this up by cutting a slab from one of the halves with which to make the actual grips. The slicing of the stone is accomplished

*The roughed out grips now are ready for rounding over,
then the drilling of the screw holes and the finishing.*

*Rounding over the grips is accomplished on a silicon
carbide grinding wheel. One must take care to leave
the grips slightly oversize for their final fitting.*

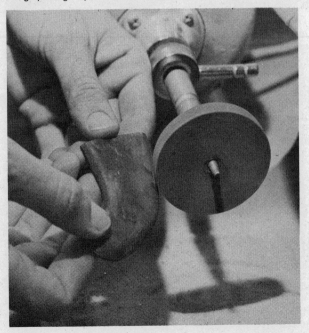

with an eight inch diamond rock cutting saw using a
light oil mixture as a coolant. This coolant consists of
one part thirty-weight motor oil to three parts kerosene.
The thickness of the slab to be used for pistol grips will
depend on the needs of the individual builder. If you
want thick grips, cut the slab thick. If thin grips are
desired for small automatic pistols — cut the slab about
a quarter-inch thick.

The outline of the grips is traced from the grip section of the pistol itself onto a piece of heavy cardboard,
then this outline is transferred to the jade slab, using
an aluminum or silver-leaded pencil. Lay out the grips
on the jade slab so that each may be rough-cut from
the slab with the diamond saw. The inside curve of the
grips — which is the hardest to work — is repeatedly
chip cut, then finished for contour on a silicon carbide
stone grinding wheel.

Once the outer contour of the grips has been cut
up to the penciled outline of the grips, it is time to begin
the actual rounding over of the exterior surface of each
grip. This is done on a carborundum grinding wheel
while using water as a coolant.

Jade, being extremely hard, requires several hours
of actual grinding before the outer surfaces of the grips
are sufficiently rounded and ready for final polishing.
Once rounded, the grips then are ready for drilling to
accept the retaining screw and escutcheons.

Jerry accomplished this chore by drilling the screw
holes with a diamond-tipped dental burr, then finishing
the mortise to accept the escutcheons with a carbide drill
chucked in a drill press at low speed. Once again, water
was used as a coolant during these drill operations.

At this point I suggested that a backing of some
sort should be utilized on the jade grips to prevent their

breakage should they be dropped from the work bench. This backing would strengthen the grips on the pistol once they were permanently attached. For this backing Lowdermilk used a 1/16th-inch thick piece of plastic used as a spacer on recoil pads of rifles and shotguns. This spacer is epoxied to the back of the grips, the epoxy allowed to harden, then is disc sanded until flush with the grip outline. During the final polishing and fitting, this spacer is dressed down along with the jade and becomes a permanent part of it. The escutcheons also are epoxied into the grips, making certain that each is in perfect alignment with the other. These are dressed down until flush with the surface of the jade during the final polishing.

The final polishing and fitting of the grips to the pistol frame is a complex affair. It requires that a

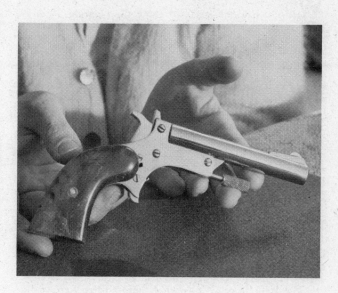

The escutcheons are epoxied in place, allowing the grip retaining screws to seat below surface of the jade.

Final fitting of the grips to the frame of the pistol is done on stone cutting emery wheel, cooling with water.

The escutcheon hole first is drilled with a diamond-pointed dental burr, then is finished for exact size on a drill press, using a carbide drill and water to cool it.

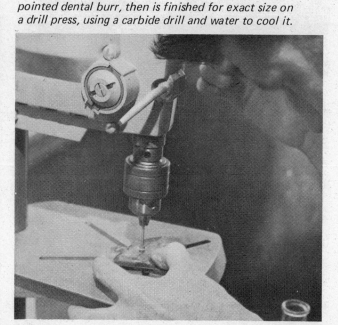

variety of silicone carbide sanding discs in grits from 120 on through 400 be utilized — from coarsest to finest —until a satiny surface is achieved. The final polishing is done by reversing a sheepskin buffer pad, applying a thick paste of tin oxide and water to the leather surface, allow this to dry out and become slightly powdery, then by applying fairly heavy pressure, thoroughly buff each grip at the same time occasionally giving the grips themselves a coating of the tin oxide mixture. After sufficient buffing, the jade will take on a mirror-like sheen. The higher the polish, the more beautiful will be the finished grips.

If this all sounds complicated, it's only because it is! Making a set of jade pistol grips isn't something a hobbyist can knock out in an evening or over the weekend. It's a job that requires a lot of patience, a lot of hard work and a certain amount of specialized machinery and tools. However, when finished, a set of jade grips on almost any pistol will certainly raise the value of that gun by a couple of hundreds dollars. Jade pistol grips are rare and most certainly unique. I only know of one set in existence today, those made by Jerry Lowdermilk, DDS.

119

GOLD PLATING

WHENEVER one starts to think of replating a gun with silver — or less likely — with gold, it generally becomes a matter of hedging when you learn the price, thinking of how many more guns you could make a down payment on with that loot, or how many boxes of ammo the sum would buy.

If you take a gun to a gunsmith and tell him you want it plated, you're generally talking in terms of fifty or sixty bucks, and ninety percent of the time, he won't even be able to do the job himself, but will have to send it out to an electro-plating specialist.

So, when I chanced to see an advertisement that read: "Plate your own gun with gold, silver or nickel — No experience necessary — all equipment furnished," my first reaction was that this was bound to be some kind of a make-a-quick-buck gimmick.

But I was intrigued by the possibilities, and I rushed off a letter for the kit to Wisconsin Platers in Madison, Wisconsin.

A few weeks still later, a small package arrived from the firm. Upon opening the parcel, I found five small glass bottles with various paste-like substances within. Two were labeled copper, one held gold, another silver, and the last, nickel. Along what these bottles were two twelve-inch wires with spring clips attached, a pair of

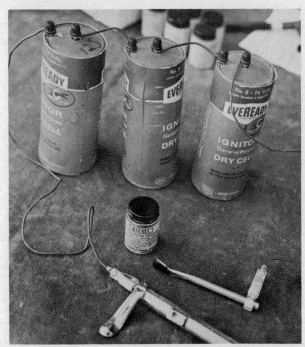

This shows proper sequence for wiring the batteries. Lead wire is attached to plating brush, while other wire is attached to metal item that is to be plated.

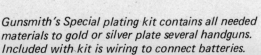

Gunsmith's Special plating kit contains all needed materials to gold or silver plate several handguns. Included with kit is wiring to connect batteries.

shorter wires, several brushes and sheet of instructions: that was all.

I was especially anxious to see just what one could do with this seemingly scanty kit. As I never had plated anything before, I was sure the boast of the advertisement that one needed no experience would be put to the supreme test.

After purchasing the trio of number 6 1½-volt dry cell batteries called for in the instructions, I wired them up in unison as the direction sheet specified. I could have gambled and used only two batteries, but played it safe and went for three.

I had a gun on hand in its original, unblued finish. It was decided that this would make an excellent gun upon which to try my hand, since it had been purchased at a reasonable price; if I goofed, it wouldn't be like ruining a more expensive model.

I disassembled this gun, laying out the various parts,

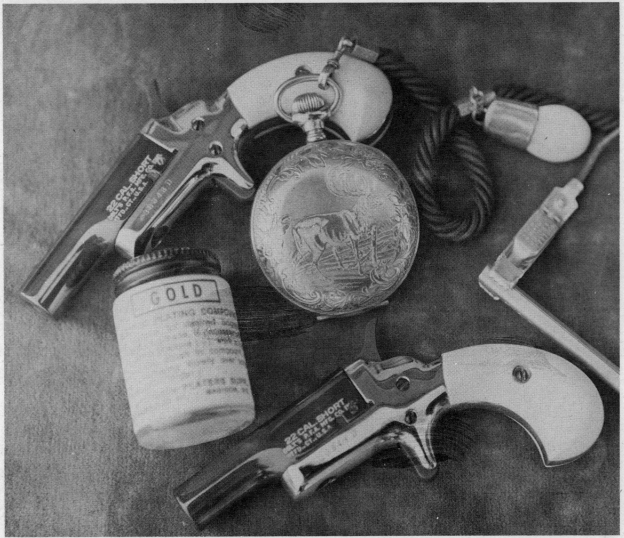

Gold plating worn from even some heirlooms can be replated in a professional manner with this kit.

Bolt handle of rifle is one of the many gun parts that can be plated. Best for this is nickel, as gold, silver wear quickly, unless lacquer-coated.

then buffed the back strap to a high polish before I proceeded to attach the longer wires, one to the brush that was to be dipped into the gold plating solution, the other to the backstrap, itself.

With the electric current running in some semblance of ordinary electro-plating methods, I dipped the brush into the gold material bottle and began to move a liberal amount of it in a circular motion over the metal of the highly polished but raw backstrap.

Almost immediately, the backstrap began to absorb the gold, and the longer I rotated the solution-ladened brush, the brighter and thicker became this yellow plate.

When I decided enough gold had been transferred to the backstrap, I washed it in cold water to remove the solution, then polished the gun part lightly with a soft cloth. To my amazement, the backstrap had taken on a fine and expensive looking plate. After over thirty years in the gun business, I can say it offers a fine, even high gloss plate that is equal to any professional job I have ever seen.

Satisfied — but guarding against overconfidence at this first success — my next step was to experiment with the silver plate, using it on the handgun's cylinder.

Attaching a clean brush to the spring clip on the wire, I repeated the operation as before, but this time using

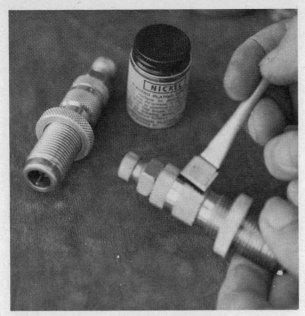

Author even found that reloading dies can be plated on exterior surfaces with nickel, silver to prevent rust. Plating interior would ruin the dimensions.

luster and evenness that was downright amazing after our initial bust.

I tried the nickel compound on the barrel bushing of a GI .45 automatic, also plating the slide lock and the bottom plate of the magazine. Since this gun is built with a rough, non-glare finish, it was necessary to do some pretty extensive buffing first, but the brightness of the plating, when done, was enough to really give the old lead thrower a personalized touch.

And there can be plenty of other uses for this inexpensive little kit besides guns, I found. Following the spree with the gun parts, I proceeded to plate everything around the house, including the cases of a couple of old watches. Besides the gold, silver and copper mixtures, the nickel compound can be a real boon around your gun shop. The bolts holding the reloading presses on my work bench now are nickeled real jazzy, as are any number of the specialized and valuable gunsmithing tools I keep.

The main trick in attaining an excellent plating job with this kit is to have all metal highly polished and absolutely clean; the higher the polish, the better the plating. It is best to wear a pair of cheap cotton work gloves while holding the metal. This assures that the metal will not come in contact with oily skin, which could cause a goof in your plating.

In spite of my initial fears that I'd be buying the proverbial pig-in-a-poke and throwing away money on this kit, a little investigation showed that I had no reason for my doubts. The kit has been assembled by professional metal plating people who know what they are doing, and from my own amateurish experiments, it is pretty well established that you can do a perfect job no matter how little your experience. The kit takes up a minimum of space for storing and little time in using. As I stated earlier — and repeat for emphasis — the only requisite for a good job is that the metal must be polish-

the compound from the bottle marked, silver.

I won't try to keep you in suspense with a lot of adjectives on this phase. It's simple enough to say it didn't turn out on a par with our initial success. But checking back, it seemed reasonable that the copper compound must have some function, so I tried this first, then put the silver on top of it. After giving the cylinder a coating of copper that turned out so beautifully that it seemed a shame to cover it, I tried the silver again; this time it seemed to literally flow onto the metal with a

In the case of custom rifle sets, accessories such as cleaning rods and screw drivers may be gold-coated, as this adds both to beauty and the value of such cased sets.

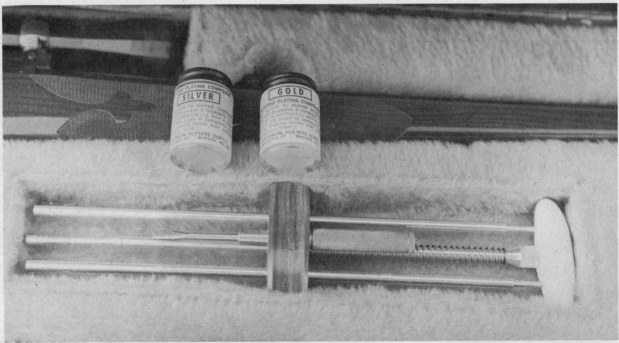

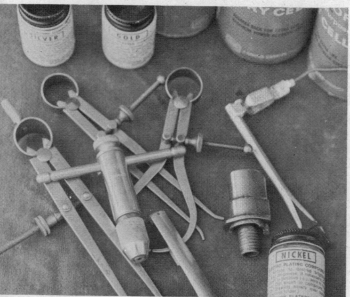

Shop tools can be plated with any of the materials. This is a good idea with precision tools such as micrometers, calipers, dividers, to prevent rust.

Brass guard and butt of custom Bowie knife have been gold plated to prevent tarnishing in display case.

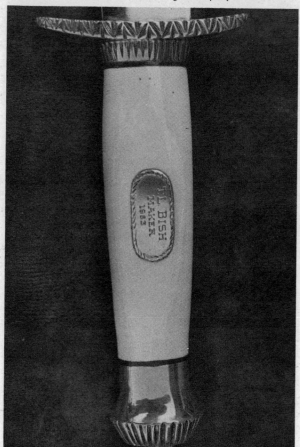

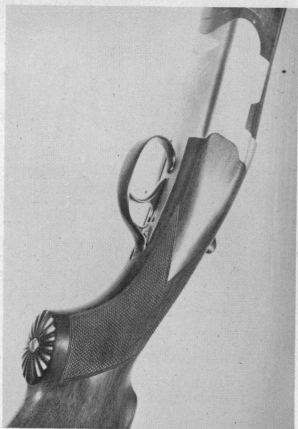

Gold on trigger of Golden Snipe shotgun had become worn. This was repaired with this simple plating kit, then screw on grip cap was plated to match.

ed to a high sheen; the higher the polish, the better the plating appearance.

As you might have guessed, this plating outfit is particularly handy for the shooter who desires to dress up a rifle or handgun as a display or show piece. Screw heads, triggers, hammers, bolt handles and other small parts can be beautifully plated in a matter of seconds after being polished. A blued pistol with gold-plated screw heads, trigger hammer and ejector rod makes a beautifully attractive show gun. However, it must be kept in mind that both gold and silver are exceptionally soft metals and will wear away quickly under hard use. Nickel, on the other hand, is hard and durable for years of hard use. If your gun is to be used a great deal, it would be better not to plate it with the softer precious metals.

Cost of the set, which is known as the Gunsmiths Special, is nominal. The batteries are extra. According to Wisconsin Platers Supply Company, it contains enough material to plate three guns with 24-karat gold, a trio with silver and the same number with nickel.

Another set offers only gold and will plate three complete guns, if the manufacturer's claims are true and still another set has enough silver for three guns. Each of these also has enough copper undercoating for all of the guns mentioned. The firm also sells refill compounds, ranging from the gold compound down to the less precious metals.

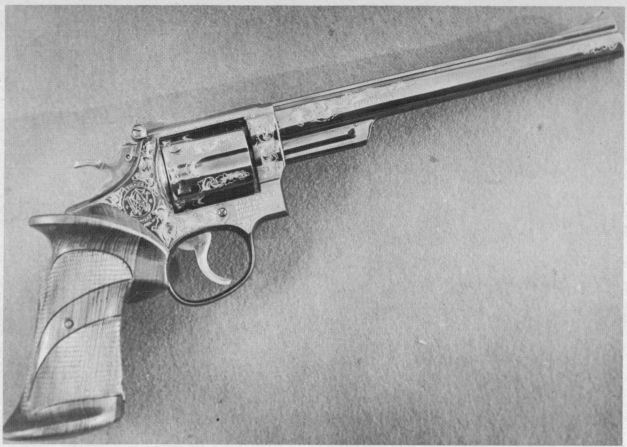

Handguns such as custom-engraved Smith & Wesson can be inlaid in gold with process, increasing the value.

**DRESS-UP
YOUR FAVORITES**

GOLD INLAYING

Gold or silver plating any sporting firearm can be an expensive proposition, if done by professional platers. A hundred dollars would about cover it! However some types of firearms can be enhanced both in beauty and value by a new kit available to the gun enthusiast.

Engraved firearms can now be inlaid with 23-karat, genuine gold, using the Gold Lode engraving inlay kit, marketed by Gold Lode, Incorporated, of Addison, Illinois. Price of this kit is $12.95 and includes enough pure gold compound to inlay a profusely engraved rifle, shotgun, pistol or revolver. However, this is not a job for the impatient. It requires careful workmanship and patience, if perfect appearance is to result. Properly done, the engraved firearm, with its pure gold inlay

The Gold Lode kit contains all necessary materials for inlaying in gold even profusely engraved arms. Disassembled firearm is ready for inlaying process.

work, can be upped considerably in value. The inlaid gold will enhance the engraving, bringing forth its elegance.

There are no complicated wiring diagrams, no batteries, acids or other paraphernalia to complicate the job. The kit consists of nothing more than a small jar of liquid called Agent No. 1, an eye dropper, a small bristle brush, clean-up cloth and a felt pad.

The procedure, while simple, must be followed to the letter. A complete instruction sheet accompanies each kit.

The basic procedure is this: The area to be inlaid with gold must be cleaned thoroughly, using Agent No. 1 in small quantities. Work a portion of the cleaning cloth, saturated with Agent No. 1, over the engraved surface to remove any oil, dirt or residue. Then allow the metal to dry for at least one minute.

Following the cleaning procedure, mix the gold with a measured amount of the agent. Using the eye dropper, add forty drops of Agent No. 1 into the container of gold. Mix thoroughly with the small brush and allow it to set for five minutes, then add ten more drops of the agent. Stir again until you have a smooth, well mixed liquid, which you can flow readily into the cuts of the engraving. It is better to have the mixture a trifle too thin than too thick and it may be necessary, from time to time, to add a few drops of Agent No. 1 to maintain the proper consistency.

It is important to brush the mixture into the engraving cuts in a light application. It is best to select one panel of engraving at a time for this phase.

When the specific panel of engraving has been filled with the gold, allow the area to dry for about three minutes. Be careful during this operation not to slop an excess of the gold liquid onto the smooth, unengraved surfaces. This would be a waste of the gold.

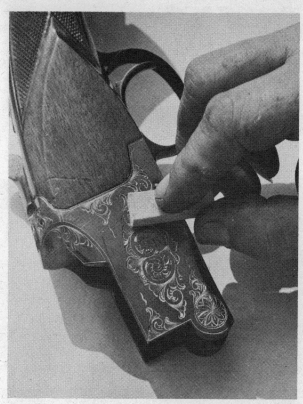

After cut is filled with gold, surface of metal is rubbed lightly with felt block that is furnished with the kit. For this, pad is moistened with agent.

Presentation-engraved silver plates such as this pistol grip cap can be gold inlaid for more clarity.

After a thorough cleaning, using the agent in kit, the well mixed gold solution is brushed into cuts of engraving, allowed to set, then rubbed to work in.

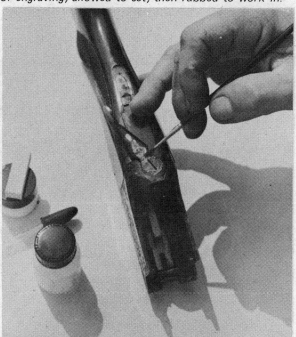

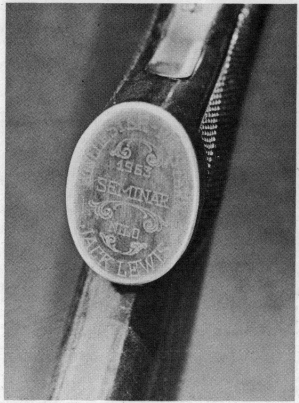

Names, model numbers, calibers and gauges that are stamped in barrels can be filled easily with gold.

After allowing the gold to dry for three minutes, a small portion of Agent No. 1 is poured into a dish, the index finger is moistened with the agent and rubbed in a circular motion over the entire gold-treated surface. The circular motion will work the gold into the engraving cuts from the smooth surfaces, eliminating an unnecessary waste of gold. During this, be sure to keep your finger moist with the agent to assure thorough and equal distribution of the gold.

When you have worked as much gold into the engraving as possible, allow the area to dry for ten minutes.

Phase three is possibly the most important of the entire operation. This includes cleaning the excess gold from the top unengraved surfaces of the metal, leaving the engraving cuts filled with the gold inlay. Wrap a portion of the wiping cloth around the index finger and dampen only with Agent No. 1. This is accomplished best by dipping the cloth into the dish containing the agent, then touching the cloth to another cloth or paper to remove excess liquid. Too much Agent No. 1 applied to the gold inlaid surface at this point will loosen or remove it from the engraving cuts.

With the dampened cloth, carefully wipe the smooth surfaces clean of excess gold. Take care to assure that not too much pressure is applied to the engraving cuts, as this could remove the gold. It is chemical action of the agent that removes the excess gold from the smooth surfaces.

Change finger positions on the cloth frequently to assure a perfect job. Agent No. 1 evaporates rapidly, so it is necessary to redampen the cloth quite often. The felt block furnished with the kit is used for cleaning up hard-to-get-at surfaces and is used the same as the cloth after dampening it with agent.

When the surface has been cleaned thoroughly, take a dry portion of the wiping cloth and polish the surface with light strokes. Check the engraved surfaces to assure that all cuts are filled properly with gold. If some of the gold has been removed during the clean-up phase, repeat the filling operation in that area.

With the engraving filled with gold, set the work aside for about twenty minutes. After that time, smooth, unengraved surfaces may be polished back to a clean, blued finish.

Special care should be taken to clean even smallest amount of excess gold from area surrounding inlays. After gold has set for 20 minutes, this can be accomplished by buffing surface with soft cloth.

Model 101 Winchester shotgun, which has been inlaid with gold, is compared to illustration on package for Gold Lode kit. Engraving is filled, metal clean.

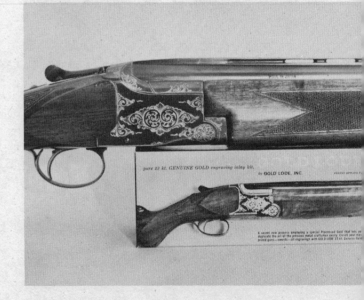

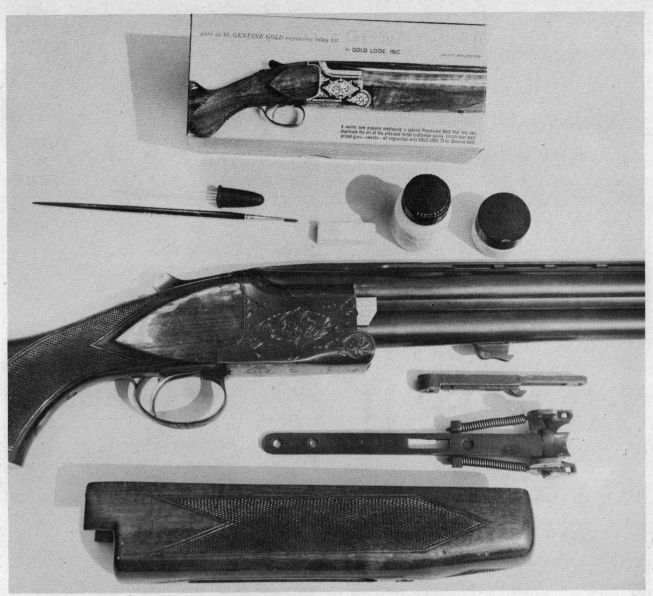

Metal parts of forearm are removed from wood prior to inlaying with gold. This should assure smooth job and make cleaning up wood afterward unnecessary.

Careful Workmanship Can Enhance The Beauty And Value Of That Firearm – But Don't Get Carried Away!

I found that some engraved surfaces are easier to inlay with gold than are others. Heavy, dish-bottomed chisel-cut types of engraving are especially difficult to fill in that, during the clean up operation, most of the gold is removed easily from these large cuts, unless special care is taken. On the other hand, the more intricate, finer engraving is filled and cleaned up with little difficulty.

It is best, when inlaying such items as shotgun forearm latches, to remove them from the wood. This makes the job easier and hastens the cleaning process. I found that it is unnecessary to remove most actions from their stocks to perform inlaying, providing care is taken to prevent the gold solution from contacting the wood. While the gold may be cleaned from the stock, it is a waste of the valuable solution.

Properly done, gold inlaying of this type should last the life of the firearm. Clean the arm in the usual manner, but use only popularly recognized gun cleaners, such as oils, solvents and waxes. Never use chlorinated cleaners or degreasers on the inlay area.

Preparations of this type can cause removal of the gold from the engraved surfaces!

DRESS-UP
YOUR FAVORITES

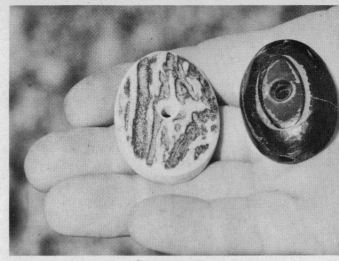

Stag antler (left) is one of numerous materials that can be used in making new pistol grip caps to replace the battered original also shown here.

CAP IT & KEEP IT

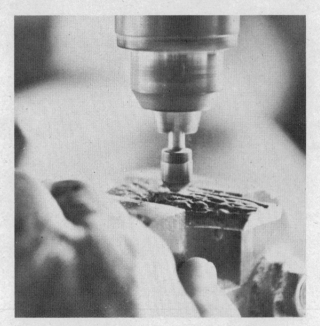

The retaining screw hole is counter-sunk for flat head screw by drill press, hand-held electric drill.

WHEN I acquired one of the Brno 7mm caliber sporting carbines, it was in a condition bordering on "near new," but had a black plastic pistol grip cap that was in sad condition. The badly worn pistol grip cap detracted greatly from its overall appearance.

Shortly after putting this carbine through the customary ritual of completely cleaning every new or used gun I acquire, I took it into my modest workshop for the purpose of replacing the unsightly, much marred pistol grip cap.

Personally, I have a great preference for elephant ivory as a material from which to make grip caps. However, everyone isn't fortunate enough to have access to a supply of this semi-precious, hard to get material. Others are available that will do the job just as efficiently, and just as attractively. Rare woods such as lignum vitea, rosewood, ebony, zebrawood, and even a small section of elk, cow or buffalo horn can be fashioned into a unique and different pistol grip cap in but a few minutes, adding a unique, custom appearance.

The shaping and finishing of such materials as elephant ivory, rare woods, or even a piece of cow or buffalo horn, are accomplished in basically the same manner. However, should a section of elk antler be utilized, it is best to select a section of the antler that has the most attractive configuration on its surface. This mottled surface should be left unfiled

and unsanded following the initial shaping of the new cap to fit the stock. Following the precise fitting of the elk antler cap, it is thoroughly polished around the edges and on the exposed, mottled surface until it takes on a high luster.

The first step in manufacturing a new pistol grip cap is, quite naturally, to remove the old one from the stock, being extremely careful not to chip the stock should the old cap be cemented to the wood. The material selected for the new cap is sanded or milled on one side so that it will seat perfectly on the flat area of the stock which was covered by the old cap.

The old cap then is placed on the flat surface of this new material and the screw hole precisely marked with a lead pencil and a matching hole is drilled and counter sunk to accept the original screw.

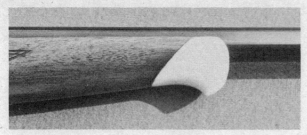

Forends of stocks such as this Model 99 Savage can be capped with exotic rare woods or even with ivory.

The new material is placed on the stock and with the use of the original screw, it is drawn down snugly onto the flat surface of the stock to prevent it from slipping during the outline tracing operation that follows.

With the material held firmly in place with the screw, the contour of the rounded pistol grip section of the stock is traced onto the new cap material with a sharp-pointed lead pencil. It is necessary for the pencil to be sharp in order for the final fitting to be accomplished with a minimum of effort.

Remove the new material from the stock and mark it on one end to assure that it does not become reversed, end for end, when replaced on the stock. With the use of first a coping saw to remove the bulk of excess material, then a fine file or disc sander to remove the remaining material down to — and including — the pencil mark, the new cap will begin to take shape.

Care must be practiced in removing the excess material, including the outlined pencil mark, to assure that the cap will be a perfect fit. This done, replace the new cap on the stock and re-mark any

Using the old grip cap as a pattern, the shape and size are transferred to the new material, which can, in most cases, be cut with nothing but coping saw.

spots that might still overhang the wood of the pistol grip section. Remove this new cap from the stock and remove any final remaining material.

With the cap perfectly fitted to the flat of the stock, its exposed surface may be finished in any of many designs to suit the individual. It may be rounded, pyramid-shaped, scalloped, or even cross-cut with the use of files, after which it is buffed on a muslin buffing wheel treated with white buffing compound, until it takes on a high polish.

The new pistol grip cap now is ready for final installation. This is best accomplished by applying a thin coating of a transparent-drying glue, such as **Glue-Bird** brand.

This old rubber cap, victim of time, bad treatment, is replaced with one of ivory (right) that has been carved attractively to add to appearance of rifle.

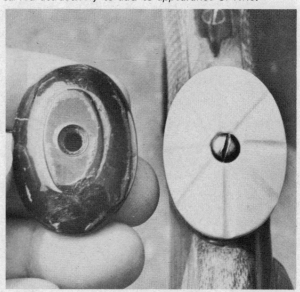

Tightening the new cap into place with the original screw, make certain that it seats in perfect alignment and has not been reversed end for end. Excess glue may ooze from the two contacting surfaces and should be carefully wiped free of both the stock and the grip cap.

The cap, if made from any one of the materials mentioned earlier, will take far more abuse and wear-and-tear than did the much softer plastics or hard rubber material that it replaced. Should it become dull looking, merely buff it to renew its attractive appearance.

Spacers of such materials as brass, copper, aluminum or sterling silver may be placed between the new cap and the wood of the stock. These spacers should be cemented to the unfitted pistol grip cap, then these two parts dressed to proper and exact size as one unit prior to final installation on the rifle.

Should you wish to go whole hog, an initial plate — with your initials hand engraved — of either silver or gold may be easily installed over the grip cap retaining screw with a little soft solder and a pistol-type electric soldering iron. The head of the screw will act as the contact point for the solder between the initial plate.

If properly done, the addition of a custom-made pistol grip cap on almost any rifle will add that look to set it apart from all others of even the same make.

TEST, EVALUATE, REPAIR YOUR HANDGUN

Tips On The Easy Way To Protect That Favored Firearm

*The easiest test is to shake the gun.
If it rattles, it needs attention.*

Chapter 18

IN frequenting pistol ranges over the years, one of the most amazing things I've found is that there are plenty of shooters, but few of them are fully familiar with their own personal guns. In fact, no matter how much they shoot over a given period, the majority don't even know how good — or bad — a gun they have.

Strangely, in shooting with a handgun, some of these individuals are inclined to blame a bad shot upon their own poor marksmanship. It comes as a surprise to them — if they learn at all — to find that the gun often is less accurate than the shooter.

I'm going to be stepping on some toes in saying this, too, but all too often, the fault of the gun is ultimately the fault of the owner. He may be a good shot, but doesn't know how to take care of a gun properly. In time, that gun will let him down, and he'll have no one to blame but himself. In numerous cases, I've run across seemingly "hot shooters" whose guns were filthy and had undergone undue abuse and wear. When asked why, they simply reply: "I never clean a gun till it won't shoot anymore."

A filthy gun, in the majority of cases, can be cleaned up and put back in perfect — or near perfect — condition, but undue wear and abuse is another combination.

It has been quite common, since the days of Cagney and Bogart gangster movies, to see a cocky pistol shooter press the cylinder latch of a double action Colt or Smith & Wesson revolver with his thumb, give the gun a twisting flip and snap the cylinder from the frame of the gun until it is stopped with a crunching snap against the lower section of the frame housing.

This same type, with a sudden snap of his wrist, returns the cylinder to the frame with so much force that the cylinder crane is sprung out of alignment with both the frame and the bore of the barrel. With the cylinder crane sprung, the cylinder no longer will lock in proper alignment; this can result in the shaving of lead from the slug each time the gun is fired. This means a lop-sided bullet and this is no answer for accuracy.

A side-break revolver always should be broken using both hands; one to hold the gun and release

(Center photo) Hammer at left has been designed for easier cocking. (Bottom) If steel checkering on the hammer spur is worn down, retrace lines with Swiss needle file to cut lightly, evenly over each line. It then is reblued with a cold blue.

the cylinder catch, the other to ease — and I said *ease* — the cylinder out of the frame to the ejecting position.

The analysis of a gun purchased second hand or one that has "just been lying around the house" is simple if one knows exactly what to look for. For that matter, if you have just purchased a new gun, it behooves you to check it out and learn exactly what you can expect of it, whether you want to use it for target work, hunting or just plain plinking.

A lot of your investigations can be conducted in your own kitchen. For example, one of the simplest ways of checking the weight of a gun's trigger pull is with a simple ten-quart bucket. Such a container will weigh roughly half a pound, varying little.

Make certain the gun is not loaded. Run a heavy cord over the trigger and attach both ends to the pail. The cord should cross the trigger at the point normally touched by the trigger finger. Hold the gun by the muzzle, with the barrel vertical and add water to the bucket, using a kitchen measuring cup. A pint of water weighs close to one pound and there are two cups to the pint, sixteen cups to the gallon. Thus, each cup will weigh about one-half pound. As you pour water into the pail, keep a count of the number of cups required to trip the trigger. For example, if six cups do the job, add the half-pound for the weight of the bucket plus six half-pounds for the water: the pull would be seven halves, or three and one-half pounds.

With a single action gun, you would, of course, cock the gun first, but if your pistol is double action and you want to test the trigger pull on this, the same system may be used.

If you want to get some idea of the penetration qualities of your handgun, get half a dozen pieces— or more—of pine board, measuring seven-eighths inch in thickness and build yourself some baffles, centering the boards three inches apart.

You'll be able to follow the channel left by the bullet in its route through the boards, and if you want to take the slug out of the last one in which it lodged, it's usually an easy chore to dig it out relatively undamaged with a pocket knife.

But if you're using a magnum for this test, you'll be safer with nine or ten boards. For example, the smallest of the current magnum crop, the .22 Rem-Jet, will go through five boards, lodging in the sixth. This gives you some sort of a norm by which you can compare your own handgun.

And if you're wondering just what the explosive effect of your gun may be, get your hands on a half-ripe watermelon. This is roughly the same consistency of a man's head. By firing into the melon, then cutting it apart (if it hasn't exploded under the impact), you'll get a fair idea of what the gun can do to tissue. The same effect can be gained by

(Left) The trigger pull is weighed with commercial weights, but text outlines other ways of measuring it.

With automatic, loose barrel linkage often is corrected by hard-chroming these parts, masking off surrounding areas to prevent plating. The barrel bushing (right) also can be built up with hard chrome internally. Thickness of the plating will determine tight fit of the working parts of the auto.

Distorted ears of cartridge magazine often account for malfunction in automatic pistol. Above, (from left) ears are bent too much, causing round to sit too low; ears are too open, causing cartridge to ride too high for proper feeding, while at right, the ratio is correct, the cartridge seated to feed. Realignment of magazine ears can be accomplished easily by reshaping to correct contour with pliers.

firing into a huge lump of modeling clay, which is available at any shop supplying artists. You can then cut apart the clay, being careful not to destroy the bullet channel, and learn what the bullet does on the inside.

Sights, of course, are one of the most important facets of good handgunning. In many cases, a shooter will have an inadequate set of sights, yet not realize it.

To check them, hold them up first against the light, and see how clearly they are defined; then aim them against a dark surface. It will be tougher to find the sights, of course, but if there is no clear definition, it might be well to blacken the sights a bit, using some of the commercial concoctions, or you can do this temporarily by simply holding the front, then the rear sight over an ordinary candle, allowing soot to build up on them.

Assuming that your gun — new or old — is in seemingly fine condition; the action works fairly smoothly and it seems to be "a pretty good gun." But "pretty good" is not enough; any firearm that is to shoot gunpowder or cartridges should be in absolutely perfect condition both from the standpoint of safety and to assure the shooter that quality known as peace of mind.

In analyzing a revolver as to safety, shooting qualities and reliability, it is best to section off the various parts containing working parts, then methodically examine each and every part in that section for wear, defects and cleanliness.

For example, the aforementioned cylinder crane is one of the most vital mechanisms on a double action revolver. It can be checked for both tightness or alignment without removing it from the gun. With the cylinder locked in the frame, grasp the grip of the pistol firmly with one hand; with the other hand, exert pressure against the right side of the cylinder, pressing to the left. If looseness is felt and a crack appears where the crane contacts the front section of the frame, then undue wear is present.

This does not necessarily mean that the crane is sprung; it can be caused by wear at one or the other of two points in the cylinder locking mechanism. This usually can be remedied by a light and careful peening of these areas, expanding metal into the section where it has been worn away. This peening of worn areas is only a temporary cure for crane looseness, but is effective; it may have to be repeated from time to time, depending upon how much firing you do with the gun.

The action of a revolver that seems silk-smooth to the novice may be as rough as the Grand Teton range to a more experienced shooter. This, again, is an obstacle easily overcome by the man who wants the satisfaction of knowing his gun is as perfect as he, himself, can make it. The honing of the action will result in a satiny smooth performance.

Honing consists of simply removing all of the microscopic burrs and rough edges from the action. These burrs, for the most part, are not visible to the naked eye, but can be detected by running a fingernail over the metal edges of all moving or working parts. If the nail catches and a sawing effect is felt, this area should be honed with an Arkansas hard stone of proper size and shape.

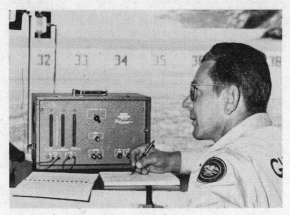

Above: Owning your own chronograph is ideal but expensive. Many gun clubs, ranges have facilities for checking velocities for small fee. (Right) To get correct feel in your grips, it often helps to rub down uncomfortable high spots with sandpaper.

Arkansas hard stone is a form of oil stone with a cutting quality so fine that it leaves a highly polished surface as it cuts, causing the removal of only the most minute burrs. With the removal of these tiny saw-like protrusions, the gun's action is freed of unnecessary drag and scraping. This means better scores on the range or better hits on game.

The rear sights of better revolvers can be adjusted for both windage and elevation, but with constant use, these sights can become loose and an accumulation of dirt and grease may build up in the recesses beneath so that the sight no longer can be adjusted effectively.

It is a simple chore to remove the entire sight mechanism and wash it in lacquer thinner; this will remove all of the residue of past years.

If this same sight is installed on the pistol by means of a slot in the top strap and has become loose, it is a simple matter to remove the sight, lightly peen the protruding edges of the slot with a small ballpeen hammer, then redrive the sight back into place from the right side. Always install sights of this type from the right side of the gun, as some have a tapered base; to drive them from the opposite side will result in complete distortion of both the sight and the slot in the gun frame.

Quite often, the ejecting potential of a side-break revolver is not what it should be. When pushing the ejection rod, it has a tendency to hang up, to work hard, to seem to bind on some unseen obstacle. There are several possible causes for this malfunction, but the most common is that dried dirt and grease have worked their way into the sleeve of the ejector rod housing and are acting as a coarse abrasive on the interior parts.

This is best remedied by completely dismantling the ejector assembly, giving it a thorough cleaning, reassembling, then reinstalling it on the gun.

Still another common cause of ejection trouble is caused by a bent ejector rod, which can be caused by a bad bump or fall. This is easily repaired by removing the rod and straightening it by lightly tapping it with a lead or brass hammer while slowly rolling it on a flat steel plate. If you don't have a steel plate, I know of one man who uses the bottom of his wife's electric iron!

One of the questions which comes our way most often has to do with the muzzle velocity of a given gun. There are two ways of figuring this. You can take the manufacturer's word for it, but this is not necessarily true, for most ballistics information issued by makers of arms and cartridges is based upon chronographed shots from an eighteen-inch barrel. Needless to say, a four or six-inch barrel on your hand-gun won't make this good a showing. Also, if it's an old gun, there are other problems that lower velocity such as too much head space, worn lands or those that are badly pitted.

But a good many ranges now have chronograph equipment which is available to the public. At a cost of as low as a buck, you can chronograph your own gun and find out exactly how well it will shoot. And this is the end result for which you are aiming in putting the gun in the best shape you can.

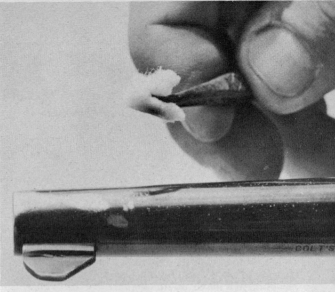

Worn blue has been caused by wear in holster. The problem is remedied by application of cold blue.

(1) With cylinder locked in place, detect excess play by moving cylinder back and forth, from side to side. If give or looseness are present, gun needs repair.

(2) Looseness of cylinder crane can be detected by moving cylinder from side to side. If crack shows as shown in photo, cylinder crane needs adjustment.

(3) The cylinder latch (note arrow), being made of hardened steel, seldom causes looseness in cylinder or crane. It is snug in relation to ejector, ratchet.

(4) The well in the ejector and ratchet assembly accommodates cylinder latch in tight lock-up of the cylinder. If this becomes worn, cylinder is loose.

(5) To correct looseness of ratchet well, cylinder latch assembly, peening ratchet area may be needed. Peen only enough to replace worn away metal in area.

(6) Cylinder locking notches may be enlarged through long, hard use, causing cylinder play. To correct, lightly peen metal back into place, reducing the enlarged notches to original shape. Worn cylinder surface is spruced up with cold blue application.

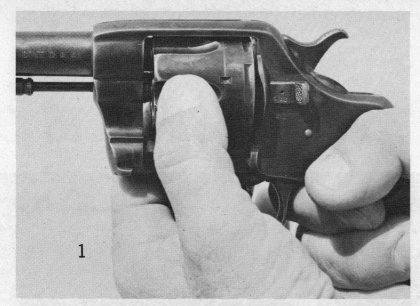

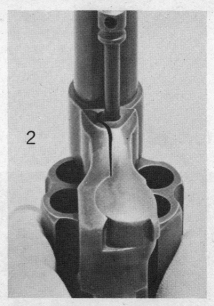

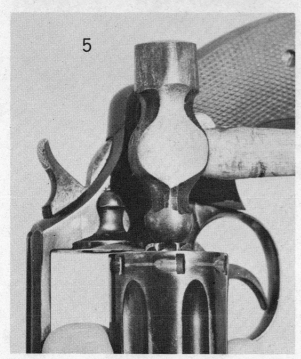

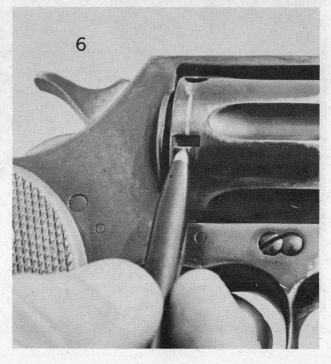

135

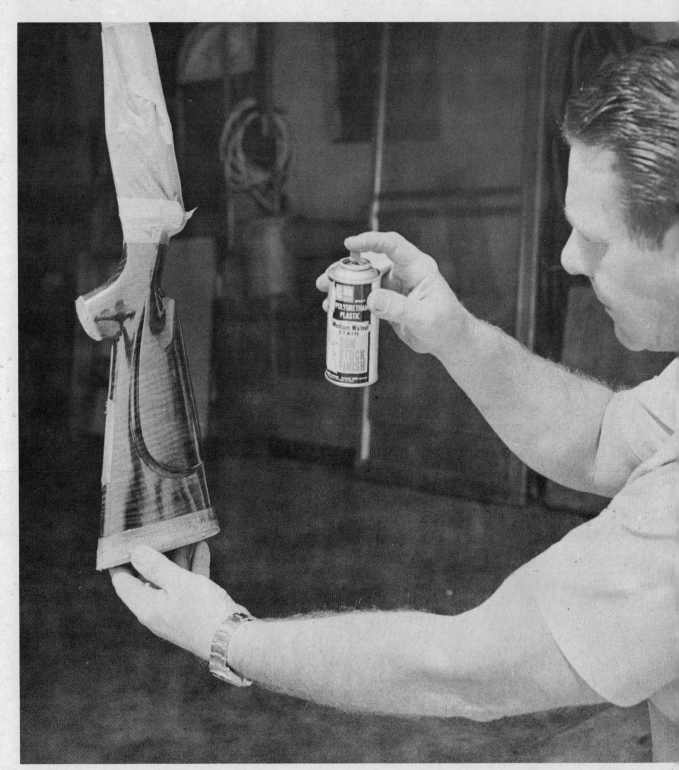

GUN STOCK FINISHING

Plastic type gun stock finish in aerosol can is far cry from ancient mixtures, methods that required days of work.

Patience And Drying Time Are The Difference Between Success And Failure!

There is little doubt — at least, in my own mind — that one of the most perplexing problems facing the majority of amateur gunsmiths building their first sporting rifle is finishing of the stock.

This is well borne out by the number of letters I have received on this one subject. The majority of these letters ask, "How do you get such a glassy finish to your stocks?" or "My stock is of the finest walnut, but I can't bring out its full beauty. I've tried everything!"

The final finishing of a gun or rifle stock is an art, requiring infinite patience and careful workmanship. But it goes beyond that.

The most important phase in stock finishing is in the thorough sanding prior to applying the liquid finish. The wood must be sanded glassy smooth, until absolutely free of even the most minute defects or scratches.

Following the sanding, which is climaxed with the use of 400-grit Wet-Or-Dry abrasive paper, the next phase is to fill the pores of the wood. This is the prime secret in obtaining that glassy appearance on the finished stock. If the pores of the wood are not filled properly, the finished stock is sure to have a pitted appearance overall.

Now comes the problem of what finishes to use. On the market today are any number of commercial stock finishes capable of producing a perfect and durable protective coating for the wood. After all, the basic reason for applying any stock finish is to protect the wood from natural elements, such as rain or snow and to toughen the wood against possible scratching by brush and tree limbs.

The stockmaker never had it so good! Years ago, finishing a stock often required weeks of labor to produce a finish that was both beautiful and durable. Today, this same job may be done in as little as a day, depending upon which commercial finish is used.

There are two different types of finishes being utilized by custom rifle makers. The first of these involves specially prepared oil finishes such as those produced by G-96 Birchwood-Casey, Herter's, Brownell's and Williams.

While most of these prepared oils are capable of completely filling the pores of the wood — provided sufficient applications are applied to the surface — I have found that

Available today are any number of commercially made preparations for producing high finish on stocks.

Filler is applied with felt pad, rubbing it in a circular motion; pores filled, dry wood 24 hours.

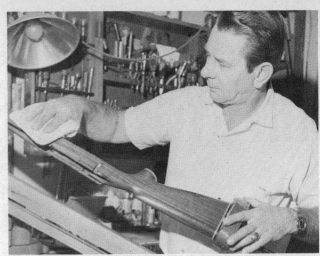

Completely dry, excess filler is wiped from surface of wood with soft cloth moved across the grain.

the use of a good wood filler, such as that from Birchwood-Casey, not only speeds up the job, but results in a perfect finish.

On the other hand, polyurethane and plastic finishes have become popular in recent years. These require no filler, if sufficient applications are made. They result in a surface that is extremely tough and durable. Products of this type also are produced by the firms mentioned above, in addition to a new product known as ADSCO Plastic Gunstock finish. All of these products are available at most well equipped gunshops or sporting goods houses.

One of the biggest mistakes made by the novice gun maker in finishing a stock is not allowing sufficient drying time for either the oil finish or the filler. The majority of commercial gunstock fillers are available in either a clear type or walnut color. The clear type is used on light-colored stocks such as maple, while the tinted fillers should be reserved for use on the darker walnuts.

While full directions are found on all commercial fillers and finishes, many hobbyists completely ignore these directions and proceed haphazardly with the operation. The result is a sloppy job.

Let's assume that your rifle stock is sanded to flawless-

ness and ready for the filler. Thoroughly shake the container containing the filler. This is absolutely essential. Next, the liquid filler is applied generously to the surface of the stock wood, using a brush or cloth, rubbing in a circular motion. Reason for this is to work the pigments of the filler well into the open pores of the wood, thus filling them level with the surface.

Allow the filler to dry for about twenty minutes, then remove excess filler from the surface by wiping across the grain. This motion will force the filler into the pores of the wood and remove any excess.

Finally, wipe the entire surface with a fine cloth, wiping with the grain, and allow the stock to sit for at least twenty-four hours to thoroughly dry. This is important!

After the prescribed drying time, the entire stock is sanded thoroughly once more with No. 400 Wet-Or-Dry paper to assure removal of any excess surface filler. Should it be noted that even a minute portion of the wood pores are not filled completely, repeat the operation outlined above in the areas necessary.

After the filling operation, the wood will have taken on a glassy, smooth surface. All that is necessary now is to apply the commercial oil finish in as many coats as desired,

Surface is hand buffed with the cloth before the application of the final finish material to wood.

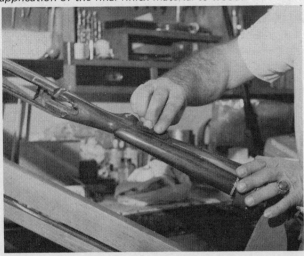

When final finish has set 24 to 48 hours, it should be rubbed down with stock rubbing compound. In this particular instance, Bish used Herter's lava stone.

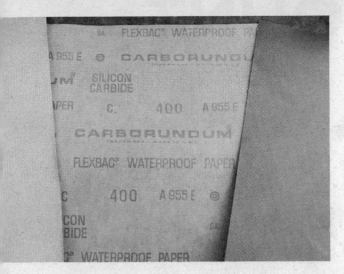

Care is necessary in selection of wood fillers. The light fillers are for use on light-colored woods, (top), while a standard walnut filler invariably works best for the darker shades of stock woods.

Rifle at top has been finished with plastic compound; wood of Savage beneath was treated with oil finish.

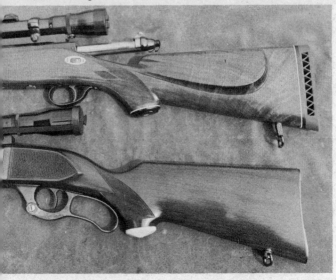

allow each coat to dry for at least twenty-four hours before the next, then rub down the entire surface with compound, such as Herter's lava stone rubbing compound, then wax and polish. If properly done and sufficient drying time has been allowed, the surface of the stock should have that glassy surface, which accentuates the grain of the wood to its full beauty.

Should a plastic-type commercial finish be used, no filler is necessary. Finishes of this type are, as a rule, capable of thoroughly filling and covering the surface of the wood in one operation. To assure positive coverage, lightly sand the first and second coats of the plastic finish, allowing each to dry overnight. Then rub it out with lava stone rubbing compound and apply wax. Plastic finishes, like oil finishes, may be applied with the fingers or a compressed air spray gun. The spray gun does a much neater and quicker job, but finger application, if properly done, is just as effective. The trick in obtaining a flawless final finish on the stock lies in just how well it was rubbed down in the final stages.

Another type of stock finish, seldom used today due to technical advances in this particular field, is the hand-rubbed or French finish. For the most part, nothing is used except raw linseed oil mixed with one-half portion of turpentine. The oil and turpentine are heated to boiling and applied to the stock with a brush or cloth swab. Linseed oil, in this form, penetrates the wood deeply and has a tendency to fill the wood to a much greater depth than do stock fillers.

After the first coat, drying time of about one hour should be allowed before the excess oil is wiped from the surface with a smooth cloth, then allowed to dry for another twenty-four hours.

Repeat this process until the wood will absorb no more oil.

I have found that, following each application of the oil, thorough hand-rubbing the entire surface greatly speeds up the transformation of the porous wood into a surface that is satiny smooth and absolutely water and heatproof. However, this method has a tendency to darken the wood to some degree. If you desire your stock to remain closer to its original color, do not use this method.

One of the greatest sins one can make in finishing a fine grain stock is to coat it with ordinary varnish. Finishes of this type have no durability, scratch easily and tend to cheapen the appearance of an otherwise fine rifle. Lacquer finishes are only slightly better and are used mostly where a real quicky finish is desired. Like varnish, lacquer too is easily marred and scratched and provides little waterproofing to wood.

It is possible to list any number of various old time concoctions that were used on gunstocks as long as a century ago. However, none of these mixtures were as durable nor as efficient as those available today. Modern technology and advanced processes have all but done away with the old method of weeks of hand rubbing to obtain an attractive, durable gun stock finish. The whole secret today is to follow the directions supplied with the product to the letter. Ignore them, and your new stock will show the effects of this oversight!

Any number of books on gunsmithing provide formulas for concocting your own stock finishes. By the time the necessary ingredients are assembled and mixed, you could have bought a far superior product at your local gunshop for as little as a buck a bottle and had it applied on the stock!

There isn't room in stock finishing for trial and error. Not only does it run into wasted time, but it can account for countless hours of hard labor. Do it right the first time and allow plenty of drying time between each coat of filler or finish.

This is the real secret to a beautifully finished stock.

SCOPE MOUNT YOUR EUROPEAN SPORTER Chapter 20

Claw Mounts Are Difficult To Find; Here's How To Make Your Own

THE old adage that "necessity is the mother of invention" has, on more than one occasion, prompted me to improvise substitute replacement parts on various firearms for which original parts were not available.

Take many of the finer sporting rifles built in Europe prior to World War II. A large number of these models were equipped at the factory with scope mount bases that accept claw-based scope rings. But these claw-type rings are all but impossible to find in the proper size these days.

For the most part, rifles having scope bases of the claw-type are of the finer grades but a great many of these rifles now in America are lacking these special rings. To utilize the existing bases that are an intrinsic part of the rifle, itself, and to alleviate the unwarranted practice of some few to drill and tap holes into the barrels and receivers to install a screw-on type scope base, it is possible, with a little ingenuity and careful workmanship, to build a new set of claws that will fit these existing scope bases without defacing the rifle.

Several months ago I acquired a German-made double-barrel rifle. This rifle was chambered for the popular 8 x 57 flanged cartridge, so I planned to use it on a hunting trip into the Sierra Nevada mountains for mule deer. A scope on this rifle would be more advantageous than open sights for the type of country that I would be hunting. Needless to say, this double rifle was permanently equipped with the claw-type scope bases and after months of fruitless searching for scope rings of the proper size and type, I had to give up.

I was still determined that this fine rifle would be scoped properly before I took it into the woods, and I wasn't about to drill and tap the barrels or center rib in order to mount a more readily available scope base.

For several weeks, available scope mounts and rings were checked and examined in trying to figure out a method in which they could be utilized in forming the needed claw-based rings. Finally a set of Buehler rings and a second-hand one-piece base, originally designed for a M99 Savage, were selected for the experiment.

It is possible that by obtaining a two-piece Buehler base, I would have saved myself considerable work, but the one-piece base was in hand and I proceeded to use it.

Prior to beginning this operation, I noted that the spring actuated thumb release button on the rear mount would conflict with the windage screws of the Buehler mount. This was easily rectified by moving the windage-screw section of the Buehler mount to the front base of the rifle. Thus, the windage could be adjusted from the front mount instead of from the more conventional rear mount.

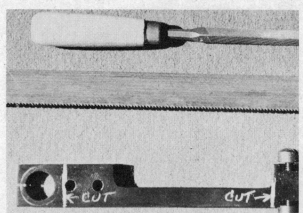

Basic requirement for constructing a set of claw mounts is minimal. Used Buehler mount was cut as explained, claws made to fit mortises on the rifle.

The first step in constructing a set of these clawed rings is to cut the socket sections from the Buehler mount with a hacksaw, being careful not to damage the sockets proper. To these sockets will be attached the claws that will hold the entire unit — including the scope and rings — to the mounts on the rifle.

The claws should be made from good tool steel measuring one-quarter inch in thickness by about three-quarters of an inch square. The claws, and how precisely they are made and fitted, will determine just how efficient the finished product will be when the rifle is fired.

With the use of a fine-toothed hacksaw, a ten-inch mill bastard file and several Swiss needle files for final fitting, the claws are formed so that they are an exacting fit into

Once the claws are rough formed, all finishing and fitting is with Swiss needle files and emery cloth.

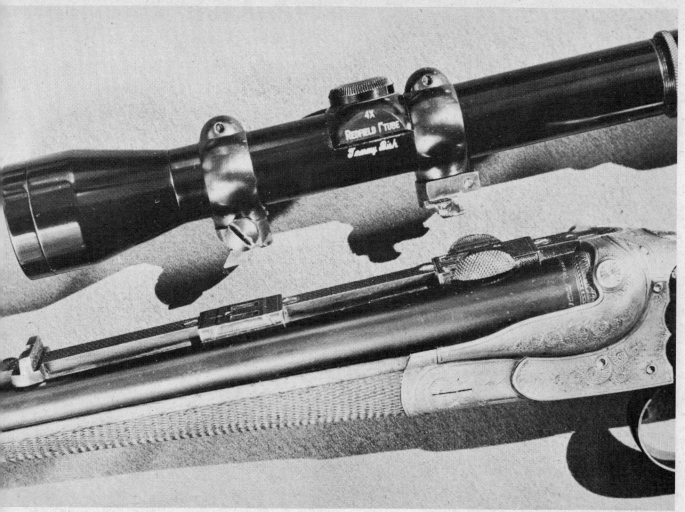

Using set of Buehler rings, cutting sections from a Buehler base to make set of claws, European rifle can be scoped without drilling or tapping.

Factory claw-type scope base, a part of the rifle, can be used by following these instructions. This is a J.J. Reebe double rifle in 8x57JR.

After fitting claws for the correct elevation, scope slides snugly into mortises of claw-type mount. Result should be accurate with fast removal.

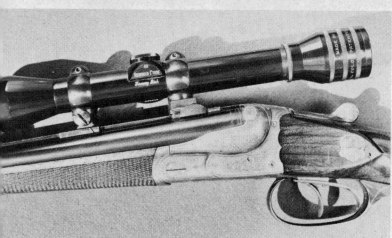

With claws clamped securely into position, torch is played over entire surface until silver solder flows. Torch is removed and unit is allowed to air cool.

to assure that only a hairline joint is visible when the job is completed. Heat with a torch only enough to flow the silver solder, no more; then allow it to air cool slowly. Do not dip the soldered parts into water or oil, as they will be hardened to the point that final filing and polishing will be impossible.

With the claw base sections securely soldered, they then are ready for final fitting and polishing. Clean all of the flux and excess silver solder from the mounts with the Swiss needle files and a fine grit emery cloth.

The care that must be exercised during the final fitting of the claw mounts cannot be stressed too highly. Should this operation be done haphazardly, the mounts will be a sloppy fit resulting in a scope that probably will change its zero each time the rifle is fired.

Any person undertaking a job of gunsmithing such as this should possess enough skill and patience to spend the necessary time to do it right. Admittedly, this is no job for an amateur.

The correct fitting of the claw bases requires that they be of such shape and proportions that they must literally be squeezed into the apertures of the permanent mount base on the rifle. At the same time, the finger-actuated locking mechanism must be free to slide forward, engaging the sloping edge of the claws and locking them tightly into the apertures.

During the final fitting, it is necessary to have the scope mounted in the rings and the rings in place on the Buehler bases to assure that perfect alignment of the scope is attained. The windage, as previously stated, can be corrected by adjusting the windage screws on the Buehler base so the most important phase of the final fitting is to concentrate on the elevation alignment of the scope. When finally mounted, the scope should be on a near-perfect plane with the axis of the rifles bored so that only minor elevation adjustments are necessary in the scope turret. Check this by bore sighting.

When you are satisfied that claw mounts are fitted to perfection, they are then carefully hand polished and either blued or plated.

This type of mount will allow one to mount any scope of your choice by using rings of the correct type and size. Another good feature is that the rings are detachable from the Buehler bases, thus allowing a variety of ring sizes to be used.

the apertures of the scope base on the rifle. The shaping of the claws is most important to assure that they lock up tightly in the apertures when the spring actuated locking device is in the forward locked position.

The socket sections of the original Buehler one-piece mount should be filed and shaped until they are on an exact plane with the axis of the bore to assure that the scope, when mounted, will be in reasonably close alignment. The windage can be corrected by the adjustment screws on the Buehler base but only minor adjustments in elevation should be made from the turret of the scope. For this reason, it is most important that the placement of the bases be as exacting as possible.

Following the rough shaping of the tool steel claws so they will slide home into the apertures of the base mount, they then are clamped into their relative positions on the Buehler bases. The claws must be in perfect alignment with the base sections when firmly clamped to assure that they remain so while being silver-soldered to the base. A minimum amount of silver solder should be used

Careful collimation is necessary prior to testing to assure as perfect scope alignment as possible.
Final adjustments through scope turret should be made, when the gun is taken to the range for firing.

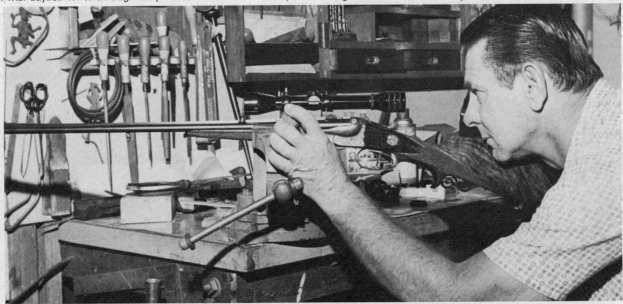

NO SQUABBLE FOR A SNOBBLE

The sleeve section of the snobble is formed on mandrel to approximate desired shape of the finished product.

Chapter 21

THE little, almost insignificant things that a rifle builder often adds to his rifles are those that receive the most attention from knowledgeable riflemen. Custom features, no matter how minor or small, that cannot be purchased from any gunsmith supply house and must be made by the individual craftsman are those features that set a rifle apart from all others as being something extra special.

A custom snobble should be just built to fit a particular rifle for which it is intended. Should snobbles of this type be turned out with production line methods, then they would cease to be "custom" and would no longer have the appeal of an exclusive item.

Custom means something special. Something that cannot be readily purchased except on special order. It may refer to a one-of-a-kind item, completely handmade and fitted for the purpose intended.

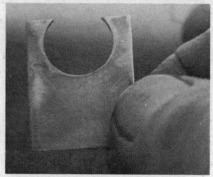

Hole about 1/16-inch smaller than outside diameter of rifle barrel is drilled in end cap for precise fit.

The end cap is attached to the sleeve by means of silver solder. Care is taken to center the cap in the sleeve.

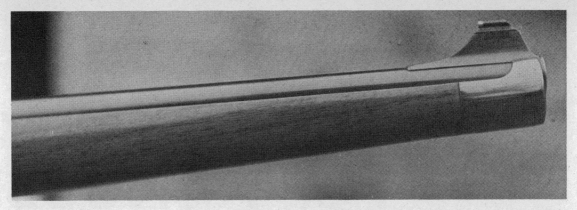

This Delicate Addition Can Improve The Appearance Of Your Favorite Mannlicher!

Construction of a custom snobble for a custom-built Mannlicher-type rifle is a fairly simple chore, requiring a minimum of tools and material. The final fitting, however, should be done with precision to assure a professional and pleasing appearance on the finished rifle. A haphazard job on this one accessory can turn a fine rifle into something that looks sloppy and amateurish.

The material needed consists of a piece of mild sheet iron measuring about one-sixteenth of an inch in thickness, 2-1/2 inches in length and 1-1/4 inches in width. This will constitute the sleeve of the snobble. Also needed will be a small piece of the same material measuring about one inch square for the end-cap.

The outside diameter of the rifle barrel at the muzzle is the deciding factor in just how small or how large the finished snobble will be. For a heavy barrel, it becomes a fairly heavy snobble; standard sporter barrel, the snobble will be slim and trim. The length of the snobble may vary, according to the builder's tastes, but I always have made it a rule to never build a snobble over 1-1/8 inches in length.

Begin the snobble by taking the larger piece of sheet iron in hand. This is bent carefully lengthwise into a semi-circle by using a piece of five-eighth-inch pipe or steel rod as a mandrel. The inside diameter of the snobble sleeve may be regulated in size to fit the barrel and stock section of the rifle by bending the ears of the

File or disc sander is used to shape ears of snobble, removing the excess metal, which is designated by shading. Ears should take on graceful contour. These are bent to the exact shape of the barrel, when finishing project.

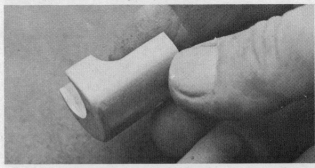

Disc sander is used to remove excess metal from end of cap. Unit then is smoothed all over in final buffing.

A hole for the retaining screw must be drilled in exact center of snobble.

Appearance of finished snobble is more pleasing, if the muzzle end can be rounded slightly before installing.

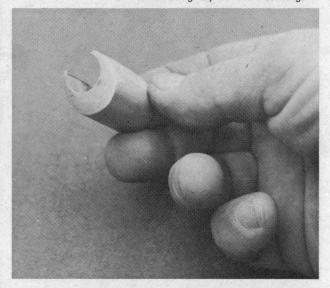

Snobble must be inletted during the final fitting to stock. Excess wood is dressed down in shaping, finishing.

snobble either in or out during their initial shaping.

Now let's set the bent sleeve aside for a few moments, while we prepare the end cap. The end cap, of the same material as the sleeve, is drilled out to about one-sixteenth of an inch under that of the actual barrel size. This is to allow for final file-fitting later.

The end of the sleeve to accept the cap is squared up with a file or disc sander until it seats on the surface of the cap in a perfect hairline fit, at the same time making certain that the hole drilled in the cap is perfectly centered with the sleeve.

These two components then are soldered together with high-temp silver solder. While this type of welding will leave a hairline of silver showing, it doesn't detract from the appearance of the finished job; in fact, enhances it as custom.

With the two components of the snobble — the sleeve and the cap — welded into a single unit, actual fitting and shaping take place. First, grind or disc sand the excess metal of the end cap until it is flush with the outer contour of the sleeve. Secondly, disc sand or file the rear portion of the sleeve to the desired length, making certain that this open end is left perfectly square for fitting to the stock. The ears of the snobble are formed by grinding and filing.

At this point, the wood forend of the stock is mortised out to accept the snobble sleeve in an exacting fit. This means that the sleeve is inletted onto the wood until it is stopped by the end cap contacting the muzzle of the barrel. This accomplished, remove the sleeve and file out the previously drilled hole in the end cap. File the lower portion of this hole until it is an exacting fit onto the barrel muzzle. A half-round Swiss needle should be used for this fitting — along with great care and precision.

The rifle barrel now should slide through the hole in the end cap in a perfect fit, leaving no gap between barrel and snobble. The rear portion of the sleeve is fitted to the adjoining wood of the stock with a little careful chisel work until it is a hairline fit. At this point, the wood of the stock is higher than that of the metal of the snobble. This is as it should be, for the wood will be dressed down to the metal of the snobble later on.

The upper portions of the snobble, commonly called the ears, are bent until they lay snugly against the outer surfaces of the barrel's contour. They then are cut in length — with a file — to allow the snobble to clear the front sight ramp.

The snobble, still in a rough state, is precisely fitted onto the stock and barrel. Remove the snobble and disc sand away all roughness, ending by giving it a thorough buffing and polishing on a cloth wheel.

Place the snobble on the stock and barrel again, then find the exact center on the bottom of the snobble and center punch about one-half of an inch from the rear edge. Drill with a one-sixteenth-inch drill through the snobble and wood of the stock, then countersink the hole in the snobble to accept the flat head of a #3-48 screw. This hole will accept the snobble retaining screw. The nut for this screw is countersunk into the barrel channel of the stock. If the rifle barrel is to be glass bedded, the snobble retaining nut should be glassed over, making it invisible.

With the snobble firmly in place on the stock, the retaining screw cinched up firmly in the nut and trimmed for length, finishing of the stock may be completed. When sanding in the area where the metal snobble adjoins the wood, use a block sander and sand both snobble and wood as a unit to assure perfect lines. Do not sand with the fingers as the wood will wear away much quicker than will the metal of the snobble, creating unsightly dips in the wood where it joins the snobble.

Chapter 22

PORTABLE FIELD REPAIR KIT

This Miniature Shop Can Save Time, Trouble When You're After Game!

A **good hunt** ruined for the lack of a seemingly insignificant tool, such as a screwdriver, a pair of pliers or adequate bore-sighting or cleaning equipment has happened to more hunters than will admit it.

Hunting rifles can be temperamental and in spite of the exacting care given them in the home, they sometimes choose the most inopportune time to kick up. Like when you are miles from the nearest town or village and the right size screwdriver could make the difference between continuing your hunt or abandoning it because of a minor malfunction of your rifle that could have been remedied quickly with a simple hand tool.

Certainly it is not feasible to carry a complete gunshop in one's pocket while hunting but remember that the majority of all gun malfunctions in the field can be attributed to some minor, simple cause. It is entirely possible for a firing pin or extractor to break at any time, but these too can be replaced in the field providing the hunter has had the forethought to include extras, along with necessary tools, if needed, in his kit.

To end possibilities of having a hunt ruined due to some minor fault — one that could be fixed quickly with simple tools — I built up a compact, portable field repair kit.

My personal kit is made of quarter-inch mahogany plywood and measures 12½ inches in width, 10½ inches in height and six inches deep. This provides more than adequate room to carry everything needed for on-the-spot gun repair in the field.

A field kit such as this should be as small as possible without sacrificing any of the essential tools needed for field gun repair.

Cost-wise, this kit can be built for only a few dollars, the most expensive part of it being the hardware. The hinges, hasps and other metal work should be of solid brass to eliminate the possibility of rusting. The kit should include at least a couple of felt-lined drawers for small tools and compartments large enough to accept a three-piece jointed cleaning rod, nitro powder solvent, patches and other essential equipment. All joints of the box should be glued firmly and bradded with one-inch steel brads, then the finished kit given several coats of spar varnish for weather proofing.

It is designed to be carried either in your car, pickup truck or jeep where it will always be handy when needed in the field.

Kit includes several drawers, compartments for tools and accessories. Entire case is of plywood that has been coated with marine varnish for more durability.

Such items as an extra firing pin, main spring and extractor should be carried on prolonged hunt trips.

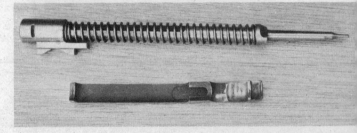

While this kit, or box, may vary in size and shape, it still should contain basic tools appropriate for working on the type of rifle or guns to be used by the hunter. If, for instance, the hunter is using a Mauser or Springfield sporting rifle, then he should include an extra firing pin, main spring, magazine spring and extractor in his kit. If a few basic screws for these rifles are available, they should be included.

Properly fitted screwdrivers for both the rifle and scope mounts should be standard equipment, and a pair of needle-nose pliers is indispensable. A soft copper or aluminum drift pin is handy where open sights are being used — just in case the sights have to be reset. A small ball-peen hammer is worth its weight in gold when needed. A small oil stone of top quality should be included — if for no other rea-

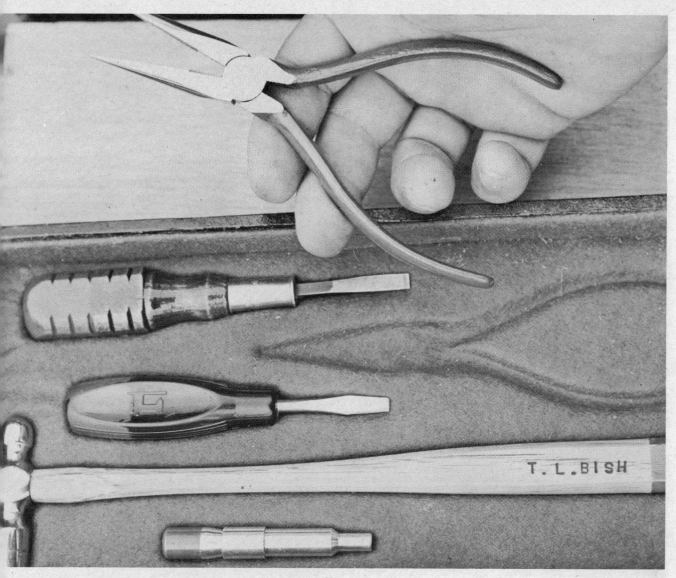

Needle nose pliers, screw drivers, a small hammer and drift punch are valuable in the remote areas.

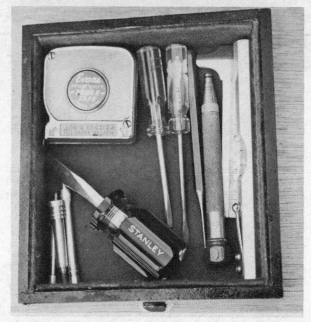

son than to sharpen your hunting knife. They are small, light in weight and darned cheap insurance!

In my personal kit I include a husky-bladed pocket knife, a couple of Swiss needle files, a ten-foot steel tape measure, a small spirit level, extra cleaning rod tips, patches, Hoppes, screwdrivers in several sizes, a three-piece cleaning rod, a pin punch and anything else that might pertain to the particular rifle I might be using — including those all-important spare parts, such as firing pins, main springs, etcetera. Last, but by no means least, I built my kit so it would accommodate a Sweany Site-A-Line bore sighting tool. A most important piece of equipment for field use.

While a field repair kit entails only a few hours of work on the part of the builder, then a couple of hours in deciding what is to go into it, it should prove to be one of the most valued pieces of gear taken afield. It is a mighty good feeling to know that should gun trouble arise, you have the means at your finger tips of correcting it.

While my kit has yet to save me a hunt, it has still helped others to continue theirs, which is some satisfaction, at least to myself. And were I to leave it home on my next hunt, I might return home with a fouled-up rifle and no meat! I'll continue to take it with me.

It's The Little Things That Make A Custom Rifle Of What Otherwise Is Just Another Gun!

I **WOULD** judge that there have been at least a jillion and two articles concerning the customizing of two of the more famous military rifles of recent history, the 1903 Springfield and the Model 1898 Mauser.

For the most part, these articles are prone to praise these great old arms, while a few have berated these fine actions in favor of some commercial version, which was nothing more than a copy of the basic Mauser action!

Over the years I have examined hundreds of fine sporting rifles built on the '03 Springfield or '98 Mauser

action. I have built several hundred myself from these actions. They both are strong enough, durable enough and accurate enough, even in their original calibers, to warrant putting a few dollars into converting them to fine big game or varmint rifles.

I've seen some real butcher jobs done on both these fine rifles in attempts to turn them into sporters. The military stocks have been cut down, built out, lopped off and even inlaid with dental silver in attempts to enhance their beauty and usefulness in the game fields. My personal opinion is that the original military stocks make excellent firewood!

If one wants to build a sporter, the first consideration should be a good commercially built stock designed specifically for sporting use. This stock — usually purchased in a semi-finished state — should receive some loving care in finishing it to the exact conformation required by the owner. It should be built to fit!

Another unpardonable sin involving sporterizing the old Springfield military rifle is to cut off the cocking

Chapter 23

SURPLUS TO SPORTER

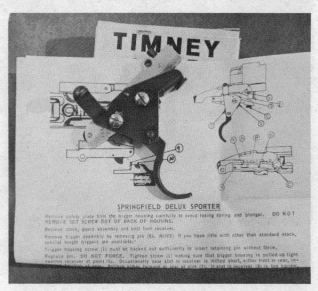

Timney's Delux Sporter trigger for the Springfield is ready to use after installation. Pull is factory-set.

knob flush with the bolt sleeve. It is the misdirected opinion of some that this reduces weight of the finished rifle and enhances its beauty, although actual weight of this knob is less than one ounce!

Its removal greatly impairs the ease with which the bolt can be disassembled and reassembled, Hacksawing this knob off the bolt merely does away with a feature that is both practical and useful.

Two of my most prized rifles are old surplus specimens that I built within the past five years. The first is an '03 Springfield built into a full-stocked Mannlicher type in .308 Norma magnum caliber. The original four-groove barrel was rechambered to the more potent magnum round and the original bolt face was opened up to accept the larger head of the belted magnum case.

To this combination, I added a semi-flat Mannlicher-type bolt handle simply because it doesn't take a door-knob to open a well honed bolt. The Fajen stock on this rifle carries a nine-panel checkering job, a silver pistol-grip cap with gold initial by Bill Dyer of Oklahoma and a hand engraved, silver likeness of a big horn sheep on the floor plate which was done by Sid Bell.

Its accuracy has been proven over and again, especially for long range work. However, something was lacking in this rifle's makeup. About a year ago, I had missed an easy shot at a blacktail deer galloping in front of me at not more than forty yards! In fact, I didn't even get off a shot and the reason was obvious.

I had installed a dog-ear safety of the type that replaces the original GI version. It was a good safety, but I wasn't use to it. My thumb automatically went to the proper position for a push-type thumb safety and it wasn't there!

I have this type safety on most of my other rifles and I have grown use to it. It was second nature for me to expect it to be there on this one occasion. It wasn't and I went home empty-handed.

Some years ago, I converted a standard Model '98 Mauser military rifle into another full-stocked Mannlicher sporter. This rifle was equipped with a Bishop stock and a Douglas Premium-grade barrel in 7mm Remington magnum. Not only does this assembly incorporate a smooth, fully adjustable trigger, but a thumb-type safety that locks both the entire trigger mechanism and the bolt, itself, by means of a hardened steel pin that is actuated by the thumb button. This pin, when installed properly, engages and seats in a hole drilled into the underside of the bolt. When the thumb lever is pressed to the rear or locked position, this steel pin enters the hole in the bolt, locking it tightly in the closed position. At the same time, the trigger mechanism is securely locked by yet another action within the trigger housing. This trigger, a product of Timney, is about as foolproof as any devised to date and is known by its trade name as the **Timney Delux Sporter trigger with pin lock.** It is priced at $18.95 and is available for both the '03 Springfield and the Model '98 Mauser.

The basic procedure is the same for installing the Timney delux trigger on the '98 Mauser and the Springfield. Installing it on a Mauser action requires only minor fitting and the drilling of the hole to accept the pin lock. This same installation on a Springfield action is a little more involved, requiring a certain amount of grinding on the underside of the rear tang and assuring that the sear slot in this tang is long enough to accept the sear of the new trigger mechanism with full clearance.

The grinding doesn't impair the safety of the rifle's action, nor does removal of metal in the tang area to accommodate the slide plate of the new trigger weaken the rifle.

Since incorporation of this trigger mechanism on a Mauser action is comparatively simple, let's concentrate

Small portion of metal must be removed from under side of tang to clear new trigger as designated by white area.

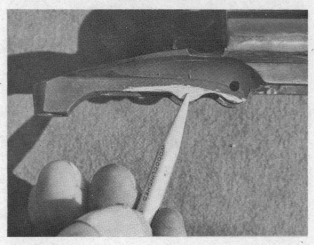

on the more complicated Springfield installation. The first step is to remove the bolt from the action. Then place the new trigger mechanism against the rifle's action in approximately the same position as when it is installed. Using a soft lead pencil, or one with silver lead, mark the exact end terminals of the side of the trigger mechanism. This is to determine the exact amount of metal to grind away on the tang to facilitate full clearance of the side plate when the safety thumb button is moved from the **on** to **off** position.

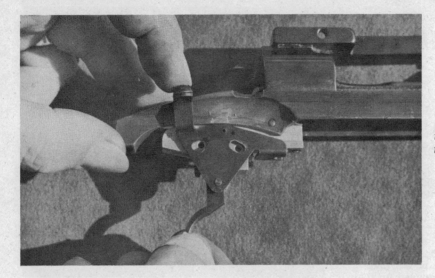

Following removal of metal from tang, the trigger assembly is set in place to check clearance of safety lever.

The best way of removing excess metal from the tang area is with an electric hand tool, using a small grinding stone. The rib on the right side of the tang is ground down slowly but accurately, until the fully assembled trigger mechanism will slide smoothly into the mortise of the tang. Additional grinding may be necessary to assure full clearance of the trigger side plate. Make certain that this plate in no way binds on the ground surface. If it does, remove more metal.

Once the tang rib has been ground to the proper contour, the trigger is installed and checked for sear clearance. Should the sear slot in the tang of the receiver be too short, binding the sear, enlarge it with either a Swiss needle file or an abrasive stone, until the sear has full freedom in the slot. Then remove the trigger.

This Timney trigger is a precision instrument. It is set at the factory for a crisp, backlash-free pull. Do not attempt to tamper with any of the adjustment screws on the trigger housing.

Crucial in the installation trigger is drilling the hole to accept the bolt lock pin. This is accomplished by first removing the side plate of the trigger. This requires

Excess metal on tang's under side can be removed by using small electric drill chucked with carbide stone.

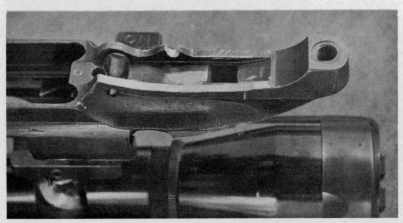

Properly ground, tang is smoothed up and touched up with cold blue where metal is removed. This is done prior to permanent installation of trigger.

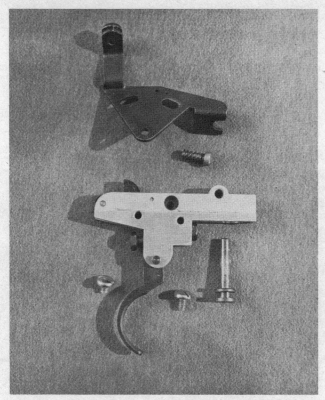

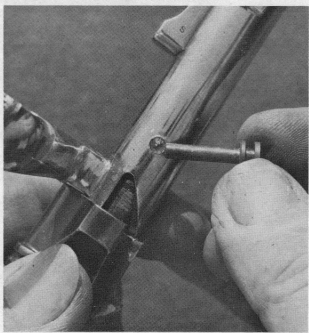

Left: Components of the trigger assembly are simple. The bolt lock and safety lever must be removed from housing, as shown, for proper fitting of trigger to rifle's receiver; a small but important detail.

Hole must be drilled in bottom section of the bolt to accept locking pin. It is best not to penetrate the thickness of bolt wall in performing operation.

removal of the two large-headed screws and carefully lifting the side plate clear of the main trigger housing. Be especially careful during this operation not to lose the small spring and plunger concealed under the side plate. Remove the side plate spring and plunger and place them in a container such as a small glass jar.

Side plate removed, the trigger housing once more is installed on the action after first thoroughly washing the action with cleaning solvent to rid it of abrasives left by the grinding. Insert the main trigger pin, then tighten the small locking screw located on the forward section of the trigger housing. The rifle bolt then is placed in the action and the bolt closed in the cocked position. Be sure that the action is cocked before proceeding further!

The receivers of most Springfield rifles, as well as those of the '98 Mausers, usually are too hard to drill with an ordinary high speed drill. In drilling for the bolt locking pin, a #20 carbide drill should be used. The hole should penetrate completely the existing metal on the lower portion of the receiver, going on into the tubular section of the bolt itself, but not completely through!

The rifle action may be clamped in a good bench vise and drilled with a small electric hand drill or it may be clamped in a drill press vise and drilled on the drill press. Either way will give the same results, if care is taken.

Before drilling, make certain the bolt is closed fully and cocked in the action. Using a #20 drill, proceed to drill the hole using the existing hole in the trigger housing as a drill guide. It is best during this operation to take it slow and easy. Check often for penetration and depth of the hole. Once the metal of the receiver has been penetrated completely with the drill, the hole in the bolt is begun. This hole, as stated, should not go all the way through. Leave a thin wall of metal intact between the hole and the interior of the bolt. This can be determined by inspecting the hole depth as it is being drilled.

While this may sound a bit complicated, the entire drilling procedure shouldn't take more than ten minutes.

Clearance on the left side of the rifle's receiver must accommodate protruding end of safety plunger. This is accomplished by filing or by grinding it.

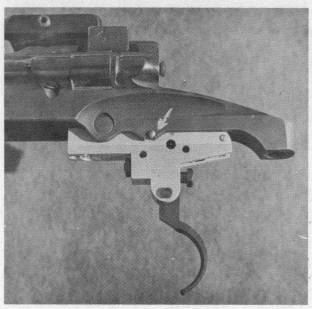

With the hole drilled, remove the trigger mechanism and the bolt from the action. Remove all burrs left by the drill from both the receiver channel and the underside of the bolt. This is done best with fine abrasive stones or an abrasive rubber wheel. If these burrs are not removed completely, a rough bolt will result.

Thoroughly clean the trigger mechanism and rifle receiver with cleaning solvent to rid it of any drilling residue or abrasives. Reassemble the side plate on the trigger mechanism, being certain to replace the small plunger and spring, as well as the bolt locking pin in their proper positions. Give all moving parts a light coating of good gun oil, then reinstall the trigger mechanism on rifle receiver.

If all went well, that old Springfield sports a new crisp trigger, plus a thumb-type safety that, when engaged, locks the entire bolt of the rifle as well as the trigger.

With the trigger, with it's pin lock installed on the Springfield action, certain modifications must be made

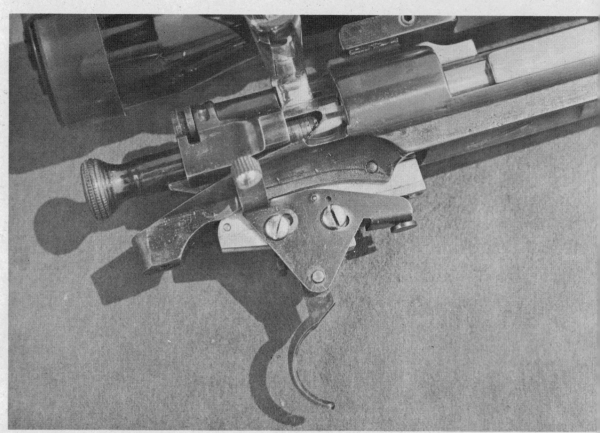

When installed properly, the thumb piece can be bent to conform to stock's contour. The slot to accept the lever of the thumb piece should be cut to the exact length, as explained in text.

Prior to the actual inletting of the stock to accept trigger mechanism, install it on action, then mark the thumb piece for necessary clearance.

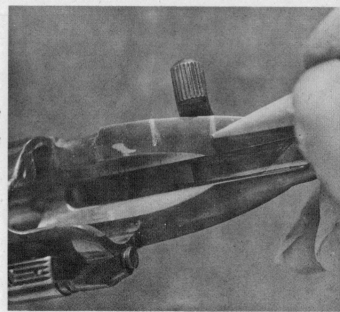

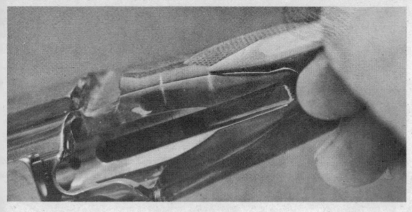

The action then is placed in stock sans trigger mechanism and stock is marked for length of safety throw. This assures exact fit in cut-out.

to the stock's interior to accommodate the new trigger and lever of the thumb piece. This is accomplished with a little careful chisel work. Should any wood bind on the trigger side plate, the safety could be made inoperable. Incidentally, proper inletting can take more time than installation of the trigger mechanism.

Modifications are unnecessary to the original Springfield safety. Just leave it alone. Flip it to the left side and forget it! It will come in handy when you disassemble the bolt for cleaning and it weighs less than an ounce!

Properly installed, the safety lever should clear tang by 1/64 inch.

The original safety may be left intact on bolt of rifle; it presents no extra bulk and weight is minor.

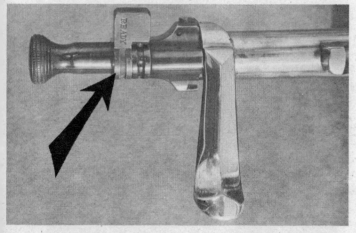

Springfield sporter in .308 Norma magnum was given treatment described here.

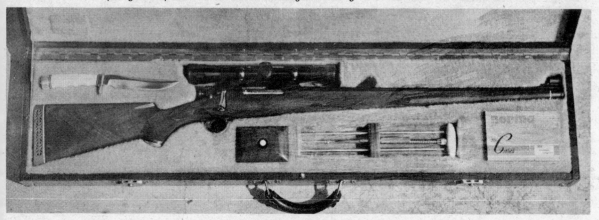

153

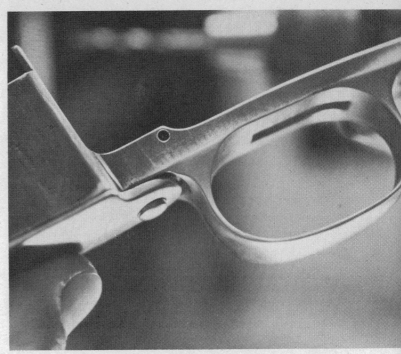

HALF A SPORTER IS WORSE THAN NONE

The simple push button floor plate release should extend above surface of the floor plate 1/32 inch.

ONE of the several nice things about the durable old Springfield rifles is the fact that there are so many of them around. Thousands of owners have acquired military models and retired to the basement or garage workshop, emerging much later with "sporterized" conversions. Some of them have been dandies, but some should have stayed in the basement forever.

It is frustrating to see a rifle that has been sawed on a little bit here, filed and sanded a trifle there, hit with a lick of bluing and stock finish and called a conversion. I have seen a great many such Springfields which sadly lacked the extra touches that make the difference between a truly custom-built sporting rifle and one that was merely converted in haphazard fashion to sporting use.

One of the often overlooked details in converting a worthy Springfield military rifle into a sporter concerns the trigger guard and floor plate section.

I have found that most people who attempt to customize the Springfield rifle ignore this facet. In most cases, they will give these components a thorough buffing, then dip them into the bluing tanks. But this isn't enough if you want your Springfield to be an outstanding example of customizing when finished. This simple job can make all the difference in the world in your rifle's final appearance and handiness. It's a job that requires a minimum of time, tools and almost no cost. It's a minor chore, but one that will add eye-appeal and dollars to the value of your finished rifle as well as giving it that distinction of a truly customized sporter.

It is necessary that you remove the entire trigger guard assembly from the stock. Remove the magazine spring and follower from the floor plate and set them aside. You won't be working on these parts.

The first item we'll tackle is the trigger guard. As issued, these guards aren't badly shaped when compared with other military rifles, but for a fully finished custom job we can grind and taper both the front and rear sections of the trigger guard until it takes on some of the grace of those guards

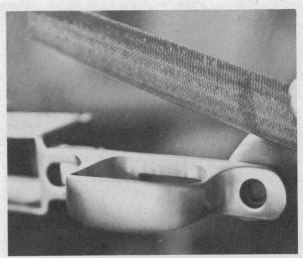

Reshaping the trigger guard is accomplished with files, emery cloth, leaving the guard wide at the front, but tapering slighlty at the rear area.

found on such fine custom rifles as the Griffith & Howe, the Holland & Holland and the Purdey.

This trigger guard shaping operation may be accomplished with a half-round file, a one-inch sanding drum or even a small grinding wheel of the type used in hand-held electric-powered tools. When a pleasing and graceful contour has been achieved, the trigger guard may be finished and polished with either emery cloth or a small abrasive rubber wheel chucked in the electric hand tool. This entire job should take no more than an hour at most.

The next operation is to make and install a push-button floor plate release. This simple button will do away with the possible deformation of the noses of your soft point bullets in attempting to release the sometimes stubborn floor plate to unload.

In making and installing one of these push-buttons, it is necessary to work on only two parts of the trigger guard assembly, the floor plate catch and the floor plate itself. Needed materials will be a

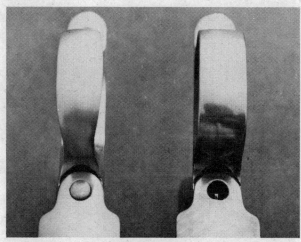

At left is the reshaped trigger guard with the push button installed. An original Springfield guard, floor plate are at right for comparison's sake.

one-sixteenth-inch steel retaining pin — for holding the new button in place — and the button itself which is made from either cold-rolled steel rod or drill rod. This button will not experience any great amount of wear — even after years of hard use — so cold-rolled, rod, or even a steel bolt of the correct size will suffice.

The push-button may be turned in a few minutes on a small lathe, or can even be shaped in a drill press with the use of files and emery cloth. I have made more of these buttons in a drill press than on a lathe simply because there were times when no lathe was available to me.

The sketch shown will give you only the general measurements, however. Due to the variances in manufacturing methods used by different producers of Springfield models, it is best that you hand-fit the new button to your particular floor plate.

The existing hole in the floor plate, for the purpose of inserting the nose of a cartridge to release the floor plate, is the exact size that the thumb-button on your new push-button should be: about seventeen-sixty-fourths-inch in diameter. The shank of the new button may vary somewhat in size, but I have found that three-sixteenths-inch is a happy medium which allows sufficient strength to be maintained in the walls of the locking stud on the inside of the floor plate. It is through these walls that the one-sixteenth-inch steel retaining pin will be pressed to hold the push-button in place. The hole in the floor plate measures about seventeen-sixty-fourths-inch in diameter, the bottom of which closes up to reveal a

mere slot through which the fin of the floor plate catch protrudes when the floor plate is in place on the housing.

The floor plate is clamped carefully into a drill press vise and the slotted bottom of the hole is drilled out to three-sixteenths-inch, making certain that this hole is dead center with the larger existing hole in the floor plate. It is through this smaller hole that the shank of the push button will extend so as to contact and depress the floor plate catch, unlocking the floor plate from the trigger guard housing.

With the three-sixteenths-inch hole drilled, the push button is inserted into the hole and the floor plate again is clamped into the drill press vise. A one-sixteenths-inch hole is drilled through the push-button shank and on through the rear portion of the floor plate locking stud. During this operation, the push-button must be held tightly in place with thumb pressure to assure correct placement of the one-sixteenths-inch hole.

The push-button now is removed from the floor plate and the freshly drilled one-sixteenths-inch hole in the shank is opened up to seven-sixty-fourths-inch. This will allow plenty of clearance for the push-but-

Although measurements shown will apply to majority of Springfield floor plates, it is best to recheck each measurement to assure perfect fit on your rifle.

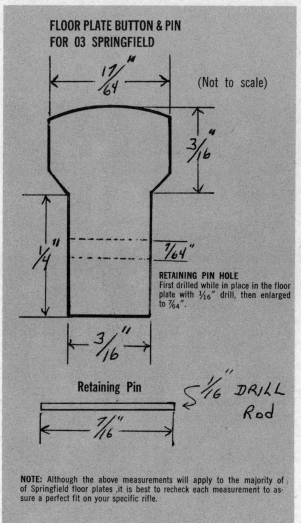

FLOOR PLATE BUTTON & PIN FOR 03 SPRINGFIELD

(Not to scale)

$\frac{17}{64}$"

$\frac{3}{16}$"

$\frac{1}{4}$"

$\frac{7}{64}$"

RETAINING PIN HOLE
First drilled while in place in the floor plate with $\frac{1}{16}$" drill, then enlarged to $\frac{7}{64}$".

$\frac{3}{16}$"

Retaining Pin

$\frac{1}{16}$" DRILL Rod

$\frac{7}{16}$"

NOTE: Although the above measurements will apply to the majority of of Springfield floor plates ,it is best to recheck each measurement to assure a perfect fit on your specific rifle.

Made from common cold rolled steel, the push button is simple to make on even the smallest shop lathe.

ton to move up and down sufficiently for it to depress the floor plate catch enough to unlock it.

The next phase is to remove the floor plate catch from the trigger guard housing. This is done by pushing out the retaining pin, making certain that the tension spring under it does not fall out and get lost. It will be noticed that this catch has a "fin" on it. This fin must be ground or disc sanded off until it is flush with the flat surface of the catch. Following this, the catch is re-installed into housing.

The push-button is once again installed into the floor plate and the one-sixteenths-inch retaining pin inserted through the shank of the button and into the locking stud section of the floor plate. It is during this phase that the final fitting will take place. The head of the push-button should protrude only slightly above the surface of the floor plate. Usually one-sixteenths-inch or so is sufficient.

Full working time to complete this simple project should take no more than a half-hour, few tools.

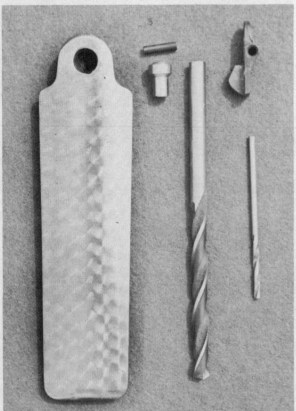

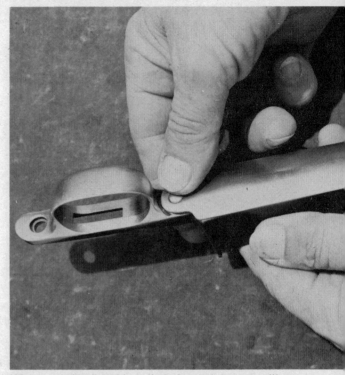

When completed and installed, the push button will release the floor plate, when pushed inward. For sake of appearance, head of button can be checkered.

While holding the floor plate in the hand, the push button is depressed. In this position, the end of the shank should be on an exact plane with that of the locking stud of the floor plate. If the shank is too long, it will be impossible to get the floor plate to lock into the trigger housing. If it is too short, it will lock into the housing but will not release the floor plate when pushed.

Make certain that this final fitting is precise. Even though this fitting is all-important, it still shouldn't require over two or three minutes of filing or honing to get a perfectly smooth operating push-button.

For those not too familiar with the operation of the Springfield floor plate, whether with a push-button as outlined here, or using the nose of a bullet, the floor plate must be pushed a sixteenth of an inch or so toward the trigger guard in order to disengage the locking lug of the floor plate from the trigger guard housing. When pushing your new push-button release, always push it slightly in the direction of the trigger guard at the same time. If properly 'tuned' the floor plate will pop right out of the housing.

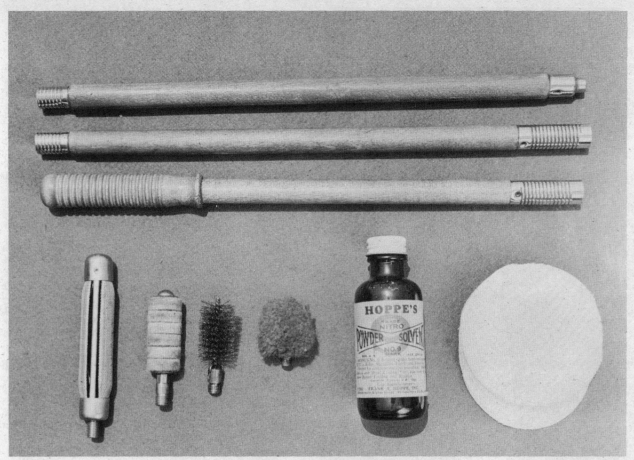

For shotgun cleaning — a repair preventative in itself — the needs are simple and inexpensive. The gear for cleaning rifles, handguns is less involved.

CLEANLINESS IS NEXT TO GUNLINESS

Chapter 24

IN RECENT years, many shooters have become overly lax in cleaning their firearms. This may be attributed to the fact that some manufacturers of cartridges and shotshells have over-emphasized in their advertising campaigns that the frequent cleaning of firearms shooting their non-corrosive ammunition is unnecessary.

Any firearm, be it a rifle, pistol, shotgun or anti-tank bazooka has to be cleaned thoroughly after each extended use, if maximum performance and accuracy are to be expected from these arms in the future.

The method of cleaning any firearm is basically the same whether it fires a shotshell or cartridge. The purpose of thorough cleaning, naturally, is to remove any and all powder residue, lead, metal foulings and other foreign matter that may have accumulated during extended use in the field.

The proper care of a firearm — and particularly the correct cleaning of the bore and action of that firearm — can extend the life of that arm into several generations of use. It is almost impossible to literally "wear out a gun" through normal, careful use, provided it has seen proper care internally as well as externally.

The shotgun is perhaps one of the most abused arms when it comes to the exercising of proper gun care. It has been my frequent observation that a great many shotguns hanging on the walls of sportsmen around the country should immediately be taken down and correctly cleaned. In many cases, these guns have been "swabbed out" with oil after a hunting season, then hung on the wall until the following season.

While the bores of these guns may have been

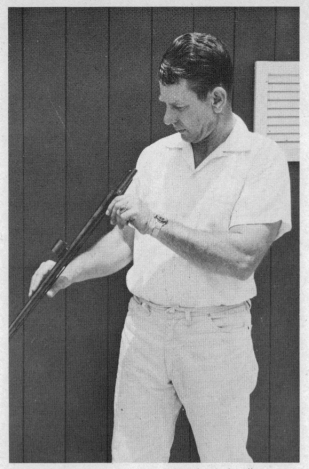

The barrels of shotguns can be examined visually for lead fouling, powder residue. Use of a nitro powder solvent, patches, bore brush eliminates this.

saturated with oil, the internal parts of the locks and actions have received no attention at all, which leads one to believe that the old adage of "out of sight is out of mind" is well practiced by many members of the shooting fraternity as far as their firearms are concerned.

Let's examine making the cleaning of any sporting arm more simple, it should either be placed in a vise with padded jaws, or on a bench or cleaning rack constructed for the express purpose of holding the gun in a stable position. It is also best to clean barrels from the muzzle but this sometimes is not possible due to the gun's design as in the case of various solid frame lever action rifles such as the Model 99 Savage, the Model 94 Winchester and others. Shotguns are cleaned from the breech.

With the gun held firmly, a patch saturated with powder solvent is swabbed through the bore to lubricate it for the next step, which consists of brushing the bore. This should consist of only a few passes completely through the bore from breech to muzzle to loosen up all residue. If using the Tomlinson Cleaner on a shotgun, one should be passed through the bore a sufficient number of times to remove all leading streaks and powder residue.

A series of clean patches, well saturated with powder solvent, should be passed through the bore, with sufficient patches being used until they no longer appear soiled or dirty when removed. The bore then is swabbed until dry of all powder solvent with clean, dry patches and closely examined. The bore, at this point, should be clean and bright and completely free from residue. If it isn't, repeat the above operation.

The chambers of shotguns and rifles alike should be cleaned thoroughly, along with bore. In this case, shotgun chamber is cleaned with nitro powder solvent.

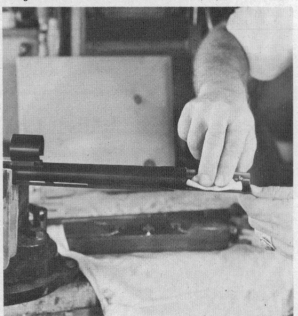

Once the bore is clean, all interior and exterior surfaces of metal should be coated with gun oil.

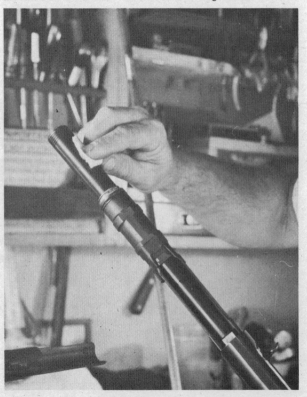

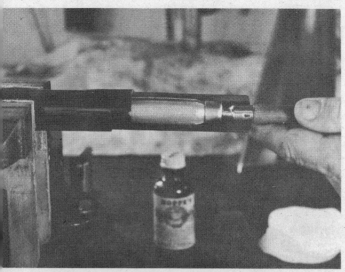

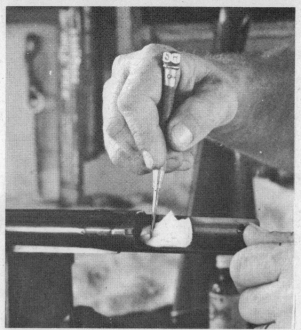

Stubborn lead fouling in shotgun bore can be removed easily with a Tomlinson bore cleaner. Implement is put through bore in scrubbing motion, removing lead.

Machined areas of action are cleaned with a patch that is saturated with bore solvent. A semi-pointed instrument is used for getting into tight areas.

Though this shotgun appeared clean, rubbing lightly with a new patch proved it was coated with dust and the residue from firing, which was months before.

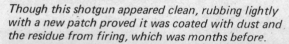

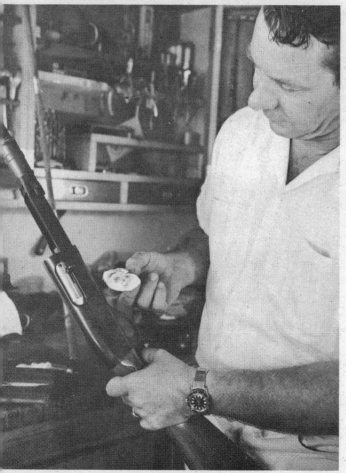

Following the final dry-bore examination and finding it to be perfectly clean, another patch is saturated with either powder solvent or a good gun grease and the bore is again lubricated.

No experienced shooter or hunter will let his firearms go with just a one-time cleaning following extended field use. Some will wash the bore first with hot, soapy water, followed by the earlier outlined procedure. This is still followed by running patches through the bore on separate occasions for a period of several days following the initial cleaning. The powder solvent will "loosen" stubborn residue remaining in the bore that is invisible to the naked eye, having found its way into the very pores of the steel and therefore must be literally soaked loose.

The day following a thorough cleaning, it usually is possible to run a patch through a rifle or shotgun bore and have it come out well crusted with both loosened leading and black residue; it is for this reason that several patches should be run through the bore each day, for several days following the use of the firearms.

Following the cleaning of the bore, the other components of the gun should be examined and cleaned. In the case of bolt action rifles, it is wise to disassemble it. The actions of all guns should receive the same attention given the bores. Where it is possible, breech blocks, trigger assemblies, cartridge magazines and receivers should be washed in cleaning solvent to remove both powder residue and collected dust and grime picked up in the field.

In other words, after cleaning a gun, it should be spotless all over — not only in the visible areas — but in those hard-to-get-at places such as around the chamber section and extractor cut-outs at the breech of the barrel.

Speaking in the terms of the old Marine Corps, of pre-WWII days, rifles were inspected by officers wearing snow white gloves, and those gloves had better not be soiled after handling as many as thirty or forty rifles.

Similar treatment of your own guns will give added life, accuracy and beauty.

Chapter 25

**This New Version Of An Old Action
Can Be Turned Into A Quality
Custom Single-Shooter!**

MARTINI
ON THE STOCKS

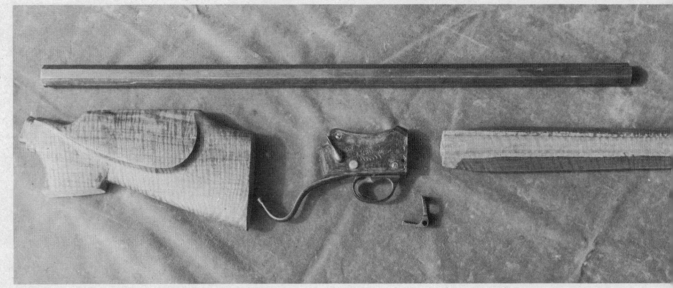

*Components for building this Martini rifle include
the BSA action from Service Armament; Numrich .444
octagon barrel and stock, plus forearm from Fajen.*

*Shown are various parts of rifle prior to fitting
stock and forearm, chambering, reforming the lever.*

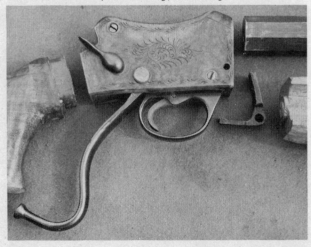

I **never was too interested** in single-shot rifles, especially those of the Martini type, until I examined one of the new commercial versions of this proven action. This action, a product of the famed BSA arms firm of England, is being imported by the Service Armament Company New Jersey and is priced at $49.50 for the plain blue version or $59.50 for the one with its color case-hardened and engraved finish.

Martini actions have done little for me in the past perhaps because the majority I had examined were half wornout military versions hardly worth the effort of converting into a sporting rifle.

This brand spanking new action has been tested by the British government to 65,000 pounds per square inch and is so proof marked. The receiver is forged machine steel and the general workmanship in its construction is exceptional. When received, this action does not have the extractor fitted. This is a tedious job that we will cover a little later in this narrative.

The Martini bug suddenly bit me, but a suitable barrel, stock and forearm were needed, plus a stock retaining bolt 7/16 — 14 and 7-1/2 inches in length. The barrel choice created a problem in that it had to be at least 1-1/8 inches in diameter at the breech to handle the threading and proper fitting to the receiver.

I couldn't think of a nicer guy on whom to shove this particular job.

The octagon barrel sold by Numrich Arms is a heavy affair. It weighs something like eight pounds before chambering and threading and probably would make an excellent tube for a heavy benchrest rifle. However, I had in mind something along sportier lines, so I asked Capone to lathe off the barrel to twenty-five inches in length, then turn it into a half octagon — half round barrel with a slight taper in order to reduce weight.

More problems arose, when Capone didn't have a finish chambering reamer in .444 Marlin, but on his advice, I called the Raton Gun Shop in Raton, New Mexico, which turns out some of the best chambering reamers in the country. At my request, they made up a finish reamer in the caliber and sent it directly to Capone to save time.

Arnold Capone prepares to chuck heavy octagon barrel in his lathe for threading, chambering, contouring.

Forearm lug is dovetail into the barrel. This lug holds forearm in place on the barrel, also acting as the screw base for the forward sling swivel screw.

I remembered that Numrich Arms had just such a barrel priced at $24.95, which they had designed principally for the Remington rolling block rifle. The caliber of this barrel is .444 Marlin, it is twenty-eight inches in length and 1-1/8 inches across the flats of the octagon tube. This barrel is unchambered and unthreaded, so it could be used with the Martini action.

With the new BSA Martini action and a fine octagon barrel in .444 Marlin, I needed suitable wood for the stock and forearm. A letter to Rick Fajen of Reinhart Fajen, Incorporated, specified that I wanted something in a nicely figured walnut and that I wanted the stock blank to be left extra full at both the pistol grip and along the comb. In short order, a stock and forearm were received, which turned out to be among the nicest figured fiddleback walnut I've ever seen. It was quite evident that both stock and forearm had been cut from the same plank.

Not having a lathe, I took the new barrel and action to a gunsmith friend whom I have known for many years, Arnold Capone of King's Gun Works in Los Angeles, California. I wasn't too surprised to learn that he never had had occasion to do such a job on a Martini in the past. The fitting of that extractor, as I well knew, could be a real pain in the neck to any gunsmith, but

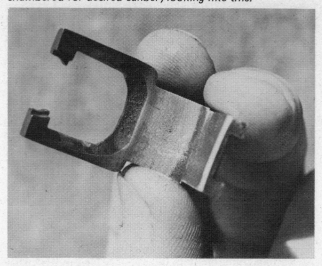

When action was received, extractor was not fitted; this must be accomplished after barrel is threaded, chambered for desired caliber, looking like this.

After weeks of getting everything together, the Martini action by Service Armament, the .444 octagon barrel by Numrich Arms and the stock and forearm by Fajen's could be wedded finally into what I hoped would be a fine single-shot sporting rifle.

However, I want to be perfectly honest in that, should any reader feel that he can build one of these new Martini rifles for peanuts, he has another thought coming! Remember that the action is priced at $49.50 for the blued version (ten bucks more for the fancy engraved job); the barrel is $24.95; the wood can vary in price according to how fancy you want it. But the cost of having the barrel chambered and fitted to the action, plus the fitting of the extractor can easily run over half a century note!

By the time sights, sling swivels and other necessities, such as stock finishing and glass bedding are

an exquisite little Martini-Henry carbine in .577/450 which fired black powder and a lead bullet. It was beautifully engraved and inlaid with gold right up to the muzzle of its short octagonal barrel. It had been built to the special order of an Indian prince just before the order prohibiting all weapons of that caliber in India."

Taylor goes on to say that he had picked up this little Martini simply because no one else in Africa wanted a gold inlaid rifle. However, his record of elephant, rhino, lion and hippo attest to the efficiency of this little rifle before he finally lost it in the Zambezi river when a hippo overturned his freight canoe. The Martini single-shot has written a lot of history as an efficient killer, so is worthy of consideration.

When Arnold Capone had finished the fitting of the barrel and extractor to the new Martini action and had

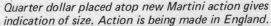

Quarter dollar placed atop new Martini action gives indication of size. Action is being made in England.

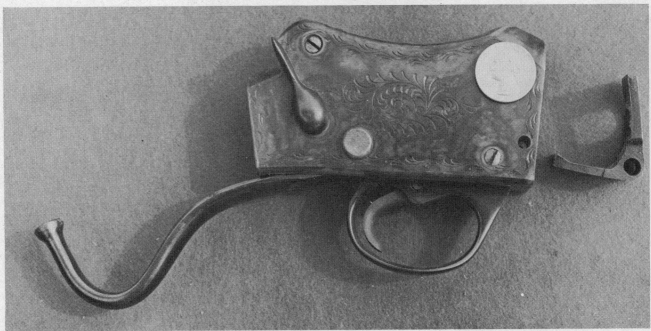

purchased, you can just bet that $200 or more will be spent. This does not include your hours of labor in assembling and tuning the finished rifle.

The single-shot sporting rifle has been around a long time. There are those who swear that such a rifle is the arm of the true marksman and this is especially true in the hunting fields where that one shot must be a perfect shot. The Remington rolling block, the Farquharson, the Semper Krieghoff, the Rigby, Holland & Holland and the various versions of the so-called Schuetzen rifles, usually of German origin, all are fine rifles. Many bring hundreds of dollars even today, though several of these rifles haven't been manufactured for years. In recent years, Ruger has come out with a single-shot rifle that knows no peer. This is one of the finest one-shots I've ever had the privilege of examining and well worth every nickel of the price tag that runs something like $280.

But getting back to the Martini: John Taylor, author of several classic and factual books on African big game hunting, including **Pondoro, Last Of The Ivory Hunters,** used a Martini single-shot rifle early in his hunting career which lasted well over thirty years. He still hunts Africa today and had this to say:" I armed myself with

turned the octagonal barrel to my specifications (half round and half octagon), I found that additional tuning of the action was necessary to assure a super-smooth operating rifle.

The mechanism of the Martini is somewhat complicated to work on, especially if one has had little occasion to work on one previously. The dismantling of this action is comparatively easy, requiring the removal of a couple of screws and one push-pin. However, reassembling the thing can be a headache on that first attempt. Some will swear that the holes in the component parts of this action are drilled crooked or off center. This certainly is not true! Reassembling this action becomes comparatively easy once you get the hang of it. It's a matter of getting everything lined up perfectly, depressing .the trigger to disengage the sear, then installing the front trigger assembly screw first.

Following this, the large pin holding the sear, lever and rear portion of the trigger housing is pressed into place, making certain that the squared portions of the shank align with the square cut-out in the sear, itself. During reassembly, always remember to have the

With barrel installed, additional work is necessary to assure positive extraction, checking the action.

breech bolt in the open or down position and the trigger depressed.

I found, at least on the Martini action with which I was working, that a good tuning up and honing made a world of difference in the smooth operation of the piece. This consists merely of smoothing up all operating parts that contact or rub on another working part. This is accomplished quickly and easily by stoning with a fine hone — a small oil stone — of appropriate shape and size. Lastly, the action is given a thorough but light coating of good gun oil and reassembled.

Not furnished with the new Service Armament Martini action is the stock retaining bolt, which may be purchased at almost any hardware store. The size is 7/16 inch — 14 (14 threads per inch on a 7/16-inch bolt). The length of this bolt should be 7-1/2 inches and it can be shortened slightly to fit the length of the hole through the stock. These bolts usually are purchased with a square head. Round this head on a grinding wheel or disc sander and cut a screwdriver slot in it with a hacksaw.

The first chore following the barrel installation should be the fitting of the stock to the receiver and shaping of the lever. The lever should be removed from the receiver during the bending and shaping operation and all bending accomplished only after sufficient heat from a blow torch has been directed at the area to be bent. To attempt to bend the lever cold could result in breaking or cracking it, necessitating a weld to the broken area.

The stock should be fitted to the action first, the pistol grip area of the stock fully finish-shaped, then the steel lever bent to the exact contour of the finished pistol grip. The lever may be mortised into the pistol grip section of the stock, creating cleaner, trimmer lines to the overall rifle.

Glass bedding stock, forearm was done with Precision Mold Epoxy Butter bedding kit from Ponderay Labs.

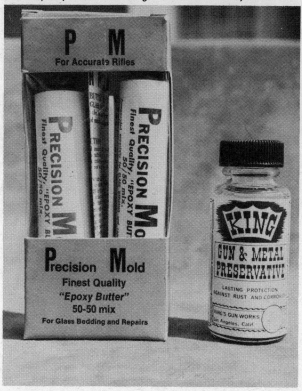

Finishing Touches
Show The Difference Between
Perfection And Adequacy!

Once the barrel is fitted properly to the new Martini receiver and the extractor tuned for easy and positive removal of a cartridge case, it is time to give fitting of the wood serious consideration.

In building a single-shot rifle, the forearm should be bedded to the barrel first, the exterior surfaces con-

The section of the stock that joins the frame must be a precise fit to assure durability. This can be reinforced by applying good stock bedding compound.

toured, then laid aside temporarily. The correct fitting of the forearm where it joins the receiver will require several hours of painstaking, precise workmanship to assure a perfect fit. The rear portion of the forearm must be fitted into circular mortises in the steel receiver. Not only do these mortises play an important part in securing the forearm to the barrel in this area, but the proper hairline fitting of wood-to-metal will determine just how custom your finished rifle will look when completed. Take your time in fitting the forearm.

The bedding of the barrel to the forearm was accomplished with the use of Precision Mold Epoxy Butter, a product of the Ponderay Laboratory in Yakima, Washington. This is priced at $3.50 for the two-tube kit.

This bedding compound is mixed in equal parts from the two tubes and worked much like any other epoxy bedding compound. I found that it does an excellent job in glass bedding rifle stocks and forearms and may be tinted to the exact shade of the wood by adding small portions of the dye furnished in each kit.

Martini action, stock must be joined in perfect hairline fit for strength. Unfinished stock is being glassed in place on the frame of the Martini.

A good releasing agent is a must when using glass bedding. That produced by King Gun Works of Los Angeles, California, and priced at $1.50 per bottle is about the best I've used. Known as **King Gun and Metal Preservative**, this liquid also is an excellent rust preventive.

If the forearm is perfectly fitted and glassed, a hole is drilled to accept the retaining screw, which, in turn, is threaded into the steel lug mounted on the underside of the barrel. All that is necessary to complete the forearm is finish sanding and application of a good stock finish.

Fitting of the stock to a Martini action must be done with precision. To do a haphazard job could result in the stock splintering and cracking under the slightest use, to say nothing of the recoil should the rifle be in one of the more potent calibers.

The stock is held to the action with one large bolt, which was described in Part I of this article. For this bolt to do its job properly, the fitting of the stock to the metal of the receiver must be perfect! As mentioned, a sloppy fit in this area is almost certain to result in either a cracked stock, chips being knocked out where the wood contacts the metal or both.

For final fitting of the stock-to-metal, the use of minute portions of Epoxy Butter is entirely permissible. The use of this compound will afford a positive, tough and durable seat between the wood and metal. The epoxy is applied to the area, the stock bolt is drawn up tight, then the whole works is set aside for about twenty-four hours to allow the compound to cure and harden.

Contour of the stock and forearm should fit the needs of the person for which the rifle is being built. The stock should fit the individual and the forearm should be contoured for comfort and ease of handling. However, fantastic shapes and bulging contours have no practical place, unless one is entering his contraption in a pop art contest! If you are building a rifle to use as a rifle, keep it sane and within the limits of good taste and practicality. A rifle is a sportsman's tool. It can be beautiful and yet one hundred percent practical without adding lines to the stock that look like something straight out of a Buck Rogers comic strip!

Installation of the Pachmayr recoil pad is the next phase of stock construction. I had originally planned on using one of the **500 Presentation** model pads but it didn't arrive in time. Therefore, I used one of the equally effective Pachmayr field pads.

The installation of the recoil pad necessitates that the stock be off the rifle receiver during initial fitting and disc sanding. The recoil pad on this rifle must be installed in such a manner as to provide access to the stock retaining bolt. Do not cement the pad to the wood too securely.

Once the pad is disc sanded to the exact contour of the stock, the stock is bolted firmly in place on the

Needed for installing front ramp and sight were the Brownell ramp soldering jig; sight pusher. Bonding was with Force 44 silver bearing solder and flux.

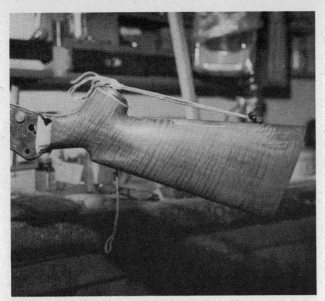

Lever properly inletted, mortise can be coated with glassing compound. Then lever is tied in position until fiberglass hardens for precise wood-metal fit.

of the European detachable type.

The installation of the Williams Guide rear sight created a bit of a problem at first. These sights are designed for use on a round barrel (though Williams does produce one with a flat base, I believe) and the barrel of the Martini is octagonal in the area where the rear sight was to be installed. In installing one of these sights, it straddled the two top ridges of the octagon barrel perfectly and seated solidly. The curvature on the bottom of the sight base was filled with epoxy bedding compound and touched up with flat black paint. It is possible to round this area of the octagon barrel over with a little judicious file work but I felt this was unnecessary as the method of installa-

Shaping of the pistol grip section is accomplished by first heating, then bending the steel of this lever, until it fits mortise cut into pistol grip.

receiver. I found that with the stock attached to the receiver, it was much easier to work on. I carefully masked off the metal of the receiver to assure its protection against even minute scratches while sanding of the stock. Using a variety of files and garnet sandpaper, the latter varying from medium coarse to extra fine, the stock is shaped to the desired dimensions while held firmly in a bench vise.

While the Fajen stock used on Service Armament's Martini was left especially full at my request, I ended up by removing the Monte Carlo "hump" from the stock, thus turning it into what I consider the most practical for my own purposes, the classic type. The cheek rest of the stock must be fitted to each individual.

But before final finishing of the stock and forearm, the lever of this Martini action should be inletted into the pistol grip of the stock for better feel and more pleasing lines. This is accomplished with careful chisel work after first tracing the outline of the lever onto the wood of the pistol grip.

Shaping of the lever, itself, is done by securely clamping the lever in a bench vise, heating the lever to a cherry red, then by carefully bending and reshaping, the lever is given the contour desired. This completed, do not quench in water but allow the lever to air cool. To use water would give the lever a glass-like hardness that would be brittle and likely to break.

The safety lever on the side of the receiver can be improved immeasurably by heating to a cherry red and bending as shown here. Following this, the thumb section of the lever may be checkered with a metal checkering file available from Brownell's of Montezuma, Iowa.

The trigger of the BSA Martini leaves a lot to be desired as to shape, and I found that by fitting and installing an Ace trigger shoe, the trigger was greatly improved.

I chose a Williams Guide rear sight and a Williams Sweat-On ramp. While it is possible to mount a scope on the Martini, I never have been able to convince myself that either an off-set scope or one that sits half way down the barrel is practical. The most practical sling swivels that can be installed on any rifle are those

tion just described was rock-solid and neat looking.

The pistol grip cap may be of any so-called exotic material such as ivory, stag horn, rare woods and the like. However, I used one of the engraved silver caps produced by Bill Dyer of Oklahoma. Regardless of the type of material used as a pistol grip cap, it should be grooved out to accept the lever of the action in a perfect fit.

In addition to the silver grip cap, I installed a spring-lidded cartridge trap in the stock.

As a final touch, I gold plated both the safety lever and the cartridge trap, using one of the plating kits

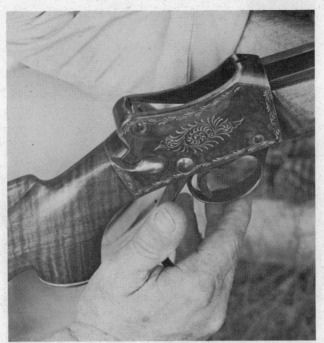

With safety lever in safe position, it still is possible to open action of the gun with the lever.

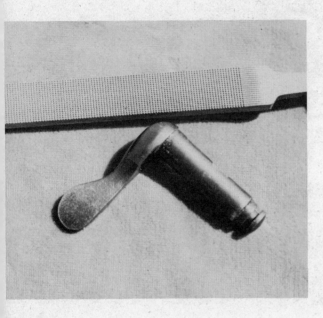

Above: Safety lever, as received, is semi-rough casting. (Below) It was bent upward slightly, then checkered on the thumb piece as described in text.

as sold by the Wisconsin Platers Supply of Madison, Wisconsin. This kit is priced at $15 for the **Gunsmiths Special** with which one may gold or silver plate several complete guns. All that is necessary to use this kit is to purchase three inexpensive dry cell batteries.

The final finishing of the stock and forearm of the BSA Martini being imported by Service Armament Company of Ridgefield, New Jersey, can be done with any good stock finishing material such as **Tru-Oil** by Birchwood-Casey or a spray can container of polyurethane stock spray such as G-96 brand. I decided to give this new G-96 polyurethane spray a trial, and I found it to produce a fine and lasting finish on walnut providing it is used exactly as directed. I made the mistake of holding the can too close to the wood and got some runs the size of tidal waves! Hold the can twelve to fourteen inches from the work and spray sparingly and you'll have no trouble.

When this finish has dried for at least twenty-four hours, it is thoroughly rubbed out with stock rubbing compound to bring out the beauty of the wood.

Prior to final assembly of the finished Martini rifle, all screws in the receiver — somewhat rough when received — should be buffed and blued along with the reshaped lever. I polished these components to a luster — not a high polish — then blued them with repeated coatings of G-96 gun blue until they were the shade desired. While this is a cold bluing paste, it is one of the most durable available today and if given a good coating of paste wax, will hold up quite well under normal use. In fact, the stock and forearm should be given a thorough rubdown with paste wax and polished to a sheen before being taken afield for actual firing.

Bish checks fit of reload in gun's chamber, still eying target downrange. Reloads, factory both worked well.

Some of the products utilized in the completion of custom Martini were a stock finish, gun blue, gun treatment.

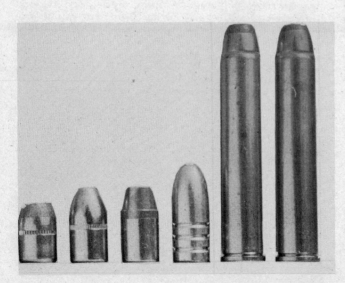

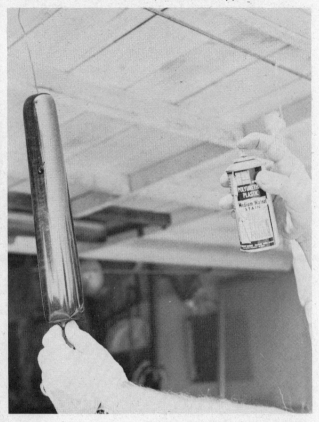

Beavertail forearm requires fitting where it contacts the frame. Then it is sanded, final finish applied

of the handcast lead bullets about which Grennell was curious. I have frowned on using cast bullets in any good rifle, because I felt it was defeating the rifle's overall efficiency. The Martini may be an exception, but I found that I attained excellent groups to one lead bullet that had fallen down when used in the Marlin, lever action with a slower barrel twist than that of the Martini.

I also learned that the Martini action would accept much hotter loads — with no flattened primers — than those recommended as maximum for the Marlin.

In building up fodder for the Martini, I first loaded up a quantity of the heavy cast bullets thrown from a Lyman #427103 mould. These bullets were cast by Grennell and weighed an average of 363.5 grains each after lubricating.

Behind these elongated lead bullets I used CCI #200 rifle primers and 42.5 grains of 3031 powder. This heavy bullet got up to a whopping 1850 fps and was amazingly accurate at one hundred yards. This would be the heavy bullet I would use in this rifle for brush busting.

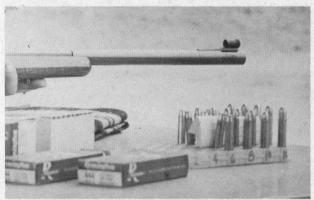

In testing reloads, they were carefully cataloged, information being retained on each round, then a comparison made between reloads and factory ammo.

The proof of any newly built rifle is in the shooting tests. During this session, the actual mechanics of any new rifle are tested for smoothness of operation, durability and accuracy. This initial test should bring out any bugs that might be hidden within the bedding or in the action, itself. Ejection of fired cartridges should be smooth and the action should feed new rounds into the chamber smoothly. It had to be field tested before I would consider it a finished rifle.

During construction of the Martini, staffer Dean Grennell was interested in its progress. He had some pet cast lead bullets he wanted to put through it. These same cast bullets hadn't performed too well in the Marlin .444 magnum he had field tested some weeks earlier, so he was somewhat anxious to see what they would do through the Martini, as its barrel has a much faster twist than that of the Marlin.

Upon completion and time for testing with a variety of handloads Grennell was involved in testing a new desk. My wife and I were heading into the High Sierras of California to a friend's ranch, so I took the Martini along for plinking purposes. The serious testing could wait until both Grennell and I could arrange to be on the rifle range at the same time. It was during this outing that the first bugs showed up that had to be corrected.

Some weeks later, Grennell and I met at the rifle range at the foot of the rugged San Gabriel Mountains. I had loaded up eight variations, including a number

Although it cannot be seen here, area of safety to be contacted by thumb was checkered using a metal checkering file. This was after reshaping safety.

Highly figured walnut stock incorporates such features as silver pistol grip cap, a sculptured cheek piece and cartridge trap holding four rounds.

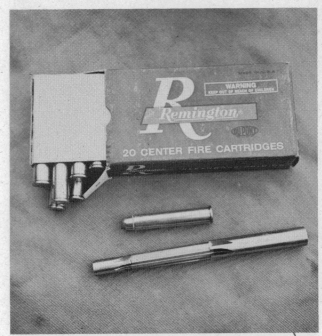

There was difficulty in obtaining correct chambering reamer in .444 Marlin. Once chambered, barrel was finished to accept standard Remington cartridges.

Author's wife grimaces under full recoil from .444 Marlin. Load used for this photo was especially hot and was concocted as a special test round for gun.

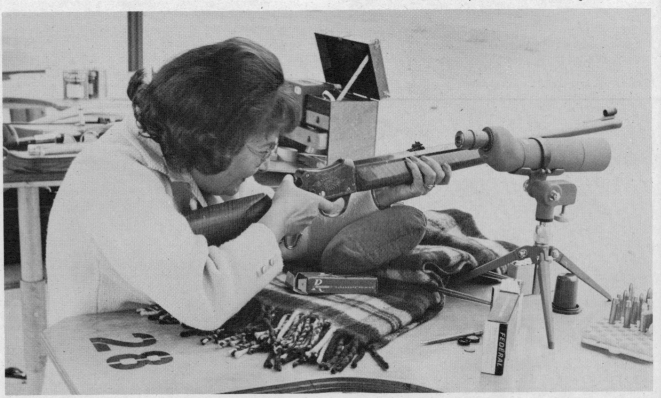

Bish and Dean Grennell discuss potential reloads for .444 Marlin. Wide spread of handloads were used, some of which proved excellent, others quite poor.

In the jacketed bullets, I stuck to Norma's 240-grain soft point and Hornady's 265-grain S.P., feeling that these would give the best performance. Using 50.4 grains of 3031 and a #200 CCI primer behind the 265 grain Hornady bullet, we got 2100 fps. However, accuracy left much to be desired.

Later, in working with various loads, I found that 52 grains of 3031 was about ideal in the accuracy department for this particular rifle and the velocity jumped to 2250 fps., with inch and a half groups at a hundred yards possible.

The 240-grain Norma bullet proved a chore in figuring out a proper load for it. After much trial and error, I found that 47 grains of IMR 4198 powder gave the best results accuracy and velocity-wise. This load got up to 2360 fps and two-inch groups were possible at one hundred yards.

These were the three loads that proved most efficient in the Martini and I have no doubt that each is safe and sane for this action.

During initial tests, on numerous occasions the rifle failed to fire. Close inspection proved that the firing pin was too blunt to detonate the primer properly. This was corrected by stoning the firing pin to a more precise point. However, after this correction, the rifle

on occasion still would fail to properly fire. With no round in the chamber, the action worked perfectly, but when a cartridge was loaded into the chamber and the breech block closed, often the firing pin was not being released instantaneously by the sear. This resulted in the firing pin striking the primer so lightly that it wasn't even dented!

I finally decided that this malfunction must, in some way, be connected with the safety lever located on the right side of the action. I removed the safety and the rifle fired perfectly! I elaborate on this particular malfunction simply because it is one that might be experienced by other Martini builders. I found that the clearance slot cut into the shank of the safety wasn't cut deep enough; when the safety was disengaged and the trigger pulled, the sear would hit and bind up on the not-deep-enough slot of the safety.

Using an electric hand tool, I ground this slot just a little deeper to allow the sear full clearance. While this malfunction was of a simple nature, it still required a thorough study of the rifle's action to pinpoint the trouble. It is hoped that these few extra lines will help others who might experience the same difficulties. It's simple to correct once you know what to look for; a real headache if you don't!

Chapter 26

THE BITELESS BROWNING

After bobbing, smoothing up and touching up with cold blue, hammer now is pinch-proof and graceful.

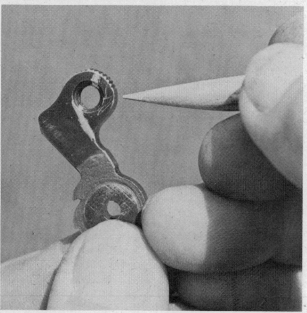

Lines for cutting are marked on hammer surface with white lead. Cuts with wheel are inside these lines.

In place of a regular hammer spur, the Browning is equipped with a circular affair with a hole in the center. This is to accept a lanyard cord, but it's a poor system!

That pinching and nipping is caused by insufficient space being allowed between the bottom of the circular hammer spur and the rear grip housing, when the hammer is in full cocked position. As the hammer is slammed to the rear during firing, it has a tendency to grab a portion of the shooter's hand. The pinch is enough, in some instances, to raise blood blisters.

So it was old Doc Bish to the rescue. I told one individual experiencing discomfort in shooting his Browning that I could eliminate the trouble in either one of two ways. Amputate that section of his hand that was giving the trouble, or do a bob job on the Browning itself! He selected the latter, a sure cure for Brownings that bite.

This operation requires dismantling the gun to a point that the hammer can be removed from the frame. This is accomplished by removing the slide from the housing, then the grips. Remove the pin holding the sear, then the hammer pin and the rest will come out easily.

With the hammer removed from the gun, two lines are

The small section behind the pencil line is removed with carbide cut-off wheel, cutting each section.

The Belgian-made Browning 9mm Hi-Power semi-automatic pistol is a great gun — except for a few hundred thousand manufactured under Nazi supervision during the German occupation of Belgium during World War II.

Many of these particular guns were sabotaged deliberately by the Belgian workers, so if a person has one of doubtful lineage, it's best to have it checked by a competent gunsmith.

This semi-auto, the last design of John Moses Browning, is a fine gun! However, as many shooters will admit, it does have its drawbacks, the most noticeable of which is its nasty habit of pinching, nipping and pounding that fleshy part of the hand located between the thumb and the index finger each time the gun is fired and the hammer automatically thrown back to the full cocked position.

Care must be taken in cutting lower section of the hammer ring to prevent accidentally cutting into the lower section or possibly overheating the metal.

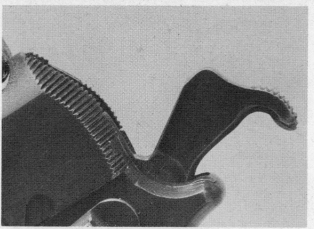

The lower portion of the ring-shaped hammer spur removed, it is not possible for the hammer to pinch.

The Browning ringed hammer spur is notorious as a hand pincher. This occurs when the slide drives to the rear and recocks the hammer as the gun is fired.

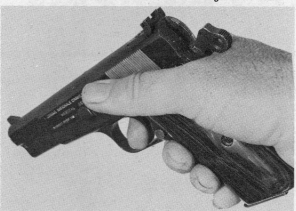

Its lines streamlined, the functioning of Browning automatic is impaired in no way by this alteration.

For this operation, simple as it really is, the pistol is dismantled in order to remove the hammer.

drawn with a white lead pencil, as illustrated, to act as guides for the next operation.

The bobbing operation on the Browning hammer is simple, requiring only the use of a narrow cutoff abrasive wheel and finally a pecay wheel for polishing.

The first cut with the wheel is made along the extreme back side of the rounded hammer section. Cut until the wheel enters the holed section of the hammer spur. Now make another cut on the under side of the rounded spur. When this final cut is made, a small section of the rounded spur will fall free of the hammer. The only thing left to do now is dress-up the cuts with a pecay wheel, polish and touch up with cold blue. The Browning now has a regularly shaped hammer spur. Round this over neatly to eliminate any sharp edges left by the cutoff wheel.

While this operation is definitely not recommended for collector quality Browning Hi-Powers, it can be a boon to those who shoot their Brownings regularly. No longer will the rounded section of the hammer bite and pound that fleshy part of the hand.

One last word of advise: When cutting the section from the hammer, do not allow the hammer to become overly hot. Should it become too hot to hold in the bare hand, it should be quenched in water immediately. The reason for this is obvious: The hammer is of hardened steel; keep it that way by not overheating!

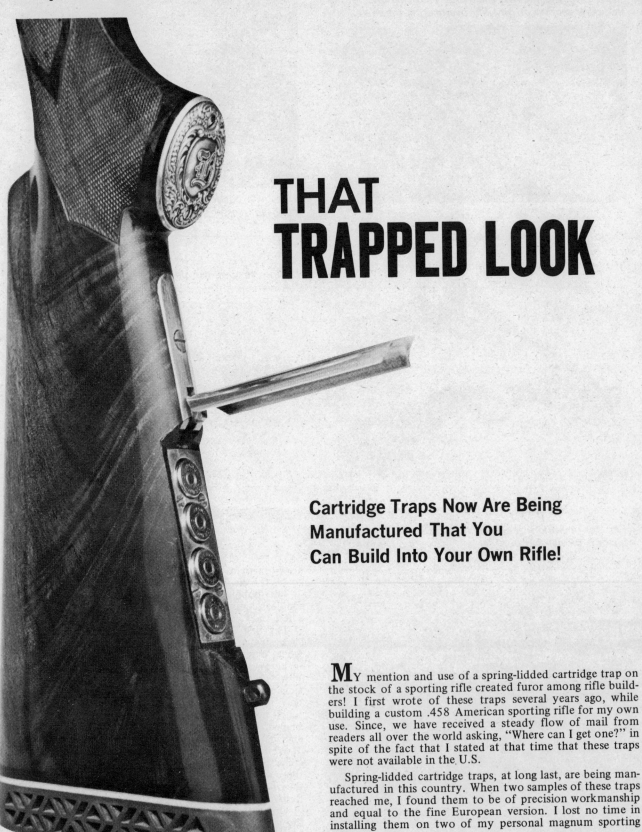

Chapter 27

THAT TRAPPED LOOK

**Cartridge Traps Now Are Being
Manufactured That You
Can Build Into Your Own Rifle!**

MY mention and use of a spring-lidded cartridge trap on the stock of a sporting rifle created furor among rifle builders! I first wrote of these traps several years ago, while building a custom .458 American sporting rifle for my own use. Since, we have received a steady flow of mail from readers all over the world asking, "Where can I get one?" in spite of the fact that I stated at that time that these traps were not available in the U.S.

Spring-lidded cartridge traps, at long last, are being manufactured in this country. When two samples of these traps reached me, I found them to be of precision workmanship and equal to the fine European version. I lost no time in installing them on two of my personal magnum sporting rifles.

Machined of fine steel, these traps are a product of N.H. Schiffman, Custom Gun Service up in Murray, Utah While installation of one of these traps into a rifle stock

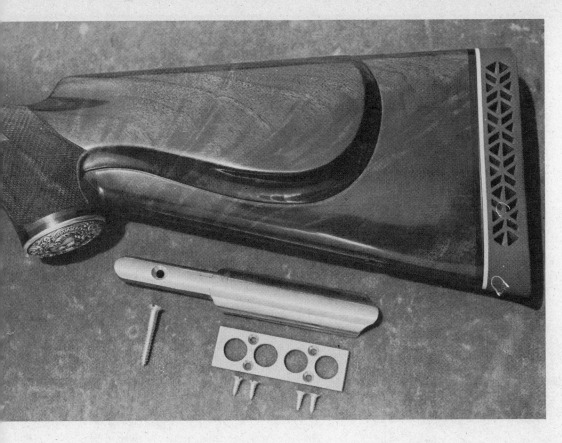

The cartridge trap is unpolished, but after installation and fitting, entire unit can be blued or plated.

involves a certain amount of precise workmanship, it can still be accomplished by the gun owner himself.

Fitting and installation of a trap into an unfinished stock is a fairly simple chore, when compared to the same installation in a fully finished and contoured stock. On the unfinished version, the trap is inletted midway between the toe of the stock and the pistol grip during the early stages of stock contouring. Finally, during the finish shaping and sanding, both the wood of the stock and the rounded contour of the cartridge trap are blended into one flawless surface. The same operation on a finished stock is something else!

Let's assume that you are installing the cartridge trap on a stock that has a beautiful finish. This can be done only if careful workmanship and forethought are exercised. Attempt to rush the job or overlook any phase and you are apt to end up with a piece of walnut that would make excellent kindling wood.

The first consideration is the stock itself. An installation such as this requires that a certain amount of fullness be present in that section of the stock located between the toe and the rear portion of the pistol grip. If this area has been filed and sanded excessively, the stock may not accept the installation. While the hinged lids of the new Schiffman cartridge traps are purposely left much thicker than the Europen version to allow for shaping and contouring, they require a certain amount of wood in the prescribed area for a perfect job.

The heavy spring that actuates the lid of the trap is held in place by an Allen head screw. Remove this screw and lay it and the spring aside for the time being. Locate and center the trap midway between the pistol grip and the toe of the stock. Should a sling swivel be in the way, remove it, to be reinstalled later.

The area of the stock to accept the trap then is covered with masking tape, making certain that the tape lies smoothly over the surface of the wood and is long enough. Lay the trap on the surface, making certain that it is in dead center of the stock area. Carefully trace the outline of only the tang section of the trap onto the masking tape.

The tang of the trap must be inletted fully before any chisel cuts are made to accept the lid itself. This is to assure perfect alignment of the tang with the stock, so that the lid will close in perfect alignment.

The masking tape serves at least three purposes: as a template for laying out the trap contour, to prevent minute chipping of the edges of the wood during the actual chisel inletting and to prevent bedding compound from marring the surface of the stock.

The outline of the trap tang traced onto the masking tape should measure exactly one-half an inch wide by 2-1/8

The lid spring and screw are removed prior to initial layout of the conformation of the tang on the stock.

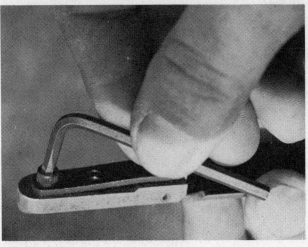

The tang of the trap is placed in perfect alignment on the stock, then outlined with a soft lead pencil.

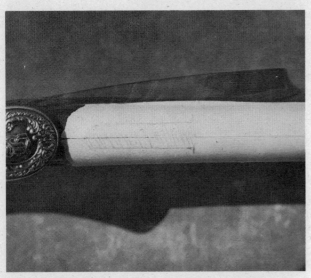

Area of the stock in which trap is to be inset is covered carefully with masking tape, allowing room to accept the conformation of the metal trap.

inches in length.

The handiest chisels I have ever owned for inletting are produced by Miller Falls Tool Company. Fairly inexpensive, these chisels are unsurpassed for chores such as minor inletting and fitting. Costing about ten dollars for a set of six in varying shapes, this is the chisel used in this job.

The outline of the trap tang traced on the masking tape now is chisel cut, completely penetrating the tape and the surface of the stock wood. The wood within the outline is chiseled away carefully, until the desired depth is reached. During fitting the tang section to the stock, use the lid of the trap as a handle. Insert only the tang into the mortise constantly to assure a perfect fit, making chisel cuts only where necessary.

When the tang had been fully inletted, the Allen screw and spring are reinstalled on the trap. The mortise in the

Tang section is inletted for depth and width with small chisels. Then the lid spring is replaced on trap and additional inletting is done to accommodate both spring and screw.

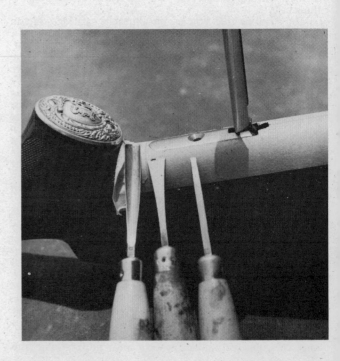

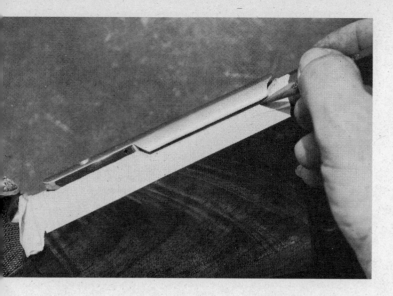

Tang in place in the mortise, lid is outlined onto the masking tape. Allow one-eighth inch extra depth for full seating of lid, with tang in mortise.

stock then is cut to accommodate these. During inletting, to accommodate the spring, make certain to allow sufficient room for the spring, as the trap is opened and closed.

At this point, the entire tang section of the trap is inletted into the stock.

Now to the crucial job of mortising the stock to accept the lid section in a perfect fit!

With the lid in the closed position on the tang, the unit is placed on the stock, making sure that the trap is on a perfect line with the stock edge. Trace an outline of the trap lid onto the masking tape. During this phase, the trap sits about one-eighth of an inch above the surface of the stock. This must be taken into consideration when tracing the lid outline. Add that eighth of an inch to the bottom of the traced line, thus allowing the lid to drop to its proper depth, when the mortising is completed.

While the entire section to accommodate the lid may be chisel cut, the use of a coping saw greatly speeds up the operation in removing excess wood from the area. With this wood removed, the surfaces to accept the seating edges of the lid are filed carefully to a perfectly flat plane. This particular operation will determine just how attractive and custom-like the job will look when completed. The lid should fit onto the stock surface in a hair line fit.

The entire trap section installed on the stock, the next operation involves installation of the cartridge plate to accept four rounds. This plate is centered on the lid seat, its outlined traced. Using a sharp chisel, the wood is relieved about one-sixteenth of an inch to accommodate the thickness of the plate, after which the four screws are installed, securing the plate to the stock.

As received, the Schiffman cartridge trap plate is drilled

Excess wood in the lid area is removed best with coping saw; allowing at least one-sixteenth inch of wood to be filed for a perfect hairline fit.

Care must be taken in filing flat to accept lid. This makes difference between good or amateur job.

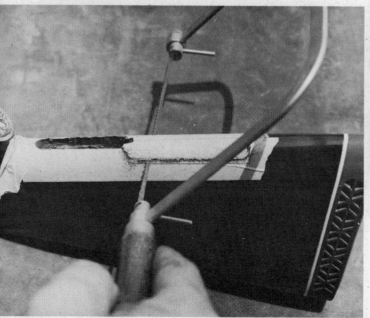

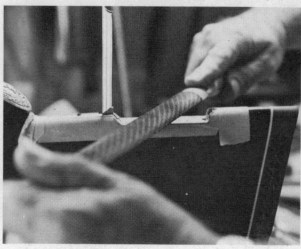

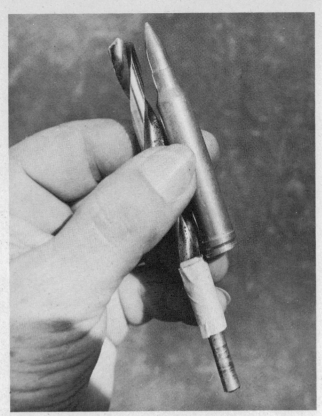

Drill, larger in size that bullet, is marked for depth with masking tape. It is used for hole that will accept only bullet section of cartridge, but also acts as guide for next phase of completion.

Drilling holes to accept the case part of round is done with a drill that is slightly larger than case. It also is marked for the proper depth of the hole.

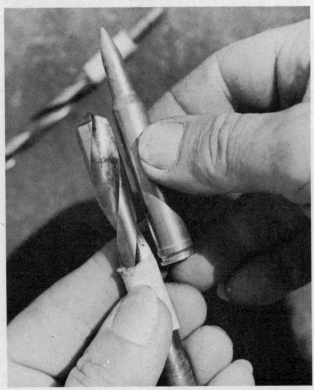

to accept cases such as the .243 or .30/06. However, by drilling these holes out, these traps will handle cases of the larger magnum sizes. I have mounted five traps involving such calibers as .458, .308 Norma magnum, .300 Winchester magnum and 6.5mm Remington magnum. All have worked out perfectly and strength and durability of the stocks have not been impaired. Should you alter the cartridge plate to accept the larger magnum rounds, do this prior to inletting it into the stock.

The most crucial task in the installation of a cartridge trap is drilling the holes into the stock to accept the four extra rounds of ammo. These holes must be in perfect alignment to each other to assure that perfect partitions of wood exist between each round. To cramp a steel drill in one of these holes during the drilling operation could tear out the partition. The procedure goes like this:

First determine the caliber or bullet size of the round to be used. Let's assume that it is .30 caliber. Prior to drilling, find the exact center of the holes in the cartridge plate (now held with four screws in the stock). These centers are well marked and center punched. Using a three-eighth-inch drill, the length of the proposed cartridge is determined, less the rimmed head area. This length, in turn, is marked on the drill with a short section of masking tape wrapped around the drill. This is to prevent drilling the hole too deeply.

The drill then is chucked into either a drill press or an electric hand drill. Being extremely careful as to exact angle and pressure on drill, the holes are drilled to the exact depth marked by the masking tape.

When the four holes are drilled, all slightly larger than actual bullet size, the drilling to accept the cartridge cases begins.

These holes should be drilled to the same sizes as the

Properly drilled, only the rims of the cartridges should protrude above the cartridge plate's surface.

Using cartridge plate and the holes that are larger than bullet as guide, finished holes have partitions.

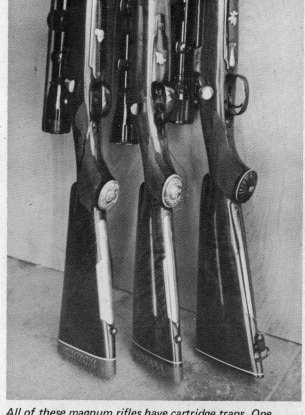

All of these magnum rifles have cartridge traps. One is silver-plated, one with gold, third has been blued.

Lid in closed position, it should seat on the stock in perfect fit. If edges of trap extend beyond plane of stock, file or sand to exact fit before bluing.

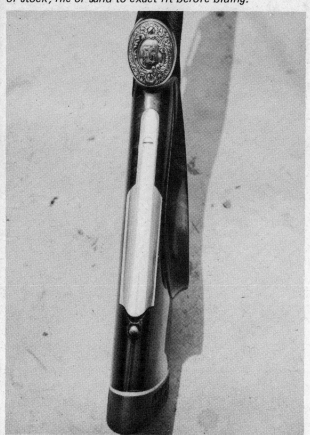

holes in the cartridge plate. Once again, the length of the large portion of the cartridge case is measured. This length is marked on the steel drill with masking tape. Again, this is to assure that the hole is drilled only as deep as necessary to accept the cartridge case. Drill each of these holes, using the smaller, larger-than-bullet-size holes as drilling guides.

With the holes cleaned of drill dust, the cartridges should slide into the holes freely, only the rimmed sections protruding above the surface of the steel cartridge plate. These holes now should be sealed with any good stock sealing compounds.

Should there be minute imperfections in the inletting around the tang section, these may be filled with Micro-Bed stock bedding compound, then be allowed to cure and harden for at least six hours. In the majority of cases involving the installation of a cartridge trap on a fully finished stock, it is necessary to do minute dressing down of the wood in the area of the tang. This will leave small areas of raw wood that will require refinishing. A small dab of Tru-Oil will do the job perfectly in a few moments.

Once fully installed, the lid of the trap may overhang the wood of the finished stock slightly. This can be remedied by removing the trap from the stock and filing or disc sanding these surfaces to a perfect fit. As these traps are supplied purposely only in bare metal, they may be polished and blued or gold or silver-plated.

Chapter 28

BUILD YOUR OWN CARTRIDGE TRAP

I CERTAINLY cannot take credit for invention of the spring-lidded cartridge trap that was discussed at length in the last chapter. Most of those I have seen hold four extra rounds so that they can be extracted and used quickly.

This innovation was perfected — and used — long before I was born and originally was designed for use on German-made drillings, as I understand it. Until recently, it has been a rare situation, when one was found incorporated in the standard type of bolt action sporting rifle.

A drilling, as most shooters are aware, is a combination rifle and shotgun, that incorporates as many as four barrels in a single cluster. Three usually is the limit, however, with a rifle barrel mounted exactingly beneath two shotgun tubes.

The spring-lidded cartridge trap was designed originally for this type of gun and was meant to hold extra rounds for the rifle barrel. Such traps were manufactured by various German firms and, since World War II, some have arrived in this country from West Germany. The high tariff, however, made this economically

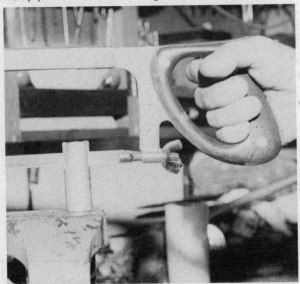

Components of cartridge trap are cut from one-inch iron pipe. Lid section is being sawed from the pipe.

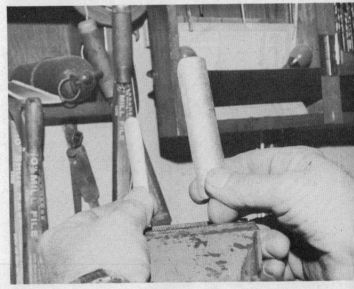

The spring base, also cut from pipe (left), trap lid should be slightly oversize to allow filing.

CARTRIDGE TRAP LID

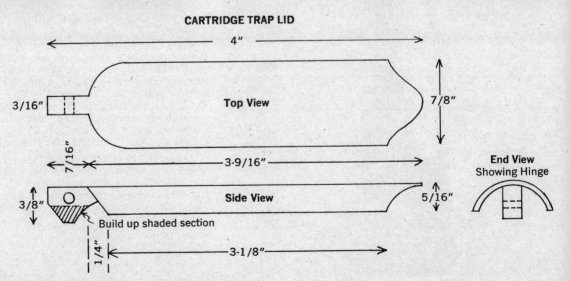

4"

3/16" Top View 7/8"

7/16" 3-9/16"

3/8" Side View 5/16"

End View
Showing Hinge

Build up shaded section

1/4" 3-1/8"

unfeasible and, to the best of my knowledge, they no longer are being imported, although at least one U.S. distributor is making his own.

I obtained some of the German-made styles several years ago. I never had seen one used on a conventional bolt action sporting rifle up to that time, but I used one in a little 7mm Mauser that I built up as a Mannlicher-type sporter several years ago. Later, I incorporated traps in some of my other rifles, including a .458 American.

To put it simply, if you want to install one of these cartridge traps on your personal rifle, I would recommend that you buy one of those American-made types now being marketed.

After those opening words of advice — and before you rush out to buy the materials and ignore these same words — a few more well chosen syllables: The spring-lidded cartridge traps are tough to build, if you are going to insist upon putting together your own. If you are the low-on-patience type, not familiar with exacting precise and tedious work, it may be best that you forget the thing.

Hinge section of lid is built up in thickness, shaped.

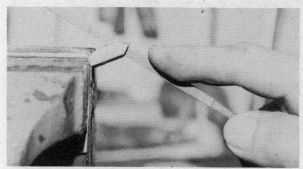

Spring base hinge mortise is rough cut with a hacksaw, is finished carefully with mill, Swiss needle files.

Left: The shaded portion of lid is ground and filed to conform with the dimensions shown in the plans.

SPRING BASE

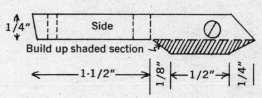

1/2" Top 3/16"

2-3/8"

LAY-OUT OF CARTRIDGE PLATE

3-1/8"

1/4" Side **End View**

Build up shaded section 3/8"

1-1/2" 1/8" 1/2" 1/4"

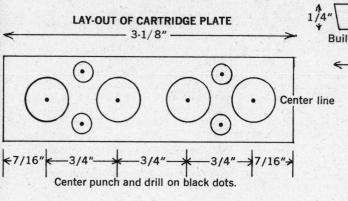

Center line

7/16" 3/4" 3/4" 3/4" 7/16"

Center punch and drill on black dots.

Author's sketch shows placement of holes to be drilled in steel plate. The small holes are counter-sunk to accept small, flathead retaining screws. Larger holes vary in size, according to cartridge used. The plate is one-sixteenth-inch thick and is of cold-rolled steel plate.

But on the assumption that you have ignored that suggestion, too, let's get the most simple part of the chore out of the way first:

The cartridge plate acts as the reinforcement on which the lid of the trap will sit under spring tension. It is through the holes drilled in this plate — and into the wood of the stock — that the cartridges will be inserted for safe-keeping later.

This plate may be made either from cold-rolled steel plate or tool steel measuring 1/16th of an inch in thickness, 3-1/8 inches in length by 7/8ths in width.

Fitted, with the hinge pin in place, the lid and spring base of cartridge trap should look like this.

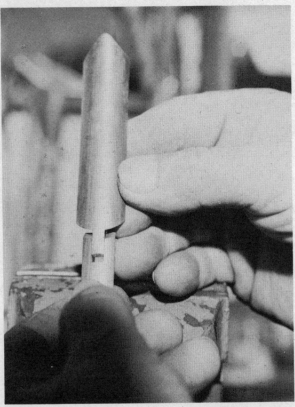

Hinge sections of lid and base must be hand-fitted in exacting slide fit between two; it's hardest part.

After precise fitting, both of the components are drilled to accept hinge pin, using 3/32-inch drill.

After cutting and squaring up the plate, draw a pencil line through the exact center of the plate lengthwise. Measure off the cartridge holes and center-punch them. First drill these four holes with a one-eighth-inch drill, then open up to the exact size of the cartridge case to be used. This size is determined by miking the diameter of the case immediately below the rim.

The four smaller holes are for the retaining screws that will hold the plate to the stock, when it is installed. These holes are drilled first with a one-sixteenth-inch drill, then countersunk to accept small, flatheaded wood screws. Be sure to countersink the screw heads below the surface of the plate to assure an exacting fit of the spring-loaded lid later on.

The manufacture of the cartridge plate shouldn't require over an hour or so. The holes through which the cartridges will be inserted must be of an exacting size to assure that the cartridge cases will slide freely through them with no binding. These holes also will act as a drill guide, when the trap has been installed and the stock is to be drilled to accept the rounds of ammunition. When finished, this plate should be polished, then laid aside.

The next chore is the really big one: construction of the hinged lid and the spring base. Both must be made more or less as one unit to assure a perfect fit of the hinge section of the lid into the hinge mortise in the spring base.

After discarding all other possibilities, I finally settled on a short length of black iron water pipe as the ideal basis for our cartridge trap. Being of iron, it will blue or plate beautifully when the trap is finished. A word of caution concerning your selection of a piece of water pipe. Make sure it is of black iron; not galvanized. Galvanized iron will not accept bluing solutions nor will it plate satisfactorily.

The pipe must measure one inch on the outside diameter and should be six inches in length. This will allow for plenty of room from which to hacksaw out our lid and spring base.

First, let's tackle the lid. Secure the pipe in a bench vise, then measure in from the side a good full three-eighths of an inch. Take your hacksaw and start cutting lengthwise down the pipe for slightly over four inches. This will allow plenty of room for filing and trimming. When cut, set the roughed-out lid aside and cut out the spring base from the remaining piece of water pipe.

We now have the two basic sections, excluding the spring, of the cartridge trap roughed out. From now on the job will require the use of various files, sweat and possibly a few tears! Take the lid in hand and file and shape it exactly as shown in the sketched diagram. This is a job that can require several hours of careful workmanship with a variety of files. The main hinge section on the rear of the lid must be built up slightly either by welding or by silver soldering a small piece of iron or steel in place. It is here that the tension spring will make contact to hold the lid firmly closed or in the open position.

Disc sand, file and shape both lid and spring base sections to the exact proportions shown on the accompanying sketch. The mortise cut-out in the spring base, plus the hinged section of the lid, is a job of precision fitting that will make the difference in just how attractive your finished trap will be. This fitting must be flawless and is best accomplished with a flat Swiss needle file. These two units must be a tight slide fit into each other with no gapitis apparent. Fitting of the lid hinge into the mortise of the spring base accomplished, the two units are taken to the drill press, firmly held together, then drilled to accept the hinge pin. To make this job more simple but just as effective, install a steel pin through the hinge in lieu of the threaded screw found in the orginals. The drilled hinge-pin hole should be 3/32 inch in diameter. From this point on, the two units will be worked and finished as one, being held together with the hinge pin.

The next step is to drill both the retaining screw hole and the hole that will accept the threaded screw which holds the spring to the base.

This is accomplished first by making a center-punch mark in the exact center of the spring base. This mark then is drilled with a three-sixteenth-inch drill and countersunk to accept a filister-head wood screw. This done, make a second center-punch mark on the spring base, this time measuring in from the end one-half inch. This punch mark then is drilled with a No. 29 high speed drill, then tapped out to 8-32. This threaded hole will accept the screw holding the spring in place on the base.

All that is necessary now, prior to the actual installation in the stock, is to manufacture the spring and smooth up the entire trap making sure that the hinged lid works smoothly and that the spring is strong enough to hold the trap closed under normal use.

Manufacture of the lid spring is a simple matter provided you possess a working knowledge of how to properly temper a piece of spring steel.

Most steel spring material first must be annealed before it can be worked properly and bent to the desired shape. This is accomplished by heating the spring stock

Using existing holes in cartridge plate as drill guides, stock is drilled to accept the cartridges. The holes vary in depth, diameter for the caliber.

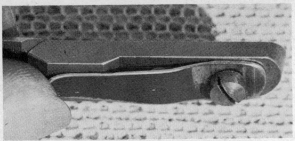

Spring is formed and shaped to exert pressure on raised camming surface of lid hinge. This surface is shaped to hold lid open, closed under tension.

Two holes are drilled through spring base. One is for spring retaining screw, the other to accept the screw holding the trap to the wood of the stock.

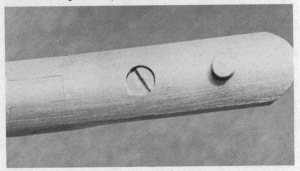

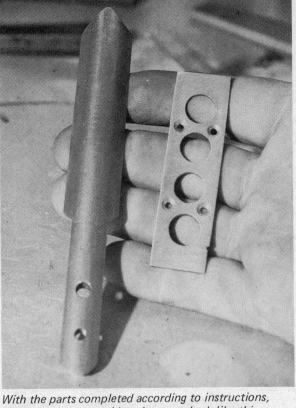

With the parts completed according to instructions, lid, spring base, cartridge plate now look like this.

With two holes drilled through spring base, the spring is tightened in place, drilled to accept the wood screw, using larger hole as a drilling guide.

Contour of the trap is transferred to position on stock, using soft lead pencil to outline for size.

to a cherry red, then allowing it to cool slowly. The slower it cools, the easier it will be to work. Once annealed, the spring material may be bent, shaped and filed to the exact proportions desired.

Material needed for the cartridge trap lid spring will be a piece of spring stock measuring two inches in length by 7/16 in width by 3/32 inch in thickness. Once annealed, the material is bent and shaped to the desired proportions, then is drilled in the exact location with a No. 17 drill to accept the retaining screw. Through this hole goes the 8-32 threaded screw to secure the spring to the base.

A second hole must be drilled through the spring to accept the shank of the filister-head wood screw that will hold the trap to the stock. This is accomplished by attaching the spring in place on the base with the 8-32 screw, tightening it, then drilling the second hole in the spring by using the large, unthreaded hole in the spring base as a drill guide.

Once drilled, this hole in the spring must be opened up in size for proper clearance, assuring that the spring does not bind up on the shank of the screw when under tension. If this all sounds somewhat complicated, remember what I said about shedding a few tears. It is slightly complicated!

We now have all the components ready for final

finishing. The spring is shaped, drilled and ready for re-tempering.

This is accomplished by once again heating the spring to a cherry red, then quickly dousing it in water. The spring now should be glass-hard and the temper must be drawn before it can be used. It will be noted that the spring is now a grayish color.

A torch is played over the entire spring, until it turns a straw color, then a light blue. The instant it turns blue, submerge it completely and quickly in an oil bath, then remove and allow it to completely cool. If properly done, the spring now should be tough, yet flexible enough to properly operate the trap lid. The spring should have enough strength to hold the trap lid shut, requiring little finger exertion on the part of the shooter to open it.

With the spring tempered, the trap is completely assembled and checked for operating smoothness. The lid should open and stay open until actually closed. It should close with a snapping sound, when it is inletted into the stock.

Until now, we have ignored the outer surfaces of the new cartridge trap. These surfaces must be dressed down after the trap is installed in the stock to assure perfect conformation of both trap and stock.

The inletting of the trap into the stock can be the cause of some more of those shed tears. Precision chisel work must be exercised during this job or a good stock can be ruined. Take your time and think in advance. Inletting of the cartridge trap requires that the craftsman plan his mortises far in advance of the actual work. Exact locations to accept the protruding head of the spring retaining screw and the spring itself must be figured out to assure that they seat perfectly into the mortises. The spring itself must be free to operate when the lid is opened with no wood to bind it. Then the retaining screw — the one that holds the trap to the stock — must be aligned perfectly so that the trap sits absolutely square with the stock's conformation.

Much of what I am saying here already has been said in Chapter 27. However, I am repeating it for the sake of continuity. If more details concerning inletting for the cartridge trap are required, refer to the preceding chapter.

You finally have your trap inletted. The lid works perfectly with good spring clearance and the thing looks good. Now we draw file and sand the outer surfaces of the trap and stock until they actually blend into each other in perfect unison. During this phase the exposed surfaces of the lid and the cartridge plate are dressed with a fine file until both the wood of the stock and the metal of the trap are absolutely flush with each other. From this point on, until the stock is ready for its final coating of stock finish, both it and the trap are sanded and finished as one unit.

When the above has been accomplished, the trap is removed from the stock, given a good buffing, then is blued or plated. Then the trap is reinstalled in the finished stock.

It is time to drill the four holes in the stock to accept the extra rounds of ammunition. The cartridge plate has been installed into the stock along with the trap and is held firmly in place with the four flathead wood screws. The large holes in this plate act as guides through which one drills the holes to accept the four cartridges. Each hole must be drilled to a pre-determined depth to properly accommodate the specific cartridge for which it is intended. The rim of the cartridge should extend just above the surface of the plate, not below it! Each of the four holes must be drilled at exactly the same angle to assure perfect partitions of the wood between them.

And to do the job up pink, one might install small coil springs at the bottom of each of these holes, cementing them in place with epoxy. This will allow the cartridges to pop up, ready for use, each time the lid is opened.

Once inletted, surfaces of trap and the cartridge plate are filed to the surface of the walnut. The trap then is finished, sanded as part of the rifle.

Completed trap — gold-plated on the finished stock — is a functional addition, adding value to rifle.

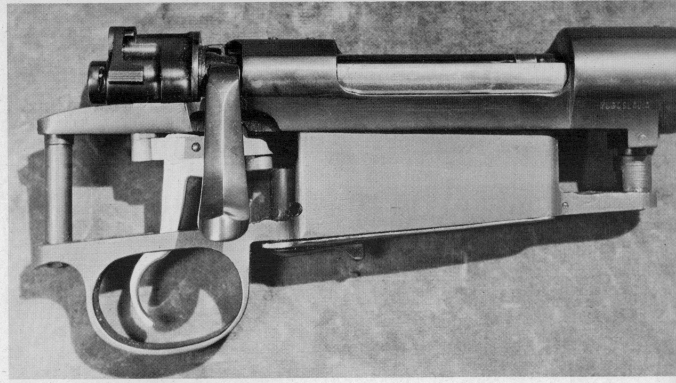

This is the way the Yugoslavian-made Mauser action, a medium length version of the Model 1898, looked at the time it was received by Bish from the importer.

Chapter 29

LET'S BUILD A .458 AMERICAN

Here's A Versatile Caliber That Can Be Built From Many Actions, But Still Has Punch!

In 1962, Frank C. Barnes developed a new cartridge which for some unknown reason is all too little known today. This cartridge was designed to fill a dubious need for a big bore rifle capable of taking the largest game found on the entire American continent without going into calibers which had been designed strictly for use on elephant, rhino and Cape buffalo.

In developing this cartridge, Barnes began by shortening the Winchester-developed .458 magnum to exactly two inches from its original length of 2.500 inches. This produced a cartridge that would feed through either standard or medium length rifle actions and was even used successfully in the short action of the Model 722 Remington. Barnes named this cartridge the .458-2-inch American and it should prove to be a dream come true for buffs of the big bores.

Ballistically — considering the heavy bullets used — this round is capable of some respectable velocities with big 350 or 405-grain bullets. And 52 grains of 4198 pushes a 350 grain soft-point bullet up to velocities of over 2200 fps and giving a muzzle energy of close to 4000 pounds! Using the big 405 grain bullet with 49 grains of 4198 powder, muzzle velocities of over 2000 fps develop a muzzle energy of over 3800 pounds!

With ballistics like this it is quite evident that this cartridge can be potent medicine for the Kodiak bear or bull moose, and the beauty is that this potent rifle, with a little planning, may be built up into a sporter weighing only a fraction over seven pounds due to its large bore.

While the .458-2-inch American dosen't have the trajectory nor range of a caliber like the .375 H&H magnum, neither does it have the weight so necessary in a heavy, expensive magnum receiver. The American can be built on any good surplus military Springfield or Mauser action, and there is no reason why it wouldn't work beautifully in even the little Model 600 Remington action.

The American was primarily designed as a short to medium-long range sporting rifle for use in either close

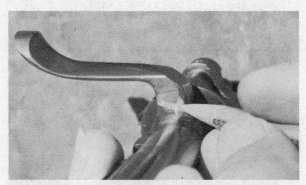

Spoon-handle bolt handle is removed by cutting at the angle marked. Abrasive cut-off wheel was used, although hacksaw will do if the bolt is annealed.

cover or open terrain. And more in its favor is the fact that it can be built inexpensively, has moderate recoil when compared to other similar magnums and the cases can be formed by shortening any of the large belted magnum cases to two inches. The first twenty rounds which I formed were once-fired .264 Winchester magnum brass. After cutting to two inches, the brass then was full-length sized in RCBS dies designed specifically for this round.

To my knowledge, RCBS has been the only company carrying the .458 American dies, however, it is my understanding that Eagle Die Company intends to produce these dies.

I saw my first rifle chambered for the .458 American

After the weld has been smoothed and polished, the insert of ivory can be epoxied into hollow head.

This action comes equipped with a standard Mauser bolt sleeve. It can be replaced with more racy FN version shown. The original sleeve is at top.

about three or four years ago and since that time it has been one of those rifles that I intended to build someday. While I was a little in the dark concerning the full potential of this caliber, I have found that the best way to get the facts is to build such a rifle then take it on a hunt. There generally are too many old wives' tales surrounding a comparatively new caliber such as this and generally these tales are carried by those who have never fired the rifle!

An excellent example of these unwarranted tales was prevalent when the M/600 Remington carbine was introduced in both the .350 Rem. magnum and the 6.5 Rem. magnum calibers. I was told "...the muzzleblast from that cartridge from that short barrel will knock your eardrums out!" Hogwash! I also was told that this little carbine in these magnum calibers "has a kick like a mule." This was an overestimate! For such reasons, I like to prove things to myself when it comes to sporting rifles in some controversial new caliber, hence my desire to build the American.

As the basis for this rifle, I decided to use the currently available VZ 500 Mauser action produced in Yugoslavia. This is the medium-length version of the famed '98 Mauser and is a commercial product, not a war surplus item. It is available in good quantities from Harry McGowen in St. Anne, Illinois, and is available in either barreled or unbarreled. Calibers available through McGowen in barreled actions cover everything from the .22/250 on through all of the short magnum cartridges.

The VZ 500 Yugoslavian Mauser action is well made and as strong as any. However, as with the majority of

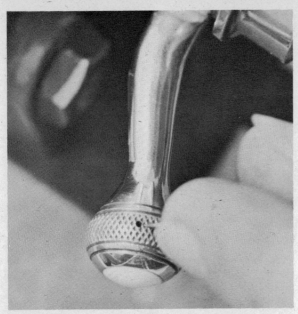

A small hole should be drilled in the back of bolt knob to relieve pressure that might loosen plug.

Author felt original trigger guard was too broad. He tapered, rounded it for more pleasing appearance.

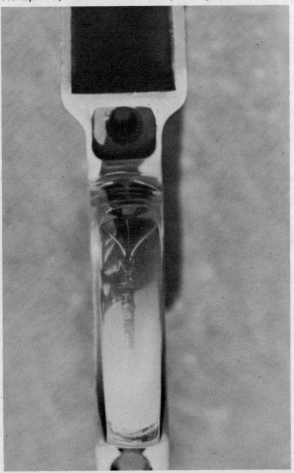

such commercial actions, I found it necessary to completely hone and lap the bolt into the receiver to assure it being glassy smooth. The action received from McGowen was equipped with a Mannlicher-type spoon bolt handle and while I have long favored this type of bolt, maintaining that you don't need a door-knob to open any rifle bolt if it is properly honed, I decided to remove this spoon and install a hollow-head, knob-type bolt handle.

For the novice who never has done any welding, I strongly suggest that any bolt welding be done by a competent gunsmith familiar with the exacting procedure. The new bolt handle usually can be obtained from the gunsmith for installation.

After welding, the new bolt handle is smoothed and polished and the bolt extracting cam surface and the cocking cam surface is rehardened by heating to a cherry red then quenching in oil. This, of course, will be done as a part of the job if the bolt is welded by a gunsmith.

I have made it a practice, when using a hollow-head bolt handle, to plug the hollow in the knob with such exotic material as elephant ivory, beautifully grained rosewood or horn.

This decorative plug adds both a touch of customization to the finished rifle and prevents foreign matter, such as rain, dust, even mud, from getting into the hollow, creating hard-to-get-at rust. The purpose of the hollow head bolt handle is basically to reduce weight in the finished rifle, but there are those who maintain that it is to provide a lighter lift to the bolt handle itself. If a hunter isn't strong enough to lift a normal bolt handle, he should take up knitting to put some muscle in his fingers.

The plug for the hollow head of the bolt handle is formed from any of the materials mentioned into a round and slightly tapered dowel. The taper of the material should be such that the material will touch the bottom of the hollow when firmly pressed in, and, at the same

In tapering the trigger guard, no metal should be removed from area covered by stock. To assure this, one should draw guide line before reshaping begins.

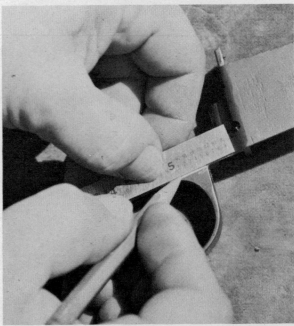

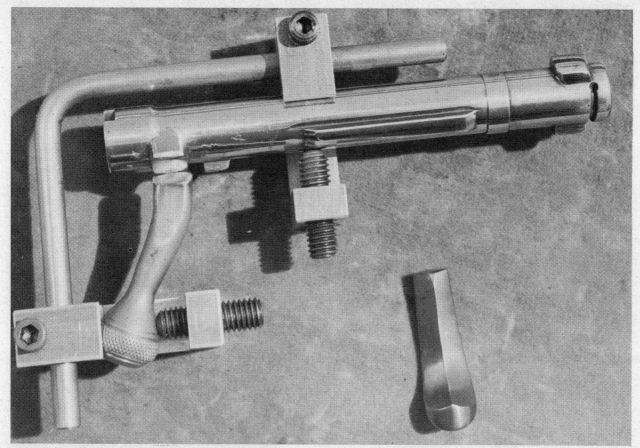

The new bolt handle can be welded to the bolt best by using a bolt welding jig such as one shown with bolt.

The .458-2 American cartridge is compared with case of .264 Winchester, which was used to make initial rounds. Also shown are .300 Weatherby and bullets for the custom rifle in the 350-405-grain range.

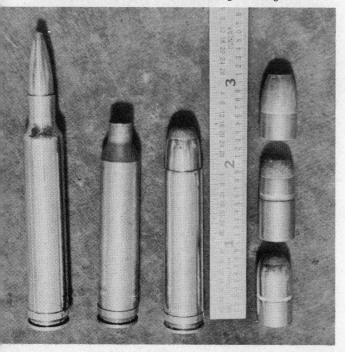

time, making a tight contact with the outer edge. A small portion of epoxy cement is mixed and applied to the inner surfaces of the void that will contact the plug. A small drain hole should be drilled on the back side of the hollowed bolt knob with a No. 58 drill to assure that the sealed hollow does not become an air-tight pressure chamber which might, in extremely hot weather, cause the plug to loosen and drop out. This small hole will not allow foreign matter or water to enter the bolt knob.

While the epoxy cement is drying, make sure that the drain hole is kept open to allow for expansion and contraction of the drying cement. Once the cement is dry the plug may be sanded and buffed to a luster. This plug adds only a fraction of an ounce to the weight of the finished rifle, but don't install it until the bolt is completely finished. If the bolt is to be heat blued, then install the plug afterwards. I doubt that any of the materials would stand up under the heat of a bluing bath.

There are a hundred and one little things of consequence that might be done to a rifle action before the actual building is started. These include honing the working parts of the bolt release until it works with perfection; polishing and lapping the inner parts of the bolt itself, such as the firing pin and even the threaded section of the bolt sleeve that screws into the bolt.

Hand honing and lapping the guide rails on which the bolt slides through the receiver is easily accomplished with silicon carbide flour until the bolt slides effortlessly through the receiver, as it should on any well built, custom rifle. All of these little things take time and most people are reluctant to pay the price asked for such a job by a professional gunsmith, but they can be done by anyone building his own rifle in spare time. It is just such a job as this that we will do in building the American.

Fred Huntington, president of RCBS, informed me that they have carried a good stock of reloading dies, case trimmers and reamers for this caliber almost from its inception back in 1962. My basic purpose in attending this seminar was to learn all I could about the .458-2-inch American cartridge and its popularity with shooters. It was gratifying to learn that RCBS has sold a great number of reloading components for this round which clearly indicates it is not the orphan some people might think it is.

But little has appeared in print concerning this big bore cartridge. Some have referred to it as a hop-

Inletting of the bolt handle into the stock should be done with care to avoid gaps. Removal of too much wood results in unsightly cracks around handle.

Appearance of the reshaped trigger guard is less blunt and military looking, as shown at this angle.

The trigger guard must be inletted precisely and slightly below wood's surface to assure a perfect fit, when stock undergoes final shaping, sanding.

ped-up, belted .45/70. Personally, I prefer to regard it as an African cartridge that has been tamed for use on the American Continent. But let's get on with building this rifle.

The VZ 500 action used in this article was sent up to P. O. Ackley in Utah for installation of a barrel for the .458 American round. The new barrel is exactly twenty-two inches with the outward appearance of a shotgun tube! Quite naturally, the outside diameter of this barrel is of respectable size. It measures something like eleven-sixteenths of an inch across the muzzle (outside diameter) but is still surprisingly light in weight due to the large bore. This large bore size makes it ideal for building into a super lightweight sporter.

The selection of a stock should be a matter of personal choice and taste for each individual building his own rifle. One might prefer an expensive piece of

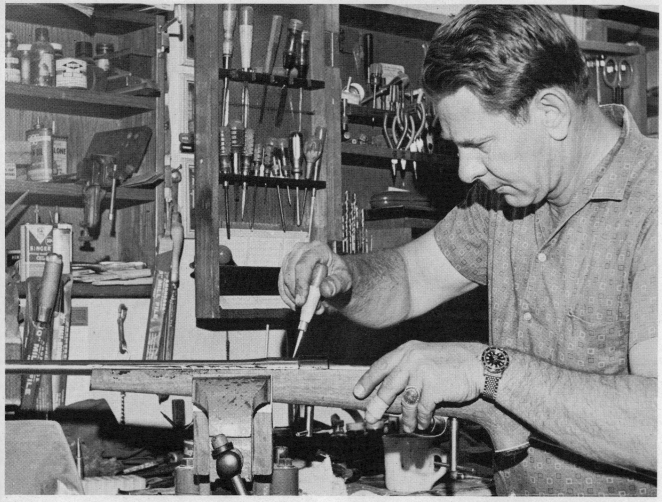

Barreled action in newly glassed stock, held with stockmaker screws, the excess fiberglass compound is scraped away as it seeps from beneath the action.

wood costing as much as a hundred bucks or more. However, there are excellent semi-finished stocks available from such stock-making concerns as Fajens, Incorporated, or Bishop Stocks, both located in Warsaw, Missouri. These are priced from about $13 for the utility grade to $50 or more for a semi-finished

Adding extra custom look is pistol grip of buffalo horn in sunburst design. It is attached to wood of stock before major shaping, dressed with the wood.

stock with superb fancy grain. Should these same stocks be hand-fitted to what is referred to as "shop rifles" by either Fajen or Bishop, there is an additional charge for this service. For hand-fitting to your personal barreled action these prices are about doubled.

The wood used in this article is a modified version of Fajen's *Plainsman* stock from which I removed the Monte Carlo. When received, the barrel channel was un-cut, which necessitated the use of stock rasps and a variety of stocking chisels to bed the new Ackley barrel.

The inletting of the barreled action into a new stock is an exacting chore and should be done with the greatest of care to avoid cracking the stock and yet assure a perfect fit overall.

There are two means by which an action might be inletted into a stock properly. The first is accomplished only after many hours of tedious workmanship with barrel inletting rasps and chisels and is the method utilized by most professional gunstockers in turning out high quality, expensive rifle stocks. It is a method used by those who specialize in this type of work and perfection is acquired only after years of practice. As

Stocking Can Make
The Difference Between Hit
And Misses In This
– Or Any – Custom Rifle!

a result of this exacting professionalism, little or no glass bedding is necessary.

Realizing that most of us are not Al Lindens or Monte Kennedys, the second method is to inlet the barreled action as close as is personally possible into the semi-finished stock, then end up by giving it a precise glass bedding. This second method is particularly desirable when using a semi-finished, over-the-counter rifle stock where the tolerances in inletting are somewhat erratic.

Personally, I prefer to glass bed each rifle I build simply because, in my own mind, this is the best way to do the job. I feel that glass bedding is superior to bare wood being left in the barrel channel of any stock. Regardless of how careful a man might be or how skilled he might be in hand inletting a stock, it would be almost impossible to duplicate the absolutely perfect job of which glass bedding is capable. More

Bolt release lever can be outlined by epoxying thin layers of black fiberglass in this area. When the cement dries, these are dressed to surface of the wood with careful use of files and garnet sandpaper.

During inletting and glass bedding, author feels that stockmaker's screws are an invaluable asset.

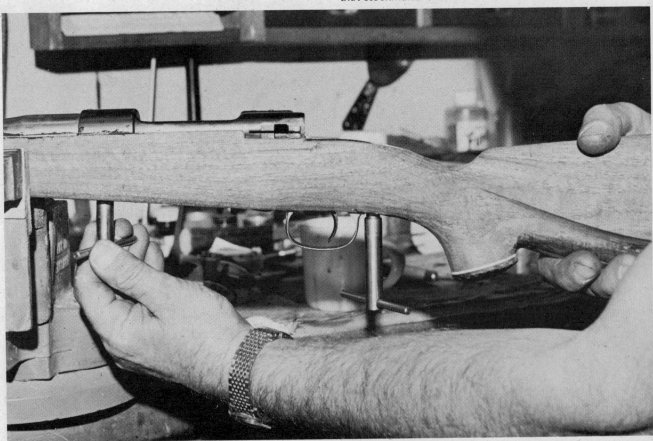

in its favor is the fact that glass or epoxy bedding compounds both strengthen the stock and make it waterproof.

In building the .458 American, it is the wise man who takes the necessary time to reinforce the recoil lug section of the stock with a steel plate well glassed into place. This rifle is capable of being built into a super-lightweight sporter due to its large bore and moderate recoil. However, it is a big bore, so all stress points should be reinforced where possible to safely absorb the pounding from recoil it is certain to receive. This is especially true if the stock is to be slimmed down to reduce weight of the finished rifle.

The type and design of the stock used must be left to each individual's own tastes and needs. Some may prefer a thumbhole varminter type stock while others might prefer an ultra modern stock, such as the *Regent* produced by Reinhart Fajen, or a more conservative stock of the *Classic* design as shown on these pages.

Should one prefer to more or less design his own stock, then Fajen has just introduced what they call the *Stockmaker's Special* which is shown in their latest catalog. This stock is left especially full to allow plenty of wood for custom shaping to the individual's specific tastes. It is priced from $17.95 for the supreme grade to $57 for the ultra fancy-grained AAA grade.

The selection of stock accessories such as recoil pads, butt plates, pistol grip and forend caps are again items that must be left to each individual building his own custom rifle. After all, one rifle copied from another is not exactly individualistic nor does it reflect the creativity of the builder. A custom rifle should reflect the ideas of what each person would like to see most in a rifle for his own use. For these reasons, I will merely suggest items that might be incorporated into a custom rifle.

As a rule, and especially on a high-powered rifle having considerable recoil, I usually install a Pachmayr recoil pad. However, on the .458 American being built for this article I decided to use one of the fine genuine buffalo horn butt plates sold by Brownell's of Montezuma, Iowa. These horn plates add a desirable customizing feature to any rifle and are available with corrugated, basket weave or checkered finish and are priced at $2.50 each.

The pistol grip cap can be of many types of materials in countless designs and finishes. Elephant ivory, rare woods and other semi-precious materials might be installed as a pistol grip cap. Too, finished caps in silver with gold initials may be obtained from Bill Dyer of Oklahoma at reasonable prices and are possibly the ultimate in custom pistol grip caps. Incorporated into the rifle shown on these pages I used still more buffalo horn in the form of a pistol grip cap having a sunburst design on its face. These are also available from Brownell's at $1.50 each.

One of the most distinguishing features that can be added to a custom rifle — and it is seldom done — is a cartridge container in the stock. Perhaps the rea-

son more of these containers are not used is because they are exceptionally hard to find and when one is located, it can be expensive. However, I recently was fortunate in locating two of these cartridge containers in two different designs so am incorporating one into my own version of the .458 American.

The containers are of steel with a hinged, spring-loaded cover. They are inletted about mid-way between the toe of the stock and the pistol grip during the early stages of stock shaping, then filed and sanded down as a part of the stock to assure a perfectly

For sake of comparison, .458 bore (left) is shown beside the muzzle of commercial Norma .308 magnum.

flush fit with the stock contour. Finally, when the stock is finish-sanded and ready for the final finish of oil, the steel cartridge container is removed from the stock and given a blue job along with the barrel and receiver and other metal parts. After the stock has received its final finish of oil, lacquer or varnish, the container is re-installed into the stock. It holds four extra rounds of ammunition and adds no noticeable weight to the finished rifle. It's a custom feature found only on a handful of highly custom-built European rifles, but a desirable feature should you be fortunate enough to locate one for your own use.

In shaping the stock, use your own imagination, but keep it sane and within the limits of good design. Make certain that the stock fits as it should when thrown to the shoulder. Determine that the cheek rest is not too thick, which would result in neck craning for proper sight alignment. The length of the stock in proportion to your stature and arm length is all important for good marksmanship and ease of handling, so spend some extra time on this and make it fit.

Once the stock is semi-finished and the barreled action inletted and glassed to perfection, we will go into those final touches that make the difference between a common every-day stock and one that is custom built.

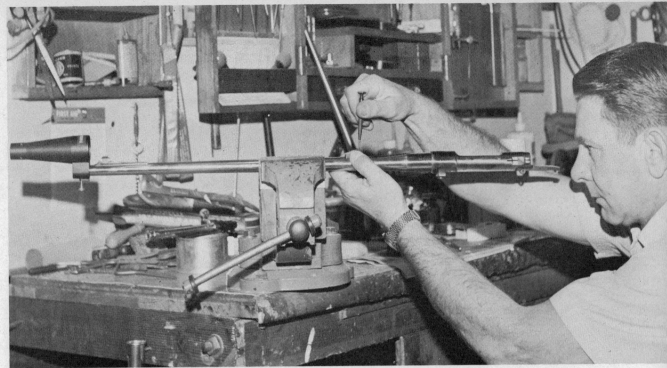

In affixing the sights to the barrel, Bish used the Sweany Site-A-Line for initial line-up of sights.

The final design, shape and finish of a custom stock is certain to reflect the craftmanship and knowledge of good gun design by its builder. Should the stock take on fantastic, unsymmetrical lines foreign to good gun design, or should the builder fail to properly sand and finish the stock, the finished product can be little source of pride.

It is the practice of some stockmakers to leave all squared edges of a stock — such as the outer rim of the cheek rest — with a sharp edge. This is fine if you like it that way. However, I have made it a practice to round over these edges slightly with No. 400 grit paper during the final sanding. In my book there is nothing more miserable or as uncomfortable to carry and handle as a rifle with sharp corners on either the wood or metal. A rifle should be built for comfort and ease of handling.

And those forward slanting forend tips are one of my pet peeves in modern rifle design! Have you ever attempted to buck your way through a thick growth of manzanita or aspen with a rifle equipped with one of these brush hooks? If so, you recall that a good share of your time was spent in guiding that hook-like affair through the thicket to avoid snagging every twig in sight! A forend tip of this type is against all sane rules of good rifle stock design and their only purpose is to cause a serious hunter no end of trouble on a stalk through heavy cover. Too, they add a few ounces of unnecessary weight to the stock.

A nicely rounded forend tip of either rare wood or the plastic type as sold by Fajen on certain models of their semi-finished stocks, is ideal for any hunting rifle. To keep the finished weight of the .458 American to a minimum, I chose to utilize the existing wood of the stock for the forend tip by rounding it over.

The selection of sighting combinations deserves serious thought in building your own .458 American. Open sights for this block-buster are ideal but should you decide to install a scope, then this too must be given added consideration. I feel that both open sights and a

Before being blued, position should be determined, then the barrel drilled for Williams open rear sight.

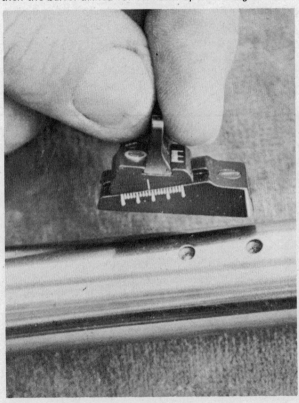

Screwed into place on the barrel, the sight used is adjustable for windage, elevation, although actual use in the field probably will necessitate a scope.

For ornamentation without great cost, one can use engraved animal heads fashioned of sterling silver.

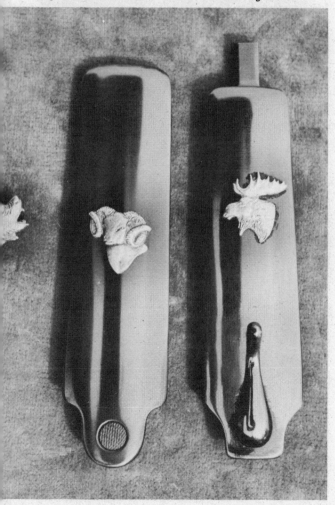

These Finishing Touches Leave This Custom Rifle Ready To Fire And Prove Itself!

good scope would prove advantageous under the varying conditions that might be encountered in stalking and hunting America's largest game with this particular rifle. In heavy cover the open sights would be ideal for close shots. In open terrain where the shots might be from medium to long range, the scope would prove invaluable.

It must be remembered that the .458 barrel is considerably larger in diameter than that of almost any other popular caliber. Where ordinarily a front ramp will measure about seven sixteenths of an inch in height, the .458 barrel will require a lower ramp to compensate for thickness of the barrel.

After much figuring, I chose to install open sights of medium height. With the use of my Sweany Site-A-Line, I found that a five-sixteenth-inch sweat-on-type Williams streamlined ramp topped with a Williams gold bead front sight .312 inch in height, and with a three-thirty-seconds-inch bead, proved a perfect combination with the Williams Guide open sight installed on the rear. The

Front sight clamped to barrel with soldering jig, ramp is heated with torch until the silver solder flows under the ramp. During this, ramp must be square on barrel, in alignment with rear sight.

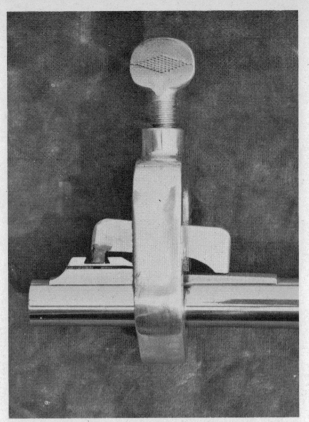

Used in this instance was a Williams sweat-on type front sight. Soldering jig simplifies soldering it.

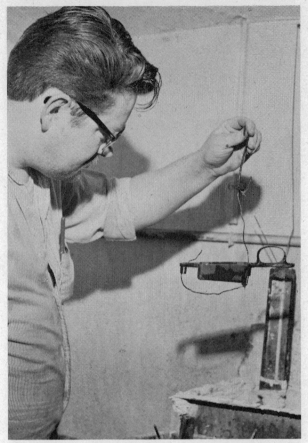

Dave Mateer checks color of the trigger guard by withdrawing it from the bluing tank for a moment.

Guide sight is topped with a one-quarter-inch blade with a U notch aperture.

The installation of the sweat-on type ramp is accomplished best by using the ramp soldering jig produced by Brownell's, Montezuma, Iowa. The ramp is soldered to the barrel before the final polishing. Once the ramp is installed, the barrel and ramp are finish-polished and blued as a unit. To install the new ramp on an already blued barrel could result in conflicting shades of color.

In the scope department. I chose one of the new Redfield 4x-12x variable scopes mounted on JR mounts with medium height split rings. This scope is equipped with parallax-focus from fifty yards to infinity. While the price tag on this scope, complete with rings and mount, comes to almost $150, it is shooting gear for the serious hunter.

While it is not practical for most of us to spend the kind of money it takes to have a rifle completely engraved, there are other decorations that I feel are effective for less dough. Sid Bell of Tully, New York, does some of the finest hand-engraving I have ever seen, and the beauty of his type of engraving is that it can be afforded by most gun builders to add that final touch of customization to their cherished sporting rifles. For some years, Bell has been doing miniature animal heads in sterling silver. These heads are equipped with studs in the back for easy attachment to stocks or floorplates of rifles. These heads are engraved in minute detail, each

The barrel was chambered to author's specifications by P.O. Ackley; is marked with his name, the caliber.

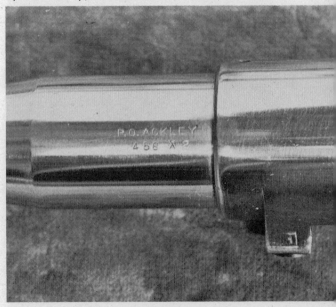

it's time to give bluing of the metal parts and checkering of the stock some thought.

While some have the ability to properly polish all metal parts for bluing, it isn't practical for the sportsman-rifle builder to be equipped with a complete bluing tank set-up necessary for a perfect job. Too, necessary equipment for properly buffing the component parts of a rifle can prove a problem to the man building his first sporting rifle.

Should you feel that you have the ability to correctly polish the metal parts of your rifle, do so, then take them to someone having a bluing tank set-up for dipping. The most important part of a good blue job is in preparing the metal for bluing. Many established

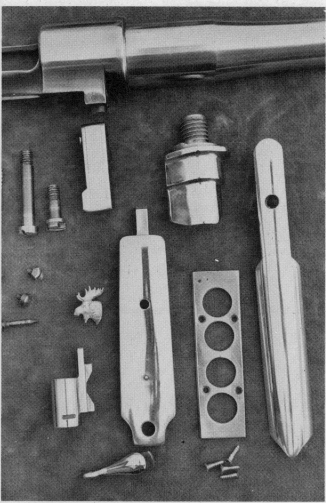

Prior to bluing, all parts were polished thoroughly. Silver moose head, however, was not installed on the floor plate until rest of parts had been blued.

Installed prior to bluing process was the Timney Model 98 Mauser trigger, which has a thumb safety.

hair and fang in place. These heads must be viewed through a magnifying glass to be fully appreciated. Including moose, grizzly bear and big horn sheep these heads are hand finished by Bell and are priced at $10 and up.

Mention was made earlier in this series concerning replacement of the original Mauser bolt sleeve with one of the racy FN types. While the FN bolt sleeve is certain to give the finished rifle a more custom and trimmer look, it has no provisions for a safety, therefore it is necessary when using one of these sleeves to install a custom trigger with a thumb-type safety.

An excellent choice in a custom trigger with a thumb type sliding safety is the Timney Sportsmaster, when used in conjunction with the FN bolt sleeve. These triggers are available with or without the bolt locking feature.

However, installation of this bolt lock requires special milling work on the receiver tang to accept the bolt locking lever of the Timney trigger. The one I used has no bolt lock.

When your .458 American is nearing the final stages,

gunshops have no bluing tank set-up, sending out such work to those fully equipped for bluing.

Chapter 8 concerns do-it-yourself checkering. All that is necessary is a starter set of Dem-Bart checkering tools costing only a few dollars and the ability to draw a straight line, then to follow it with these tools. If you never have done any checkering, don't practice on your new rifle stock! Instead, do your practicing on a smooth

piece of scrap walnut until you feel that you have mastered the handling of the tools.

Should you care to go whole hog, one of the Dem-Bart electric checkering tools would be the answer. It is possible with one of these mechanical marvels to checker a complete rifle in about one-fifth the time it requires by hand, regardless of how complicated the pattern. Once the stock is finished, give it a thorough waxing with a good stock wax such as that produced by Birchwood. Should you decide to checker your stock, give the new checkering a good swabbing with lemon oil for lasting beauty. For a high luster, G-96 offers a poly urethane plastic spray finish.

I chose European-type sling swivels for installation on my .458 American and from these hangs one of the Cobra slings manufactured by Bianchi Holsters of Monrovia, California.

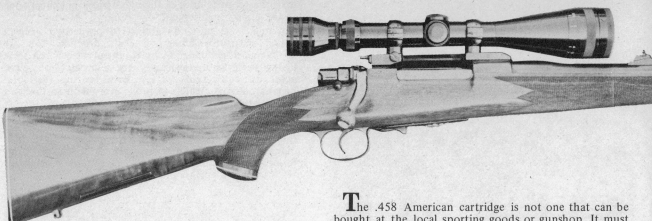

For This Boomer
You Have To
Make Your Own Ammo!

The .458 American cartridge is not one that can be bought at the local sporting goods or gunshop. It must be made and loaded as a custom cartridge.

Building ammunition for this rifle entails the three essentials mentioned earlier: tools, material and a little know-how.

Let's take the tools first, then gradually work into the materials. The know-how will take care of itself as we progress with each step in assembling the potent, powerful .458 American cartridge.

But let's assemble the tools and materials necessary. First, a good reloading press such as produced by RCBS, Pacific, C-H and others is a must. Second is a complete set of dies, a neck reamer and case trimmer are necessary for forming the cases. These are available only from RCBS. Third is a good quality powder scale for weighing each initial charge and finally, and this is very important, a good lube pad for lubricating each case as it is run through the various dies.

The materials needed for building the .458 American round include a quantity of cases — more on this — a supply of IMR 4198 powder, CCI No. 250 magnum rifle primers, a quantity of 350-grain soft-point Hornady bullets and the same in Winchester 405-grain soft point bullets.

Cartridges for the .458 American can be made from any of the large belted magnum cases based on the

Needed for reloading .458 American are (from left): RCBS file-trim die with chamfering tool, neck reamer and die, full length resizing die, as well as the expanding and bullet seating dies mentioned in text.

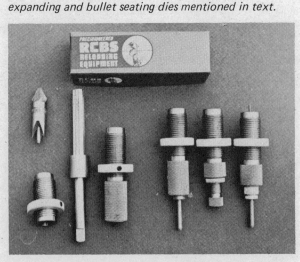

For reloading, Norma cases were used, with IMR 4198 powder, CCI 250 magnum rifle primers, as well as bullets by Winchester and Hornady, good lube pad.

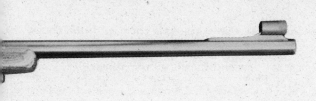

cut-off wheel or a disc sander. The new cut then is chamfered to rid the case mouth and rim of burrs. The shortened case then is well lubricated and run into the RCBS trimming dies where it is cut to exactly two inches with the use of a fine file. Before removing the freshly filed case from the trim die, it is best to once again chamfer the mouth of the case, remove it from the die, then chamfer the outer edge. This will assure smoother operations when the case is finally full-length resized.

The case now is shortened to exactly two inches, the mouth and rim cleanly chamfered. The next step is reaming. This operation may not be necessary, but there are several factors involved that will determine whether a case has to be reamed. Should the walls of the case be too thick at the mouth, the seating of a bullet in the case will distort this area to the point that slight bulges in the case are visible to the eye. Quite often the cartridge will not feed into the chamber of the rifle or will chamber tightly. When this happens, the case most definitely needs reaming. On the other hand, I found I got excellent rounds from most of my brass by not reaming at all. Some however, had to be reamed due to the bulges in the case. I would suggest that, after cutting to proper length, several cases of a specific make be full length re-sized and bullets seated to the proper depth in them. This will immediately show you whether the cases need reaming.

The reaming operation is thus: size cases in the trim die to two inches. Using expander die, expand case neck, but do not run into die far enough to bell mouth. Run the lubricated cases into the neck reamer die and proceed to ream out case neck. During this operation, be sure to remove reamer at least twice during the operation to clear it of cuttings. This reamer loads up fast, so clear it often. When finished, clean each case of all brass cuttings.

At this point, the cases are ready for full length re-sizing, priming, powder charge and seating the bullet. During the re-sizing operation, the case is primed with a NO. 250 CCI magnum primer. The powder charge will be determined by the weight of bullet used.

While the .458 American cartridge performs well with bullets in weights from 250 grains up to and including 405-grain jacketed soft points, I always have felt that shooting light bullets in a large bore rifle was defeating the purpose for which the rifle was originally designed. For this reason I have stuck to 350 and 405-grain bullets in reloading this caliber for my own use.

After much trial and error, I finally settled for the 350-grain Hornady jacketed soft point bullet as about

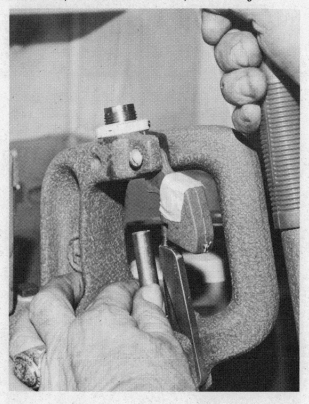

The cases first are shortened to slightly more than two inches, then run into trim die, filed to length.

design of the .300 H&H magnum. In my particular case, I started by using once-fired .264 Winchester, .338 Winchester and even a few .300 Weatherby cases which were cut to exactly two inches in length, then neck-reamed and sized in the special dies mentioned above. Later, I obtained a quantity of new, unformed, unprimed Norma cases which were a snap to form into .458 Americans by merely shortening them to the required two inches. Instead of being stamped with a specific caliber designation, these new Norma cases are stamped Special, which is more ideally suited to the purist ammo builder in forming a cartridge of exclusive caliber.

The cases, whether new Norma cases or once-fired rounds in other large magnum calibers, are cut to slightly over two inches in length with the use of an abrasive

Filing mouth of the case is a process that requires care in order that all cases will be uniform length.

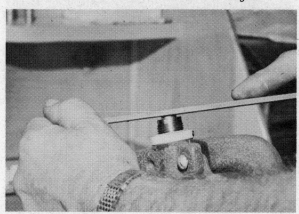

On left is the malformed 405-grain bullet that is mentioned in text. This was eliminated by seating these big bullets out beyond cannelure of the case.

Research of Austin, Texas. This compact, little instrument weighs in at only a couple of pounds, measures 8x5x4 inches and is housed in a rugged steel case with a permanently engraved aluminum front panel.

This chronograph measures the velocity of all small-arms bullets accurately and is powered by three standard flashlight batteries. It is highly portable and when in use the controlling crystal vibrates at 400,000 cycles per second. The reading is taken by rotating the dial, or knob, through twelve positions marked from 1 to 2048 in powers of 2. These numbers are written down each time the Yes-No meter indicates Yes and these figures are totaled up and the final count is referred to the table of velocities furnished with the chronograph.

Extensive tests conducted by Kenneth L. Oehler, PhD and Colonel Charles Askins have proved that, while the "laboratory" chronograph measured time only to the nearest ten microseconds, the Oehler chronograph consistently measures time to the nearest 2.5 microseconds.

In testing this new chronograph I had brought along my pet .308 Norma magnum with a supply of ammunition, the velocities of which had been chronographed in the past on some of the best known instruments. After firing a number of rounds through the screens of the Oehler chronograph, I was completely satisfied that it was as accurate, as other instruments I have used in the past. It is a chronograph within the reach of all serious shooters. whether black powder muzzleloading or magnum enthusiasts.

The first rounds through the .458 American were loaded with 52 grains of IMR 4198, a CCI No. 250 primer and a 350-grain Hornady soft point bullet. These

ideal for loading into the .458 American. While the 405-grain bullet performs well, I found it difficult to seat into the case over the recommended powder charge of 49 grains of IMR 4198. This was due to the longer bullet compressing the powder to such an extent that the nose punch of the bullet seater mushroomed and distorted the soft lead nose of the bullet to the point it had to be pulled and discarded. This malformation occurred only when the bullet was seated to the cannelure. If the cannelure of the bullet was discounted and the bullet seated to a shallower depth, this malformation of the lead bullet ceased.

I now had a fine, new rifle of my own make, a quantity of cartridges with varying powder charges and in two bullet weights and I was ready to wring the whole works out.

I loaded up the car with a new Oehler Digital Chronograph, the rifle and ammunition, a canteen of water and headed into the nearby San Gabriel mountains.

At this point it might be wise to describe the new Model 10 digital chronograph, a product of Oehler

Winchester, Norma, Remington and even Weatherby's brass were utilized in loading the initial rounds. Note similarity of .264 Winchester, Norma's case.

These ten cases now have been cut and trimmed to proper length, outer rims chamfered for reaming.

averaged out at a reading of 874 on the Oehler chronograph and, when referred to the table, meant a muzzle velocity of 2288 fps. The cases used for these loads were Winchester once-fired .264 cases cut to two inches and resized to .458 American.

Changing over to Norma cases loaded as above, the velocities dropped slightly on each shot to an average of 2276 fps for three shots. Similar loads, but dropping the powder charge to 50 grains, lowered the velocity to 2123 fps. So two grains of IMR 4198 in the .458 American case, whether Norma or Winchester, can make a lot of difference in velocity. However, the basic purpose of chronographing this particular rifle was to

Redfield 4-to-12X scope was mounted on new custom rifle for initial range tests on accuracy, velocity.

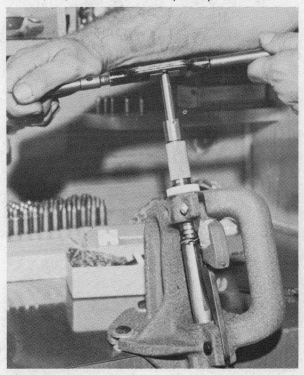

Cases were reamed to the exact thickness with RCBS reamer, die, which were made especially for round.

satisfy my own curiosity as to what the big bullets would do with varying powder charges. Too, I wanted to determint the most accurate and potent loads for safe hunting purposes. I have never been one to go on a high velocity binge as far as any rifle or caliber is concerned and the .458 American cartridge at 2288 feet per second is plenty powerful enough for any animal that walks the American continent.

The final loads to be run through the Oehler chronograph were the 405-grain Winchester soft points. As stated, it was necessary to seat these bullets out beyond the cannelure to avoid malformation of the soft lead noses, but this didn't seem to have any effect on the accuracy or velocity of these big bullets when backed with 49 grains of IMR 4198. A three-shot string of these rounds averaged out at 2155 fps from Norma cases and I feel this velocity could be upped safely by adding an additional grain of powder. The powder behind these 405-grain bullets was compressed to some extent. but no blown or flattened primers were evident when closely examined.

In all, forty-seven shots were put through the .458 American in two bullet weights and varying powder

Bish fires through Oehler chronograph screens from kneeling position.

Evelyn Bish shows that recoil of the .458 American is not as rough as one might imagine.

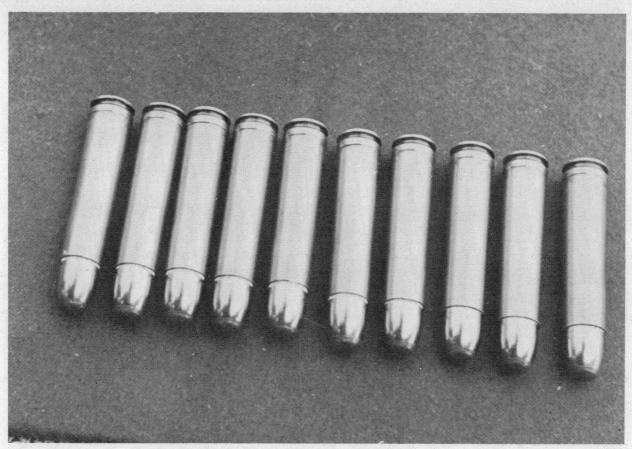

The ten rounds with which the initial experiments in reloading for wildcat were made ready to fire.

charges during this initial testing. The rifle performed like a dream. Extraction and feeding were glassy smooth and accuracy, especially with the 350-grain Norma bullet, left little or nothing to be desired in a hunting rifle of this bore size.

Possibly the accuracy attained from this rifle on its initial testing can be attributed, at least in some part, to the new Redfield 4x-12x variable scope — which was set at four-power for these tests — and the smooth pull of the Timney Sportsmaster trigger.

Dial of the Oehler digital chronograph is made of aluminum with the figures etched into the surface.

It's a mighty good feeling to take a new rifle afield that one has built himself — then have it perform to perfection from the first shot. It's still a better feeling, while shooting this new rifle, to know that even the ammunition being shot is more or less exclusive and that it too was formed and built by the shooter.

In taking the .458 afield for the first time, it was with no litte amount of pride that I removed it from its case, slipped off the protective Storm Queen scope caps from the new Redfield 4x-12x variable scope and prepared the Oehler chronograph for actual testing.

About this time other shooters in the area wandered down the canyon following that first shot from the .458 American.

"What in 'ell you shooting there?" inquired one grizzled oldtimer.

"Just a .458 American," I returned.

"Sounded like a mountain howitzer going off! Gad, look at the size of that bore!" one of my audience remarked.

"Bet it kicks like 'ell," another offered.

I casually handed the "tamed African" to my wife, who matter-of-factly chambered a 350-grain Norma-cased torpedo into the rifle. Raising the rifle to her shoulder, she aimed at a tin can across the canyon. All eyes were watching.

The rifle recoiled against her shoulder and the tin can jumped into the air. Chambering another round, she once more let fly and once more the tin can flew into the air as the 350-grain Hornady bullet literally tore it to pieces. After four shots, she casually handed me the hot-barreled rifle with bolt open and unconcernedly went about her self-appointed chore of placing new screens in the chronograph.

The crowd that had gathered slowly drifted away, shaking their heads!

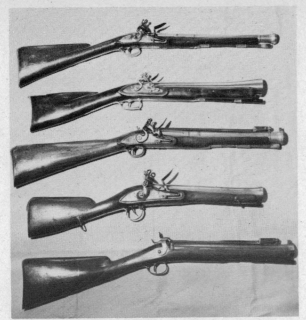

Four of these are genuine. The fifth, second from top, is the one built from kit as described here.

Chapter 30

BUILDING THE BLUNDERBUSS

This Big Bore Blunderbuss Will Fire Almost Anything But The Gunner!

NOW I need a blunderbuss like I need a hole in the head! But when I became aware of the fact that my old friend, Turner Kirkland of the Dixie Gun Works down in Union City, Tennessee, was offering a complete do-it-yourself kit for constructing one of these unique Eighteenth Century flintlock weapons, I became interested.

After all, one can get a little weary of building modern sporting rifles — especially when the gun cabinets are overloaded already. Too, one of these flared-barrel coach guns would make a nice decorator for the den.

An airmail letter to Kirkland brought a prompt reply from his head man, Ernest Tidwell, in the form of a package containing all of the components necessary for constructing a faithful replica of the Blunderbuss coach gun. Included was the flintlock action — complete with two flints, a brass trigger guard and butt plate, a nicely countoured steel barrel which flares out to two inches at the muzzle and is stamped with Belgium proof marks, a stock of some sort of blonde hardwood, all necessary screws, pins, trigger plate and trigger, ramrod thimbles and a steel ramrod. The last I immediately discounted as a part

As received, the kit contains all necessities for construction of shooting replica of the antique blunderbuss. However, some substitutions were made.

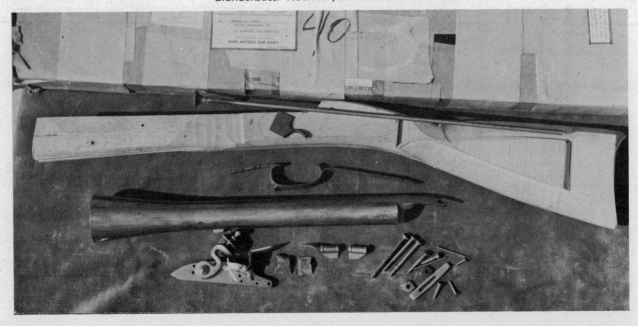

With the barrel inletted, shaping and contouring can begin. Reference should be made to the old, genuine pieces in order that authenticity can be maintained.

of my finished gun. Instead, I would make a tapered hardwood ramrod and tip it with buffalo horn, as the majority of the originals were equipped.

It didn't take long to ascertain that the stock shaping and the mounting of the brass hardware and inletting of the lockplate and barrel would be the major operations in putting this gun together. The lockplate would require some major finishing and polishing as would the trigger guard and butt plate, both of them rough brass castings.

The first step in assembling this unusual weapon is to inlet the barrel into the stock. This stock is semi-countoured but the specimen that I received was inletted for neither the lockplate or tang, nor for the flared muzzle of the barrel. While the stock is channeled out, it must be precisely inletted to accept the breech plug section of the barrel and rasped out to accept the barrel flare at the muzzle. This chore is a simple one and requires an hour at the most to complete so that the barrel seats smoothly and evenly into the stock. It is an absolute necessity to seat the barrel into the stock before the lockplate can be correctly positioned and inletted so the touch hole in the barrel — already pre-drilled — aligns perfectly with the pan of the flintlock.

The brass butt plate is the next to receive attention. This component is a rough casting which should be smoothed up before attempts are made to fit it to the stock. This is accomplished easily with a disc sander and a little judicious fitting with the aid of a fine mill bastard file. The heel of the stock must be cut away to accept the upper tang of the brass butt plate in a precise fit, then the curve of the butt plate is fitted to the pre-cut curve of the wood stock. Once the butt plate has ben fitted and screwed into place, the excess overhanging brass may be trimmed off with either a file of a disc sander.

The next step is to position and inlet the lockplate. This may prove to be one of the biggest headaches for those attempting to build their first arm of this type. It must be remembered that the pre-drilled touch hole in the barrel should be in the precise center, and in the lower portion of the powder pan of the lock when the lockplate is inletted finally and permanently.

The inletting of the lockplate is more easily accomplished if the lock is completely disassembled. The lockplate is positioned on the stock and precisely outlined with a sharp lead pencil. Follow this outlining, small inletting chisels are brought into play

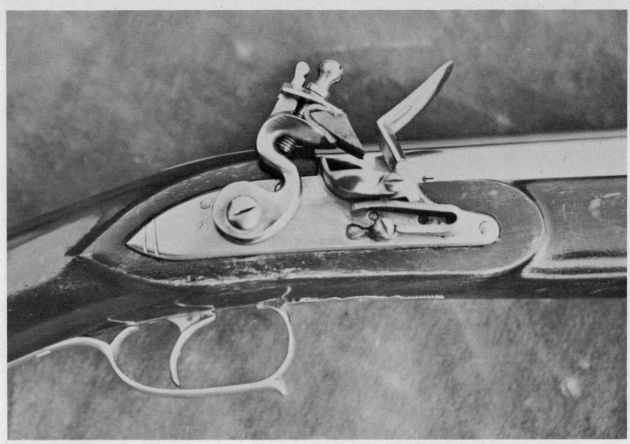

Prior to the final inletting, the lock should be polished to a dull luster, honed for smoothness.

The trigger guard tang is outlined onto the stock, then inletted in a precise fit, pinned in place.

to remove just enough wood over the entire area to allow the lockplate to seat about 3/32 inch into the wood. When this has been accomplished, and the lockplate is a precise fit in its mortise, the entire lock is assembled and the inletting of the wood to accept the sear, bridle, mainspring and other lock components is accomplished.

Remember during this operation that only enough wood is removed to allow the entire lock to seat into its mortise, at the same time allowing all components to work freely when the lock is cocked. The arm of the sear is that part of the lock contacted by the trigger so make certain that this arm is not bound by excess wood. I use a quarter-inch drill to inlet

Installation and placement of the trigger and trigger plate require a minimum of ordinary horse sense and reasoning. The trigger is inletted so that only the rear portion of the fin of the trigger will contact the bar or arm of the sear, at the same time making sure that the cast of the trigger is such that it will allow the brass trigger guard to be installed without undue bending for clearance. With the trigger properly placed and the pin hole drilled so that the supplied pin holds it in place, the trigger plate then is inletted into the stock in perfect relationship to that of the trigger.

The brass trigger guard is a rough casting which should be smoothed up and polished before attempting to inlet it into the stock. Files and an electric hand tool chucked with abrasive drum sanders are excellent for removing the coarse finish from the trigger guard casting; a final buffing on a small muslin wheel dressed with white rouge will give the guard a high polish and smoothness.

The trigger guard tangs should be inletted slightly below the surface of the wood in order to allow a blending of the brass and wood into a perfect union as the stock is given its final shaping and contouring with both files and garnet sandpaper. In other words, file and sand the tangs of the trigger guard along with the surrounding wood of the stock for a better looking finish and more precise fit.

As stated, I had decided not to use the steel ramrod furnished with the blunderbuss kit. Instead I formed and shaped a tapered wooden ramrod from hickory then added a buffalo horn tip. Most of the original ramrods common to this type of firearm are of ebony and horn-tipped, so I used some black harness dye to turn my hickory ramrod into one that looks passably like ebony. It was necessary to enlarge the ramrod thimbles furnished with the kit to accept the larger pseudo ebony ramrod, but this was accomplished by merely bending and reshaping the thimbles until the new ramrod slid through them in a snug fit. The thimbles then were installed in the ramrod channel of the stock.

It goes without saying that in building a firearm such as this, there are numerous little items that must be done before the arm can be called finished. There are such necessities as tuning the flintlock so it will throw a show of sparks over the powder filled pan, the installation of protective escutcheon plates for the lock retaining screws, the correct contouring of the stock to coincide with the period and dozens of other little things that go into the building of a firearm of almost any type. With careful workmanship, it is possible to produce a blunderbuss that might fool even the most knowledgeable gun crank into believing it is the real McCoy!

To eliminate the possibility that the specimen I built ever should be mistaken for a genuine antique,

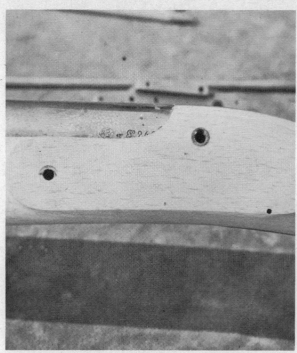

Lock retaining screw holes are drilled as outlined in text to assure alignment with the lock plate.

When finished, the lock retaining screws are seated in the metal inserts that are imbedded in the stock.

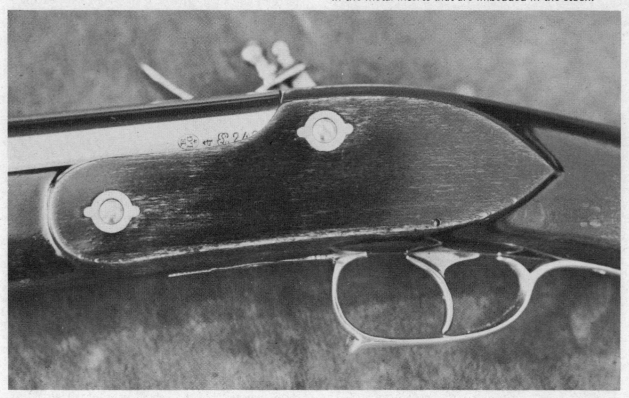

Mixture of granite pebbles and empty .22 brass cases provided makeshift load for initial firing of arm.

Effects of the charge are evident, as the coffee can is knocked high in the air at about ten feet.

I stamped the face of the breech plug with both my name and the date. These markings are clearly visible by looking down the .95 caliber bore.

Nor did I construct this arm strictly as a display piece! I intend to give it a thorough workout by at least patterning it on large pieces of paper at distances of ten yards or so. The originals of these flared barrel arms were intended as coach guns or as boarding arms on sailing vessels. As such, they were short range weapons and it was common to load them with rocks, sand, even dirt, when lead pellets were not available.

Upon completing the blunderbuss and tuning the flintlock action to give off a good shower of sparks, when the flint struck the frizzen, I began to wonder about it's shooting qualities.

Not having any FFFFg black powder handy, it wasn't possible to pre-test the ignition system, but the shower of sparks produced by the flint as it struck the frizzen assured me that the sparks would ignite the black powder in the flash pan. This would, in turn, ignite the charge of coarse black powder loaded down the barrel, this by burning through the touch hole located in the barrel at the bottom of the flash pan.

The next step was to take this compact replica — it measures only 27¾ inches overall — into the San Gabriel Mountains to spot I refer to as Jackass Gulch. It is only a fifteen minute drive into the mountains and the canyon.

Selecting a spot where my back was to the rocky mountainside, I proceeded to ready the blunderbuss for its initial firing. As it was beginning to sprinkle a little, I wanted to test the gun before the heavens opened up with a cloudburst. Shooting a flintlock in fair weather is a cinch, but to attempt to load and fire one in a driving rain can create some problems. It's a matter of literally keeping your powder dry, especially in the flash pan.

I figured that a powder charge of four drams of FFg black powder should be about right for the initial firing.

This charge was topped off with a wadding of paper napkins — for the lack of something better. As I had been unable to locate 00 buckshot in any quantity, I decided to substitute a handful of pebbles selected from the canyon floor. This charge of pebbles was, in turn, topped off with a tight wadding of more paper napkins. After all, history bares the fact that blunderbusses were designed so that almost anything could be fired from them: broken glass, chunks of iron, rocks, nails or whatever else that was handy.

Prior to loading the flinter, I took the necessary safety precuations of placing the hammer on the safety notch and closing the frizzen. The main powder charge was then poured down the barrel after a slight charge of FFFFg super-fine powder first had been poured. This assures that the touch hole in the barrel will be filled with a fine powder, assuring positive ignition. Following the charging with powder and shot, the frizzen is opened, the flash pan is filled to level with the FFFFg fine powder and the frizzen closed. All that is necessary for firing is to draw back the flint hammer, squeeze the trigger and, amid a cloud of white smoke, you will hear the distinct ka-boom so familiar to a large bore black powder gun.

A half-inch wooden dowel was used to pack the load in the barrel. The load was an unlikely concoction consisting of newspaper for wadding, rocks, .22 brass.

The recoil is considerable as evidence in this moment of ignition. Recoil is upward, not to rear.

The coffee can was perforated with the .22 brass cases, although granite rocks only scratched paint.

This stump wasn't riddled by the blunderbuss load, but by others shooters using it as their backstop.

I had selected an empty two-pound coffee can as a first target at about ten yards. Incidentally, the blunderbuss is strictly a short range weapon. My purpose was to see just how badly the can could be sieved by a charge of pebbles. The trigger was pulled, an instantaneous flash and a cloud of white smoke drifted down the canyon, accompanied by a bellowing boom that reminded one of a three-inch mortar going off.

The coffee can sailed into the air and across the canyon, but when retrieved, was found to be intact except for a few minor scratches. As it turned out, I found that the pebbles I was using were of soft granite that pulverized easily against the tough sides of the coffee can.

Concerning our lack of suitable fodder for the blunderbuss, I eyed some fired .22 rimfire cases lying on the ground. Gathering a handful of the empty brass, I again loaded the flared barrel with four drams of FFg and the paper napkins for wadding, then topped this off with the .22 brass and more wadding.

It was decided that the tin can should be weighted to offer more resistance to the fired projectiles. I placed a couple of fist-sized rocks inside the can, primed the pan, cocked the flint hammer and once more let go at the target. This time, with the impact, the can tipped sideways and fell off the stump on which it sat.

The .22 empties not only had penetrated the coffee can in numerous places, but many of the brass cases had gone completely through the metal sideways, piercing both sides of the can. I found that at short range those empty rimfire cases could be more deadly possibly from the blunderbuss than they ever were in loaded, unfired condition!

In all, I fired some thirty or more shots from the flintlock blunderbuss and experienced not one misfire. It's a unique curiosity and anyone owning or planning to build one of these bell-muzzled scatterguns can depend on having a throng of curious onlookers each time it is taken out for firing in public.

Tests included attempts at patterning the various charges of pebbles and .22 brass cases on a paper target, but due to wind and rain, this proved impossible. However, I found that any projectiles fired from this blunderbuss began spreading the minute they left the barrel. At about ten yards the spread is approximately eight feet!

It was asked if the pebbles and brass cases didn't play havoc with the bore of the blunderbuss. Not at all! In fact, the bore actually is better polished now than prior to field testing. No scratches or gouges are apparent anywhere in the bore. The only real damage suffered was to the finish of the stock in the vicinity of the lock where the flash of black powder slightly scorched the surrounding wood.

Incidentally, four drams of black powder is about maximum for this blunderbuss. With this charge, topped with tight wadding and powder, some sort of projectile is needed. Either No. 5 or No. 6 shot would be fine. This .95 caliber flinter does let you know that you are shooting a big bore. It has a respectable kick and is designed to be fired from the hip or chest rather than the shoulder.

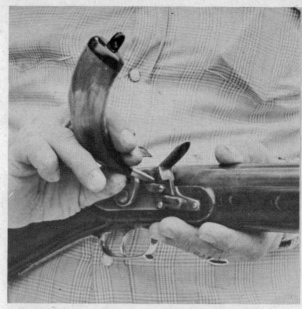

Using small priming horn, the pan is charged with FFFFg black powder just before initial test shot.

Comparing the old and new, the blunderbuss in the background is some 200 years, other two days old.

Chapter 31

LEOTARDS FOR YOUR RIFLE

This Material Can Camouflage And Protect Your Rifle

"WHAT'S THAT? Leotards for a one-legged mistress?" my wife wanted to know, glaring down at the material I was working on her sewing machine.

"When I am done, this device will probably prove a boon to the hunter," I assured her. "It is a camouflage suit for my rifle."

She sniffed at that and went off to the closet to see whether I had raided her wardrobe for the cloth I was using. But I had told her the truth. A camouflage sheath was exactly what I was making.

Why camouflage a sporting rifle in this day and age, when the necessity for bright red clothing is preached to all hunters to possibly prevent oneself from being mistaken for fair game by some neophyte hunter across the canyon? What benefits can be derived by camouflaging a rifle?

Such ideas have been used by guerrilla forces and select military units for years, but could it be practical for the hunter?

After sleeping on the possiblities for several nights, I arrived at the conclusion that a camouflaged sporting rifle would have merit for certain types of hunting. For the past few years, varmint hunters have gone in for camouflage in a big way, even to painting their faces like warring Comanches and wrapping their rifle barrels with black tape to break up the reflection. As varmint hunting is conducted for the most part in isolated desert regions, camouflaging one's rifle is in keeping with the rest of the varmint hunter's technique and the likelihood of being mistaken for a coyote by another hunter is somewhat remote.

A well camouflaged rifle could serve well in hunting pronghorn antelope, desert and rocky mountain sheep and any of the other animals that must be stalked over open terrain for a killing shot. Such camouflage could prove an asset in those types of game hunting where the field is not crowded with hunters stumbling over each other in their efforts to fill their licenses.

Many of the modern re-blue jobs on sporting rifles today are so bright and so shiny, the stocks so highly finished with shiny lacquers or plastic coatings that they can be spotted for miles by the sparkle of reflected sunlight. Any wild animal is aware that a sudden reflection from a bright surface in his domain can mean only one thing! The presence of his worst enemy — Man!

For simplicity and efficiency, it seemed the best

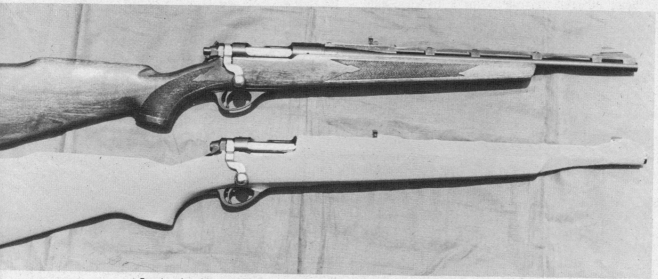

Production Model 600 Remington carbine at top is compared to camouflaged version for appearance. The cloth covering can be advantageous in game fields.

type of camouflage should be a snug-fitting sleeve made from a material with a good deal of elasticity. Thus, when sewn into a pre-shaped sheath, it would contour to the rifle with no slop or bulk left over.

The type of material for such a project constituted a problem until a shapely young thing strolled past my window, wearing a pair of those skin-tight leotards. Here was a material that had plenty of stretch. This much was obvious by the way the garment clung to this form that was fast retreating from my view. This fact was further impressed upon me later that afternoon when I was at the local super market and spotted a woman who would weigh a healthy two-hundred pounds or so. She also was wearing stretch pants, as I believe one variety is called. Again it was obvious that the material can be stretched to any contour, although in this instance I must admit it was a bit of a shame. No matter what, or how much, you put into it, the material retained the quality of elasticity that would cover. would mold to each and every curve and bump of a girl — and I hoped, a rifle — in a snug fit.

First off, I asked my wife whether she had any worn out leotards. This resulted in a raised eyebrow.

There followed many calls to yardage houses in

search of "the type of material used in leotards," and always the standard reply: "Sorry, we don't have any."

Ray Rich finally located a sufficient amount of this material to do the job through a maternity clothing manufacturer. Just why a maker of maternity clothing should find this stretch material beneficial I'll leave to your imagination, but I was happy to get a yard or so of this cloth which seems to be a type of jersey woven from one of the synthetics such as nylon.

I had decided to use the Model 600 Remington carbine in 6mm caliber as a sort of guinea pig in my camouflage efforts. This little firearm is short and compact, and since I'm no professional with a sewing machine, I figured I could save some stitches.

The actual making of such a sleeve to fit any rifle shouldn't take much over half an hour. Simply have your wife sew up a sleeve that will slide over the entire rifle, from muzzle to butt, in a snug fit. It might be well to keep in mind that this light weight material can be stretched to twice its normal size, so have the little lady make the sleeve so that it will provide a snug stretch fit, Also, in sewing

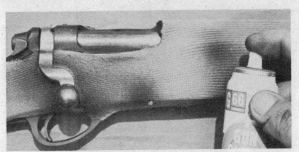

Once in place, the slip cover can be camouflaged with aerosol can of sight blackener, colored paint.

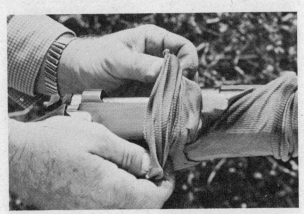

Fashioned of jersey, the slip cover can be easily installed or removed from the rifle's contours.

this material, it is best to sew it while stretching the cloth in the area being sewn. Thus, when done, the material will return to its original size and the sewn seam will not rip out. Be certain, too, that a fine needle is used in the sewing machine, as a heavier one will tend to cut the threads in the cloth.

With the sleeve snuggly encasing the rifle, you can use a sharp pair of scissors or a razor blade to make a small slit for the front and rear sights to come through. In the case of a rifle scope, slit the material just enough for the lenses to be exposed. If you plan to use this camouflage suit more than once, it might be well to lap over a fold of the material in these areas and sew a hem to protect the loose strands against raveling. If you sew a good button hole stitch, this will probably do well, and at the same time, you can show your wife that you know as much about sewing as she does. The danger, of course, is that you may soon be doing your own mending!

Next, make appropriate cuts in the material in the vicinity of the receiver section to allow free functioning of the action, whether it be a bolt action or semi-automatic model. With a little experimentation here and there, and with the realization that the

slits must be made quite small to compensate for the tension in the material, you should soon have a well fitting and sexy set of "tights" for your favorite hunting rifle. And you can carry it in a watch pocket — this material folds up that compactly.

In addition to this camouflage sleeve preventing reflected light from your rifle, it will protect it from brush scratches and will be especially appreciated, as far as your hands are concerned, should the weather be extremely cold.

Should the bolt on your rifle be highly polished as so many are, you can apply a light coating of **Gun Sight Black**, which comes in an aerosol can produced by the Jet-Air Corporation of Paterson, New Jersey. A light spraying from this can will eliminate all bright surfaces of the rifle's action that might be exposed through the slits you have cut in the material. The real advantage of **Gun Sight Black** is that it may be easily removed with lighter fluid or cleaning solvent when you are ready to put the rifle back in your gun rack until next hunting season. In addition to blackening the bright metal surfaces, the camouflage sleeve, itself, may be spotted here and there with the spray to add to the camouflage effect, breaking up the outline.

In various parts of the country, the color of these camouflage sleeves might vary to fit with the terrain being hunted, if you're no particular believer in science, but more of that in a moment.

In snow country, a white sleeve should be most effective, while in mountainous country with a good deal of greenery, the color of the sleeve should be green. Olive drab is particularly suited to the desert regions of the Southwest, where it fits in well with the various hues of sagebrush and cacti. I feel that a set of rifle tights such as this should not be used in heavily hunted areas where hunters are thicker than the animals being hunted, if it matches the terrain.

But that's where we get to that interest in science mentioned a few lines back. It might also be a practical use for that pair of red worn out stretch pants your wife has been hoarding.

Scientists allege that animals are color blind. If you believe it, this bright red material, mottled by applying a few drops of bleach here and there to break up the pattern, might be put to practical use.

Then, you have to hope that other hunters in the area aren't color blind, too!

Chapter 32

Building The U9

THE building of a custom sporting rifle can take many forms. Some craftsmen may use nothing but Mauser actions in their custom jobs, while others will run the gamut from Springfields through the Enfields and Japanese actions that are readily available. Others constantly are on the lookout for something a little more exotic or more precisely engineered before attempting to spend hours at the work bench in turning out a truly custom-built sporting rifle.

This is not to say that Mausers, Springfields and similar actions are not worthy of utilizing on a sporting rifle. In fact some of the finest rifles in my personal battery were turned out from war weary Springfield and Mauser actions. However, within the lifetime of most professional builders of custom sporting rifles, there is always that urge someday to build a special

First step in building this rifle is inletting of trigger guard, floor plate. Both must be let into wood below surface to allow for shaping and sanding.

It's a long haul from start to finish of this job, but author admires Mannlicher-stocked U9 big game rifle built on English Birmingham Small Arms action.

rifle that will surpass all turned out previously. Perhaps this urge is motivated when a new or revolutionary type action is introduced. In my case this came about, when I closely examined one of the rifle actions being offered by Herter's of Waseca, Minnesota.

This rifle action, a product of the famed Birmingham Small Arms of England, is the precisely engineered BSA bolt action used the world over by hunters of everything from varmint to elephant. This importer calls it, though, the Herter's Mark U9 Custom model.

The U9 barreled action is an exquisite affair available in calibers ranging from .222 up to and including the monstrous .458. It is beautifully blued and priced at a modest $64.50. It also is available with either a grooved receiver or the new round type. Scope mounts for either are readily available.

One of the many refinements of this action is in the bolt itself and consists of a red cocking indicator which protrudes from the bolt sleeve when rifle is cocked. When bolt is in the fired, or uncocked, position, the red indicator is flush with the outer surface of the bolt sleeve.

All in all, the U9 is an action worthy of anyone's consideration for incorporating into a custom built rifle. All that is necessary is to build a stock worthy of carrying such an elaborate piece of iron.

When I decided that I would build one of these rifles, a letter to Myron Barrie of Herter's brought a prompt reply including an itemized list of accessories for building the stock, since everything needed could be purchased from Herter's. As a result, I ordered the following:

U9 Barreled action in .300 Winchester	$64.50
Custom American walnut stock (Mannlicher)	19.95
Herter's glass bedding kit	2.60
Herter's recoil pad w/spacer	1.50
Herter's stock finishing kit	1.25
Herter's pistol grip plate w/spacer	1.37
Herter's sling swivel set	2.75
Herter's barrel band (inside type)	1.20
Total	$95.12

On top of this was added a few dollars for postage and insurance, the total of which still came to less than a hundred dollars.

As the barreled action required only minor touching up in the area of the safety — the safety button rubbed slightly on the bolt — the main job would be fitting the stock to the action, glass bedding it, then finishing.

Deciding to build this U9 rifle as a Mannlicher, I decided to reduce the length of the barrel from its original 23-1/2 to exactly twenty-two inches by lathe cutting one and-a-half inches from the muzzle. This reduction in length in no way impairs the ballistics of the .300 Winchester magnum and adds no notable muzzle blast.

The Mannlicher-type stock received from Herter's was of American walnut and incorporated a roll-over cheek-piece. As I never have had any fondness for this type of cheek rest, maintaining that they are just a waste of good walnut, I planned to eliminate it completely with a good sharp wood plane. But let's not get ahead of the various steps.

When the U9 components are received, the stock, quite naturally, will receive one's initial attention. The

The amount of labor that lies ahead is evidenced in various parts of the U9 kit as they come from box.

With use of Prussian blue, components of trigger guard assembly, floor plate are pressed into mortise. All contact points then are relieved by chisel cuts.

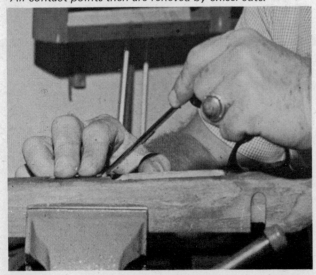

first step is to bed the trigger guard and floor plate. This is accomplished with an assortment of small inletting chisels and Prussian blue. The chisels are used to relieve the wood from areas where the trigger guard and floor plate bind up when firmly pressed into place in the mortised cut-outs of the stock. These areas are determined easily by giving the guard and floor plate a slight coating of Prussian blue at the contact points. The Prussian blue will leave its mark on the wood to be relieved. Remember to remove only slight scrapings at any one time with the chisels to prevent **gapitis** between the edges of the metal and the wood.

Correct inletting of the trigger guard, floor plate and tang is most important. If the job is done correctly, there will be no unsightly cracks visible around the outer edges. Trigger guard and floor plate should be snug, slide fits into the mortises and, in the initial fitting, should be set slightly below the surface of the unfinished wood of the stock. This allows ample wood for sanding and shaping later.

The U9 trigger guard and floor plate assemblies are separate units, unlike those of either the Mauser or Springfield, which are single units. As a result, it is necessary to inlet the trigger guard of the U9, then proceed to inlet the floor plate and tang, making certain that the rear edge of the floorplate engages the locking lever of the trigger guard in an exacting fit. This assures, that when both components finally are

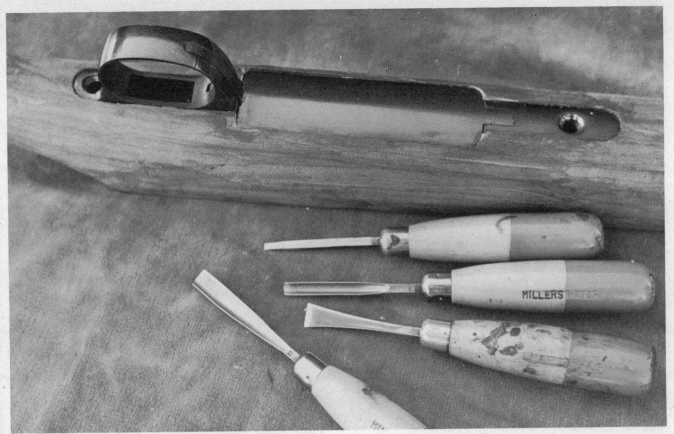

Correctly inletted trigger guard and floor plate are set below stock surface for exact fit. Excess wood is left for work in final finishing of stock.

Stockmaker screws for the BSA-made action aren't available commercially, but can be made from cold-rolled steel rod to seat barrel in stock channel.

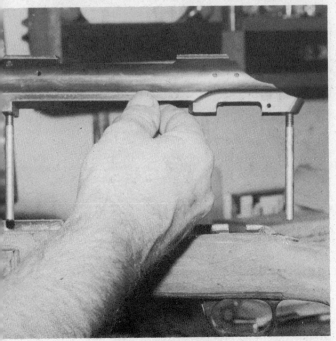

set into the stock, the floor plate will lock up smoothly with no binding.

Once the trigger guard and floor plate are inletted, should you find that the two screw holes in the stock are not exactly in line with those of these two components re-drill the holes in the stock, thus aligning them, with a 17/64-inch drill. These holes are re-drilled by using the existing holes in the trigger guard and floor plate as guides.

Now we turn our attention to the vital job of inletting the barreled action. Needless to say, this job is perhaps the most important in building an accurate, strongly constructed sporting rifle. This phase of rifle construction can mean the difference between a rifle that is accurate and rugged or one that never places a bullet in the same place twice and is apt to literally fall apart with each shot! This is especially true if one is building a magnum with heavy recoil.

Herter's stocks are furnished with the major part of the inletting done in the receiver area of the stock. However, final and precise fitting must be done by the builder himself. The barrel channel, especially on the Mannlicher-type stock, must be cut and finished almost in its entirety.

One of the most often used basic tools for inletting a barreled action is a set of stockmakers' screws. However, these screws are available for only a few standard rifles such as the Mauser, Springfield, Krag, Remington and Winchester. I know of no source for these screws for the U9 or BSA rifle but should one have a small lathe handy, I would suggest that a pair of these screws be made.

We'll assume that you have made a set of stockmakers' screws from common cold-rolled steel to fit your BSA action. These will be used to assure perfect align-

The barreled action is inletted into the stock, as Prussian blue is used to mark obstructive areas. Only finger pressure should be used in seating the stock. Never press with a vice or stock will crack.

With action inletted, it was found the safety thumb piece rubbed slightly on the bolt. This edge was rounded slightly in order to correct the problem.

Knurled area on thumb button was not deep enough, so it was recut to afford better contact with thumb.

ment with the holes in the stock that will accept the front and rear trigger guard screws, both of which hold the barreled action to the stock.

With the stockmakers' screws in place in the receiver the barreled action is lowered carefully onto the stock until each of the screws slides into the holes in the stock. Allow the action to seat as far as possible onto the un-inletted barrel channel section of the stock. At this point the barrel should be in perfect alignment with the dead-center of the stock from the rear tang on out to the muzzle. Carefully trace an outline of the barrel's contour onto the stock holding the pencil in a perpendicular position. Remove the barreled action.

If correctly done, the contour of the barrel now is transferred to the wood of the stock's forearm. It is here that the wood must be removed with rasps and routers until the barrel will slide into place in a slightly loose fit. At the same time the barrel is being fit to the stock, the receiver section of the action will need attention, too.

As the barrel is recessed into the forearm, it will be noticed that certain areas of the receiver will tend to bind up in the mortises of the stock. Once again Prussian blue is used to mark the binding areas, just as it was used on the trigger guard and floor plate. The high, or binding areas are relieved with a sharp chisel, allowing the receiver section to settle slowly to full depth in the stock.

The bedding of the barreled action into the stock is not a chore requiring only a few minutes. If a perfect job is expected, several hours will be expended before this precise operation is even begun. Once started with chisels and rasps, several more hours of exacting work can be expected. The inletting of the action into the stock is the heart of a strong and accurate rifle. Do the job poorly and you end up with a good club!

Glass bedding a barrel and action is one of the surest ways of completing a rifle that can be both accurate and rugged. However, like any phase of building a custom sporter, this job must be done perfectly. The U-9 by BSA of England has a fine rifle action, but its shooting qualities will be only as good at its woodwork. If the stock is wrong, the entire rifle is wrong!

Let's assume that you have bedded the trigger guard, floor plate and barreled action into the semi-finished stock correctly. At this point nothing is really bedded, its merely fitted into the wood.

The secret of correctly glass bedding the barrel lies in the theory that no wood of the stock's forearm should be touching the barrel at any spot ahead of the forward receiver ring. Using barrel inletting rasps and chisels the barrel literally is free-floated, allowing at least one-sixteenth of an inch free space between barrel and forearm.

To make certain that there are no high spots in the barrel channel of the stock, I wrap a piece of cardboard about one-sixteenth-inch in thickness around the barrel and slide it down the full length of the barrel.

As mentioned in other sections of this book, a strong steel insert, glassed in place, should be mandatory in custom building all magnum rifles.

Enough clearance is allowed between barrel and stock channel to permit a section of a business card to slide freely the length of the barrel.

If it should hang up this identifies a high spot in the channel and must be hit with a rasp once more. When the cardboard slides down the barrel unobstructed, the channel is ready for glass bedding. However, we still have a minor but important, chore to perform on the stock before mixing our Herter's glassing compound.

It long has been habit with me to install a small steel plate in the area of the recoil lug of the stock. This operation takes only a few minutes to accomplish but assures that the stock is amply reinforced in the area where it takes the most recoil. This is especially needed for the larger magnum calibers.

The steel plate mentioned is a safeguard against the stock splitting as it prevents the barrel from sliding rearward with recoil, which often results in a chunk of stock being knocked out by the rear tang of the receiver. The steel plate should measure about one-eighth-inch in thickness, half an inch in width and a fraction over an inch in length. This plate is inletted by removing sufficient wood from the forward section of the recoil lug, inserting the plate, then glassing the whole works, including the barrel, in one operation. The plate

should be mortised into the recoil lug area deep enough to allow at least one-sixteenth-inch of glass bedding compound to completely cover it thoroughly.

The barrel channel, at this point, is free-floated with at least one-sixteenth-inch clearance, the recoil plate is installed and we are ready for the actual bedding.

The barreled action and the front trigger guard screw are coated liberally with the releasing agent supplied with all Herter's stock bedding kits. This agent will assure that the barrel and receiver may be removed easily from the stock once glass has set. Failure to use the releasing agent could mean that the barrel and stock would bond so securely that the only way to get them apart would be to chisel the stock off the metal! Use releasing agent liberally!

An instruction manual is furnished with each Herter's glass kit. Follow it to the letter during the mixing procedure and during application. Only practice will teach one to mix just the right amount for the job, so during this initial trial, mix a little more than you feel you actually will need. It is better to have more than enough and this will prevent the necessity of possibly having to patch up the job later.

With the glass compound mixed, it then is applied to the channel of the stock, starting in the recoil lug area and working it forward. It is best to apply the compound equally along the bottom of the barrel channel of the stock. Thus, when the barreled action is squeezed into place and the guard screws tightened, the compound will have a chance to bleed off any trapped air below the barrel and distribute itself uniformly over the entire channel surface.

As a rule, this will eliminate completely air bubble holes often found in the bedding when a barrel is removed. When sufficient glass compound has been applied to the channel, the barreled action is placed onto the stock and pressed firmly into place with the hands, then the front and rear trigger guard screws are tightened to their fullest.

Once the barrel is tightened into place, excess glassing compound will ooze from beneath the barrel due to the pressure. Allow this substance to continue for a few minutes, then wipe off the excess with a scraper made of wood. Do not use metal for this clean-up job as the blue of the barrel may be scratched. The glass compound will continue to ooze from beneath the barrel until the glass begins to set and harden. Keep the excess glass wiped free of the barrel which will result in easier separation of the barrel from the stock when the glass has hardened. Do not attempt to do more work on the rifle until the glass has set completely. Instead, put it aside for at least twenty-four hours to completely cure.

After twenty-four hours of curing, the barrel is ready to be removed from its precise bedding of glass. The trigger guard screws are removed, the stock grasped firmly in one hand while the other hand strikes the barrel smartly. This blow should loosen the barrel and receiver section from the glass after which it is removed from the stock. All glassing compound is removed from the stock with mild rasps and files.

Should any glass be stuck on the metal parts, it usually can be removed easily with the finger nail, or in stubborn cases, with a piece of brass or aluminum used as a scraper. Do not use iron or steel as a scraper on the blued barrel or receiver.

Once the barreled action is placed in newly glassed stock, then tightened, all of the excess fiberglass should be wiped away from metal surface with care.

It often is best to glass bed the receiver section just as the barrel was bedded. However, this should be done after the barrel has been bedded. To begin this, clean up the hardened glass from the barrel bedding. After this has been accomplished, the entire receiver section is given a thorough coating of releasing agent, then the glass is mixed and applied to the receiver area of the stock. The barreled action once more is tightened into place with the guard screws and allowed to cure for another twenty-four hours.

In bedding the receiver section, be certain that the rear tang mortise of the stock also is glass-bedded. This adds considerably to the strength of the stock in this area and results in a more exacting fit of tang-to-stock. Be sure to apply releasing agent to both trigger guard screws during this operation.

Herter's recoil pad with its lightning-streaked spacer is attractive and, when properly installed, adds to both the eye appeal and value of the finished rifle. As received, the Herter semi-finished stock measures exactly 13-1/2 inches from the toe to the trigger. This is about standard for a stock for a man six feet in height. A man having short arms will have to shorten the stock accord-

ingly. However, we will proceed to install the recoil pad in what is generally considered to be the standard length of 13-1/2 inches.

The recoil pad is one-inch thick, which means that this amount of length must be removed from the stock before installation of the pad. The stock is marked

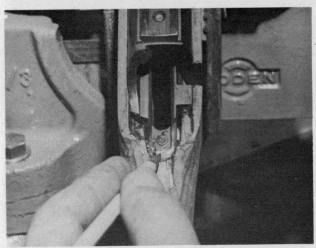

The rear tang of the majority of big game rifles should be glassed along with the barrel and action.

around its circumference with a soft lead pencil, measuring up exactly one-inch. A mitre saw is used to cut this inch-thick section from the stock. The recoil pad then is placed on the butt of the stock and the spacing of the screw holes in the pad transferred to the stock by means of a sharp awl pushed through the pad. These two holes are drilled to a depth of about one-inch using

This easily built stock marking block is used to mark off stock section to be removed for recoil pad.

a one-eighth-inch drill A coating of good cement is applied to both contacting surfaces of the stock and recoil pad. The two retaining screws are pushed through the rubber pad and firmly drawn up tight with a screwdriver into the wood of the stock.

The correct grinding of a recoil pad to exact stock contour can be no little headache to the novice. However, if this job is done on a disc sander, and the build-

The recoil pad should be installed prior to final shaping, sanding to assure correct pad-stock contour.

Shaping of Mannlicher forearm should receive extra attention to assure it is straight, sans dips, bellies.

er takes his time, it shouldn't prove to difficult. Just remember to carry out the original lines of the stock into the recoil pad. Don't round over the toe or cup-out the heel of the pad.

In the pistol grip department, there are any number of unusual caps that might be utilized. Some might want to make theirs of staghorn or ivory, while others may prefer to use rare woods or any one of the custom caps available. Herter's supplies a large black tear-drop cap with a diamond-shaped insert that covers the retaining screw head. However, I decided to use one of the new blued steel engraved caps by Bill Dyer of Oklahoma City, Oklahoma. These caps sell for $5 each, but with a fourteen-carat gold initial, another five bucks is added.

Engraved blued steel pistol grip caps are available from Bill Dyer of Oklahoma. Gold initials are extra.

The installation of a pistol grip cap amounts to finding the exact center of the pistol grip, marking it, then installing the cap with the screw or screws provided.

The procedure for shaping and finishing a sporting stock, whether a Mannlicher-type full-stock or a sport-

ing half-stock, is basically the same. The major wood removal is done with a variety of files and rasps followed by sanding, first with a medium coarse garnet paper, then a fine garnet paper. Finally the stock is well rubbed with a 400 grit paper until it takes on a glassy smoothness.

Should the stock be finish-sanded in a haphazard manner, and the stock itself ill-shaped, a sloppy rifle will result. Should one be building a Mannlicher-style stock, the forearm should be slimmed down considerably more than that found on a half stock sporter, then a metal snobble installed on the tip of the forearm. While Herter's have available a couple of different models of these snobbles, I have always preferred to make my own from sheet black iron. The process for building these customized snobbles has been covered.

Custom snobble, discussed in chapter 21, can be constructed, installed on the unfinished stock.

During the final finish sanding great care must be taken in removing the excess wood from the area of the trigger guard and floor plate. The wood should be sanded **exactly flush** with the surfaces of the metal. However, this is a tricky job to assure that the blue of the floor plate or trigger guard is not scratched by the sandpaper.

221

Care And Consideration In Final Finishing Makes The Difference in Customizing!

I N turning one of the excellent Herter's U-9 barreled actions into a custom stocked sporting rifle, it has been brought out in the first two segments that everything necessary for the job, be it for a half-stocked sporter or a full-stocked Mannlicher type, can be obtained from Herter's Incorporated of Waseca, Minnesota.

Thus far the trigger guard and floor plate have been inletted, the barrel has been free-floated prior to glass bedding and the recoil pad and pistol grip cap have been installed. This brings us to final shaping and sanding of the stock and final application of the filler and finish.

The lines and conformation of the stock should be kept within the limits of good gun design. Should custom features such as inlays, stock carvings or checkering be desired, then these should conform to the overall concept.

One possible custom feature is the insertion of some exotic material into the hollow head of the bolt handle. I prefer elephant ivory but any of the semi-rare materials such as rosewood, a small section of finely grained staghorn, bone, buffalo or even cowhorn, might be inserted into the hollow of the bolt handle and epoxied in place to add a novel touch. The addition of a cartridge trap in the stock usually is limited to European sporting arms of the drilling-type of shotgun-rifle combination but I have found that it is also an extremely useful feature for any sporting rifle.

Prior to final finishing of the stock, silver or gold initial plates, inlays, cartridge traps, other desirable adornments can be inletted into the stock and finished along with the surrounding wood. The cartridge trap I used is not available from any source in the United States today.

During the final phases of stock shaping, it might be necessary to reduce the thickness of the cheekrest. The majority of semi-finished stocks are supplied with the cheekrest left full to allow for proper fitting to each individual. Correct fitting is best accomplished by closing both eyes, placing the stock to the shoulder in a normal, comfortable manner without craning the neck, then opening the eye used for sighting the rifle.

The aiming eye should be looking straight down the center of the barrel. Should the barrel be off to the right — for a right-handed shooter — of the aiming eye, the cheekrest is too thick and must be rasped and planed down until the eye opens in perfect alignment with the barrel. The neck never should have to be craned to align the sights on any rifle or shotgun!

During the final phases of stock finishing, and prior to the final sanding with #400 paper, the holes for the sling swivels should be drilled into the stock. I always have preferred to place the butt swivel approximately three inches from the toe of the stock (if a one-inch rubber recoil pad is installed) or two inches from the toe if no recoil pad is used.

The forearm swivel should be placed approximately fourteen inches forward of the front bow of the trigger guard. If a Mannlicher-type stock is used, the forearm swivel should be placed as near the center of the barrel length as possible. Quite naturally, the placement of the forward swivel on a Mannlicher-type stock might vary according to whether a barrel band or a stock stud is

Herter's stock finish kit includes all needs for a durable, professional-looking finish. Included are grades of sand paper, pore filler, Liege finisher.

Above: Stock filler, applied with a felt pad, is allowed to dry slightly, then wiped off across the grain. (Below) Forearm of stock is slotted under barrel to accept barrel band that is supplied with kit. This is done after the glassing of the stock.

Squared edges of barrel band can be rounded over for more pleasing appearance. This was accomplished with a disk sander, but can be done with mill file.

When finished, the mounted front sight ramp and the snobble should look like this, following instructions.

After slotting the stock for the barrel band and rounding edges of band, it will offer sleeker look.

Using system explained in text, hollow of the bolt handle is plugged with ivory for decorative touch.

used. As a rule, when a band is used, the swivel is slightly forward of the center of the barrel.

Make absolutely certain, when laying out the placement of the swivel screws with a soft lead pencil, that they are dead-center of the stock.

On the U-9, I completely removed the roll-over Monte Carlo-type hump in the stock. I prefer a classic stock because it fits me better, even when using a scope. It always has been my contention that if a rifle stock is built correctly, with the proper amount of drop at the heel and the cheekrest fitted as already outlined, that extra lumber and weight is unnecessary! Accentuated Monte Carlo stocks, hook-shaped pistol grips and forearm caps that are nothing more than glorified brush

hooks, as well as gaudy inlays, are not my idea of a good, reliable sporting rifle.

Once the stock is shaped to your satisfaction, begin the finish-sanding. The stock finishing kit produced by Herter's includes everything necessary for the initial and final sanding, the filling of the pores in the wood and the application of the tough, durable Leige finish. Included are sixteen sheets of the finest quality garnet paper and extra-fine grit wet or dry paper. These papers are used progressively from the most coarse to the finest to give the wood a glassy smooth surface. The quality of the final finish will depend entirely upon just how well the stock was sanded.

When the stock has become glassy smooth, with no

minute file or sandpaper marks, the stock is ready for pore sealer and filler. Herter's stock finishing kit contains a bottle of **French Red Liquid.** This liquid imparts a rich French walnut color to the wood, while sealing and filling the pores, when used as directed. Allow the sealer to dry at least overnight before the next step.

The Leige finish supplied in the finishing kit may be applied with either a spray gun or by brushing it on with a fine camel hair brush. I have had the best luck applying such finishes by hand, but this takes a lot of practice to assure a reasonably perfect job. Following the directions on the bottle, one might apply as many as three or four coats before a glassy appearance is attained. Set it aside in a dust free area for at least thirty-six hours to set and harden.

Final rubbing down is accomplished with the imported lava stone found in the Herter's kit. Known as Greek Lava Stone, this product cannot be compared to common rotten stone, which, in most cases, removes far more stock finish than it polishes. This lava stone, properly used, produces a soft eggshell luster to the wood.

During the final rubbing with lava stone, do not scrub the finish but wipe firmly with the grain of the wood. Minute brush marks left on the surface will disappear and the finish soon will take on the luster of polished jade and will feel about the same.

The stock is given a good coat of paste wax of the type specifically made for rifle stocks or fine furniture, then is buffed carefully with a soft cloth. With the stock finished, it may be checkered or carved.

In assembling your finished rifle, give all surfaces of the barrel, receiver, trigger guard and floor plate a thorough coating of silicone grease where it contacts the wood, but wipe off any excess before assembling. This will act both as a preservative and a lubricant between the surfaces of the metal and wood. Herter's No. 629 silicone lubricant is available at eighty-five cents for three bottles.

The barrel band for Mannlicher-type stocks furnished by Herter's has squared edges. I rounded these over on the upper half of the band by beveling them on a disc sander, repolishing them prior to rebluing. This requires only a few minutes but adds to the look of the finished rifle. It is necessary to bevel only the upper portions of the band that are exposed above the stock, leaving the lower portions in their original squared shape.

It is only necessary now to build some handloads for the Herter's U-9 sporting rifle, take it afield for testing and zeroing of the scope or sights prior to taking it on a hunting trip for game.

My test firing of the U-9 in .300 Winchester magnum was done with bullets in weights from 150 grains up to 180 grains of both Sierra and Hornady vintage. All rounds were handloaded in Federal cases. While I stuck pretty close to data furnished in the Speer Reloading Manual, I still concocted some off-breed loads of my own proportions to determine the limitations for this particular rifle. When slightly flattened primers occurred, I backed off.

Even with maximum loads, extraction was easy. The U-9 bolt is one of the smoothest I've ever used and the red cocking indicator encased in the bolt sleeve is handy.

In mounting a scope on this new rifle I ran into difficulties. I had planned to use one of the new Redfield 4x12x variables but didn't care to drill and tap the grooved receiver to accept a bridge-type mount. I could not find suitably high mounts to fit the grooved receiver and had to settle for standard BSA mounts which were too low to accept the large bell of the variable's objective lens housing. I finally settled for a Redfield 4x scope which is suited to the BSA rings I had on hand.

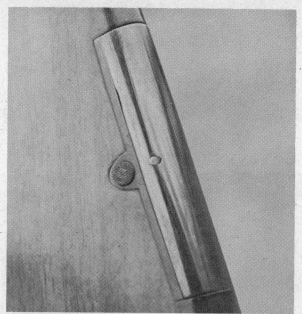

Inletted properly, the cartridge trap in the stock adds both to value and appearance of custom rifle.

For Herter's U9 rifle, the Williams Guide rear sight was chosen for an excellent scope/open sight combo.

While the commercially built cartridge trap used on the U9 opens from the side, this type, hinging at the end, also can be incorporated in the design.

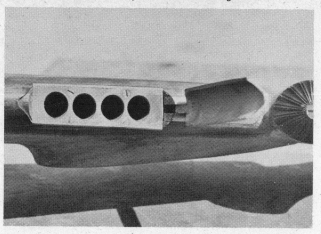

Chapter 33

It's the Little Marks That Are Most Simple
To Fix, Unless You're A Well Equipped Expert!

GUNSMITH BLUES

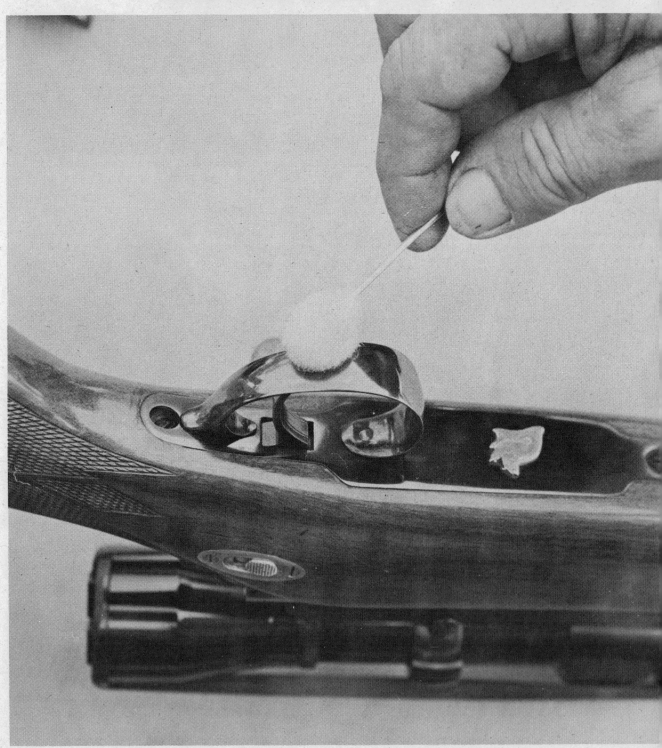

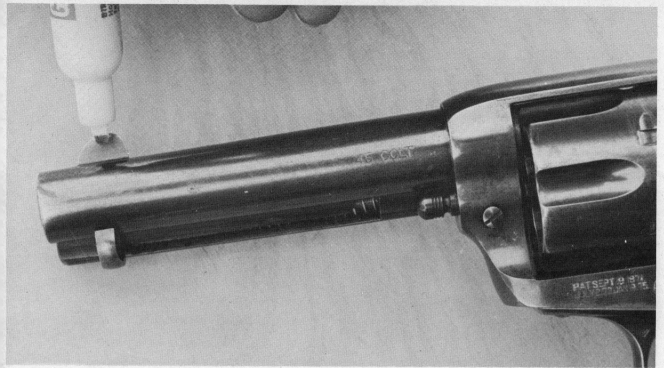

Using the G-66 Blue Stick, such components as sight blades can be touched up to kill glare of worn metal.

The use of cold blues for touch-up on expensive guns doesn't impair value, if common sense is used.

I doubt that there is a gunsmith anywhere, providing he is honest, who won't admit that, on at least several occasions during his career as a gun mechanic, he has had some lousy blue jobs come out of his tanks!

Catastrophes such as this can be due to several factors. Either the bluing salts have lost their oomph, some oily matter has gotten into his bluing tanks or possibly, due to a rush order or customer interference, the metal of the gun wasn't really ready for the bluing tank. It's happened in the best shops and undoubtedly will continue to happen on remote occasions.

Not generally known among the gun fanciers' fraternity is the fact that the major work of rebluing any gun doesn't occur in the bluing tank. It's getting the metal ready for the tank that is the real job. Only when the metal is prepared properly through buffing to a high luster and thorough degreasing is it ready for the rather simple matter of dipping it in a hot solution of bluing salts for the prescribed time.

Most home gun craftsmen are not set up to reblue a firearm properly due to the complex equipment needed. The first necessity would be a complete buffer setup. This would include various types of wheels and buffing compounds in at least three grits. But most of all, a thorough knowledge of gun buffing is mandatory! More guns are ruined at the buffing wheel by novices than through almost any other cause.

In addition to buffing equipment, at least four separate tanks — large enough to accept rifles and shotgun barrels — are needed.

The first of these tanks will contain a hot degreasing solution that will leave the gun metal almost microscopically clean. The second tank contains the hot bluing solution. The parts to be blued first are degreased and heated in the hot solution in tank No. 1. Then they are dipped into the bluing tank, being held suspended in the hot salts with wires.

During the actual bluing process, the parts are raised for visual inspection occasionally, until the desired shade of blue is reached. It is then that tanks 3 and 4 come into use. When the desired shade of blue is attained, the gun parts are immediately transferred to tank 3, which contains a scalding hot rinse of pure water.

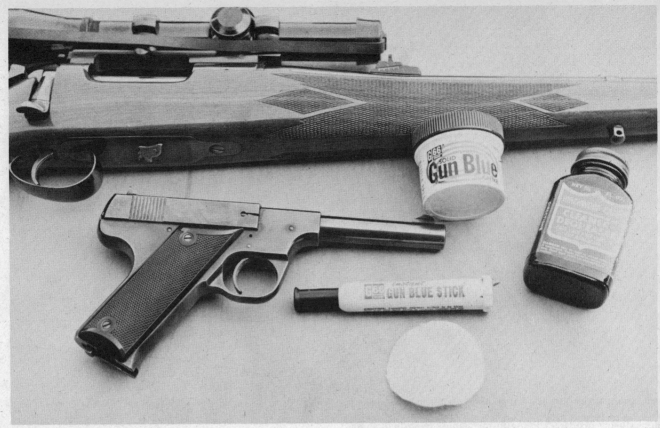

The materials required for successful application of cold blue preparations are few, simple to use.

Some of the preparations being marketed today must be rinsed with water after applying to stop action.

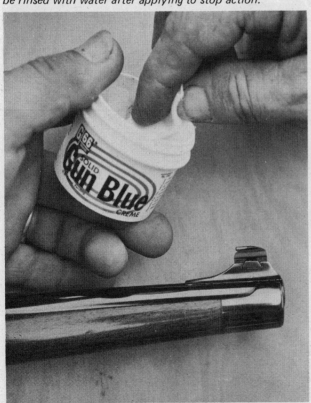

After a thorough rinsing, the parts are placed in tank 4, which contains neutralizing oil. This oil completely kills the action of any remaining bluing salts that might be on the metal parts.

An elaborate system of burners is necessary for heating each individual tank — and all at the same time. The gunsmith has a sizeable investment in this one phase of gunology alone!

Complete volumes have been written concerning the many and varied methods that one might use to blue or reblue a firearm. There is the hot solution dipping method just described and the rust method, where heated solutions are swabbed onto the preheated gun metal, then allowed to set until a rust film covers the surface.

After a prescribed period, this rust is removed, leaving a deep, beautiful and durable blued surface on the gun. This method is one of the best known, but it takes a lot of the gunsmith's time, hence it is fairly expensive.

Last, there are the so-called cold bluing solutions that have become popular among gun working novices in recent years. These solutions require no elaborate equipment or setups to use. They do the job quickly and, in most cases, efficiently. However, these solutions never should be used for completely bluing any firearm simply because they are not durable enough, regardless of what the advertising says on the bottle or container! I have yet to see or use a cold blue that couldn't be removed or blotched by simple hand rubbing or by wiping with an oily cloth.

This doesn't mean that cold blues aren't good; used properly, they are. I have used any variety in my own shop for years. I wouldn't be without them, but not for complete blue jobs.

Take, for example, an incident concerning a valuable

The paste bluing solutions now available to the home gunsmith are used in the same manner as liquids.

Pencil-type bluing applicators are ideal for any touch-up of small scratches on surface of any gun.

engraved and gold-inlaid sporting rifle. This rifle had been purchased in used condition by a friend of mine. It had been to Africa on two safaris and had been jousted around on the back of an elephant, while on shikar in India. Still in excellent condition, it nonetheless showed the effects of these hunts in worn areas of blue at the muzzle and around the breech section.

My friend had investigated the possibility of having the entire rifle reblued, but what would this do to the engraving and gold inlays?

Certainly the process of buffing the gun would indeed make a notable difference in the appearance of the overall rifle. The engraving would be blunted, especially on the gold surfaces, despite careful workmanship on the part of the gunsmith.

I talked my friend out of having the rifle reblued com-

It may take an eye for color, but bluing solution
is applied to worn area until color is fully restored.

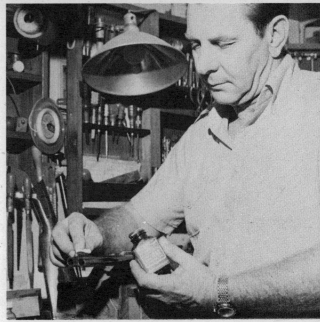

When area has been re-blued to match the original,
metal is cleaned of solution, then is waxed lightly.

Bish works over an expensive English-built double
rifle. He re-blued small areas where it had worn off.

pletely and asked him to leave it with me for a few days. In
a couple of days, he returned and I handed him the rifle. He
refused to believe that I hadn't completely reblued the rifle,
so I enlightened him.

I had taken the rifle into my shop and thoroughly cleaned the exterior surfaces with solvent. Following this, I
briskly wiped the surface of the metal, removing any film
left by the solvent to assure a positive, clean surface. With
an ordinary round gun cleaning patch and a bottle of cold
bluing solution, I went to work.

It is fairly well known that most cold blues will react on
some precious metals. It will turn sterling silver coal black
and, in many cases, will tarnish gold. The rifle I was touch-

Trigger guards and floor plates often become worn,
scratched. This is remedied easily with cold blue.

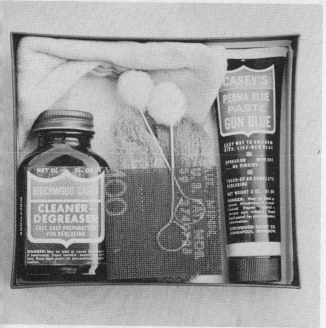

Bluing kits now are available from several makers, for the complete job, including Birchwood-Casey.

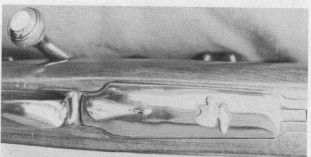

Above: Front sight worn to bare metal, should be reblued to kill glare. (Below) Scratched trigger guard has been refinished with cold blue solution.

ing up was literally crusted with both precious metals. But this was no deterrent.

I applied the cold bluing solution only to the worn areas of the original blue, ignoring for the moment the gold and silver inlay work that abutted the blued surface. The whole secret of a job such as this is to have the metal absolutely clean and grease-free. Even hand or fingerprints should be removed thoroughly, if a perfect touch-up job with cold blues is expected.

Finally, when I had all worn surfaces of the blue touched up, I lightly buffed the areas with a soft cloth, then used a jeweler's silver cloth, which is treated with red jeweler's rouge.

Winding this cloth tightly around my finger, I lightly

Cold blue materials come in various forms, including tubes, bottles and pencil-like sticks, but all seem to work equally well if the directions are followed.

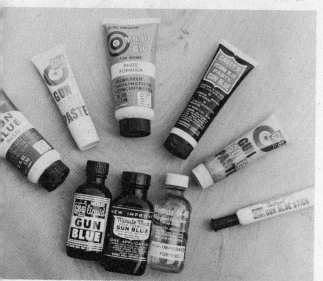

buffed the gold and silver surfaces tarnished by the bluing solution. The tarnish almost immediately disappeared and the precious metals took on a beautiful luster once more.

The last step was to give the entire metal surfaces of the rifle a thorough coating of Birchwood-Casey's stock wax. This was allowed to dry to a film, then was buffed lightly with a soft, hand-held cloth. The surface of that expensive inlaid rifle never looked prettier! There were no worn spots in the blued surface visible to the eye and a fraction of a penny's worth of cold bluing solution had done the job!

I still maintain that the cold bluing solutions should not be used for complete bluing jobs, but they are unsurpassed for touching up worn areas of blue on any gun, providing these areas aren't too large.

Take, for example, any handgun that is carried in a leather holster. In a short time, the sides of the barrel at the muzzle begin to show bright spots as a result of rubbing against the abrasive surface of the leather. If the holster is lined with a soft kid or calf leather, this is prevented to some extent. Eventually, though, there will be worn areas on the blue, both at the muzzle and possibly on the sides of the cylinder. Touch it up with cold blue and give it a coat of wax!

Shotguns and rifles that are carried in leather scabbards create the same problems. Before the wear gets too bad, touch them up with cold blue and wax.

There are any number of excellent cold bluing solutions on the market today, including Formula 44-40, the several different types of bluing solutions and pastes produced by the Jet-Air Corporation under their G-66 brand and the excellent bluing preparations produced by Birchwood-Casey.

The basic secret to a good looking and durable touch-up job using cold bluing solutions is to seal the finished surface with a good paste wax once the touch-up is completed. To leave the raw metal surface open to the air could result in rust forming over the entire surface, then having to do the job all over again.

Completely rebluing any firearm correctly is an art that only experience can master. If a really good gun needs blue, let an experienced gunsmith do the job for you. If your gun shows only minor holster or scabbard wear, then touch it up yourself.

Chapter 34

CHECK: DON'T WRECK THAT TREK

These Safeguards Can
Make Your Hunt A Success!

Almost without fail, hunting season after hunting season, and from one hunters' camp to the next, are heard the moanings of no few rimrods-of-the-tall-timber complaining that their hunting trip was a bust, because of some failure or malfunction of that most important piece of equipment, their rifles.

In the majority of these cases, the malfunctions are a direct result of hap-hazard preparations on the part of the individual hunter. He just didn't give his rifle the careful checking over that it needed for a successful hunt. His most important piece of equipment was taken for granted as being in top condition, since this same rifle had, in most cases, seen hard usage in past years with never a hint of trouble.

Speaking from experience, I will never forget the fruitless hunt that occurred in the wilds of eastern Oregon where I and some hunting compadres had gone for elk. I had brought along my favorite rifle, the make of which I will not mention here for fear that my own stupidity might reflect upon this particular gun's quality. At any length, I thought that I had been careful in checking and rechecking the gun before leaving the ranch — the bore was spotless; the action worked like that of a fine watch, as it had for several years.

The trip into the elk country by pick-up truck was made in the dead of winter through blinding snowstorms and on icy roads at the end of which was a long cold hike over exceedingly rough terrain and through thick masses of buckbrush and heavy timber. But we finally arrived in a beautiful snow-covered valley through which ran the trails taken by the regal elk in their migration from the high country.

At the moment when one of the most beautiful hatracks I have ever seen came within range, I attempted to jack a cartridge into the chamber only to have the lever literally fall out of the receiver! The screw holding the lever had in some way loosened and dropped out somewhere along seven hard miles of rough, icy trails to our rear.

In the event that hunting is to be done in extremely

Before any hunt, all scope screws should be checked and tightened to prevent scope slipping. Loc-Tite or shellac on threads also prevents loose screws.

Pistol grip checkering should be examined prior to an extended hunt. Should it be too smooth, it can be gone over, renewed, as explained in Chapter 6.

cold country, it is best to remove all existing oil or grease from the gun's mechanism to prevent it from freezing up when it is needed most. Make certain that the firing pin is oil and grease-free in sub-zero temperatures, as this one part is most likely to freeze tight in the bolt or breech block. A rifle with even a partially frozen mechanism becomes useless.

If you're going to be hunting with a lever action in cold weather, keep in mind that this model is particularly sensitive to a mixture of frigid weather and grease. Get down to the zero mark on the thermometer and you can have all sorts of unexpected mishaps. I know of at least one incident in which a friend missed his big chance after he borrowed my Savage 99, because he didn't heed my advice to take the grease out of the firing pin spring before leaving for the high country.

As it resulted, he crept up on a big buck, then a couple of rounds failed to fire, because the grease about the spring had congealed. This resulted in the pin striking the primer with reduced potency; not enough force to cook off the round.

This review of a fruitless hunt is by no means remote. It happens each year and in every part of the country, where hunters go afield. To profit from the mistakes of others and to prevent this possibility of traveling hundreds of miles to good hunting country and expending hard dollars for a sightseeing trip, let's consider some of the advance remedies.

There are numerous mechanical occurrences which can render a rifle useless for anything except a club on a tough hunt. This can be particularly true of some of the vintage military rifles that have been sporterized. Screws may loosen and drop out; extractors and firing pins may break at the crucial moment, when they are needed (a common happening with some older military bolt actions).

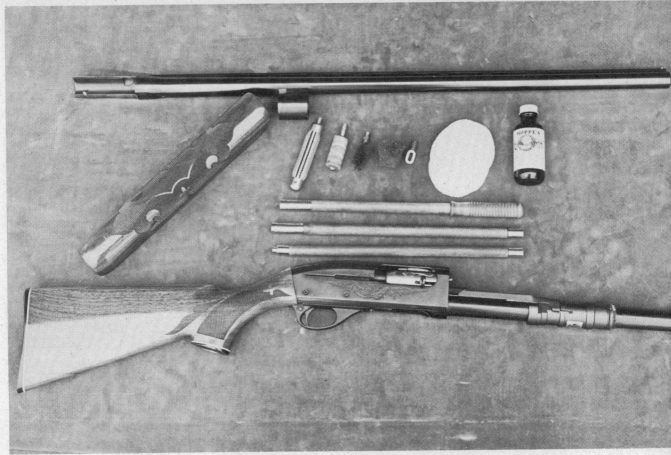

Shotgun cleaning equipment can include special bore buffers and polishers shown here. Rifles, handguns require less complex gear for a thorough cleaning.

Malfunctions in modern, commercially manufactured sporting arms can happen, but are not seen nearly as often as with older converted military models. The reliability of converted military jobs depends to a degree upon who did the conversion and in what manner.

In the case of foreign rifles and parts of military origin, some have seen improper storage for many years and may be so eaten by rust and erosion that they no longer are reliable on a serious hunting expedition.

There are many facets to the thorough preparation and checking of a rifle prior to taking it into the deep woods on a hunting trek, but most can be accomplished in a matter of minutes. If the chore is undertaken with the thought that "without a working rifle, my hunting trip is a complete failure," fewer hunters would come back to the old homestead empty-handed.

A few of the more important check points are:

A. Make certain that bore and mechanism are clean and unobstructed.

B. Check all screws for tightness. In some cases, the new Ny-Lock washers may be used, but a slight coating of shellac on threads will prevent them from becoming loose.

C. In the case of home-converted military rifles, it is best to have the head space checked by a competent gunsmith. This operation takes but a few minutes and may prevent a serious accident. Carry an extra firing pin and extractor.

D. A good woods rifle should have a passable blue job; the worn spots should be touched up with a cold blue solution to prevent reflected sun light. Reflected light from a gun barrel will spook wild game.

E. If using older military rifles and as-issued ammunition, make certain that ammo is safe to shoot and that tracers have not found their way into the batch. It isn't necessary to cook your game on the spot and tracers have started forest fires!

F. It is a safe bet, if one is hunting in remote areas and far from his car or truck, to carry along a few basic tools such as a small three-way Colt-type screwdriver and a thong-type cleaning outfit for the rifle bore. This consists of a strong piece of cord slightly longer than the barrel length with a weighted end that may be dropped through the bore to remove snow or mud that may have found its way there.

In the woods a hundred and one things can happen to bring to a close what could have been a bountiful hunting trip. A sudden slip on a steep bank with a scoped rifle can ruin the scope in the resulting fall, or at least jar it so far out of zero that a trip to the workbench, then to the rifle range for resighting would be necessary.

If you hunt with a scoped rifle — and who doesn't these days — you will do well to check all of the screws in your mounts before you go out to hunt. These have a tendency with some models to work loose and a loose scope can throw your aim off by several feet, even yards, if you're zeroing in on a trophy at two or three hundred yards.

Also, if you find that such screws in your mounts are loose and you tighten them, you may have to zero in the scope again on a range to be certain you haven't changed the adjustment of those delicated crosshairs.

Les Bowman, who ran the LB Bar Ranch up in Cody, Wyoming, and who was one of the best known outfitters and guides in the country before his retirement, reports, "More hunters seem to be working at being better shots, but most could do a lot more practice on one phase that can be practiced at most any time and place. This is the

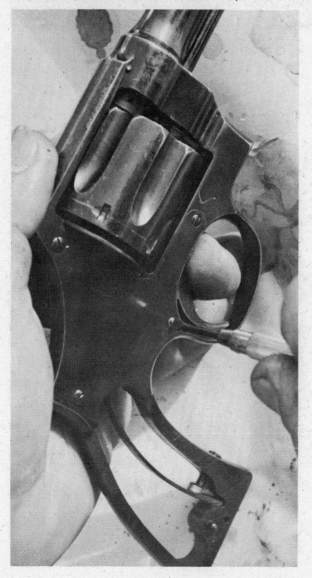

When a handgun is carried as a back-up arm for any semi-dangerous game, it is best to check it for loose screws, as well as for smoothness of operation.

practice of locating the target rapidly and accurately in your sight scope.

"Most all hunting is done out here with a scope sighted rifle and it takes practice to locate a target quickly and positively in a scope. Check your rifle — be sure it's not loaded — look at a sight point, throw the rifle to your shoulder, smooth and naturally. The reticule should be nearly on sight point, and for sure, the sighting point should be in the range, without any jiggling around to find it; just a slight correction so the reticule centers on the target. Practice this type aiming as much as possible. You will be surprised at how much it improves your gun handling and how much quicker you are at game for hunters than any other one thing."

The most frequent mishap with hunters' rifles occurs through lost or broken parts. You can avoid losing parts by thoroughly checking the rifle before leaving home. In the case of broken parts, it is best to carry a spare or two of those parts that are know to be breakable in the rifle that you are using.

If that quality known as "pride of ownership" is present in the hunter, then it is a good thought to have the stock of the rifle well finished with one of the better known stock finishes in order to protect it from damaging moisture and rain. A good coating of Birchwood-Casey stock wax helps protect the finish of varnished or lacquered stocks from scratches and mositure.

It's also a good idea, if you're going to be out in wet weather or deep snow, to waterproof the barrel channel and the other cuts in the stocks. True, a custom rifle probably will have this done when it's delivered to you, but the less expensive models will have only raw wood beneath the barrel.

Take the barrel and action out of the stock and use several coats of linseed oil or one of the commercial derivatives. In extreme cases, you can even use a good grade of furniture wax. This serves as a protection to the wood at the moment and may keep your stock from warping after the hunt is done.

A good sling equipped with quickly detachable mounts is a must on long, hard hikes in hunting country. This sling, if of leather, should be kept well dressed with Lexol or some other mild leather dressing. Never use oily dressings on older leather, as these have a tendency to rot it. Neatsfoot oil is fine for one coating on new leather, but will cause older leather literally to fall to pieces.

And of course, the heart of any gun is the bolt. If you use a bolt action rifle, my advice is to remove the bolt and strip it down, soak all of the parts in some type of good solvent, remove the gum and grease and scrub down all of the parts with an old toothbrush or similar implement. When you lubricate it, use a light oil and use it sparingly. I personally prefer either a grease like Lubriplate, which can stand extreme temperature changes, or even powdered graphite. The latter gives a smooth movement of parts, yet protects them from undue wear.

The powdered graphite is excellent for moving parts of the action, too, if you're going to be in cold weather. There are those who will disagree, but I feel it has all of the advantages and none of the disadvantages.

When hunting season is here, take stock of your armament to make certain that it is "woods worthy" and won't let you down just as that trophy-size head appears in your sights. Your rifle is a full partner in your hunt and, without its helps, you will go home empty handed.

*Unorthodox methods, usually born of lack of training,
are used in all phases of gun destruction among
those who profess to be fully qualified gunsmiths.*

Chapter 35

A WHACK AT THE GUN QUACK

Thousands Of Guns
Are Damaged
Each Year By Gun Butchers
— But You Can
Avoid Their Traps!

A friend of mine recently sent an 1851 Navy Colt with a square back trigger guard—an extremely valuable antique—to a comparatively new gunsmith for slight repairs. This workman, hoping to make a hit with the gun dealer, and possibly gain additional business, proceeded to completely buff the pistol, then give it a beautiful new blue job!

The dealer, upon reclaiming his pistol, literally was ready to sit down and cry. The gun's antique value had been completely ruined.

This may be an extreme case of the damage being done every day by gun quacks, but similar professional obscenities are being committed continually, and it is the gun owner who suffers in the long run. Even if he refuses to pay for the privilege of having had his gun butchered, it still has been a costly experience.

Webster defines the word, quack, thusly: *"A person who, with little or no foundation, pretends to have knowledge or skill of a particular field."*

The rare Henry rifle at top of photo has been buffed until almost worthless. Same model beneath it shows clean sharp corners common to an unbutchered Henry.

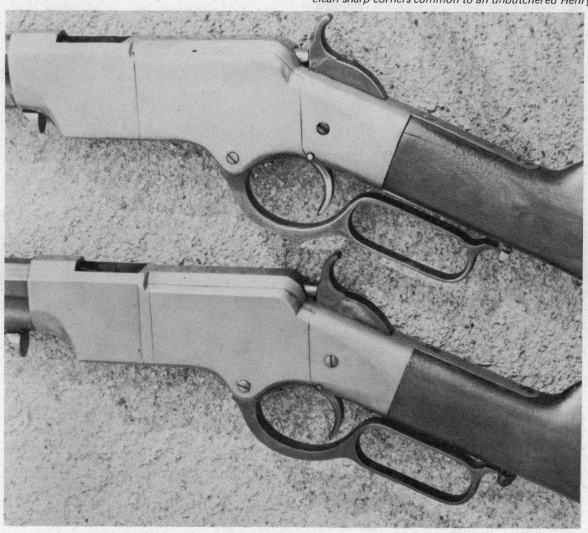

Forend cap of rifle illustrates poor workmanship. Oak is not a good wood for such adornment and cap fell off – literally – after rifle's first shot.

With the increasing interest in guns and shooting in this country, the gun quack is becoming an ever increasing menace; there are undoubtedly some in the business who will feel that this article should not be written; that we are aiming at them. On the other hand, there are those artisans and perfectionists in the gunsmithing field who will feel it is long overdue!

In something like a quarter of a century in the gun field, I have seen far too many of the "hacksaw and hammer" boys enter business, claiming to be crackerjack gunsmiths, while as a rule, they may never have worked on any firearm other than those they might have in their own collections. Generally speaking, their own guns are so loused up that all that is necessary to put them back in good shape is to jack up the front sight (providing that hasn't been ruined, too) and roll a new gun under it!

The most discouragingly pitiful aspect of this situation is that most of the psuedo experts are not intentionally doing harm; posing as charlatans of the firearms trade. They usually feel that they are good enough to work on someone else's guns; they simply fail to realize their own ignorance, depending upon ego for the technical answers.

Let's take the case of one so-called gunsmith, for instance, who is doing business strictly on the basis of one year and seven months experience in Army Ordnance. His attitude is, "the Army said I was a gunsmith, and by gummies, I'm a gunsmith!"

The only problem is that his entire nineteen months of military experience were devoted to the relatively simple chore of field stripping and cleaning countless cases of .45 automatic pistols, Thompson submachine guns and other miscellaneous small arms.

We'll agree that someone has to clean weapons even on the home fronts, but his experience hardly qualifies him to take advantage of his field stripping experience by opening a gun shop and begin butchering other people's property out of ignorance and at far higher prices than the Army was paying!

And this man is not alone; there are plenty of others without even his military experience, who having set themselves up as experts, now are hacking, cutting and chiseling their way into the hearts of good American guns!

I recently was in the shop of a new gunsmith who was in the process of mounting a scope on a brand new sporting rifle. He had drilled and tapped the necessary four holes into the receiver to accommodate the scope mount and was attempting to place the mount in position, but not one of the holes in the weapon lined up with those of the mount!

As I watched, this neophyte wrecker filled the holes with plastic wood and drilled four new ones!

Words cannot express the contempt I felt for this butcher after watching a beautiful new rifle ruined, and you can rest assured that neither I nor anyone of even my most casual acquaintance will be taking him business if word of mouth advertising is as powerful as the experts claim!

The mounting of rifle scopes has been one of the more abused practices among men who haven't the slightest idea of the art. To them, mounting seems to

This custom stock has been nearly cut in two at the pistol grip and could endanger the shooter. It can shatter or splinter under recoil, causing injury.

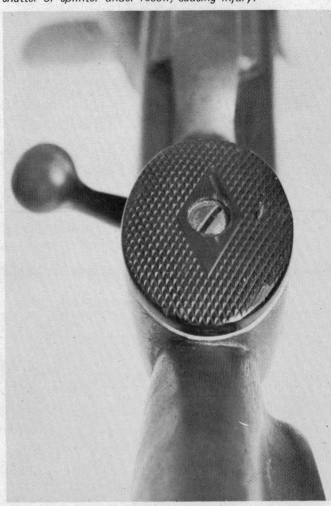

mean nothing more than screwing the mount into place on the rifle receiver, placing the scope in the rings, tightening it and tagging the gun as ready to go when the bill is paid!

Invariably, the owner takes his piece to the range to do some shooting only to find that he isn't even hitting in the same county with his target. He begins adjusting his windage and elevation knobs to bring the scope onto the target, but after he has used up all of his clicks and his scope reticles are adjusted almost out of the tube, he is still trying to find the target!

Had the scope been mounted by a competent man in the first place, it would have been guaranteed to be within at least four inches of dead center at a hundred yards.

I know of a recent case in which a friend took a Colt's SAA to a shop for minor repairs. This revolver is one of the most easy ever made to repair and correctly tune, and in this situation, the trigger would not stand in the safety notch in the hammer in spite of the fact that both trigger and hammer were new parts and had been originally fitted correctly to the gun.

The psuedo gunsmith spent almost two hours in his attempt to correct the fault, then handed the gun back to its owner, saying, "Two dollars and a half, please."

"Two and a half for what?" was the critical demand. "You didn't fix the gun!"

This erstwhile expert became quite irate at the logical question, declaring, "I spent a couple of hours on it, didn't it? My time's worth money!"

The gun owner paid the sum and made his disgusted exit with the words, "Thanks for exactly nothing!" never to return. He also went out to spread the word among his gun fancying friends that a butcher who was also a sharpy was in the neighborhood.

As an anti-climax to this tale, he took the gun to a qualified man and found that the only trouble with his pistol was that the trigger in some manner had been bent at the point where it engages the hammer. This fault was corrected in less than five minutes by a competent man and at *no* charge to the customer!

This incident, while minor, if multiplied many times, does create a gigantic loss to the gun owner, who is certainly deserving of getting some value received for the money he is willing to spend on his arms.

In my mind, there is no doubt that these quacks do have, in their own dubious ways, affection for guns. It is their lack of mechanical skill and know-how, to say nothing of natural ability and patience, that marks them as gun butchers.

This statement, as well as the illustrations offered here may sound strong, but any qualified gunsmith, if

Poor inletting and fitting on the receiver of this sporterized Enfield show shoddy workmanship, as does quickie lacquer job, evidence of backyard butchery.

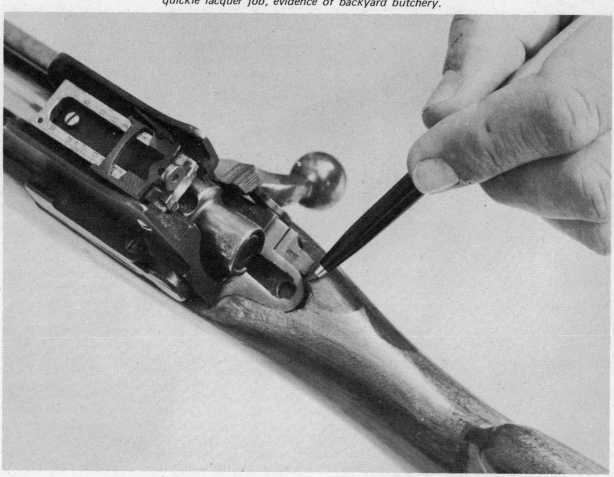

Outdoorsy workbenches are nice, but not when fine guns are left outside, winter and summer, to rust.

questioned, will tell you that hardly a day passes in which he does not receive firearms that have in some way been damaged, ofter ruined beyond repair, by some backyard expert.

As a result, the quack fees, then the costs of honest repairs, often run as high as the original price of the guns themselves. Whereas the needed repair might have been minor in the beginning, the cost of repairing the repairs often is terrific!

The seemingly lesser crime regarding the butchery of obsolete arms that no longer are manufactured may seem trivial to some, as in the case of the man who re-blued the 1851 Navy Colt, but to an avid collector such as myself, this can be far worse than the abortive efforts performed against currently manufactured pieces. When an obsolete or antique gun is altered or butchered in any way, a bit of American history goes down the drain!

Gunsmithing is an ancient and honorable profession and requires years of training and is long in the requirements for experience, patience and precision. Unlike most other fields, no two jobs are exactly alike. When it is considered that there are several hundred variations in gun actions, it is more easily seen that experience and this alone is necessary to repair these sometimes intricate mechanisms.

In the moments when even an experienced gunsmith runs into a repair problem that is either beyond his comprehension or the tooling facilities of his shop, he will invariably tell you and suggest factory service where the work can be handled correctly. On the other hand, the hammer hack will accept the job and you may well have a loused up gun!

Volumes could be written on the atrocities performed daily upon firearms by the hosts of shop quacks and backyard experts but no amount of writing will end this situation. However, it is hoped that those who read this will be on their guard henceforth, not being subject to spur of the moment selections in choosing the man to work on their guns. It can be less expensive to learn of the man's background and qualifications and find what he offers in the way of guaranteed precision work.

Bear in mind that not even a well tooled shop means the best in craftsmanship. It isn't the amount or costliness of the tools a man owns that makes him an excellent gunsmith. Money can buy all of the tools in the world, but only time can purchase the knowledge, experience and precision of the true gunsmith!

The answer to the problem of gun butchery is difficult and must be solved by gun fanciers themselves. You can talk to those who have utilized the services of a given gunsmith and evaluate their opinions, of course. As a rule, a competent sporting goods store or retail gun outlet in your vicinity may be helpful in recommending one who has done satisfactory work for them.

But to carry the program a few steps further, such organizations as the National Rifle Association; the United States Revolver Association, and the leading collectors and firearms groups might license or approve craftsmen who have shown the proper qualifications and have garnered the necessary degree of experience. However, to be so approved, the gunsmith should be required to pass extensive practical examinations as proof that he is qualified.

FIELD DRESS FOR THE BUGGY BOOMER

This Replica
Of An Oldtimer Can Be
Made More Functional
For Hunting Use With A Bit Of
Thought And Labor!

Numrich's black powder rifles and carbines come in varying lengths, but the Deluxe Buggy carbine is fitted with a short twenty-inch barrel. More standard, perhaps, is another Numrich rifle of the same basic design with thirty-two-inch barrels. Both are available either in .36 or .45 caliber. The carbine with which we are dealing here weighs approximately 5½ pounds, while the rifle is 8½ pounds.

The Deluxe Buggy carbine is of the same basic design as the rifle used by Goerg on his successful Hawaiian hunt, but instead of the thirty-two-inch barrel, the carbine is fitted with a short twenty-inch barrel. Both the rifle and the buggy carbine sell for about $64.50 and both are available in either .36 or .45 caliber. The carbine weighs approximately 5-1/2 pounds while the rifle weighs in at 8-1/2 pounds.

Besides the lack of sling swivels — or provisions for them — I noticed that the small of the stock was too small to provide a good handhold. The wrist of this stock is about the same size as a broom handle and needed something at least to provide a better holding surface for those of us with large hands. The forearm wasn't too bad, but as thin as it is, it doesn't lend itself to the treatment that I intended to give the small of

the stock: a checkering job, using a Dem-Bart electric checkering machine, cutting eighteen lines per inch.

The addition of sling swivels to the Hopkins & Allen bottom bangers calls for a little thought. The butt swivel provides no problems as almost any standard swivel screw can be installed in a few minutes. The forend creates the problem in that a conventional swivel screw cannot be installed without obstructing the ramrod channel. Too, the wood of the forearm is too thin to stand any strain put on it by even the swivel screw. It would pull out.

Knowing that it would be fruitless even to attempt buying a sling swivel that would work in the forearm of this carbine, one either must be made from scratch or converted from something else.

In going through what I call my goodie box containing hundreds of old and obsolete gun parts and

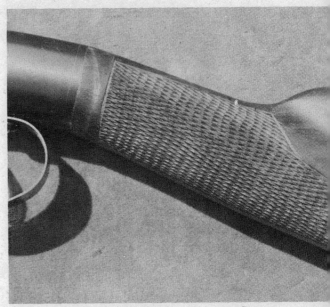

A plain but effective checkering pattern was used on small of the stock. Dem-Bart electric checkering tool was used to do the 18-lines-to-an-inch pattern.

Rear sling swivel installation creates one problem, as standard screw eye obtainable at sporting goods stores is installed in wood to accept hooked swivel.

components, I came across an old magazine band originally designed for the Model 1892 Winchester carbine in either .32 WCF or .25-20 caliber. This band was designed so that it replaced the standard magazine band and provided a loop for a hook-type sling swivel. The inside diameter of this band was made to order to accept the ramrod of the H&A bottom banger. The only thing necessary was to cut a dovetail slot into the underside of the barrel just forward of the wooden forearm. Then the ramrod could slide through the band and on into the slot of this forearm.

Not everyone has access to a Model 1892 Winchester swivel-type barrel band but one using this same principle may be made by hand by any home mechanic. The basic idea is that, since you cannot go directly through the forearm with a swivel attachment, you must go around it with a band, then have your swivel attached in some way to this band.

In getting this particular new muzzleloading carbine model ready for the field — following the installation of the sling swivels and checkering the small of

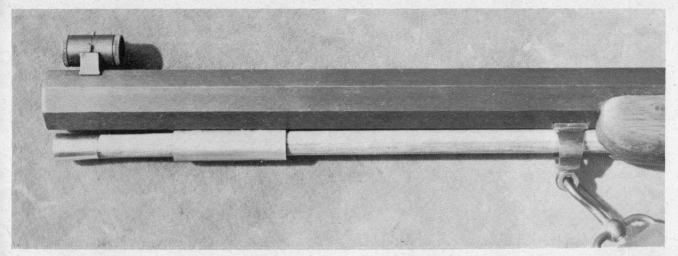

Salvaged sling ring from old Winchester rifle was dovetailed into barrel, provides ideal set-up for a hook-type swivel. Ramrod tip also is reinforced.

the stock — I checked out the sights with my Sweany **Site-A-Line** collimator to assure that they were reasonably close for hunting purposes. I have no pipe dreams about this muzzleloader being anything but a short range arm — especially with a twenty-inch barrel — so I took care to zero this particular carbine for one hundred-yard shooting.

Experience in shooting these front-loading charcoal burners has shown that they definitely are not for long range shooting; this is especially true if one is attempting to bag game of any size. They will reach out; there's no doubt about that, but by the time that black powder-propelled lead ball has traveled any great distance, it hasn't enough poop left to make a clean kill.

In the initial test firing, I found that the wooden ramrod was taking quite a beating in pushing the lead ball down the barrel and seating it tightly on the pow-

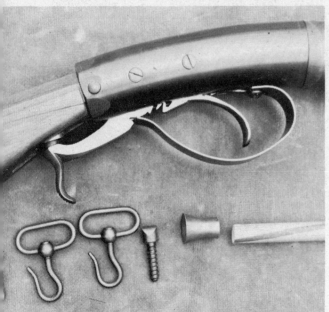

Equipment required for improving Numrich carbine for field use includes front swivel base, pair of hook-type swivels, swivel screw, brass ramrod tip.

der charge. I remedied this situation by installing a brass tip on the ramrod with epoxy cement and a brass pin. This brass tip is drilled out to accept the wooden ramrod end after it has been cut-down, or stepped, so that both brass tip and ramrod might be dressed down together, forming a smooth union of the two components.

The brass tip should be just under bore diameter in size, and the end used in pushing the ball down the barrel should be concaved slightly to form a perfect seat in which the ball rides as the ramrod pushes it down the barrel.

Experience also has taught me that powder in too coarse a grain is no good in a muzzleloader if the gun has a short barrel. The powder coarseness must be regulated to the length of the barrel, assuring that all of the powder is burned within the barrel. Should the powder be too coarse for the barrel length, an unignited portion of the powder charge will be blown out of the barrel. I have proved this point many times to doubters when there was snow on the ground. I would load the rifle with FG or FFG powder — which is too coarse for a .45 caliber muzzleloader — fire the rifle, then show the doubting Thomases as much as fifteen grains of unburned powder lying in the snow directly in front of the rifle's muzzle!

The little DeLuxe Buggy carbine, produced by Numrich Arms shoots well with a loading of 63 grains of FFFG black powder and a tightly patched .45 caliber lead ball seated firmly on the powder charge. This carbine also is available from Numrich in .36 caliber.

This black powder carbine can be shot all day for a few pennies worth of powder, percussion caps and lead balls. However, if it is to be used for serious short range hunting on such animals as deer, the owner should familiarize himself thoroughly with its potential as a big game rifle. A few hours of steady shooting on a rifle range should bring out any idiosyncrasies of any particular firearm and this carbine is no exception.

This carbine can be improved greatly with the innovations mentioned here, especially if it is to be carried for serious hunting. This carbine has a good set of sights but even these should be checked out before the carbine is taken on a hunt.

The trigger mechanism, while primitive, on the specimen used in these tests was reasonably smooth and crisp, needing no honing. The cap nipple, being on the underside of the barrel, eliminates the possibility of percussion cap fragments injuring the eyes or stinging the face. However, it still is an excellent idea to wear a good pair of shooting glasses when firing.

Chapter 37

FRONTIER GUNSMITHING

The complete story of gunsmithing is a long one and it would require several large volumes to adequately cover the overall picture, as it predates the Middle Ages when the crossbow and stone catapults were the most formidable weapons of the day.

The story of gunsmithing contains too many phases, too many eras and too many modes of manufacture to completely catalog them all on these pages. It is a profession that has helped protect nations from aggression and delivered others from beneath the heel of dictatorial rulers. It is a profession that played no little part in the winning of wars and the keeping of the peace.

During the early years of young America, when firearms were as necessary as food on the table, the gunsmith was a man held in highest esteem by his fellow townsmen; a man of stature, who could be depended upon to hang the village bell (many early gunsmiths were also bellhangers), repair the steeple clock or manufacture, by hand, keys for the local jail. He was a man who had a complete knowledge of hand tools and their use, but more important, his hands were highly trained by years of apprenticeship to guide those same tools to the completion of any job that he undertook. To use an ancient gunsmith slogan, these jobs were "finished in the finest manner."

The apprenticeship of an early American gunsmith was usually for a term of from four to six years during which time he was expected to pay "tuition" to the skilled gunsmith teaching him the trade. It was a rare case where an apprentice received any wages whatsoever. During this apprenticeship period, the neo-gunsmith not only was taught the correct use of tools in relation to the gunmaking trade, but was given a thorough course in

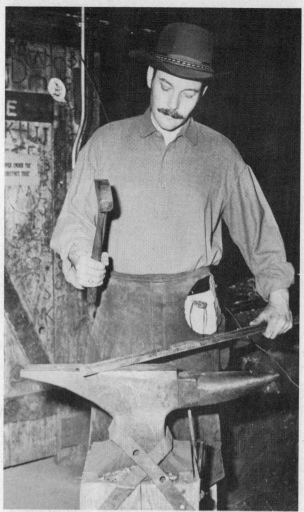

Barrels were anvil-forged to shape, then bores were formed by hand beating flat iron stock around dowel of hardened steel. When finished, this dowel was removed, leaving a perfect tube ready for rifling.

Top and bottom screws are handmade in their entirety from bits of scrap iron. Modern screw is in center.

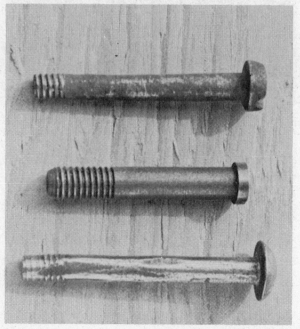

metallurgy. He was able to manufacture from raw materials almost anything that he may need, whether in the complete assembly of his entire shop, all of his own tools, or the complete manufacture of a firearm by hand down to the smallest spring and the finest screw.

The gunsmith and gunshop of a hundred-odd years ago is a far cry from the modern automated shops of today. The use of electric motors, milling machines, automatic lathes and drill presses were as foreign to the old gunshop as is common courtesy on a crowded streetcar today.

Each and every piece of equipment needed by most frontier gunsmiths was manufactured, for the most part, entirely by his own hands. His shop was, if at all possible, located beside some stream or flowing body of water from which the gunsmith could, by the use of water wheels and wooden gears, furnish himself with a source of power to run a part of his primitive equipment.

Other less fortunate gunsmiths, who had to locate far from such a source of power, depended on other means with which to mechanize their equipment. Such methods as treadle devices were worked out and installed on lathes, which had been constructed with a fly-wheel cut from a section of a hardwood tree. The bed-ways were of any metal available as were the jaws of the wooden lathe chuck. All cutting on these lathes was

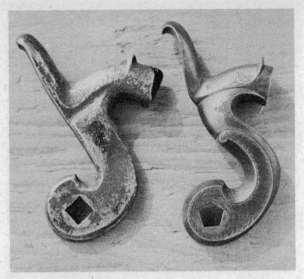

Hammer at left was hand-forged, then finished by a backwoods gunsmith. Both are of the same vintage, but hammer on the right is European, machine-made.

performed by holding the cutter in the hands due to the instability of a tool post on these wooden contraptions. Such other tools were handmade and included files, reamers, cherries for making bullet molds,taps and dies for threading barrels and breech plugs. Even complete barrel rifling guides and tools where hand manufactured from any available material. Cutters for these rifling guides were made from hickory rods with a small metal cutter inserted in one end; these cutters were inserted into the round smooth bore of a newly hand-formed rifle barrel and were worked slowly back and forth, so each pull and push would allow the cutter to eat into the metal of the bore ever so slightly. The cutters were guided by a grooved, cylindrical wooden guide which gave the lands and grooves being cut into the barrel a perfect pitch or twist. Later these newly cut lands and grooves were smoothed up and polished by a process known as "hand lapping."

The making of screws, an important factor in gunsmithing, was accomplished by first heating a small piece of scrap steel to a cherry red in the forge, then beating or anviling it out to the desired diameter. The head of the screw to-be was formed in a like manner, then slotted, while still hot, with a slotting chisel. This crude, preshaped piece of steel then was forced through a "screw plate," a piece of steel with various sized threaded holes. This plate had been case hardened with any one of several old time case hardening formulas.

The workbench of the frontier gunsmith was anything but elaborate. Here, gunsmith is fitting original stock to the action of antique percussion shotgun.

After a barrel has been formed and welded by hand, the round steel rod was removed, leaving a bore that was ready for hand cutting lands and grooves.

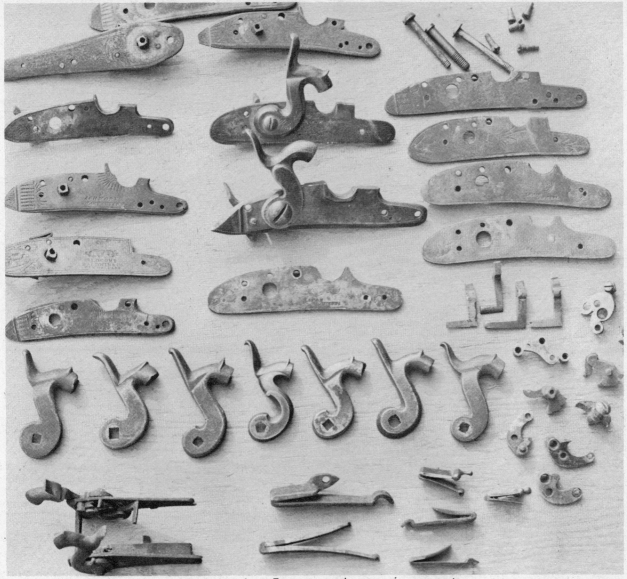

*Both American, European-made percussion gun parts
are in this collection, although most are handmade.*

Being hardened, the plate would cut the semblance of a thread on the shank of the milder steel of the hand-wrought screw. Crude though the screws may seem, there are hundreds of beautiful Kentucky-type rifles still in existence today that are held together by just such screws.

Not only was the gunsmith of a century or more ago a master armsmaker, but usually it was imperative that he master several other trades as well to successfully fulfill his commitments as a gunsmith. Silversmithing, brass casting, steel forging and engraving were all as much a part of the gunsmithing profession as the guns themselves.

Barrel and lock making were phases of gunsmithing commonly taken for granted as a part of the gunsmith's job, but many smiths would purchase ready-made locks, barrels and other needed hardware from foreign markets or sources in the larger cities. These parts then were merely assembled by these so-called experts. The true gunsmith of the old frontier made his arms in their entirely, even to hand forging the steel barrels by many hours of beating and welding the barrel from flat

steel stock. This process was accomplished by anvil forming the flat steel bar, at cherry red heat, around a small round steel rod. This round rod was approximately the same size — slightly less — than the caliber of the intended rifle; this difference is size was to allow for cutting of the lands and grooves into the bore of the finished barrel.

The making of gun springs was a process that required no little knowledge of steel. This phase is one that is sorely lacking in even the most modern so-called gun shops. It is an art in itself and one that can be perfected only through actual practice; the tempering of gun springs cannot be learned from books.

The gunsmith in the wilderness area of young American forged his own springs from the scraps of steel available, heating and anviling this metal to just the correct thickness and density, then dousing it expertly into tallow, fat or other animal grease. The more accomplished used nothing more than plain water to temper springs that were to last well over a century.

Many early gunsmiths, upon completing their apprenticeships, headed for the wilderness settlements of

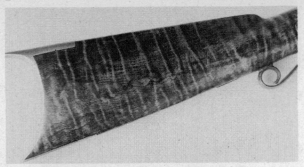

Tiger striping is art accredited to early American gunsmiths. It adds beauty and value to frontier rifles. It's done today by only a few specialists.

The locks are of 1839-1860 period and are typical of Kentucky-type rifles of that era. Lock at top is of European origin; other was forged, handshaped.

the West. They first constructed a shelter in which to live, then threw up seldom more than a crude lean-to in which to practice their chosen profession. Some of these frontier gunshops still are standing throughout the U.S. and are a tribute to the masterful pieces of workmanship in firearms that once were produced in them. There were no such luxuries as air-conditioning; the floor was of earth, in winter they were cold and in summer hot. All tools that graced the walls and work bench were crude by today's standards, but the number and quality of the tools certainly did not indicate the ability of the workman.

The frontier gunsmith, after getting his living quarters and shop constructed, almost immediately would begin

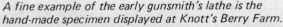

A fine example of the early gunsmith's lathe is the hand-made specimen displayed at Knott's Berry Farm.

searching for a source of well seasoned and aged planking or log wood for use in the manufacture of stocks for his rifles. This wood was preferably well seasoned maple, but due to location, the smith often resorted to other less desirable woods such as walnut and even oak. If no source was available for seasoned stock wood, he would cut wood of his choice from living trees and pile it where it would cure and age properly, to be used in a matter of several years. The drying time of wood greatly depended upon the location and climate of the area.

The stocking of a rifle was painstakingly accomplished with the use of special stocking tools and chisels, all of the gunsmith's own manufacture. Wood bits or drills, often over four-feet long, were completely hand made. These were used in the primary stages of inletting the stock to accept the barrel and were used much as was the lands and grooves cutter mentioned earlier.

When the stock of a rifle was semi-finished, it often was given a "tiger striping" by means of dipping a string of spun wood or flax into a container of pitch or tar. This string then was set afire and allowed to burn into the stock slightly. This left the stock covered with a series of burnt rings more or less equally spaced the full length of the wood.

The stock then was worked down with fine sandstone or other abrasives and finally given a coat of stock varnish mixed with burnt umber or other coloratives. This type of finish on a gun stock is known as "tiger striping" and was applied almost exclusively to maple. One of the most beautiful finishes ever applied to a gun stock, it is strictly an American frontier gunsmith's innovation.

The seat of the gunsmithing profession in America for many years was in the vicinity of Lancaster County, Pennsylvania, so this spot is generally conceded to be the birthplace of the art in this country. In the beginning, it consisted of gun artisans of Dutch and German ancestry. These highly skilled workers soon taught their arts to native American youths who were to be the nucleus of the frontier gunsmith.

Such names as Golcher, Settle, Brooke, Tryon, Deringer and many others had added their illustrious names to a long list of men who were pioneers in the gunsmithing industry. Men who, if handed a block of steel and a stick of wood, could in a short time hand you back a complete shooting gun. These artists accomplished works of the finest form in firearms with seemingly the crudest of tools.

Chapter 38

FORGOTTEN FIREARMS FORMULAE

FOR every problem that may arise in repairing, altering or simply beautifying a gun in this day and age, it is a good bet that a solution was worked out many years ago by some long forgotten village gunsmith in his quest for a better way of doing a job with the primitive tools at hand.

And this knowledge can be of value to the gun fancier of this day, who is interested in working over his own firearms. The very simplicity of many of these forgotten formulas and methods, plus the fact that they could be done with the simplest of tools, makes these processes a natural for the do-it-yourself addict in the arms field.

Some of these formulas still are in daily use and some are even turned out commercially solely for those who revel in refinishing, rebuilding or just plain common every day upkeep of the arms in their shooting arsenal. But, the particular formulae described here have all but been forgotten in this modern age.

For the most part, the older methods are simple to understand and are easy to use, yet have been completely overlooked in the past fifty years or more. These old gunsmithing expedients were concocted and perfected

Section of pipe large enough for gun part, quantity of bone meal and a furnace are needed in order to produce colors in durable case hardening process.

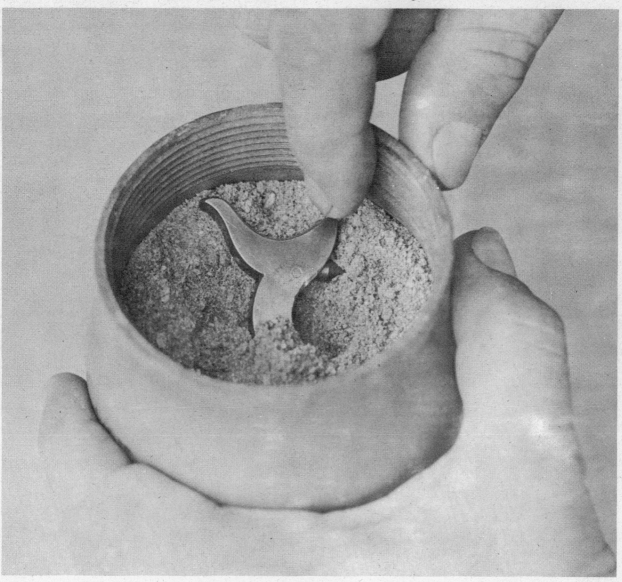

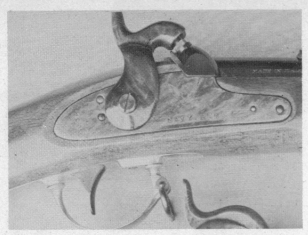

Some replica antique firearms of modern manufacture are beautifully case-hardened in color in Europe. Work usually is accomplished in old-fashioned way.

Few older guns can match beauty of older revolvers from Colt's, which were charcoal blued, the frames case-hardened, using charred leather or bone meal.

they were fired. Barrels and cylinders should be of a tough grade of steel that is flexible enough to withstand expansion and contraction. If the metal is case hardened, this expansion and contraction is minimized. Case hardening should be reserved for such parts as revolver frames, hammers, sears and tumblers and some screws. To case harden other parts of the gun would be inviting trouble.

The processes used many years ago in case hardening are many and greatly varied, but all have the same basic purpose: to make a gun part more durable. Some of these processes are extremely simple and require a minimum of time and effort. Many of the oldtime gunsmiths would heat the particular gun part to a cherry red in a forge or furnace, brush it or dip it in a mixture of cyanide of potassium, then toss it into a tub of water. This process usually was used by the backwoods smithy, whose source of supply was limited, but the craftsman who had better access would endeavor to attain better results. The above formula will perform the job of case hardening, but the finished product is not nearly as durable as others and will wear away with much use of the gun.

One of the older and better formulas for case hardening, one that may be used by the home craftsman is as follows: Obtain a short section of heavy iron pipe which is threaded on both ends to accept a pipe cap; screw one of these caps onto the pipe very tightly. (The pipe should be about three inches in diameter and approximately six inches in length for pistol frames and parts.) Into the open end of the pipe are packed the gun parts to be hardened. The packing is composed of bone dust or meal such as that used by farmers for fertilizing, each part packed in its own section of bone dust with no parts touching each other.

When all parts are well packed into the pipe, the other cap is screwed into place, but not tightly. The entire container then is plunged into hot fire and allowed to remain under a red heat for about fifteen minutes or so, after which the cap is unscrewed and the entire contents dumped into a water bath.

If bone meal or dust are unobtainable, there is another method which consisted of wrapping the gun hammer or parts inside of several layers of leather. Over this was applied a wet compound of salt and sand mixed in equal proportions. Finally, the packet was coated with an inch-thick layer of clay. This was placed in a hot fire and allowed to "cook" under a cherry red heat long

through dire need and in areas where only nature, for the most part, was the source of supply.

One of the most asked questions with regards to old-time formulas has to do with the process for case hardening gun parts; how was it done, and with what materials or equipment?

First, it probably should be explained exactly what case hardening is and the purposes for which it is used. The simplest definition for case hardening is that, through a process of heating and quenching and by the use of certain chemicals or materials, the outer surface of cast or malleable iron or steel is given a tough, wear-resistant coating; a shell of protective highly carbonized steel or iron. This coating will vary in durability with the process and materials used.

Not all guns parts should be given the case hardening treatment for to harden such parts as a revolver cylinder or gun barrel could lead to their shattering when the gun is fired. Barrels and cylinders have been case hardened in the past by certain individuals, and there are instances of these same guns literally disintegrating the first time

Browning solution must be kept in glass container during use. Swab is saturated during the process.

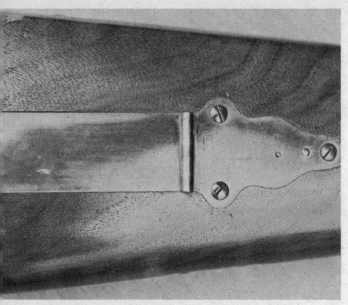

The patch box of this Sharps rifle is beautifully case-hardened, retaining rainbow hues for years.

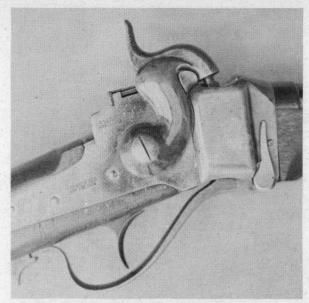

The hammer and lock mechanism, as well as entire frame of this Sharps rifle was color case-hardened, using time-consuming methods that now are obsolete.

enough to consume the leather, after which the parts were dropped into water.

The principle of "browning" a firearm is simply the even rusting of a barrel with the use of certain chemicals. One of the best of these oldtime processes is to make a solution of three-quarters ounce of spirits of nitre; an equal amount of tincture of steel; one-quarter ounce of black brimstone (crude sulphur), one-half ounce of blue vitriol, one-quarter ounce of corrosive sublimate, one drachm of nitric acid and a quarter ounce of copperas. Mix these with a pint of distilled water in a glass bottle (keeping it away from your good tools) and it is then ready to use.

After the barrel has been cleaned thoroughly and glossy polished, making certain that all foreign substances have been removed to prevent spotting of the rusting solution, swab or wipe the solution over the entire barrel and set it in a cool place for at least twenty-four hours. At the end of this time, a rust coating will have formed on the barrel. This is removed with either a

Metal to be browned must be free of dirt or grease before browning solution is even applied to it.

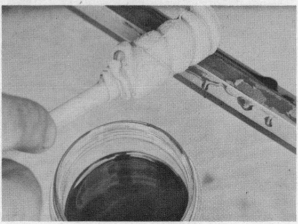

steel brush or steel wool and finally burnished with a woolen cloth. If, at the end of the twenty-four hour period, you find that the coloring is not dark enough, repeat the procedure, swabbing the barrel with solution, then steel wooling it again at the end of the second twenty-four hours. When the correct coloring has been achieved, wash the barrel in clear water, dry thoroughly, then rub it down with linseed oil to prevent further rusting. This formula produces a beautiful finish, if care is taken, and is especially fine for damascus or twist steel barrels as it will bring out the design.

In most of the old formulas, chemicals are mentioned under names which are unfamiliar to many present day pharmacists, but a little checking into a dictionary usually will solve the problem. Several old recipes mention "brimstone" as a component. This is an old term for common sulphur, while black brimstone refers to crude sulphur. Another stumper is the term "dragon's blood," which is nothing more than a colorative derived from vegetable roots that is used in dyes and tints. This term is quite often mentioned in the preparation of stock finishes.

The term, copperas, as used in barrel browning, is nothing more than sulphate of iron, which in turn, is brought about by dissolving iron or iron pyrites in oil of vitriol (more commonly called sulphuric acid). It is interesting to note the change that has undergone in the wording of these chemicals in the last fifty to seventy years. It also brings out the fact that the oldtime gunsmith, out of necessity, did have to know about other things than just working on firearms; his knowledge of chemicals and their uses was an important part of his job.

There are formulas for every phase of gunsmithing, from removing badly rusted nipples and screws from gun frames to sharpening files with diluted acids. There are formulas for the treatment of stock woods and for the casting of brass and iron; formulas for the tempering of gun springs. In fact, the oldtime gunsmiths had a formula for every phase of their works, including the mixing of their own lubricating oils and bore cleaners.

As stated, some of these have been handed down through the years; others have been lost with the passing of their inventors.

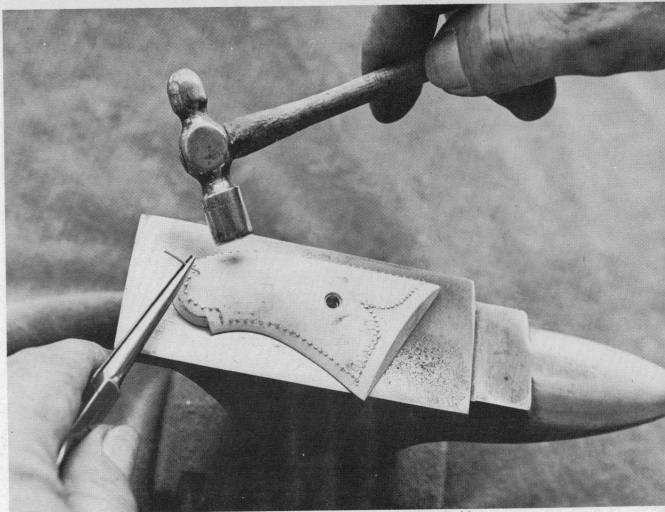

Each of the silver wire pegs must be aligned with
the hole into which it is to be driven; it then
is tapped into place with ballpeen hammer, cut off.

Chapter 39

SILVER PEG IN A ROUND HOLE

A Simple But Attractive Method Of Adding Beauty To Your Handgun Grips

For centuries, armorers have attempted to create the different, the outstanding in arms decoration. A visit to almost any museum will bear out that armament, from crossbow to halbert, blunderbuss to percussion pistol often was literally crusted with ornamentation of some type. Everything from bone and ebony to gold and silver have been used in this form of art.

In past chapters, I have mentioned some of the rare, unusual or exotic materials that might be used in making a pair of pistol grips. But one type of pistol grip decoration, while old, is seen only on rare occasions today! This is silver pegging.

Before going into silver pegging procedures, let's consider grips, themselves, and materials from which they might best be made.

Quite naturally, one doesn't start with a piece of cull wood obtained from an apple crate for a job such as this! The material can be anything in the so-called rare or exotic line of materials. Included may be finely figured French or burl walnut, coca-bola, cherry wood, bubinga, zebra wood, striped maple, ivory and others too numerous to mention. The basic theory in turning out a set of custom grips is to make them beautiful, unusual and unique. The term, "custom," means exclusive and something that cannot be purchased on

sharp awl or scribe for marking the locations of the silver pegs; a steel drill, the size of which will be discussed; a small ballpeen hammer, a pair of small wire cutters and a pair of diminitive needle-nosed pliers. For final finishing, a ten-inch mill bastard file, a small piece of fine garnet sandpaper and an electric buffer will be needed.

Silver pegging is simple, but requires drilling hundreds of small holes in a precise and decorative design. The exact number of holes depends upon the complexity of the design sketched on the grip with a lead pencil. Into each of these holes is tapped a section of silver wire, after which the wire is nipped off at the surface of the grip material with wire cutters.

The only materials needed are a set of grips and a section of silver wire. This sterling silver wire is available at most lapidary supply shops and usually is sold by the foot. Cost depends upon the gauge desired. I used 24-gauge silver wire, which cost about fifty cents a foot. A foot or so of this wire should be sufficient for several pairs of grips, even if complex designs are utilized. If using 24-gauge wire, a No. 57 steel drill will provide the tight holes into which the silver wire is driven.

The first phase is to lay out a design to your liking on the rounded surface of the grips with a sharp lead pencil. The design completed, take the sharp awl or scribe and center-punch the entire design outline, spacing punched holes one-eighth-inch or less apart. This center-punching is to provide a starting dent for the point of the steel

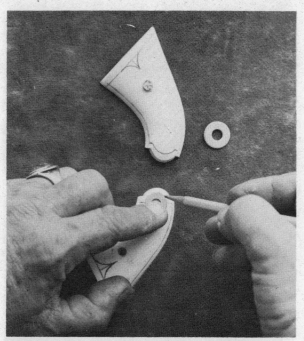

If grips are new and fitted to gun's frame, they are left unpolished for layout of the desired design. The outline can be drawn on surface with soft pencil.

With a hand-held awl or one chucked in drill press, penciled design can be outlined with a series of shallow dents. An ordinary punch also can be used.

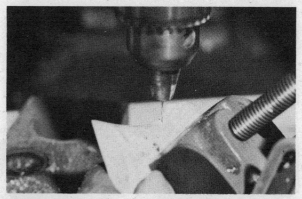

Drilling holes is done with a hand-held electric drill or grips can be held in vise with a tilting base. The holes then are made at an angle to grip.

the general market. If the grips aren't made neatly and precisely, the exclusive term hardly applies.

The pegging method of gun ornamentation can be applied by any substance of reasonable texture and hardness. While elephant ivory is used here, it is only because the author had just finished the grips and decided to trim them up a bit with silver. However, the only source of ivory of which I know is from ivory dealers on the east coast of Africa and I do not know the addresses!

The tools needed for the job are few and simple: a

drill. This prevents the drill from possibly walking away from the pencil line.

Drill out each of these dents to no more than one-eighth-inch in depth. In drilling around the edges of the grips, where the material is thinnest, be sure to guide the drill straight in toward the center of the grip. This prevents the drill from completely penetrating the thickness. This is done best on a drill press with each grip held in a drilling vise capable of being tilted to the proper angle for each series of holes.

If all holes have been drilled in each of the two grips, all are in perfect alignment with the original pencil sketched design and each is cut cleanly and free of drill dust and cuttings, we are ready to do the actual pegging.

Due to the softness of sterling silver wire, I have found it best to cut a quantity of short pieces about three-eighths of an inch in length. These short wire sections are held easily in the jaw of the needle-nose pliers and will not bend to any extent, when tapped gently into the drilled holes. Each of these short wires will provide sufficient material for about three pegs. The peg of silver wire is cut off flush with the grip material the moment after it is tapped into the hole, the remaining portion of the wire is carried to the next hole and tapped into place.

Each silver peg is tapped gently into each of the holes, until it seats on the bottom of the hole, then is

The butt section of the grip also can be pegged, using exactly the same working methods described.

With pegs driven into the grip, the entire surface is filed to blend the material into smooth finish.

Coverage for pegged silver depends on individual taste. Conservative border, silver shield were used.

In this instance, more modern sights were installed on gun after pegging. This is discussed elsewhere.

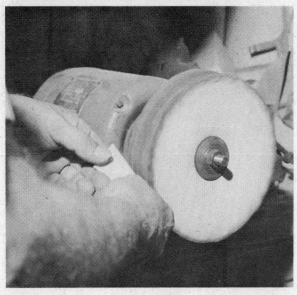

After filing and sanding until smooth, grips are buffed with muslin wheel, white buffing compound.

nipped off with the cutters. Use a light hammer for this purpose and tap — do not pound — the silver wire into place!

When all pegs have been tapped into place and the design completed, the protruding stubs of the pegs are filed, until they are flush with the surface of the grip material. The grips are sanded thoroughly with fine garnet sandpaper until both the grip material and the silver pegs are blended into a flawless, smooth surface. The grips now should be buffed on a muslin wheel. In the case of semi-precious woods, such as walnuts, the entire surface should be coated with a good stock finishing preparation.

Should the grips be of ivory or other similiar animal matter, a coat of paste wax is all that is necessary for the final finish after buffing.

Designs with silver pegging are limited only by the scope of one's imagination. There is no limit to the extent to which one might go in producing unique floral or scroll designs. The heads of trophy game animals or the owner's initials might be reproduced in sterling silver in a set of pistol grips or even the stock of a rifle or shotgun. However, silver pegging consumes far more time to execute than does inlaying sheet silver.

The ivory grips made by the author were for a replica 1858 Remington .44 revolver to show what can be accomplished on the grips of any handgun, regardless of make, model or age. The principles of silver pegging are the same for all. Just use your own imagination in creating your own designs.

Chapter 40

HORN OF PLENTY

Building This Powder Horn Should Help The Black Powder Shooter Keep Smoking!

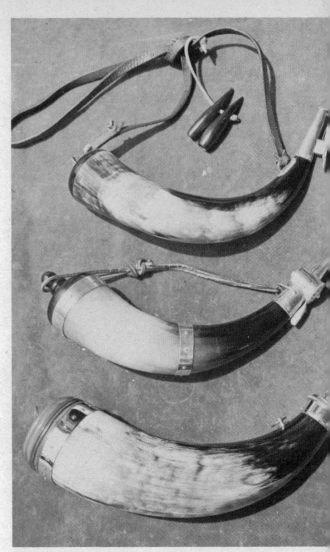

The powder horn is almost as old as gunpowder itself. When gunpowder was adopted as a means of hurling a projectile through space to down game or an enemy, a means of carrying powder was essential. This container had to be impervious to the weather, watertight and of a substance that didn't contract moisture or sweat in humid climates, clotting the powder and making it useless.

Black powder containers of both wood and leather have been used in countries all over the world. Someone thought of using either hollow cow's horn or a section of stag antler for storing and carrying the supply of powder. Horn and antlers are waterproof and will not sweat under any weather conditions. For centuries horn and antler have been carved into works of art.

Properly constructed, the powder horn could be sub-

The type of spout incorporated in a powder horn can be drawn from any number of varieties, as shown.

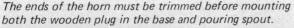

The ends of the horn must be trimmed before mounting both the wooden plug in the base and pouring spout.

merged in water for considerable time without seriously affecting it contents. Cow horn will not absorb moisture, although stag antler will to some extent.

In later years, elaborate flasks were manufactured in Europe and America of brass and copper. These flasks usually were adorned with elaborate hunting or patriotic scenes, floral patterns, basket weave designs and others. However, the old powder horn made from one of Bossie's protective projections continued the favorite among frontiersmen where hard use was the order of the day. The brass and copper flasks were subject to smashing and denting, while the horn was of a more resilient nature. The natural curve of the horn itself made it ideal for carrying, and if properly shaped, it rode naturally and comfortably on either hip.

The powder horn still is very much in use today by the clan of modern muzzleloading marksmen.

With the current firearms laws being what they are, muzzle gun shooting has taken on new life. Thousands of shooters, both target paper punchers and hunters, have taken up the front loader and the era of the charcoal burner is far from being over!

Other than the rifle or pistol, one needs a bullet mould and a powder horn.

Building a powder horn requires few tools and materials.

Installation of the pouring spout requires that the small end of the horn be filed and sanded until the spout is a snug slide fit, then attached with screws.

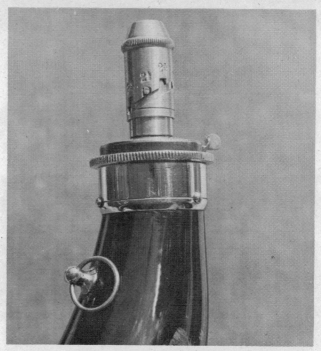

Adjustable powder measure incorporated on the spout is available from Dixie Gun works. However, a less elaborate type can be built by individual craftsmen.

A horn can be obtained from the Dixie Gun Works of Union City, Tennessee, for a couple of dollars. The only others needs are a wooden plug and a spout or measuring device to be attached to the small end of the horn.

The first chore is to file, sand, scrape and finally polish the horn to a luster on a muslin buffing wheel treated with white compound.

Next, cut, install and shape the wooden plug that fills the base of the horn. This is cut perfectly circular in shape

The wooden base plug can be turned on wood lathe or simply by spinning on a steel bolt chucked to electric motor. Numerous designs thus are possible. This particular design is known as the beehive type.

and slightly larger than the outside diameter of the horn's base. The edges of the plug then are tapered — somewhat cone-shaped — to the point that it can be forced into the base of the horn. Should the base be irregular in shape, submerge this section of the horn into scalding hot water for a few minutes. When the horn has softened, the plug is forced into the void as far as it will go, leaving a portion of the wood extending beyond the edge of the horn, this excess will be rounded and polished during actual finishing.

Woods such as figured walnut, curly or birdseye maple can be used for this plug. Once the horn has cooled with the plug in place, the plug then is removed and the edges coated with waterproof cement or epoxy. The plug is replaced in the base of the horn and bradded in place with small nails of solid brass. (Steel or iron nails will rust quickly and erode). The horn then is set aside to allow the cement to dry thoroughly.

The excess wood still protruding from the horn base is filed or disc sanded until round. It is sanded with various grades of paper until smooth, then is finished in the same manner as would be a gunstock.

The smaller end of the horn may be treated in several ways. It may be filed for various ornamental shapes and a small wood peg used as a stopper or one may manufacture his own pouring spout from brass or copper. A flask-type top is available from Dixie Arms Company that has an automatic shut-off thumb-piece and a graduated measuring spout attached. This is of solid brass and is the type found on early brass and copper powder flasks.

It is possible that the hollow may not run far enough up the horn to provide an opening at the small end. If such is the case, drill out that section of the horn, using a quarter-inch drill. Run the drill in, until it meets the hollow of the horn.

Some provision should be made for attaching a carrying cord or strap. A powder horn may be etched with names, places, events and dates or mounted with ornamentation in silver or brass, such as eagles, buffalos or elk and the like. When completed, the horn once more is buffed on a soft muslin wheel, then waxed to a high gloss.

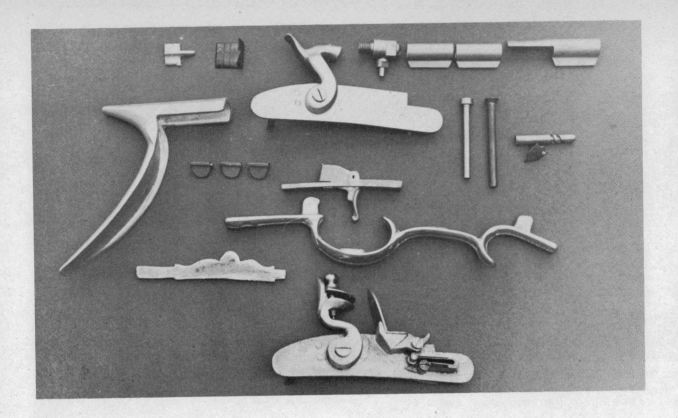

Chapter 41

BUILD YOUR OWN KENTUCKY RIFLE

When a new build-it-yourself kit for a Kentucky-type rifle was delivered to my doorstep, I realized it was from Turner Kirkland, who operates the Dixie Gun Works down in Union City, Tennessee. He had mentioned plans for such a kit earlier, wondering whether he should go into production. The decision had been made, if the receipt of this kit was an indication!

In no uncertain terms, a kit such as this requires far more than mere assembly. Hours and hours of hard work, plus a little know-how in the proper use of hand tools and a reasonable knowledge of Kentucky rifle design is necessary. But in the end, there is the potential of a rifle that, in addition to being a beautiful firearm to hang on the wall, can also be a fine, vintage-type hunting arm for the muzzleloading enthusiast.

In this and subsequent articles. we will attempt to show how this kit should be assembled, affording the student of gunsmithing a step-by-step program.

Should a person not possess a thorough knowledge of the use of common hand tools, files and chisels in particular, and have an understanding of the basic Kentucky Pennsylvania rifle design — to say nothing of infinite patience — it is my confirmed opinion that he will be far better off not to attempt the building of this, or any other, type of rifle.

To undertake the building of this Kentucky-type rifle kit will literally tie a person to a work bench in all of his spare hours for several weeks.

In unwrapping the old newspapers that held the many and varied unfinished parts, I was somewhat surprised to note that the lock plate and tang screws were mere blanks. They weren't threaded nor were the screw driver slots cut into the heads. This was a minor problem however as my small but adequate shop is well supplied with threading taps and dies

— and a hacksaw would cut the screw driver slots in a few moments.

The butt plate and trigger guard were unfinished brass castings which would require a couple of hours of hand filing and polishing. The trigger and trigger-plate were of cast iron but with minor filing and cleaning up, they would prove adequate.

The pre-turned stock was of plain, tough maple, strong and straight grained and reasonably well inletted along the barrel channel. The ramrod slot, a big job when building a stock such as this from scratch, is nicely pre-cut and requires little or no revamping.

Included in this kit is a forty-inch octagonal barrel and while these barrels are available in some five calibers, from .32 up to .50 caliber, the one furnished in our kit is of .40 caliber and measures thirteen-sixteenths of an inch across the flats. These barrels are fitted with pre-installed breech plugs and are beautifully rifled with one turn in forty-eight inches. Made of carbon manganese steel, these barrels alone make the job of building one of these rifles well worthwhile.

All in all, this Dixie Rifle kit contains the nucleus of what can be turned into a fine Kentucky-type rifle. Just how fine the finished rifle is depends upon the man making it, and how many long hours of labor he is willing to donate to its construction.

In building one of these rifles it is well to remember that there is no set pattern for the final design or decorations that may be incorporated into the building of these vintage-type weapons. Every genuine Kentucky rifle has its own characteristics of design and no two are ever exactly alike, so you may let your imagination run rampant should you care to go the limit as far as inlays, patch boxes et cetera are concerned. Let's proceed with the actual building of the rifle from this kit.

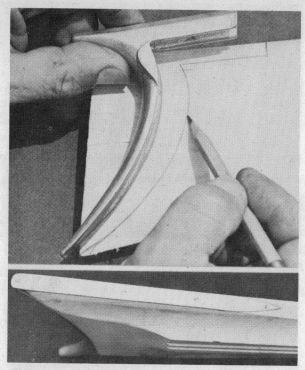

The contour of the brass butt plate is transferred to stock with soft lead pencil, cut with coping saw.

Installed, the butt plate is filed or disc sanded to the contour of the adjoining wood of the stock.

Step One — Installing the brass butt and toe plate:

In building one of these rifles, it is proper procedure to begin the construction by working from the butt plate forward, completing each phase to the best of your ability, then moving on to the next section to be shaped, installed or worked upon.

Installation of the brass butt plate may seem a simple chore but can prove to be a headache to even the most practiced gunsmith. The butt end of the maple stock first must be cut to the exact shape of the brass butt plate after first, and very carefully, drawing the contour of the butt plate onto the stock with a soft lead pencil. This section then is carefully removed by cutting with a coping saw. It is finished to exact shape with the use of a half-round file until the brass butt plate seats perfectly in place.

Following the precision fitting of the butt plate — an operation that requires the greatest of patience in order to assure a perfect fit — the butt plate then is drilled and counter sunk to accept the two retaining screws that will hold it in place on the stock. The butt plate is placed on the stock and the two holes transcribed with a pencil mark onto the wood, then drilled to a depth of approximately one inch with a one-eighth of an inch drill.

Following the drilling of these holes, the butt plate is screwed onto the stock, using brass screws, where it will remain permanently. After installation, the excess brass of the butt plate that extends beyond the wood of the stock is filed or disc sanded until it is flush with the wood. At this point, we will merely get various components installed; later we will return to them for final polishing and dressing down to final shape.

Installation of the toe plate is a fairly simple chore in that a strip of 18-gauge brass is inletted and secured with small brass screws, after which it is dressed down as was the butt plate. This toe plate may be of any length desired by the individual; there is no set length, the purpose being to protect the toe of the stock from chipping should the rifle be accidently dropped on the butt. The toe plate end may be cut or filed into various designs but a plain pointed design is used in the illustration.

Step Two — Inletting the barrel:

It is necessary now to inlet the barrel into the pre-cut channel of the stock before proceeding to the installation of other components such as the lock, trigger and trigger guard.

It will be found that the pre-cut barrel channel of the stock requires only minor fitting in the section that accepts the barrel tang and the rear lower portion of the breech plug. This section of the stock must be chiseled out to accept the tang in a snug, even tight, fit.

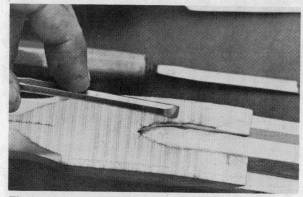

The barrel tang is inletted below the surface of the wood to allow for exacting shaping and fitting.

Following the careful inletting of this section, it will now be possible to slide the barrel into the entire channel in a tight squeeze fit, making certain that the barrel is fully seated into the channel until an equal amount of side-flat of the octagon barrel is visible for the full length of the stock. Do not drill a hole in the tang to accept the tang screw. This will be done, after trigger plate is installed. The tang screw will be threaded into, and anchored at the trigger plate after this plate is installed.

Step Three — Inletting and Installing the Lock:

This one phase of building a rifle of this type, whether in flint or percussion lock, is one of the most important and is certainly one that can make that big difference in a rifle that is well built and one that has been cobbled together in a hurry.

The placing of the rifle lock is all important in that the hammer nose must be in perfect alignment with the correctly placed drum and nipple — or in the case of a flintlock, the touch hole. The ·drum and nipple of the percussion lock, or the touch hole of the flintlock must be so placed as to be no more than one-fourth of an inch ahead of the breech plug face which extends into the barrel roughly about one-half to five-eighths of an inch.

Some years ago, I owned a fine Bedford County, Pennsylvania flintlock rifle. In addition to its many distinguishing features, it had a lock plate that was outlined with a border of inlaid brass. I never ceased to admire the intricate workmanship that went into the inlaying of the brass around the lock plate, and I decided to attempt just such a job myself in the building of this Dixie rifle kit. Needless to say, this one job was no little chore so I do not recommend the novice, undertaking it unless he has had extensive practice in inlaying and shaping of metal of this type.

With the barrel tightly in place in the stock, and after pre-determining the exact location of the breech plug face and marking its location on the stock with a pencil, one should make another mark as to the exact location where the drum and nipple assembly or touch hole will be placed. The lock then is disassembled completely and the bare lock plate is placed on the flat of the stock. It is carefully traced with a soft lead pencil for outline while making certain that the hammer face will correspond exactly with the alignment of the touch hole or drum and nipple.

With the lock plate traced onto the flat surface of the stock in the exact correct position with regard to hammer — touch hole or drum and nipple alignment, an assortment of sharp chisels is used to inlay the lock plate into the wood until the reinforcing bar, that thick portion of the lock plate, lies snuggly against· the side flat of the barrel.

Again, the neatness of this lock plate inlaying will determine the final appearance of the finished rifle, so take your time here and do a precise job of inletting that lock plate until it is a snug fit into the morticed-out section.

With the lock plate inlaid into the stock, it is again fully assembled. It is now time to do the inletting for the lock's working parts, or "innards" so that the lock, when fully assembled, will slide into the inletted section in a snug fit.

Careful note must be made of each lock part and its relation to the stock cut-out after which a drawing is made of these parts on the bottom of the new cut-out in the stock. Each screw head, springs and

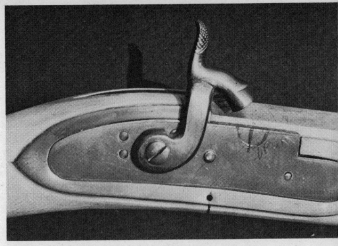

Once inletted, lock plate is placed in the stock mortise, marked so that there will be no problem in proper placement of drum, nipple, touch hole.

bridle must be given consideration in relation to the depth that they will require for·full clearance in the cut-out, or inletted section that accepts the fully accepted lock plate.

Following this position marking for the lock's working parts, the chisels are again brought into use to remove the necessary wood. During this operation it will be necessary to drill a clearance hole with a one-fourth of an inch drill for the sear. This hole should not be much over the total length of the sear (about one inch) in depth; just enough to give it sufficient clearance to operate and no more.

The working parts of the lock mechanism should be polished and honed before final assembly of the the rifle when finished but this will be left up to the individual builder as to just how finely finished he might want the overall rifle when completed.

With the lock inletted into the stock, the builder may then proceed to shape the area around the lock plate to suit his own tastes. If a design such as is shown in the accompanying photographs is desired, this may be accomplished with the use of large rat-tail files and a half-round file. As stated before, no

When kit was received, spur of the hammer (left) was smooth, was checkered with three-corner file (right).

For proper inletting, the lock should be dismantled, lock plate used as a template to mark the outline.

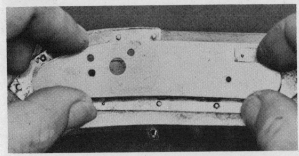

two Kentucky-type rifles are alike in finish or design, so use your own imagination here.

On the opposite side of the stock from the lock plate, you also may create a design to border the reinforcing plate that accepts the lock plate screw. This screw, a blank, unthreaded and with no screw driver slot when received, may be threaded with a 10-24 threading die and the head slotted with a hack saw. A hole then is drilled in an appropriate location on the left side of the rifle, through the reinforcing plate, and a hole drilled and threaded with a 10-24 tap into the lock plate to accept, in perfect alignment, the lock plate screw. This is the screw that will hold the lock plate to the rifle during its entire life time, so make certain that it, and the drilled hole for it, are perfectly aligned and true.

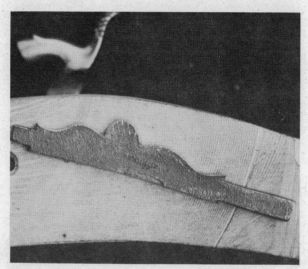

When received, lock reinforcing plate is rough and not drilled. It must be placed exactly to assure proper alignment with proposed screw holes in lock plate located on the right side of the stock (below). It is inletted as shown and filed flush with stock.

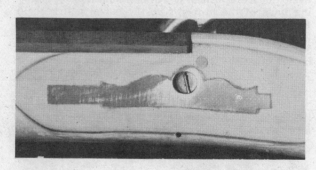

The side plate is inletted into the left side of the stock directly opposite the lock plate, and will serve as a reinforcing bar as well as a decorative inlay through which the two lock retaining screws will pass. Keep in mind that this side plate may vary in design with each builder's taste as there are no hard-set rules for its design, whether large of small, nor its depth of inletting.

Some builders prefer to leave this plate extending slightly above the surface of the wood, beveling its edges, thusly creating a more individualistic appearance when the rifle finally is finished. However, and to simplify this part of the rifle's construction, we will utilize the side plate furnished with the Dixie Gun

Works Kit and inlet it flush with the wood of the stock.

The side plate is placed on the flat of the stock so that its position is in exact alignment with that of the lock plate and outlined with a sharp, soft lead pencil. The plate must be placed so that the two retaining screws that will hold the lock in place on the stock will be in perfect alignment with those areas of the lock plate that will be drilled and tapped to accept these screws.

After outlining the side plate with a sharp pencil, the area within the pencilled line then is chiselled away until the side plate may be pressed into the recess in a snug fit. The lock plate then is reinstalled on the stock and the exact placement of the two retaining screws determined. These screws must be placed so that they do not interfere with any of the lock's working parts. Center punch the location of these two holes on the side plate and drill with a #9 drill, completely penetrating the side plate and the wood of the stock until the drill is stopped by the metal of the lock plate.

Allow the drill to score a mark on the lock plate to assure that the holes to be drilled and tapped in the lock plate are properly positioned. The lock plate is then removed from the stock, the scoring mark made by the drill noted and center punched. With a #25 drill, drill these two holes completely through the lock plate and tap them out with a 10 x 24 tap.

It also is necessary to thread the lock plate screw furnished with the kit and to cut a screw driver slot in its head with a hack saw. Quite naturally you will use a 10 x 24 die to thread this screw.

Following the drilling and tapping of these holes, the lock plate is again placed into its recess in the stock, the screws inserted into the holes in the side plate until they contact the threaded holes of the lock plate and are then drawn up, with a screw driver, until the lock plate is firmly in place on the stock. It will be noted that the retaining screws must be shortened in order to be flush with the outside surface of the lock plate. This is easily accomplished by first cutting the screws to the proper length, then dressing the threaded end up with a fine file or disc sander.

In the case of the rifle being built for this article, I placed the 10 x 24 threaded screw as near the center of the lock plate as possible without interfering with any of the lock's working parts. The front screw consists of one of a smaller size (8 x 32) and acts as an added stabilizer for the lock plate.

Before going too far into the installation of the trigger assembly and trigger guard, it is best to first "dress up" all of these parts, removing all roughness left by the casting process from their surfaces. This assures a more precise and neater installation. This

In inletting trigger plate and guard, there must be proper alignment with sear bar of lock mechanism.

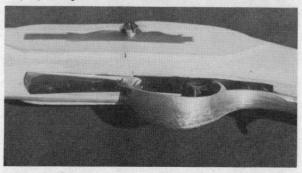

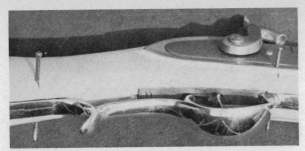

Before final installation, trigger guard is polished to luster. Temporary installation is made with nails.

is best done with the use of a variety of small files, emery cloth, buffing wheels and, if available, a disc sander.

It will be noted that the top-most part of the trigger has a bar-like extension. This bar is that part of the trigger that engages the sear bar when the trigger is pulled, thus allowing the sear to be disengaged and allowing the hammer to fall.

In the installation of the trigger plate (that part to which the trigger is attached) it is a comparatively simple matter to align the trigger bar so that it will properly engage the sear bar when all relative components are assembled into this section of the rifle.

After determining the proper positioning of the trigger plate and outlining it with a pencil, just as you did with the lock plate and side plate, a small chisel or wood router in a drill press is brought into play. A slot is cut to accept the upper part of the trigger assembly, allowing it to engage the sear bar of the lock freely. At the same time, the stock is inletted to accept the trigger plate itself after which a one-eighth-inch hole is drilled into the rear portion of the trigger plate, counter sunk, and a small wood screw is installed to hold this plate in place on the stock.

The proper positioning and installation of the trigger guard consists of inletting each end extension of the guard, itself, and providing additional inletted slots to accept the pin tabs which will secure the trigger guard to the stock.

Following this inletting, it is wise to either clamp or tightly squeeze the trigger guard extensions in the area of the pin tabs before drilling the pin holes with a three-thirty-second-inch drill. This will assure that the trigger guard and extensions are well seated and more rigid when held in place by the retaining pins which may be from common nails of the proper size.

Provided with the Dixie Gun Works kit are three barrel lugs, or tabs, used for securing the barrel to the stock. These lugs must be dressed to a shape that will readily be accepted into a dove-tail slot cut into the barrel with the use of a hack saw and a three-cornered file.

On the rifle being built for this article, the first dove-tail was cut exactly four inches to center from the muzzle and the two additional lugs were placed exactly fourteen inches to center apart, using the center of the first lug as a starting point. After cutting the slots and installing the lugs, each was soft soldered in place to assure rigidity.

Following the installation of the three lugs on the under side of the barrel, the barrel then is squeezed into the barrel channel of the stock until the lugs contact and slightly dent the wood of the barrel channel.

Remove the barrel from the stock and, with the use of small chisels, inlet the three dented areas to accept the barrel lugs. It no doubt will be necessary to replace the barrel on the stock several times to determine when the exact amount of wood has been removed to allow the lugs to seat fully into the recesses in the stock. **A series of measurements** will be necessary to determine the exact location that the holes will be drilled for the retaining pins. These holes must be drilled through the stock and barrel lugs in unison. The measurements are best made by first determining the exact center of the lugs then marking these centers onto the stock. The next important measurement is made by using the bottom flat of the barrel channel in the stock itself as the final factor in locating the exact area to drill the three pin holes with three-thirty-seconds-inch drill.

The locating of these holes, which must be exacting, is a simple matter, but it is best to be absolutely certain of their location before actual drilling. When these holes are drilled, it will be found that by inserting nails of the proper size, the barrel will be held firmly to the stock's forearm section.

The sights furnished with this kit, while usable, are quite crude. The front sight consists of a rough casting of brass, which I replaced with one of my own

Trigger assembly and plate must be placed precisely for positive contact of trigger bar to the sear bar.

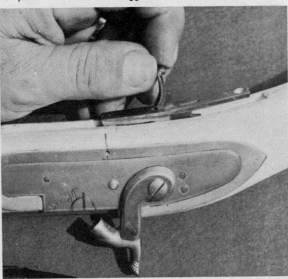

While sights were furnished like one in foreground, Bish used more refined type, shown installed.

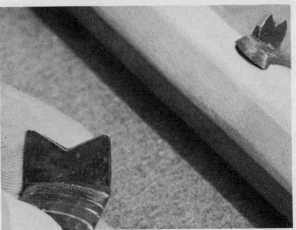

manufacture that is similar. There are any number of commercially made sights that one might incorporate into one of these replica rifles for shooting purposes.

Both front and rear sights may be installed in dovetail slots. The placement of the front sight should be within two inches of the muzzle while the rear sight should be placed 32 to 34 inches from the muzzle for the best sighting radius on a forty-inch barrel.

Precise workmanship is a prime requisite to a finely finished rifle. Where corners are meant to be square, make them square. Where curves and contours are encountered, make them graceful! Where the inletting of inlays or component parts are concerned, take your time. Make each inlay a tight fit into the chiseled out recess.

It will be necessary, before the rifle is finished, to manufacture and install such items as the fore-end cap, patch box, barrel pin escutcheon plates, ornamental inlays, ramrod thimbles and last comes the final finishing of the stock.

Barrel lugs to accept stock retaining pin are set in dovetails, then soldered in place for strength.

Dovetail slots are cut into the top flat of barrel with a variety of files, then are finished with a gunsmith's slotting file. (Below) Sight is in place.

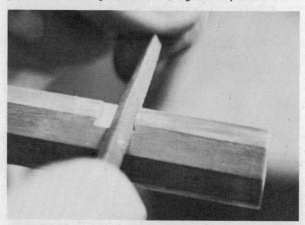

ing wood slightly so that when the stock has received its final sanding, the wood and the brass at this point will create a smooth, even surface with no lumps or bumps to detract from the rifle's overall appearance.

Whether you are building a percussion lock or a flintlock will determine the method employed in drilling the barrel to accept these locks.

With a flintlock, the hammer is already aligned perfectly with the frizzen and pan so it is only necessary at this point to drill the small touch hole which will allow the powder in the flash pan to reach the load in the barrel. This touch hole, or vent hole, should be drilled only slightly above the bottom of the flash pan in order to assure a more spontaneous detonation of the charge in the barrel, and should be no larger than three-sixty-fourths-inch in size The exact location of the breech plug must be determined prior to drilling the vent hole to assure that the vent hole enters the barrels interior just forward of the breech plug face. It is permissible to drill the vent hole on an angle in order to prevent it hitting the breech plug.

The installation of the drum and nipple on a percussion lock rifle presents a more complex problem in that the face of the hammer must be pre-aligned with the drum and nipple before the barrel is drilled and tapped to accept the drum.

Following the installation of the drum on the bar-

Brass forend cap is from sheet brass. Construction is identical Mannlicher snobble shown in Chapter 21.

The fore-end cap, not furnished in the Dixie kit, is available from this source at modest cost. Or it may be made quite easily from a small sheet of 18-gauge brass measuring approximately two inches square. This brass is bent and shaped to the rounded contour of the pre-prepared stock at the muzzle. An end piece is then silver soldered on one end of the rounded cap and later trimmed and cut, in an exacting fit, to match the size and shape of the octagon barrel. (Dixie Gun Works can furnish these barrels in various barrel sizes and calibers.)

The completed muzzle cap then is installed on the pre-prepared and shaped wood of the forearm with a good mastic cement. It makes a far neater job if the muzzle cap is inletted below the surface of the adjoin-

rel, by first drilling and tapping the barrel at the pre-determined location, and filing a half circle cut-out in the lock plate to accept the drum, the face of the percussion hammer should, if in correct alignment, seat squarely onto the mouth of the nipple. It is quite possible to bend or re-shape slightly the position of the hammer until it is in perfect alignment with the nipple but this hammer bending must be done with the hammer removed from the lock to prevent damage to the lock itself

At this point in the rifle's construction it is time to begin the semi-finish shaping of the stock, itself, a pre-requisite to the inletting of the barrel pin escutcheons, patchbox, and ornamental inlays.

Prior to this operation, however, we must install the tang screw. This screw, in addition to holding the breech section of the barrel firmly in the stock, also will be threaded into the trigger plate, holding both the tang section of the barrel and trigger plate in place.

The tang first is drilled and counter-sunk to accept the head of the tang screw after which it is placed on the stock. Using this hole as a guide for the drill, the wood of the stock is drilled downward until the drill point contacts the metal of the trigger plate at the front of the trigger. The drill again is allowed to score the trigger plate after which the trigger plate is removed, drilled and tapped until it will accept the threads of the tang screw. During this operation care must be taken to drill this tang screw hole at such an angle through the stock that it does not interfere with the lock mechanism.

Starting at the butt of the rifle, using files of various shapes and garnet sandpaper graduated in grits from medium course to extra fine, the entire stock is worked down to the desired shape and dimensions that please the builder.

The area around the lock and side plate, may be given a raised or sculptured look with the use of rat-tail files. The stock receives its final shaping during this operation, leaving only minor sanding to be done once the inlays are in the stock.

Also during this phase, thought might be given to the type of finish on the barrel and lock assembly. Most genuine rifles of this type had all steel hardware in what is known as a "browned" finish.
Actually, this type is nothing more than a well but evenly rusted coating applied to the steel parts with a chemical solution. The Dixie Gun Works can furnish this solution at a buck a bottle. It is easily applied and will leave a lustrous red finish.

I chose to blue both the barrel and the flintlock assembly. For this chore I utilized a product of the Jet-Aer Corporation, of Paterson, New Jersey. Their excellent Solid Gun Blue Creme is easily applied in a few minutes for a most beautiful deep blue finish to the steel.

If you are after authenticity, then by all means brown it. But should you be wanting this rifle strictly for hunting and shooting purposes, then you cannot go far wrong by bluing it.

The installation of the barrel lugs and retaining pins which hold the barrel firmly to the stock were

The raised portion of the stock around the lock plate is shaped with rattail files, elbow grease.

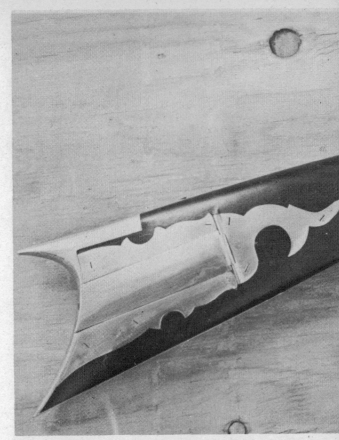

The brass trim on the rifle, including the butt plate, the patch box, trigger guard and the inlays add greatly to the overall appearance, but to be fully effective, they all must be properly fitted.

explained earlier in this chapter. The barrel retaining pins, utilized on many of the early rifles of this type built in the Southern states, were left unsupported by escutcheon plates. However, it is best to support these pins by adding this vital reinforcement to prevent undue wear to the pin holes in the stock.

These escutcheon plates may be cut from sheet brass with a jeweler's saw or may be ordered from the Dixie Gun Works at a nominal price. They are not included in the kit.

Correct installation of the escutcheon plates requires that one plate be center punched and drilled to the same size as the barrel retaining pin. Then place this plate directly into position on one side of the stock, letting the slightly protruding barrel pin hold it in place. It then is outlined with a sharp pencil and inletted until its surface is flush with that of the wood. This plate will act as a guide in drilling the hole through the opposite plate which is installed in the same manner. All inlays may be cemented in place or they may be held with tiny wood screws. This procedure is repeated with all six of the barrel pin escutcheon plates. The pins holding the ramrod thimbles in place do not require these plates as the thimbles are a part of the rifle that need never to be removed.

For installation and inletting of various hex or good luck inlays, such as the eight-pointed star, the crooked heart, the fish or other inlays commonly found on rifles of this type, all are easily cut from sheet brass, then finished with small files prior to the inletting.

While I utilized a patch box, which I altered somewhat, that Turner Kirkland sent along, these can be made quite easily by the tool-wise craftsman in designs to suit his own tastes.

The inletting of the patch box can prove to be the biggest headache in building the entire rifle. Should the patch box selected have numerous cutouts, or open work, the job of inletting is multiplied greatly. The patch box should be extremely well fitted and contoured to the rounded shape of the stock and butt plate so as to not be a nuisance when the rifle is handled and fired from the shoulder. Some modern-made replica Kentucky rifles I have seen have patch boxes installed in such a manner that they flip open each time they are brushed against a coat or shirt sleeve. When you install your patch box, make it snag proof!

In installing the patch box, make careful measurements of that section where the hinge and spring are located. This will be inletted into the stock first and will allow the patch box to lie perfectly flat on the wood for tracing.

Crooked heart was popular hex sign during the era of popularity for Kentucky rifle, research shows.

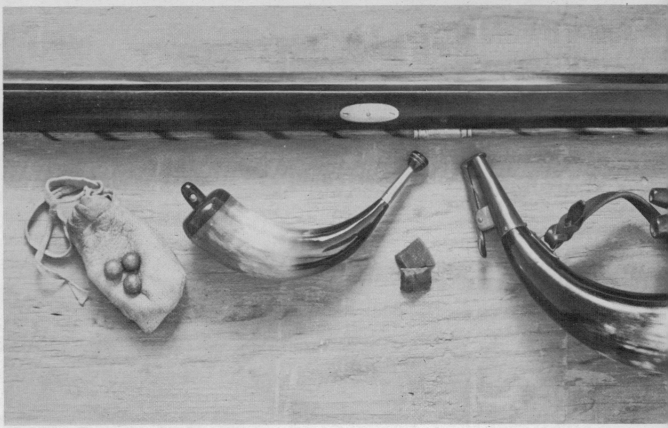

The finished rifle, complete with priming horn, a powder horn and buckskin bullet pouch, makes ideal combination for hunter wanting to try black powder.

Sufficient clearance must be allowed for the spring bending as the patch box is opened and closed. Insufficient clearance will result in the gate of the patch box either binding or rendered incapable of being opened at all.

During the inletting for the patch box, where large, but thin, sections of the wood must be precisely removed, I have found that a set of small wood carving chisels manufactured by the Miller Falls Tool Company is well suited to the chore. They

Inlaying of the stock decoration is accomplished with sharp chisels, inletting metal below surface.

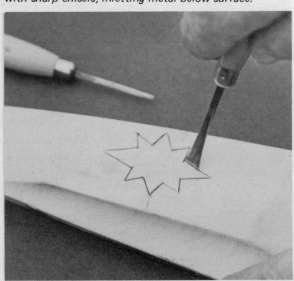

The inlay then is sanded to the exact surface of the stock, finished along with stock in final phase.

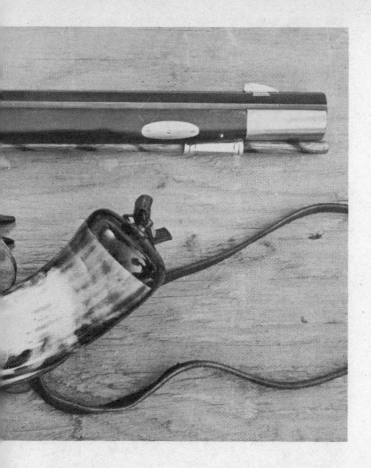

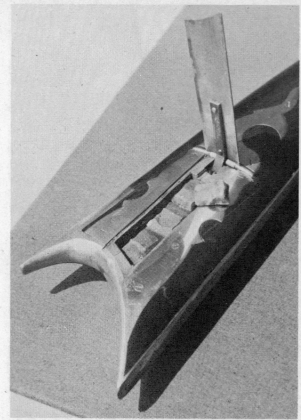

Patch box should be recessed enough to accept extra flints or patches. The lid of box is spring-loaded.

are kept sharp on a good oil stone, and by buying several sets, I have been able to reshape, grind down in width and thickness, a number of them in order to have a more diversified selection for the more minute cuts in inletting intricate designs.

Following inletting of the patch box, it is possible there are slight over-cuts where the wood of the stock lacks only fractions of touching the metal of

End of loading rod can be finished with attached jag to remove unfired loads from the rifle's bore.

Each metal accessory must be inletted precisely to assure the attractiveness of rifle, when completed.

When the final finish has been applied to the stock, metal inlays are cleaned of stock finish materials. For this, use fine steel wool, taking extreme care.

A rough casting when received, trigger guard must be worked down with disc sander or a file until it is semi-smooth, then sanded, buffed to luster.

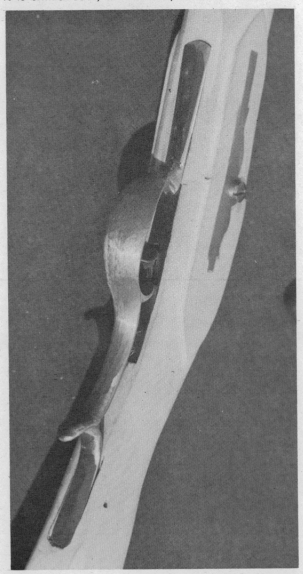

the patch box. If so, slightly steam the wood in these areas as you would steam the dents from a gun stock. This will cause the wood to swell against the metal of the inlay after which it is sanded with a fine-grit garnet paper. In the case of extra-large overcuts, it may be necessary to fill these in with a wood dough. This is easily made by mixing sandpaper wood dust from the stock itself with any transparent-drying wood glue, filling in the cracks thoroughly, allowing to dry, then sanding until smooth.

The striping of a muzzle loading rifle ramrod is said to have originated with the American Indian who, to more easily locate lost arrows, would stripe the shaft in barber pole fashion, so that they would be more distinguishable.

Originally this was accomplished by wrapping the arrow shaft with a strip of rawhide, then hanging the wrapped shaft from the top of the center pole of a tepee where it would be smoked by the fumes sucked upward through the vent hole. The arrow shaft nicely cured, this rawhide wrapping left a spiral marking the full length of the shaft.

In recent years this striping has been accomplished by other methods including the use of iodine and wood dyes as staining agents. I use the age-old method of rawhide and fire but have by-passed the top-o-the-tepee method in favor of first wrapping the ramrod with rawhide, equally spaced, then applying a torch flame to the exposed areas of the wood, striping the full length of the ramrod. It then is coated with a good paste wax and buffed on a soft wheel until glossy.

Following inletting of the ornamental inlays and patch box, the entire stock is given a final sanding with 6/0 garnet sand paper. Care should be taken

It is possible to construct this rifle either in flint or percussion lock styles. Both types are available from the source mentioned in the text.

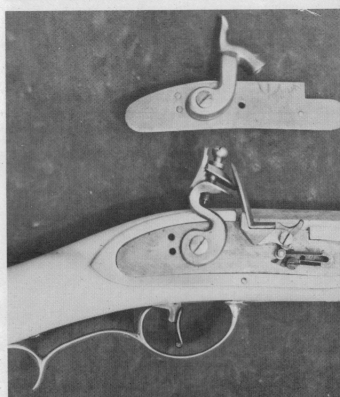

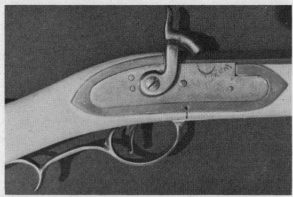

Outlined with inlaid brass, the lock now is fully inletted into stock, ready for the drum and nipple.

Made to use with the flintlock rifle were powder and priming horns, hunting bag, horn powder measure.

that all inlays have been dressed to the surface of the wood and all scratches removed from their surfaces with a fine file and emery cloth. Should even slight scratches remain in the stock, these will be magnified greatly when the finish is finally applied.

There are any number of commercial gunstock finishes which may be utilized to finish a modern Kentucky-type rifle. The stock supplied with the Dixie Gun Works rifle kit is a dead white maple color.

When oiled, this wood takes on a pleasing golden maple color but should one prefer a darker finish,

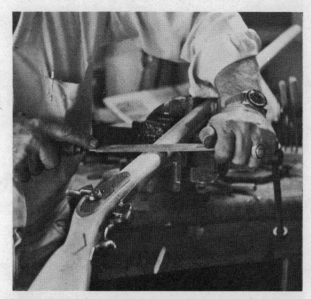

When all hardware has been mounted on the stock, shaping and finishing the wood can begin. Remove as much wood as possible to retain traditional lines.

a bottle of gunstock stain can be ordered from this same firm. This stain will satisfactorily color this hard maple and apparently consists of Feibing's harness and saddle dye, which I had occasion to use for several years in a saddle shop.

In application the color may be regulated from light to dark reddish color. The more applications, the darker will be the wood. Should the color become too dark, the surface may be swabbed with a damp cloth to lighten the color. When the desired color has been achieved, the stock is laid aside for at least twenty four hours to dry, then again lightly sanded.

A sealer of some type should be applied to the surface of the wood. For this, I chose a plastic-based preparation produced by Jet-Aer. This finish comes in an aerosol spray can, which makes application a simple matter. When dry, this preparation, called G-66 Stock Finish, produces a tough, protective coating.

Following application of the sealer the brass inlays, as well as the ramrod thimbles, forend cap, trigger guard and other brass parts may be daubed with stock finishes. This can be removed with fine steel wool. Finally, after the countless hours of labor, the rifle is ready for its first firing. All that is needed are lead balls of the appropriate size, black powder and a good flint installed in the hammer jaws, or, in the case of a percussion, the proper sized percussion caps.

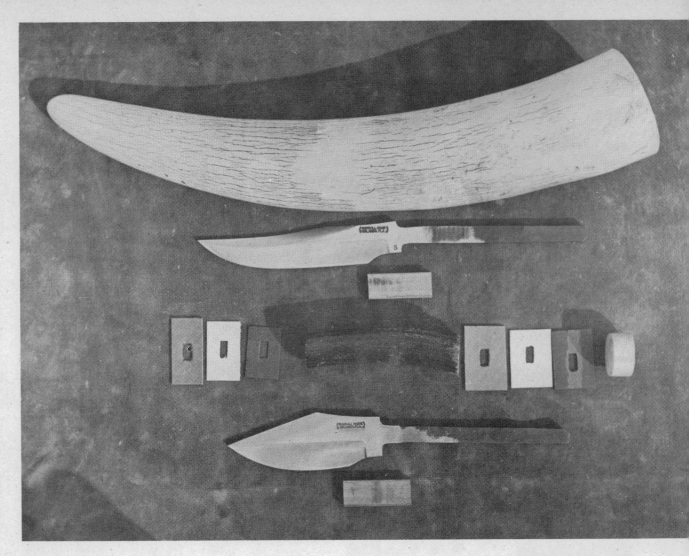

Chapter 42

FOR NEED OF A KNIFE

The Best Blades Can Be Those You Build Yourself

One of the most important pieces of equipment one can take with him on a hunt is a good belt knife. This knife may vary in type and style from one hunter to the next, but it should be of a design best suited to the particular hunt. If one plans to have his guide skin out his game, then an all-purpose knife, such as the Randall Little Bear will serve the purpose. However, if the hunter makes it a practice to skin out his own big game animals, a knife designed for this purpose, such as the Randall Bushmaster big game skinner is just the ticket. Each is designed for a specific purpose; the Little Bear for general all around use and the Bushmaster for heavy duty big game skinning.

While both of these fine knives may be purchased from W. D. Randall, complete with leather handles and sheath, a waiting period of a year or more must be experienced before delivery can be made, due to the tremendous backlog of orders.

However, it is possible to build either of these knives almost immediately by ordering either in kit form. These kits include a finished blade, hilt and butt cap material and other material for producing a knife with a leather handle. Should the builder prefer a stag horn or ivory handle, these may be purchased from Randall at extra cost. The complete price list covering all Randall do-it-yourself knife kits is available from W. D. Randall, Jr. in Orlando, Florida, for fifteen cents and includes such extras as ivory, rare woods and stag horn for handles, nickel silver for hilt or butt caps and all other necessary material for building a custom hunting knife.

In selecting both the Bushmaster skinner and the Little Bear all-purpose hunting knife, I felt that one or the other would fill the bill for most outdoorsmen. In ordering the two kits I wanted to make, I informed Randall that I planned to build one with a stag horn handle, the other with an elpehant ivory handle. The stag horn he was to furnish, while I would supply my own ivory.

The blades of the Randall kit knives are completely finished except for threading the tangs to accept the handles. However, as I planned to bond the stag horn handle to the tang of the Bushmaster — which would require no retaining nut — it was necessary to anneal and thread only the tang of the Little Bear knife on which the ivory handle would be placed.

The preparation of the tangs is the first step in preparing either of these knives for installation of the hilt, spacers and handle material. If the handle is to be bonded to the tang, the only preparation necessary is to shorten the tang to exactly four inches. This will allow for a finished handle of 4½ inches and still allow room for placing a compass in the butt.

Should one prefer to have the handle material held in place with a threaded nut, the tang must be shortened to 4¾ inches, annealed and threaded with a 10/32 die. The steel in Randall blades is tough, so the annealing of the tang is accomplished by cutting it to proper length, then grinding the portion to be threaded until it will accept a 10/32 die.

Using a torch, a small quantity of charcoal is fired until it glows with a white ash covering. The tip of the tang then is heated to a bright cherry red with the torch and immediately placed in the glowing charcoal. The tang is left in the hot coal until both are cold. This process requires several hours but is the only successful way to properly anneal this steel so that it might be threaded. Do not attempt to thread the tang without first annealing it as outlined here. To attempt to do so would result in a ruined die.

Included in the knife kit are several fiber spacers in red, white and black colors, a heavy brass hilt and an aluminum butt cap. The brass hilt material first is drilled with a three-sixteenths-inch drill, then filed until it slides onto the tang of the knife blade in a tight fit. I make it a practice to make the tang cut-out in the hilt such a tight fit that it must be tapped with a hardwood mallet to make it seat firmly on the shoulders of the blade. Once seated, the brass hilt then is soft-soldered in place from the tang side and all excess solder wiped away while still in the molten state.

With the brass hilt in place, we now turn our attention to the colored fiber spacers. These may be used in any combination. The color combinations of the spacers must be left to each individual's own tastes, but it is better not to place a white spacer next to a light-colored handle nor a black spacer next to dark handle material.

Possibly the most exacting chore in building one of these Randall kit knives is in drilling the handle material to accept the tang of the blade. While elephant ivory may be cut in a more or less straight block to provide handle material, staghorn usually is slightly curved, thus creating somewhat of a headache in drilling the tang hole.

I have found that by clamping the material firmly in a drill press vise, carefully checking it to make certain that it is as perpendicular as one can determine, I then can

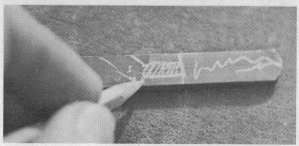

Section of tang to be threaded is laid out to show the work necessary after area has been annealed.

A torch is applied to the tang section until cherry red. Then it is plunged into hot charcoal to cool.

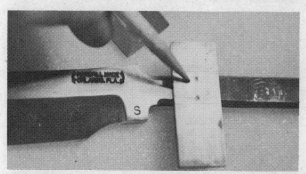

The brass hilt first is marked to exact width of tang, then is center-punched. Drill three side by side holes, which measure three-sixteenths inch each.

After drilling the cut-out in the hilt, it is shaped with a small square file, until it is a tight fit on the tang. It is soldered permanently in place.

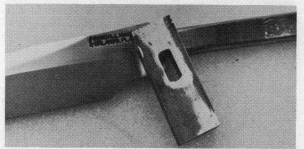

With hilt soldered in place, spacers on the blade,
handle section then is installed with epoxy cement.

drill the two three-sixteenths-inch holes side by side.
These two holes are drilled completely through the
handle material — whether it be ivory, a rare wood or
staghorn — lengthwise. With these two holes drilled, I
then knock out the partition between them with a
rotary rasp chucked in the drill press. Finally, a rattail
file is used to finish the slotted hole until the handle will
slide onto the tang snuggly.

At this point, the hilt is soldered in place, the fiber
spacers are slid on the tang in contrasting combinations
of red, white or black. With the handle material drilled
and ready for installation, we follow the step in installing a bonded handle, which requires no retaining nut at
the butt-end.

In experimenting with various bonding materials, I
have found that Micro-Bed, an epoxy stock bedding
compound, a product of the Micro Sight Company in
Belmont, California, is about the best available. This
compound, correctly mixed according to instructions
on the box, is liberally smeared over the entire tang of
the knife blade and, at the same time, a portion of the
mix is forced into the tang slot of the handle material.
The handle then is pressed tightly onto the tang until
fully seated against the laminated spacer material of the
guard. Following this, all excess epoxy that oozes from
the handle should be wiped off, making the clean-up job
of the handle easier during the final shaping operations.

Put the knife away for at least twelve hours for the
epoxy to harden. Once hardened, the handle material

becomes permanently bonded to the knife tang and
should not loosen even under severe climatic conditions
or hard usage. Later, the butt-end of the bonded handle
may be dressed up by installation of a compass, thus
concealing the oval-shaped, epoxy-filled hole in the butt
of the handle.

The Little Bear knife which I built has an elephant
ivory handle that incorporates a threaded retaining nut
on the tang to hold it in place on the blade. A butt cap
of aluminum furnished with all kits serves as a base for
the retaining nut.

The aluminum butt cap furnished with the kit must
be drilled to accept the threaded section of the tang and
an oval cut-out made to accept at least a small portion of
the larger tang section not ground for threading.

This oval-shaped cut in the butt cap needn't be over
one-eighth inch in depth and will assure that the
aluminum cap, when permanently installed, will not
rotate or turn when the nut is tightened. The retaining
nut may be screwed down tightly on the existing surface
of the cap itself, or the cap may be counter-drilled so
that the nut is counter-sunk below the surface where it
will receive little wear from hard use.

In drilling and installing the handle, be certain that
the handle goes onto the tang straight. Should it be off
to one side, a sloppy job will result. Should you find
that the handle is a little lop-sided on the tang, a little
work with a rattail file usually will straighten it up. If,
after this operation, you find that the handle material is

Bushmaster Skinner model has stag handle epoxied in place sans butt cap. The other knife, Randall Little Bear style, is ready for its ivory handle.

Handle material is drilled best, while held firmly in drill press vise. The two holes, side by side, are necessary for creating slot for tang of blade.

a loose fit on the tang, then it may be shimmed with slivers of hardwood. A perfect job of drilling will prevent a lop-sided handle but just in case you should have trouble with this exacting job, that's one remedy. After straightening, should the handle still be too loose, then epoxy-bond it on and forget about the threaded nut.

With a bit more detail on the nomenclature of each of these knives, you can be the judge as to which will best suit you. The Bushmaster Model 19 has a 4½-inch blade of quarter-inch high carbon steel. The top cutting edge is sharpened for about 2½ inches and is intended for cutting or hacking through bones of the largest game animals. The

cutting edge of the blade is curved for fast, easy skinning. This knife is designed as a heavy duty big game skinner.

The Little Bear Model 12 is designed for those desiring a general purpose hunting knife. It has a six-inch blade of the finest high carbon steel. The top cutting edge is sharpened for about 4½ inches. This knife makes a good skinner as well as serving as a general purpose camp knife.

Up to this point in the construction of these two knives, they have, for the most part, been held in the jaws of a bench vise. From this point on, both of these sharp blades will see considerable handling. To prevent any mishaps, such as a couple of detached fingers, preventive measures become necessary.

By folding a strip of thin tough leather over the cutting edges of the knife, then securing the leather in

With the ivory handle securely in place, using the butt cap nut and epoxy cement, the handle now is ready for the final shaping and finishing process.

place with several wraps of masking tape, there is no chance of getting a gashed hand, while buffing or grinding the semi-finished handle section. Should a buffer grab one of these blades, it can be thrown with considerable force. So be sure to wrap the blade with leather or some other tough material before attempting to disc sand, buff or grind the handle section.

With the handle sections installed on the tangs of the blade, in rough form, we must shape these handles to comfortable proportions to fit our own hand. Should you have a large hand, leave that handle large. But if your hands are small, or the knife is being built for your wife or girl friend, cut it down to fit.

Needed for this operation will be a disc sander for the major removal of excess material, a one-inch drum sander for cutting in the optional finger grooves and a couple of files, one a half-round, the other a fine-cut mill bastard. A few pieces of fine garnet paper are necessary for removing the file marks prior to buffing on a muslin buffing wheel.

There is no set rule for shaping a knife handle and this is especially true, when one is building a custom knife for his own use. Just let your conscience be your guide. Keep it in good taste, comfortable to handle and, by all means, make it fit your hand.

Knife in hand, the blade is carefully wrapped as outlined earlier with leather and masking tape. Remove all excess material from the handle section. During this operation, I find that using a disc sander is the best method for removal of excess material and rough-shaping the handle.

When the handle has taken on a pleasing appearance, but is as yet a little over-sized, a rattail file in employed to shape that section of the handle that adjoins the hilt. In filing this section, be sure to blend the material of the fiber spacers, the brass of the guard and the handle material into a graceful arc. The best gauge for this arc is

Prior to finishing the handle, wrap entire blade in leather, then tape it to protect your hands.

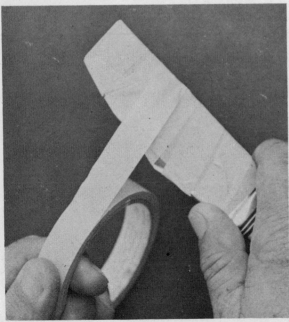

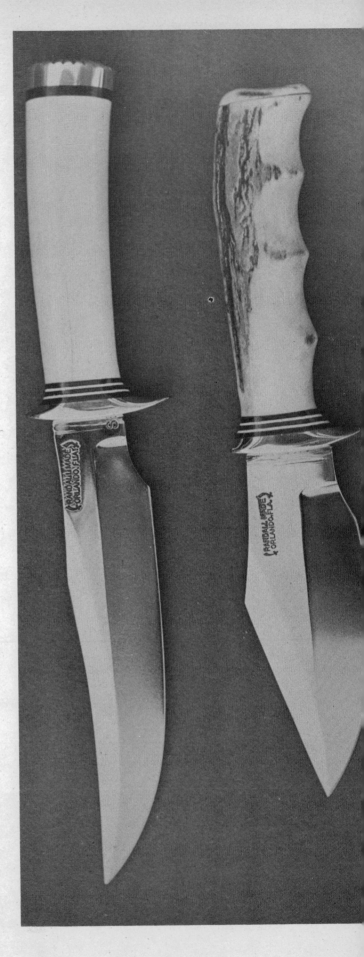

The guard or hilt is shaped to fit the index finger, using a rattail file or half-round file, as shown.

the first finger of the hand in which you normally use a knife. Make this curve fit this finger for a perfect fit.

The handle section should have a gentle curve downward toward the butt to more naturally and comfortably fit the hand. Once the hilt or guard section of the handle is shaped, the bulk of the handle now should be finish-filed to the exact size desired. This is followed by a thorough sanding with fine garnet sandpaper until all file marks have disappeared. Lastly, the complete handle section is buffed thoroughly with white buffing compound until the handle material, whether leather, staghorn, ivory or rare wood, takes on a gleaming luster and is glassy smooth.

The butt cap can be of aluminum or brass stock that is threaded to the tang of the blade. After the final shaping, it then is polished on the buffer.

In absence of drum sander, the finger grooves are cut with half-round file, finished with emery cloth.

Best way to cut finger grooves is with one-inch drum sander chucked in drill press. The final finish should be done with garnet paper, then the buffer.

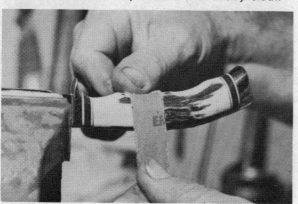

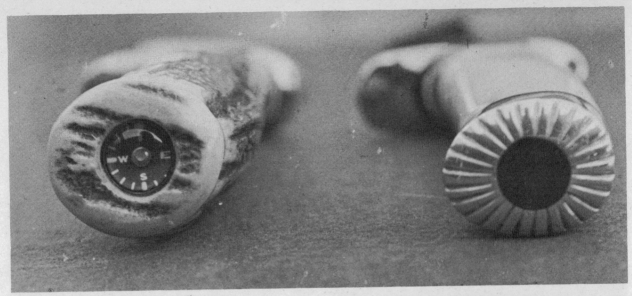

A fluid compass can be incorporated in the butt of the knife handle, minus the butt nut. The knife on left has inset butt nut sealed in place with epoxy.

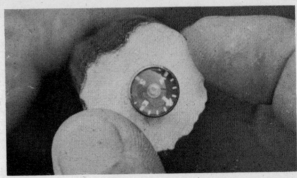

Installation of compass conceals the hole drilled in handle material to accept the tang of blade. It can be cemented in place with a clear epoxy cement.

I decided to install a fluid compass into the butt of the stag-handled Bushmaster. This is possible only on a knife on which the tang has been cut about one half-inch shorter than the length of the finished handle. The handle then is epoxied onto the tang in lieu of the threaded nut, as on the ivory-handled Little Bear. When the epoxy has set and hardened, the butt is drilled out to accept the compass in a snug fit. Finally, as on the knife built for this article, a well figured piece of staghorn is cut to a thickness of about one-eighth inch and drilled to the compass size. This is epoxied over the butt of the knife and centered to fully reveal the compass face. While this last cap of staghorn is not necessary, it adds a nicer appearance to a finished knife.

The cutting of finger grooves in a handle of ivory, staghorn or other suitable material is a somewhat touchy job. Care must be taken not to cut too deeply into the handle material. To do so could result in a nasty, jagged hole in the handle where the file or drum sander had cut into the tang holes of the handle material. The cutting of the finger grooves, which is optional with the builder, is best accomplished with either a small drum sander one inch in diameter or a half-round file.

The finger grooves are laid out by holding the unfinished knife in the hand in the normal cutting position. Then, with a sharp lead pencil, draw a line between each of the four fingers by forcing the pencil between the fingers and scribing a line onto the handle material. These lines will act as guides for cutting the finger grooves. It will be noted that the fingers are laid at an angle on the handle material. Cut the grooves on this angle for a better fit, but don't cut too deeply or your knife will need a whole new handle!

The selection of handle materials may vary from leather, ivory and staghorn to exotic hardwoods such as ebony or rosewood. All are available at extra cost from Randall and all have their good points and their bad.

Elephant ivory probably is the most desired so-called exotic material for a knife handle. However, under certain conditions, such as dry, hot weather, ivory has a tendency to crack. The ivory to be used for a knife handle should be prime and not dried out. Using ivory too old or dry will result in a handle that is sure to crack and chip. Compressed leather handles are attractive and durable, but under extensive use have a tendency to become rough and swollen, especially after being exposed to either damp weather or to repeated washings. Ebony and rosewood make fine durable knife handles, but lose their luster after extensive use and are subject to line-cracking similar to that of elephant ivory.

Staghorn is perhaps the most durable of all handle materials in that it becomes more beautiful with age and is not subject to cracking or becoming rough. The best staghorn for knife handles comes from India and is available from Randall in a section big enough for even the longest knife handle.

At this point, your knife should be about finished. If, after the initial buffing operation, you notice stubborn file marks still in the material, sand them out and rebuff. Use your own imagination in creating the handle section, but keep it within the limits of good knife design.

Shown are four different types of skinning knives which can be constructed from kit described here.

Four types of general purpose camp knives are (from top): Bowie-type knife made by the author; an all-purpose knife; a smaller type with stainless steel blade and general purpose camp and skinner style.

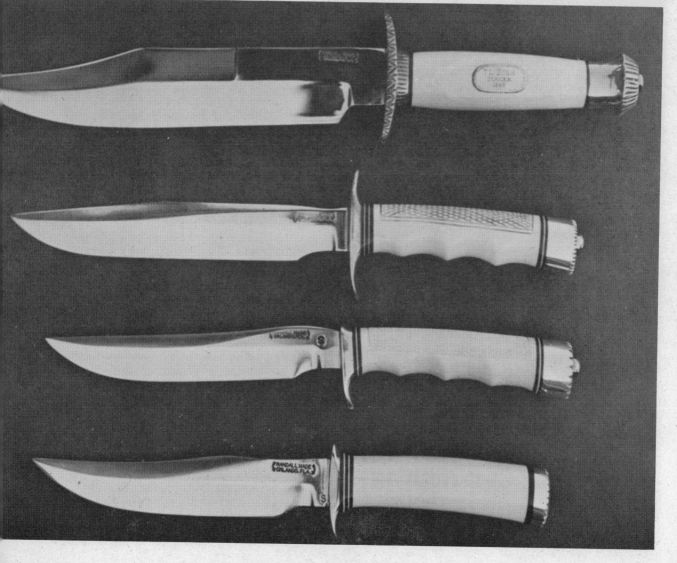

Holster should allow pistol or revolver to enter freely. Tightness can cause abrasive action of the leather against blued metal; result is undue wear.

Chapter 43

FORM FIT YOUR LEATHER

These Instructions Save On Bluing And Cost Nothing!

Years ago, in the Old West, water — and water alone — was considered the best "custom fitter" of anything that required fitting. If a cowboy could afford the price of a new pair of boots or a new Stetson hat, he would immediately head for the nearest horse watering trough where he doused them throughly, then would wear them until they were dry.

The theory behind this process was to get a custom fit of apparel molded exactly to his size and shape. As extreme as this measure may seem, it has proved itself to be so successful that it is carried on to this day by many people who liberally dampen a new pair of pinching shoes, then suffer the torments of wearing them until dry, knowing that the final result will be a pair of shoes that are both comfortable and non-pinching.

In spite of this being the Space Age in which the majority of oldtime methods for getting things done have been outmoded, there still is only one way to properly shape leather successfully; to make it fit the job it is to perform; to mold it to the shape of the items on which it is to be used. Pistol holsters, cartridge belts, rifle scabbards and all of the complicated parts of the so-called western saddle have received repeated soakings in water during the varying phases of their manufacture. Water has been the only substance found that will successfully render ready-tanned leather to a moldable state.

On the market today are numerous of holsters in all designs designated for various models of revolvers and automatic pistols. Most of these holsters are manufactured from the fine materials and workmanship, but others are made from modern, inexpensive, synthetic leathers comprised of a combination of pressed cardboard and leather shavings.

The genuine leather holsters, while of the finest materials and workmanship, still must be fitted to each individual gun in order to eliminate undue holster wear and friction that, in time, will strip the blue from any gun.

We will assume that a new holster has been purchased. This scabbard is of fine quality, but still is found to be a little too snug fitting and creates undue friction on the gun in certain spots. These spots will, in time, act as a fine abrasive on the gun and will eventually strip the blue from that area.

There are two remedies for removing undue snugness from a new holster; both are accomplished with nothing more than water, using the gun itself or a "molding form" made from wood, which is of the approximate size and shape of the gun to be used in the holster.

The first method is to place the holster in a bath of water at about room temperature (never use hot water, as this will ruin the leather beyond repair) for fifteen minutes or so, or until the leather is completely saturated. The time element will vary with the oil content of the leather.

After the leather has become thoroughly soaked, it is removed from the bath and wiped dry of all excess water. The gun, in the meantime, has been given a coating of good gun grease, wrapped in a thin shell of plastic sheeting (such as that is which the laundry returns your finished shirts), then is slid tightly into the holster and the actual chore of finish fitting begins. Such fitting is accomplished by "boning-down" all known tight spots of the holster with the use of an old toothbrush handle, a piece of ivory or even a smooth piece of rounded hardwood. This boning-down operation consists of rubbing the entire outer surface of the holster briskly, literally molding the damp leather to the exact contour of the gun's frame. The plastic sheeting in which the gun is wrapped will allow just enough clearance for the holster to be friction free and yet not cause a sloppy fit.

The second method of obtaining a perfect friction-free holster, which is particularly adaptable for automatic pistols, is to first shape a piece of wood into a comparable contoured facsimile of the gun, leaving this molding block slightly larger in contour than the frame of the gun. This compensates for shrinkage as the leather dries. This molding block is pushed tightly into the wet holster after which the holster is boned down, as previously described. The blocked holster is set aside then to dry, after which the holster is given a liberal coating of saddle soap or several applications of the leather preserver.

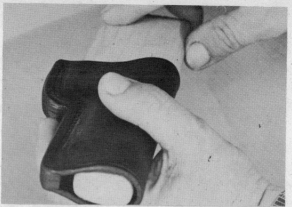

With holster well dampened, a slightly oversized form of pre-shaped wood is slid into place. The leather then is allowed to dry while on the form.

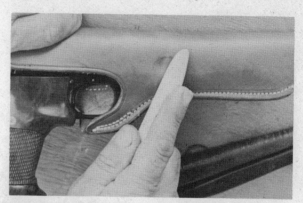

Once dry, leather again is dampened, the pistol or revolver slid in and holster rubbed thoroughly with hard material like toothbrush handle, piece of ivory.

Restoring leather that has lost its body or stiffness is accomplished by the process known in the leather working trade as "casing." This restores the heavier leathers used in holsters, belts and saddles to their original tough, semi-stiff state.

This is accomplished first by soaking the leather in water as described, then drying very slowly. The slower and longer the drying period, the more body the leather will have at completion of the process. In casing new leather, it is best to give it a good coating of neatsfoot oil when thoroughly dry, then use only saddle soap or Lexol from then on. On leather that has seen many years of use, never use neatsfoot oil as it has a tendency to "burn" it and greatly hastens deterioration. Neatsfoot oil, likewise, should not be used on any leather which the owner wishes to buff or polish to a luster. In short, neatsfoot should be used only on new leather and for only one good coating.

Following the remolding of a new holster, it is best to rerub the outer edges that have been roughened by the water. This is accomplished first by coating these edges with wax or appropriately colored shoe polish, then rubbing briskly with a denim or canvas cloth or the toothbrush handle.

This will restore these edges to a smooth, highly polished surface, adding greatly to the finished appearance of what now is a custom-fitted holster.

Chapter 44
A SIGHT TO BEHOLD
Modern Accessories On Black Powder Guns Can Up Your Score

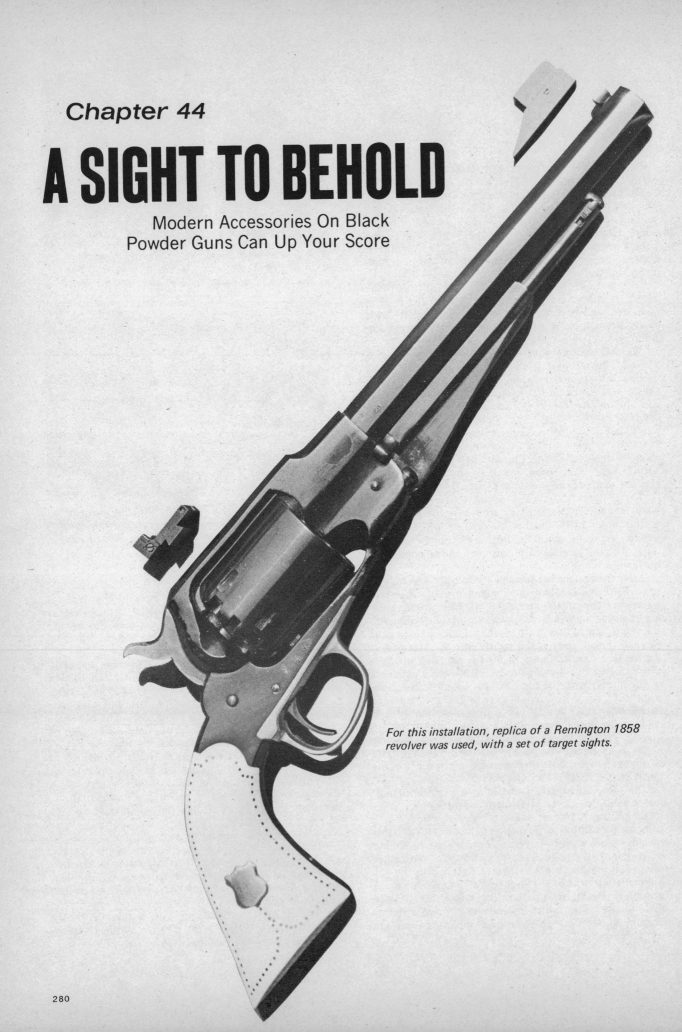

For this installation, replica of a Remington 1858 revolver was used, with a set of target sights.

The first step is to remove original front sight. It is filed down to surface of the barrel so that there is provided a perfect seat for new ramp type.

Like most revolvers designed for modern metallic cartridges, the percussion handgun must meet certain specifications to qualify as a potentially accurate handgun. The cap and ball revolver can provide hours of shooting for mere pennies and is capable of firing respectable groups within its limitations.

Excellent percussion replicas are being manufactured for shooting purposes. Some of these replicas are stronger in construction than the genuine oldtimers. Constructed of modern steels, they are less apt to suffer from overloads.

The .44 New Model Army revolver, produced by the Navy Arms Company of New Jersey, is an exact replica of the 1858 Remington percussion revolver.

The first of these Navy Arms .44 revolvers that I fired was about ten years ago, when I decided to give the big Remington replica a severe field test, duplicating the torture tests given the original guns by the U.S. Army testing Boards of the 1850s. The revolver was loaded and capped, then thoroughly doused with water to simulate a rain storm. Caked deliberately with sand and dust while still wet, the gun continued to fire smoothly. Now, ten years later, I wanted to accurize one of these handguns into a precise shooter for my own use.

As received, the Navy Arms Remington replica is ready to fire after minor cleaning. However, I wanted a gun that would boast accuracy, looks and overall mechanical perfection.

The Navy Arms replica, like the original 1858 Reming-

ton Arms revolver, comes equipped with a set of sights that date from the earliest hand cannon and are about as accurate.

These sights consist of a stud-type front sight and a V rear sight cut into the upper cylinder strap.

Once the action was smoothed to perfection with hones, I considered the sights. Experience had taught me that sights of this type, were a by-guess-and-by-golly affair, with plenty of Kentucky windage and elevation thrown in!

First, I considered a Williams Shorty ramp backed up with one of the excellent Williams Guide rear sights, which is adjustable for both windage and elevation. However, as both of these sights were designed chiefly for use on rifles or carbines. I decided to stick to combinations designed for handguns.

I called George Thannisch of Micro-Sight Company in Belmont, California, after I had decided that the set of Micro sights designed for the Colt Single Action Army revolver might be just the ticket for installation on the Remington. The basic design of the frame, hammer and other components were about the same. With a few alterations in dovetailing and adjusting, I felt this combination would be about ideal.

However, Thannisch had other ideas. Because the frame of the Remington is slotted to accept the long blade-like firing pin extension, he didn't think it would work out satisfactorily. Finally I selected a Micro rear sight designed for the Colt M1911 automatic and a front ramp five-eighths

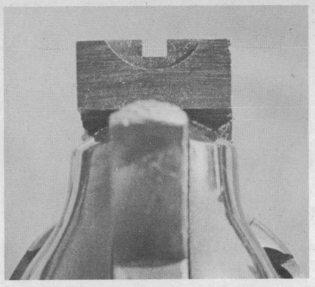

Above: Installed, the rear sight must be level with the frame of the gun and not tilted. (Upper right) Bottom of ramp is tinned first with solder, then is put straight on barrel secured with ramp soldering jig. Heat is applied with the torch, until the solder melts, after which the entire unit is allowed to cool.

Right: Correctly installed, new ramp is attached solidly to barrel. It is square and straight to the axis of the bore, if it is to prove its accuracy.

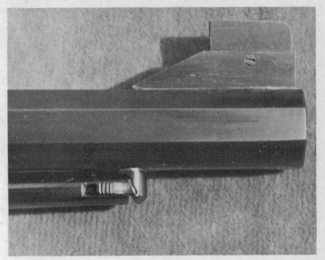

of an inch in height and having a blade one-eighth-inch in thickness. This ramp had a flat bottom. This provides a perfect fit to the top flat of the pistol's octagon barrel.

As stated, the front sight of the M1858 type Remington revolver is nothing more than a rounded stud set into a blind hole drilled into the top of the barrel. Instead of removing this stud to leave a gaping hole open on the barrel top, I filed this stud flush with the barrel flat, providing a perfect and solid surface to which to solder the new ramp.

The front ramp soon was installed by sweating it to the barrel top, using Brownell's Force 44 silver bearing solder.

It is essential that the ramp be held firmly dead-center to the barrel with a ramp soldering jig or its equivalent.

Attaching the Micro rear sight is more complex in that a dovetail slot must be cut, filed or milled completely across the rear portion of the top strap. This is between the barrel breech and the recoil shield of the revolver frame.

I located this slot so that the rear portion of the dovetail slot was situated exactly five-eighths of an inch from the rear of the top strap. This means that the rear of the dovetail is exactly 9½ inches from the barrel muzzle, if one is to avoid cutting into the frame slot provided for the hammer. With this precaution, operation of the hammer was in no way impaired and easily cleared the rear section of the Micro sight by a full one-eighth-inch.

If a milling machine is available, the dovetail cut is easy.

But while the steel in the frame of the Navy Arms .44 revolver is tough, it still can be cut with a sharp file. This is accomplished by roughing the slot out with the narrow, flat edge of a mill file to the approximate depth, then finishing with a three-corner Swiss needle file to a perfect fit.

The dovetail cut must be a perfect fit to accept the Micro sight; snug enough that the Micro sight can be installed by tapping it lightly from right to left in the slot with a soft-faced brass hammer. To have this slot too tight could result in serious damage to the new sight as it is pounded into place. If it won't go, remove more material from the slot with the Swiss needle file.

Most important is that the rear sight be absolutely level with the revolver's frame. A canted or twisted rear sight can play havoc with accuracy. Several hours of careful hand-work can be spent in hand filing this slot. When finished, the base of the sight should fill the newly cut slot completely. There should be no gaps between sight and slot.

When the new slot accepts the sight in a perfect fit, it should be touched up with a cold bluing solution and coated with a preservative gun oil. The new sight permanently installed, the two retaining screws in the Micro sight are cinched down snugly. These small screws prevent the sight from shifting position should the gun or sights be bumped. A good precaution is to seal the sight in place with a small dab of Loc-Tite. It is smeared into the dovetail

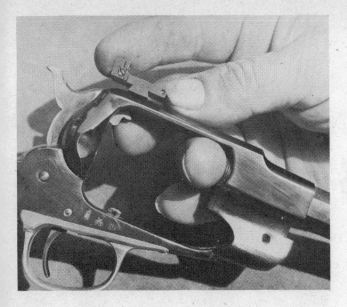

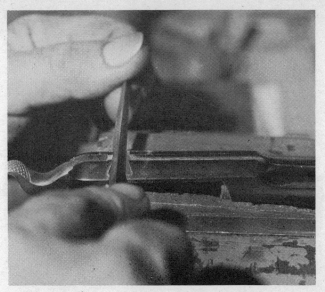

Above: The slot is cut out with the edge of 10-inch mill bastard file, then finished for perfect fit with Swiss needle file, dovetailing or slotting file. (Upper left) Installing Micro rear sight requires filing dove slot in top strap. Judge the correct location by holding sight on frame, mark position.

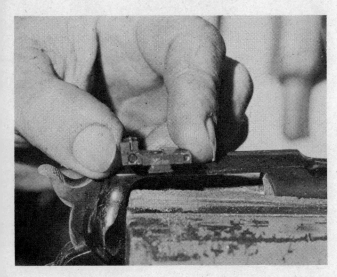

Left: Care is taken to assure finished dovetail will accept the Micro sight in a perfect tight fit.

groove prior to final installation.

Sights installed, the revolver should be placed in a vise with padded jaws and the new sights collimated to the axis of the bore. As a rule this will put you on target at twenty-five yards or so and will allow for final sight adjustment when the gun is fired from a rest on the range. As stated earlier, the Micro rear sight is fully adjustable for both windage and elevation by quarter-minute adjustment screws slotted for screw driver use.

As a direct result of pre-firing collimation, the only adjustment I needed on the revolver was to raise the rear sight four clicks to put it dead center on the target at twenty-five yards.

In firing revolvers of this type, I use sufficient FFg powder in each chamber of the cylinder to allow only enough room for full seating of the lead ball without undue compression of the powder. When loaded, each ball is topped with a thorough coating of a good high-temp grease to prevent chain firing. The percussion caps are installed on each nipple last. I cannot remember ever having a misfire with one of these guns, except through the use of faulty percussion caps.

Any gun is something that should be kept immaculately clean at all times and checked regularly for possible defects resulting from normal wear. This is especially essential insofar as black powder guns are concerned. Unlike smokeless powders, black powder is highly corrosive. It can build up and cake hard on certain vital gun parts, rendering the gun useless until cleaned.

Following each shooting session with a black powder gun, it should be stripped, the metal parts and bore throughly washed in hot, soapy water, rinsed in scalding water, then dried and oiled. The bore of any black powder shooter should be cleaned thoroughly for at least three days running after a shooting session, the first day with hot water and the second and third day with gun patches saturated with a nitro powder solvent such as Hoppe's No. 9. About a week after third cleaning the bore should be checked once more for possible corrosive action.

There are any number of sighting combinations that might be incorporated into any black powder gun to make it shoot more accurately, whether rifle or revolver. However, I certainly do not recommend altering for such installations on genuine antique guns of any type. Such installations should be reserved for modern-made replicas, which are better for shooting purposes due to better steels used in their construction.

To alter a genuine antique gun would be to ruin its historical value, to say nothing of knocking dollars off its potential value.

Chapter 45

DON'T BLEED FOR A BEAD

Replacing That Broken Sight Is Simple And Requires Minimum Tools

*Shaped to the correct size, the bead made of bronze
or brass brazing rod is tinned, soldered in position.*

*The repaired sight, the new bead now reinstalled,
is ready for more years of use in the game fields.*

Probably the most overlooked of all phases of gun maintenance concerns the iron front sight, This small, seemingly insignificant piece of steel is taken for granted or is given no thought at all! At least this is true, until it gets knocked off from hard use!

Granted, should a front sight bead become damaged, it is a matter of only a few dollars to have it replaced. However, if most gun owners are like me, they like to keep their sporting equipment in perfect condition at all times at as little cost as is possible.

Over the years, I have seen perhaps several hundred good usable front sights discarded simply because they were damaged in a minor way or had the beads knocked off. I would estimate that over ninety percent of these could have been put back in use had just a few minutes of workmanship been expended on them.

Take, for example, a popular rifle in current production. This rifle is well built and thousands of them have been sold. However, one major fault is the fact that the gold — actually copper — bead on the front sight can be flicked off with the fingernail! I have had numerous friends bring these rifles to me for repair, since these sights are of a special design for this particular rifle and cannot be bought at any gun shop. The actual job of replacing these sight beads requires half an hour at most. And the replacement bead cannot be knocked off without completely ruining the front sight ramp!

It would require a book to detail replacing beads on all types of front sights. There are just too many styles, designs and variations. However, the basic methods pertain to all sights, whether they have ivory, gold, brass or copper beads.

The metallic beads, usually of non-ferrous metal, such as brass or copper, may be replaced on the iron sight by means of a good silver-bearing solder, such as Force 44 sold by Brownell's of Montezuma, Iowa. The plastic inserts or ivory beads are reinstalled with a good epoxy cement, which is allowed to cure for at least twenty-four hours before the gun is used.

Some Smith & Wesson revolvers, such as the Model 29 .44 magnum and the Model 57 .41 magnum, have red inserts in the front sight blades. It is not uncommon for this red plastic material to become damaged or lost from the revolver completely.

However, it is a minor matter to replace these inserts in only a few minutes. Your local drug store carries inexpensive toothbrushes with brightly colored plastic handles. Some have florescent handles that gather light rays to result in a fantastically clear front sight bead. It is best to purchase a toothbrush with either a bright orange or red handle for this purpose. The handle is cut into small sections, then filed to exact replacement size in the S&W sight blade. Make it a snug, slide fit and add a small drop of epoxy to secure it in place. One toothbrush handle will provide hundreds of this type of front sight bead.

*The brazing rod, as explained in the text, can be
formed to proper shape, size with file, disc sander.*

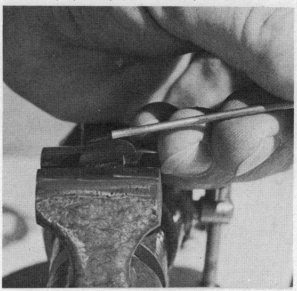

The surface of the sight blade from which the bead has been lost must be cleaned and brightened with a small file before the new bead can be soldered.

Once oversize bead is soldered in place, it is cut to size and correct length with jeweler's saw. It then is finished off with one of Swiss needle files.

Brass beads in any of the various sizes needed can be turned out from bronze or brass brazing rod. Use the one-sixteenth-inch rod for the small beads and the one-eighth-inch rod for larger sizes. The bead is shaped carefully to its correct size, while still a part of the brazing rod. Once the proper shape and size are attained, the bead is cut from the rod and tinned with silver-bearing solder. It is held in place on the steel front sight with a pair of machinist's tweezers, then soldered in place with either a small torch or a soldering iron. Once the bead had been replaced, it either is buffed lightly or sanded to remove the tinned coating of solder, revealing its true surface. Properly done, this new bead should be as good as the original.

In some cases, front sights are constructed so that the bead must have a tapering shank that inserts into a hole bored into the blade of the steel sight itself. If this is the case, it is best to clean out any segments of the broken bead that might remain in this hole, taper the shank of the new bead accordingly, tin it lightly with solder, then solder it in place. While beads with tapered shanks are a bit harder to make and install, the entire job still shouldn't require more than half an hour.

Some shooters never are satisfied with the type of front sight beads furnished on over-the-counter rifles. As

The various sizes and types of front sight beads run from 1/16-inch brass and ivory to those made of copper with elongated shapes in varying sizes.

After soldering in place, cutting to correct length, bead is brightened with garnet paper, crocus cloth.

Replacement beads can be finished with either flat or rounded surfaces in final phases of the work.

a rule, these beads are round and vary in size from 1/16 up to about 3/32 of an inch. Perhaps the customer wants a sourdough-type of bead. In many cases the existing front sight can be altered successfully to the sourdough Patridge design simply by filing the bead-accepting surface to a forty-five-degree angle and soldering on a new bead, square in shape, that measures .070 in width. However, an alteration such as this is only possible where the width of the steel blade is also .070 inches. Thin, narrow-bladed front sights are not practical for installation of sourdough beads.

While it is possible to have a broken shotgun bead replaced for as little as fifty cents per bead, plus labor, these too may be made by the individual in his own workshop. Some shotgun beads are merely pressed into a tight fitting hole in the barrel, but the majority of these beads are threaded to either 2x56 or 6x48. This means that it wouldn't be practical for the home gun mechanic to attempt to make a threaded bead, when one can be purchased for about fifty cents.

The press-in type shotgun bead may sound like a simple matter to make, but they require painstaking workmanship. The best material that I have found for this type of sight is close-grained elephant ivory, obtainable only from the Congo. While East African ivory may be used for shotgun beads, it is somewhat coarse and much more easily broken than the Congo ivory. This is especially true, as the bead is being pressed into the hole in the barrel. As previously stated, the press-in type of shotgun bead is the exception rather than the rule and a job of this type is rarely encountered today, unless the gun is quite old and of European origin.

Repair of front sights is a fairly simple chore for anyone familiar with the simplest handtools, a working knowledge of soldering and the use of epoxy cements.

Chapter 46

USE YOUR TROPHIES

Here Are Means Of Putting Those Hunting Results To Practical Use In Daily Life.

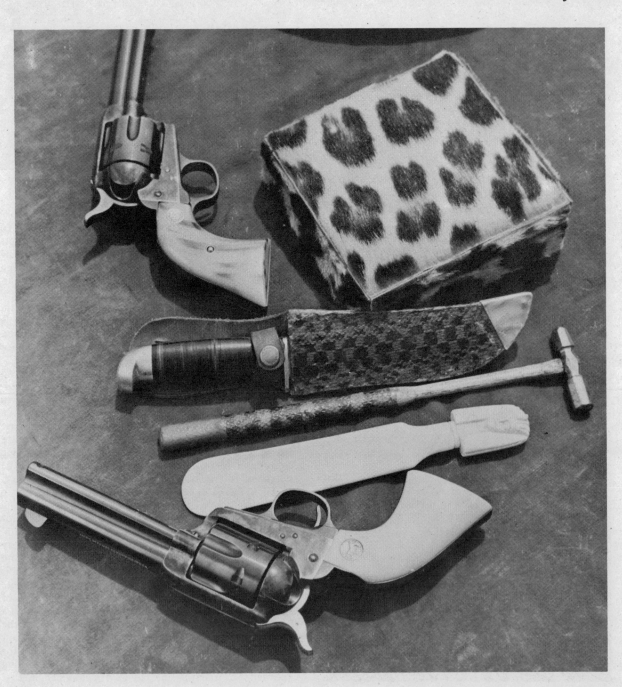

FOR almost a year the large fangs of a trophy jaguar had rested on the green velvet lining of a glass display case in my den. I had carefully removed them from the bullet-shattered skull shortly after the kill in that steaming section of the Yucatan jungle. Upon returning home, I had cleaned and buffed them until they had taken on the appearance of highly polished ivory. They looked great — at least I thought so — but for some reason I wasn't satisfied with having those two large cuspids merely as display pieces. I wanted to wear them!

After all, one doesn't bag a jaguar every day, and taxidermists seldom if ever use the original skull and teeth in mounting an animal nowadays. Why couldn't those teeth be made into an attractive and unusual bolo tie slide? After all, the current trend for unusual bolo tie slides runs rampant among the ranks of sportsmen and hunters these days.

So I finally turned those chompers into a real conversation piece; a bolo tie slide of jaguar fangs mounted in hand engraved and initialed sterling silver. The whole job, including the engraving, took less than two hours to complete.

A great number of combinations can be utilized in making bolo ties and slides from those parts unused by the taxidermist. Buckskin from your tanned deer hides may be cut into narrow strips and used as the tie, while the slide may be made from any unusual section of a horn or antler. A friend of mine up in Montana made a most attractive bolo tie slide by mounting a cluster of some twenty elk teeth in plastic of some sort, and while this particular slide is quite large, it is by no means out of proportion to some that I have seen worn by sportsmen and hunters. One bolo slide I saw recently was made from the complete hoof of a good-sized mule deer. Beautifully polished, it was most attractive, unusual — and heavy!

In the past I have enjoyed making all sorts of things from miniature stagecoaches and Bowie knives to sporting rifles that have been turned out in their entirety on my work bench. I get a real kick out of creating useful items from unusual materials, and I am sure that many sportsmen, at one time or another, have at least attempted to turn some of the by-products of their trophy game into useful, attractive mementoes.

To mention just a few of the items that can be made from the spare parts of game would be to list such items as cuff links, tie clasps, key chain hangers, bracelets, ring settings, buttons and others made from such materials of the hunt as animal teeth, deer and elk antler, elephant ivory, animal claws, fur and hides, hooves and horns, even bone. Certainly our pioneer forefathers, as well as the American Indian, utilized every part of wild game possible for their subsistence, but the modern hunter has a tendency to discard a good portion of his hard earned trophy as useless.

While this article isn't meant to be a step-by-step do-it-yourself on any single item that may be made from animal by-products, it is to suggest a number of items that may be made — and worn — by the sportsmen who enjoy tinkering around a workshop. The tools are basic and your game animal "spare parts" will provide the material.

Horn, antler, bone, hooves and ivory are most easily cut with a hacksaw after which the saw cuts are smoothed up with a mill bastard file and fine garnet sand paper. Finally, the finished product should be given a thorough buffing on a loose muslin buffing wheel dressed with white buffing compound.

Where cementing or gluing is necessary, it is best to use an epoxy-type cement which is exceptionally strong, water-proof and durable. I have found Epoxy 220, produced by Hughes Associates of Excelsior, Minnesota, to be excellent. However, nearly all epoxy cements perform the same basic purpose of providing a strong bond between two materials.

If one is reasonably good at using a sewing machine —

Threaded bolts can be epoxied into cured deer or elk legs to provide means of fastening to racks.

Elk hooves and even bear paws, properly cured, can be made into unique ash trays or lamp bases. This one has been fashioned from hoof of Cape buffalo.

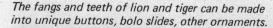

The fangs and teeth of lion and tiger can be made into unique buttons, bolo slides, other ornaments.

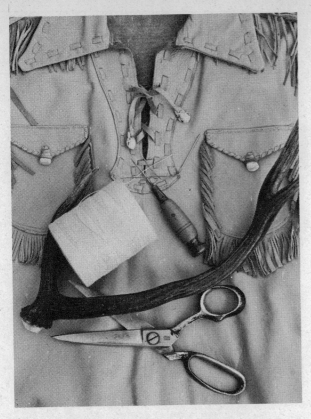

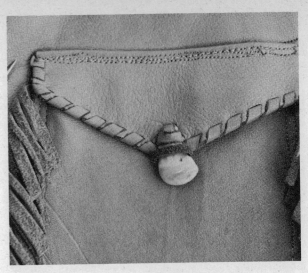

All edges of seams were laced with buckskin lacing made from scraps. Note the button from elk tooth.

Left: Author made this buckskin shirt, using elk's teeth as buttons and for lacing ends. The project required three good-sized hides, though, to finish.

providing his wife will allow it — wearing apparel such as buckskin gloves, shirts, jackets, vests, caps and other items may be turned out from the tanned hides of wild animals that the hunter has bagged himself. Patterns are available in most department stores covering all of these items, so all that is required of the sportsman is a little imagination and ingenuity to make any of these wearable trophies.

In working with tanned hides such as buckskin and other soft leathers, the only tools necessary are a good sharp pair of scissors, a sewing machine, in some cases a pair of leather sewing needles and an awl, and a quantity of linen thread of good quality for stitching those portions of the leather too thick for the usual home-style sewing machine.

Attractive and unique buttons from such materials as horn, antler, ivory and bone are made easily and may be utilized on such items of apparel as sports jackets, buckskin shirts, vests — even on the rear fly of your long john underwear in a pinch. These buttons are cut from that section of the horn, antler or bone closest in diameter to the size of button desired. They should be cut to a thickness of approximately three-sixteenths of an inch, then filed and sanded smooth only on the parts scarred by the hacksaw. Leave the outer edges in their natural state as this is what adds character to these buttons. Either two or four holes are drilled through the center of the button to accommodate the thread that will attach each of them to the garment. These thread holes should only be large enough to accept, with slight clearance, the needle used in sewing. Finally, the buttons are buffed to a high luster and given a coating of thinned brushing lacquer. When dry, they may be sewn to the garment.

One hunter I know is the proud owner of a pair of trophy boots to end all trophy boots! Made to his order and covered with the skin from a giant-sized anaconda snake from South America, these boots are possibly the only ones of their type in existence.

While on the subject of boots, a friend of mine recently visited me from Arusha, Tanzania (formerly Tanganyika), East Africa. He showed me his pair of mosquito boots, the tops of which were covered with the most beautifully figured leopard skin I have ever seen, a trophy of one of his hundreds of hunts into the bush veldt of East Africa and from a leopard that gave him no end of trouble before it was finally bagged. Truly a conversation piece.

The application of trophy hides and solid matter to wearing apparel is limited only by the scope of one's imagination. Noting that I had sundry pieces of jaguar hide left over from a purse and shoes I had made for my wife, she persuaded me to cover a number of buttons with small pieces of the hide from the head section of el tigre. In this area on a jaguar's body, the spots are quite small and lend themselves beautifully to covering buttons. In addition to the buttons, I was persuaded to make a set of additional buttons which were epoxied to earrings.

Trophy hat bands are worn by many hunters today. This probably originated in Africa where a leopard skin band has become almost commonplace. However, many hunters in areas of North America, where bobcats are more or less common, may be seen wearing attractive hunting hats of the felt brimmed variety banded with a colorful strip of bobcat hide. Snakeskin, too, can be made into colorful hat bands, but its use doesn't end there. For many years, I have owned a hunting knife sheath that I covered with snakeskin as well as a waist belt. Both are well over twenty years old and simply refuse to wear out!

The curing of a snakeskin is a simple matter and may be accomplished by the hunter in the field, providing he has warm sunshine and a small quantity of salt in his possession. The snake is skinned by slitting it the full length down the belly. The hide then is stretched, both in length and width, as it is tacked to a board longer in length and wider in width than the stretched skin. Small nails or brads should be placed about an inch apart and driven securely into the board along the outer edges of the hide as it is stretched. Quite naturally the fleshy side

Python hide was used to make this unusual pair of cowboy boots, but it cracked as it dried in time.

Hat bands and covered cigarette boxes are items that can be fashioned from leftover jaguar, leopard hide.

Author had this purse made in Mexico, using part of one of the jaguar hides taken during Yucatan hunt.

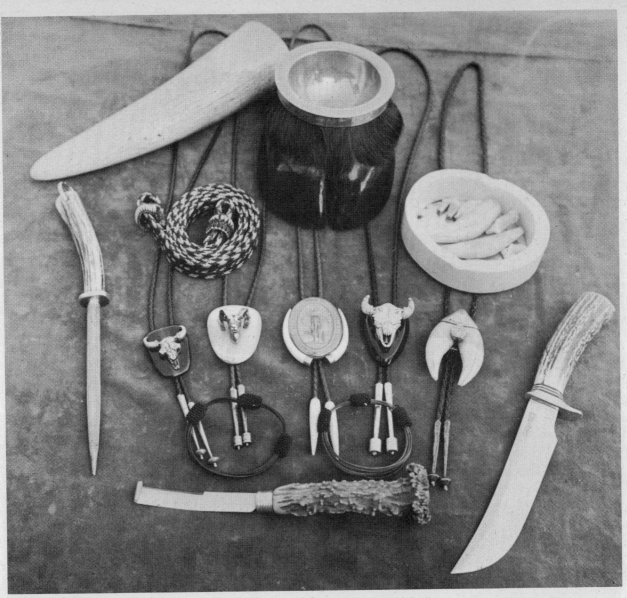

These are some of numerous items that author made from hunting trophies. Included are bolo ties, knife handles, ivory ash trays, ash trays from the hooves of game, bracelets made from elephant hair.

of the skin is left up and, after stretching and nailing, all excess fat is removed with a knife and the skin is thoroughly salted down and placed in the sunshine to dry. About two days in the hot sunshine usually is sufficient to completely cure a snakeskin, after which it is removed from the board, the salt brushed off completely. Depending upon size, the snakeskin now is ready for cementing to almost anything. It may be applied to cigarette lighters, ash trays, belts, hat bands, knife sheaths, yes, even to boots and hammer handles. In cementing snakeskin to any flexible item such as waist belts, a good flexible saddlemaker's cement should be used. To use a hard-drying glue on such items requiring flexibility would be to have the snakeskin come loose in short order.

Should one be fortunate enought to have a quantity of trophy elephant ivory on hand, there are numerous useful — and valuable — items that can be made from this semi-precious material. Again, the craftsman-sportsman is limited only by the scope of his own imagination as to the uses for his raw ivory.

An extremely interesting conversation piece is a set of salt and pepper shakers from either deer or elk antler. The most interesting figured sections of antler are cut into two sections, each measuring approximately three inches in length. These sections then are drilled out — but not all the way through — with a half-inch drill from the largest ends, or bases, of the proposed shakers.

The top of the shaker is drilled out with a small drill in a series of holes to permit either the salt or pepper to flow. The drilled base then is plugged with a cork. The shakers, thoroughly buffed and lacquered, are ready for use.

Sure, the mounted head of a trophy game animal does look great hanging on the wall of any sportsman's gunroom or den. But what happened to the rest of that trophy? The part that the taxidermist didn't need for the mount? What about those hooves, hides and even teeth that were a part of the animal at the time it was bagged? All of these items are certainly trophies of the hunt just as much so as the head.

In many cases the hunter will by-pass having even

This ash tray has been fashioned from jaguar hide, brass, copper and large cartridges for African guns.

Right: Pistol grips are fashioned of elephant ivory and bighorn sheep horn as mementoes of the big hunt.

Elk teeth can be used for many purposes. The ends for lacings add to unique appeal, value of shirt.

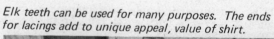

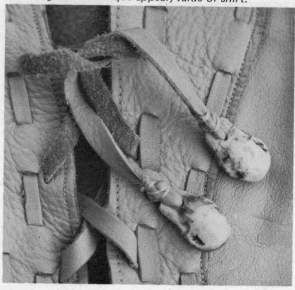

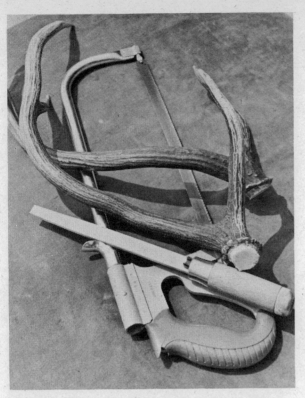

Antlers from deer, elk, caribou, even moose can be used for lamps, knife handles, pistol grips and any number of unusual items for sportsman or his den.

The author prepares to cut a section from an India stag antler to make handles for custom-made knives.

the head of his trophy mounted, settling only for a tanned hide — which he usually rolls up and tosses into a closet — while the horns, antlers, hooves, teeth and other components of his trophies either go begging in the rafters of his garage or are relegated to the smelly confines of a garbage pail for disposal.

There are numerous other useful items that may be made by the enterprising sportsman-hunter in utilizing those left-overs.

Take the cloven hooves of such animals as deer, antelope, wild boar and elk. These hooves — with short sections of the hide covered legs left attached — can be made into countless attractive and unusual items, especially if the job is done shortly after they are removed from the carcass. The freshly removed leg and hoof sections are placed into a brine of salt water for about a week or more — after which they may be removed from the brine, bent to the desired angle then placed on a board and with the aid of nails driven into the board to hold the bent legs in the proper position, allowed to thoroughly dry in the sun. Usually about a week of drying is sufficient. Less, if the sun is warm.

When thoroughly dry, these hoof-leg sections may be made into such items as rifle racks, table lamps, letter opener handles, legs for stools and any number of other practical things.

Hooves from larger animals, such as buffalo, elk and large mule deer may be utilized as pin cushions, ash trays, bases for table lamps and containers for paper clips and other necessities on the sportsman's desk.

Tanned hides may be used in covering den chairs, cigarette and cigar boxes, ash trays, photo albums, coffee table tops, humidor covers and even wastebaskets. Should you have a trophy rhino hide or two

lying around, then these make into most unique table tops that are real eye-stoppers.

Elk and deer antler provide ideal material for such things as pistol grip and forearm caps on rifles, hunting knife handles, pistol grips, chair and stool legs, unique table lamps, and even ash tray holders may be made from sections of the larger horn or antler by hollowing out the center to accept a brass or copper ash tray.

It is sometimes desirable to combine hide, horn, antler and hooves in creating an interesting item for the trophy or gunroom.

Take for instance a coffee table that I constructed some years ago — still a prized possession in my den. This table has four legs made from the horns of Texas steers while the top is of carved Texas steer hide depicting a Wells Fargo stage coach crossing the plains. The carved leather top is encircled with a section of top-grade manila lariat rope. Pieces of furniture like this certainly cannot be bought at any local furniture store and therefore are rare, unusual and unique.

Possibly some of the more unusual den trophies are those made from the skulls of dangerous animals. **After boiling,** cleaning and bleaching in the sun, skulls may be trimmed in either brass, copper or sterling silver and made into outstanding ash trays or other useful items in the trophy room. The use of skulls in this matter should be limited to those of dangerous animals having impressive-sized fangs or chompers such as lion, jaguar, leopard or wild boar. The use of non-dangerous animal skulls, such as deer, antelope etc. are neither impressive nor decorative in the den or trophy room.

Some years ago, I purchased a small, hinged box of sandarac wood in Mogador, French Morocco, and

The skin and rattles from rattlesnake can be made into attractive hatband with minimum preparation.

Author took his jaguar in Yucatan, uses the fangs to create handsome bolo tie bearing silver cap and the cartridge case from round that downed the cat.

Epoxy cement can be used extensively in bonding animal matter of all types. In this instance, a slide is being cemented to a piece of buffalo horn.

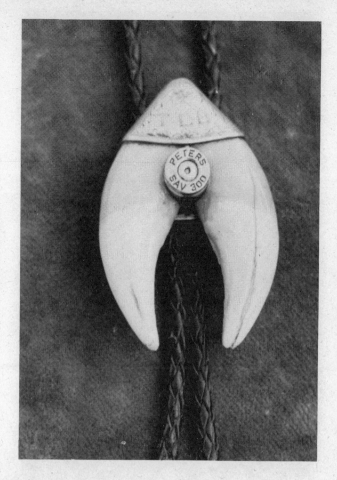

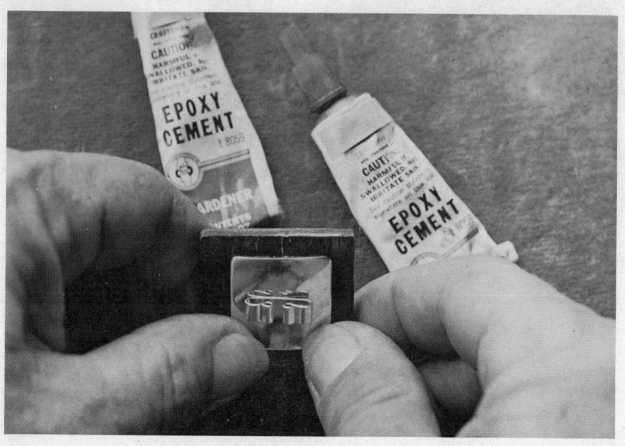

Author made rug of this jaguar's tanned skin. Skull was made into ash tray, while the fangs went into one of the bolo ties, illustrated elsewhere in story.

This hoof knife for the horseman is mounted with a section of axis deer antler. The rifle sling has been laboriously braided of varied color horsehair.

Made in Africa by tribesmen, these elephant hair bracelets are considered acme of trophy materials among big game hunters, who have shot an elephant.

Elephant ivory, one of the most sought semi-rare materials is used for handle of custom-built knife.

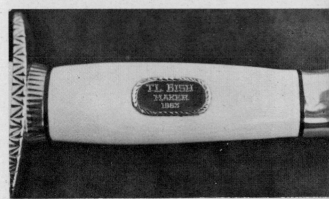

while this box wasn't too impressive to those not familiar with its origin, I valued it as a trophy of my travels. I since have covered this box, the hinges of which were made by the Arabs from discarded beer cans, with leopard skin and it seldom fails to draw favorable comment from visitors whereas in the past it was hardly noticed.

Strips and scraps of tanned hide from game animals may be cemented to a large variety of equipment, thus giving them both value and attractiveness. Cigarette lighters, letter openers and even picture frames can be greatly enhanced in appearance by the simple application of a strip of wild animal hide. Where in the past these same items had no appeal, you will notice that they become real conversation pieces among friends, guests and visitors to your gunroom or den after gluing on a small piece of colorful animal hide.

Some years ago, I was given a number of sizable elk antlers, all of which had lain exposed to the elements for some years. While these antlers were bleached by years of exposure to all kinds of weather, I found that by carefully staining them with mahogany-colored wood stain, they again took on their original rich color. Following the staining, I coated those antlers with a thinned-down brushing lacquer until they were glassy smooth.

Over a period of approximately four months, I managed to turn that pile of elk antlers into what is probably one of the most unusual items that I ever

Unusual coffee table was constructed by the author, using horns from Texas steers as legs. The top is leather carving depicting stagecoach on the prairie.

Select sections of deer or elk antler can be made into variety of items, including fancy pistol grips.

Elk and deer legs are easily cured and made into rifle racks or lamp bases by tool-handy hunters.

attempted, a Chair! When finished, the chair weighed something like ninety-six pounds, stood over five feet in height and was four feet in width! This chair was surprisingly comfortable and as rugged as a Sherman tank! Today this same chair is in a museum in Oregon with a placard that reads: **Made By An Early Oregon Pioneer!** ?????

The number of useful items that can be constructed by the sportsman-hunter from antlers, horns, hides and other by-products of the hunt is almost endless but you can rest assured that these same items will be unique, unusual, rare and real functional pieces. They will be a constant reminder of those hunts that you have made in the past.

As brought out earlier, the tools needed for building or assembling these mementoes of the hunt are simple. A hacksaw for cutting the hard material, garnet or sand paper and a file for smoothing-up and a buffer for polishing are about all that are needed in working with antler, horn, bone or hooves. Epoxy cement should be used exclusively in joining any of the above together or to a base of wood. In covering various items with animal hide, the only necessities are a sharp pair of scissors and a bottle or can of good rubber cement or saddlemaker's glue.

As stated, the craftsman-sportsman is limited only by the scope of his own imagination as to the uses he might put the surplus "spare parts" from his trophy game.

GUNSMITH SUPPLIERS' DIRECTORY

CLEANING & REFINISHING SUPPLIES

ADSCO, Box 191, Ft. Kent, Me. 04743 (stock finish)
Ed Agramonte, 41 Riverdale Ave., Yonkers, N.Y. 10701
 (Ed's cold blue)
Allied Products Co., 734 N. Leavitt, Chicago, Ill. 60612 (Cor-O-Dex)
Ammodyne, Box 1589, Los Angeles, Cal. 90053 (Gun Kote)
Backus Co., 411 W. Water St., Smethport, Pa. 16749
 (field gun-cleaner)
Birchwood-Casey Chem. Co., 7900 Fuller Rd., Eden Prairie, Minn.
 55343 (Anderol, etc.)
Jim Brobst, 31 S. 3rd, Hamburg, Pa. 19526 (J-B Compound)
Geo. Brothers, Great Barrington, Mass. 01230 (G-B Linspeed Oil)
Bullet Pouch, Box 4285, Long each, Cal. 90804 (Mirror Lube)
Burnishine Prod. Co., 8140 N. Ridgeway, Skokie, Ill. 60076
 (Stock Glaze)
Chopie Tool & Die Co., 531 Copeland, La Crosse, Wis. 54601
 (Black-Solve)
Clenzoil Co., Box 1226, Sta. C, Canton, O. 44708
Commercial Chemical Co., Inc., Box 711, Houston, Tex. (bore oil)
Dex-Kleen, Box 509 Des Moines, Ia. 50302 (gun wipers)
Dri-Slide, Inc., Industrial Park, Fremont, Mich. 49412
Forty-Five Ranch Enterpr., Box 1080, Miami, Okla. 74354
Frye Industs., Box 1244, Laguna Beach, Cal. 92652
Fur Fame Bait Co., Route 1, Lindsay, O. 43442 (U.S. Bbl. Blue)
Gun-All Products, Box 244, Dowagiac, Mich. 49047
Percy Harms Corp., 7349 N. Hamlin, Skokie, Ill. 60076
Hell Mtn. Gun Shop, R.D. 2, Lebanon, N.J. 08833 (Moose Milk)
Hi-Speed Patch, 1488 N. Glen, Fresno, Calif. 93728 (oiled patches)
Frank C. Hoppe, P.O. Box 97, Parkesburg, Pa. 19365
Hunting World, 247 E. 50th St., N.Y., N.Y. 10022 (P-H Safari Kit)
Jet-Aer Corp., 165 3rd St., Paterson, N.J. 07514 (blues & oils)
LPS Res. Labs. Inc., 2050 Cotner Ave., Los Angeles, Calif. 90025
Carl Lampert Co., 2639 So. 31st St., Milwaukee, Wis. 53215
 (gun bags)
Lehigh Chem. Co., Box 120, Chestertown, Md. 21620 (Anderol)
LEM Gun Spec., Box 31, College Park, Ga. 30022 (Lewis Lead
 Remover)
Liquid Wrench, Box 10628, Charlotte, N.C. 28201 (pen. oil)
Lynx-Line Gun Products, Box 3985, Detroit, Mich. 48227
Marble Arms Co., 1120 Superior, Gladstone, Mich. 49837
Mill Run Prod., 1360 W. 9th, Cleveland, O. 44113 (Brite-Bore Kits)
Mint Luster Cleaners, 1102 N. Division, Appleton, Wis. 54911
Mistic Metal Mover, Inc., 19 E. Peru St., Princeton, Ill. 61356
Mitchell Chemical Co., Wampus Lane, Milford, Conn. (Gun
 Guard)
New Method Mfg. Co., Box 175, Bradford, Pa. 16701 (gun blue)
Numrich Arms Co., West Hurley, N.Y. 12491 (44-40 gun blue)
Nutec, Box 1187, Wilmington, Del. 19899 (Dry-Lube)
Outers Laboratories, Onalaska, Wis. 54650 (Gunslick kits)
Glen A. Pemberton, 260 Macedon Center Rd., Fairport, N.Y. 14450
Polyform Mfg. Corp., Box 305, Escondido, Calif. 92025
R.E.I., 101 Wolpers, Park Forest, Ill. 60466 (whale oil lube)
Radiator Spec. Co., Charlotte, N.C. 28201 (liquid wrench)
Realist Inc., N. 93 W. 16288 Megal Dr., Menomonee Falls, Wis. 53051
Riel & Fuller, 423 Woodrow Ave., Dunkirk, N.Y. 14048 (anti-rust oil)
Rig Products Co., Box 279, Oregon, Ill. 61061 (Rig Grease)
Rocket Chemical Co., Inc., 5390 Napa St., San Diego, Calif.
 92110 (WD-40)
Rusteprufe Labs., Box 333, Sparta, Wis. 54656
Seatex Corp., 6400 Westpark Dr., Houston, Tex. 77027
Service Armament, 689 Bergen Blvd., Ridgefield, N.J. 07657
 (Parker-Hale)
Sheldon's Inc., Box 508, Antigo, Wis. 54409 (shotgun brushes)
Shirtpocket Gun Rod, 1518 Alabama St., Vallejo, Calif. 94594
Shooters Specialties, Box 264, LaMirada, Calif. 90638 (Schukra rod)
Silicote Corp., Box 359, Oshkosh, Wis. 54901 (Silicone cloths)
Silver Dollar Guns, 7 Balsam St., Keene, N.H. 03431 (silicone oil)
A. D. Soucy, Box 191, Ft. Kent, Me. 04743 (stock finish)
Sportsmen's Lus., Inc. Box 732, Anoka, Minn. 55303 (Gun
 Life lube.)
Sun Ray Chemicals, 371-30th Ave., San Francisco, Calif. 94121
Taylor & Robbins, Box 164, Rixford, Pa. 16745 (Throat Saver)
C. S. Van Gorden, 120 Tenth Ave., Eau Claire, Wis. 54701 (Instant
 Blue)
W&W Mfg. Co., Box 365, Belton, Mo. 64012 (shotgun cleaner)
Webber Gage Division, 12900 Triskett Rd., Cleveland, O. 44111
 (Luger oil)
H. M. Whetstone & Co., 282 St. George St., St. Augustine, Fla.
 32084
Williams Gun Sight, 7389 Lapeer Rd., Davison, Mich. 48423
 (finish kit)
Winslow Arms Co., P.O. Box 578, Osprey, Fla. 33595 (refinishing kit)

GUN PARTS, ANTIQUE

Bannerman, F., Box 26, Blue Point, Long Island, N.Y. 11715
Shelley Braverman, Athens, N.Y. 12015 (obsolete guns)
Carter Gun Works, 2211 Jefferson Pk. Ave., Charlottesville, Va. 22903
Dixie Gun Works, Inc., Hwy 51, South, Union City, Tenn. 38261
Ellwood Epps Sporting Goods, 80 King St., Clinton, Ont., Canada
Golden Eagle, 36 E. Brown St., West Haven, Conn. 06516 (list 25c)
International Gunmakers, 12315 Newburgh, Livonia, Mich. 48150
Edw. E. Lucas, 32 Garfield Ave., Old Ridge, N.J. 08857 (45-70)
R. M. Marek, Rt. 1, Box 1-A, Banks Ore. 97106 (cannons)
Thomas I. Mazzola, 6937 54th Ave., Maspeth, N.Y. 11378
Numrich Arms Co., West Hurley, N.Y. 12491
Robert Patton, Box 13155, San Antonio, Tex. 78213
 (Obsolete Win.)
A. Sheldon Rich, 114 Franklin St., Revere, Mass. 02151
Norman S. Romig, 910 Fairmount Ave., Trenton, N.J. 08629
S&S Firearms, 88-21 Aubrey Ave., Glendale, N.Y. 11227
H. M. Schoeller, 569 S. Braddock Ave., Pittsburgh, Pa. 15221 (ML)
Rob. Thompson, 844-14th Ave., So., Clinton, Ia. 52732 (Win. only)
R. M. Verner, 263 Kurtz Rd., Marietta. Ga. 30060
C. H. Weisz, Box 311, Arlington, Va. 22210

GUN PARTS, U. S. AND FOREIGN

Badger Shooter's Supply, Owen, Wisc. 54460
Shelley Braverman, Athens, N.Y. 12015
Philip R. Crouthamel, 817 E. Baltimore, E. Lansdowne, Pa. 19050
Charles E. Duffy, Williams Lane, West Hurley, N.Y. 12491
Federal Ordnance Inc., P.O. Box 36032, Los Angeles, Calif. 90036
Greeley Arms Co., Inc., 223 Little Falls Rd., Fairfield, N.J. 07006
Gunner's Armory, 186 Dartmouth St., San Francisco, Calif. 94124
H&B Gun Corp., 1228 Fort St., Lincoln Park, Mich. 48166
Hudson Sporting Goods Co., 52 Warren St., New York, N.Y. 10007
Hunter's Haven, Zero Prince St., Alexandria, Va. 22314
Inter-American Co., P.O. Box 8022, Sacramento, Calif. 95818
Bob Lovell, Box 401, Elmhurst, Ill. 60126
Numrich Arms Co., West Hurley, N.Y. 12491
Potomac Arms Corp. (see Hunter's Haven)
Powder Horn, Box 545, Pt. Pleasant, N.J. 08742
Reed & Co., Shokan, N.Y. 12481
Martin B. Retting, Inc., 11029 Washington, Culver City, Cal. 90230
Santa Barbara of America, Ltd., P.O. Box 925, So. Houston,
 Tex. 77587 (barrels and barreled actions)
Sarco, Inc., 192 Central, Stirling, N.J. 07980
R. A. Saunders, 3253 Hillcrest Dr., San Antonio, Tex. 78201 (clips)
Schmid & Ladd, 14733 Hwy. 19 So., Clearwater, Fla. 33516
Shooters Specialties, Box 264, LaMirada, Calif. 90638
Clifford L. Smires, R.D., Columbus, N.J. 08022 (Mauser)
Spokane Sporting Goods, 1702 N. Monroe, Spokane, Wash. 99205
N. F. Strebe, 4926 Marlboro Pike, S.E., Washington, D.C. 20027
Tilden Mfg. Co., 607 Santa Fe Dr., Denver, Colo. 80204

GUNSMITH SCHOOLS

Colorado School of Trades, 1545 Hoyt, Denver, Colo. 80215
Lassen Junior College, 11100 Main St., Susanville, Calif. 96130
Oregon Technical Institute, Klamath Falls, Ore. 97601
Penn. Gunsmith School, 812 Ohio River Blvd., Pittsburgh, Pa. 15202
Trinidad State Junior College, Trinidad, Colo. 81082

GUNSMITH SUPPLIES, TOOLS, SERVICES

Adams & Nelson Co., 4125 W. Fullerton, Chicago, Ill. 60639
Alamo Heat Treating Co., Box 55345, Houston, Tex. 77055
Alley Supply Co., Box 458, Sonora, Calif. 95370
American Edelstaal, Inc., 350 Broadway, New York, N.Y. 10013
Anderson Gunshop, 1203 Broadway, Yakima, Wash. 98902
 (tang safe)
Armite Labs., 1845 Randolph St., Los Angeles, Cal. 90001 (pen oiler)
B-Square Co., Box 11281, Ft. Worth, Tex. 76110
Benrite Co., 353 Covington, San Antonio, Tex. 78220
Brown & Sharpe Mfg. Co., Precision Pk., No. Kingston, R.I. 02852
Bob Brownell's, Main & Third, Montezuma, Ia. 50171
W. E. Brownell, 1852 Alessandro Trail, Vista, Calif. 92083
 (checkering tools)
Maynard P. Buehler, Inc., 17 Orinda Hwy., Orinda, Calif. 94563
 (Rocol lube)
Burgess Vibrocrafters, Inc. (BVI), Rte. 21, Grayslake, Ill. 60030

M. H. Canjar, 500 E. 45th, Denver, Colo. 80216 (triggers, etc.)
Centerline Prod. Box 14074, Denver, Colo. 80214
Chicago Wheel & Mfg. Co., 1101 W. Monroe St., Chicago, Ill. 60607
(Handee grinders)
Christy Gun Works, 875 - 57th St., Sacramento, Calif. 95819
Clymer Mfg. Co., 14241 W. 11 Mile Rd., Oak Park, Mich. 48237
(reamers)
Colbert Die Cast Co., 10107 Adella, South Gate, Calif. 90280 (Panavise)
A. Constantine & Son, Inc., 2050 Eastchester Rd., Bronx, N.Y.
10461 (wood)
Dayton-Traister Co., 7028 164th St., S.W., Edmonds, Wash. 98020
(triggers)
Dem-Bart Co., 3333 N. Gove St., Tacoma, Wash. 98407
(checkering tools)
Die Supply Corp., 3173 E. 66th St., Cleveland, O. 44127
Wm. Dixon, Inc., Box 89, Newark, N.J. 07101
Dremel Mfg. Co., P.O. Box 518, Racine, Wis. 53401 (grinders)
Chas. E. Duffy, Williams Lane, West Hurley, N.Y. 12491
Dumore Co., 1300 - 17th St., Racine, Wis. 53403
E-Z Tool Co., 918 Douglas, Des Moines, Ia. 50313 (lathe attachment)
Edmund Scientific Co., 101 E. Gloucester Pike, Barrington, N.J. 08007
F. K. Elliott, Box 785, Ramona, Calif. 92065 (reamers)
Foredom Elec. Co., Rt. 6, Bethel, Conn. 06801 (power drills)
Forster Appelt Mfg. Co., Inc., 82 E. Lanark Ave., Lanark, Ill. 61046
Keith Francis, Box 343, Talent, Ore. 97540 (reamers)
G. R. S. Corp., Box 1157, Boulder, Colo. 80302 (Gravermeister)
Gold Lode, Inc., P.O. Box 31, Addison, Ill. 60101 (gold inlay kit)
Grace Metal Prod., Box 67, Elk Rapids, Mich. 49629
(screw drivers, drifts)
Gopher Shooter's Supply, Box 246, Faribault, Minn. 55021
(screwdrivers, etc.)
H. & M., 24062 Orchard Lake Rd., Farmington, Mich. 48024
(reamers)
Hartford Reamer Co., Box 134, Lathrop Village, Mich. 48075
R. E. Hutchinson, Burbank Rd., Sutton, Mass. 01527 (engine
turning tool)
O. Iber Co., 626 W. Randolph, Chicago, Ill. 60606
The Joplings, Box 483, Bellevue, Neb. 68005
Kasenite Co., Inc., 3 King St., Mahwah, N.J. 07430 (surface
hrdng. comp.)
Lea Mfg. Co., 238 E. Aurora St., Waterbury, Conn. 06720
Lock's Phila. Gun Exch., 6700 Rowland Ave., Philadelphia, Pa.
19149
Marker Machine Co., Box 426, Charleston, Ill. 61920
Viggo Miller, P.O. Box 4181, Omaha, Neb. 68104
Miller Single Trigger Mfg. Co., Box 69, Millersburg, Pa. 17061
Frank Mittermeier, 3577 E. Tremont, N.Y., N.Y. 10465
Moderntools Corp., Box 407, Dept. GD, Woodside, N.Y. 11377
Karl A. Neise, Inc., 5602 Roosevelt Ave., Woodside, N.Y. 11377
P & C Tool Co., Box 22066, Portland, Ore. 97222
P.G.E. Products, 6700 Rowland Ave., Philadelphia, Pa. 19100
Palmgren, 8383 South Chicago Ave., Chicago, Ill. 60167 (vises, etc.)
C. R. Pedersen & Son, Ludington, Mich. 49431
Penn Ind., Box 8904, Philadelphia, Pa. 19135 (contour gauge)
Ponderay Lab., 210 W. Prasch, Yakima, Wash. 98902 (epoxy
glass bedding)
Redford Reamer Co., Box 6604, Detroit, Mich. 48240
Richland Arms Co., 321 W. Adrian St., Blissfield, Mich. 49228
Riley's Supply Co., Box 365, Avilla, Ind. 46710
(Niedner buttplates, caps)
Roderick Arms & Tool Corp., 110 2nd St., Monett, Mo. 65708
Rob. A. Saunders, 3253 Hillcrest Dr., San Antonio, Tex. 78201
(45 conversion kit)
Schuetzen Gun Works, 1226 Prairie Rd., Colo. Springs, Colo. 80909
Silver Grip Caps, Bill Dyer, 503 Midwest Bldg., Oklahoma City,
Okla. 73102
Shooters Specialties, Box 246, La Mirada, Calif. 90638
Silken Compass Cutter Co., Box 242, Oceanside, N.Y. 11592
A. D. Soucy Co., Box 191, Fort Kent, Me. 04743 (ADSCO stock finish)
L. S. Starrett Co., Athol, Mass. 01331
T.D.C., Box 42072, Portland, Ore. 97242
Timney Mfg. Co., 5624 Imperial Hwy., So. Gate, Calif. 90280
(triggers)
Stan de Treville, Box 2446, San Diego, Calif 92112 (checkering
patterns)
Twin City Steel Treating Co., Inc., 1114 S. 3rd, Minneapolis,
Minn. 55415
Ward Mfg. Co., 500 Ford Blvd., Hamilton, O. 45011
Will-Burt Co., Box 160, Orrville, O. 44667 (vises)
Williams Gun Sight Co., 7389 Lapeer Rd., Davison, Mich. 48423
Wilson Arms Co., Box 364, Stony Creek, Branford, Conn. 06405
Wilton Tool Corp., 9525 W. Irving Pk. Rd., Schiller Park, Ill.
60176 (vises)
Woodcraft Supply Corp., 71 Canal St., Boston, Mass. 02114
Wright Gun & Tool Co., Box 245, Bloomsburg, Pa. 17815

HANDGUN GRIPS

Beckelhymer's, Hidalgo & San Bernardo, Laredo, Tex. 78040
Belmont Products, 415—2nd Ave. N., Twin Falls, Ida. 83301
Caray Sales Co., 2044 Hudson St., Ft. Lee, N.J. 07024
Cloyce's Gun Stocks, Box 1133, Twin Falls, Ida. 83301
Enforcer Prod. Div., Caray Sales Co., 2044 Hudson St., Fort Lee,
N.J. 07024

Fitz, Box 49797, Los Angeles, Calif. 90049
Herret's, Box 741, Twin Falls, Ida. 83301
Mershon Co., Inc., 1230 S. Grand Ave., Los Angeles, Calif. 90015
Mustang Grips, 13830 Hiway 395, Edgemont, Calif. 92508
Safety Grip Corp., Box 456, Riverside St., Miami, Fla. 33135
Sanderson Custom Pistol Stocks, 17695 Fenton, Detroit, Mich. 48219
Jay Scott, 81 Sherman Place, Garfield, N.J. 07026
Sile Dist., 7 Centre Market Pl., New York, N.Y. 10013
Sports, Inc., 5501 Broadway, Chicago, Ill. 60640 (Franzite)
John W. Womack, 3006 Bibb St., Shreveport, La. 71108

METALLIC SIGHTS

B-Square Eng. Co., Box 11281, Ft. Worth, Tex. 76110
Bo-Mar Tool & Mfg. Co., Box 168, Carthage, Tex. 75633
Maynard P. Buehler, Inc., 17 Orinda Highway, Orinda, Calif. 94563
Chicago Gun Center, 3109 W. Armitage, Chicago, Ill. 60647
Christy Gun Works, 875 57th St., Sacramento, Calif. 95819
Clerke Technicorp., 2054 Broadway Ave., Santa Monica, Calif. 90404
Art Cook Supply, Rte. 2, Box 123B, Laurel, Md. 20810 (Illum. gunsight)
Firearms Dev. Lab., Box 278, Scotts Valley, Calif. 95060
Freeland's Scope Stands, Inc., 3734-14th Ave., Rock Island, Ill.
61201
P. W. Gray Co., Fairgrounds Rd., Nantucket, Mass. 02554 (shotgun)
Hi Lo Sights, P.O. Box 131, Lyndon Station, Wis. 53944
International Guns, 66 Warburton Ave., Yonkers, N.Y. 10701
Lyman Gun Sight Corp., Middlefield, Conn. 06455
Marble Arms Corp., 1120 Superior, Gladstone, Mich. 49837
Merit Gunsight Co., P.O. Box 995, Sequim, Wash. 98382
Micro Sight Co., 242 Harbor Blvd., Belmont, Calif. 94002
Original Sight Exchange Co., Box J, Paoli, Pa. 19301
C. R. Pedersen & Son, Ludington, Mich. 49431
Precision Gun Sight Co., Box 2143, West Hartford, Conn. 06117
(shotgun)
Redfield Gun Sight Co., 1315 S. Clarkson St., Denver, Colo. 80210
Schwarz's Gun Shop, 41 - 15th St., Wellsburg, W. Va. 26070
Simmons Gun Specialties, Inc., 700 Rodgers Rd., Olathe, Kans. 66061
Slug Site Co., 3835 University, Des Moines, Ia. 50311
Stokes Ent., 5290 Long Beach Blvd., Long Beach, Calif. 90805
Wm. Tell Gun Sight, Inc., Rte. 1, Wilder, Ida., 83676
Trius Prod., Box 25, Cleves, O. 45002 (bi-ocular)
Williams Gun Sight Co., 7389 Lapeer Rd., Davison, Mich. 48423
W. H. Womack, 2124 Meriwether Rd., Shreveport, La. 71108

MUZZLE LOADING BARRELS OR EQUIPMENT

Luther Adkins, Box 281, Shelbyville, Ind. 46176 (breech plugs)
Jesse F. Booher, 2751 Ridge Ave., Dayton, Ohio 45414
G. S. Bunch, 7735 Garrison, Hyattsville, Md. 20784 (flask repair)
Pat Burke, 3339 Farnsworth Rd., Lapeer, Mich. 48446 (capper)
Challanger Mfg. Co., 105-23 New York Blvd., Jamaica, N.Y. 11433
(H.&A. guns)
Cherry Corners Gun Shop, Rte. 1, Lodi, Ohio 44254
Earl T. Cureton, Rte. 6, 7017 Pine Grove Rd., Knoxville, Tenn. 37914
(powder horns)
John N. Dangelzer, 3056 Frontier Pl. N.E., Albuquerque, N. Mex.
87106 (powder flasks)
Ted Fellowes, 9245 16th Ave. S.W., Seattle, Wash. 98106
International Gunmakers, 12315 Newburgh Rd., Livonia, Mich. 48150
JJJJ Ranch, Wm. Large, Rte. 1, Ironton, Ohio 45638
J. Lewis Arms Mfg., 3931 Montgomery Rd., Cincinnati, Ohio 45212
(pistol)
Log Cabin Sport Shop, R.D. 1, Lodi, Ohio 44254
Jos. W. Mellott, 334 Rockhill Rd., Pittsburgh, Pa. 15243 (barrel blanks)
W. L. Mowrey Gun Works, Inc., Box 711, Olney, Tex. 73674
Numrich Corp., W. Hurley, N.Y. 12491 (powder flasks)
Penna. Rifle Works, 319 E. Main St., Ligonier, Pa. 15658
(ML guns, parts)
H. M. Schoeller, 569 So. Braddock Ave., Pittsburgh, Pa. 15221
C. E. Siler, 9 Sandhurst Dr., Asheville, N.C. 28806 (flint locks)

REBORING AND RERIFLING

A & M Rifle Co., Box 1713, Prescott, Ariz. 86301
P. O. Ackley, P.O. Box 17347, Salt Lake City, Utah 84117
Bain & Davis Sptg. Gds., 559 W. Las Tunas Dr., San Gabriel, Calif.
91776
Carpenter's Gun Works, Rt. 32, Plattekill, N.Y. 12568
Fuller Gun Shop, Cooper Landing, Alaska 99572
Ward Koozer, Box 18, Walterville, Ore. 97489
Les' Gun Shop, Box 511, Kalispell, Mont. 59901
Nu-Line Guns, 3727 Jennings Rd., St. Louis, Mo. 63121
Al Petersen, Riverhurst, Saskatchewan, Canada
Schuetzen Gun Works, 1226 Prairie Rd., Colorado Springs. Colo.
80909
J. Hall Sharon, Box 106, Kalispell, Mont. 59901
Smith's Gun Shop, Box 486, East Tawas, Mich. 48730
Snapp's Gunshop, 6911 E. Washington Rd., Clare, Mich. 48617
R. Southgate, Rt. 2, Franklin, Tenn. 37064 (Muzzleloaders)
J. W. Van Patten, Box 145, Foster Hill, Milford, Pa. 18337

RIFLE BARREL MAKERS

A & M Rifle Co., Box 1713, Prescott, Ariz. 86301
P.O. Ackley, P.O. Box 17347, Salt Lake City, Utah 84117
Apex Rifle Co., 7628 San Fernando, Sun Valley, Calif. 91352

Christy Gun Works, 875 57th St., Sacramento, Calif. 95819
Clerke Technicorp., 2054 Broadway Ave., Santa Monica, Calif. 90404
Cuthbert Gun Shop, 715 So. 5th, Coos Bay, Ore. 97420
G. R. Douglas, 5504 Big Tyler Rd., Charleston, W. Va. 25312
Federal Firearms Co., Inc., Box 145, Oakdale, Pa. 15071 (Star bbls., actions)
Gibbs Rifle Prod., Viola, Ida. 83872
A. R. Goode, 3306 Sellman Rd., Adelphi, Md. 20783
Hart Rifle Barrels, Inc., RD 2, Lafayette, N.Y. 13084
Wm. H. Hobaugh, Box 657, Philipsburg, Mont. 59858
Intern'l Gunmakers, 12315 Newburgh Rd., Livonia, Mich. 48150
Jim's Gun Shop, 715 So. 5th St., Coos Bay, Ore. 97420
Johnson Automatics, Box 306, Hope Valley, R.I. 02832
Les' Gun Shop, Box 511, Kalispell, Mont. 59901
L. E. Nauman, 1048 S. 5th, Douglas, Wyo. 82633
Nu-Line Guns, Inc., 3727 Jennings Rd., St. Louis, Mo. 63121
Numrich Arms, W. Hurley, N.Y. 12491
SS & D, Inc., Clinton Corners, N.Y. 12514 (cold-formed bbls.)
Sanders Cust. Gun Serv., 2358 Tyler Lane, Louisville, Ky. 40205
J. H. Sharon, Box 106, Kalispell, Mont. 59901
Ed Shilen Rifles, 4510 Harrington Rd., Irving, Tex. 75060
Bliss Titus, 70 E. 2nd No., Heber City, Utah 84032
Walker Machine Tool Co., 4804 Pinewood Rd., Louisville, Ky. 40218
M. G. Watts, 5627 Euclid, Kansas City, Mo. 64130
Wilson Arms, Box 364, Stony Creek, Branford, Conn. 06405
Realist, Inc., N. 93 W. 16288, Megal Dr., Menomonee Falls, Wis. 53051
Redfield Gun Sight Co., 1315 S. Clarkson St., Denver, Colo. 80210
S & K Mfg. Co., Box 247, Pittsburgh, Pa. 16340 (Insta-mount)
Sanders Cust. Gun Serv., 2358 Tyler Lane, Louisville, Ky. 402305 (MSW)
Savage Arms, Westfield, Mass. 01085
Scope Inst. Co., 25-20 Brooklyn-Queens Expressway West, Woodside, N.Y. 11377
Sears, Roebuck & Co., 825 S. St. Louis, Chicago, Ill. 60607
Selsi Co., 40 Veterans Blvd., Carlstadt, N.J. 07072
Southern Precision Inst. Co., 710 Augusta St., San Antonio, Tex. 78215
Southwest Cutlery, 1309 Olympic, Montebello, Calif. 90640 (lens cap)
Stoeger Arms Co., 55 Ruta Ct., S. Hackensack, N.J. 07606
Swift Instruments, Inc., 952 Dorchester Ave., Boston, Mass. 02125
Tasco, 1075 N.W. 71st, Miami, Fla. 33138
Tradewinds, Inc., Box 1191, Tacoma, Wash. 98401
Trueline Instruments, Box 1357, Englewood, Colo. 80110
John Unertl Optical Co., 3551-5 East St., Pittsburgh, Pa. 15214
United Binocular Co., 9043 S. Western Ave., Chicago, Ill. 60620
Universal Firearms Corp., 3746 E. 10th Ct., Hialeah, Fla. 33013
Vissing Co., Box 437, Idaho Falls, Idaho 83402 (lens cap)
H. P. Wasson, Box 181, Netcong, N.J. 07857 (eyeglass apertures)
Weatherby's, 2781 Firestone, South Gate, Calif. 90280
W. R. Weaver Co., 7125 Industrial Ave., El Paso, Tex. 79915
Williams Gun Sight Co., 7389 Lapeer Rd., Davison, Mich. 48423
Carl Zeiss Inc., 444 Fifth Ave., New York, N.Y. 10018 (Hensoldt)

STOCKS (Commercial and Custom)

W. S. Abe, 5124 Huntington Dr., Los Angeles, Calif. 90032
R. E. Anderson, 706 So. 23rd St., Laramie, Wyo. 82070
G. & S. Bartlett, 23004 W. Lancaster Rd., Lancaster, Calif. 93534
John Bianchi, 212 W. Foothill Blvd., Monrovia, Calif. 91016 (U. S. carbines)
Al Biesen, West 2039 Sinto Ave., Spokane, Wash. 99201
E. C. Bishop & Son Inc., Box 7, Warsaw, Mo. 65355
Wm. Buchele, 2832 Sagamore Rd., Toledo, O. 43606 (ML only)
Cadmus Ind., 6311 Yucca St., Hollywood, Calif. (U. C. carbines)
Calico, 1648 Airport Blvd., Windsor, Calif. 95492 (blanks)
Chuck's Custom Gun Stocks, P.O. Box 1123, Frederick, Md. 21701
Mike Conner, Box 324, Cedar Crest, N.M. 87008
Crane Creek Gun Stock Co., Box 268, Waseca, Minn. 56093
Charles De Veto, 14087 Irene Rd., Lyndhurst, O. 44124
Reinhart Fajen, Box 338, Warsaw, Mo. 65355
N. B. Fashingbauer, Box 366, Lac Du Flambeau, Wis. 54538
Ted Fellowes, 9245 16th Ave. S. W., Seattle, Wash. 98106
Clyde E. Fischer, Rt. 1, Box 170-M, Victoria, Tex. 77901
Jerry Fisher, 1244—4th Ave., Kalispell, Mont. 59901
Flaig's Lodge, Millvale, Pa. 15209
Horace M. Frantz, Box 128, Farmingdale, N.J. 07727
Freeland's Scope Stands, Inc., 3734 14th Ave., Rock Island, Ill. 61201
Frontier Gunshop, 3584 Mt. Diablo Blvd., Lafayette, Calif. 94549
Aaron T. Gates, 3229 Felton St., San Diego, Calif. 92104
Dale Goens, Box 224, Cedar Crest, N.M. 87008
Gould's Myrtlewood, 1692 N. Dogwood, Coquille, Ore. 97423
Rolf R. Gruning, 315 Busby Dr., San Antonio, Tex. 78209
Gunstocks-Rarewoods, Haleiwa, Hawaii 96712
Gunwoods (N.Z.) Ltd., Box 18505, New Brighton, Christchurch, New Zealand (blanks)
Hank's Stock Shop, 1500 Mill Creek Rd., Ukiah, Calif. 95482
Harper's Custom Stocks, 959 Lombrano St., San Antonio, Tex. 78207
Harris Gun Stocks, Inc., 12 Lake St., Richfield Springs, N.Y. 13439
Elden Harsh, Rt. 4, London, O. 43140
Hal Hartley, Box 147, Blairsfork Rd., Lenoir, N.C. 28654
Hayes Gunstock Service Co., 914 E. Turner St., Clearwater, Fla. 33516
Edward O. Hefti, 300 Fairview, College Sta., Tex. 77840
Herter's Inc., Waseca, Minn. 56093

Howard's, Box 1133, Twin Falls, Ida. 83301
Hurst Custom Gunstocks, 917 Spotswood Ave., Norfolk, Va. 23517
Jackson's, Box 416, Selman City, Tex. 75689 (blanks)
Paul Jaeger, 211 Leedom ST., Jenkintown, Pa. 19046
Bob Johnson, 1730 E. Sprague, Spokane, Wash. 99200
I. D. Johnson, Rt. 1, Strawberry Point, Ia. 52076 (blanks)
Monte Kennedy, R.D. 2, Kalispell, Mont. 59990
Dale M. Larsen, Box 123, Niagara, Wis. 54151
Leer's Gun Barn, Rt. 3, Sycamore Hills, Elwood, Ind. 46036
LeFever Arms Co., Inc., R.D. 1, Lee Center, N.Y. 13363
J. L. Lyden, 1516 Chelton, Pittsburgh, Pa. 15226
Maryland Gun Exchange, Rt. 40 W., RD 5, Frederick, Md. 21701
Maurer Arms, 2366 Frederick Dr., Cuyahoga Falls, O. 44221
Leonard Mews, 6116 Hollywood Blvd., Hollywood, Calif. 90028
Robt. U. Milhoan & Son, Rt. 3, Elizabeth, W. Va. 26143
Mills (D.H.) Custom Stocks, 401 N. Ellsworth Ave., San Mateo, Calif. 94401
Nelsen's Gun Shop, 501 S. Wilson, Olympia, Wash. 98501
Niemiec's Gun Shop, 7507 Lillian Lane, Highland, Cal. 92346 (blanks)
Oakley and Merkley, Box 2446, Sacramento, Calif. 95801 (blanks)
Ernest O. Paulsen, Chinook, Mont. 59523 (blanks)
Peterson Mach. Carving, Box 1065, Sun Valley, Calif. 91352
Roberts Wood Prod., 1400 Melody Rd., Marysville, Calif. 95901
L. B. Rothschild, 4504 W. Washington Blvd., Los Angeles, Calif. 90016
Royal Arms, Inc., 10064 Bert Acosta Ct., Santee, Calif. 92071
Sanders Cust. Gun Serv., 2358 Tyler Lane, Louisville, Ky. 40205 (blanks)
Saratoga Arms Co., R.D. 3, Box 387, Pottstown, Pa. 19464
Roy Schaefer, 965 W. Hilliard Lane, Eugene, Ore. 97402 (blanks)
Shaw's, 1655 S. Euclid Ave., Anaheim, Calif. 92802
Thomas Shelhamer, Rt. 3, Box 189A, Dowagiac, Mich. 49047
Walter Shultz, R.D. 3, Pottstown, Pa. 19464
Sile Dist., 7 Centre Market Pl., New York, N.Y. 10013
Ed Sowers, 8331 DeCelis Pl., Sepulveda, Calif. 91343
Sportsmen's Equip. Co., 915 W. Washington, San Diego, Calif. 92103 (carbine conversions)
Stag Custom Stocks, 1430 So. Gilbert St., Fullerton, Calif. 92633
Keith Stegall, Box 696, Gunnison, Colo. 81230
Stinehour Rifles, Box 84, Cragsmoor, N.Y. 12420
J. R. Sundra, 683 Elizabeth St., Bridgeville, Pa. 15017
Swanson Cust. Firearms, 1051 Broadway, Denver, Colo. 80203
V. S. Swenson, Rt. 1, Ettrick, Wis. 54627
D. W. Thomas, Box 184, Vineland, N.J. 08360
Roy Vail, Rt. 1, Box 8, Warwick, N.Y. 10990
John E. Warren, Box 72, Eastham, Mass. 02642
Weatherby's, 2781 Firestone, South Gate, Calif. 90280
Western Stocks & Guns, Inc., 2206 E. 11th, Bremerton, Wash. 98311
Orland Wheeler, 405 W. 10th St., Holden, Mo. 64040
Joe White, Box 8505, New Brighton, Christchurch, N.Z. (blanks)
Fred Wranic, 6919 Santa Fe, Huntington Park, Calif. 90255 (mesquite)
Paul Wright, 4504 W. Washington Blvd., Los Angeles, Calif. 90016
Wyatt's Gunshop, Kosciusko, Miss. 39090

SURPLUS GUNS, PARTS AND AMMUNITION

Allied Arms Ltd., 655 Broadway, New York, N.Y. 10012
B. P. Caldwell, Jr., 211 E. Chicago Ave., Chicago, Ill. 60611
Century Arms, Inc., 3-5 Federal St., St. Albans, Vt. 05478
W. H. Craig, Box 927, Selma, Ala. 36701
Cummings Intl. Inc., 41 Riverside Ave., Yonkers, N.Y. 10701
Eastern Firearms Co., 790 S. Arroyo Pkwy., Pasadena, Calif. 91105
Fenwick's, P.O. Box 38, Weisburg Rd., Whitehall, Md. 21161
Hudson Sptg. Goods, 52 Warren, New York, N.Y. 10007
Hunter's Lodge, 200 S. Union, Alexandria, Va. 22313
Inter-American Imp.-Exp. Co., P.O. Box 8022, Sacramento, Calif. 95818
International Guns, Inc., 66 Warburton Ave., Yonkers, N.Y., 10701
Kadet's Arsenal, 7388 N. Center, Mentor, O. 44060
Lever Arms Serv., 771 Dunsmuir St., Vancouver, B.C., Canada
Mars Equipment Corp., 3318 W. Devon, Chicago, Ill. 60645
National Gun Traders, 251-55 W. 22nd, Miami, Fla. 33135
P & S Sales, Box 155, Tulsa, Okla. 74102
Plainfield Ordnance Co., Box 281, Dunellen, N.J. 08812
Potomac Arms Corp., Box 35, Alexandria, Va. 22313
Ruvel & Co., 707 Junior Terr., Chicago, Ill. 60613
Service Armament Co., 689 Bergen Blvd., Ridgefield, N.J. 07657
Z. M. Military Research Co., 9 Grand Ave., Englewood, N.J. 07631

LOAD TESTING & CHRONOGRAPHING

Carter Gun Works, 2211 Jefferson Pk. Ave., Charlottesville, Va. 22903
Custom Ballistics' Lab., 3354 Cumberland Dr., San Angelo, Tex. 76901
Horton Ballistics, North Waterford, Me. 04267
Jurras Co., Box 163, Shelbyville, Ind. 46176
Kennon's, 5408 Biffle, Stone Mountain, Ga. 30083
Plum City Ballistics Range, RFD 1, Box 128, Plum City, Wis. 54761
R & M Chronograph Serv., 9882 E. Manning, Selma, Calif. 93662
Shooters Service & Dewey, Inc., Clinton Corners, N.Y. 12514
H. P. White Lab., Box 331, Bel Air, Md. 21014

TOOLS OF THE TRADE

Among craftsmen — be they jewelers, masons, auto mechanics, cabinet makers or gunsmiths — the proper tools for a specific job can make the difference between one that is done well in the shortest possible length of time and one that is botched.

Gunsmithing possibly requires a larger assortment of specialized tools than any other trade. There are even a few basic tools that are mandatory for even those maintaining their own hunting batteries, small though they might be, or building sporting rifles from obsolete military models. It is possible, in many instances, to improvise some non-gunsmithing tools, although it is best always to have the proper tools on hand, if a first class job is expected.

This catolog of gunsmithing tools is by no means complete, but it does cover a number of tools considered essential to even the home gun craftsman, who takes pride in his workmanship. These tools are not for the amateur alone, though. All are journeyman gunsmith tools in every sense of the word and specifically designed for the purpose intended. However, the wise man should obtain catalogs listing such tools from such suppliers listed elsewhere to be certain of current prices.

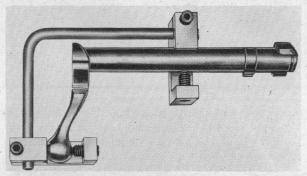

BROWNELL'S BOLT WELDING JIG

This jig employs a different approach to aligning the handle to the bolt; that by use of a protractor supplied with the jig kit. Full and complete instructions are supplied with each jig set. Properly used, this jig assures a perfect bolt handle weld. . . . . Each: $6.75

BROWNELL'S HYDRAULIC DENT RAISER

Removes dents from shotgun barrels hydraulically in a few minutes. A must tool for the man specializing in shotgun repair and maintenance. No hammering or peening of barrel is necessary with this tool. Available in 12, 16 & 20-gauge sets. . . . . Per Set: $22.50

BROWNELL'S NYLON/BRASS DRIFT PUNCH

Knurled handle is of high impact steel. Interchangeable nylon tip is steel reinforced to prevent bending or breaking. Interchangeable brass tip is used for more solid impact.
Each drift punch with brass and nylon tip $1.00
Each tips, brass or nylon .25

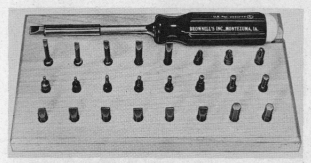

BROWNELL'S GUNSMITH SCREWDRIVER

These Magna-Tip screwdrivers are true hollow ground to transmit all the twist (torque) evenly and smoothly up the shank of the bit. Assures positive contact between tip of bit and the entire screw slot. Thus maximum power can be exerted.
Magna Tip screwdriver, each, with one bit . . . $ 3.15
Assortment of 24 bits 13.68
Assortment with block 15.18

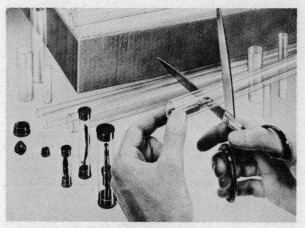

BROWNELL'S CELLUPLASTIC

Consists of plastic tubing in varying sizes from 3/8 up to 7/8 inches in 18-inch lengths. Complete with neoprene caps to fit all sizes, tubing can be cut to any length desired. Ideal for storing precision tools, taps, reamers and expensive files and chisels. Kit contains large assortment of all sizes of tubing and 150 caps in assorted sizes. . . . . Per Kit: $3.00

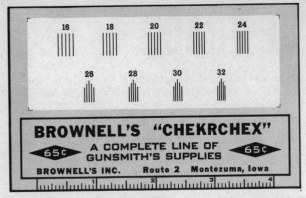

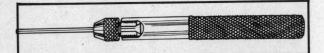

BROWNELL'S CHEKRCHEX

A proven measuring instrument for the professional or hobbyist gunsmith. Quickly determines the lines-per-inch of any checkering job, old or new. Includes spacing from 16 to 32 lines-per-inch on transparent, see-through material. For use on flat or curved surfaces. Includes 4-inch ruler. . . . . Each: $ .65

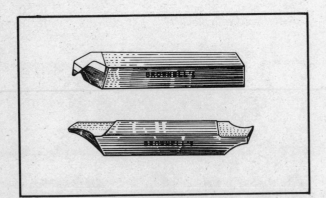

BROWNELL'S REPLACEABLE PUNCH SET

Designed exclusively for the gunsmith with pin punch troubles. The steel punches may be replaced instantly should they become damaged or broken. Available in three sizes: .039 for 3/64; .060 for 1.16; .091 for 3/32. (Special handle is needed for each size.)

Set of three sizes	$3.25
2-inch replaceable pins, 6 pins your choice	1.00
2½-inch replaceable pins, 4 pins your choice	1.00

BROWNELL'S BOLT FACING, CROWNING BITS

For the gun worker with a lathe. The bolt facing lathe bit is for opening up bolt faces to magnum dimensions. Each is ground professionally to give best performance on bolt steels. Carbide tip is securely brazed. Barrel crowning bit is professionally ground to give maximum cutter strength and proper clearance as cutter enters bore and shank approaches barrel. Two radii are cut on each bit, one for .210-inch the other for .250-inch radius cut.

1/4-inch square Barrel Crowning Lathe bit	$4.20
3/8-inch square Barrel Crowning bit	4.75
1/4-inch square bolt facing lathe bit	3.75
5/16-inch square bolt facing lathe bit	4.15

BROWNELL'S SIGHT SCREW COUNTER-BORES

Available in either 6 x 48 or 8 x 40 Filister with 90-degree shoulder or Weaver with 45-degree shoulder.

In 6 x 48 Filister or Weaver	$ 3.25
In 8 x 40 Filister or Weaver	3.50

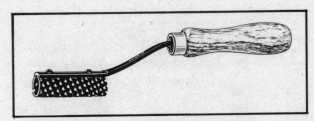

BROWNELL'S QUICKUT INLETTING TOOL

Quickly removes excess wood from barrel channel during inletting operations. Easy to use for both the professional and beginning gunsmith. . . . . Each: $2.90

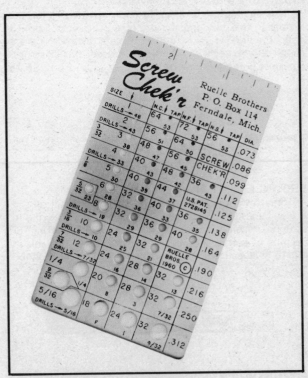

BROWNELL'S SCREW CHEK'R

Cuts the thread size on marred screws or cut unhardened screws to correct length. Tells correct size, threads per inch of screws, tap series, body drill size and tap drill to use for each screw. Does not include 6 x 48 or other bastard sizes. . . . . Each: $3.95

BROWNELL'S SIGHT BASE CUTTER

High speed steel, 60-degree cut, .020" undersize to compensate for milling tolerances. For standard front/rear sight bases. Higher priced than competitive cutters because: 1) Lips of cutter have radial ground relief - 2) Vapor honed for ultimate sharpness - 3) Center relief hole only .052" as compared to others' .082" diameter; thus giving many times more flute strength for longer money-saving life. Engineered for maximum production with least investment.

60-degree Sight Base Cutters .... Each: $5.25

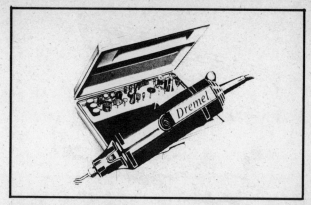

DREMEL MOTO TOOL

This tool is one of the handiest pieces of equipment one can own around a gun or hobby shop. Capable of completing jobs no other tools can master.

Model 270 .... $29.95
Model 280 with bearings 39.95

BROWNELL'S GUNSMITH LEVEL

A magnetic protractor level designed especially for the gunsmith. Assures that gun is absolutely level with drill press table, workbench or surface plate. Ideal for mounting front or rear sights. Will automatically hold position anywhere on barrel or action of steel or cast iron. Easily adjusts for any degree of angle reading.

Each: $3.20

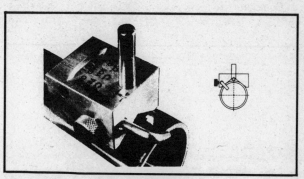

BROWNELL'S DEAD-CENTER PUNCH

A rugged, foolproof tool for finding the dead center of rifle or pistol barrels for purposes of drilling for sight installations. Fitted with bubble level and center punch for exacting work. .... Each: $8.75

BROWNELL'S GUNSMITH BRUSH

Of special value for cleaning hardened grease and caked dirt from gun mechanisms. Brush is stainless steel, uneffected by bluing solutions or the various cleaning agents used in the gun trade. .... Each: $ .90

BROWNELL'S SHOTGUN BEAD INSTALLER

For positive, easy installation of aluminum or brass shotgun beads. An instrument with precision holding jaws which are ground and lapped to assure a positive holding surface without marring or defaceing the bead. Available in three sizes for small, medium and large beads.

Each: $1.75
Set of two 3.25
Set of three 4.50

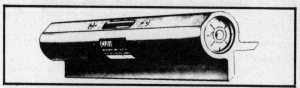

BROWNELL'S GUNSMITH V-LEVEL

Precision-ground level with heat treated alloy frame. Ideal for barrel and action work where guess work is taboo for a precision job. May be used on drill press for scope and sight mounting jobs. .... Each: $16.00

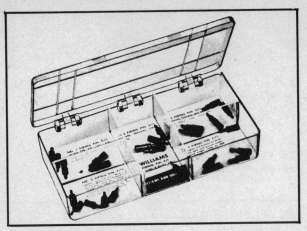

WILLIAM'S FIRING PIN KIT

This kit takes care of ninety-five percent of all single and double barrel shotgun firing pin replacements. Contains 25 numbered firing pins of different styles for such guns as Stevens, Svage, Iver Johnson, Montgomery Ward, Western Field brand, Harrington & Richardson.
Complete kit $18.75

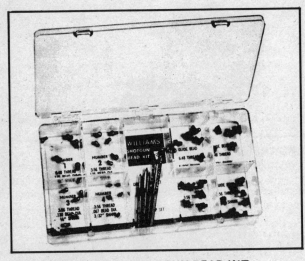

WILLIAM'S SPECIAL SHOTGUN BEAD KIT

Contains a complete assortment of beads in various styles and colors. Will fit any shotgun. Included are two drill and tap sets, the 6-48 and 3-56. There are 48 beads in all in varying sizes.
Complete kit $63.70

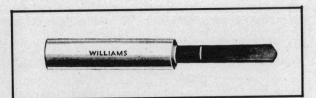

WILLIAMS CARBIDE DRILLS

For drilling hard receivers such as the M/70 Winchester, Springfield and Mauser. In two sizes to cover the majority of scope mounting chores, these carbide drills are available in No. 28 and No. 31. Are capable of cutting through the toughest case hardening.
No. 28 Carbide drill . . . . Each: $8.00
No. 31 Carbide drill . . . . Each: 7.50

WILLIAM'S SERVICE KIT

This kit contains screws and taps most used by the working gunsmith. The 6-48, 8-40 and 10-32 screws and taps are the general repair standbys. Replacement screws and taps for kit are available.
Complete assortment $17.50

WILLIAMS SIGHT BASE CUTTER

This special four-fluted 3/8-inch dovetail cutter is of special high-speed cutting steel. Made .010 undersize with a plus or minus .005 tolerance so that the slot can be precision cut to the exact size on the second cut.
Each: $5.50

RICHLAND SHOTGUN CHAMBER REAMER

New type three-quarter cut chamber reamer and polishing tool with long forcing cone and brass pilot. Excellent for trimming chamber bushings and new ejectors and extractors to exact chamber size of 12 or 20 gauge.
Each: $15.00

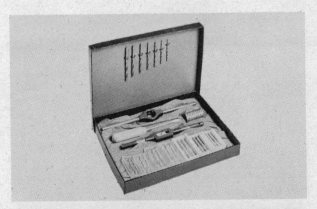

RICHLAND METRIC DRILL, TAP AND THREADING

With this kit, it is possible to make any screw used for European shotguns or for plugs covering the hinge bolt. Contains all necessary taps, dies, die wrenches, screw driver and drills : . . . . Per Kit: $29.95

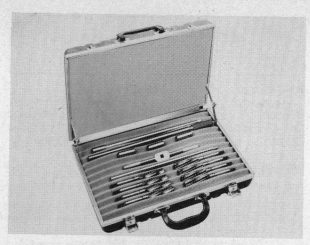

RICHARD C-300 CHOKE REAMER KIT

For the advanced gunsmith, is available in 12 or 20 gauge. Each kit consists of eight choke reamers, three bore bushing guides, one two-piece rod and handle and carrying case. Left-hand spiral, right-hand cut. Assures that parallel planes of the choke are parallel to the bore.
Complete kit $85.00

BROWNELL'S TRIGGER PULL GAUGE

Made by Schrader, this is one of the best trigger pull gauges on the market today. Calibrated from 4 to 80 ounces in 2-ounce graduations. Small in size, it is accurate and precision-made. . . . . Each: $6.25

WILLIAMS COUNTER BORE

For boring and counter boring sling swivel in stock and for machine swivel in forend.
Sling Swivel Counter Bore, with No. 17 drill. . . $6.50

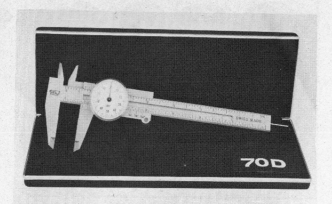

SCHLESINGERS CALIPER

Swiss precision made Model No. 70D Dial Caliper measuring in .001-inch graduations. . . . . . . Each: $5.95
Velvet-lined case 2.55

BROWNELL'S CHOKE COMPARISON CALIPER

A high precision instrument designed to give the amount of choke change within a few ten thousandths of an inch. For actual bore measurement they are accurate within plus/minus of .002. Used where change in shotgun chokes by honing is done to assure precise work. Long enough to reach cylinder bore of all American made shotguns, including the three-inch Browning magnum. . . . . .Each: $8.25

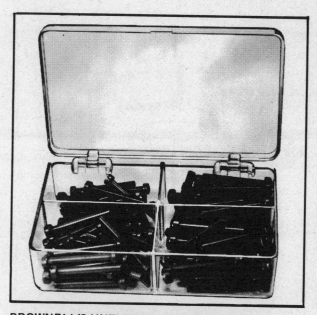

BROWNELL'S UNTHREADED SCREW KIT

One of the handiest kits for the working gun craftsman. Contains about 80 unthreaded screws in varying lengths and sizes, most adapted to gun work. Thread them yourself to proper size.
Complete kit $3.15

CLAMDOWN TOOL

This handy little bench clamp for holding small parts during soldering or cementing operations can be used for setting small stock and pistol grip inlays. . Each: $10.50

DETROIT TAC RAG

An absolute necessity for stock woods requiring a high grade finish. Completely removes all lint, dust and fine sanding particles from wood surface prior to final application of finish. Non-inflammable and a must in any gun shop where wood work is done. Brownell's.
Each: .... $ .30

BROWNELL'S SANDING PADS

Constructed of heavy felt backing with fold over canvas flap. The handiest knuckle and finger saver for all wood sanding needs. Works good on metal, too.
Each: .... $ .75

DURITE WATERPROOF SANDPAPER

Can be used either wet or dry. Is the exact type used on all projects found in this book. For putting the glassy smooth finish on stocks prior to application of liquid finishes. Available in 220A (very fine), 320 (extra fine) and 400 grit (super fine). From Brownell's.
Five sheets: .... $ .90

WILLIAMS FRONT SIGHT PUSHER

The modern way to install front sights on ramps without damage to ramp or sight. Equalized pressure assures that sights slide into dovetail slots smoothly without pressure on ramp itself. .... Each: $12.50

BROWNELL'S ENGINE TURNING ABRASIVE, BRUSH

For applying the jeweled effect to rifle bolts, revolver hammers and other gun components where applicable. The wire bristled brush is chucked in the drill press, an application of oil and 120-grit engine turning abrasive is applied to the surface to be jeweled in paste form.
3 engine turning brushes $1.15
1 pound can, 120-grit abrasive 1.55

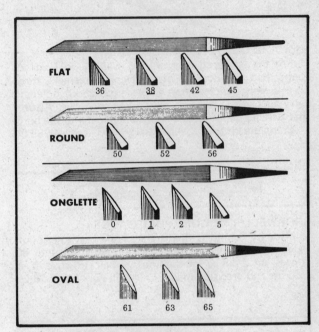

BROWNELL'S ENGRAVING TOOLS

Gravers of every type are available from this source. Shown are but a few of the types most used by professional gun engravers.
Each .... $ .70

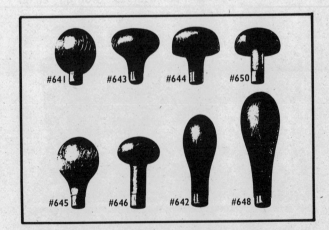

BROWNELL'S CHISEL AND GRAVER HANDLES

For the man doing metal engraving. Available in a variety of sizes and shapes, for the beginner and professional alike.
Ten handles, your assortment: $1.50

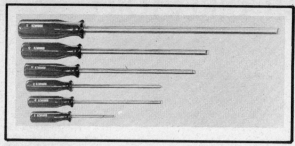

BONANZA SCREW DRIVERS

A variety of fifteen screw drivers especially ground to fit screws in specific guns such as Winchester, Remington, Sako. Savage, Mauser, Charles Daly, Browning, as well as scopes by Lyman, Leupold, Redfield, Williams and B&L. Invaluable to the gunsmith doing general gun work on all types of guns.

$1.50 to $2.25 each.

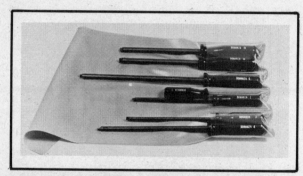

BONANZA GUNSMITH SCREW DRIVER KIT

Set of seven of the most popular sizes complete with a compartmented roll. . . . . .Per set: $10.00

BROWNELL'S STEEL BENCH BLOCK

Handy gunsmith bench block for drill or knocking out pins etc. in round or flat work. Holes vary from 1/8 to 5/8 inches. V in center for holding odd-shaped material, indispensable for gun work. . . . . Each: $8.50

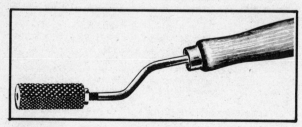

BROWNELL'S INLETTING RASPS

Grobet barrel inletting raps. A must for any one building a sporting rifle using semi-inletted stock. Imported from Swiss. Available in two sizes:

One-half-inch $6.35
Three-quarter-inch 6.95

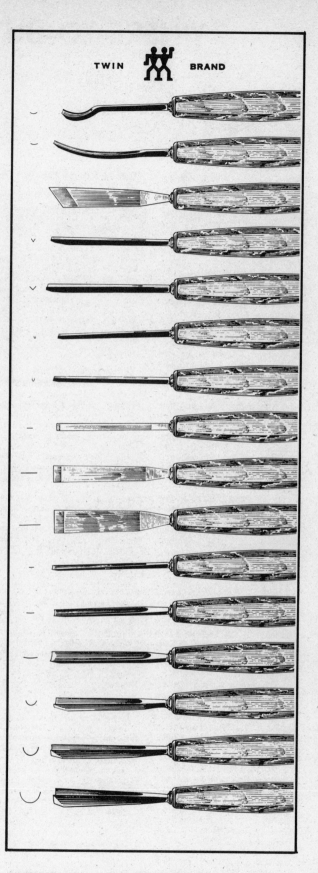

TWIN BRAND

BROWNELL'S INLETTING CHISELS

Twin Brand by J. A. Henckel of Germany, the Cadillac of inletting chisels. Preferred by leading gunsmiths. Price varies according to style needed.

$2.35 to $3.30

WHERE-TO-BUY-IT-DIRECTORY

Accessories and Gunsmithing Services

Alabama

Albertville . . . . Crickett Hall
Alexander City . . . City Home & Auto
Alexander City . . . . Ray Voss
Andalusia . . . . . . Ye Old Gun Shoppe
Anniston . . . Anniston Sporting Goods
Anniston . . . . Carter Gun Shop
Anniston . . . . Tornado Supply
Atmore . . . . Rex's Sporting Goods
Bay Minette
   Builders Hardware & Supply
Bessemer . . . . . Long Lewis Hdwe. Co.
Bessemer . . . Traywick Sporting Goods
Birmingham . . . . Lovemans
Birmingham . . J. L. Quick & Son Co.
Birmingham . . . Stewarts Sport Shop
Birmingham . . . . The Gun Shop
Centre . . . . . Tabs Sporting Goods
Childersburg . . . . Limbaugh Hardware
Clanton . . . Western Auto Assoc. Store
Coden . . . . Olde Fort Alabama
Columbia . . . . Orr's Gun Shop
Columbiana
   Western Auto Assoc. Store
Cullman . . . Mary Carter Paint Store
Cullman . . . Harold Mayo's Gun Shop
Decatur . . . . Garrison Boats & Motors
Decatur . . . . Sandline & Sons
Decatur . . . . Wiley Sales Co.
Dothan . . . . Pake McKeen
Dothan . . . . . . Target Arms Company
Enterprise . . . . Joe C. Jones Hardware
Enterprise . . Moose Hope Sports Shop
Florence . . . . Roberts Hardware
Gadsden . . . . Schwartz Gun Shop
Gadsden . . . . Fred Singtons
Georgiana . . . . . . Jim Johnson Sons
Guntersville
   Paul's Stop & Swap Gun Shop
Huntsville . . . . House of Guns
Huntsville . . . . Hutchens
Huntsville . . . Johns Guns & Camping
Huntsville . . . . Wiley Sales Co.
Jasper . . . . Parkland Hdwe. Co.
Mobile . . L. G. Adams Sporting Goods
Mobile . . . . B & W Sport Shop
Mobile . . . . . Brannan Sporting Goods
Mobile . . . . Downtown Hardware
Mobile . . . . . Eugene Thoss Jr. & Sons
Montgomery
   Montgomery Sporting Goods Co.
Montgomery . . Relfe Shotshell Supply
Montgomery . . . . The Gun Shop
Montgomery . . . . Woolco Dept. Store
Opelika . . . . Penny's Store
Phenix City . . . Davis Sporting Goods
Prichard . . Eddie's Pawn & Gun Shop
Russellville
   W. R. Alsbrooks Guns & Ammo
Russellville Dependable Service Center
Saraland . . . . Coastal Hdwe. & Supply
Scottsboro . . . . W. J. Word
Selma . . . . Benderskys
Sheffield . . . . Martin Marine
Sylacauga Arnold Hardware & Supply
Talledega . . . . Barton Co., Inc.
Tuscaloosa . . . Circle Wood Gun Shop
Tuscaloosa . . . Hanly's Pawn Shop
Tuscaloosa . . Allen Jemison Hardware
Tuscaloosa . . . . . Mack's Bait Shop
Tuscaloosa . . . . Pake McKeen
Tuscaloosa . . . . . . Woolco Dept. Store

Alaska
Anchorage . Bob Seaman's Sport Shop
Anchorage . . . . Caribou Ward
Anchorage . . Custom Bluing Gun Shop
Anchorage . . . . . Great Northern Guns
Anchorage . . . . . . Gun & Ammo Shop
Anchorage . . . . Howard's Gun Shop
Anchorage
   Mountain View Sport Center, Inc.
Anchorage . . . . J. C. Penney
Clear . . . . O. A. Mooney & Sons
Cordova . . . . Karl's Gun Shop
Fairbanks . . Frontier Sporting Goods
Fairbanks . . Penska's Outdoor Store
Fairbanks . . . . . . Shebal's Gun Shop
Juneau . . . . . . Brownie's Gun Shop
Juneau . . . . . . Skinner's Gun Shop
Juneau . . . . . Totem Bay Associates
Ketchikan . . . . . Tongass Trading Co.
Palmer . . . . Kosloskys
Sitka . . . . Tackle Shop

Arizona
Douglas . . . Frank Fair Sporting Goods
Flagstaff . . . . . Andy's Sporting Goods
Flagstaff . . Babbitt Bros. Trading Co.
Glendale . . . . Sport Center
Globe . . . . Unique Sporting Goods
Kingman . . . . Central Commercial Co.
Mesa . . . . . . M&S Sporting Goods
Mesa . . Mesa Hdwe. & Sporting Goods
Mesa . . . Petersons Sporting Goods
Mesa . . . . O. S. Stapley Co.
Nogales . . . . Ace Electric
Nogales . . . . . . Brackers Dept. Store
Phoenix . Bohn's Handloading Supplies
Phoenix . . . . Jewel Box Loan
Phoenix . . . . . . Quillens Gun Shop
Phoenix . . . . Stop & Swap
Prescott . . . . . Prescott Gun & Tackle
Prescott . . . . Rifle Ranch
Prescott . . . . . . The Sportsmans Shop
Scottsdale . . . . Averys
Scottsdale . . Gunsmoke Sports Center
Show Low . . . . A & A Sporting Goods
Tucson . . . . Lathrop's
Tucson . . . . Steinfelds
Tucson . . . . . Super City Dept. Store
Winslow . . . . Hutch's Sporting Goods
Yuma . . . . Frank's Gun Shop
Yuma . . . . Marine & Sport Supply
Yuma . . . . Mesa Sport Shop
Yuma . . . . Starlite Gun Shop

Arkansas
Batesville . . . . Airport Sports Mart
Batesville . . . . Parks Hdwe. Co.
Benton . . . . . . Smith's House of Guns
Camden . . . . Lloyd's Bait Shop
Crossett . . . . Jordans Sporting Center
Crossett . Homer Pierce Sporting Goods
De Queen . . . . Wilson Hardware
Des Arc . . . . Eddin's Hardware
DeWitt . . . Bill's True Value Hardware
De Witt . . . . Schall Horn Hdwe.
Earle . . . . Bruce's Repair Shop
El Dorado . . Cawvey Fix It Shop, Inc.
El Dorado . . . . Lewis Sporting Goods
Fayetteville . . . . Park's Place
Forrest City . . . . Havens
Ft. Smith . . . Midwest Hdwe & Supply
Harrison . . . . Holt, Inc.
Heber Springs . . . George's Sport Shop
Helena . . . . C. E. Mayer Co.
Hope . . . La Grone Williams Hdwe.
Hot Springs . . . . Bob's Gun Shop
Hot Springs . . . Albert Pike Supply Co.
Jonesboro
   Charlie Keller's Sporting Goods
Lake Village . Livingston Sport Center
Little Rock . . . . Blass Park Plaza
Little Rock . . Pfeiffers Sporting Goods
Little Rock . Star Sporting Goods Co.
Magnolia . . . . . . Olive Sporting Goods
Malvern . . . . Quality Hardware
Mc Ghee . . . . The Sportsman's Center
Mena . . . . Ellis Goss Hdwe.
Mountain Home The Sportsman's Shop
Newport Farm & Ranch Sporting Goods
North Little Rock . . . R. E. Phillips Co.
North Little Rock
   Razorback Shooters Supply
Paragould . . . . Pete Gregory Hdwe.
Paris . . . . Paris Hardware
Pine Bluff . . . . Arkansas Worm Ranch
Pine Bluff . . . . . Grady Newton, Inc.
Prescott . . . . Prescott Hdwe. Co.
Russellville . . . . Rush Sporting Goods
Searcy . James For Guns-Western Auto
Siloam Springs
   Blackie's Army-Navy Store
Springdale . . . Jack's Loading Supplies
Springdale . Laymans Shopping Center
Star City . . . . Beesons
Stuttgart . . . . Macks Sport Shop
Trumann . . . . Dudley Hardware
West Memphis . . . . Ray's Electric
West Memphis . . Sportsmans One Stop

California
Alameda . . . Alameda Sporting Goods
Alhambra . . . . Butler Bros.
Alpine . . . . Alpine Trading Post
Alturas . . . . Ingrahams Hdwe.
Anaheim . . . . Elz Fargo Gun
Anaheim . . . . Gemco
Anaheim . . . Gun Refinishing & Repair
Anaheim . . . Sportsmans Workshop
Anaheim . . . Wisser Sporting Goods
Anderson . . . . . . Army Navy Store
Anderson . . . . . Bert's Sporting Goods
Apple Valley . . Valley Sporting Goods
Arcata . . . . A. Brizard, Inc.
Arlington . . . Stewart's Sporting Goods
Artesia . . . . . Leach's Sporting Goods
Auburn . . . G. E. Lukens & Sons, Inc.
Azusa . . . . . . Bill's Sporting Goods
Bakersfield . . . Snider's Sporting Goods
Bakersfield . . . . Vincent's, Inc.
Barstow . . . . Platt's Gift & Sport Shop
Bellflower Shenk Bros. Sporting Goods
Bell Gardens
   Newport Koch Hdwe & Sports
Berkeley . . . . Earl E. Buchanan
Beverly Hills . . . . . Kerrs Sport Shop
Bishop . . . . . . Brucks Sporting Goods
Bishop . . . . Mac's Sporting Goods
Blythe . . . Farm Fresh Sporting Goods
Blythe . . . . Imperial Hdwe. Co.
Brawley . . . . . . Imperial Hdwe. Co.
Bridgeport
   Eatons Redwood Sporting Goods
Bridgeport . . . . Ken's Sporting Goods
Burbank . . . Humes Sporting Goods
Burney . . . Vaughn's Sporting Goods
Calexico . . . . . . Imperial Hdwe. Co.
Camarillo . Camarillo Sporting Goods
Cambell . . . . Heller's Camp
Canoga Park . Canoga Sporting Goods
Carmichael . . . Bicks Sporting Goods
Carmichael . Lombard Sporting Goods
Cayucos . . . . Stovnis Sporting Goods
Ceres . . . . Bilson Sport Shop
Chester . . . . M. D. Ayoob Dept. Store
Chico . . . . A. Barth Sporting Goods
Chico . . . . Chico Gun Shop
Cloverdale . . . . . Glenns Rifle Shop
Clovis . . . . Preuss Gun Shop
Colusa
   Chick Montgomery Sports Equipment
Compton . . . Woody's Sporting Goods
Concord . . . Concord Sports & Service
Concord . . . . Diablo Sports Center
Corcoran . . . . . F. G. Gross Hdwe Co.
Corcoran . . . . Woody's
Corona . . . Stutsman Sporting Goods
Costa Mesa . . . . . . Grant's Surplus
Costa Mesa . . . F. W. Woolworth Co.
Covina . . . . . Chick's Sporting Goods
Culver City . . . Sportsman's Exchange
Cypress . The Powderhorn Gun Shop
Davis . . . . Cookes Gunsmithery
Delano . . . . Delano Hdwe.
Del Paso Heights . Al's Sporting Goods
Dinuba . . . . Woodhouse Cyclery
Dos Palos . . . . Roberts
Downey . . . . Matheus & Sons
Downey . . . . The Sportsmans Supply
Duarte . . . . Campers Haven
Duarte . . . . Harry's Gun Shop
Dunsmuir . . . . . . Big Sporting Goods
El Centro . . . . . . Ace Sporting Goods
El Centro . . . . . . Imperial Hdwe. Co.
El Cajon
   Stanley Andrews Sporting Goods Co.
Encino Pony Express Sport Shop, Inc.
Escalon . . . . Ray's Sporting Goods
Esparto . . . . Esparto Gun Shop
Eureka . . . Bucksport Sporting Goods
Eureka
   Steelhead Louie Sporting Goods
Fairfield . . . . Fairfield Sport Shop
Fall River Mills
   Summers Sporting Goods
Folsom . . . . W. M. Rumsey
Fontana . . . . Lazio's Sporting Goods
Ft. Bragg Tom Cooney Sporting Goods
Fortuna . . . . Grunert Sporting Goods
Fremont . . . Alameda Sporting Goods
Fremont . . . . K-Sports
Fresno . . . Advance Reloading Supplies
Fresno . . . . Hanoians Sporting Goods
Fresno . . . Herb Bauer Sporting Goods
Fresno . . . . Johnson's Gun Shop
Fresno . . . . Roos Atkins
Fresno . . . . . . Vettling Sporting Goods
Fullerton . . . . . . Neal's Sporting Goods
Garberville . . . . The Tackle Shop
Garden Grove . . Grove Sporting Goods
Gilroy . . . . Jim's Sport Shop
Gilroy . . . . Ray's Sportland
Glendale . . . . . Alaskan African Arms
Glendale . . . . Cornwall & Kelty
Granada Hills Wm. Gammill Gunsmith
Grass Valley . . . General Gunsmithing
Grass Valley . . . . . . Tom's Gun Shop
Gridley . . . . . . Bromer Hardware Inc.
Guerneville . . . . . . Ferenz Sport Shop
Hanford . . . . Sports Center
Hanford . . . . . Tulare Sports Center
Hawthorne . . Perry's Sporting Goods
Hayward . . . . . G and H Sports Center
Hayward . . . . Skaggs Hardware
Hemet . . . . . Jim Cain Sporting Goods

Hollister .... The Outdoorsman
Hollywood Brass Rail Sporting Goods
Hollywood Hollywood Gun Shop, Inc.
Holtville .... Imperial Hdwe. Co.
Indio .... Imperial Hdwe. Co.
Indio .... The Outdoorman
Inglewood ... AB & S Sporting Goods
Inglewood .... Cole's
Inglewood ..... Mel's Sporting Goods
La Crescenta .... Liberty Arms Corp.
La Crescenta
    Viking Leather Specialties
La Fayette ...... Frontier Gun Shop
Laguna Beach
    Bill & Al's Sporting Goods
La Habra .... A & A Athletic Supply
La Habra .. Johnson's Guns & Ammo
Lakeport ..... Pete's Sporting Goods
Lakewood .... Butler Bros.
Lakewood
    Lakewood Center Sporting Goods
La Mesa ..... La Mesa Sporting Goods
Lancaster .... The Gun Shop, Inc.
Lancaster .... Rowell's Shoe
Lemon Grove
    Berry's Lemon Grove Sptg. Goods
Lemoore .... Lowes
Livermore .... Minoggios Sport Center
Long Beach .... Shore Sporting Goods
Long Beach . Thompson's Sptg. Goods
Los Alamitos .Harrison Sporting Goods
Los Angeles .. Blaine's Sporting Goods
Los Angeles .... FEDCO
Los Angeles .... G. W. Arms Sales Co.
Los Angeles ...... King's Gun Works
Los Angeles Lees Sportsmans Exchange
Los Angeles ...... New York Hdwe.
Los Angeles ... Pachmayr Gun Works
Los Angeles
    Richey's Cameras & Sporting Goods
Los Angeles .... Sportsmen's Den
Los Banos ..... San Luis Sport Shop
Los Gatos .... Wild Cat Sport Shop
Marysville .. Gordons Sporting Goods
Marysville .... Randolph's
Marysville .... Ray Gouge Firestone
Merced ..... Whitehouse Gun Shop
Middletown ...... The Corner Store
Midway City ...... Crest Carving Co.
Modesto ...... Argonaut Gun Shop
Modesto ..... Ed. F. Lacque & Sons
Modesto .... Turners Hardware
Mojave .... Carol's Dept. Store
Montebello ...... The Outdoorsman
Monterey ..... Rasmussen & Moody
Montrose .... Solingen Cutlery
Morgan Hill .. Squeri Bros. Hardware
Mountain View .... Eddys Sport Shop
Mt. Shasta .... Bob's Gun Shop
Napa .... Georges Gun Shop
Napa .... Glaziers Supply Store
Napa .... Yates Cochrane
National City
    J. N. Weisser Sporting Goods
Nevada City .... Alpha Hardware Co.
Norco ..... L. C. Davidson Company
N. Sacramento ..... Swarts Hardware
Norwalk ..... Western Gun Exchange
Novato .... Jim's Sport Shop
Oakland .... Grand Auto Stores
Oakland .... Reilly's Gun Shop
Oakland .... Siegles Guns
Oakland .... Simon Hardware
Oceanside . Johnson's Sporting Goods
Ojai .... Messer's Sports Center
Ontario ...Bumsteads Sporting Goods
Orange .... Fowler Gun Room
Orland .... Buckes
Oroville .... Curriers Appliance
Oroville .... R. C. B. S.,Inc.
Oxnard .... Oxnard Sporting Goods
Oxnard .....Sportsmen's Exchange &
    Western Gun Traders
Oxnard .... Walker's Gun Shop
Pacifica ..... Pacifica Sports Center
Pacific Beach
    Jim & John's Sporting Goods
Palmdale ..... Gibbs Sporting Goods

Palm Springs ..... Frontier Gun Shop
Palo Alto .... Spiro's Sport Shop
Palo Alto .... Stanford Sport Shop
Paradise .... Edd Marty Chaplin
Pasadena .... Harrys Gun Shop
Paso Robles .... Halls Sporting Goods
Paso Robles ..Paso Robles Mercantile
Petaluma .... Mike's Gun Shop
Pittsburg .... Imperial Gun Shop
Placerville ...... Placerville Hardware
Pleasant Hill .... Hogan's Stores, Inc.
Pomona ... Beamon's Sporting Goods
Pomona .... Pomona Gun Shop
Pomona .... Rod Gun & Hobby Shop
Porterville .... Sportsman
Quincy ...... Mike's Sporting Goods
Red Bluff ...... Army & Navy Store
Red Bluff .... Bob's Sport Shop
Redding .... Army-Navy Stores, Inc.
Redding .... Vern's Sportshop
Redlands ..Pratt Bros. Sporting Goods
Redondo Beach
    Shooters-Hunters-Reloaders
Redondo Beach .... Sportsville U.S.A.
Redwood City .... B & D Sport Shop
Rio Dell . Grundmans Sporting Goods
Rio Vista .... Oilwell Materials
Riverside ... Bob Stewart's Gun Shop
Riverside ... Pratt Bros. Sporting Goods
Riverside ...Threshers Sporting Goods
Rosemead .... Parry's Sporting Goods
Sacramento .....Christy Gun Works
Sacramento .... Ed's Sporting Goods
Sacramento .... Murphy's Gun Shop
Sacramento .... Jack Shauls
Sacramento .... Simms Hardware Co.
Sacramento .... Tower of Sports
Salinas ...... Sherwood Sport Shop
Salinas ..... StanLisk Sporting Goods
Salinas ..... Star Fish Sporting Goods
San Andreas ....Treats General Store
San Bernardino .. Gene's Trading Post
San Bernardino ..... Hunters Supply
San Bernardino ... P Q Sporting Goods
San Bernardino
    Pratt Bros. Sporting Goods
San Bruno ... Ellingson's Sport Center
San Clemente .....Harry's Gun Shop
San Diego .... Frontier Gun Shop
San Diego .... Krasne's Gun Shop
San Diego ...... Pacific Surplus, Inc.
San Diego
    Stanley Andrews Sporting Goods Co.
San Fernando ... Ed Sowers Custom
    Gun Stocks & Shooting Supplies
San Francisco . Abercrombie & Fitch
San Francisco ......Joe Cuneo Guns
San Francisco
    Park Prosidio Sporting Goods
San Francisco ... Fred Rush Gunshop
San Francisco
    San Francisco Gun Exchange
San Gabriel . Bain & Davis Sptg. Goods
San Gabriel ..... Jeffs Sporting Goods
San Jose .Guerra Bros. Sporting Goods
San Jose .... The Gun Exchange
San Jose ...... Paul's Custom Rifles
San Jose ...... Reed Sporting Goods
San Jose ...... F. Schilling & Son
San Leandro .... Jim's Bait Shop
San Leandro ..... Kodiak Gun Shop
San Leandro .... The Traders
San Luis Obispo
    Stewart & Sons Gun Dealers
San Mateo ... Ellingsons Sport Center
San Rafael ...... Western Sport Shop
Santa Ana ... Neal's Sporting Goods
Santa Ana .... Santa Ana Gun Room
Santa Barbara
    All-American Sporting Goods Co., Inc.
Santa Barbara .... J. J. Jenkins
Santa Barbara .... Ott's
Santa Clara ... Cope & McPhetres, Inc.
Santa Cruz .... Grays Gun
Santa Cruz .... Sportsman's Shop
Santa Fe Springs ...... Paul Purdum
Santa Maria ...... Farmers Hardware
Santa Maria ....Glenn Roemer Hdwe.

Santa Monica .... Ames Guns
Santa Monica ... Bay Sporting Goods
Santa Rosa Joseph Cuneo Sport Shop
Santa Rosa .... Lou's Sporting Goods
Santa Rosa ..... Perkins Sport Shop
Santa Susana . Simi Valley Gun Service
Scotia .... A. Brizard, Inc.
Seaside .... A to Z Sport Center
Sebastopol .... The Rifleman
Sonoma .... Ed. Peterson, Inc.
Sonora .... Alley Supply
Sonora .... The Sportsman
South Gate
    Weatherby's Sporting Goods
Stockton .... Davenport Arms Co.
Stockton . So. McKinley Bargain Store
Stockton
    Reloading & Ammunition Shop
Stockton .... Turner Hdwe. Co.
Studio City
    Early & Modern Firearms Co., Inc.
Suison .... Paul's Boat Harbor
Sunland ..... Shawnee Sports Center
Sunnyvale .... Ted's Gun Shop
Susana Knolls .... Cienega Gun Shop
Susanville ...... Millar Hardware
Susanville .... The Sportsman
Taft .... Taft Sporting Goods
Tahoe Valley ... The Outdoorsman
Topanga .... Hutton Rifle Ranch
Torrance .... Torrance Cycle
Tulare .... Linder Hardware Co., Inc.
Tulelake .... Tulelake Hardware
Turlock .... Bilson Sport Shop
Turlock ..... Turner Hardware Co.
Ukiah .... Palace Sport
Upland ..... Ralph's Sporting Goods
Vallejo .... Al's Sport Shop
Van Nuys .... Barkley's Gun Shop
Van Nuys .... Butler Bros.
Ventura
    All American Sporting Goods Co., Inc.
Ventura .... Shaffers
Victorville ..... Victorville Hardware
Visalia .... Cross Horlock Co.
Visalia .... Dale's Sporting Goods
Watsonville ...... Valley Sport Shop
Weaverville .. Walters Sporting Goods
West Covina ...... The Gun Room
Westwood .... Lassen Sport Shop
Whittier .... The Accuracy Shop
Whittier .... Hinshaw's Dept. Store
Williams ....The Boat Fair
Willow Creek
    L. E. Blasch Sporting Goods
Willows .... Valley Firestone
Willows ..... Willows Sporting Center
Woodlake .... Boas Minnow Farm
Woodlake ... Woodlake Hardware Co.
Woodland ... Georges Sporting Goods
Woodland ..... Henigan and Shull
Yreka .... Bish's Gun Shop
Yreka .... Don's Sporting Goods
Yuba City ..... Bromer Hardware, Inc.
Yucaipa .... Olive's Gun Shop

Colorado

Arvada .... Al's Sporting Goods
Arvada .... Sportline Gun Dept.
Aurora .... Arlans
Aurora .. Gart Bros. Sport Goods Co.
Aurora .... Sports Villa
Boulder ... Arapahoe Sporting Goods
Boulder .... Gamelines, Inc.
Canon City ..... Jimmy's Sport Shop
Climax .... Leighton Co., Inc.
Colorado Springs
    Blick Sporting Goods Co.
Colorado Springs Campbell's Gun Shop
Colorado Springs
    Dave Cook Sporting Goods Co.
Colorado Springs Suters House of Guns
Cortez ..... Howards Sporting Goods
Craig .... Craig Sports
Delta .... Murphy's Sport Shop
Denver .... Ace Sporting Goods
Denver Dave Cook Sporting Goods Co.

Denver ..... Gart Bros. Sport Goods
Denver ..... Martins Gun Shop
Denver .... Rhine Products Corp.
Denver .... Sports Villa
Englewood .... Arapahoe Gun Shop
Englewood ... Gart Bros. Sport Goods
Englewood .... Sivey's
Ft. Collins ..Ed Deans Sporting Goods
Ft. Collins .... House of Guns
Ft. Morgan .... Coast To Coast Store
Ft. Morgan ..... The Clatworthy Co.
Glenwood Springs
    Bob's Sporting Goods
Glenwood Springs
    Van's Highway Shop
Grand Junction
    L. Cook Sporting Goods
Grand Junction .... Rod & Gun Shop
Greeley ... Jones Co. Sporting Goods
Greeley .... Sargents Sport Shop
Gunnison .... Mac's Marine Service
Hotchkiss ...... Stengel's Gunshop
Lakewood . Lakewood Sporting Goods
Littleton
    Andrews Ammunition and Arms
Littleton .... B & H Ski
Longmont . Arapahoe Sporting Goods
Loveland .... Draper Drugs
Naturita ..... Naturita Shooting Shop
Pueblo .... Johnson Hardware
Rifle .... The Sports Shop
Salida .... The Magnum
Salida .... Tuttles Trading Post
Sterling . Dollerschell's Sporting Goods
Sterling .... RL's Gun Sales & Service
Sugar City . Ye Gunne Butcher Shoppe
Westminster . Denver Sporting Goods
Westminster .... Gambles
Westminster Westminster Sptg. Goods
Wheatridge .... Sports Unlimited

Connecticut

Bridgeport Dick's Sport and Cycle Shop
Bridgeport .... Pasieka Bros.
Bridgeport .... People's Hardware
Bridgeport ...... Sportmens Den, Inc.
Danbury ...... Jade Custom Guns
Darien .... Bob's Guns Division
Darien .... Darien Sport Shop
Deep River ... Johnny's Sport Center
East Hartford A. V. Bryant, Gunsmith
Glastonbury Glastonbury Sport Center
Groton ...Campbell's Sporting Goods
Guilford .... Pioneer Gunshop
Hamden .... Cook, Newton & Smith
Hamden .... Piscitellis Gun Shop
Ledyard .... Chappy's Gun Shop
Manchester ....Banville's Gun Center
Manchester ...... Nassiff Arms Co.
Marion ... Elwood V. Tainter & Sons
Middletown .. Middlesex Sport Center
Monroe .... Sports World
New Britain .. Hoffman's Sport Center
New Britain .. Young's Guns & Ammo
New Canaan ....Bob's Sports, Inc.
New Haven ....Antique Guns & Parts
New Haven ....New England Armory
New London .... J. L. Raub
New Milford .... Valley Sport Center
New Preston ....Antique Armory
North Canton . D. R. Custer Gunsmith
North Haven .... Lal's Gunshop, Inc.
Norwalk .... Sportland, Inc.
Norwich . Campbell's Sporting Goods
Norwich ....Walenda's Studio of Guns
Oakville ....Midway Sporting Goods
Old Saybrook Middlesex Sport Goods
Orange ... Yankee Gun Shop, Inc.
Portland .... Zah's Sporting Goods
Putnam .... Bob Racine Sports
Ridgefield ..... Safari Outfitters, Ltd.
Rockville .... Fire Arms, Inc.
Roxbury ...... J. Dewey Gun Co.
Sandy Hook ...Garrison Firearms, Inc.
Seymour ...... Seymour Sport Shop
Shelton .... The Gun Rack
Stamford .... Bob's Sports, Inc.
Stamford .... George A. Pecot

Stamford . . . . Village Sport Shop
Stratford . . . . Stan's Gun Shop
Stratford . . . . . . Stratford Gun Shop
Torrington . . . . . Frank's Sport Store
Torrington . . . . . . Sportsmens Paradise
Torrington . . . . . . Sport Traders, Inc.
Uncasville . Fort Shantok Trading Post
Warehouse Point . C. Ray Boudman, Jr.
Watertown Watertown Shooters Supply
West Hartford . . . . Clapp & Treat, Inc.
Willimantic . . . . Nassiff Arms, Inc.
Windsor . . . . Victor A. Positano
Windsor . . . . Townline Marine
Winsted . . . . William Rosgen
Wolcott . . . . . Anzes Fire Arms Supply
Woodbury . Judson Darrow Gunsmith

Delaware
Dover . . . . Buchanan Service
New Castle . . . . Miller Gun Shop
Seaford . . . . . . Y & M Sporting Goods
Smyrna . . . . . Smyrna Sporting Goods

District of Columbia
Washington . . . . Atlas Sport Shop

Florida
Apopka . . . . BJP, Inc.
Arcadia . . . . Tinsley's Feed Store
Boynton Beach . . Boynton Gun Shop
Bradenton Wm. Henry Sporting Goods
Clearwater . . . . The Big Store
Cocoa . . . . Belk-Lindsey Dept. Store
Clearwater Hayes Gunstock Service Co.
Dade City . . . . . . Dade City Hardware
Dania . . . . . . H. M. Nierling Gunsmith
Daytona . . . . Buck's Gun Shop
Deland . . . . Angevine Gun Shop
Deland . Nordmann's Hdwe. & Supply
Delray Beach . . . . Rods and Guns
Eau Gallie . . . Southern Gun Exchange
Eau Gallie . Eau Gallie Gun-Pawn Shop
Ft. Myers . . . . Bulls Eye Sport
Ft. Myers . . . . Davis Gun Sales
Fort Walton Beach
          Vernon Gun Consulting
Frostproof . . . . Allison T. French
          Reloading Supplies
Gainesville . . . . Gulf Hardware
Gainesville . . . . . Rice Grose Hardware
Gainesville . . . . The Rancher
Haines City . . . . Buff Sales Co.
Havana . . . . Moreland's Gunshop
Hollywood . . . . Chira's
Hollywood . . . . Hollywood Gun
Hollywood . . . Jones Equipment Co.
Hollywood . . . . Tom's Gun Shop
Inglis . Backwater Sportsmen Club, Inc.
Jacksonville . . . . Skip's Gun Shop
Jacksonville . . . . Towers Hardware
Key West . . . . . . Charlie's Gun Shop
Kissimee . . Tom Addison's Gun Shop
Lake Geneva . . . . . Slim's Fish-N-Stuff
Lake Wales . . . . Bill's Gun Shop
Live Oak . . . . Mack's Sport Shop
Mango . . . . Frank Wm. Coutcher
Marianna . . Russell Sports Distributors
          and Gun Shop
Miami . . . . Bensons Loan Co.
Miami . . . . Peter Bataskov Firearms &
          Shooting Supplies
Miami . . . . Bullseye, Inc.
Miami . . . . Century Arms
Miami . . . . Europa Corporation
Miami . . . Flagler Jewelry & Loan Co.
Miami . . . . National Gun Traders
Miami . . . . Seminole Gun Shop
Miami . . . . Southern Gun Distribs.
Miami . . . . Tamiami Gun Shop
Miami . . . . The Fix-It Swap Shop
Miami . . . . The Gun Shop, Inc.
Miami Shores . . The Gun Shop, Inc.
Miami . . . . . . Traeger Bros. & Assocs.
Mt. Dora . . A. W. Peterson Gunshop
Naples . . . . . . Sunshine Ace Hardware
Nokomis . John W. Norman, Gunsmith

Ocala . . . . Marion Hardware Co.
Ocala . . . . Pasteur's Sport Shop
Opa-Locka
     Art Lawson Custom Firearms, Inc.
Orlando . . . . Gun Traders
Orlando . . . . Triggermart
Palatka . . . . . . Motes Hardware Store
Palatka . Taylor's Westgate Ace Hdwe.
Panama City . . C & G Sporting Goods
Parker . . . . Rush Gun Shop
Panama City
     Montin Hardware & Sporting Goods
Pensacola . . . . . Biggs Sporting Goods
Pensacola . . . . Pennys
Plant City . Plant City Growers Assoc.
Riviera Beach Custom Gunsmiths, Inc.
St. Petersburg . . Kenneth D. Clothier
St. Petersburg . Gulfshore Sport Center
St. Petersburg . . . . Bill Jackson
St. Petersburg . . . . Ed. Maier
Sanford . . . . . Robson Sporting Goods
Sarasota
     Alton Horne Custom Gunsmith
Sarasota . . . . Tucker Sporting Goods
Starke . . . . . . Starke Builders Supply
Stuart . . . . McDonald Repair
Tallahassee . . . . Downtown Hardware
Tallahassee . . . . F. M. Poggie
Tampa . . . . Jesse E. Harpe
Tampa . . . . Kenfix Company
Tampa . . . . Pioneer Tire Co., Inc.
Tarpon Springs . John K. Gentry & Son
Titusville . . . Belk-Lindsey Dept. Store
Warrington . . . . Gator Sport Shop
Wildwood . . . . . . Clarence L. Howard

Georgia
Albany
     Albany Sporting Supply Co., Inc.
Albany . . . . . . City Loan & Music Co.
Albany Owens Sporting Goods & Hdwe.
Albany . . . . . . The Albany Gun Shop
Ashburn . . . . Barker Hardware
Athens . . . . Athens Firearms, Inc.
Atlanta Atlanta Armory Company, Inc.
Atlanta . . . . Bates Hardware
Atlanta . Brooklyn Loan & Jewelry Co.
Atlanta . . . . Deans, Inc.
Atlanta . . . . King Hardware Co.
Atlanta Everett Roach Sporting Goods
Atlanta . . . . Surplus Guns, Inc.
Atlanta . . . . The Gun Room, Inc.
Augusta . . . . Frye's Guns
Augusta . . . . Georgia Sporting Goods
Bainbridge . . Frank's Gun-Sport Shop
Bainbridge . . . Jakes Pawn Shop
Barnesville . . . . Keadle Hardware
Blakely . . . . Foster's Gun Shop
Cairo . . . . . . Roddenberry Hardware Co.
Cartersville . . . . . Abercrombie's, Inc.
Cedartown . . . . Casey's Sporting Goods
Chickamauga . . . . Tri-State Arms
Claxton . . . . . . Kicks Sports Center
Columbus . Citizen Jewelry & Loan Co.
Columbus . . . . Richardson Home
Columbus . . . . The Accuracy Gunshop
Cordele . . . . The Gun Shop
Cornelia . . . . Modern Gun Shop
Covington . White's Tire & Auto Supply
Cumming Holbrook Hardware & Supply
Dalton . . . . Lackey Marine
Decatur . . . . The Gun Corral
Decatur . . . . Sportsmens Paradise
Donalsonville
     Hatcher Sporting Goods Co.
Doraville . . . . Old Sarge Army Surplus
East Point . . . . The Gun Room
Fitzgerald . Western Auto Assoc. Store
Forsyth . . . . Chambers Sporting Goods
Gainesville . . . . . Stancil Martin Sports
Greensboro . . . . P & S Pawn Shop
Hartwell
     James J. Morsey Custom Gunstocker
Kathleen . . . . Whites Gunshop
Kingsland . . . . . Bush Sporting Goods
Lawrenceville
     Western Auto Assoc. Store

Mableton . . . Mableton Sporting Goods
Macon . . . . Averys
Macon . . . . . R. L. Dunn Hardware Co.
Macon . . . . . . Weaver's Sporting Goods
Macon Westgate Firearms & Accessories

Macon . . . . Willingham, Inc.
Marietta The Mountain View Gun Shop
McDonough Sportsman Gun Shop, Inc.
Milledgeville . . . . Cooks
Milledgeville
     Frank Hines Sporting Goods
Montezuma . . . Tindol Sporting Goods
Moultrie . . . . Baell Mercantile Co.
Newnan . . . . . . Johnson Hardware Co.
Nicholls . . . . Bickley Farm Supply
Pinehurst . . . . Raymond E. Davis Guns
Rentz
     Ronnie Horne's Handloaders Supply
Rome . . . . Owens Hardware Co.
Rossville . . . . Peerless, Inc.
Savannah . . . . Cranmans
Savannah . . . . Ed's Reblueing
Savannah . . . . . . Stubbs Hardware Co.
Smyrna . . . . Home & Hobby Hardware
Statesboro
     W. C. Akins & Son Hdwe. Co.
Statesboro . . . . Roy Smith's Gunshop
Summerville . . Summerville Gun Shop
Swainsboro . . . . The Sports Shop
Tennille . . . . . . McMaster Supply Co.
Thomaston . O. W. Jones & Sons Hdwe.
Thomasville . . . . . Knapp Hardware Co.
Thomasville . . Vaughns Sporting Goods
Valdosta . . . . The Sports Center
Warner Robins
     Blackwater Sporting Goods
Waycross . . . . . . Mayo Bros. Hardware
Waycross . . . . Okefenokee Gun Service
Waycross . . . . The Sport Shop
Waynesboro . . . . . Goodyear Tire Co.

Hawaii
Honolulu . . . Honolulu Sporting Goods
Honolulu . . . . . King's Sporting Goods

Idaho
Blackfoot . . . Alaskan Sporting Goods
Blackfoot . . . . Just's Army Store
Blackfoot . . . . Sam's Sport Center
Boise . . . . Grand Central Market
Boise . . . . Gerald K. King
Boise . . . . Moons Gun & Tackle
Boise . . . . Purcell Sporting Goods
Boise . . . . Skaggs Drug Center
Boise . . . . The Bon Marche
Burley . . . . Morgan Hardware
Caldwell . . . . . . Becker Hardware Co.
Caldwell . . . . Pennywise Drug Store
Coeur D'Alene
     Lighthouse Sporting Goods
Emmett . . . . Dill's Sporting Goods
Gibbonsville . . . . Broken Arrow
Grangeville . . . . . Western Outfitters
Idahoe Falls . . . . Bon Marche
Idaho Falls . . . . Bukys Village
Idaho Falls . Northway Sports Center
Idaho Falls . . . . The Mart
Idaho Falls
     The Outdoorsman Sporting Goods
Idaho Falls . . . . Woodys, Inc.
Kooskia . . . . Brownie's Service
Lewiston . . . . L&B Supply
Lewiston . LoLo Sporting Goods, Inc.
Lewiston . . . . Reed Hardware Co.
Lewiston . . . . . . Warrens Sport Shop
Moscow . . . . Tri-State Store
Mountain Home . . . . Gem State Loan
Nampa . . . . Herb Carlson Sport Shop
Nampa . . . . Ken's Jewelry & Loan
Nampa . . . . . . Pennywise Drug Store
Pierce . . . . . . X. E. Durante Hardware
Pocatello . Bistline Lumber & Hardware
Pocatello . . . Crockett Sporting Goods
Pocatello . . . . Freddy's Sport Shop
Pocatello . . . . . . Getty's Sport Center
Pocatello . . . . . . Pocatello Gun Shop
Pocatello . . . . . . Roy's Sporting Goods

Pocatello . . . . . . Sam's Loan & Jewelry
Pocatello . . . . . Sunset Sporting Goods
Rexburg . . . . . . Rainbow Sport Shop
Rexburg . . Thompson Sporting Goods
Rigby . . . . Marv's Sport Shop
Rupert . . . . Western Auto Store
St. Anthony . . . Ives Sporting Goods
Salmon . . . . Buckhorn Gun Shop
Salmon . . . . Havemann Hardware
Salmon . . . . . Lock, Stock and Barrel
Sand Point . . . . The Pastime
Twin Lakes Blue Lakes Sporting Goods
Twin Falls . . . . Gerrish Sporting Goods
Twin Falls . . . . . Pennywise Drug Store
Twin Falls . . . . Red's Trading Post
Twin Falls . West Point Sporting Goods

Illinois
Abingtdon . . . . Winkless Sport Center
Addison . . . . Puccini's
Alton . . . . . Klump Boat & Motor Co.
Alton . . . . Wittel's & Co.
Anna . . Union County Sporting Goods
Anna . . . . A. W. Walter Jr. & Co.
Antioch Gibbs & Jensen Sporting Goods
Aurora . . . . Arenkills Loan Bank
Aurora . . . . . Aurora Main Store, Inc.
Aurora . . . . Crosby's Sport Shop
Aurora . . . Lake States Gun Exchange
Aurora . Precision Shooters Supply Co.
Barrington . . Darkens Sporting Goods
Bartonville . . Ed Rebbec's Sport Shop
Belleville . . . . Belleville Hardware
Belleville . . . . Kiefer Stocks
Belvidere . . . . . Garrigan's Sport Shop
Berwyn . . . . Mages Sport Center
Bloomington
     J. Howard Rose Sporting Goods
Blue Island Blue Island Gun Shop, Inc.
Broadview . Hildebrand Sporting Goods
Brookfield . . . . Jerry's Gun Shop
Cairo . . . . Metheny's Gun Shop
Calumet City . . . Arco Sporting Goods
Calumet City
     Calumet Marine & Sports Supply
Canton
     Duryea's Trading & Sporting Goods
Carbon Cliff
     Carbon Cliff Bait & Tackle Shop
Carbondale . . . . C & F Boats & Motors
Carbondale . . Jim's Sporting Goods
Carbondale . . . . . Veath's Sports Mart
Casey . . . . Stifal Hardware
Centralia . . . . Dwight F. Cross
Centralia . . . . . . Hanseman Gun Shop
Centralia 20th Century Sporting Goods
Champaign . . . . . Bailey & Himes, Inc.
Champaign Curly's Gun and Pawn Shop
Chester . . . . Parker Hardware
Chicago . . . . Abercrombie & Fitch
Chicago . . . Chicago Archery Center
Chicago . . . . . . Chicago Gun Center
Chicago . . . . Clip Master
Chicago . Community Discount Center
Chicago
     Gabby Hartnett Recreation, Inc.
Chicago . . . . Gitter & Siovic, Inc.
Chicago Jack Gundlach Sporting Goods
Chicago . . . . H. Harris
Chicago . . . Henry's Sport & Bait Shop
Chicago . . . . Hi-Way Sport Shop
Chicago . . Klein's Sporting Goods, Inc.
Chicago . . . . . . Mages Sporting Goods
Chicago . . . . Marshall Field & Co.
Chicago . Marquette Sports Equipment
Chicago . . . . Roseland Sports Center
Chicago . . . . Sam Santo Sport Store
Chicago . . . . Scaramuzzo & Sons
Chicago N. H. Schulkin Sporting Goods
Chicago . . . . Sevic Sport Shop
Chicago . . . . . . Simmon's Sport Shop
Chicago . . . . . . Sportsman's Center, Inc.
Chicago . . . . Superior Sport Store
Chicago . . . . . . Varsity Sporting Goods
Chicago . . . . Vim Sports Co., Inc.
Chicago . . . . Wielgus Sport Shop
Chicago . . . . E. H. Winkler

Chicago Heights .Vicari's Gunshop, Inc.
Chicago Ridge
　　　Chicago Ridge Gun & Range, Inc.
Cicero .... Cicero Sporting Goods
Cicero ...... Novak Sporting Goods
Clinton .... Rolofson Sporting Goods
Collinsville .... L. J. Williams, Jr.
Crystal Lake
　　　Dave's News & Sport Store, Inc.
Danville ...... Bott's Sporting Goods
Danville
　　　Cleve Alexander Sporting Goods
Decatur .... Bill Dotsons, Inc.
Decatur .... Frank's Sport Shop
Decatur ....Ray Myers Sports Center
Decatur .... Rupert's Sport Shop
Deerfield .... Custom Load
Deerfield
　　　Deerfield Bicycle & Sport Shop
DeKalb ...... Tommy's Sport Shop
Des Plaines
　　　Johnson Sporting Goods Co., Inc.
Dixon .... D. C. Long's Sportsman
Dundee .. Fox Valley Rifle Range, Inc.
Du Quoin .... Maclin Westside Drug
East Peoria ... K. C. Fish & Sports Co.
Edwardsville .... Kriege Hardware
Effingham . Vogt Bros. Sporting Goods
El Dorado . El Dorado Sporting Goods
Elgin .... Keeney Sporting Goods
Elgin .... Sportsman's Lodge
Elk Grove Elk Grove Village Sports, Inc.
Elmhurst ... Chipain's Sporting Goods
Elmhurst ... Elmhurst Pro Sport Shop
Evanston
　　　Angler's Supply & Sporting Goods
Evergreen Park
　　　Klein's Sporting Goods, Inc.
Flora .... Gambles
Forest Park
　　　Ray Hanson's Favorite Sport Shop
Fox Lake .....Homan Sporting Goods
Fox Lake ..... Lechner's Tackle Box
Franklin Park
　　　Bell's Gun & Sport Shop, Inc.
Freeport .... Ciganek Sporting Goods
Freeport ... Freeport Sporting Goods
Freeport
　　　Messing & Becker Sporting Goods
Galesburg . Dom's Sporting Goods Co.
Galesburg .... Nelson Sporting
Galesburg ..Gale Ward Athletic Goods
Geneseo ....Cherry's Sporting Goods
Geneva .... Geneva Sport Shop
Glencoe .... Ray's Sport Shop
Glen Ellyn . Glen Sport & Camera Shop
Glen Ellyn .... The Powder Horn
Glenwood ..Bill's Trap & Skeet Supply
Granite City ..Fahnster Tire & Supply
Greenville ...... Main Tire & Battery
Hanover .... Sullivan's Hardware
Harvard .... Carlson's Sporting Goods
Harvard .... Re-Bild Gun Shop
Havana .... Zempel Hardware
Henry .... Perdew Gun Shop
Herrin ....Church Sporting Goods
Highland .... Broadway Tire
Highland Park Greenwald's Sport Shop
Highland Park
　　　Highland Park Sport Shop, Inc.
Hillside .. Klein's Sporting Goods, Inc.
Hoffman Estates .. Omega Sport Shop
Hoopeston .Country Shooters Supply
Jacksonville ......D&D Sports Center
Jacksonville ... Gene's Sporting Goods
Jacksonville .Spaulding Sporting Goods
Jerseyville .... Norton Hardware
Joliet
　　　Bowl Rite Bowling & Sporting Goods
Joliet .... Stukel's World of Sports
Joliet .... AH. Swanson Co.
Kankakee .... Hank's Sporting Goods
Kankakee
　　　Salkeld & Sons Sporting Goods
Kewanee
　　　Breedlove Sports & Hardware Store
Knoxville .... Gil Hebard Guns

La Grange .... Lockhart's Sport Shop
Lake Forest .... Koppens
Lake Zurick ..... Village Sport Center
Lanarle .... Kroll Repair Service
Lansing .... Lansing Hardware
Lemont .. Southwest Shooters Supply
Libertyville .... Suburban Sportsman
Lincoln .... Vic's Sports
Lincoln .... Werth Gun Shop
Lombard ...... Lombard Sport Shop
Loves Park .... Blackhawk Small Arms
Lyndon ....Johnson Roller Mill
Lyons
　　　Midwest Sporting Goods Co., Inc.
Macomb .... Dannys
Macomb ... Feathers Sport Center
Markham ..... Ed Shirley's Sports
Mattoon .... Bob's Gun Shop
Mattoon
　　　Oakley & Son Cycle Hobby & Marine
Mattoon ....Paullins
McHenry .... Ernie's Sport Center
McHenry ...... McHenry Gun Center
Melrose Park ..Mages Sporting Goods
Melrose Park .... Mercury Sports
Melrose Park
　　　Rubin Sporting Goods Co., Inc.
Melrose Park Suburban Sporting Goods
Millstadt
　　　Broken "L" Gun & Saddle Shop
Monmouth .Mitchell's Sporting Goods
Morris .... Redfern Hardware
Morton .... Sander's Gun Shop
Morton Grove ... Dempster All Sports
Morton Grove
　　　L&B Schulkin Sporting Goods
Mt. Carmel ...... E. D. Walter Sports
Mt. Prospect Maxon Shooter's Supplies
Mt. Prospect
　　　Randhurst Sports Chalet, Inc.
Mt. Prospect .... Wille, Inc.
Mundelein ..Suburban Sportsman, Inc.
Murphysboro Bowers & Sons Hardware
Naperville ...... Master Shooters
Naperville ..... Naperville Sport Shop
New Berlin ...... Bernie's Gun Shop
Newton .... Franke Recreation Parlor
Niles .... Klein's Sporting Goods, Inc.
Normal .....Gibson's Sporting Goods
Northbrook
　　　Stark's Northbrook Sports Center
Northfield ... Bess Hardware & Sports
Oak Lawn .... Associated Guns
Oak Lawn
　　　Oak Lawn Gun & Sports, Inc.
Oak Lawn ....Sundeen Guns
Oak Park .... Breit & Johnson
Oak Park ... Cunningham-Reilly, Inc.
Olney ..Bauman True Value Hardware
Olney ...... Richland County Tire
Oregon .... Doeden's
Palatine ....Pro Sport Center
Paris .... Steffeys
Park Forest ... Sports & Hobbies, Inc.
Park Ridge .... Blyth Enterprises, Inc.
Pekin .... Bob's Rod & Gun Shop
Pekin ... Buckley Brothers Sport Shop
Pekin ....Shipman Sport Center
Peoria .... Hinman Outfitters
Peoria .....Jack's Hunter's Supplies
Peoria ...... Keenan Sporting Goods
Peoria Heights .. Heights Hardware Co.
Pinckneyville ... Hicks Trading Station
Pinckneyville ..Mann's Sporting Goods
Plainfield ...... Van's Gun Shop
Pontiac ...... Shepherd's Pet Shop &
　　　　　　　　　　Sporting Goods
Princeton ...Ky-Wa Acres Sport Shop
Quincy .... Merkel's, Inc.
Quincy ...... Snowhill's Sports Shop
Rantoul ...... Litchfield Hardware
Richmond .... Oakdale Sports
Riverdale ...... Chuck's Gun Shop
Roberts .... Harold's Firearms
Rockford Humpal Sporting Goods Co.
Rockford .McNames Gun Repair Service
Rockford Mortenson's Sporting Goods

Rockford Rockford Sports Center, Inc.
Rockford .... Sterns
Rock Island .... 44th Street Bait Shop
Rock Island ... Freelands Scope Stand
Rolling Meadows ...... Sports Chalet
Round Lake ...Avon Hardware, Inc.
Round Lake . Cross Sport & Gun Shop
Sandwich
　　　R. G. Seitzinger Sporting Goods
Savanna .... Pitts Sport Store
Shabbona ....Carter's Gun Shop
Shabbona .... T & J Shop
Shelbyville ... Rose Center Rifle Shop
Sparta ...... Henderson's Equipment
Springfield .....Sportsman's Center
Sterling ...... Rock River Sport Shop
Streator .....Christoff's Hardware
Sycamore ......Hagen Ace Hardware
Toulon ....John's Gun Room
Urbana ... Lorry's Favorite Sport Shop
Vandalia ....The Sports Center
Villa Park
　　　Community Discount Center, Inc.
Watseka .... G & M Sports Center
Wauconda ....Dorkens For Sports
Wauconda ....Herb's Sport Shop
Waukegan .. Downtown Sports Center
Waukegan .... Grand Sporting Goods
Waukegan ... Shaw Bros. Gun Center
Waukegan .... Smoke 'N Gun
Wheaton ..... Wheaton Sport Shop
Wilmette Wilmette Bicycle-Sport Shop
Winnetka .... Fred's Bicycle Shop
Woodstock ....P. O. Knuth Company
Wyanet ..Hickory Grove Hunting Club

Indiana

Anderson .... Gun Barn
Aurora .... Kennedy Sporting Goods
Avilla .... Riley's, Inc.
Bloomington .... Schmalz Dept. Store
Bloomington
　　　University Sporting Goods
Boonville..............Addingtons
Brazil .... Clarks Sporting Goods
Chesterton .... Jack's Gun Shop
Columbus .... Marlin Sporting Goods
Columbus .....Ron's Reloading Shop
Columbus Thompson's Sporting Goods
Connersville
　　　Knight's Custom Gun Shop
Corydon ... Lamon & Davis Hardware
Crawfordsville ... Ben Hur Sport Shop
Crown Point . R. E. Safford Enterprise
Dyer ... Schereville Bait & Sport Shop
East Chicago .... J. P. Davis & Co.
Edwardsport Edwardsport Lumber Co.
Elkhart ... Berman Sporting Goods
Elkhart . Sportsman's Enterprises, Inc.
Evansville ....B&S Sporting Guns
Evansville ..... Beards Sporting Goods
Evansville Gus Doerner Sporting Goods
Evansville .... Franklin Drug Co.
Evansville .... Rajo Gun Shop
Ft. Wayne ..Buchwald Sporting Goods
Ft. Wayne ... Cashman's Sporting Goods
Frankfort . Conkright Sporting Goods
Galveston
　　　J. L. Jones Firearms & Ammunition
Gary .... Broadway Sports & Marine
Gary .... Griffin Sport & Marine, Inc.
Goshen ... Goshen Rod & Gun Shop
Goshen ...... Phil's Sporting Goods
Greensburg Doerflinger Sporting Goods
Griffith .... Blyth's Sport Shop
Hammond .... The Sportsman's Store
Hartford ...... Suite Sporting Goods
Indianapolis Broad Ripple Sports Shop
Indianapolis . Em-Roe Sporting Goods
Indianapolis .....Shaw's Gulf Service
Indianapolis . Vonnegut Hardware Co.
Kokomo ....The Gun Room
LaFayette .... A. F. Herbst
Lafayette ...... The Sportsman, Inc.
Lafayette .... Trader Horn Co.
La Porte ... Bob's Custom Handloads

La Porte ....La Porte Sporting Goods
Lawrenceburg ... Triangle Sport Shop
Lawrenceburg ... Triangle Sport Shop
Linton .... Wright's Bait Shop
Madison ..... Bill's Sporting Goods
Marysville ... Marysville Hardware Co.
Michigan City ..... Bob's Sport Shop
Muncie Dick's Antique & Modern Arms
Muncie .... Dustin Waymire
Muncie ....Kirk's Sporting Goods
Muncie ....Retz Sporting Goods
Muncie .....Sheward's Gun Repair
New Albany .... Bush Keller Co.
New Albany ....Combs Custom Guns
New Castle ...... Ramrod Gun Shop
North Manchester ... Schutz Brothers
North Vernon . J. R. Greathouse & Son
Osgood .... Gloyd Hardware
Paoli .... Boule Sporting Goods
Peru .... Yentes Sporting Goods
Plymouth .....Don's Sporting Goods
Rensselaer .... Hudsons
Richmond
　　　Cooper & Evans Sporting Goods
Richmond .... Phil's Sport Shop
Rochester .... Baileys Hardware
Rockport .... Schoenfeld Rexall Drug
St. Paul
　　　Settle's Antique & Modern Firearms
Seymour ....Stewarts Appliance
Shelbyville ....Cartridge Cabin
Speedway City Vonnegut Hardware Co.
Syracuse ..Wawasee Sportsman Center
Terre Haute . McMillan Sporting Goods
Terre Haute .. Paitsons Bros. Hardware
Terre Haute .... Poffs Sporting Goods
Valparaiso .... Bernard Gotaut
Valparaiso .... Johnstons Sports
Veedersburg .... J. C. Sport Shop
Vincennes .... Tresslars
Vincennes ..Vanmeter Sporting Goods
Winchester ..... Keener Sports Store
Winchester .... Sports Center

Iowa

Ames .... Long's Specialties
Ames .... Nims Sportsman
Ames ..... Woods Shooting Supply
Anamosa ....R. L. Flaucher & Son
Aurelia .... Menetee Hardware
Boone ......Red Fox Sporting Goods
Britt .... Kreitinger Hardware
Burlington .... Dehner Seed
Burlington .... Lloyds Surplus
Carroll ...... Uptown Sporting Goods
Cedar Falls .... Olsen's Boat House
Cedar Rapids ....Coast To Coast Store
Cedar Rapids ....Drews
Centerville .... Favorite Sports
Charles City .. Monroe Sporting Goods
Cherokee .... Doors Sport Service
Clarinda .... Campbell Farm
Clear Lake Clarks Sport & Hobby Shop
Clinton .... Lateke Marina
Clinton .... R. D. Letch Co.
Corning .... Ashenfelter Leather
Council Bluffs ....Peoples Dept. Store
Creston ....Dreys Sporting Goods
Davenport ... Cratons Sporting Goods
Davenport ...Credit Island Sport Shop
Davenport .... Don's Sport Shop
Davenport .. Kunkel's Sporting Goods
Decorah ......Lange Sporting Goods
Denison ...... Denison Sporting Goods
Des Moines ....Betts & Son Hardware
Des Moines .... Central Hardware Co.
Des Moines
　　　Des Moines Pawn-Sporting Goods
Des Moines .... Gun Craft
Des Moines .... Hog Gun Shop
Des Moines ..... Ted Holm Gun Sales
Des Moines
　　　Hopkins Sporting Goods, Inc.
Des Moines ....Jay's Sales Co.
Des Moines ... Thode Sporting Goods
Dubuque ...... Central Hardware Co.
Dubuque .... Junie's Tri-State

Dubuque
Bob Zehentner's Sporting Goods
Emmetsburg Johnsons Sporting Goods
South English . . . . Slates Service
Estherville . . . . Lees Sport Shop
Evans Dale . . . . Cedar Sport Shop
Fairfield . . . . The Sport Shop
Farmington . . . . Bob's Shop
Ft. Dodge Kautzky Sporting Goods Co.
Ft. Dodge . . . . Nordquist Sports
Ft. Madison . . . . Burgunds
Glenwood . . . . . Coast To Coast Store
Grinnell . . . . Harry's Sport Shop
Grundy Center . John High Hardware
Independence . . Coast To Coast Store
Independence
Freeman's Sporting Goods
Iowa City John Wilson Sporting Goods
Laurens . . . . Laurens 5 To 1 Store
Leon . . Leon Concrete & Bldg. Supply
Le Mars . . . . Adler Sporting Goods
Manchester . . . . Cassel & Cassel
Manchester . Hawkers Sporting Goods
Manchester . . . . Saunders
Maquoketa . . Casady's Sporting Goods
Marengo . . Style & Economy Clothiers
Marshalltown . . Hays Sporting Goods
Marshalltown . . . . . Turners Gunshop
Mason City . Bobs Shooters Supply Co.
Mason City . . . Decker Sporting Goods
Mason City . . . . Greischar
Muscatine . . . Carlisle Sporting Goods
Muscatine . . Safley's Sporting Goods
Mystic . . . . Hampton's Gun Shop
Newton . . . . Coast To Coast Store
Oelwein . . . . Coast To Coast Store
Osceola . . . . Clark Sporting Goods
Oskalooza . . . . Firestone
Oskaloosa . . . . Upton & Colville
Perry . . . . Al's Sporting Goods
Perry . . . . Walt's Sport Shop Inc.
Sac City . . . . Art's Sports
Shell Rock . . . . Pruin Body Shop
Sioux City . . . . Olson Sporting Goods
Sioux City . . . . . . Riverside Hardware
Spencer . . . . Sportsmans
Storm Lake . . . . . Coast to Coast Store
Waterloo . . . . Coburn Sporting Goods
Waterloo . . . . Winder Sport Shop, Inc.
Waverly . . . . Dales Sport Shop
Waverly . . . . Sportsmen's Corner
Webster City . . . Jones Sporting Goods

Kansas

Abilene . . . . R. H. V. Store
Arkansas City . . Arkche Supp. & Serv.
Ashland . . . . Sportsmans Supply
Atchinson . . . . Rudolph's
Chanute . . . . Sportsmans Supply
Clay Center . . Ward's Sporting Goods
Coffeyville . . . . Frazee's Firestone
Coffeyville . . . . Schille's
Colby . . . . Pratt Hardware
Columbus . . . . Hurst Firestone
Concordia
F. D. Everitt & Son Hardware
Dodge City Pennington Sporting Goods
Downs . . . . 181 Gun Shop
Emporia . . . . Emporia Sport Shop
Eureka . . . . Gambles
Ft. Scott . . . . Central Gun Shop
Garden City
Western Kansas Sporting Goods
Goodland . . . McClure Sporting Goods
Goodland . . . . Myers Sporting Goods
Great Bend . . . . Brant's Sporting Goods
Great Bend . . . . Field & Lake Sports
Great Bend . . . . . . Gibsons Products
Great Bend . . . . Phillips Sporting Goods
Hopewell . . . . Curtis Gun Shop
Hoxie . . . . Mickey Hardware
Hugoton . . . . Floyds Hardware
Hutchinson . . . Boren Sporting Goods
Hutchinson . . . . . Reno's Ace Hdwe.
Independence . Kansan Boat & Marine
Iola . . . . Wilson Hdwe.
Junction City Ski's Shooting Supplies

Junction City . . . . Waters, Inc.
Kansas City . . . . Gateway
Kansas City . . . Schrader's Sport Shop
Kansas City . . Smitty's Boats & Motors
Lawrence . . . . Ernst & Son Hardware
Lawrence . . . Wilson Supply & Service
Leavenworth . . . . Gateway
Leoti . . . . Y & S Camper Sales
Liberal . . . . Chaffin Hardware
Manhattan Smith Bros. Sporting Goods
Mankato . . . McCarthy Hardware Co.
Merriam . . . . B. E. Hodgon
Newton . . . . Graber's Hardware
Norton . . . . Horneys
Oberlin . . . . Guinns
Ogden . . . . Main St. Pawn
Ottawa . . . . Brown Hardware Co.
Overland Park . . . . Lucky's
Parsons . . . . . Farran's Sporting Goods
Phillipsburg . . . . Finkbeiner's
Russell Friesen Army & Sporting Goods
St. Francis . . . . . St. Francis Hardware
Salinas . . . . Cleves Marine
Scott City . . . . Bryan's, Inc.
Scott City . . . . . Claycomb-McDaniel
Topeka . . . . G. F. Y.
Topeka . . . . Maverick Gun Works
Topeka . . . . Topeka Sporting Goods
Ulysses . . . . . Gish Sporting Goods
Wathena . . . . Kaelins
Wellington . . . . Cooley's
Wellington . . . . Lawrence Drug
Wellington .Wellington Sporting Goods
Wichita . . . . Hesse Sporting Goods
Wichita . . . . Lewis Bros.
Wichita . . Wichita Sporting Goods Co.
Winfield . . . . . Hyter Sporting Goods
Winfield . . . . Shooters Supply

Kentucky

Ashland . . . . Jay's Loan Co.
Bardstown . . . . Swap Shop
Berea . . . . Coffey's Gun Shop
Bowling Green
Aspley & Aspley Hardware
Brandenberg
Brandenberg Sporting Goods
Campbellsville . . . . Crabtrees
Covington . . . . Egelston Maynard
Elizabethtown . . . . Surplus, Inc.
Fulton . . . . Bennett Electric Co.
Fulton . . . . Railroad Salvage Co.
Glasgow . . . . Bob's Gun & Tackle
Glasgow . . . . Sports Shop
Greenville . . . . . . E. A. Cohen & Sons
Hazard . . . . Sterling Hardware
Henderson . . . . Paynes
Henderson . . Reynolds Sporting Goods
Hopkinsville . . . Cayce Yost Hardware
Independence . . . Cleveland Gun Shop
Lexington J. T. Barrick Sporting Goods
Lexington . . . . Phillip Gall & Son
Lexington . . . . Rosenberg Bros.
Liberty . . . . Reid's Gun Shop
Louisville Blue Grass Shooters Supply
Louisville . . . . S. E. Davis Co.
Louisville . . . . Davis & Son, Inc.
Louisville . . . . Sutcliffe
Louisville . . . . The Oakwood
Louisville . . . . Tinsley Gun
Louisville Umberger's Sporting Goods
Loyall . . . . Harco Distributors
Madisonville . Arnold Sporting Goods
Mayfield Look of Sky Sporting Goods
Mayfield . . . . . W. Kentucky Hatchery
Maysville . . . . . . Maysville Sport Shop
Melbourne . . . . . . Jack's Sports Shop
Middlesboro . . Middlesboro Hardware
Moorehead . . . . Perry Hardware
Owensboro . . . . Cox Gun Shop
Owensboro . . . . L. Mahlinger
Paducah . . Ray Gage Sporting Goods
Paducah . . . . Jones Marine
Paducah . . . . . Sportsmans Paradise
Paris . . . . . Ben Cohen Sporting Goods
Plesor Ridge Park
Sumners Sporting Goods

Louisiana

Abbeville . . . . Landry Stores
Alexandria Briston Marine—Hardware
Bastrop . . . . . . Alan's Sporting Goods
Bastrop . . . . Bastrop Feed
Baton Rouge . . . . Bonfanti
Baton Rouge . . . . Sport Shop
Baton Rouge Steinberg's Sports Center
Bogalusa . . . . Land Of Sports
Bunkie . . . . Kenards
Crowley . . . . . Morrows Sports Center
De Ridder . . . . Kerns
Eunice . . . . Johnson, Inc.
Gonzales . . . . . . Gonzales Sport Shop
Houma . . . . . . Jones Sporting Goods
Jena Jimmy Wallace Sporting Goods
Lafayette . . . . Southern Arms
Lafayette . . . . The Sportsman
Lake Charles . . . . Buster Keaton, Inc.
Lake Charles . . . . . E&M Sports Center
Lake Charles . . . . House For Sports
Lake Providence . . . . Schneider's, Inc.
Manx . . . . Boyens Hardware
Minden . . . . Goodwill Hardware
Monroe . . . . . Gene's Sporting Goods
Monroe . . . . Haddad Hardware
Monroe . . . . Hunt & Whitaker
Morgan City . Spanish Trail Arms, Inc.
Natchitoches . . . . . Deblieux & McCain
New Iberia . . . . Comptons
New Orleans . . . . Crescent Gun
New Orleans . . New Orleans Arms Co.
New Orleans . . . . Rolands
New Orleans . . . . Security Co.
Shreveport . . . . Arms Center
Shreveport . . . . Evans Sporting Goods
Shreveport . Harbuck Sporting Goods
Shreveport . . . . Lorants
Shreveport . . . . . Otto Sport Center
Shreveport . . . . Turbocraft, Inc.
Shreveport W. H. Womack Riflesmith
Sterlington . . . . DeFee's
Tallulah . . . . Crawford Feed
Tallulah . . . . . . Johnson's Firestone
Thibodaux . . . . N. J. Gaubert
Ville Platte . . . . G. Ardoin & Co.
Westwego . . . . Coulon's

Maine

Ashland . . . . . . Ashland Hardware Co.
Auburn . . . . . . Higgins Sport Center
Augusta . . . . . . Ft. Western Tire Co.
Bangor . . . . W. T. Grant & Co.
Bangor . . . . . Morrison's Gun Shop
Bangor . . . . . F. L. Wight Co, Inc.
Belfast . . . . Hall Hardware Co.
Belfast . . . . . Home Furnishing Co.
Belfast . . . . Wm. B. Keswick
Biddeford . . . . Major Frank R. Irving
Brunswick . . . . Atlantic Tire & Supply
Brunswick . . . . MacIntosh Outfitters
Brunswick . . Pelletier's Outfitters
Caribou . . . . . Briggs Hardware Co.
Caribou . . . . Nelson & Page
Dixfield . . . . Drury's Gun Shop
Dover, Foxcroft . Western Auto Store
East Orland . . . . R. W. Neider
East Wilton . . . . Rolfe Maingas
Ellsworth . . . . Maddock's Sport Shop
Ellsworth . . . H. F. Wescott Hardware
Co., Inc.
Fairfield . . . . Joseph's Outlet
Farmington . . . . Pearson's
Fort Kent . . . . A. J. Neadeau & Son
Fort Kent . . . . . A. D. Soucy Co.
Freeport . . . . . Freeport Hardware Co.
Greenville . . . . Sander's Store
Halldwell . . . . H. L. Nilson
Houlton . . . . . Almon H. Fogg Co.
Houlton . . . . Rod & Gun
Kennebunk . . . . R. W. Libby & Son
Kittery . . . . . . Kittery Trading Post
Kittery . Tom Taylor Sporting Goods
Kittery . . . Webber's Sporting Goods
Lewiston . . . . Wise Pawn Shop
Lincoln . . . . Lincoln Sport Shop

Livermore Falls . . . . . . Ed's Gun Shop
Livermore Falls
C. H. Newcomb Sporting Goods
Madawaska . . Madawaska Sport Shop
Milford . . . . Gun-Craft
Millinockett
Hikel Bros. Sporting Goods
Milo . . . . Milo Sport Shop
Norway . . . . Woodman's
North Windham . Sebago Trading Post
Old Town . . . . . Ross Sporting Goods
Pittsfield . . . . White's Gun Shop
Portland . . . . . . Carl's Sporting Goods
Portland
Porteous Mitchell Sporting Shop
Portland . . . . Tommy's Hardware Co.
Portland . . . . Whitmore's Gun Shop
Presque Isle . . . . Roy's Army & Navy
Rockland . . . . H. H. Cree & Co.
Rumford . . . . Hamannes
Rumford . . . . . . Rumford Surplus
Saco . . . . Kennedy's Tackle
Saco . . . . King's Fly Shop
Skowhegan . . . . Cross Hardware
South Waterford Yankee Gunsmith Co.
Topsham . . . . Dick's Gun Repair
Waterville . . . . W. T. Grant Co.
Westbrook . . . . Knight's Hardware
Westbrook . . . . Paul's Gun Shop
Westbrook Tom Taylor Sporting Goods
Winslow . . . . Proctor & Bowie Co.
Winthrop . . . . Audette's
Wiscassett . . . . Flood's Hardware
Wiscassett . . . . Harvey's Gun Shop

Maryland

Annapolis . . . . Bataskou Firearms
Baltimore . . . . . . Baltimore Gunsmiths
Baltimore . Edmondson Hardware Co.
Baltimore . . . . Miller's Guns
Baltimore National Sporting Goods Co.
Baltimore . . . . . Peltzer's Sport Shop
Baltimore . . . . Schreiber & Jones
Bethesda . . . . The Sportsman
Brooklyn Park Marvin's Sport City, Inc.
Chevy Chase . . . . . . Colony Arms Co.
Chillum . . . . . . Apple Hardware, Inc.
Cumberland . . . . Sport Shoppe
Denton . . . . Will's Sporting Goods
Easton . . . . Shanahan & Wrightson
Elkton . . . . . . Herbert F. DeWitt, Inc.
Elkton . . . . Elkton Supply Co.
Essex . . . . . . Bayside Sporting Goods
Essex . . . . . . Marvin's Sport City, Inc.
Frederick . . Maryland Gun Exchange
Frederick . . . . Shipleys Inc.
Frostburg . . . . Prichard Corp.
Gaithersburg . . . . Robert L. Lindsay
Garrison Maryland Sporting Goods, Inc.
Hillcrest Hights
Marvin's Sport City, Inc.
Indian Head
Indian Head Sportmen's Den
Jefferson . . . . The Trading Post
Laurel . . . . Voss Sporting Goods
LaValle . . . . . . LaValle Sport Center
Mt. Ranier . . . . Bob's Gun Shop
Oakland . . . . . . Carroll's Sport Shop
Ocean City . . . Elliott's Sports Marina
Pasadena . . . . . Bart's Sporting Goods
Quantico . . . . Dave's Sport Shop
Riverdale . . . . Atlas Sport Store
Rockville . . . . Custom Gun Service
Rockville . . . . . . Rockville Trading Post
Salisbury . . . . . . Morris O. Hammond
Silver Springs . . . . Atlantic Guns
Silver Springs . Potomac Trading Post
Towson . . . . Ponentos Supplies
Towson . . . . Valley Gun Shop
Upperco . . . . Duffy's Gun Room
Upper Marlboro . . . . . Bud's Gun Shop
Woodbine . . Carroll Shooters Supply
Worton . Robt. Elliott Sporting Goods

Massachusetts

Agawam . . . . Agawam Assocs.

Andover .... Dana's Sport Shop
Arlington ...... Holovak & Coughlin
Athol .... Epquoig Firearms
Attleboro .... Klebe Sport Shop
Ayer .... New England Arms
Bedford .... Jordan Marsh
Beverly .... Johnny Appleseed
Billerica .... Quirion's Rod & Gun
Boston .... Giordani Bros.
Boston ......Ivanhoe Sports Center
Boston ...... Jordan Marsh Co.
Boston .... Kirkwood Bros.
Boston ... Bob Smith Sporting Goods
Brockton .... A. C. Grady Co.
Brockton .... Mammoth Marts
Brockton ....Sports World
Brockton .... Wetzell's
Burlington ...... Middlesix Gun Serv.
Buzzards Bay Red Top Sporting Goods
Cambridge ...... Harvard Gun Shop
Cambridge .... Lechmere Sales
Cambridge ... Roach Hardware Co.
Canton .... Cline's Gun Room
Chelmsford .J. E. Dominicis Gunsmith
Chicnpee ...... Kenneth R. Stich
Concord .... Macone Sporting Goods
Dalton .... Dalton Gun Shop
Dedham .. Dedham Sportsmen Center
Dedham .... Lechmere Sales
Dighton .... Carr's Trading Post
East Longmeadow .... The Gun Barrel
East Springfield . Thomason Gun Shop
Fall River ....Al Dexter's
Fall River ... Russ Gold Sporting Co.
Falmouth .... Gun & Tackle
Fitchburg ....Jake's Sport Center
Fitchburg ...... Peter Whitney Guns
Framingham .... Bretts
Framingham .Lew Horton Sport Shop
Franklin
   Franklin Reservoir Sport Center
Gardner ..... General Sporting Goods
Greenfield .... Clark Sport Shop
Greenfield ...... Geo. R. Jonelunas
Groton ....Frank's Sport Shop
Holland ..... Holland Sports Marina
Holyoke .... Ward Two
Hyannis .... Puritan Clothing
Lawrence ....Al's Rod & Gun
Lawrence .... Tom's Gun & Sport
Leominster ....The Sport Mart
Leominster . Werner's Sporting Goods
Littleton .... Frank's Sport Shop
Littleton Nashoba Valley Sport Center
Lowell ....:.Schulman's
Lynn ....Jerry's, Inc.
Lynn ....Pennyworth's
Malden ...... Day's Sporting Goods
Marlboro ....The Gun Shop
Mattapoisett .. Capeway Sport Center
Maynard ....Victor Brociner
Medford ..... Bernie Gould Guns
New Bedford ....McGees
New Bedford .. Smith Athletic Store
Newburyport . Chas. A. Carroll & Co.
Newburyport ... Narrow's Gun Shop
North Adams ... Bill's Sporting Goods
North Adams .. Center Sporting Goods
North Dartmouth ..Smith Mills Sports
Norwell ....Bradberry's
Norwood .... Ortin's Sport Shop
Norwood ...Sandell's Sport Center
Orleans ....Goose Hummocks
Pittsfield ....Ernie's Sporting Goods
Pittsfield . Dick Moon Sporting Goods
Pittsfield .. Pittsfield Sporting Goods
Plainville .... Custom Sporting Goods
Plymouth ....M&M Sporting Goods
Salem ....Salem Army-Navy
Seekonk ...Thompsons Sport Shop
Shrewsbury .... Underwood Arms
Somerville ....Detras
South Dartmouth ....J. M. Arsenault
Springfield ....Blair's Range
Still River ...... Bucky's Sport Shack
Stoneham ....Al's Gun Shop

Stoughton .... Corcoran's
Stoughton ... Stoughton Trading Post
Sudbury .... H. P. Stratemeyer
Swansea ....Thompson's Sport Shop
Taunton .. Pierce Taunton Hardware
Townsend .. The Trading Post
Tyngsboro .... Forest Marine Co.
Wakefield ....Mike's Gun Shop
Waltham .... Scott's Surplus
Ware .... Sporting Goods & Blrds.
Wareham ....American Arms Co.
Watertown ....Ivanhoe Sports Center
Westboro .... Hawill's
West Boylston ....Never Fail Products
Worcester ..... Ivanhoe Sports Shop
Worcester ...MacBen Sporting Goods
Worcester .... The Fair
Worcester .... The Rod & Gun

Michigan
Ada ....Gilmore's Sporting Goods
Adrian .... W. Johnson Service
Adrian .... Mau Mee
Adrian .... Noveskys
Allegan .... Stone's Sport Shop
Alma ....Don Elsea Sports
Alma .... Van Attens
Alpena ......Alpena Sporting Goods
Alpena .... Neuman's Tire
Ann Arbor
   Ann Arbor Arms & Sporting Goods
Ann Arbor ...... Fox Tent & Awning
Armada .... Mac's Firearms
Auburn ..... Auburn Hts. & Hardware
Baldwin ....Eds Sport Shop
Battle Creek .... Frosty's
Battle Creek ... Lakeview Hardware
Battle Creek ...... Marine-Gun Shop
Bay City .... Breen's Sport Shop
Bay City .... Leo D. Goddeyne
Bay City ...... Jennison Hardware
Beaverton .... Morris Hardware
Beaverton ....White's
Bedford .... Bedford Bait Shop
Benton Harbor .... Gardner's
Big Rapids .... Grunst Bros.
Bridgman .... Al's Sport Center
Bridgeman .... Daves All Sport
Buchanan .... Allen Hardware
Buchanan .... Sullivan Bros.
Cadillac .... Johnson Hardware
Cedar Springs
   Log Cabin Sporting Goods
Charlotte ...... Munger's Sports
Clare .... Grove Brothers
Clarkston ..... Lawson's Gun Shop
Clio .... Water Wonderland
Comstock Park
   Comstock Park Sports & Hobby
Crystal Falls .... Bauman Sports Inc.
Davison ...... Williams Gun Sight Co.
Dearborn .... Kenneth J. Budney
Dearborn .... Nichols Sport
Dearborn ...... Wyoming Hardware
Dearborn .... Zims Sports
Detroit .... B&M Firearms
Detroit .... "EPPS"
Detroit ..... Gell's Sporting Goods
Detroit ..... Griswold Sporting Goods
Detroit .... Gun Rack
Detroit .... Maurie's Gun Serv.
Detroit .... Stephen T. Milford
Detroit ...... Neumann's Gun Shop
Detroit ...... Wessel Gun Service
Eaton Rapids ..... Appleby Gun Shop
Eaton Rapids .. Keeler's Trading Post
Escanaba .... Jerry's Sport City
Farmington . Budde's Sport Shop, Inc.
Fennville ......Dickinson's Hardware
Ferndale . Greakes Sporting Goods
Flint .... Art Beauchamp
Flint ..... Allsports Sporting Goods
Flint .... C-W Arqunco Co.
Flint ...... Flint Tent & Awning
Flint .... Goods Sporting Goods
Flushing ..... Central Distributors
Fremont ....Sherman Sport Shop

Gaylord .... Marzof's Alphorn
Gibraltar ....Dick's Gun Shop
Grand Haven . Hoby Bell's Sport Shop
Grand Rapids ...Al & Bob Sport Inc.
Grand Rapids .... Bobs Gun Shop
Grand Rapids . Buikema Sport Center
Grand Rapids .... Custom Gun Shop
Grand Rapids .Davis Bros. Gun Shop
Grand Rapids .... Godwin Sport Shop
Grand Rapids .Kent Block Hardware
Grand Rapids Olsen Bros. Sport Center
Grand Rapids ....Peck's Bait Shop
Grand Rapids ....Roy's Sport Shop
Grand Rapids .... Wurzburg's
Greenville ...Daniel's Sporting Center
Greenville ...... Jack's Bait & Tackle
Grosse Pt. .... Detroit Gun Sight
Grosse Pointe Park ... B. McDaniel Co.
Hamtrack ...... Jack Roy's Gun Shop
Harbor Spring ..... Harbor Gun Shop
Haslett ....William C. Roege, Jr.
Hastings .... Leary's Sport Ctr.
Hazel Park ...... Gun Bugs Haven
Hillman ....Hillman Hdwe.
Hillsdale ....Tolan's Gun Shop
Holland ....Bobs Sport Shop
Holland ....Main Auto Supply
Holland ....Prins Gun Shop
Holland ....Superior Sport Store
Holly .... Cliff Dreyer
Houghton Lake Hgts ... Tuck's Hdwe.
Indian River ...... Northland Sports
Ionia .... Tom's Tackle Shop
Iron Mt ....Bert & Harvey's
Iron Mt .... Izzys Ski & Sport
Iron Mt .... Smittys Spt. Gds.
Ironwood .... Ben's Rod & Gun Shop
Jackson ... Beach & Heuman Sptg. Gds.
Jonesville .... H & S Hobby Shop
Kalamazoo ... Eastwood Plaza Sports
Kalamazoo ..
   Miller & Boardman Sporting Goods
Kalamazoo .... Schau Powell, Inc.
Kalkaska .... Vallaro Sport Shop
Keego Harbor ...... Briggs Sptg. Gds.
Lambertville ..... Wolverine Arms
Lansing ..Beck Bros. Sport Shop, Inc.
Lansing ...Britton's Sport Store
Lansing ..... McCloud's Gunsmithing
Lansing ......Norton's Firearms
Lansing ....Sportland
Lansing ....Vander Voort's
Lakeview ....Lakeview Sport
LaPeer .... LaPeer Hardware
Lincoln Park ......Hoods Gun Shop
Linwood ....Bid Pen Sptg. Gds.
Livonia ....Gell's Civilian PX
Ludington .... C. R. Pederson & Son
Ludington ......Tuck Sport Shop
Mancelona ....Rays Sport Shop
Manistee .... Freidrich Sport Shop
Marquette ...... Gibb's Sptg. Splys.
Marshall .... Marshall Sport Shop
Menominee .... Lou's Sport Shop
Michigan Center O'Briens Trading Post
Midland ....Al's Sport Shop
Monroe ....Cooks Sportland
Morley .... Franks Sport Shop
Mt. Clemens ..... R. Krieger & Sons
Mt. Clemens .....Prevost Spt. Gds.
Munising ....Madigan Bros.
Muskegon ....The Outdoorsman
Newberry ....Dukes Sport Shop
New Buffalo ....Al's Gun Shop
Niles .... James Kehrer Guns
Novi .... Trickey's
Owosso .... Johns Sports & Marine
Owosso ...... Shippee & Smith
Paw Paw .... Sportsman's Corner
Pentwater ..Bob Maynards Gun Shop
Petoskey ....Bremmeyer Bain Co.
Pontiac ...S. C. Rogers Sptg. Goods
Pontiac .... Simms Bros.
Pontiac .... Ralph E. White
Port Huron ....Docks Sptg. Gds.
Port Huron .. Northgate Sports Ctr.
Rochester ... Harold Freeborn & Son

Saginaw .... Moreley Bros.
Saginaw .... Peters Gun Shop
Saginaw .... Sam's
Saginaw .... Shea's Allsports
Saginaw .... Smith Hardware
Saginaw .... Vic's Sport Shop
St. Clair Shores ..... Dunhams, Inc.
St. Johns .... Allen Dean Sport Center
St. Johns ...... A. R. Dean Hrdwe.
Sawyer ...... Peterson's Gunshop
Scottville .... Scott's Sport Store
Southfield .... Dunhams, Inc.
Southfield ... M. T. Sportsman Center
South Haven ....McKimmies, Inc.
Spruer ....Wills Gunshop
Sturgis .... Sportsarama
Sturgis ..... Sturgis Sporting Goods
Traverse City .... Hampels Gun Shop
Traverse City ..... Vaneenaam Hdwe.
Union City ...... E. W. Merchants
Union Lake .... Dunhams, Inc.
Union Lake .... Simms Bros.
Utica .... Heide & Kidd
Warren ....Gell's Sptg. Goods
White Cloud ....Bob Osborne
White Hall ....Duck Lake Gun
Whitehall ....Vern Scholl Sport Shop
Wyandotte ... G. C. Reloading Service
Wyandotte ... Ken's Gun Shop
Wyoming .... Bentley's Gun Shop

Minnesota
Alexandria .... Sports Center
Anoka .... Great North Trading Post
Austin .... Dugans Sport Shop
Bagley ....Northland Sport Ctr.
Baudette .... Gambles
Bemidji ..... Coast to Coast Store
Bemidji ....Lakeland Sptg. Goods
Brainerd .... King's Sptg. Goods
Breckenridge ....Scheel's Hardware
Caledonia ...... Coast to Coast Store
Calidonia ...... Otterson's Reloading
Deerwood ....Deerwood Sport Shop
Detroit Lakes .. Coast to Coast Store
Detroit Lakes ......Lake Sport Shop
Duluth ....Pike Lake Gamble
Duluth .... Reliable Co.
East Grand Forks Giese Hardware Co.
Ely .... Coast to Coast Store
Eveleth ...... Arrow Head Gun Shop
Fairmont .... Coast to Coast Store
Fairmont .... Mahowald's
Faribault .... Mahler Hardware
Faribault ....Mahowald's Sptg. Goods
Farmington Farmington Shooters Sply.
Fergus Falls .....Ottertail Ski & Sport
Fergus Falls ....Vores
Forrest Lake Bob Johnson's Sptg. Gds.
Fridley .... Traders Den
Hastings .... Gamble Store
Hibbing .... Big V Dept. Store
Hibbing .... Guy's Sptg. Goods
Hibbing ....Hyde Supply
Hutchinson .... Quade, Inc.
International Falls .Riley's Sptg. Goods
International Falls .... Totem Pole
Little Falls ....Pap's Sport Shop
Long Prairie .... Vic's Sports
Mahtowa
   Arrowhead Ammunition-Firearms
Mankato .... Mahowald's
Marshall ...... Kenney's Sport Shop
Minneapolis .... Christys
Minneapolis .... Corries
Minneapolis ....Donaldsons
Minneapolis ...George's Gunsmithing
Minneapolis . Golden Valley Sports Ctr.
Minneapolis ...... Guns Unlimited
Minneapolis ...... Larson-Olson Co.
Minneapolis ......Lloyd's Sport Shop
Minneapolis ...... Lyndale Hardware
Minneapolis . Minneapolis Outlet Store
Minneapolis ...... Northland Sports
Minneapolis . Ostroms Sporting Goods
Minneapolis ....Warner Hdwe.
Montevideo .... Gordy's Camera
Moorehead ....Sportland, Inc.

313

Moorhead .. Valley Gun & Sport Shop
Morris .... Cruze Electric
Mound .... W. S. Candell Co.
Mountain Lake .... Jungas Hardware
New Brighton .. Twin Ski Sptg. Goods
New Ulm .... Retzlaff Hdwe.
North St. Paul ..... Olson Hardware
Ortonville .... Coast to Coast Store
Owatonna ...... Bjoraker Sport Shop
Owatonna ...... Johnsons Sport Shop
Pelican Rapids .. Coast to Coast Store
Pipestone .... Strobers Marine
Ray .... Westerburg Gun Shop
Red Wing .... Carlsons Sport
Redwood FallsNelson Schjaastad Hdwe.
Rochester .... Dale's Gun Shop
Rochester .... Dayton's
Robbinsdale .... Coast to Coast Store
Rochester ..... Frerich's Hdwe.
St. Cloud .... Pap's Sport Shop
St. Cloud . Centennial Hdwe.-Spt. Shop
St. Cloud .... Scheel's Hardware
St. Cloud .... Thielman's
St. Louis Park .... Christys
St. Paul ...... Dolan Sporting Goods
St. Paul ..... Joos Bait & Sptg. Goods
St. Paul .... Larry's Live Bait
St. Paul .... Russell Bait Store
St. Paul ...... Virales Sport Ctr.
Shakopee ... Great North Trading Post
Staples .... Anderson's Hdwe.
Stillwater .... Stillwater Surplus
Taylors Falls .... Rivard's Sptg. Goods
Thief River Falls . Coast to Coast Store
Tracy .... Rignell Ace Hdwe.
Virginia .... Biss Repair Shop
Wadena .... Coast to Coast Store
Wadena .... Merickel Lumber
Wadena .... Wadena Hdwe.
Watseka .... Herter's
Wells .... Gun Exchange
West St. Paul
    Suburban Hardware & Marine
Willmar .... Bill's Gun & Tackle
Willmar ... Nelson Hdwe.–Sptg. Gds.
Winona Blackhawk Shooters/Trappers
Winona .... Graham & McGuire
Winona .... Out-Dor Store
Worthington .... Coast to Coast Store
Worthington .. B. Lundgren Sptg. Gds.
Worthington .... Rickbeil's Hdwe.

Mississippi
Aberdeen ...... City Sporting Goods
Batesville .... Mize Hardware
Biloxi .... Pat O'Neal's Buy & Sell
Brookhaven .... Davis Sporting Goods
ClarksdaleCompassi Sptg. Gds. & Hdwe.
Cleveland ..... Dunlap's Hardware
Columbus . Chick Sharp Sporting Gds.
Corinth .... Clausel Brothers
Durant .... Waller Hardware
Greenville .... Riverside Hardware Co.
Greenwood ...... Glovers Spt. Goods
Grenada ..... Collins Sporting Goods
Gulfport .... Loflin's Gun Shop
Hattiesburg .... Hattiesburg Hardware
Hattiesburg ...... Smokie's Spt. Gds.
Jackson .... Barfield Hardware Co.
Jackson .... Tatum Brown
Kosciusko .... Attala Sporting Center
Lauderdale ... La Geose's Gun Repair
Laurel .... Sid's Trading Post
Laurel .... Frank Gardner
Laurel .... Thaxton's Sporting Goods
Lucedale .... R. F. Ratliff, Jr.
Meridian ..... Hammond Gun Shop
Meridian .... Maxey's
Natchez .... Rex Sptg. Gds.
Natchez ...... The Sport Center
Pascagoula ..... City Pawn & Gun Shop
Pascagoula .... Monti Market
Pascagoula .... Sportsman Center
Port Gibson .. Claiborne Hardware Co.
Sardis .... Hearn's Trading Post
Starkville .... Smith Hdwe. Co.
Vicksburg .... The Sport Shop

Winona .... Shooks
Yazoo City ..... Planter's Hdwe. Co.

Missouri
AdvanceRichmond Hardware & Lumber
Ballwin ...... Depco Sport Supplies
Bel Ridge . Bailey's Outdoor Supply Co.
Bethany ...... B & J Sporting Goods
Brookfield
    Beach's Sporting Goods Corp.
Cabool ..... Durnell Sports Shop
Cameron .... Hawkins Store
Cape Girardeau ... Beards Sport Shop
Cape GirardeauSouthern Boat & Motor
Carthage .... Carthage Hdwe.
Chaffee .... Whitaker Hardware
Chillicothe .... Frost Hdwe.
Clayton .... Kelly Sptg. Goods
Creve Coeur .... Essen Hardware
Dexter .... Chrisman Hdwe.
Edina ..... Patterson & Rose Hdwe.
Elvins .... Edgar Sporting Goods
Fenton .... Dennis Hdwe.
Gladstone ...... George Rogers, Guns
Hermann ...... Gosen's Sptg. Goods
Independence . Maywood Sptg. Goods
Jackson .... L. C. Jenkins
Jefferson City Goodins Sporting Goods
Jonesburg .. Taynor's Sporting Goods
Joplin .... Carlson's Hdwe.
Kansas City .... Bargain City
Kansas City . R. S. Bar Gun Collection
Kansas City .. Binting Hardware Co.
Kansas City ..... C. R. Specialty Co.
Kansas City ... R. S. Elliott Arms Co.
Kansas City ... Gateway Sptg. Goods
Kansas City ... J. S. Palmer, Gunsmith
Kansas City ... Parkview-Gem Inc.
Kansas City ...... Troost Gun Shop
Kirkwood ..... Casey's Sport Stores
Kirkwood ..... Central Hardware Co.
Kirkwood ..... Kip's Sporting Goods
Lebanon
    Pearce Home & Auto Supply, Inc.
Lebanon .... Perry's Firestone
Lees Summit Seerban Yamaha & Sports
Lexington .. Pat's Army & Sptg. Goods
Liberty .... Boggess Hardware
Liberty ...... C. & C. Sporting Goods
Maryville ..B. & W. Sporting Goods Co.
Memphis .... Gundys Gun Shop
Merigold .... Hoyt C. Daves
Mexico .... Graf & Sons
Moberly .... Connorstire
New Hampton
    C.C. Wilson Discount Sporting Gds.
Neosho ...... Hickory Hill Ranch
North Kansas City .... Guns Inc.
Overland .... American Arms
Poplar Bluff .... 303 Sporting Goods
Raytown .... The Sport Spot
Richland Gunrunner Gun & Saddle Co.
Rockport .. Opp & Prime Sptg. Goods
Rolla ...... Bruce A. Betts, Gunsmith
Rolla . Twitty True Value Home Center
St. Charles ...... Faerber Sptg. Goods
St. Clair .... Custom Gunworks
St. James .... Plemmons Hardware
St. Joseph ... Hatfield Sporting Goods
St. Joseph .. Harry Heiten Sptg. Goods
St. Joseph .... Mr. B. Hardware
St. Louis ...... A.A.A. Sptg. Goods
St. Louis ..... Cassani Sptg. Goods
St. Louis ..... Central Hardware Co.
St. Louis ...... Ernie's Gun Shop
St. Louis . Floyd's Auto & Home Sply.
St. Louis ..... Goodmans for Guns
St. Louis ..... K's Sporting Goods
St. Louis . Kay's Photo & Optical Co.
St. Louis . Tom Mc Gregor Sptg. Goods
St. Louis .... National Sptg. Goods
St. Louis .... Nu-Line Sptg. Gds.
St. Louis .... Tom's Guns
Salem ...... Malone's Sptg. Goods
Sedalia .... Cash Hardware
Springfield .... Consumer's Hardware
SpringfieldJay Key & Gun Shop Service

Springfield .... Plaza Hardware
Sullivan .... Bruce's Gunshop
Summit .... J. Scott Jr.
Trenton .... Dean's Gun Shop
Trenton .... Guns
Villa Ridge
    Farmers Wayside Stores, Inc.
Warrenton .... Eagle Point Farm
Wellston
    Pearlman's Sporting Goods, Inc.
Willow Springs ..... Dave's Gun Shop

Montana
Billings .... Qs Sport Shop
Billings .... Reiters Marina
Billings .... Rerneking Gun Shop
Billings .... Scheel's Hardware Co.
Bozeman .... The Beaver Pond
Bozeman .... The Powder Horn
Butte ...... Franks Gun & Cycle Shop
Butte ...... Fran Johnson Sport Shop
Butte ...... Phil Judd Hardware, Inc.
Butte .... Lucky Bug Shop
Butte ..... The Sportsmen of Butte
Columbia Falls O'Neal Sporting Goods
Cut Bank
    Davenport & McAlpine Hardware
Dillon ...... Sneed's Sporting Goods
Fort Benton ...... Harry's Gun Shop
Glasgow ...... D. & G. Sport Center
Glasgow ...... Jim's Husky Super Stop
Glasgow .... Tag-Markle
Glendive .... Coast to Coast Store
Glendive .... The Beer Jug
Great Falls .... Alsports Supply
Great Falls .... Coast to Coast Store
Great Falls . Great Falls Sporting Goods
Great Falls .... Morris Sporting Goods
Great Falls .... Osco Drug 931
Hardin .... Clarence Beck
Havre ...... Bing & Bob's Sport Shop
Havre .... Buttreys
Helena .... Army Navy Stores
Helena .... The Four Seasons
Kalispell ...... Capps Sporting Goods
Kalispell .... Gamble Store
Kalispell .... Kalispell Mercantile Co.
Kalispell ..... Read's Sporting Goods
Lewistown .... Don's
Lewiston .... The Sport Center
Lewiston ..... Van's Sport Center
Libby .... Sports Center
Libby ...The Caribou Sporting Goods
Livingston .... R. E. Dickensheets
Miles City .... The Sports Center
Missoula All American Sporting Goods
Missoula ....Mau-Jones Sptg. Goods
Missoula .. Missoula Merchantile Co.
Missoula ..... Playmore Sporting Goods
Missoula ..... Spears Sporting Goods
Missoula .... Bob Ward & Sons
Plentywood ..... Smith Farm Supply
Polson .... Polson Sports Center
Rudyard .... Sanvik Bros. Inc.
Shelby .... Hardware Hank
Shelby .... S. & Q. Hardware
Sunburst .... Big Sky Blue Shop

Nebraska
Alliance .. Professional Gun Shops, Inc.
Auburn .... Heskell Implement
Beatrice .... Uhl's Sporting Goods
Bellevue .... Woodle Hardware
Blair .... Scheffler's Sporting Goods
Broken Bow .... Coast to Coast Store
Columbus ..... Carlson's Gunshop
Columbus ..... Persons Sport Shop
Crofton .Marlon Smith-Gambles Dealer
David City .... Vern's Gun Shop
Fairbury ....Bedlan's Sporting Goods
Falls City .... Lorenzo's Shoe
Fremont ..... Baker's Sporting Goods
Fremont ..... Bennett's Gun Shop
Fremont .... Thompson's Sport Shop
Grand Island .... Dubs Inc.
Hastings .... Sporting Goods, Inc.
Holbrook ...H. D. Minnick Hdwe. Co.
Holdrege .. Hilsabeck Sporting Goods

Kearney . Pollat's Sportsman Hangout
Lexington .... Ed's Sptg. Gds.
Lincoln .... Central Gun Inc.
Lincoln .... Golds
Lincoln .... Gun Rack
Lincoln .... Lawlors
Lincoln ... Western Gun & Supply Co.
Madison ...... W. A. Lafleur & Son
McCook ....Joe Moskal Sptg. Gds.
McCook .... Rutts Store
Norfolk .... Gambles Store
No. Platte .... Boldt's Rod & Gun
No. Platte .. Glenary Gun & Gift Shop
No. Platte ... Young's Sporting Goods
Ogallala ..... Coast to Coast Stores
Omaha .... Bahnsen's, Inc.
Omaha .... Brandeis
Omaha ..... Canfields Dept. Store
Omaha ....Guncraft
Omaha .... Gun Haven
OmahaMertz & Sons Dealers-Gunsmiths
Omaha Mondo's Sptg. Goods & Service
Omaha ...... Moneymaker Guncraft
O'Neill ...... Montgomery Hardware
Plattsmouth ..W. A. Swatek Hardware
Sidney ...Haworth Hdwe. & Sptg. Gds.
Sidney .... Reads Army Store, Inc.
Scotts Bluff
    Lordino's Sports Products
Scotts Bluff ...... Sports Center, Inc.
Scotts Bluff ... Valley Sporting Goods
Trenton ....Trenton Sptg. Goods
Valentine ...Sandhills Sports Center
Wakefield .....Fullerton Lumber Co.
Wayne .... Coast to Coast Store
Wisner .... Becker Hardware
York ....Toms & Sons Sptg. Goods

Nevada
Boulder City ...... M. & T. Gun Sales
Elko ... Wallace's Western Sportsman
Fallon .... Fallon Sptg. Goods
Gardnerville ....The Outdoorsman
Hawthorne ......A. J. Park Gunshop
Las Vegas ..... Christensen Shooters
    Supply & Spt. Gds.
Las Vegas ....The Outdoorsman
Las Vegas ...... Vegas Gun Traders
Las Vegas .....Vegas Village Dept.
Lovelock .... Davins
Reno .... Markfore
Reno ....Mount Rose Sporting Goods
Reno .... The Sportsman
Sparks ....Block Sporting Goods
Sparks ......Greenbrae Sports Center
Sparks .... Saturn Sports, Inc.
Tonopah ... Wolfe's Desert Hdwe. Co.
Winnemucca .... C. B. Brown
Winnemucca ....The Reliable Co.
Yerington ....The Westerner
Zephyr Cove ......The Outdoorsman

New Hampshire
Bartlett ..... The Bartlett Trading Post
Bethlehem ......H. & H. Outdoorland
Berlin ....King's
Bradford . Dickie's Bait & Tackle Shop
Center Ossipee
    The Gun Rack and Sport Shop
Colebrook ... Ducrets Sporting Goods
Concord . Frank & Bob's Supermarket
Concord . Haggett's Sport Shop
Concord .... Mickey Finn, Inc.
Derry .... Derry Trading Post
Derry . Great Northern Sports Center
Plymouth .... Ted Guinnan's Dugout
Dover ...... Neal Hardware, Inc.
Exeter .... Vic's Market
Grafton .... Brewster's Guns
Groveton .... Emerson & Son, Inc
    Sptg. Gds. & Hdwe.
Hampton ....K. & H. Firearms Co.
Hampton Falls .... R. P. Merrill & Son
Hanover .... Campion's Inc.
Hillsboro .... Halladay's Store
Hooket .... Riley's Sport Shop
Keene ....Gunsmith Association
Keene .... Vernon W. Maine

Keene .... Silver Dollar Guns
Keene .... Zimmerman's
Kingston ... Kingston Outboard Corp.
Laconia .... Paugus Bay Sptg. Gds. Co.
Laconia ... Shooters Service & Supply
Lancaster .... Connary's Sptg. Goods
Lebanon .... Welch's Jewelry
Manchester .... Mickey Finn, Inc.
Manchester .... Hanks Sport Ctr.
Manchester .... Lynch's
Manchester ... Bob Marks Sport Shop
Manchester .... J. J. Moreau
Manchester .... Ted's Sport Shop
Marlow .... Sand Pond Gun Shop
Milan .... Rays Gun Shop
Montvernon .... Reed B. Parks
Nashua .... Family Sports Center
Nashua .... Bob Marks Sports
Newport .... Bob's Sport Shop
Newport .... Rody's Gun Shop
No. Conway .... Robertson Store
No. Haverhill .... The Green Store
Pittsfield .... Volpe's Store
Plymouth .... Joe's Gun Shop
Portsmouth
Automotive & Electronics Supplies
Rochester .... Hooper & Carrigan
Troy .... Gus Adamson
Whitefield .... The Fournier Store
Wolfeboro ...... Lakes Region Sports

New Mexico

Albuquerque ... H. Cook Sptg. Goods
Albuquerque ..... M & W Sptg. Goods
Clovis .... Foster's Gun Shop
Clovis .... Wades Sptg. Goods
Deming .... White's Assoc. Store
Farmington .... Ross Sptg. Goods
Gallup .... Gallup Sptg. Goods
Hobbs .... Vandiver Hdwe.
Las Cruces .... Funk's
Las Cruces .... Gibson Products
Las Cruces .... Van Noys
Las Vegas .... Fur, Fin & Feather
Portales .... Nation's Gun Shop
Roswell .... House of Guns
Roswell .... Maxwell's
Roswell .... Wilsons
Santa Fe .... Tianos Sptg. Goods
Silver City .... E. Cosgrove, Inc.
Truth or Consequences
Zaid Fandey Sptg. Gds.

New Jersey

Asbury Park . Bob Kislin's Sptg. Goods
Audubon .... Polly Bros. Inc.
Belleville .... Sportsmans Haven
Bellmawr ...... The Sportsman's Lair
Belvidere ...... Jackson's Sptg. Goods
Blackwood .... Jay's Sports Center
Bound Brook .. Efinger Sporting Goods
Bridgeton ... Busnardo's Sport Center
Camden .... G & P Archery
Collingswood .... Curriden's, Inc.
Dayton .... Dayton Gun Shop
Denville .... Denville Boat
Elizabeth ...... Ross Sport Shop, Inc.
Elizabeth .... Solomon's Inc.
Flemington .... Al's Gun Repair
Flemington .. Hunterdon Sptg. Goods
Fords .... Zud Supply Co.
Frenchtown .... Art's Sport Shop
Garfield .... S. Meltzer & Sons
Glassboro .... Bob's Little Sport Shop
Hackettstown County Line Sport Shop
Harrington Pk. ..... Roehr's Gun Shop
Highland Park Paul Tellier Guns & Amm.
Highland Park
Rutgers Gun & Boat Center
Hope .... Walker's Sporting Goods
Jersey City ..... Cajo's Gun-A-Rama
Keansburg .... Yaqui Arms
Kearny .... Raven Rock Arms Co.
Kenvil .... Ammerman Sptg. Gds.
Lakewood .... S-M-A-R-T Services
Ledgewood
Ledgewood Outdoorsman, Inc.
Lindenwold .... Willis Sport Ctr.
Lumberton ..... Staley's Gun Repair
Manasquan . D. and H. Sport Shop, Inc.
Maple Shade ... Fellowship Gun Shop
Medford Lakes .... The Outdoorsman
Milltown .... Herman Treptow
Millville ...... Jim Bolton Sport Shop
Millville .... Millville Sport Center
Monclair .... George H. Mc Carthy
Montvale Standard Target Amm. Reload
Mt. Ephraim ... Woodland Gun House
Mt. Holly ...... Checker Auto Supply
Mullica Hill .... Oscar C. Jenkins
New Milford . The Arms & Amm. Shop
Newton .... Gun Repair Service
Nutley .... Frank L. Samara Jr.
Oldbridge .... Edward E. Lucas
Paramus ...... Morsan Paramus, Inc.
Paramus .... Ramsey Outdoor Stores
Paterson .... Paterson Rod & Gun
Pequannock .... Sportsmen's Den
Perth Amboy .... Fishkin Bros.
Phillipsburg ...... Falks Dept Store 7
Pine Brook ..... Wrights Gun Service
Piscataway .... Sportsman's Den
Pt. Pleasant .... The Sports Shop
Pomona .... Bernard J. Korsak
Pompton Plains Livingston Sport Center
Quinton .... Smith Gun Shop
Ramsey ..... Ramsey Outdoor Stores
Red Bank .... Kislins
Ridgefield .... Service Armament Co.
Roseland .... P.J. O'Hare
Saddle Brook .... R.J. Enoree
Saddle Brook Targeteers Sporting Goods
Salem .... G. W. Cawman & Son
Scotch Plains ...... Ray's Sport Shop
Secaucus ...... Old Mill Trap & Skeet
Toms River ...... Ficket's Gun Shop
Trenton ...... Russo Rod & Gun Shop
Union .... Morsan Union, Inc.
Union ... Rosenberg's Gun Shop, Inc.
Union City . Transfer Sta. Sptg. Goods
Vineland .... George Haughey, III
Vineland .... Petes Gun Shop
Wail .... Guy's Sport Shop
Washington ...... Hi-Way Sport Shop
Washington .. Washington Sptg. Goods
West New York .... Levy's Inc.
Woodbine Colorado Sportsmans Center
Wyckoff Tom Norman's Sport Shop, Inc.
Yardmille .... Harry's Sporting Goods

New York

Albany ...... Jim Maher's Sptg. Gds.
Albany .... Ressus Sptg. Goods
Albany .... Taylor & Vadney, Inc.
Amherst .... Al. Dekdebrunn
Amsterdam .... Guns
Amsterdam .... John E. Larrabee, Inc.
Astoria .... Sea & Land Spts. Co.
Auburn .... Byrn's Sptg. Gds.
Auburn ...... Bob Nolan's Sptg. Gds.
Auburn .... Pearson's Spts.
Babylon ...... Babylon Sport Center
Babylon .... Bill Boyce
Baldwin .... Norman Richman
Baldwinsville .... Firth's Firearms Co.
Ballston Spa ..... Wurster Sptg. Gds.
Batavia .... Batavia Marine
Batavia .... Salway's Hdwe.
Batavia .... Trading Post
Bayshore .... Al's Guns Supplies
Bay Shore .... Gem Gun Shop
Bethpage .... Gun Gallery, Inc.
Binghamton ..... Allen's Sport Shop
Binghamton .. Chenango Valley Shop
Binghamton ...... Dick's Sport Shop
Binghamton .... Parks Gun Shop
Brewerton .... Brewerton Shop
Brewster ...... John Knapp Sptg. Ctr.
Brockport .... Sportsmans Shop
Bronx .... Cromwells
Bronx .... Franks Sport Shop
Bronx ...... Westchester Trading Co.
Brooklyn .... Ambrose Outdoor Store
Brooklyn .... Fortway Camera
Brooklyn ...... Goodwear Sptg. Gds.
Brooklyn .... John & Al
Brooklyn .... Meteor Arms Inc.
Brooklyn ..... Mandall Supplies Corp.
Brooklyn .... Ed Paul's Sptg. Gds.
Brooklyn .... Triangle Stores
Buffalo .... Allsport, Inc.
Buffalo .... Angert Auto Parts
Buffalo .... Downtown Gun Shop
Buffalo .... Dick Fisher, Inc.
Buffalo .... G & R Tackle Co.
Buffalo .... Outdoor Store
Buffalo .... H. L. Peters, Inc.
Buffalo .... Ted's Sport Shop
Canadaiqua .... Cole & Rae's, Inc.
Canastota .... Blakes Lee's Gun Shop
Carthage .... Lloyd's Gun Shop
Cassville .... Wm. J. Byers III
Castile .... Castile Gun Shop
Chestertown ...... Beecher Brainard
Clarence .... Neubrand's Guns
Clayton .... Steele's Shop
Clinton Cors .... J. Dewey Service
Cohocton .... Ed. Hart's Guns
College Point ...... G & G Gunsmiths
Copiague .... Lou's Arms
Corning ..... National Sporting Gds.
Corona .... Jerome Kritz Serv.
Cortland .... Hines Service
Cuba .... Cuba Gun Shop
Deer Park ...... Galaxy Firearms Co.
Delmar .... Thomas V. Corrigan
Dunkirk ...... Lakeshore Sptg. Gds.
Dunkirk .... Walt's Sptg. Gds.
Elma .... Guy's Guns
Elmira .. Bensen, Jessup & Knapp, Inc.
Essex .... Al's Tackle Shop
Farmingdale ...... Magnum Gun Co.
Farmingdale Morsan Farmingdale, Inc.
Flushing .... B & B Sptg. Gds. Co.
Flushing .... Empire Sport Shop
Freeport .... Fishing Hole
Freeville .... Hughes Guns
Fulton .... B & T Sport Shop
Fulton .... F. O. Stanton
Garnerville .... Zugibie Bros.
Geneva .... Harmon's Sport Shop
Glen Cove .... Lemp's Gun Shop
Glens Falls .... Goldstock's Sptg. Gds.
Gouverneur .... H. H. Loomis
Gowanda .... Western Store
Grand Island .... I. Rubin
Greenvale ..... Greenvale Sport Shop
Hamburg .... Art Pfeiffer
Hammondsport .... Roy Jacobs
Harrison .... Harrison Sport Shop
Hempstead .... Hempstead Store
Hempstead .... Robin Hood Store
Henrietta .... Genesee Valley Shop
Herkimer .... C & D Sport Shop
Herkimer .... Maddy's Guns
Hicksville .... Mid Island Sports
Hillsdale .... Hillsdale Sport Shop
Holcomb .... Creekside Gun Shop
Hornell .... Scotts Gun Shop
Hornell .... Southern Tier Hobby
Horseheads . Ray Hotchkiss Sptg. Gds.
Horseheads ..... Wilkens Gulf Service
Hudson .... Steiner's Spts. Cntr.
Hudson Falls ..... Juckett Sptg. Gds.
Hudson Falls ..... Moran's Sptg. Gds.
Huntington ..... Guns & Ammo Shop
Ithaca .... Gees Sport Shop
Ithaca .... Pearson's Sports
Ithaca .... Stone's Guns
Jamestown .... John W. Bollman
Jamestown ...... Collins Sport Shop
Jamestown ..... Lundquist Hdwe. Co.
Johnson City .... Southside Hdwe.
Johnstown .... Klena Bros.
Johnstown .... Lizio's Gun Shop
Kenmore ...... Fred Hoffman Sports
Kenmore .... Loaders Lodge
Kingston .... Potter Bros.
Kingston .... Spada's Sport Shop
Kingston .... Jack L. Williamson
Kirkland .... Kirkland Armory
La Grangeville .... Kanuk Enterprises
Larchmont .... Clark & Finney
Lawtons .... Keoppen Gun Shop
Levittown .... Colonial Firearms, Inc.
Liberty .... Berner's Sptg. Gds.
Lisbon .... H. Bill Gray
Liverpool .... Wayne D. Burgess
Livingston Manor .. Willowemoc Shop
Lockport .... Cabin Range
Lockport .... John F. Collins
Lockport .. Dick Cummings Sptg. Gds.
Lockport .... Regan's Sptg. Gds.
Macedon .... Dean R. Newcomb
Mahopac .... Tom Kat, Inc.
Malone .... East End Hardware
Massena .... W. L. Smith, Inc.
Medford .... Phil Primrose
Medina .... Medina Trading Post
Melville .... Sportorama
Merrick .... The Outdoorsman
Middleton .... Gun Center
Middletown .... Bob Lounsbury
Middletown .... Royal Coachman, Inc.
Middleville ..... W. Canada Spt. Shop
Mineola .... Mineola Guns, Inc.
Monroe .... Smith & Strebel Co.
Mt. Kisco ...... C. S. Daum Sptg. Gds.
Mt. Vernon ...... Fisherman's Center
Nanuet .... Lombard's
Newark .... Gerry's Trading Post
Newburgh ...... Conover's Sptg. Gds.
Newburg .... M. C. Kinney Corp.
Newburgh .... Shapiro Sptg. Gds.
New Hartford .. Mohawk Trading Post
New Hyde Park ... Jericho Canvas Co.
New Rochelle .. Allen Sport Shop, Inc.
New Rochelle .... Parker Dist.
New York ..... Abercrombie & Fitch
New York ... Continental Arms Corp.
New York .... Hermans
New York .... Harry Moss & Son
New York .... Wm. Mills & Son, Inc.
New York .... Paragon Sptg. Gds.
New York .... Rex Firearms Inc.
Newport .... Wm. H. Wheatley
New York .... Zirmo Co.
Niagara Falls ..... Stanley Hohenstein
Niagara Falls . John Di Salvo Sptg. Gds.
Norfolk .... Don's Guns
North Dartmouth. Ray Pease Sptg. Gds.
Northport .. Bowman's Sptg. Gds. Co.
North Syracuse ..... Sports Mart Inc.
North Tonawanda . Otto Walther & Son
Northville ..... Rulison's Sport Shop
Odessa .... Odessa Hrdwe.
Ogdensburg .... Sports Mart
Olean .... Adams Sptg. Gds.
Olean .... Bluementhals
Olean .... Hopkins Sptg. Gds.
Oneonta .... Bill's Sport Shop
Oneonta .... Floyd's Gun Shop
Oneonta .... Stevens Hrdwe. Inc.
Oswego .... Ontario Sptg. Gds.
Oswego .... Oswego Guns
Palmyra .... Jim's Sports Un.
Parish .... Breckheimers
Parishville .... Harry Caringi Shop
Patchoque ..... Royal Fishing Tackle
Pearl River .... Art Hoffmeyer
Penn Yan .... Ron's Gun Shop
Phelps .... De Vito's Sptg. Gds.
Phelps .... Tate's Sptg. Gds.
Pine Bush .... Town & Country Corp.
Plattekill .... Carperter's Works
Plattsburgh .... Larkin Camera
Plattsburgh .... Ray's Gun Shop
Port Jervis .... Deer Park Gun Shop
Port Jervis .... Tri State Sply.
Poughkeepsie ... Arlington Sptg. Gds.
Poughkeepsie ... Big Indian Gun Shop
Poughkeepsie .. M. Douglas Campbell
Poughkeepsie .... John N. Lucas
Poughkeepsie ..... Wolf's Sport Shop
Prospect .. Prospect Reloaders Supply
Ravena .... Sportsmen's Trading Post
Remsen .... Robert Ainley
Rensselaer ...... Jerry's Gun Exchange
Riverhead .... Edward's Disc. Ctr.
Riverhead ..... Riverhead Sports, Inc.
Rochester .... ABC Sport Shop

Rochester . Commercial Sptg. Gds. Co.
Rochester .... Robt. W. Eve Guns
Rochester .... Dick Fischer, Inc.
Rochester .... Gun Shop
Rochester .... S. J. Hunting Lodge
Rochester .... Naum Bros, Inc.
Rochester ...... Slim's Sport Supply
Rome .... Mike's Sport Shop
Rome .... Wells Boat Shop
Rome ...... Dick Wilson's Sptg. Gds.
Saratoga Springs .. Savard's Gun Shop
Saratoga Springs .... R. W. Walton
Schaghticoke .... Beecroft's Gun Shop
Schenectady .. Goldstock's Sptg. Gds.
Schenectady .... Guns
Seneca Falls .... Hadley's Hrdwe.
Seneca Falls ..... Moulton's Sptg. Gds.
Sherrill .... Sykes Sales
Sidney .... Marcy's Sport Shop
Silver Creek ... Frank Chiappone Store
Silver Creek .... Stoll's Gun Shop
Smithtown .... Smithtown Spts. Inc.
Sodus .... Cooks
Sparrow Bush .... Phil Bob Sptg. Gds.
Spencerport ... Big Ridge Sport Shop
Spring Valley ...... Palmach Shooters
Staten Island .... Harry Kaplan
Staten Island ...... Nick's Gun Repair
Syracuse .... Gem Spt. Supply Co.
Syracuse .... W. T. Grant Co.
Syracuse ...... Mulligan's Sport Shop
Syracuse .... Reliable Loan Co.
Syracuse .... Vad's Sport Shop
Ticonderoga ...... David Avery Guns
Tonawanda ...... Dick Fischer, Inc.
Tonawanda ...... Seeger's Gun Shop
Tonawanda .... Sportsman's Paradise
Tonawanda .... E. L. Sweet & Son
Troy .... Andy's Sptg. Gds. Inc.
Troy .... Tigars Sptg. Gds.
Utica .... Highland Gun Shop
Wantagh .... Voehringers
Wantagh .... Woodside Studios
Warsaw .... W. W. Griffith Oil Co.
Waterloo .... Jarvis Auto Supply
Watertown ...... W. W. Conde Hdwe.
Watertown ...... Seaway Sport Shop
Watervliet .... Gun Shop
Waverly .... Jim's Sptg. Gds.
Wawarsing .... Geary's Sport Shop
Webster .... J. R. Rieger
Wellsville .... Carter Hardware
W. Hurley ...... Numrich Arms Corp.
Westport .... Marshall F. Fish
Westport .... 'Trader' Robinson
West Sand Lake ... Miller's Gun Works
West Seneca .... Al. Dekdebrunn
White Plains .... Clark & Finney
White Plains .... Maletown, Inc.
White Plains .... Shooter's Shop
Wolcott .... Pettit's Gun Shop
Yonkers .... Ed. Agramonte, Inc.
Yonkers .... Vic De Mayos Inc.

North Carolina

Albemarle .... Lowder Hdwe. Co.
Albemarle ..... Stanley Hardware Co.
Albemarle ..... Bill Tobias Gun Shop
Asheville .... Don's Gun Shop
Asheville .... Doug's Gun Shop
Asheville .... Finkelsteins Inc.
Asheville .... Hunting & Fishing Splys.
Beech Creek .... Patrick's
Bostic .... F. E. Biggerstaff
Charlotte .... Builders Hdwe. Co.
Charlotte ...... Carolina Police Supply
Charlotte .... Collias-Lawing & Co.
Charlotte .... Collins Dept. Store
Charlotte .... Faul & Crymes, Inc.
Charlotte .... The Sportsman Inc.
China Grove .... Guns
Concord ..... Ritchie Hdwe. Co. Inc.
Conover .... Charlies Bait Shop
Davidson .... Dancy Arms
Durham .... Durham Sptg. Gds.
Elizabeth City ... Froggy's Sport Shop
Ellerbe .... Horton's
Fayetteville . Cumberland Pawn & Loan
Fayetteville ..... A. K. Mc Callum Co.
Fayetteville ..... Pine State Gun Shop
Franklin ...... Macon County Hdwe.
Gaston .... Carsons Spt. Gds.
Gastonia .... Akers Center Hdwe.
Gastonia .... Franklin Hdwe.
Gastonia .... Southern Supply Co.
Goldsboro McBride & Herring Sptg. Gds.
Goldsboro ...... Music & Sports, Inc.
Greensboro
Dockery Lumber & Hardware
Greensboro .... Phipps Hardware
Greensboro .. Southside Hardware Co.
Greenville .... H. L. Hodges
Hazelwood .... Cline Bradley Co.
Hendersonville
Sherman's Sporting Goods
Hickory ...... Clark Tire & Auto Sply.
Hickory ...... Hickory Sptg. Gds. Co.
Hickory ... The Sportsman of Hickory
Hickory .... Walter Motors, Inc.
High Point .... Beeson Hdwe. Co.
Jacksonville ... Boom Town Furn. Co.
Jacksonville . Furniture Fair Sptg. Gds.
Kannapolis .... Ritchie Hdwe. Co.
Kings Mountain ..... Phifer Hdwe. Co.
Lenoir .... Winkler Gun Shop
Long Beach ...... Save-U-Stores, Inc.
Morgantown ..... The Hobby Center
New London .... Pickler Arms Co.
Newport .... Eubanks & Co.
North Wilksboro ..... Swaffords, Inc.
Raleigh .... Hackneys, Inc.
Raleigh .... Hill's Inc.
Raleigh .... Thornes, Inc.
Raleigh .... Village Pharmacy
Roanoke Rapids
Harris Joyner Sptg. Gds.
Robbins .... Central Hardware
Rocky Mount ...... Jim's Sport Shop
Rocky Mount . Joyners Athletic House
Salisbury ...... Goodman's Gun Shop
Salisbury .... Salisbury Sptg. Gds.
Sanford .... Carolina Sptg. Gds.
Sanford .... Doyce Gregson
Sanford .... Mann's Hardware
Spring Lake ...... Woody's Gun Shop
Statesville .... Adams Sptg. Goods
Valdese .... Major Electric Co.
Wadesboro .... Cowick Porter Hdwe.
Walnut Cove .... Reynolds Gun Shop
Williamston . Griffin's Shooting Center
Wilmington .. Miller Trading Company
Wilson .... Stephens Hdwe.
Winston-Salem ... Bocock-Stroud Co.
Winston-Salem ..... Ken's Gun Shop
Winston-Salem .. Pleasants Hdwe. Co.
Winston-Salem .. Wilson-Pleasants Co.
Zebulon .... J. W. Perry Jr. Store

North Dakota

Bismarck .... Roy's Gun Shop
Bismarck ...... Sioux Sporting Goods
Columbus .... Miller Hardware
Cooperstown ... Tims Oil & Supply Co.
Devils Lake .... Gerrells
Edgeley ...... Ron's Sales and Service
Fargo .... Als Sport Shop
Fargo .... A. Beckers Sporting Goods
Fargo .... Scheels Our Own Hardware
Garrison ...... Robinson Sport Shop
Grand Forks ..... Tremys Sport Shop
Jamestown ... Gun & Reel Sport Shop
Leeds .... Miller Drug
Minot .... Dakota Firearms
Minot .... Gun Schmidt
Minot .... Harvey Enterprizes
Minot .... Northland Sptg. Gds.
Minot .... Northwest Sporting Goods
Minot .... Saunders
Riverdale ... Riverdale Sporting Goods
Rugby .... Bucks Sport Shop
Williston .... Coast to Coast
Williston .... Pangers Sporting Goods

Ohio

Akron .... Boyles Hunting
Albany .... Coe's
Alliance ...... Alliance Gun Exchange
Alliance ...... Dicken & Marshall, Inc.
Ashland .... D. E. Satterfield
Ashtabula .... William Limback
Athens . Swearigen Sporting Goods Inc
Aurora .... Joseph Prenosil
Austintown .. Sportsmans Trading Post
Avon ...... Avon Hardware, Gunshop
Barbberton .... A. E. Bechter
Baltic .... Levi Yoder
Bedford ...... Bedford Gun & Tackle
Bellefontaine .... Paul Wammes
Bellevue ... Fennwood Shooting Park
Bucyrus .... Parsel's Gun Shop
Butler .... Main Hardware
Cambridge .... Vance Sporting Goods
Canal Fulton
Hillview Sportsman Supply
Canton ..... Buckeyee Sports Supply
Canton .... Canton Hardware Co.
Canton .... Field And Stream
Canton ...... John's Sporting Goods
Canton .... Real Live Bait
Celina .... Heckler Hardware Co.
Celina .... Whitacre Gun Shop
Chesterland .... Hart Arms Co.
Chillicothe .... John S. Cole Shooters
.... Supplies
Chillicothe .. Hornstein Hardware Co.
Cincinnati Brendamour Sporting Goods
Cincinnati
Cincinnati Gun Specialists, Inc.
Cincinnati .... Pioneer Guns
Cincinnati .. Queen City Fire Arms Co.
Cincinnati .... Shillito's
Circleville .... Pettits Sport Shop
Cleveland .... A. A. Rod & Gun Shop
Cleveland .... Abele Davis Corp.
Cleveland . Clark Gun & Supply Goods
Cleveland Cleveland Custom Gun Shop
Cleveland .... Higbee Company
Cleveland .... Nash Shooting Supplies
Cleveland .... Newman Stern Co.
Columbus . Columbus Sporting Goods
Columbus .... Daves Gun Store
Columbus .... Federated Dept. Stores
Columbus . Graceland Sporting Goods
Columbus .... Kennedy & Son
Columbus .... Linden Hardware
Columbus .. Outdoors Sporting Goods
Columbus .... Zanes Gun Rack
Coshocton . Coshocton Sporting Goods
Coshocton .... Roscoe Hardware
Crestline ..... Fisher's Sporting Goods
Crestline .... Shot & Shell
Dayton .... Cole Sporting Goods
Dayton ... Dayton Gun Headquarters
Dayton .... Jim Flynn Inc.
Dayton ...... M & M Sporting Goods
East Cleveland .... Heckman Arms Co.
Eastlake .... Imperial Firearms
Elyria .... Mens Shop
Fairborn .... George's Arsenal
Fairview Park .... The Dodd Co.
Findlay .... Douglas Gun Shop
Findlay ...... Jacqua Sporting Goods
Findlay .... Rose Sporting Goods
Fostoria ..... Veres Sportsman Shop
Fremont .... Bruce Custom Guns
Fremont .... Fremont Gun Store
Fremont ..... Wassermans Gun Store
Freeport . Freeport Sportsman Supply
Gallipolis ... The McKnight Davies Co.
Garrettsville .... Fays Gun Shop
Glouster .... The Economy Store
Greenfield .... Greenfield
Grove City .... Pat's Gun Repair
Hamilton . C. A. Clark's Sporting Goods
Hamilton .... Roemer Hardware
Hanoverton .... Grant Dicks Gun Shop
Heath .... Rex's Gun Shop
Huron .... Lander Company
Ironton .... Bob Linn Sporting Goods
Kenton .... Kenton Surplus Store
Kinsman .... Virgils Gun Shop
Kinsman .... Yorktown Gun Shop
Lancaster City News & Sporting Goods
Lebanon ... Bashfords Sporting Goods
Lima .... Crows Gun Shop
London .... Thomas Hardware
Louisville .... J. B. Metzger Hardware
Lowell .... John Huges Service Station
Madison ..... Erbackers Sport Center
Mansfield .... Diamond Hardware Co.
Mansfield ...... Goetz Hardware Co.
Marion .... Hintons Sport Shop
Marietta ...... Hoffs Sporting Goods
Marietta .... John Yost
Marion .... Idle Hour Sports
Massillon .... Hal's Sport Shop
Maumee .... Bobs Marathon
Maumee ..... Fleegers Pro. Hardware
Medina ... Albrights Sportsmans Shop
Middletown .... Allsports Inc.
Middletown .... Roberson
Middletown
Streifthaus Sporting Goods
Milford . Charlie Grossman's Gun Shop
Mt. Blanchard
Foster Hardware & Sport Shop
Newark ..... Farquhar & Steinbaugh
Newcomerstown .... Bill Heifner
New Phildelphia
Sam Bond Sportsmans Supply
North Bend .... K. & W. Gun Shop
North Lawrence . Schrader's Gun Shop
Norwalk .... P. H. Fulstow Co.
Norwood ...... Geo. C. Burrier, Guns
Norwood .... Pioneer Guns
Orrville .... Martheys Sporting Goods
Orwell .... Huntley Jewelry
Oxford .... Ronnies Bait
Painesville ... Atwells Sporting Goods
Parma .... The Gun Shop
Peebles .... Lucas Hardware
Peninsula ..... Buckeye Sports Center
Perrysburg ... Lake Erie Marine Corps.
Piqua .... Davis Gun Shop
Ravenna .... Minards Sporting Goods
Rittman .... Chief Coins
Salem .... Williams Guns and Supplies
Sandusky .... Bogert Gun Store
Sandusky . Herb's Sportsmans Supply
Scio .... Scio Pottery Museum
Seville .... Jone's Store
Sharon Center .... Stauffers Inc.
Shelby .... Shelby Sporting Goods
Springfield .... George Meek Co.
Springfield .... Reco Sporting Goods
Tallmadge ... Yorktown Custom Arms
Thornville ..... Gary Smith-Firearms
Tiffin .... Baik Bros. Co.
Toledo .... Gedert Gun Shop
Toledo .... Gross Photo Mart Inc.
Toledo .... U. Janney
Toledo .... Lickendorfs
Toledo .... Tackle Box-Inc.
Toledo .... Trilby Sport Center
Toledo .... Van Burens Gun Shop
Trenton .... Young's Gun Shop
Troy .... Jerry Dye, Gunsmith
Troy .... Troy Sports Center
U. Heights ..... Dratler Custom Guns
Upper Sandusky ... Lees Trading Post
Upper Sandusky
V. A. Mennigen Sporting Goods
Urichsville .... Bills Gun Room
Vandalia
Miami Valley Shooting Grounds
Van Wert .... The Gunsett Co.
Van Wert ...... Tex Gun & Coin Shop
Wadsworth .... Russ Bordner Inc.
Waldo ... McClarens Sportsman Store
Warren .... Elm Road Sport Shop
Warren .... Sport Land
Waverly .... Hawley's Gun Shop
Westerville .... Accent Guns
Woodsfield .... Modern Hardware
Woodsfield . Schwalls Sporting Goods
Wooster .... Forest Atland, Gunsmith
Wooster ...... Pierces Sporting Goods
Xenia .... Dan Prindle
Youngstown ...... Austintown Tool
Zanesville .... Bonifield Hardware Co.
Zanesville ...... Glossman Hardware
Zanesville .... Niebel Sporting Goods

Oklahoma

Alva .... Gibson Products
Ardmore .... Lukes
Bartlesville . Lehman's Sporting Goods
Bartlesville .... The Sport Shop
Broken Arrow .... Hoods Sales
Chandler ...... Lawrence Hardware
Claremore .... .Wilson Hardware
Clinton ... Shamburg Sporting Goods
Drumright .... Smitty's Gun Shop
Duncan .... .Murf's
Duncan ..... Woolworth Dept. Store
Enid .... Larry Black's
Enid .... Zaloudek's
Frontier City .... .Service Arms
Guthrie .. Bill Nelson Sporting Goods
Guthrie ..... Martin's Sporting Goods
Guymon .... Kingsland
Hartshorne .... Hartshorne Hardware
Idabel .... Idabel Hardware
Mangum .... Cox Auto Supply
McAlester ...... Diamond Hardware
Miami .... Beacon Hardware
Miami ...... Forty Five Ranch Ent.
Miami ...... Williams Hardware
Midwest City ...... Service Arms Co.
Muskogee .... Oak Gun Shop
Muskogee .. V. F. Smith Sport Shop
Norman ... Norman Import/Export
Norman .... Sports Center
Nowata .... Titsworth Motor Co.
Oklahoma City
    Andy Anderson Sporting Goods
Oklahoma City .... Ed. L. Kloss
Oklahoma City ..... Mashburn Amrs
Oklahoma City .S. W. Shooters Supply
Oklahoma City .... Underwater Sports
Ponca City .... Chittum Gun Shop
Sands Springs .... Service Arms
Sapulpa ..... Sapulpa Sporting Goods
Shawnee .... Baptist Hardware
Stillwater .... Murphy's
Tulsa .... Davis Stores
Tulsa .... Dong's Sporting Goods
Tulsa .... Froug's Dept. Store
Tulsa .... The Sportsman

Oregon

Astoria ..... Kaufman's Sport Center
Astoria .... McGregor Supply
Bend .... Bob's Sporting Goods
Bend .... Ken Cale Hardware
Chiloquin ...... Kircher Hardware
Cloverdale .... Bill's Guns
Coos Bay .... Fithian's Gun Shop
Coos Bay .... Stewart Sport Shop
Coquille ...... Taylor Sport Shop
Corvallis ...... Nixon Sports Center
Corvallis .... Les & Bob's
Elgin .... Houser Hardware
Enterprise ...... Weaver Hardware
Eugene .... Eugene Gun Shop
Eugene .... Maxon's Gun
Florence .... The Sportsman
Gold Beach ..... Morrie's Outdoor
Grant's Pass
    Grants Pass Sporting Goods
Grants Pass .... Milo's Sporting Goods
Gresham ..... Bonnell's Sport Center
Hood River ...... Franz Hardware
John Day .... John Day Hardware
Klamath Falls
    Joe Green Sporting Goods
Klamath Falls ...... Hal's Sport Shop
Klamath Falls ...... Sierra Gun Shop
Klamath Falls ...... The Gun Store
Klamath Falls .... Totem Sptg. Goods
LaGrande .. W. H. Bohenkamp Hdwe.
LaGrande .... Choates
LaGrande ...LaGrande Outdoor Sply.
LaGrande ...... Zimmerman Hdwe.
Madras ...... Oscar's Sptg. Goods
Medford ...... Lamport Sptg. Goods
Myrtle Pt. ...... Suncrest Gunstock
Newport .... B and B Sports Center

Oregon City .... Coleman Electric
Oregon City ..Oregon Cty.Sptg. Goods
Pendleton ...... Coast to Coast Store
Pendleton ......Darrel's Gun Shop
Portland ....Allison & Carey
Portland .... Bazar
Portland .... Bwana Junction
Portland ....Meier & Frank
Portland .... Nick's Guns
Portland ...... Roberts Gunstocks
Portland .... St. John's Sptg. Goods
Portland .... Serafin's
Portland ....The Gun Room
Portland .... The Gun Trader
Prineville ....Bill's Sport Shop
Prineville .... Ernie's Sport Shop
Roseburg .... Umpqua Gun Store
Salem ..... Anderson's Sptg. Goods
Salem ...... Cascade Merc. Co.
Springfield .... Fireside Sports
The Dalles .... Mer's
Tillamook .... Hawkins & James
Toledo .... B & B Sport Ctr.
Union .... Reuter Hardware
Wallowa ....Wallowa Hdwe.

Pennsylvania

Aliquippa ....Sol's Stores
Allentown ... Nestors Sporting Goods
Allentown ...... Phillips Dept. Store
Altoona ....Burkett Gun Shop
Altoona .... Helsel Hardware
Altoona .... Pioneer Gun Sales
AmbridgeAmbridge Army & Navy Store
Ambridge ....Sol's Stores
Andalusia .... Robert S. Kraus
Ardmore .... Eylers Sport Shop
Beaver Falls
    Valley Sportsmans Supply Co.
Bedford ..... Beegle's Sporting Goods
Belle Vernon ....The Gun Rack
Bellwood .... Cornmesser Hardware
Benleyville .. Bentleyville Sport Shop
Berwick .... Cons. Supply Store
Bethlehem .... Marcus Sporting Goods
Bethlehem ..F. E. Weinland Hardware
Bloomsburg .... Lamatia Sport Goods
Blue Ball ..... Shirks Saddle Shop
Braddock .... Wally's Gun Shop
Bradford .... Beezer Appliance
Bradford .... Lundins Sporting Goods
Bridgeville ......Stone's Sport Center
Bristol .... Aquarium Hobby Shop
Brookville ....Chestnut Gun Shop
Brookville .... Demans
Broomall ..... Gordon's Sporting Goods
Butler ... Kirkpatrick Sporting Goods
Butler ... I. G. Klugh Gun Shop
Butler .... Kopies Gun Shop
Carbondale
    Mermelsteins Sporting Goods
Carlisle ...... J. B. Bixler & Son
Carlisle Sheaffer Bros. Sporting Goods
Carnegie .... R & D Gun Shop
Catawissa ... Susquehanna House
Chambersburg
    Gale Diehl Sporting Goods
Clarendon .... Robert P. Ferry
Clarion .... Variety Dist. Co.
Clearfield .... Grice Gun Shop
Clearfield .... Paul T. Yoder
Clifton Heights .. Antique Firearms &
                    Military Equipment
Clifton Heights .... Brooks
Clymer ....H & H Gun Shop
Coatesville
    Commonwealth Firearms & Supply
Coatesville .... East End Hardware
Columbia Uncle Nev's Sporting Goods
Connellsville .. Edenbo Sporting Goods
Conshohocken ...... Walt's Sport Shop
Coraopolis ..... West Hills Sport Shop
Corning Height ...... Polly Bros, Inc.
Crum Lynne .... Joseph D. Dvornicich
Curryville ...... Burgets Hardware Co.
Dauphin .... Wilson's Gun Store
Doylestown
    Meininger's Sporting Goods

Easton ....Falk's Dept. Store
Easton . Grube & Betts Sporting Goods
Edensburg .... Shopp Sporting Goods
Elizabethtown ....Tropical Treat
Elverson ....Warwick Gun Shop
Emporium .... Grimones
Ephrata ..... Ernie's Sporting Goods
Erie .... Decoys Unlimited
Erie .... Erie Sport Store
Erie .... Gorenflos
Erie .... Lighthouse Arms
Erie .... Kuharsky Bros., Inc.
Erie .... The Sportman, Inc.
Fairless Hills
    Lower Bucks Safety Brake, Inc.
Farrell ....Sport Center
Feasterville
    E. J. Malone Sporting Goods
Ft. Loudon .... Walker's Trading Post
Franklin .... Rearm Sport Center
Girrard ....Jim's Gun Shop
Glenshaw .. Kleber's Sporting Goods
Hanover ... W. E. Sell Sporting Goods
Harrisburg
    Percy Hoffman Sporting Goods
Hatboro ... Chick's Archery Supplies
Hawley .... J.W. Nichols
Herman .... Eichenlaub Sport Shop
Huntingdon .... C. H. Miller Hardware
Indiana .Markles Sporting Goods Store
Ingram ... Sam F. Simpson & Sons
Jacobus .... Smith Village
Jacobus .... Straley's
Jeannette ... Mac's Auto & Sport Store
Jenkintown ...... Paul Jaeger, Inc.
Jersey Shore .National Sporting Goods
Johnstown ....W. T. Grant Co.
JohnstownGresh's Guns & Ammunition
Johnstown ....Overdorff Bros.
Johnstown . The Swank Hardware Co.
King Of Prussia .... Brooks
Kittanning ... McConnell & Watterson
Kutztown ...... Beck Sport Shop
Lancaster ...... Hoak & Yarnall, Inc.
Lancaster .... Reilly Bros. & Raub
Lancaster .... Shenk Bros.
Lancaster ...... The Sportsman's Den
Lansdale .... Weingartner Sport Shop
Latrobe ....Army & Navy Store
Lebanon ..... Parson's Sporting Goods
Leechburg ..... Service Book Store
Lehighton ....Drumbore Gun Shop
Levittown ...... Gateway Gun Shop
Lewistown .... Aurand's For Sports
Lititz ...... The Lititz Sports Center
Lititz .... Wholesale Shooters Supplies
Littlestown
    E. B. Geiman Sporting Goods
Lockhaven .... E. H. Draucker & Son
Logantown ....Dean's Place
Loganville ..... Klinedinst & Hopper
Lyndora ...... Kopies Gun Shop
Mahanoy City
    Varanavage's Shooting Supplies
McClellantown .... 21 Super Market
McKeesport ..... Leonatti Bros., Inc.
McKeesport .. Shader's Sporting Goods
Meadville ... Meadville Sporting Goods
Meadville ... Robbie's Sportcenter
Meadville Selby Almon Sporting Goods
Meadville ....Wolffs
Mechanicsburg . Ritter's Hardware Co.
Milford .... Sportsman's Rendezvous
Millvale .... Flaigs
Milton ....Milton Sports Center
Monroeville ... Jacobs Sporting Goods
Morgantown .. Muehlenberg, Hardware
Mt.Joy ... Ray Knorr Sporting Goods
Mountaintop .... Davis Gun Shop
Mount Union
    D. C. Goodman & Sons, Inc.
Nanticoke .... Crawford's
Nanticoke .... D & R Discount House
Natrona Heights ..... Joseph Horne Co.
Nazareth .... Nazareth Sporting Goods
New Berrytown
    L. Guiswhite Sporting Goods
New Bethlehem .Evans Sporting Goods

New Bethlehem .. Forrester's Antiques
New Bethlehem ... Sayer's Truck Stop
New Britain .... Arts Surplus
New Castle .....Sporting Goods Co.
New Freedom
    Young & McNew Sporting Goods
New Holland .. The Sportsman's Shop
New Kensington
    Jacobs Sporting Goods Co.
New Oxford ....Joe's Gun Shop
New Providence
    Scott's Trap & Skeet Supplies
Norristown ....Nesters Toys
NorthhamptonWas Den Sporting Goods
North East .... Hogue Gun Store
Northumberland .. Andrews Hardware
Northumberland .... Gun Rack, Inc.
Oil City .... Oil City Army Store
Oil City .... Sportsmens Den
Osceola Richardson's Sportsmans Store
Philadelphia .... Brooks
Philadelphia ...... Colosimo's Guns
Philadelphia
    James E. Duffy, Jr. Gunsmith
Philadelphia
    Locks Philadelphia Gun Exchange
Philadelphia ... M&H Sporting Goods
Pitcairn .... Esman's
Pittsburgh .... Bolton Sporting Goods
Pittsburgh .. DeBay Sports Center
Pittsburgh .... E.J.H. Gunshop
Pittsburgh ...... Martin's Gun Shop
Pittsburgh ...Myers Sporting Goods
Pittsburgh .. Firearms Unlimited, Inc.
Pittsburgh .... Honus Wagner Co.
Pittsburgh .... Joseph Horne Co.
Pittsburgh .... Huch Sport Shop
Pittsburgh .... Ideal Sport Shop
Pittsburgh .. Jerry's Shooters Service
Pittsburgh .... Kaufman's
Pittsburgh .. South Hills Sports Center
Pittsburgh ....Tackle Service
Pittsburgh .... The Swap Shop
Plymouth ....F. W. Woolworth
Polk .... Roy's Gifts & Firearms
Pottstown .... A. P. Giangiacomo
Pottsville .... George Derbes
Prospect Park Prospect Sporting Goods
Punxsutawney .. Williams Sport Center
Reading .. Bill's Bait & Sporting Goods
Reading ....Boscous East
Reading .... Kagens, Inc.
Rochester .... Smith Bros. Gun Store
Sandy Lake .... Lakeview Sport Shop
St.Mary's .... Dauers Sport Shop
St.Mary's .... Smith Sport Store
Scranton .... Evers Gun Shop
Sewickley .... Dempsey's Gun Shop
Shamokin ...... Jones Hardware Co.
Sharon ....Beckdol's Sporting Goods
Sharon .... Gene's Gun Repair Shop
Sharon .... The Sportsman's Shop
Sharpsburg .... L. B. Arms
Shippenville ....Bill's Sport Shop
Shippenville
    Chamberlain Sporting Goods
Slippery Rock ....Big Buck Gun Shop
Somerset ...... Somerset Sport Shop
Springfield .... Earl Freas
Stahlstown ....Dicks Barber
State College ... Waltz Sporting Goods
Tamaqua ..... P. & B. Sporting Goods
Telford .. Indian Valley Sports Center
Telford .... Shooters Den
Tionesta . Forest County Sport Center
Titusville ...... Bryan Hardware, Inc.
Titusville .... S. C. Hopkins
Tremont .... Tremont Hardware, Co.
Tyrone .... Burley Bros.
Upper Darby .... Brooks
Upper Darby ...... Joffe's Gun Shop
Upper Darby .... Llanerch Gun Shop
Warren .... Farr's Sporting Goods
Warren ...... Finley Sporting Goods
Warren .... Goosheven Gun Shop
Washington .... Ace Auto
Washington .... Coen Oil Co.
Washington .... National Retail Stores

Washington . . . Reeves Sporting Goods
Waynesburg . . . . Mac's Hardware
Waynesburg . Joe Riggs Sporting Goods
West Chester . . . Briggs Sporting Goods
West Chester . . . . The Gun Shop
West Reading . . Wiests Sporting Goods
Whitehall . . . . Joseph Horne Co.
Wilkinsburg . Braverman Arms Co. Inc.
Williamsport
     E. L. Blair & Co Sporting Goods
Williamsport . . Handy Home & Sports
Williamsport
       Harders Sporting Goods Co.
Williamsport . . . . Lenny's Sports
Willow Street . . . . Clair Frank
Willow Street . . . Don Greenawalt Guns
          & Shooting Supplies
Windber . . . . Good Shooting Supplies
Wyncote . . . . Polly Bros.
Wyoming . . . . Carey's Sporting Goods
York . . . . Lincoln Hiway Garage
York
     C. Patterson & Son Sporting Goods
York . . . Scott Stevens Sporting Goods
York . . . Stonybrook Sporting Goods
York . . . . . Wolfgang's Sporting Goods

Rhode Island
Coventry Ctr., ... Wm. G. Gessner, Sr.
Cranston . . . Champ's Custom Loading
Cranston . . . . . . Elmwood Sport Shop
Cranston . . . . Quick Sports Haven
East Greenwich . . . . Sportsmen's Shop
East Providence . . . G & M Sport Center
Hope . . . . Lowell Gun Shop
Newport . . . . Don's Sports
Newport . . . . . Ryan's Sporting Goods
North Kingston . Quonset Sports Haven
Portsmouth . . . . R. M. Keshura
Providence . . . Jimmy's Custom Guns
Providence . . . . . . Malt's Gun Service
Smithfield . . . . Hunting Lodge
Warwick . . . . Commander Bob's

South Carolina
Aiken . . . . Hobby House Marine
Anderson . . . Anderson Hardware Co.
Anderson . . . . Grady's Sport
Barnwell . . . . 300 Gun Shop
Charleston . . . . Norvell's
Columbia . . Columbia Gun Exchange
Columbia . . . . S. B. McMasters
Dillon . . . . Winesett's
Easley . . . . Pepper Hardware
Florence . . . . Barringer Hardware
Greenville . . . . Belk Simpson
Greenville . . . . Putnam's
Greenwood . . . . Jack Ellenberg
Marion . . . . Manning Jolly, Jr.
Mt. Carmel . . . . D. J. McAllister
North Charleston . . . S & S Gun Shop
Newberry . Frank Lominack Hardware
Orangeburg . . . J. W. Smoak Hardware
Spartanburg . . . . Hoffman Fur
Summerton . . . . Grayson-Elliott
Summerville . . Old River Rd. Antiques
Sumter . . . . Carolina Hardware
Ulmer . . . . Palmetto Antiques
Westminster . . Randy's Gun Exchange

South Dakota
Aberdeen . . . . . . Coast To Coast Store
Aberdeen . . . . Leftys Bait
Arlington . . . . Maxwells
Belle Fourche . Pioneer Sporting Goods
Brookings . . . . Bills Sport Shop
Chamberlain . . Trusty's Gun Shop
Clark . . . . Kyles Hardware
Deadwood . . . . Olson's Gun
Deadwood . . . . Stearn & Shedd
DeSmet . . . . Ollies Auto Electric
Howard . . . . Dons Sporting Center
Huron . . . . Huron Surplus & Guns
Huron . . . . Mahowald Hardware
Huron . . . . U. S. Army Surplus
Minot . . . . Saunders Sporting Goods
Mitchell . . . . Leader Hardware

Pierre . . . . Coast To Coast Store
Pierre . . . . Hinseys Oahe Sport Shope
Rapid City . . . . Du Ell Sporting Goods
Rapid City . . . . . . Robbies Gun Shop
Rapid City . . . . Sport Club
Rapid City . . . . . . The Powder Horn
Sioux Falls . Hunting & Fishing Supply
Sioux Falls . . . . Johns Sporting Goods
Sioux Falls
      Olsen Marine & Sporting Goods
Sioux Falls . . . . West Sioux Falls Hdwe.
Valley Springs . . . . . Big 45 Gun Shop
Vermillion . Thompson O. K. Hardware
Watertown . . . . Nelson Ace Hardware
Yankton
     Kennys Service & Sporting Goods

Tennessee
Bristol . . . . Bristol Hardware Corp.
Athens . . . . Cherokee Hardware
Cerro Gordo . . . . . . Harbour Pitts Co.
Chattanooga . . Olson's Gun & Supplies
Chattanooga . . . Terminal Loan Office
Chattanooga . . W. A. Wood Supply Co.
Clarksville . . . . . Kennedy's Gun Shop
Clarksville . . N. P. C. Sportsman Store
Cleveland . . . Economy Auto Supply
Cookeville
     Brown & Watson Sporting Goods
Cookeville . . . . Mid-State Sport Shop
Cowan . . . . Sport City Sales
Crossville . Crossville Surplus & Salvage
Dickson . . . . . Nick's Hardware Co, Inc.
Dickson . . . . Roger Hamilton
Elizabethton . Mack Roller Sport Shop
Fairview . . . . M. T. Wallace & Son
Fayetteville . . . . . Goodrich Hardware
Franklin . . . . Sparkman-Ethridge
Gallatin . . . . . . Ed Mack Sport Center
Greenville . . . . . Richards Trading Post
Harriman . . . . Harrison Sporting Goods
Hendersonville . . . Russell's Gun Shop
Hohenwald . Ray Grimes Hardware Co.
Jackson . . Ham Howse Sporting Goods
Jackson
     Travis Johnson's Sporting Goods
Johnson City . . . . Ben's Sport Shop
Johnson City . . . . Londons
Kingsport Dobyn's-Taylor Hardware Co.
Kingsport . . . . Lynn Garden Hardware
Knoxville . . . . Athletic House
Knoxville
     Fowler & Irick Sporting Goods
Knoxville . . . . Millers
Knoxville . . . . United Loan Co.
Knoxville . . . . Zayres
Lawrenceburg . . . . Rayfield Hardware
Leach . . . . Goodsuns Sporting Goods
Lewisburg . . . . . Turner Auto Supply
Livingston . . . . Roberts Hardware
Livingston . . . . . Speck Bros. Hardware
Loudon . . . . Greer's Inc.
Maryville . . . . Mosers
McMinnvillee . Brown Reloading Center
McMinnville . McMinnville Boat Center
McMinnville . . . . Sportsman Den
Memphis . . . . B & B Sales Co.
Memphis . . Mid-Continent Armament
Memphis . . . . University Arms
Memphis . . . . York Arms Co.
Morristown . . . . . Cox Sporting Goods
Morristown . . . . Firestone Store
Morristown Hasson Bryan Hardware Co.
Nashville . . . American Firearms, Inc.
Nashville . . . . . . Bob's Sporting Goods
Nashville . . . . . Clay's Sporting Goods
Nashville . . . . . Gun City U.S.A. Inc.
Nashville . . . . Sportsman Store
Newport . . . . Buck's Pawn Shop
Oak Ridge . . . . Oak Ridge Disc. Store
Pulaski . . . . Abernathy Hardware
Pulaski . . . Blue Bird Sporting Goods
Santa Fe . . . . Leon's Gun Shop
Savannah . . . . Tenn Tusky Fisherman
Sevierville . . . . . Carl Ownby Hardware
Shelbyville . . . . Martin & Price
Signal Mountain . . . . . . Brown Bros.

Sparta . . . . . . Jimmy's Sporting Goods
Tullahoma . . . . Whit's Sport Shop
Union City . . . . . . Turner Kirkland
Wartburg . . . . Shannon's
Waynesboro . . Waynesboro Hardware
Whitehaven . . . . York Arms Co.
Winchester . . . . Judges Gun Shop

Texas
Abilene . . . . Bible Hardware
Abilene . . . . The Mackey Co.
Alice . . . . Alice Hardware Co.
Amarillo . . . . Amarillo Traders
Amarillo . . . H&H Sporting Goods
Amarillo . . . Tom & Roy's Gun Shop
Amarillo . . . Vance Hall Sporting Goods
Athens . Montgomery Sporting Goods
Atlanta . . . . . . Price Hardware Co.
Austin . . . . Chuck's Gun Shop
Austin . . . . . Chas. P. Davis Hardware
Austin E. R. Haire Custom Stockmaker
Austin . . . . McBride Gun Shop
Austin . . . . Oshmans
Austin . . . . Petmeckys
Bandera . . . . B. F. Langford
Bay City . . . . Denn Bros.
Bay City . . . . Oshmans
Beaumont . . . . Kyle's Inc.
Beaumont . McKnights Sporting Goods
Beeville . . . . . . Burrows Hardware Co.
Beeville . . . . Roberts & McKenzie, Inc.
Big Springs . Big Springs Hardware Co.
Borger . . . . Wicks Sporting Goods
Brownsville . . . . . J. H. Batsell & Sons
Brownsville . . . Brownsville Hardware
Brownwood . . . . . . Weakley Watson
Center . . . . . Payne & Payne Hardware
Cleveland . . . . . Cleveland Hardware
Colorado City . . . . Taylor Hardware
Corpus Christi
     Connally's Shooters Supplies
Corpus Christi . . . . Oshmans
Corpus Christi . . . . Texas Gun Clinic
Corpus Christi
   Wehring-Matthews Hardware Co.
Cuero . . Wagner Hardware & Machine
Dallas . . . . Buckhorn Trading Post
Dallas . . . . Cullum & Boren Co.
Dallas . . . . Gibson
Dallas . . . . Ketchum & Killum
Dallas . . . . Bill Lundgren's Guns
Dallas . . . . Moore-Ehler Co.
Dallas . . . . Navy Exchange
Dallas
     Ray's Hardware & Sporting Goods
Dallas . . . . Wiley's Gun
Del Rio . . . . Shively's Gun Shop
Del Rio . . . . Russell Hardware
Denison . . . . . . Dusek Sporting Goods
Denton . . . . . . Denton Sports Center
Denton . . . . Pierces
Dumas . . . . Phillips & Sons
Eagle Pass . . . . Eagle Hardware
El Campo . . . . The Sports Center
El Campo . . Mack J. Webb Hardware Co.
El Paso . . . . Beav's Sport Shop
El Paso . . . . El Paso Sporting Goods
El Paso . . . . Firearms Inc.
El Paso . . . . Hellier Co.
El Paso . . . . . Orville C. Kuberski
El Paso . . . . . Popular Dry Goods Co.
Falfurrias . . . . Forsyths
Floydada . . . . . Kirk & Son Hardware
Ft. Worth . . . . B-Square Company
Ft. Worth . . . . Cross Gun Shop
Ft. Worth . . . . Knights Gun Store
Ft. Worth . . . . Leonard's Dept. Store
Ft. Worth . . . . Lowell Pruett
Ft. Worth . . . . Manning's Disc.
Ft. Worth . . . . Noble Firearms
Fredericksburg . . . . Probst
Fredericksburg . . . . The Sports Center
Freeport . . . . Firestone Store
Galveston . . . Skains Sporting Goods
Gatesville . . . Jim Miller's Army Store
Goliad . . . . Ramseys Inc.
Grand Prairie . Henry's Sporting Goods

Grapevine
     Jess Stockwell Shooters Supply
Groves . . . . Keith Hardware
Hamilton
  George W. Chambless Sporting Goods
Halingen . . . . The Sportsman
Hearne . . . . Gables Auto Supply
Henrietta . . . . Moore's Hardware
Hillsboro . . . . House Lumber Co.
Hondo . . . . Gaines Store
Houston . . . . Britts
Houston . . . . Consolidated Aero
Houston . . . . Deep River Armory, Inc.
Houston . . . . Foleys
Houston . . . . Heights Tackle House
Houston . . . . W. A. Holt Inc.
Houston . . . . Houston Sport Shop
Houston . . . . Joskes
Houston . . . . Oshmans
Houston . . . . Texas Gun Clinic
Houston . . . . Zero Gun Shop
Junction . . Chenault's Sporting Goods
Katy . . . . Gene's Sport Shop
Kermit . . . . Blakes Sport Goods
Kerrville . . . . Chas. Schreiner Co.
Kilgore . . . . . Adams Sporting Goods
Kingsville . . . Ed Byrne Furn. & Appl.
Laredo . . . . Beckelhymers
Laredo . . . . Guerra Hardware
Longview . . . . H & T Sporting Goods
Los Saenz . . Gonzales Merchantile Co.
Lubbock . . . . A. Acme Pawn Shop
Lubbock . . . . Farmer's Exchange
Lufkin . . Abney & Medford Hardware
Lufkin . . . Haygood's Sporting Goods
Marshall . . . . Logan & Whaley
Marshall . . . . Manlys
McAllen . . . . Broadway Hardware
McAllen . . . . J.B. Guthrie Co.
McAllen . . . . The Sportsman
McAllen . . . . . . Valley Sports Shop
Mercedes . . . . . Borderland Hardware
Mineral Wells . Davidson Hardware Co.
Mission Mission Hardware & Supply Co.
Monahans . . . . . Lyle's Sporting Goods
Nacogdoches . . . . . Cason Monk & Co.
Nacogdoches
      Nacogdoches G. I. Supplies
New Braunfels . . . . . . Louis Henne Co.
Odessa . . . . Ace Pawn Shop
Odessa . . . . . Roberts Hardware Supply
Odessa . . . . . Texas Wholesale Supply
Orange . . . . Guns' N Gadgets
Orange . . . . The Sportsman Shop
Pampa . . . . Addington's Western Store
Paris . . . . . . Williams Sporting Goods
Pasadena . . Pasadena Sporting Goods
Pleasanton . . . . . Fred Krause Supply
Port Arthur . . . . Kens Gun Clinic
Port Arthur Wil Moritz Sporting Goods
Port Arthur
     Bill Warren's Sportsmans Shop
Port Lavaca . . . . Oshmans
Richardson
  Hank's Sporting & Shooting Supplies
Rockdale . . . . Spuds Gun Shop
Rosenberg
  Rude & Sons Hardware & Sporting
San Angelo . . . . . . B & B Trading Co.
San Angelo . Sammons Sporting Goods
San Antonio Bowman Sporting Goods
San Antonio . Dillard's Sporting Goods
San Antonio . . . . Kaufmans Inc.
San Antonio . . . . Joskes
San Antonio . . Nagel's Sporting Goods
San Antonio . . . . Potchernicks
San Antonio . . . . Topperweins
San Antonio
     Gene Toudouze Hardware Co.
San Juan . . . . Valley Hardware
San Saba . . . . San Saba Hardware
Seguin . . . . . . Sageveil Sporting Goods
Seguin . . . . Vivroux Hardware Co.
Sherman . . . . . Sanders Sporting Goods
Snyder . . . Fish Newton Hardware Co.
South Houston . . . . K-M Shooters
Sweetwater . . . . Turner Hardware

318

Texarkana .... Riley's Sporting Goods
Texas City .... Busbee's Hardware
Texas City ...Trout's Sporting Goods
Tyler .... Mac's Gun Shop
Tyler . Bob Reynolds Custom Gunshop
Victoria .... Firestone Store
Victoria .... Zac Lentz Hardware
Victoria .... Victoria Hardware
Waco .... Cogdells
Waco .... Holt's Sporting Goods
Weslaco .... Borderland Hardware
Wichita Falls ... G & C Sporting Goods
Wichita Falls ... Holt's Sporting Goods

Utah

American Fork
Robinson Sporting Goods
Brigham City Thompson Sporting Goods
Cedar City .... Hunter Hardware
Heber City .... Ashton Pro
Lehi .... Hutch's Pro
Logan .... Al's Sporting Goods
Logan .... Sunset Sporting Goods
Magna .... Falvo's Sporting Goods
Moab .... Custom Ammo
Moab .... Miller's
Murray ...... Jerry's Sporting Center
Murray .... Trail Sports Center
Ogden .... Armstrong Sporting Goods
Ogden .... Gift House
Ogden .... Kammeyer's
Ogden .... Kent's Shooters Supply
Ogden .... Sunset Sporting Goods
Ogden .... Williamson's Sports
Orem .... Burr's
Orem .... The Sportsman
Price .... Price Trading Co.
Provo .... Innes Sporting Goods
Provo .... Provo Sporting Goods
Roy .... Sunset Sporting Goods
St.George .... Nelson Supply
St.George .... Pickett Lumber
Salt Lake City .... Auerbach's
Salt Lake City ..... Beehive Antiques
Salt Lake City .... Chris & Dick's
Salt Lake City .. Duce Sporting Goods
Salt Lake City .... Gallenson's
Salt Lake City ...... Guns Unlimited
Salt Lake City .. Joe's Sporting Goods
Salt Lake City .... P. M. Guns
Salt Lake City ...... Red Front Store
Salt Lake City .... Shopper's Discount
Salt Lake City ... Skagg's Drug Center
Salt Lake City .... West Side Drug
Salt Lake City
Wolfe's Sportsman's Headquarters
Salt Lake City .. Zinik Sporting Goods
Tooele .... Sunset Sporting Goods
Vernal .... Sunset Sporting Goods

Vermont

Arlington .... Wisewood
Bennington
Ted DeMarco's Sporting Goods
Bennington .... Gun Rack
Brattleboro ..... Burrows Sport Shop
Brattleboro Clapp's Sporting Goods Co.
Brattleboro .... Sam's Dept. Store
Burlington .... Linden Gun Shop
Burlington .... L. P. Woods, Inc.
Enosburg Falls .... A. Brown
Fairhaven .... W. S. Lloyd
Lyndonville .... Edmund's PHC
Manchester Center ..... Cartridge Box
Morrisville .... A. Brown
Morrisville .... Thomas D. Hirchak, Jr.
New Haven Jct.
Lathrop Sporting Goods
Norich .... Devaux's Gun Shop
Rutland ...... Lindholm Sport Center
Rutland .... Wilson's Sports
St.Albans .... Bushey Sporting Goods
St. Albans .... Sports Shop
St.Johnsbury .... C. H. Dana, Jr.
Shelburne .... White's
West Danville .... W. D. Hall
Windsor .... Joseph C. Meyette, Jr.
Woodstock .... W. H. Shurtleff
Woodstock .... Woodstock Sports

Virginia

Alexandria ...... Potomac Arms Co.
Alexandria .... Interarmco
Altarista .... Altarista Hardware
Annandale .... Dawson's
Arlington .... Sport Fair Inc.
Ashburn ..... Forest Farm Gun Club
Baileys Cross Roads . Atlas Sport Store
Bridgewater .. Rockingham Milling Co.
Bristol .... DeVault's
Buena Vista .... Douty Hardware
Buena Vista .... White's Hardware
Charlottesville .... Carter's Gun Works
Charlottesville . Wayne Greene's Sports
Charlottesville .... Chuck Kraft
Chase City .... Jeffrey-Lambert
Chesterfield .... Fred L. Cook, Jr.
Danville .... Booth White Sports Shop
Fairfax .... Jay Lee Sports
Falls Church .... Davis Gun Shop
Falls Church .... Kuhn's
Floyd .... Phipps
Franklin .... Whitley Hardware
Fredericksburg ..... Abels Gun Shop
Fredericksburg Fredericksburg Center
Galax .... J. C. Matthews
Galax .... Vass Kapp Hardware
Gladys .... Suddith's Gun Shop
Glen Allen .... Green Top Service
Harrisonburg ..... Landes Enterprises
Harrisonburg . Rockingham Milling Co.
Harrisonburg ... Rocking R. Hardware
Hopewell .. Carmany's Sporting Center
Keysville .... Hamner Bros.
Leesburg .... Thomas F. Stewart
Lovingston .... Eugene J. Baker
Manassas .... J. E. Rice Co.
Marion .... Robinson's
Martinsville Bryant's Sporting Center
Newport News .... Long's Sport Shop
Newport News Sherwood Hobby House
Norfolk .... Blaustein & Reich
Norton .... Nards Appliance
Petersburg ..... Dixie Sporting Goods
Poquoson ...... PoQuoson Gun Shop
Portsmouth ..... Harrell's Sport Shop
Richlands ..... Nat'l Sportsman Shop
Richmond .... Carwich Marine
Roanoke .... Colonial Gun Supply
Richmond ...... Harris Flippen & Co.
Richmond .... Sportsman's Shop
St.David's Church Kings Crossing Store
Salem .... Creasy's Gun Shop
Smithfield .... Allen P. Thacker
South Hill .... Jeffrey Lambert
Staunton ..... Worthington Hardware
Timberville ..... Rockingham Milling
Va. Beach .... Sportsman's Shop
Warrenton .... Clark Bros.
Warsaw .... Irondale
Winchester .... Braddock Sport Shop
Winchester ..... David A. Falmestoch
Woodstock ..... Western Auto Dealer

Washington

Aberdeen .... Failors Sporting Goods
Aberdeen ...... Reiners Sports Shop
Anacortes .... Bryant's Sporting Shop
Bellevue .... Ernst Hardware
Bellevue .... Vernel Sport Shop
Bellingham .... H & H Sporting Goods
Bellingham Ira Yeager's Sporting Goods
Burlington ...... Kesselring Gun Shop
Castle Rock
Four Corners Sporting Goods
Chehalis .... Two Yard Birds
Chehalis .... Wisner's Gun Shop
Cle Elum .... Victory Sporting Goods
Colville .... Rambles Sport Shop
Deer Park .... Weber Hardware
Edmonds .... Custom Gun Service
Ellensburg
Will Strange Sporting Goods
Everett .... Everett Sport Shop
Longview .... Ed's Gun Shop
Longview .... Manchesters
Longview .... Spikes Sporting Goods
Longview .... Ted's Rifle Shop
Millwood .... Ed. Karrer's Guns
Moses Lake .... Tri State Store
Omak ...... Hendrickson Sport Shop
Oroville .... Fleishmans
Port Angeles .... Katz's Gun Shop
Port Angeles ... Mel's Sporting Goods
Port Angeles .... The Mart
Port Orchard .... Pete's Gun Shop
Raymond .... Odell's Gun Shop
Pasco .... Barrie's Sporting Goods
Puyallup .... Stoners
Renton ...... Seattle Sporting Goods
Richland .... B B & M Sporting Goods
Seattle .... Bon Marche
Seattle .... Ernst Hardware Co.
Seattle ..... Keth Peabody's Sport Inc.
Seattle ...... Seattle Sporting Goods
Seattle .... Sportsman Supply Co.
Seattle .... Waffenfabrik-West
Seattle ...... Warshals Sporting Goods
Seattle .... Webbs Gun Shop
Shelton .... Guns
Spokane .... Amer. Int. Co.
Spokane .... Crescent Dept Store
Spokane .... Ed's Gun Shop
Spokane .... Sportsmans Surplus
Spokane .... Trap House
Spokane .... Two Swabbies
Sunnyside .. Amundson Hardware Co.
Sunnyside .... Killingstad Bros.
Tacoma ...... Deritis Sporting Goods
Tacoma .... Chet Paulson, Inc.
Tacoma .... Totem Guns
Toppenish .... Roeberry's Rec. Center
Walla Walla .. Brock's Sporting Goods
Walla Walla Drum Heller Hardware Co.
Walla Walla ..... Thrifty Drug Center
Wenatche .... Adams Sport Shop
Wenatchee .. Stallings, Adams, Conway
West Seattle ... Seattle Sporting Goods
Winslow ...... Anderson's Hardware
Yakima .... Anderson's Guns
Yakima .... Jerry's Gun Shop
Yakima .... Lewis & Sears
Yakima ..... Mellotte Sporting Goods
Yakima .... Ted's Sporting Goods

West Virginia

Beckley .... Keatleys Inc.
Bradshaw .... Davis Photo Service
Buckhannon A. G. Shannon's Hardware
Charleston .... The Gun Store
Dellslow .... Ed. Galasky
Elkins .... The Sport Shop
Elm Grove .... Millikens Gun Shop
Fairmont .... Lipsons
Fairmont .... The Sport Store
Ft.Ashby .... Dave's Gun Shop
Gassaway .... Byrne Hardware
Gassaway
Gassaway Hardware & Furniture
Huntington ...... Mac & Daves Loans
Keyser .... Graysons
Madision ..... Spencer's Sport Center
Marlington C. J. Richardson Hardware
Milton .... Morris Watch Shop
Morgantown .. McPhersons, Gunsmith
Moundsville ... Sullivan Gun Specialty
New Martinsville ..... Allen O. Pinner
New Martinsville ..... The Sport Shop
Nitio .... Amlo Corp.
Nitro ... Nitro Hardware & Supply Co.
Oak Hill .... New River Supply co.
Oak Hill . Roy's Loan & Sporting Goods
Parkersburg . Chancellor Hardware Co.
Philippi .... Wolfe & Co.
Princeton Douglas Sporting Goods Inc.
Richwood .... Coe's Sport Shop
Romney .... Bob Mar Sport
Shady Spring ..... Ray's Leisure Time
Spencer .... Eddie's Sport Shop
Stumptown ...... Williams Gun Shop
Summersville .... Herold & Herold
Vienna .... Opha B. Poling
Webster Spring ... Damron Hardware
Weirton .... Weir Cove Sporting Goods
Wellsburg ...... Schwarz's Gun Shop
West Columbia ...... Paul Fitzgerald
Weston .... Dave's Sport Shop
Wheeling .... Banov Sports Center
Williamson ..... Alberts Loan Office
Williamson . Hatfield's Sporting Goods

Wisconsin

Antigo .... Sport Marine Inc.
Appleton ... Schieder Mayer Hardware
Baraboo .... Baraboo Sporting Goods
Baraboo ..... Premo's Service Store
Beaver Dam ...... Beaver Sport Shop
Beloit .... Beloit Sport Center
Beloit .... Krueger Sport Shop
Berlin .... Cunningham Hardware
Berlin .... Curly's Sport Shop
Black Earth ...... Bill's Shoe & Sport
Brandon .... Brandon Sport Shop
Brillion .... Brillion Sports
Brookfield .... Brookfield Ind.
Cashton .... Hundt Imp. Co.
Chilton .... Farm & Home Supply
Chippewa Falls ..... Bill's Sport Shop
Chippewa Falls .... Mac's Marine
Cumberland . Indian Head Sport Shop
Eagle River .... Speiss Sporting Goods
East Troy .... The Trading Post
Eau Claire ...... Outdoor Sport Shop
Edgar .... Kresbach's
Elkhorn .... Pat's Sport Shop
Fond Du Lac .... The Sport Shop
Fontana .. Fontana Army-Navy Store
Ft. Atkinson ... Lakeland Sport Shop
Franksville .... Bodven's
Glenbeulah .... Dick's Gun Shop
Green Bay ...... Bertrand Sport Shop
Green Bay .... Denis Sport Shop
Green Bay .... Gordon Bent Co.
Green Bay ..... Prange Budget Center
Hager City .... Prairie View Gun Shop
Hartford .... Johns Sport Shop
Iola .... C. Neil Krause
Iron Ridge
Earl Sportsman's Trading Post
Janesville ...... Janesville Sport Shop
Kaukana .... Dave's Sport Shop
Kenosha .... Bogard's Gun Shop
Kenosha .... Tyson's, Inc.
LaCrosse .... Bills Sport Shop
LaCrosse
Tausches Retail Hardware Inc.
Land O'Lakes .... Eberly's
Lomira .... Bill's Sport Shop
Madison .... Berg Pearson
Madison . H. H. Petrie Sporting Goods
Madison .... Rush Gun Shop
Madison . Wisc. Felton Sporting Goods
Manitowoc .... Finders Keepers
Manitowoc ... Sporting Goods Supply
Marinette ..... Marinette Sport Shop
Marshfield .... Miller's Sport Shop
Mazomanie .... W. J. Ewald
Menomonee Falls ...... Jay's Sports
Menomonee Falls .. Sports Unlimited
Menomonie .... The Sport Shop
Merrill .... Dukes Sport Shop
Milwaukee .... A. B. C. Supply
Milwaukee .... Casanovas Inc.
Milwaukee .... Dean's Sport Shop
Milwaukee .... Flintrop Arms
Milwaukee ... Johnson Sporting Goods
Milwaukee .... Ken's Gun Center
Milwaukee .... Kess Arms
Minocqua ..... Lakeland Sport Shop
Monroe .... Martins Sport Shop
New London .... Sport O Lectric
Oconomowoc
Stevens Sporting Goods, Inc.
Oshkosh .... A-1 Service
Oshkosh .... Hergert Sport Center
Oshkosh .... Joe's Sport Shop
Oshkosh ..... Spanbaur Sport Shop
Oshkosh .. Valley Arms & Equipment

Park Falls ....Scullys Inc.
Pepin............. Pepin Hardware
Peshtigo .... Pete's Sport Shop
Phillips .... Martwick's
Plymouth ....Langjahr's
Portage ....Coast To Coast Store
Portage ....Portage Sport Shop
Port Washington
               Schiller's Sporting Goods
Prairie DuChein ... Richard Stark, Inc.
Racine ....Fodor's
Racine .... Higgin Sporting Goods
Racine ....The Trading Post
Reedsburg ....Fred F. Haugh
Reedsburg ....Tom's Gun Shop
Rice Lake .... Lou's Sport Shop
Richland Center ...A. H. Krouskop
Ripon ....Ripon Sport Shop
Shawano .... Fritz's Gun Repair
Shawano ....K&G Sport Shop
Solon Springs ......Al's Gun Repairs
South Milwaukee ..... N. Hints Sports
Stetsonville ....Mundt "Jeep"

Stevens Point .... Boyers Sport Marine
Stevens Point ....Sport Shop
Sturgeon Bay ... Em's Sporting Goods
Sun Prairie .... Klein's
Superior ....The Mareus Co.
Tomah ....Coast To Coast Store
Tomahawk .. Bennett Sporting Goods
Viroqua .... K&L, Inc.
Waterford ...... Jensen's Sport Shop
Watertown .. Hemp's Sporting Goods
Waukesha .... Becker Sporting Goods
Waukesha ...... Jim's Sports Heaven
Waukesha .....Jim's Streams & Field
Wausau
     Shepherd & Schaller Sporting Goods
Wausau ....The Gunsmith
Wauwatosa ..... Schelkles Gun Shop
West Allis .... Bob's Bait Shop
West Allis .... Don's Gun Shop
Wilmot .... Gander Mountain
Wisconsin Rapids .. Johnson Hills, Inc.
Wisconsin Rapids .. Perry's Sport Shop

Wyoming
Buffalo .... Sullivan's Sport Shop
Casper ....Ideen's Repair
Casper .... K. Mart 4069
Casper .... Sunset Sporting Goods
Cheyenne ..... Grand Central Market
Cheyenne ....Peoples
Cheyenne .... Tempo
Cheyenne ......The Supply Sergeant
Cody ....The Fishhook
Cody .... The Gun Hawk
Douglas ....The Saul Co.
DuBois .... Welty's General Store
Evanston ....Nevilles
Gillette .... Gambles
Gillette .... Sport Shop, Inc.
Lander ....Lander Saddlery
Laramie ......Linde's Sporting Goods
Pinedale ..Wind River Sporting Goods
Rawlins .... Birite Drug
Rawlins .... Gambles
Rawlins ...... Gene's Sporting Goods
Riverton Hartman Co. Sporting Goods

Riverton ..... The House Of Muskets
Rock Springs .. Mike's Sporting Goods
Sheridan .... Ritz Sporting Goods
Sheridan ....Sheridan Gun Shop
Torrington .... Gambles
Worland ....The Outdoorsman

Canada
Campbell River F. H. Camp, Gunsmith
Hamilton .... The Cartridge Club
Hamilton ....Gunsports Co.
Hamilton ...Snider, Custom Gunsmith
Peterborough .... Trigger Talk
Toronto ......Sole's Sporting Goods
Vancouver ....Hough Custom Guns
Victoria .... Robinson's

Puerto Rico
Rio Piedras ....Sports Shop 1967
    LAST MINUTE LISTINGS
Olathe, Kansas
.... Simmons Gun Specialties
Wichita, Kansas ...... The Gun Shop
Salem, Ohio .... Fisher's
Beaumont, Texas .... Oshman's